Students & Families

One-Stop Internet Resources

ubpl.glencoe.com

Self-Study Tools

- Chapter Overviews
- Homework Hints
- Legal Web Links

Self-Assessment Tools

- Self-Check Quizzes
- Interactive Unit Tests
- Real Cases
- Landmark Cases

Content Enrichment Tools

- Service Learning
- A Global Perspective
- Career Information

GLENCOE Understanding Business & Personal Law

ubpl.glencoe.com

Web site includes:
• Interactive quizzes and tests
• Real and landmark cases
• Chapter overviews and legal links

Glencoe: Your *Real* Business Choice

Gordon W. Brown, J.D.
Member of the Massachusetts Bar
Professor Emeritus of Law
North Shore Community College
Beverly, Massachusetts

Paul A. Sukys, J.D.
Member of the Ohio Bar
Professor of Law and Legal Studies
North Central State College
Mansfield, Ohio

Glencoe

New York, New York   Columbus, Ohio   Chicago, Illinois   Peoria, Illinois   Woodland Hills, California

Program Components

Program Components

Your *Understanding Business and Personal Law* program provides a rich and diverse offering of resources for learning, teaching, reinforcing, and enriching the individual and classroom learning experience.

Program Resources
- Student Edition
- Teacher Wraparound Edition

Reinforcement
- Student Activity Workbook
- Supplemental Cases
- PuzzleMaker

Enrichment
- Enrichment Masters
- Internet Resources
- Ethics and Business Law Activities
- Business and Competitive Events in Law
- Poster Package

Teacher Resources
- Student Activity Workbook TAE
- Lesson Plans
- Transparency Binder
- Blackline Masters
- Reproducible Tests

Technology-Based Resources
- Interactive Lesson Planner (ILP) CD-ROM
- Assessment Binder (**Exam***View* ® Pro Testmaker CD-ROM)
- PowerPoint® Presentation
- National Mock Trial Championship Video
- CourtTV Trial Stories Video Package
- Glencoe Business Video Package
- *Understanding Business and Personal Law* Web site **ubpl.glencoe.com**

 **Glencoe**

The *McGraw-Hill* Companies

Send all inquiries to:
Glencoe/McGraw-Hill
21600 Oxnard Street
Suite 500
Woodland Hills, California 91367

ISBN: 0-07-861878-9

2 3 4 5 6 7 8 9 10 11   027   09 08 07 06 05

TABLE OF CONTENTS

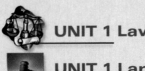
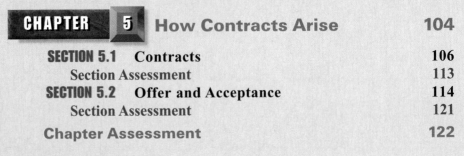

UNIT 5

Using Your Purchasing Power   480

UNIT 6

Starting a Business   580

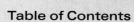

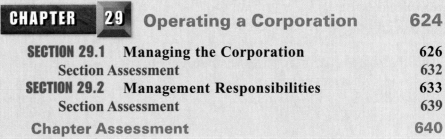

Exploring Your Book

Exploring the Unit

Understanding Business and Personal Law is organized into seven units, each beginning with a unit opener. The unit opener uses visuals and activities created to simulate thinking about the topics that will be covered in the upcoming chapters.

Unit Overview
The Unit Overview offers a brief summary of the topics covered in the unit and provides insight into how these concepts affect your life.

Your Justice Journal
This feature presents the opportunity for you to reflect on specific legal, ethical, and civil situations through written activities.

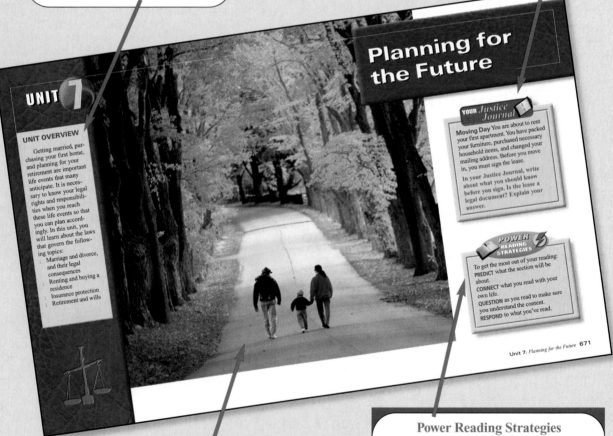

UNIT 7

Planning for the Future

UNIT OVERVIEW

Getting married, purchasing your first home, and planning for your retirement are important life events that many anticipate. It is necessary to know your legal rights and responsibilities when you reach these life events so that you can plan accordingly. In this unit, you will learn about the laws that govern the following topics:
- Marriage and divorce, and their legal consequences
- Renting and buying a residence
- Insurance protection
- Retirement and wills

YOUR *Justice Journal*

Moving Day You are about to rent your first apartment. You have packed your furniture, purchased necessary household items, and changed your mailing address. Before you move in, you must sign the lease.

In your Justice Journal, write about what you should know before you sign. Is the lease a legal document? Explain your answer.

POWER READING STRATEGIES

To get the most out of your reading:
PREDICT what the section will be about.
CONNECT what you read with your own life.
QUESTION as you read to make sure you understand the content.
RESPOND to what you've read.

Unit 7: *Planning for the Future* 671

The Unit Opening Photograph
This photograph appeals to the visual learners in your class, providing connections to daily life that will stimulate memory and reinforce concepts that are covered in the chapter.

Power Reading Strategies
These strategies challenge you to strengthen your active reading skills to increase retention, generate interest, and foster creative and critical thinking.

Exploring Your Book

Exploring the Chapter

Each chapter of *Understanding Business and Personal Law* provides an opening structure that is both visually appealing and easy to comprehend. It prepares you for learning and sets the stage, both visually and textually, for new concepts that will be covered in the chapter.

The Chapter Opening Photograph
This photograph provides a visual stimulus, provoking thought and reflection about the events depicted and how they relate to the chapter topic.

The Opening Scene
The Opening Scene is a vignette that presents a dynamic real-world situation that you may encounter in your own life. It introduces key legal and ethical issues to be covered in the chapter and offers insight into how law affects the real world in which you live.

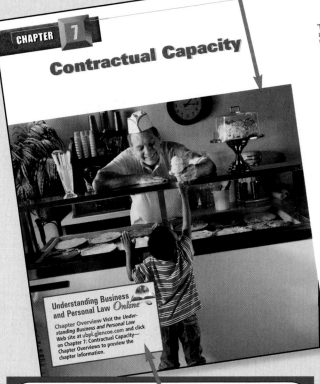

CHAPTER 7

Contractual Capacity

Understanding Business and Personal Law *Online*

Chapter Overview Visit the *Understanding Business and Personal Law* Web site at ubpl.glencoe.com and click on Chapter 7: Contractual Capacity—Chapter Overviews to preview the chapter information.

The Opening Scene
It's Saturday morning, a few days after Jake bought his "new" car. Alena, Viktor, Jake, and their college friend, Arkadi, are at the used car lot.

A Minor's Major Return
ALENA: You've dreamed up a crazy plan, Arkadi. I don't think this is going to work. The dealership is not going to return Jake's money. Maybe he doesn't even deserve to get it back. His decision was pretty stupid.

JAKE: Thanks a lot, Alena. Why do you always have to act like such a know-it-all?

ARKADI: Trust me. When I was a kid like Jake, a similar thing happened to me. We'll get Jake's money.

JAKE: Who are you calling a kid? I'm not in elementary school.

ALENA: (Ignoring Jake.) But you were 14 when you bought that defective stereo system, Arkadi. Jake is 16 right now.

ARKADI: It doesn't matter. Jake's still a kid. (Turning to Jake.) Are you ready? Do you have the paper we talked about?

JAKE: I'm prepared. Here it is. And stop calling me a kid. I'm not a kid.

(A salesperson in a cheap suit approaches the group. He grins broadly and greets the group with excessive enthusiasm.)

MR. BARENBLATT: Hello there, boys and girls. Barenblatt's the name. Cars are my game. We have a lot of good deals today—plenty of used cars and trucks that are perfect for first-time buyers. How'd you like to take this little beauty for a spin?

JAKE: I know who you are. You sold me a bogus vehicle the other day.

(Mr. Barenblat takes a closer look at Jake, recognizes him, and smiles.)

MR. BARENBLATT: Oh yeah. I thought that I knew you from somewhere. I sell a lot of cars. Sometimes

It's hard to remember everyone. Hi there, kid. How's your car running?

JAKE: It's not.

MR. BARENBLATT: What are you trying to say? It's not running?

JAKE: No. It's not my car anymore. Here you go—I guess you'll want to read this.

(Jake hands him the paper. Mr. Barenblatt reads it quickly.)

MR. BARENBLATT: What is this, some kind of stupid joke?

ALENA: It's no joke, friend. He's a minor, and he wants out of the bogus deal that you forced him into. Next time, you'll think twice before you try to hustle a minor.

MR. BARENBLATT: You can't do that! We had an agreement, and you can't just change your mind and pull out of it now. You signed a contract!

JAKE: (Smiling.) It makes no difference. After all, I'm just a kid.

What Are the Legal Issues?

1. When is a person considered a minor?
2. Why does the law permit minors to void their contracts?
3. Are there any exceptions to the rule that says that minors can void their contracts?
4. What individuals, besides minors, can void their contracts?

Chapter 7: *Contractual Capacity* **145**

Understanding Business and Personal Law **Online**
This feature directs you to the Chapter Overview that is found on the *Understanding Business and Personal Law* Web site at **ubpl.glencoe.com**. You will find a great deal of interesting and useful material on the Web site, including new features, study resources, and enrichment activities.

What Are the Legal Issues?
This feature expands upon the The Opening Scene by challenging you to critically examine the legal issues that appear in the vignette. You are asked to hypothesize about the answers to legal questions, stimulating your thought on the legal terms and concepts that are involved in the scene. This feature also helps you to focus on the important topics that are discussed in the chapter.

Exploring Your Book

Exploring the Section

Chapters of the *Understanding Business and Personal Law* text are divided into easy-to-grasp sections of information. An organized flow of concept development, punctuated by point-of-use assessment opportunities, helps you build new knowledge in easily managed increments.

What You'll Learn
Each section lists the most important concepts and highlights the skills and knowledge that you will master after study of the section is completed. Establishing these goals helps you engage the materials in an active manner. You can also use these bulleted items as study guides to the important concepts covered in each section.

Why It's Important
This feature explains the relevance of the section. It helps you connect concepts to your daily life, business relationships, society, and the legal system as a whole.

Legal Terms
Each section includes a list of the vocabulary terms that are introduced in the section discussion. These terms are printed in boldface type and highlighted in yellow the first time they are introduced in the text. Clear and contextually relevant definitions accompany each term. Studying these legal terms is an excellent way to prepare for quizzes and exams.

SECTION 13.1 The Sale and Lease of Goods

What You'll Learn
- When to apply the law of sales in your daily life
- How to describe the special rules for sales contracts
- How to determine when sales contracts must be in writing
- How to explain the rules for auctions and bulk sales

Why It's Important
As you learn more about the law of sales, you will be better able to protect your legal rights and your money when buying or selling a product.

Legal Terms
- sale
- price
- goods
- Uniform Commercial Code
- contract to sell
- merchant
- usage of trade
- firm offer
- output contract
- requirement contract
- auction with/without reserve
- bulk transfer

Sales

In the previous eight chapters, you studied general contract law, which governs contracts for such things as real estate, employment, and personal services. This chapter explains a different type of law—the law of sales—that governs contracts for the sale and lease of goods. A **sale** is a contract in which ownership of goods is transferred from the seller to the buyer for consideration. The consideration is also known as the **price**, or the money that is paid for goods. **Goods** are all things that are moveable, such as your clothing, books, pens, food, car, and even the gas you put in your car. Money, stocks, and bonds are not considered goods.

The law of sales grew from the practices of business people, merchants, and mariners in early English times. In those days, merchants administered the law in their own courts. As time went on, the early law of sales combined with English common law and eventually was put into a code (a collection of laws) called the English Sale of Goods Act.

In 1906, a code of law called the Uniform Sales Act was introduced in the United States. It was similar to the English Sale of Goods Act, and over a period of years, was enacted by the legislatures of 35 states. However, it proved to be inadequate. As interstate commerce (trade between the states) developed, the need arose to make uniform the many commercial laws in effect among the states. The result was the development of the Uniform Commercial Code (UCC) in 1952. The **Uniform Commerical Code** is a collection of laws that governs various types of business transactions. When you enter a contract involving goods, the UCC will apply.

Example 1. Malika got a summer job at a Smoothie Shop on the same day that her parents bought a new house. To celebrate, her family went out to dinner. The day's activities involved three different contracts. Malika's oral employment contract and her parents' written contract to buy the house are governed by the law of contracts discussed in Unit 2. In contrast, the family's oral contract with the restaurant for dinner is a sale of goods and is governed by the UCC.

One purpose of UCC is to combine the laws relating to commerce into a single uniform code. Another purpose of the UCC is simplify,

268 Unit 3: *Understanding Consumer Law*

Exploring Section Assessment

Each section and chapter ends with assessment questions and activities designed to evaluate your understanding of the section material. The Section Assessment provides you with a chance to review and evaluate your comprehension of the important topics immediately before moving on to new concepts.

must sell the goods to the highest bidder. The goods cannot be withdrawn from bidding unless no bid is made. An auction sale is with reserve unless it is expressly stated that it is without reserve.

Have you visited an online auction Web site when searching for a new CD or plane tickets? Internet auctions have become increasingly popular. They offer opportunities to buy and sell goods locally and worldwide. Internet auctions can be person-to-person or business-to-person. In person-to-person auctions, sellers offer items directly to consumers. The highest bidder must deal directly with the seller to arrange for payment and delivery. In contrast, operators of business-to-person auctions have control of the items and handle the payment and delivery of goods.

Internet auction fraud is a concern. Sometimes sellers don't deliver the goods, or they deliver something less valuable than the item they advertised. At other times, sellers fail to deliver an item when they say they will. The Federal Trade Commission (FTC) provides information about Internet auctions in its free brochures and at its Web site.

Bulk Transfers

Sometimes a business transfers all merchandise and supplies at once, known as a **bulk transfer**. The UCC rules require that the buyer of the bulk goods notify all of the seller's creditors at least 10 days before the transfer will take place. The creditors then have the opportunity to take legal steps to get the money that is owed them before the transfer of the goods. Before this rule existed, merchants owing money could sell out their entire stock for less than it was worth.

Law & Academics

Social Studies
Before people exchanged money for goods, people traded goods for goods. This type of sale is called barter. The discovery of nonlocal objects at many archaeological sites suggests that barter existed in prehistoric times.

Research Activity
Anthropologists have found bartered goods throughout the world. Research a country that still uses barter as an important method of exchange. Find out what types of goods are bartered and how a value is placed on those goods. Write a one-page paper that explains your findings.

Section 13.1 Assessment

Reviewing What You Learned
1. When do you use the law of sales?
2. What special rules apply to sales contracts?
3. When must sales contracts be in writing? What are the exceptions?
4. What are some rules for auctions and bulk sales?

Critical Thinking Activity
Law of Sales When you contract for something that includes both goods and services, such as having wall-to-wall carpeting installed in your home, how should you determine whether to apply the law of sales?

Legal Skills in Action
Auctions Conduct a two-part mock auction of music CDs in front of your class. Have your classmates bring in CDs to be auctioned. (Be sure to mention that everything will be returned to the rightful owners after the auction.) Arrange for the first part of the role-play to be an auction without reserve and for the second part an auction with reserve.

Chapter 13: Contracts for the Sale of Goods **275**

Reviewing What You Learned
These questions require you to recall important section materials and key terms.

Critical Thinking Activity
This activity requires you to demonstrate an understanding of the concepts introduced in the section by interpreting, analyzing, comparing, or making judgments.

Legal Skills in Action
This question focuses on using basic mathematical, communication, interpersonal, writing, language arts, and thinking skills to explain concepts studied in the section.

Exploring Your Book

Exploring Chapter Assessment

Chapter Assessment activities are designed to be flexible and to address the multiple learning styles of your students.

Chapter Summary
The Chapter Summary provides a concise overview of the main concepts of the chapter. Organized by section, bulleted points highlight the main learning objectives of the material. You can use the summaries to prepare for exams and ensure that you understand the important concepts introduced in each of the chapters.

Using Legal Language
Using the legal vocabulary terms introduced in the chapter, you are asked to complete written, oral, and creative activities that require recollection of the terms and their definitions. Many of these activities require you to work as part of a team and participate in classroom activities.

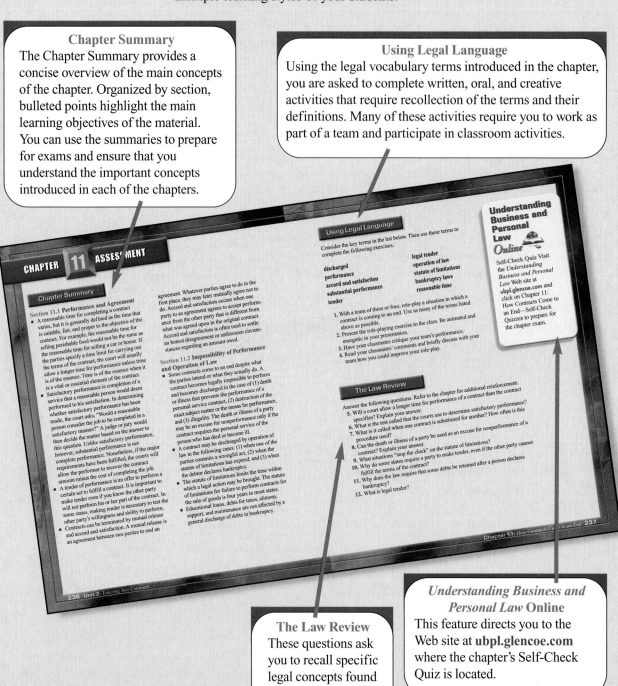

The Law Review
These questions ask you to recall specific legal concepts found in the chapter.

Understanding Business and Personal Law Online
This feature directs you to the Web site at **ubpl.glencoe.com** where the chapter's Self-Check Quiz is located.

Exploring Your Book

Linking School to Work
This feature is designed to relate legal studies to your work experiences and to those of your family, friends, or community members. For this feature, you are required to apply practical and analytical legal skills.

Grasping Case Issues
These cases present scenarios in which you are asked to interpret business or personal situations, identify a legal principle that applies, and state a decision on the issue. These case studies are hypothetical.

Analyzing Real Cases
This real-world feature challenges you to read and interpret actual cases, identify the legal issues at work, and apply applicable laws.

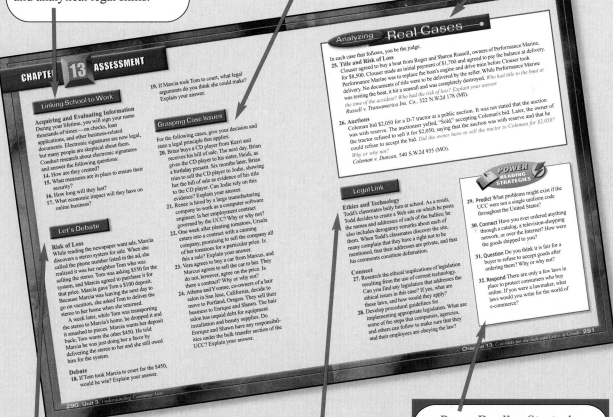

Let's Debate
This advocacy-related feature integrates critical thinking and communication skills into the exploration of legal issues introduced in the chapter.

Legal Link
This technology feature consists of a two-part activity designed to enhance your Web skills. The first part establishes a scenario or fact that relates to the legal issues introduced in the chapter. The second part asks you to research elements of the scenario and present your findings in written or oral formats.

Power Reading Strategies
These strategies incorporate active learning methods into your assessment experience. Predict, Connect, Question, and Respond questions extend learning by asking you to reflect on newly learned materials, relate this material to previous knowledge, and add personal conclusions to the discussion.

Exploring Your Book

Exploring the Law Workshops

Law Workshops are presented at the close of each unit of your book. These workshops focus on a legal issue presented within the unit. Hands-on application of the concept provides for active learning and fosters a deeper understanding of the materials presented.

Step A: Preparation
This part of the workshop introduces you to the problem and objectives of the workshop. You are also provided with effective strategies that will be employed to complete the activity.

Step B: Procedure
This section provides you with specific instructions for completing the workshop.

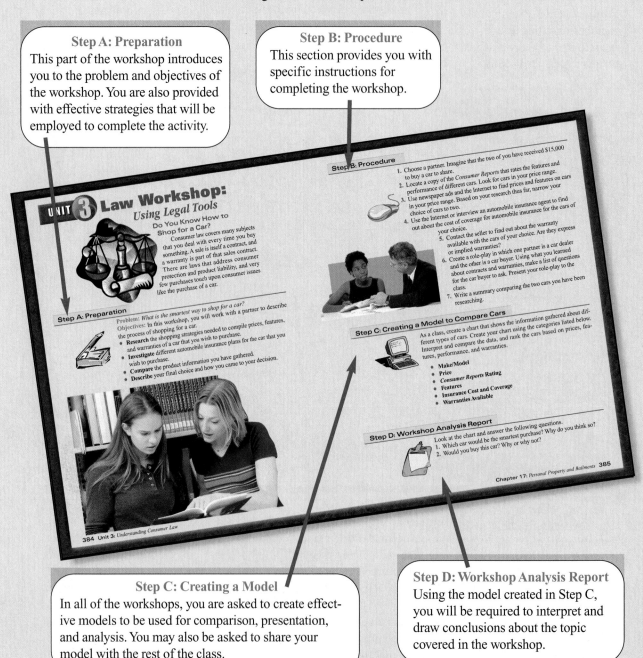

UNIT 3 Law Workshop:
Using Legal Tools

Do You Know How to Shop for a Car?
Consumer law covers many subjects that you deal with every time you buy something. A sale is itself a contract, and a warranty is part of that sales contract. There are laws that address consumer protection and product liability, and very few purchases touch upon consumer issues like the purchase of a car.

Step A: Preparation

Problem: *What is the smartest way to shop for a car?*
Objectives: In this workshop, you will work with a partner to describe the process of shopping for a car.
• **Research** the shopping strategies needed to compile prices, features, and warranties of a car that you wish to purchase.
• **Investigate** different automobile insurance plans for the car that you wish to purchase.
• **Compare** the product information you have gathered.
• **Describe** your final choice and how you came to your decision.

384 Unit 3: *Understanding Consumer Law*

Step B: Procedure
1. Choose a partner. Imagine that the two of you have received $15,000 to buy a car to share.
2. Locate a copy of the *Consumer Reports* that rates the features and performance of different cars. Look for cars in your price range.
3. Use newspaper ads and the Internet to find prices and features on cars in your price range. Based on your research thus far, narrow your choice of cars to two.
4. Use the Internet or interview an automobile insurance agent to find out about the cost of coverage for automobile insurance for the cars of your choice.
5. Contact the seller to find out about the warranty available with the cars of your choice. Are they express or implied warranties?
6. Create a role-play in which one partner is a car dealer and the other is a car buyer. Using what you learned about contracts and warranties, make a list of questions for the car buyer to ask. Present your role-play to the class.
7. Write a summary comparing the two cars you have been researching.

Step C: Creating a Model to Compare Cars
As a class, create a chart that shows the information gathered about different types of cars. Create your chart using the categories listed below. Interpret and compare the data, and rank the cars based on prices, features, performance, and warranties.
• **Make/Model**
• **Price**
• **Consumer Reports Rating**
• **Features**
• **Insurance Cost and Coverage**
• **Warranties Available**

Step D: Workshop Analysis Report
Look at the chart and answer the following questions.
1. Which car would be the smartest purchase? Why do you think so?
2. Would you buy this car? Why or why not?

Chapter 17: *Personal Property and Bailments* **385**

Step C: Creating a Model
In all of the workshops, you are asked to create effective models to be used for comparison, presentation, and analysis. You may also be asked to share your model with the rest of the class.

Step D: Workshop Analysis Report
Using the model created in Step C, you will be required to interpret and draw conclusions about the topic covered in the workshop.

Exploring Your Book

Exploring the Landmark Cases

Landmark Cases are extensive, two-page case studies found at the end of each unit. Actual cases have been selected that feature legal issues covered in the unit. These cases are also presented in a way that helps you understand the study of case law by clearly identifying the issue, facts, opinion, and holding in each case.

Holding
The holding identifies the final ruling of the court in the case. It answers the question(s) identified in the issue.

Issue
The issue explicitly identifies the legal question(s) that the court must resolve in the case.

Facts
The facts present the relevant information and sequence of events involved in the case.

Opinion
The opinion section of the case explains the court's interpretation and application of the law. It also gives you the court's reasoning and allows you to understand the grounds for their holding in the case.

Web Resources
This feature directs you to the course Web site, where you can find additional resources on each of the Landmark Cases.

Questions for Analysis
These questions ask you to understand the specifics of the case, identify the legal issues, and explain how the court interpreted and applied the law.

Features

Your *Understanding Business and Personal Law* book includes several features, each varying in length, scope, and focus. The purpose of these features is to enrich your learning experience, help you understand the practical applications of the concepts and skills you learn throughout this program, and encourage your curiosity, critical thinking, and creativity. They also connect what you learn to legal careers and to other academic disciplines, encourage you to become actively involved in your community, and suggest a variety of research projects to extend, enrich, and assess your understanding of business and personal law topics.

Community Works

These features focus on law and community involvement. They introduce you to issues such as volunteer work, neighborhood watches, substance abuse, graffiti, and handicap accessibility laws, among many others. A suggested activity at the end of each feature will give you ideas for becoming more involved in your community and in community service.

Community Works

Gifts
A gift is something that is given freely without consideration. Gifts can come in the form of money, time, or valuable items such as clothes, books, or supplies. Giving gifts is a wonderful way to enrich the lives of others. *What kind of gift do you give regularly?*

Get Involved
Give the gift of shelter. Contact organizations like Habitat for Humanity, which builds homes for low-income families, and find out how you can get involved.

Careers in Law

Learn more about the law from an actual practitioner who works in a legal field. In this feature, you will be introduced to their career in their own words and learn about their motivations and interests. You will also learn about the constructive role they play in the profession and in the community, and find information about the personal and educational requirements for pursuing a similar career.

Careers in Law

District Court Judge

At age 12, Annette Scieszinski knew that she wanted to be part of the legal system. "I thought that lawyers should do the right thing and serve the public," she says from her office in Ottumwa, Iowa. "I still think that."

Today, Scieszinski is a district court judge who presides over a wide range of civil and criminal cases. She spends about half of her time handling trials and the proceedings leading up to them. One day she may be in her chambers, helping lawyers resolve issues in a contract dispute. The next day she may be in court, instructing a jury about a murder case.

The other half of Scieszinski's time is spent researching the law, updating judicial forms, and deciding what documents she needs to help settle a case. In nonjury trials, she also devotes at least one afternoon to "ruling time."

"'Ruling time' is kind of like study hall," she says. "When I preside over a nonjury trial, I'm the one who decides the verdict. So after I've taken evidence and heard testimony, I use ruling time to study the law and write my opinion."

Scieszinski says that judges can make a difference in peoples' lives. "This is a great job," she says. "It gives you an opportunity to creatively help people solve their problems and understand that even if they lose their case, justice is done."

Skills	Oral and written communication, logic, library and database research, interpersonal
Personality	Even-tempered, self-motivated, conscientious
Education	Many undergraduate majors, but English and economics are particularly useful; law degree; broad practice (not just trial work)

For more information on district court judges, visit ubpl.glencoe.com or your public library.

A Global Perspective: Laws Around the World

As businesses expand and people travel, it is important to learn about other countries and cultures. This feature will spotlight the judicial system or other legal facts of interest in other countries and societies. The purpose is to provide you with insight into other cultures and how those cultures are organized and expressed in law. You will also learn basic facts about the countries profiled, including their population, geographical area, capital, language, religion, and life expectancy. The feature will also include a critical thinking question to encourage further exploration of the country and legal issues discussed.

A Global Perspective: Laws Around the World

Russia

What if you were forbidden to listen to your favorite music, read a popular book, or attend church? Suppose you weren't even allowed to express your opinions. For much of the twentieth century, Russian citizens were denied these basic rights. In the late 1980s, however, under the leadership of Mikhail S. Gorbachev (1985–1991), the policy of Glasnost (openness) was officially adopted by the former Soviet Union. In an effort to free up many aspects of Soviet life, Glasnost removed bans from books, movies, and plays, and even permitted criticism of the political system. In 1990, the former Soviet Union promised religious freedom. The parliament also passed a new press law banning manipulation of the mass media, including newspapers, radio, and television. For many Russians, freedom of expression still comes at a high price. Nevertheless, says Gorbachev, "tremendous gains allowed Russia to go forward. It will never return to the past." Here's a snapshot of Russia.

Geographical area	6,592,692 sq. mi.
Population	144,978,573
Capital	Moscow
Legal system	Based on civil law system
Language	Russian
Religion	Russian Orthodox
Life expectancy	67 years

Critical Thinking Question Is censorship of public information and restriction of social or political activities ever appropriate? List several examples. For more information on Russia, visit ubpl.glencoe.com or your local library.

Touring the Features

It's a Question of Ethics

This feature presents real-life situations relating to topics covered in your book and raises ethical questions (and the dilemmas they often present) for you to consider and discuss. You are encouraged to think not just about what the law says and how it applies, but also to identify the ethical issues involved and ethical courses of action. The feature encourages you to think critically and creatively, and to apply your problem-solving skills to circumstances in which clearly right or wrong solutions may not be available.

It's a Question of Ethics

Gestures of Kindness

Michael Baird's car would not start. He was stuck in the parking lot of Turner Field at 11:00 P.M. with a dead battery. As Rich and Marg Spratling drove by, they offered to help by jump-starting Michael's car. The jump-start worked, and the engine of Michael's car came to life. As Rich was disconnecting the jumper cables, Michael asked for their address. He wanted to send them $25 for their trouble. *Is Michael legally or ethically obligated to send the money?*

Touring the Features

Law & Academics

The law is related to a variety of other academic disciplines, and this feature draws connections between business and personal law and other interesting areas of the curriculum. Examples include business, social studies, mathematics, and anthropology, to name only a few. The interdisciplinary approach of this feature will help you perceive and pursue interesting links between the law and other academic fields. Each feature also includes a research activity for you to pursue individually or in a group.

Law & Academics

Language Arts

Many screenwriters for movies and television develop story lines that revolve around legal situations. For example, screenwriters might depict a person entering into an agreement under duress as part of a story line. In old western movies, ranches were often sold for a fraction of their value because of duress. Many movies about organized crime depict small business owners who are forced to turn over part of their earnings to the "family" to stay in business.

Research Activity

With a partner, write a mini-screenplay with a story line involving duress.

Touring the Features

Laws in Your Life

Have you ever wanted to start a band? When you get in trouble, do you wish that you could be judged by a court of your fellow teens? Are you curious about minimum wage laws, or whether you are bound by your promises? These questions and countless others like them point to the fact that the law is an integral part of your daily life. These features emphasize the diverse ways in which the law is part of your life, and they encourage you to think about its real-world applications. Each feature also includes critical thinking questions for you to consider or a research activity for you to pursue.

LAWS in Your Life

Extended Warranties

Almost any time you purchase stereo or electronic equipment, the salesperson will encourage you to buy an extended product warranty or service contract. The sale of such warranties represents big profits to the merchant. Profit margins can be up to 50 percent of the price of the extended warranty contract.

The value of buying an extended warranty can be debated. Original product warranties cover any breakdowns that might occur early in the life of the product. Most of the time, major defects will show up within the period covered by the original warranty.

If the item breaks after the original warranty expires, most states offer recourse under certain conditions. If you had repairs made under the original warranty, the seller or manufacturer must extend your warranty to cover the defect if it happens again. This is true even if the original warranty has expired.

Compare and Contrast Visit a local electronics or appliance store. Ask to see an original warranty. Then ask to see an extended warranty contract. Does the cost seem worthwhile in relation to the risk of breakdowns beyond the original warranty period?

Touring the Features

Legal Briefs

Legal Briefs

A multimillion-dollar masterpiece painted by Monet entitled "Nympheas, 1904" that had been plundered by the Nazis during World War II was identified by the granddaughter of its rightful owner when it was displayed at the Boston Museum of Fine Arts in 1998. The museum had borrowed the painting from a French museum. Upon learning that it was stolen, the French government returned the painting to the heirs of its rightful owner.

These short features discuss fun, interesting facts that add to your understanding of legal or law-related issues. They may also add background or context to the chapter material, or encourage thought-provoking classroom discussions.

Your Justice Journal

To be successful in a legal profession, you must have excellent writing skills. For this reason, you will be asked to keep a journal throughout this course. This feature appears with every unit in your book. Its emphasis is writing in your journal and how important it is for you to be able to clearly and effectively communicate your ideas in written form. The subject matter of your journal is diverse; you may be asked to write on some aspect of the law, something you learn in the unit, or something pertinent to your daily life. You will be required to solve problems, think creatively, and critically examine the law and related issues.

YOUR Justice Journal

Buyer Beware Your best friend bought a used car. From the day he bought the car, he has had nothing but problems. Now he needs a new transmission. He would like to take the car to the junkyard, but he still owes $900 on it.

In your Justice Journal, write about precautions your friend could have taken to be a better consumer and what you think he should do now.

Touring the Features

Virtual Law

Technology is becoming an increasingly common and important part of everyone's life. With computers, cell phones, the Internet, and other technologies have arisen new and exciting issues in the law. Do you have a right to privacy over the Internet? How safe is it to shop online? Are contracts made over the Internet binding on the parties? These and many other intriguing issues are the focus of these features. You will be asked to research issues involving law and technology, and to utilize current technology in developing and managing legal documents.

Virtual Law

E-Book Publishing Rights

Until recently, few book contracts specified who owned the rights to publish electronic versions of printed books. This issue has become increasingly important because income from the sale of electronic books has grown as this format has become more popular. Publishers argue that they own the right to sell digital editions of printed books, even when their contract with an author might not address the issue. Publishers compare their industry to the film industry, where studios have the right to sell videotapes of movies. Publishers have started to change their contract language over the past several years to refer specifically to electronic books. Most authors argue that there is no genuine agreement on this issue until such language is included. (Source: *New York Times*, February 28, 2001, p. C5)

Connect Go to the Web site for Text and Academic Authors (TAA) and see what this group has to say about electronic rights.

GORDON W. BROWN studied law to become a more knowledgeable teacher with expertise in the legal field. He attended Suffolk University Law School, Boston, MA, at night for four years, while teaching during the day. After law school, he became a member of the Massachusetts Bar and took a position as a professor at North Shore Community College, Danvers, MA, where he taught for the next thirty years. Before ending his thirty-eight year teaching career, he taught business, secretarial, and paralegal subjects at Pepperell High School, Pepperell, MA; Endicott College, Beverly, MA; and North Shore Community College. In addition to teaching, he also opened a law office in Beverly,

MA, and enjoyed a full-time career of practicing law, writing textbooks, and being a husband to his wife Jane, the father of six very special children, and a grandfather to twelve grandchildren. In 1998, Mr. Brown was awarded the Outstanding Educator Award from his alma mater, Salem State College. In addition to this text, Mr. Brown is the author of *Legal Terminology*, published by Prentice Hall, and *Administration of Wills, Trusts, and Estates*, published by West, Legal Studies. He is also co-author of *Business Law with UCC Applications*, published by Irwin/McGraw-Hill. Currently, Mr. Brown continues to be a practicing attorney and is an active member of the Massachusetts and Federal Bars.

PAUL A. SUKYS is professor of humanities, law, and legal studies in the Arts and Sciences Division of North Central State College in Mansfield, OH. In addition to teaching business law courses at North Central State College, he specializes in teaching interdisciplinary courses including, "The Legal and Ethical Aspect of Health Care," Science, Art, and Literature, "The History of the Future," "Contemporary Ethical Issues," and "The Philosophy of Technology." In

2001, he received the Pushing the Envelope Award at North Central State and in 1998 was named North Central's Outstanding Teacher of the Year. He is the author of *Lifting the Scientific Veil: Science Appreciation for the Nonscientist* and co-author of two additional books, *Business Law With UCC Applications* and *Civil Litigation*. He was chairperson of the Business Law Committee in the development of the National Standards for Business Education established by the National Business Education Association (NBEA). Along with Cynthia Redmond of Bozeman High School in Bozeman,

MT, he developed the business law lesson plans for *Entrepreneurship Teaching Strategies*, jointly sponsored by the NBEA and the Kauffman Foundation. At present, he is working on the business law chapter for NBEA's *2003 Yearbook*. In 1966, he was a member of the DANTES *Ethics in America* National Writing Committee sponsored by the Chauncey Group International. A member of the Ohio Bar, Professor Sukys received his bachelor's and master's degrees from the John Carroll University in Cleveland and his law degree from Cleveland State University. He also attended additional classes at New York University and Kenyon College. He is presently working on his doctorate in applied philosophy and art history at the Union Institute in Cincinnati. He has also taught at John Carroll University, the Fairmount Center for Creative and Performing Arts, and Cuyahoga Community College. Currently he is writing a new book entitled *Quantum Relativity: The Philosophical, Artistic, and Literary Dimensions of the Theory of Everything*.

Reviewers

We gratefully acknowledge the contributions of the reviewers of this program:

Arthur James Akins
Assistant Principal
Administration of Student Affairs
Hillsborough High School
Tampa, Florida

Carmen Cantrell
Business Education Department Head and Instructor
Nampa High School
Nampa, Idaho

Deborah Clark
Business Teacher
Princeton High School
Princeton, West Virginia

Delores S. Cotton
Business Education Department Head
Henry Ford High School
Detroit, Michigan

Coralee Dahl
Business Teacher
Wells High School
Wells, Nevada

Amber Day
Business Teacher
Nova High School
Coral Springs, Florida

Claire Dillion
Business Teacher
Potomac Falls High School
Sterling, Virginia

Michael Duncan
Business and Marketing Teacher
Castle High School
Newburgh, Indiana

Jeane Geurin
Business Teacher
Mt. Vernon High School
Mt. Vernon, Indiana

Sandy Hanshaw
Business Teacher
Nicholas City High School
Summersville, West Virginia

Diane P. Hogan
Program Specialist, Business Education
Orange County Public Schools
Orlando, Florida

Lynn Huggins
Business Instructor
Institute for Global Commerce and Government
Tracy, California

Bergie R. Jones
Business Education Instructor
Jim Hill High School
Jackson, Mississippi

Francis Michelle Kirkland
Business Teacher
Vidor High School
Vidor, Texas

Patrick W. Knowles
Vocational Department Head
Marketing/Business Instructor
West Valley High School
Spokane, Washington

Ann Lori Larsen
Business Education Instructor
Sunny Hills High School
Fullerton, California

Dr. William C. Lauer
Chairman, Business Education
Ocean City High School
Ocean City, New Jersey

Richard M. Lazeroff
Business Education Instructor
Rush Henrietta Central School District
Henrietta, New York

John Marsh
Business Education Instructor
Fargo South High School
Fargo, North Dakota

Robert L. Mata
Academic Dean, Cedar Rapids Campus
Hamilton Business College
Cedar Rapids, Iowa

Trina McLean
Business Teacher
Phoebus High School
Hampton, Virginia

Judy Mitchell
Business Department Chair
Thomas More High School
Hays, Kansas

Cynthia Redmond
Business Teacher
Bozeman High School
Bozeman, Montana

Raymond P. Rogina
Chairperson, Business Education Instructor
St. Charles North High School
St. Charles, Illinois

Donna Scheuerer
Business Teacher
Farmingdale High School
Farmingdale, New York

Gardenia S. Sligh
Business Education Instructor
Columbia High School
Columbia, South Carolina

Moira Sweeting
Business Teacher
McArthur High School
Hollywood, Florida

Kay Tippett
Business Education Instructor
Bozeman High School
Bozeman, Montana

We also wish to extend special thanks to Jane A. Brown for her work on the Student Activity Workbook and for her many suggestions that helped to improve this law program.

Gordon W. Brown
Paul A. Sukys

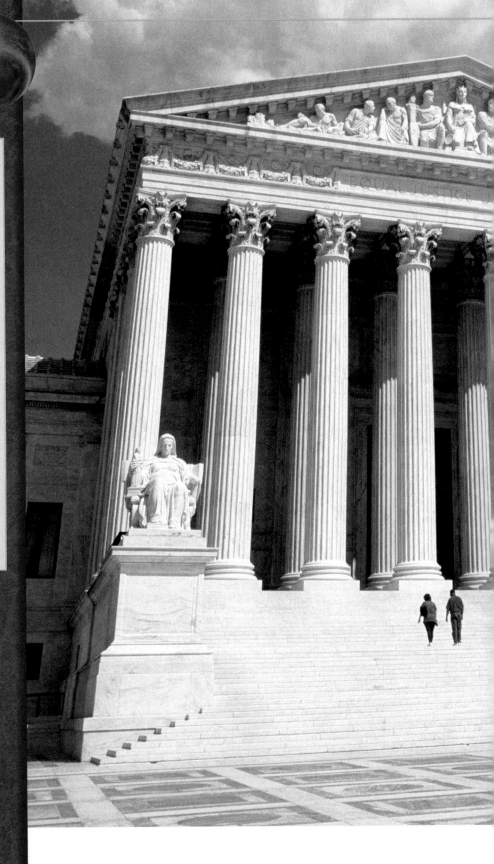

UNIT 1

UNIT OVERVIEW

Laws generally reflect and promote the values of our society. Our legal system is intended to protect the welfare, safety, and diverse interests of individuals and society more generally. Laws that protect our freedoms, encourage positive interaction with others, and prohibit harmful behavior help improve our society. In this unit, you will study:

- Ethics and the law
- The court system
- Criminal law
- The law of torts

Knowing About the Law

YOUR *Justice Journal*

Birthday Bonus You received a popular computer game for your birthday. When your friends found out, they asked you to burn a copy for them on your CD writer.

In your Justice Journal, write about the legality of copying the program, the ethical dilemma you face, and what you would tell your friends.

POWER READING STRATEGIES

To get the most out of your reading:
PREDICT what the section will be about.
CONNECT what you read with your own life.
QUESTION as you read to make sure you understand the content.
RESPOND to what you've read.

Ethics and the Law

Understanding Business and Personal Law *Online*

Chapter Overview Visit the *Understanding Business and Personal Law* Web site at ubpl.glencoe.com and click on Chapter 1: Ethics and the Law—Chapter Overviews to preview the chapter information.

The Opening Scene

Starting in this chapter, you will meet Jamila and Trai, who attend New Hope High School. They are having a discussion in their sixth-period law class, taught by Mrs. Ovelia Martinez.

A Debate about Ethics

MRS. MARTINEZ: Okay, class, let's get settled. The bell rang two minutes ago. Our first order of business today involves something a little out of the ordinary. I think many of you will find it interesting. I need volunteers! The principal wants to know if anyone in this class wants to volunteer for peer mediation.

TRAI: I volunteer Jamila.

JAMILA: Peer what?

MRS. MARTINEZ: Very funny, Trai. Haven't you heard of peer mediation, Jamila? It is when students help decide disputes. A three-day training program is scheduled next weekend at Centerburg High.

TRAI: A three-day training program? Does that mean I can miss three days of school if I volunteer to be a peer mediator? If yes, you can count me in! I could use a break from school.

MRS. MARTINEZ: If I were you, Trai, I wouldn't rush into this. The program's not a vacation—you'll be involved in some extensive training. It's not easy to be a peer mediator. Peer mediators have to make complicated decisions. Plus, it's not easy to make fair decisions when you're dealing with friends and classmates.

TRAI: Who needs training? All you have to know is the difference between right and wrong.

JAMILA: Well, not everyone knows the difference.

TRAI: That's not true. Your religion tells you the difference.

JAMILA: Not everyone is religious. You can't assume that every family is like yours, Trai.

FELICIA: It depends on how you're raised. Your parents should tell you what's right and wrong.

PEGGY: My Dad says everything I do is wrong.

DANIEL: When I do something wrong, I get a queasy feeling in my stomach.

TRAI: That's your lunch.

PEGGY: I thought right and wrong come from the Constitution—if it says something is wrong, then it's wrong.

MRS. MARTINEZ: You are partially right, but laws change. Does that mean right and wrong change?

DANIEL: Maybe right and wrong are just a matter of opinion.

JAMILA: If that's true, then maybe morality is no big deal.

MRS. MARTINEZ: Oh, I think it's a very big deal. Judging from some previous class discussions we've had, I think that you think morality is a big deal, too.

TRAI: I agree with Mrs. Martinez. For instance, I bet she would never punish somebody for something they didn't do. Isn't that right, Mrs. Martinez?

MRS. MARTINEZ: Of course. That would be wrong.

TRAI: Sweet!

MRS. MARTINEZ: Why?

TRAI: Because I didn't do my homework.

What Are the Legal Issues?

1. What is the source of morality and ethics?
2. Should ethical decisions be based on a person's feelings or opinions?
3. Do ethical and legal issues ever conflict?
4. Do ethical standards ever change?
5. Does the law ever change in the United States?

Defining Ethics

What You'll Learn

- How ethical decisions are made
- When to apply the greatest good principle
- When to apply the Golden Rule principle
- How to explain the nature of ethical character traits
- When law relates to ethics
- How to explain the importance of law
- How ethics and the law might sometimes conflict

Why It's Important

Learning how to apply ethical principles will help you make ethical decisions.

Legal Terms

- morality
- ethics
- honesty
- justice
- compassion
- integrity
- law

How Ethical Decisions Are Made

Determining the difference between right and wrong can be difficult. Individuals use different methods to choose the right thing to do in any given situation. Some people follow their conscience. Others just make certain that they always follow the rules. Some people look to religious teachings or professional codes of conduct. Others do as their parents taught them.

Defining morals and ethics can be difficult. **Morality** involves the values that govern a society's attitude toward right and wrong. **Ethics**, in contrast, are the means for determining what a society's values *ought* to be. In this text, the words *ethics* and *morality* will be used to encompass both ideas.

Throughout your life, you will face many ethical problems. Adopting a consistent ethical standard can help you deal with big or small moral problems, from deciding how much to tip a waiter to whether to support military spending.

Feelings and Opinions

In The Opening Scene, Daniel said that he knows he is doing something wrong when he gets a queasy feeling in his stomach. Later he suggests that right and wrong may be a matter of opinion. Both ideas imply that right and wrong can change depending on a person's feelings and opinions.

The view that ethics are based on changing feelings is popular in the United States. Our nation was founded on a tradition of tolerance and encourages a free exchange of ideas, feelings, and opinions on every subject, including ethics. In addition, the United States is a country of immigrants from a variety of cultures, many of which have different ethical values. In an attempt to respect all cultures, we often conclude that each culture is right, even when its values clash with others.

Some people, however, see a problem with this view. They argue that if ethics are just a matter of opinion or feelings, then no one can ever do anything that is wrong.

Example 1. Harriet comes from a poor family, but Frank's family is wealthy. Harriet believes that Frank has more money than he needs. When Frank leaves his backpack unattended, Harriet steals it. She defends her actions by saying that she needs the backpack and that Frank can buy another one.

Most of us would say that Harriet's theft is wrong, even though she thought she was right. In fact, most of us would say she is wrong even if there were no law against theft. How do we make that decision? One way is to consider how an action helps or hurts people who are affected by it. As you will learn later in this chapter, Harriet's theft is wrong for two reasons: because it hurt Frank and because it set a bad example for others.

The Greatest Good

Most people are not hermits; instead, they live and work together in society. Because of these relationships, every action has the potential to affect other people. When a person does something that hurts innocent people, many others would judge that person's action as wrong. Such a decision is based on whether an action will create the greatest good for the greatest number of people. The more good that results, the more ethical the action.

Some people see the greatest good principle as a natural way to make ethical decisions. Others, however, believe it is often misapplied.

Example 2. Alame knows that 10 of her 20 classmates cheated on their last law exam. The teacher mistakenly believes that only one innocent student is guilty of cheating. Alame decides she will keep silent because doing so will ensure the greatest good for the greatest number of people.

TAKING ADVANTAGE
Some people believe that they can do as they please because ethical standards are flexible and changing. *Why would such an attitude cause difficulties in the world today?*

Alame has misapplied the greatest good principle. Her failure to identify the 10 guilty students helps only the cheaters. Alame has also not considered the unethical example that her decision will set for the whole school or how the decision may affect the school's academic standards. In addition, Alame's decision to keep quiet is not fair to the innocent student, who must take the blame for the guilty parties.

A Global Perspective:
Laws Around the World

Ghana

A law can be a decree, a prohibition, a statue, a treaty, or any rule or principle that must be obeyed. Laws can also take the form of traditions—unwritten laws or doctrines handed down from generation to generation. In Ghana, festivals are such an important part of tradition that citizens were once given time off from work for celebrations. Fines were even levied against those who did not attend festivals.

Ghana's most important festival, Odwira, celebrates the harvest of the yams. Forty days before the festival all noise, including singing and dancing, is banned. On each day, the event follows a strict set of rules or observances—from sweeping the path to the mausoleum of the past chiefs to an entire day of silence when the whole village honors its dead. The festival's highlight, the durbar, comes on the last day. All neighboring lesser chiefs march through town escorted by drummers and servants carrying guns and swords of gold. Then with singing, dancing, and feasting, the chiefs settle in the main square and pledge their respect and loyalty to the regional chief. Odwira is a time of thanksgiving, remembrance, and fellowship. Here's a snapshot of Ghana.

Geographical area	**92,100 sq. mi.**
Population	**20,244,154**
Capital	**Accra**
Legal System	**based on English common and customary law**
Language	**English, African languages**
Life expectancy	**57**

Critical Thinking Question What are some of the reasons that people celebrate traditions? What are some of your family or school traditions? For more information on Ghana, visit **ubpl.glencoe.com** or your local library.

The Golden Rule

As commonly expressed, the Golden Rule holds, "Do unto others as you would have them do unto you." Many people prefer this rule because of its consistency and its universal appeal. Although some may identify the Golden Rule with Christianity, many religions embrace its principles. Buddhism, for example, states, "Hurt not others with that which pains thyself."

The heart of the Golden Rule is empathy, which means putting yourself in another person's position. One way to test the morality of an action under the Golden Rule is to ask yourself, "Would I want to be treated this way?" If your answer is "no," then the action probably violates the Golden Rule. The principle of good sportsmanship that you learn in athletics is an outgrowth of the Golden Rule.

Example 3. Steve is the star pitcher on New Hope High School's varsity baseball team. During a tough inning against the Vikings of St. Joseph High, Steve gets frustrated and throws two pitches at the Vikings' best batter. When the umpire ejects Steve from the game, his coach does not argue. The coach tells Steve, "You were wrong. If it's right for you to throw at their batters, then it would be right for their pitchers to throw at our batters." Steve agrees that he would not want to be a pitcher's target.

Although the Golden Rule appears easy to follow, it can be difficult to fully understand. Some people may also abuse the rule by placing their own self-interest above the interests of others.

Example 4. Stanley was judging a debate held in social studies class. He gave Abia a better grade than she deserved because he knew she might be assigned to judge his debate. He wanted her to give him a good grade in return, regardless of whether he deserved it.

Even if he does not realize it, Stanley violated the spirit of the Golden Rule.

The Golden Rule or similar moral principle has been adopted by many of the world's major religions for two reasons. First, the rule respects the dignity and worth of individuals.

THE GOLDEN RULE
The Golden Rule has been adopted as a guiding moral precept by most of the major religions of the world. *Why would most religions find it comfortable to assimilate this moral precept?*

Legal Briefs

The Golden Rule, or the ethic of reciprocity, is often regarded as the most concise and general principle of ethics.

People want to be treated with respect. The Golden Rule says that those who wish to be treated with respect must first be respectful of others.

Example 5. Vanessa's older sister, Mary Eileen, frequently goes into Vanessa's room while she is not there and borrows clothing without permission. When Vanessa approaches Mary Eileen about this problem, Mary Eileen laughs it off and points out that she is the older sister, not the one who should take orders. This upsets Vanessa because she always asks permission before she takes something from her sister's room.

Vanessa is expressing what most people consider the guiding principle of the Golden Rule—people want to be treated with respect.

The second reason the Golden Rule has been widely accepted is that, if followed properly, it can be applied in almost every situation. A rule that cannot be followed consistently may be abused by those who wish to justify their own immoral actions.

Example 6. Freida and her boyfriend, Emil, have just had a serious argument. To make Emil jealous, Freida tells Luke that she will go to the movies with him on Friday night, even though she has no intention of doing so. When Emil finds out about Freida's date with Luke, he and Freida make up. Freida then breaks her date with Luke.

Freida has adopted a rule that says, "I will make promises to get what I want even if I don't intend to keep those promises." If everyone acted in this manner, people would refuse to trust the promises of others and a complete breakdown in society would result. A world without promises would be a world without commerce, credit, law, or social engagements.

Freida's rule violates the spirit of the Golden Rule. Consider this opposite case.

Example 7. Esther likes Quon, who is Irma's boyfriend. Although Esther would love to go to the homecoming dance with Quon, she promises Michael she will go with him. Then Quon breaks up with Irma and asks Esther to go to the dance. Even though she really wants to go with Quon, she says, "Sorry, I already promised Michael I'd be going with him."

By keeping her word, Esther has adopted a principle that is consistent with the Golden Rule. If everyone acted in this manner, there would be a stable social order based on trust. Unfortunately, not everyone in our society abides by the principle of the Golden Rule.

Figure 1.1 — Ethical Characteristics

Trait	Definition
Honesty	Honesty allows a person to be open and truthful with other people.
Fairness	Fairness allows a person to treat other people with justice and equality.
Compassion	Compassion allows a person to care for others.
Integrity	Integrity allows a person to do what is right, regardless of personal consequences.

ETHICAL CHARACTERISTICS People in history and fiction who have led exemplary lives often have key ethical traits. *Who are some famous people in history or fiction who display more than one of the named character traits?*

Ethical Character Traits

In trying to determine what makes a person ethical, it helps to think of some ethical people. Many of the same names come up as answers: Abraham Lincoln, Albert Schweitzer, Mother Theresa, Mohandas Gandhi, and Martin Luther King, Jr. Fictional characters often mentioned include Don Quixote, Nick Carraway, Sherlock Holmes, Superman, and Wonder Woman. See Figure 1.1 for a list of the character traits that many of these people share. What character traits do those people have that make them ethical?

Honesty

A character trait of a person who is open and truthful in dealings with others is called **honesty**. We admire honesty because it is not easy to be honest in every situation. Most of us want to have honest friends and would like to be described by others as honest. An honest person is someone who tells the truth and can be trusted to keep his or her promises.

Justice

Another character trait ethical people share is **justice**. A person is said to be just if he or she treats people fairly and equally. Being just also means that a person is capable of treating everyone fairly, not just relatives and friends. Because most of us want to be treated with justice, it makes sense to treat others with justice as well. A just person will see that everyone gets his or her fair share of those things that are available to a group.

Compassion

Another trait attributed to ethical people is compassion. A person shows **compassion** when he or she is sympathetic to the difficulties of others and wants to help alleviate their problems. Compassion also involves a respect for other people and their right to make their own decisions. Compassionate people try to understand other people's shortcomings and forgive their mistakes.

Integrity

A person of **integrity** is willing to do the right thing, regardless of personal consequences. People with integrity stand up for their convictions, even if the majority is against them. They are willing to risk many things for the sake of their moral convictions.

The Relationship between Ethics and Law

We have already considered three ways to make ethical decisions: relying on opinions and feelings, gauging the greatest good for the greatest number of people, and following the Golden Rule. If these techniques always reached the same ethical result, and if everyone always acted by those results, there would be no need for law. In the real world, however, some people engage in certain types of conduct that most people agree are immoral or wrong.

Why Law is Necessary

Ethics tell us what we ought to do. Law is needed because people do not always do what they should. **Law** is the system of rules of conduct established by the government of a society to maintain stability and justice. It defines the legal rights and duties of the people. Law also provides a means of enforcing these rights and duties through law enforcement agencies, courts, legislatures, and regulatory agencies.

Law cannot always make people or businesses do what is best. However, law does have the power to punish people or businesses for doing things that are wrong. Consider the contrast between honest or dishonest and legal or illegal business practices.

> *Example 8.* World Cars, Inc. advertises its cars by saying "They're the best on the market!" even though it knows that, while functional and safe, they are quite ordinary. Best Auto Corp., a competitor, uses a similar slogan, but its cars violate several safety laws and are frequently involved in accidents.

Although World Cars, Inc. is in an ethical sense dishonest, their business practices are legal; the law cannot force them to make what are literally the best cars on the market. However, the law can punish Best Auto Corp., not because its slogan is dishonest, but rather because its business practice (of making shoddy cars) is illegal.

Ethical and Legal Conflicts

Because law is made by people, it is imperfect. Legislators and judges bring their personal views on ethics and morality to the law-making process. As a result, ethics and law will sometimes conflict.

Example 9. Clark is the editor of the Richmond High *Herald*. Rita tells Clark that another student is selling drugs on campus, but asks Clark not to reveal her identity in his news article or to the police. Clark agrees. When the article appears and the student is arrested, Clark has to testify at the trial. He refuses to identify his source and is held in contempt of court.

Clark has obeyed the ethics of journalism by refusing to identify the source of his story. He has, however, violated the law by refusing to obey the order of a judge.

While the law and ethical and social attitudes sometimes conflict, they also influence each other in various ways. Changes in individual or social ethics often prompt changes in the law; conversely, changes in the law that originally face resistance may gradually become generally accepted. While our ethical and social attitudes sometimes change, having law is better than letting each individual set their own rules or handle disputes in haphazard or even violent ways.

Section 1.1   Assessment

Reviewing What You Learned

1. Explain how ethical decisions are made.
2. How can the greatest good principle lead to ethical decisions?
3. How can the Golden Rule lead to ethical decisions?
4. What are four ethical character traits?
5. Analyze the effects of unethical and illegal practices on a business and on consumers. What are some consequences of such behavior?
6. Contrast honest or dishonest with legal or illegal business practices. Why are ethics and the law not always the same?
7. How might ethics and the law conflict?

Critical Thinking Activity

Ethics and Law Why is it important to distinguish between actions that are ethical and actions that are not? Why is it important to distinguish between ethics and law?

Legal Skills in Action

Business Ethics Analyze the effects of unethical and illegal practices on a business and on consumers. Create a chart with two columns. In the left column, list several unethical and illegal practices. In the right column, list the effects of such practices on a business and on consumers.

Sources of Law

What You'll Learn

- How to recognize the various parts of the U.S. Constitution
- How to explain the components of common law
- How to explain the purposes of statutory law
- How to identify the various ways that courts make law
- How the government makes administrative regulations

Why It's Important

Learning how the law is made will help you make decisions regarding your legal responsibilities.

Legal Terms

- constitution
- common law
- precedent
- statutes
- legislature
- unconstitutional
- administrative law

The Five Main Sources of U.S. Law

In general, law in the United States today comes from five main sources. Although these sources may seem different, they all pertain to the law in some way. See Figure 1.2 for a summary of these sources.

Constitutional Law

We have already defined law as rules of conduct established by the government of a society to maintain stability and justice. A country's **constitution** spells out the principles by which the government operates. In our country, the most fundamental law is the U.S. Constitution.

The Constitution of the United States Our Constitution sets forth the fundamental rights of citizens. It also defines the limits within

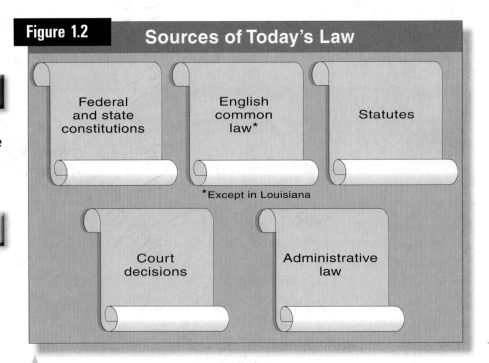

Figure 1.2   **Sources of Today's Law**

Federal and state constitutions

English common law*

Statutes

*Except in Louisiana

Court decisions

Administrative law

THE SOURCES OF U.S. LAW
The law as it exists in the United States today comes from five sources. *Which of these sources is shared by the federal and the state governments?*

Figure 1.3   United States Constitution

ARTICLE I.   The Legislative Branch

Section 1	Congress
Section 2	House of Representatives
Section 3	Senate
Section 4	Elections and Meetings
Section 5	Organization and Rules
Section 6	Privileges and Restrictions
Section 7	Passing Laws
Section 8	Powers of Congress
Section 9	Powers Denied to the Federal Government
Section 10	Powers Denied to the States

ARTICLE II.   The Executive Branch

Section 1	President and Vice President
Section 2	Powers of the President
Section 3	Duties of the President
Section 4	Impeachment

ARTICLE III.   The Judicial Branch

Section 1	Federal Courts
Section 2	Jurisdiction of the Federal Courts
Section 3	Treason

ARTICLE IV.   Relations among States

Section 1	Official Acts
Section 2	Mutual Duties of States
Section 3	New States and Territories
Section 4	Federal Protection of States

ARTICLE V.   The Amending Process

ARTICLE VI.   National Supremacy

ARTICLE VII.   The Ratification of the Constitution

Amendments to the Constitution

1st Amendment (1791)	Religious and Political Freedom
2nd Amendment (1791)	Right to Bear Arms
3rd Amendment (1791)	Quartering Troops
4th Amendment (1791)	Searches and Seizures
5th Amendment (1791)	Rights of Accused Persons
6th Amendment (1791)	Right to Speedy, Fair Trial
7th Amendment (1791)	Right to Jury Trial
8th Amendment (1791)	Bail and Punishment
9th Amendment (1791)	Rights Not Enumerated
10th Amendment (1791)	Powers Reserved to the States
11th Amendment (1798)	Suits against States
12th Amendment (1804)	Election of President and Vice President
13th Amendment (1865)	Abolition of Slavery
14th Amendment (1868)	Limitations on State Action
15th Amendment (1870)	Right to Vote
16th Amendment (1913)	Income Tax
17th Amendment (1913)	Direct Election of Senators
18th Amendment (1919)	Prohibition
19th Amendment (1920)	Women's Suffrage
20th Amendment (1933)	"Lame Duck" Amendment
21st Amendment (1933)	Repeal of Prohibition
22nd Amendment (1951)	Limit on Presidential Terms
23rd Amendment (1961)	Voting in the District of Columbia
24th Amendment (1964)	Abolition of Poll Tax
25th Amendment (1967)	Presidential Disability and Succession
26th Amendment (1971)	Eighteen-Year-Old Vote
27th Amendment (1992)	Instant Congressional Pay Raises Abolished

THE UNITED STATES CONSTITUTION
The United States Constitution consists of seven articles and 27 amendments. *Which of the amendments requires that state governments give their citizens the same rights that the federal government must give to U.S. citizens under the Fifth Amendment?*

Language Arts
The legal profession has a core of professional ethics. They are principles of conduct that members of the profession are expected to observe when they practice law. These principles stress that the lawyer's chief interest lies in serving his or her client and in securing justice.

Research Activity
What if high school students had a code of professional ethics? Work with three or four classmates to write the ethical principles that you think students in your school should observe.

which the federal and state governments may pass laws. In addition, the Constitution describes the functions of the various branches and divisions of our national government. See Figure 1.3 for an outline of the federal Constitution.

Articles I, II, and III of the Constitution set forth the structure and the powers of the three branches of the federal government. Article IV requires each state to give "full faith and credit" to the laws of all other states. That is, each state must accept the laws of other states. Article V tells how the Constitution may be amended or changed.

Article VI contains the supremacy clause. This clause states that the U.S. Constitution and the laws of the United States and treaties shall be the supreme laws of the land. Article VII, the last article, provided for ratification of the Constitution. This event took place in 1787.

The first 10 amendments, ratified in 1791, are called the Bill of Rights. They limit the powers of the government. The basic purpose of the Bill of Rights is to protect two kinds of rights: rights of individual liberty and rights of persons accused of crimes.

The Constitution now has 27 amendments. Let's take a look at one of them. The Fourteenth Amendment provides that no state shall "deprive any person of life, liberty, or property, without due process of law; nor deny to any person within its jurisdiction the equal protection of laws." This is known as the equal protection clause. As a major principle of justice, this amendment requires equal treatment of all people under the law. The Fourteenth Amendment requires state governments to give to their citizens the same rights that the federal government must give to U.S. citizens under the Fifth Amendment.

Example 10. Joe Hogan was denied admission to the Mississippi University for Women School of Nursing solely because of his gender. The university is supported by funds provided by the state government. In 1982, the U.S. Supreme Court held that the single-sex admissions policy of the state school violated the equal protection clause of the Fourteenth Amendment. The court said that the policy continued the stereotype of nursing as a woman's job. Hogan was admitted to the school of nursing.

State Constitutions   Each state has its own constitution. Although similar, state constitutions are not identical to the federal Constitution. They can be more protective, narrower, and more restrictive than the federal Constitution.

Example 11. Lawmakers in Massachusetts wanted to have a graduated income tax like the federal income tax. A graduated tax requires people with larger incomes to pay a higher tax rate than people with smaller incomes. Such a tax couldn't be passed, however, because the Massachusetts constitution requires all people to be taxed at an equal percentage rate.

Common Law

The legal system of all states, except for Louisiana, (where the influence is more French) is rooted in English common law. The early American colonists came from England, so it was natural for them to adopt the law of England in their new land.

In the early days of English history, the kings tried to centralize the English government and establish a court system. Judges, called justices or magistrates, traveled in circuits around the countryside deciding cases. Because there was no written law, judges often made decisions based on the customs and traditions of the people. Judges shared their decisions with other judges and made every effort to share the same law "in common" with everyone else throughout the country. This practice formed the basis of **common law**.

Eventually, court decisions were written down and a body of cases developed. Judges could then refer to past cases when making their decisions. This practice led to the doctrine of **precedent**. Under this doctrine, a judge is required to follow an earlier court decision when deciding a case with similar circumstances. It is also sometimes called the doctrine of *stare decisis*, which means, "let the decision stand."

Over time, the English common law eroded in the United States with the passing of state statutes and court decisions. Nevertheless, parts of the common law still exist today in some states' laws exactly as they did in England.

COMMON LAW
Common law depends on the doctrine of precedent. Under the doctrine of precedent, a judge is required to follow an earlier court decision when deciding a case with similar circumstances. *Do any parts of common law exist within the legal system today?*

Limits of Free Speech

The First Amendment guarantees Americans the right to express their thoughts and opinions. However, this freedom is not absolute. Some types of speech are not protected by the First Amendment, and engaging in such speech may result in civil or criminal penalties.

For example, you may not make any public statement on private property without the owner's permission, nor can you urge listeners to commit a crime. Also, you cannot, either publicly or in private conversations, knowingly make untrue, damaging statements about a person. Obviously, threats of violence and statements that constitute sexual harassment are not protected forms of expression, nor is obscene language in many situations.

Be aware that "speech" involves more than spoken words. Signs, posters, pamphlets, printed T-shirts, and other "writings" are among many modes of expression that the courts consider to be speech.

Ask First Would passing out flyers to advertise a school event in a store's parking lot be a First Amendment right? Call a few businesses to find out their policy regarding flyers.

Statutory Law

Statutes are laws specifically passed by a governing body that has been created for the purpose of making laws. A statute can be created to declare the law on a particular issue or governing certain circumstances. Statutes may also order people to do something. For example, a statute may require citizens to pay taxes or to sign up for the military draft when they reach 18 years of age. Other statutes forbid people from doing things. One statute prevents people from discriminating in employment or housing matters on the basis of race, color, creed, gender, or national origin.

Laws passed by the U.S. Congress, state legislatures, local city councils, or town meetings can all be called statutory law. Statutory law is found in state and federal statutes, city ordinances, and town bylaws. The different terms tell us at which level of government a law was passed.

Federal Statutes Laws that are passed by the U.S. Congress and signed by the president are called federal statutes. The United States

Congress is a **legislature**, or a body of lawmakers, that has the job of creating statutory law under the powers given to the federal government by Article I of the Constitution. These powers include such things as the power to spend, tax, and borrow money.

One important clause in the Constitution is Article I, Section 8, Clause 3. Called the commerce clause, it gives Congress the power to make laws regulating commerce among the states. Over the years, the courts have interpreted this clause very widely. This broad interpretation has given Congress enormous power, perhaps more than was originally envisioned by the framers of the Constitution in 1787.

As noted previously, the U.S. Constitution is the supreme law of the land. Consequently, Congress may not pass laws that conflict with the U.S. Constitution. The Supreme Court may declare any statute that goes against the Constitution **unconstitutional**, or invalid.

State Statutes   Each state also has its own legislature, or body of lawmakers, and most state legislatures are organized much like Congress. Ohio, for example, divides its General Assembly into a Senate and a House of Representatives. Although the names of the state legislatures may differ, their basic function is the same—to make statutory law. Like Congress, the state legislatures cannot pass statutes that conflict with the U.S. Constitution.

Court Decisions

Most people are surprised to learn that courts make law. Court-made law is often called case law, court decisions, and judge-made

Virtual Law

Whose Name Is It, Anyway?

An Internet domain name company has been taken to court, accused of tricking thousands of people. According to the Federal Trade Commission (FTC), the company sent faxes to Web site owners telling them that someone else was about to register an almost identical domain name. The purpose was to mislead people into paying a $70 fee to have the company block the domain name application. The FTC has asked the court to stop this unethical practice. They also asked that the court shut down Web sites that try to promote the activity. (Source: *New York Times*, p. C3, Feb. 16, 2001) **Connect** Search the Internet for a domain name registration, and research the site to review the processes involved.

Community Works

Adopt a Pet
Are you considering adopting a pet from an animal shelter? Don't be surprised if you must choose from many dogs or cats. Most shelters are full or overcrowded. Government shelters try to control overcrowding by euthanizing animals that are sick, dangerous, or never adopted. *Do you think euthanizing animals is an ethical issue, a legal issue, or both?*

Get Involved
Before you buy a pet from a pet store, check with your local animal shelter. Find out if your city's animal shelters euthanize animals, and if yes, under what conditions. Write a report for your class.

law. Courts make law in three ways: through the common law tradition, by interpreting statutes, and by judicial review.

Decisions made by the highest court of any state become the law of that state and must be followed by other courts in that state thereafter. In general, if not altered by statute, these precedents will continue to rule. It is possible, however, for the highest court of a state to change a line of precedent.

A second type of judicial decision involves interpreting statutes. When a statute seems to be confusing, incomplete, or unclear, it is the court's job to figure out what the statute means. A judge cannot interpret a statute, however, unless that statute is involved in a dispute between two parties in a lawsuit before that judge.

STATUTORY LAW
Statutory law is made by a legislature. The federal legislature is known as the U.S. Congress and is made up of the House of Representatives and the Senate. Statutes can order us to do something or forbid us to act in a certain way. *What are some examples of statutes that command or prohibit us?*

The courts can also decide whether laws and other government activities are consistent with the Constitution. Any laws or government actions that violate the Constitution can be declared unconstitutional by a court. The Supreme Court of the United States is the final authority regarding the constitutionality of all laws and government actions.

Administrative Regulations

Federal, state, and local legislatures sometimes find it desirable to regulate certain kinds of activities. Legislators, however, often do not have expert knowledge of a particular field. They also do not have the time to give their complete attention to any one kind of activity. For these and other reasons, legislatures often give the power to regulate a particular kind of activity to an administrative agency. Also called a regulatory agency, these agencies are departments of government formed to administer particular legislation. For example, the Federal Communications Commission (FCC) regulates broadcasting.

Administrative agencies tend to have an unusually wide range of powers. They can make their own rules, enforce their rules, investigate violations of their rules, and decide the guilt or innocence of those who violate their rules. **Administrative law** consists of those rules and procedures established by regulatory agencies.

Although regulatory agencies are constitutional, there are checks and balances on their power. The legislature that created an agency has the power to end that agency's existence or to change its powers. Any final decision by an agency can be reviewed by a court.

Section 1.2   Assessment

Reviewing What You Learned
1. What are the various parts of the U.S. Constitution?
2. What are the components of common law?
3. What are the purposes of statutory law?
4. How do the courts make law?
5. Compare common law, statutory law, and agency regulations.

Critical Thinking Activity
Sources of Law Why is it important to be able to distinguish between the U.S. Constitution and statutory law?

Legal Skills in Action
Articles of Confederation The U.S. Constitution is not the original governing document for the United States. At one time, the national government was organized and operated under the Articles of Confederation. The Articles lasted only a decade, however. With a partner, conduct a research project to uncover the weaknesses of the Articles of Confederation.

Chapter Summary

Section 1.1 Defining Ethics

- Ethical decisions can be made by relying on opinions and feelings, by applying the greatest good principle, or by following the Golden Rule.

- A decision made by applying the greatest good principle leads to an action that will create the greatest good for the greatest number of people. Although making decisions by using the greatest good principle may make many people happy, applying this principle does not always bring about ethical actions.

- The Golden Rule is traditionally associated with Christianity. However, the Golden Rule principle is present in many world religions. Applying the Golden Rule leads to an ethical decision much of the time because it requires a person to put the interests of others ahead of personal interests. The Golden Rule requires a person to "do unto others as you would have them do to you."

- Four ethical character traits are honesty, justice, compassion, and integrity. Honesty is the ability to be open and truthful in dealings with others. A person is said to be just if he or she treats people fairly or equally. A person displays compassion when he or she is sympathetic to the difficulties of others and wants to help people with their problems. Integrity refers to a person's refusal to compromise his or her values, regardless of personal consequences.

- Ethics tell us what we should do. However, ethics may be subjective, varying from person to person. People do not always do what they should do. In contrast, laws are defined. They provide an objective standard of behavior.

- Law is important because society needs a system of rules to maintain stability and peace. People need to know what their rights and duties are so that they may choose to follow them or accept the consequences for failure to follow them.

- Ethics and the law can conflict in a variety of circumstances. Professional ethics are not always consistent with the rule of law. In other cases, personal or religious ethics may conflict with the law.

Section 1.2 Sources of Law

- A country's constitution spells out the principles by which the government operates. The U.S. Constitution, which consists of seven articles and 27 amendments, enumerates the fundamental rights of citizens. It also defines the limits within which federal state governments may pass laws. The Constitution sets forth the functions of various branches of our national governing body. Each state has its own constitution.

- A body of cases called common law originates from England. These cases and their offspring can be applied to interpret statutory law. The doctrine of *stare decisis*, or precedent, is used to analogize or distinguish a case at hand from a previous case. Some parts of common law still exist today in some states' laws much as they did in England.

- Statutory law consists of rules of conduct established by the government of a society to maintain stability.

- Courts make laws through the common law tradition, by interpreting statutes, and by deciding issues of constitutionality. Decisions made by the highest court of any state become the law of that state.

- Legislatures form regulatory agencies, which have wide-ranging powers to create, enforce, and adjudicate rules and procedures. However, there are limits imposed on regulatory agencies. The legislative body that formed the agency has the power to terminate that agency. In addition, any final decision by an agency is always subject to judicial review.

Using Legal Language

Consider the key terms in the list below. Then use these terms to complete the following exercises.

morality	constitution
ethics	common law
honesty	precedent
compassion	statutes
justice	legislature
integrity	unconstitutional
law	administrative law

1. Using the key terms, pictures, drawings, and symbols, create a poster that promotes ethical and legal principles. Be creative.
2. Working with a partner, explain each of the principles depicted in your poster. Why was it selected and what messages were you hoping to convey?
3. Compare your poster with your partner's poster. In what ways are your posters similar? In what ways are they different?

Understanding Business and Personal Law Online

Self-Check Quiz Visit the *Understanding Business and Personal Law* Web site at **ubpl.glencoe.com** and click on Chapter 1: Ethics and Law— Self-Check Quizzes to prepare for the chapter exam.

The Law Review

Answer the following questions. Refer to the chapter for additional reinforcement.

4. How can the greatest good principle be misapplied?
5. Name someone you think has strong ethical principles. Which ethical character traits does this person hold? Explain your answer.
6. How can ethics and the law sometimes conflict?
7. What are the five sources of law in the United States?
8. What is the supreme law of our country?
9. What is the Bill of Rights and what is its purpose?
10. Compare and contrast common law, statutory law, and agency regulations.
11. Describe the doctrine of precedent.
12. How do courts make law?
13. Why do legislatures create administrative agencies?

Linking School to Work

Connect with Science

In March 2000, scientists in Scotland created pig clones by using genetic material taken from a cell of an adult female pig. The researchers believe that pig clones might serve as sources of organs for human organ transplants. Will this scientific advancement lead to human cloning?

14. Research the current ethical concerns surrounding human cloning.
15. Find out if there are laws being written that will regulate the cloning industry.
16. How do you feel about cloning?

Write a two-page paper stating your opinion about the future of human cloning. Include both ethical and legal implications in your paper.

Let's Debate

Animal Research

Jason, a high school senior, works at a medical laboratory near his school. He dreams of becoming a medical researcher and finding a cure for cancer.

Last week, when he arrived at work, Jason saw several animal rights activists blocking the entrance to the lab. Jason knew that his lab used animals for research and medical experiments. Although he was able to get into the lab and work that day, he began to think about the ethical issues surrounding using animals for research.

Debate

17. Should animals be used for medical research and experimentation?
18. What ethical and legal issues are involved?

Grasping Case Issues

For the following cases, give your decision and state a legal principle that applies:

19. Amy Adler is a psychiatrist and treats patients who suffer from a variety of mental illnesses. One of Amy's patients is arrested by the Secret Service for writing threatening letters to the president of the United States. When the patient goes to trial, Amy is asked to testify. However, she knows that the patient does not want her to reveal the nature of their conversations. Identify the ethical and legal conflicts that Amy faces.

20. Alex Barsky witnesses a mugging while walking home from school. He continues on his way instead of getting involved. Can the law force Alex to testify? What can the law do about the mugger? How does this demonstrate why law is necessary?

21. Lucy Demps wants to quit high school. However, a state law forbids minors from dropping out of school. The same statute gives juvenile court judges the right to suspend the driver's license of any minor who has dropped out of school. Lucy argues that statutes passed by the legislature may be able to forbid certain acts, such as stealing, but they cannot order her to attend school. Is she correct? Explain your answer.

22. Angela Gannon received a speeding ticket for driving 80 miles per hour in a 65-mile-per-hour zone. She was also cited for not wearing her seat belt, a violation of state law. One day earlier, however, the state supreme court had declared the seat belt law unconstitutional. How would you decide Angela's case?

In each case that follows, you be the judge.

23. Jurisdiction

Ewing, a medical student at the University of Michigan, failed a qualifying examination. Knowing that everyone else who had failed the test had been allowed to retake it, he also asked for a chance to take the test again. However, the university refused to allow Ewing to retake the exam. Ewing sued, arguing that the university had acted unconstitutionally, depriving him of due process as promised by the Fourteenth Amendment to the U.S. Constitution. *Can the court judge the constitutionality of a state university's action? Why or why not?*
Ewing v. Board of Regents of the University of Michigan, 742 F.2d 913 (6th Circuit).

24. Vagueness

A parent allegedly insulted his daughter's teacher in the presence of several students. The parent was charged with violating the following Kentucky state statute: "No person shall upbraid, insult, or abuse any teacher of the public schools in the presence of the school or in the presence of a pupil of the school." The parent argued that the statute is unconstitutionally vague. *Do you agree? Why or why not?*
Com. v. Ashcraft, 691 S.W.2d 229 (KY).

Legal Link

Federal Laws and Computer Crime

The Internet and other computer technologies have changed the way we live and work. Unfortunately, they have also created opportunities for criminals to commit computer crime, fraud, and abuse, including stealing personal information, destroying files, and disrupting national security. As a result, the U.S. government has begun creating laws to address Internet- and computer-related crimes.

Connect

Using a variety of search engines, research the current Internet-related legislation under discussion by the federal government. Report on the following:

25. Current and pending legislation surrounding computer crime, fraud, and abuse
26. The purpose of cookies and their impact on a computer user's privacy
27. Security and encryption policies that businesses and the government can use

POWER READING STRATEGIES

28. **Predict** How do you know the difference between right and wrong?

29. **Connect** Who is the most honest person you know? Who is the most compassionate?

30. **Question** Why do think individual states have their own constitutions, their own laws, and make many of their own decisions?

31. **Respond** How important is ethics to our legislators and other governmental decision makers?

The Court System

Understanding Business and Personal Law *Online*

Chapter Overview Visit the *Understanding Business and Personal Law* Web site at ubpl.glencoe.com and click on Chapter 2: The Court System— Chapter Overviews to preview the chapter information.

The Opening Scene

Mrs. Martinez's law class is on a field trip to the county courthouse. The students are gathered on the front steps.

A Trip to the Courthouse

MRS. MARTINEZ: *(Taking attendance.)* Where's Trai? Jamila, I thought he was supposed to ride with you.

JAMILA: He was, but that was before.

MRS. MARTINEZ: Before what?

JAMILA: Before he made other plans. He'll be along soon.

DANIEL: Hey, Mrs. Martinez. Is this a federal or state court?

MRS. MARTINEZ: It's a state court.

DANIEL: Do we have a federal court in this state?

MRS. MARTINEZ: Sure. Every state has at least one federal court.

JAMILA: Are we going to see a trial like the ones you see on television?

MRS. MARTINEZ: Yes. But it will be a civil case, not a criminal trial.

DANIEL: What's the difference?

MRS. MARTINEZ: Good question. Can anyone explain?

PEGGY: In a criminal case they can put you in jail, but in a civil trial they just take your money. Right, Mrs. M?

MRS. MARTINEZ: Well, that simplifies it a bit, but you have the right idea.

(Trai comes out of the courthouse door.)

MRS. MARTINEZ: You're fifteen minutes late, Trai. We almost started without you. Where have you been?

TRAI: I actually got here early, so I figured I'd go inside the courthouse for a little while. I was looking for my friend, Fred.

MRS. MARTINEZ: Why is your friend in the courthouse? Is he in trouble?

TRAI: He just got in a little bit of trouble a couple of months ago. Today is his juvenile court hearing. It's nothing serious.

JAMILA: My parents thought it was a big deal. They said that this isn't the first time that Fred has gotten into trouble with the law.

TRAI: Mind your own business, Jamila. I'm telling you, it was no big deal. Fred's not a troublemaker. He just came home a little late.

MRS. MARTINEZ: You mean he violated curfew.

TRAI: Something like that, yeah.

DANIEL: That's not fair. Why do we have to be off the streets by midnight?

MRS. MARTINEZ: There are different rules for juveniles.

PEGGY: That's not fair either.

MRS. MARTINEZ: No, I don't suppose it seems fair, does it?

JAMILA: So what can we do about it?

MRS. MARTINEZ: Well, first you have to know something about how the courts work. That's why we're here today. We're ready to get started. Let's go inside.

What Are the Legal Issues?

1. How is the federal court system structured?
2. How are most state court systems structured?
3. How do the courts treat juvenile offenders?
4. What is an alternate dispute resolution procedure?
5. What are the steps in a civil lawsuit?
6. What are the steps in a criminal prosecution?

A Dual Court System

The Federal Court System

The United States system of justice has two major parts—the federal system and state court systems. Federal courts hear cases involving federal matters and matters involving diversity of citizenship. State courts have their own rules.

Jurisdiction is the power and authority given to a court to hear a case and to make a judgment. Federal courts have jurisdiction over several types of cases. These cases include the following:

- Actions in which the United States or one state is a party, except those actions between a state and its citizens
- Cases that raise a federal question, such as interpreting the Constitution
- **Diversity of citizenship** cases, which involve citizens of different states and in which the amount of money in dispute exceeds $75,000
- Admiralty cases, or those pertaining to the sea
- Patent and copyright cases
- Bankruptcy cases

Example 1. Local police of a large city caught a woman breaking into a federal government building. The police arrested the woman, but because the crime was committed against federal property, she was turned over to federal authorities for trial in the federal district court.

Federal courts are arranged in three steps: U.S. district courts located throughout the United States, U.S. courts of appeals, and the Supreme Court of the United States.

District Courts

District courts have **original jurisdiction** over most federal court cases, meaning they try a case the first time it is heard. Most federal cases begin in one of the U.S. district courts, and both civil and criminal cases are heard in these courts.

Courts of Appeals

The U.S. courts of appeals, also called **appellate courts**, are **intermediate courts**, which are courts between lower courts and the highest court. They hear appeals and review cases from lower courts. Intermediate courts have **appellate jurisdiction**, meaning that any party to a suit decided in a federal district court may appeal to the federal court of appeals in the circuit where the case was tried. The United States is divided into thirteen judicial circuits. Each circuit has several district courts and one court of appeals.

A panel of three judges is responsible for rendering decisions in most U.S. court of appeals cases. No witnesses are heard, no evidence is presented, and no jury is present. Only questions of law can be raised on appeal, not questions of fact. Appellate courts only determine whether the lower court correctly applied the law in the circumstances.

Special U.S. Courts

Congress has established several special federal courts. These courts have jurisdiction in certain kinds of cases, including suits brought by citizens against the federal government, disagreements over taxes on imported goods, and disputes between taxpayers and the Internal Revenue Service.

LAWS in Your Life

Serving on a Jury

If you are registered to vote or have a driver's license, you may be called for jury duty. To serve on a jury, you must be a United States citizen and at least 18 years old. You also must understand English and not have been convicted of a felony. Should you receive a jury summons, be sure to follow its instructions. Failure to do so is a crime.

When you appear for jury duty, you become part of a pool from which jurors are chosen. During the selection process, you may be questioned by the judge and by attorneys for each side in a case. Respond honestly, even if the questions seem embarrassing or irrelevant. If you are not selected, do not be offended. Someone merely felt you were not right for that particular case.

It is possible to be excused from jury duty. However, remember that just as a jury trial is a citizen's right, jury service is a citizen's responsibility.

Interview a Juror Find people from your school or city who have served on a jury. Ask them to recall their impressions of the experience. Report your findings to the class.

Supreme Court

The U.S. Supreme Court is the highest court in the land. It has original jurisdiction in all cases involving ambassadors, consuls, other public ministers, and cases in which a state is a party. Appellate jurisdiction is the Court's main function. The Court must hear all cases that involve the constitutionality of a federal law. The Court also decides, by a vote of at least four of its nine justices, which additional cases it will hear from the U.S. courts of appeals or the state supreme courts.

State Court Systems

Each state has its own court system. However, the general pattern is the same in all states.

Local Trial Courts

Local courts are courts of **limited jurisdiction**, meaning they handle minor matters, such as misdemeanors and civil actions involving small amounts of money. Justice of the peace courts, also called magistrate's courts, were the only local courts in the early days of our country. They tried small claims and punished petty crimes in local communities, a function that they still serve today. Minor cases are also heard by traffic courts, police courts, and municipal courts. Special local courts deal with juveniles, family disputes, and small claims.

Virtual Law

"Cybercourt"

The state of Michigan has taken the novel step of creating a virtual state court in which lawyers can file briefs online and court appearances, including lawyers' arguments, can be made by streaming video. The court will not have a jury, but judges will be assigned cases by the state Supreme Court. Jurisdiction of the court is limited to business and commercial disputes that involve at least $25,000. Cases can be transferred to the state circuit court system, and like other cases, they can be contested in appellate courts. Other states, including Maryland, are also experimenting with cybercourts. (Source: *Newsbytes*, January 14, 2002.)

Connect Visit the Web site of the Michigan state courts and search for more information on the state cybercourt. Report your findings in a one- to two-page paper.

General Trial Courts

Each county in most states has at least one general trial court, or court of **general jurisdiction**. These courts, which can be called county court, superior court, court of common pleas, or circuit court, handle criminal and civil cases.

Special Courts

Courts have been established in many states to handle specialized cases. For example, probate courts hear cases involving the property of deceased persons, even if no will exists. Some probate courts also handle adoptions. A number of states have mayor's courts, in which the mayor judges cases involving traffic violations. Many states also have two other special courts: domestic relations courts and juvenile courts.

Domestic Relations Courts In most states, each county has a family or domestic relations court to handle divorce, annulment, and dissolution proceedings. The domestic relations court is also responsible for matters concerning distribution of property at the end of a marriage, including alimony and child support.

Juvenile Courts Juvenile courts have special jurisdiction over delinquent, unruly, abused, or neglected children up to a certain age. Procedures in juvenile courts differ from those in other courts, and hearings are often held in a more informal setting than a courtroom. Young people who appear before a juvenile court have no right to a trial by jury or to be released on bail. However, the Supreme Court has held that there must be proof beyond a reasonable doubt to convict a child as an adult.

Every state has passed statutes that distinguish between delinquent and unruly children. A **delinquent child** is a minor under a certain age (generally 16–18) who has committed an adult crime. Recently, some states have expanded their definitions of delinquent to include juveniles who purchase or attempt to purchase a firearm. An **unruly child** is generally a minor who has done something inappropriate that is not considered an adult crime, such as violating curfew, skipping school, or using tobacco. Many states have created a third category of children. A **neglected or abused child** is one who is homeless, destitute, or without adequate parental care. The court may make such a child a ward of the state.

Many states have imposed stricter standards for the treatment of youthful offenders, especially when drugs or violence is involved. A state may try a minor beyond a certain age (usually 14) as an adult in criminal court, especially if the minor has been in serious trouble previously or has committed a very violent offense. In deciding whether to transfer the case, the court may consider the seriousness of the offense; the minor's family, school, and social history; the minor's court record; protection of the public; the nature of past treatment; and the likelihood of rehabilitation.

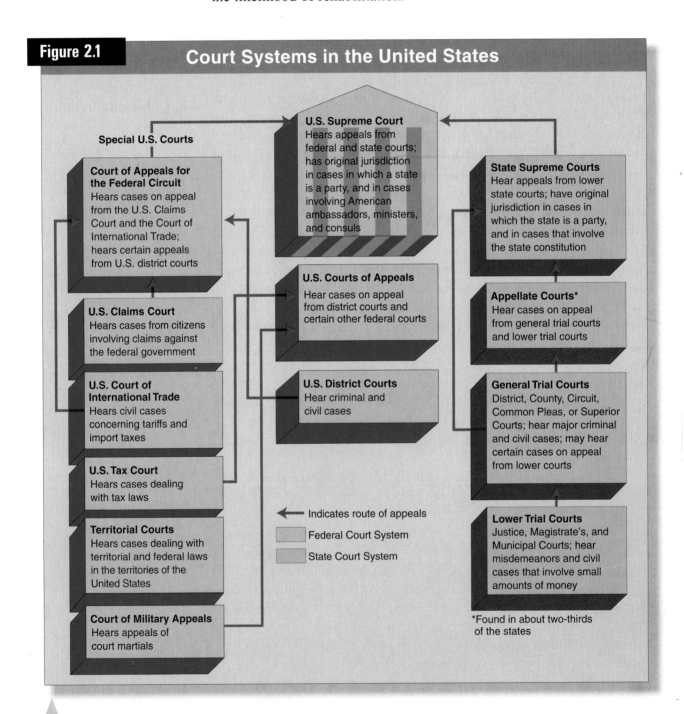

Figure 2.1

Court Systems in the United States

Special U.S. Courts

U.S. Supreme Court
Hears appeals from federal and state courts; has original jurisdiction in cases in which a state is a party, and in cases involving American ambassadors, ministers, and consuls

Court of Appeals for the Federal Circuit
Hears cases on appeal from the U.S. Claims Court and the Court of International Trade; hears certain appeals from U.S. district courts

State Supreme Courts
Hear appeals from lower state courts; have original jurisdiction in cases in which the state is a party, and in cases that involve the state constitution

U.S. Claims Court
Hears cases from citizens involving claims against the federal government

U.S. Courts of Appeals
Hear cases on appeal from district courts and certain other federal courts

Appellate Courts*
Hear cases on appeal from general trial courts and lower trial courts

U.S. Court of International Trade
Hears civil cases concerning tariffs and import taxes

U.S. District Courts
Hear criminal and civil cases

General Trial Courts
District, County, Circuit, Common Pleas, or Superior Courts; hear major criminal and civil cases; may hear certain cases on appeal from lower courts

U.S. Tax Court
Hears cases dealing with tax laws

Territorial Courts
Hears cases dealing with territorial and federal laws in the territories of the United States

← Indicates route of appeals

☐ Federal Court System

☐ State Court System

Lower Trial Courts
Justice, Magistrate's, and Municipal Courts; hear misdemeanors and civil cases that involve small amounts of money

Court of Military Appeals
Hears appeals of court martials

*Found in about two-thirds of the states

COURT SYSTEMS IN THE UNITED STATES
The courts in the United States are divided into federal and state systems. *In which court system would a criminal trial be heard?*

Intermediate Appellate Courts

In most instances, intermediate appellate courts hear appeals from courts of general jurisdiction (see Figure 2.1). Appeals may be made to a state intermediate court if the parties believe they did not have a fair trial in the lower court or that the judge did not properly interpret the law. State appellate courts hear appeals only on questions of law, not on questions of fact. Instead of hearing witnesses, appeals judges hear oral arguments from attorneys and study the documents and records in the case.

> *Example 2.* Slocum sued Archbold for injuries suffered when their cars collided. The case was tried in a county court, and the court found for the defendant, Archbold. Slocum's lawyer must look for errors in the court's interpretation of the law or the conduct of the trial to file an appeal.

Supreme Courts

The highest court in most states is known as the supreme court. A state's highest court typically decides matters of law appealed from lower courts. Supreme courts don't retry a case and reconsider the facts. Instead, they decide whether an error in interpreting or applying the law was made in the lower courts. Usually, this court chooses the cases it hears.

Section 2.1 Assessment

Reviewing What You Learned

1. What are the differences among original jurisdiction, appellate jurisdiction, limited jurisdiction, and general jurisdiction?
2. How are the federal courts structured?
3. What is the role of the United States Supreme Court?
4. How are most state courts structured?
5. Explain the differences among unruly, delinquent, and abused or neglected juveniles.

Critical Thinking Activity

Juvenile Law Why is it important to be able to distinguish among unruly, delinquent, and abused or neglected juveniles?

Legal Skills in Action

Structure of the Court System Your 30-year-old brother says he has no faith in the legal system, and for that reason, will never sue anyone. With a partner, role-play a response to your brother's argument. Explain why understanding the structure of the federal court system might benefit him, even if he never intends to be a plaintiff in a lawsuit.

Trial Procedures

What You'll Learn

- How to seek alternatives to litigation
- How to differentiate between civil and criminal cases
- How to explain the steps in a civil lawsuit
- How to exercise your rights if you're arrested
- How to explain the steps in a criminal prosecution
- How to apply court procedures to juvenile cases

Why It's Important

Learning the alternatives to litigation will help you handle disputes that arise.

Legal Terms

- alternative dispute resolution (ADR)
- complaint
- answer
- verdict
- judgment
- specific performance
- injunction
- arrest
- bail
- indictment
- arraignment
- detention hearing

Civil Trial Procedure

Criminal and civil trials begin differently. The government brings criminal cases for offenses committed against the public at large. In contrast, individuals who believe they have been injured initiate civil cases. The injured party begins the suit by filing a complaint with the court. When an individual brings a civil case to an attorney, the lawyer investigates the case, which can be expensive. As a result, people have begun to explore alternatives to lawsuits.

Alternative Dispute Resolution

Alternative dispute resolution (ADR) is an increasingly popular process that occurs when parties try to resolve disagreements outside of the usual adversarial system by using creative settlement techniques. In ADR, the methods used are relatively quick and inexpensive. They can be classified in two ways: reactive methods and proactive methods (see Figure 2.2).

ALTERNATIVE DISPUTE RESOLUTION
There are many reasons alternative dispute resolution has become increasingly popular. *Can you think of reasons why it might be preferred over litigation?*

Figure 2.2

Alternative Dispute Resolution Techniques

Reactive Methods

Mediation	Mediation happens when the parties to a dispute invite a third party into the decision-making process to help them find a solution.
Arbitration	Arbitration happens when the parties actually transfer the power to settle their dispute to a third party.
Med-arb	Med-arb combines the best aspects of mediation and arbitration.
Early Neutral Evaluation (ENE)	During ENE, an evaluator examines the facts and the law, makes an impartial evaluation of the legal rights of each party, and determines the amount of the award.
Summary Jury Trial	A summary jury trial is a short trial that runs less than a day before a real jury, which then comes up with a verdict.
Private Civil Trial	In a private civil trial, the parties can hold the trial at a time and a place of their own choosing.

Proactive Methods

Partnering	Partnering involves a process by which the parties to a long and involved contract agree to meet to get to know one another in advance.
Settlement Week	During settlement week, a court's docket is cleared of all business except for settlement hearings.
Negotiated Rule Making	During negotiated rule making, an agency that is about to create a new rule or revise existing rules meets with the parties who will be affected by the new rules. The parties then write the new rules together.
Science Court	The science court acts as a forum for disputes involving scientific and technological controversies. These disputes involve matters such as genetic engineering, nuclear energy research, and so on.

ALTERNATIVE DISPUTE RESOLUTION
This chart outlines the most popular new methods of alternative dispute resolution. *Which technique would you prefer? Explain your answer.*

Reactive Methods   These types of ADR are used after a dispute has arisen. The oldest forms of reactive ADR are mediation and arbitration. Mediation occurs when parties to a dispute invite a third party, usually called a mediator, to help them find a solution. A mediator persuades the parties to reach a compromise without making their decision for them. On the other hand, when the parties give the power to settle their dispute to a third party, the process is called arbitration, and the person engaged is called an arbitrator. A new form of ADR known as med-arb combines the best aspects of mediation and arbitration. The disputing parties first go through mediation. If the problem is not solved, they move on to an arbitration hearing.

Another new form of ADR is known as early neutral evaluation (ENE). An evaluator examines the facts, determines the legal rights of each party, and decides the amount of award that should be rendered, if any.

A summary jury trial is a short trial that runs before a real jury, which renders a verdict. The verdict is advisory but helps the parties see how a real jury would react to the case. In some states the parties can hold a private civil trial, choosing a judge whose decision is binding.

Proactive Methods   Proactive methods are discussed before a dispute even arises. These methods can be effective in preventing major disputes among parties involved in business dealings. Some businesses agree in advance to use one of the ADR tools if a disagreement between the parties arises later. An ADR contract clause says the people who are about to enter a business deal promise to use an alternative dispute resolution technique when disagreements arise. In other words, the parties promise not to sue one another. In partnering, parties to a long and involved contract agree to meet to get to know one another in advance. During this meeting, they create rules for resolving disagreements.

Some states provide a proactive ADR technique known as settlement week. During this period, a court's docket is cleared of all business except for settlement hearings, which are handled through mediation.

Another proactive ADR method is negotiated rule making. In this process, an agency that is about to create a new rule or revise existing rules works with people who will be affected.

Finally, the government might get involved in ADR through a proposed science court, which acts as a forum for disputes involving scientific and technological controversies, such as genetic engineering.

Pleadings

Civil trials begin with pleadings, the formal papers filed with the court by the plaintiff and defendant. These papers express the plaintiff's allegations, or claims, in the form of a **complaint** (see Figure 2.3). The defendant's response to those allegations is known as the **answer** (see Figure 2.4).

Methods of discovery are employed to bring facts out before trial. Methods of discovery include depositions, interrogatories, requests for documents and other evidence, physical and mental examinations, and requests for admission. If a case cannot be settled at this point, the court clerk places the case on the calendar, or court docket, for trial.

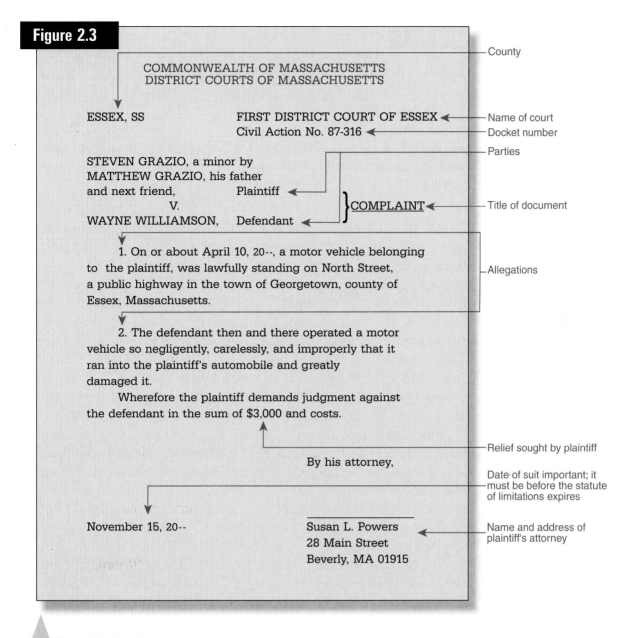

Figure 2.3

COMMONWEALTH OF MASSACHUSETTS
DISTRICT COURTS OF MASSACHUSETTS

ESSEX, SS   FIRST DISTRICT COURT OF ESSEX ← Name of court
                             Civil Action No. 87-316 ← Docket number
                                                          ← Parties

STEVEN GRAZIO, a minor by
MATTHEW GRAZIO, his father
and next friend,   Plaintiff
              V.   } COMPLAINT ← Title of document
WAYNE WILLIAMSON,   Defendant

County

    1. On or about April 10, 20--, a motor vehicle belonging
to the plaintiff, was lawfully standing on North Street,
a public highway in the town of Georgetown, county of
Essex, Massachusetts.

Allegations

    2. The defendant then and there operated a motor
vehicle so negligently, carelessly, and improperly that it
ran into the plaintiff's automobile and greatly
damaged it.

    Wherefore the plaintiff demands judgment against
the defendant in the sum of $3,000 and costs.

Relief sought by plaintiff

               By his attorney,

Date of suit important; it must be before the statute of limitations expires

November 15, 20--   Susan L. Powers
                                    28 Main Street
                                    Beverly, MA 01915

Name and address of plaintiff's attorney

A CIVIL COMPLAINT
A complaint is the first pleading that is filed in
a civil lawsuit. *Was this complaint filed in the*
federal system or in a state court?

Pretrial Hearing

Before the actual trial takes place, a pretrial hearing usually
occurs. This hearing is an informal meeting before a judge. It is
intended to simplify the issues and discuss matters that might help dispose of the case.

AN ANSWER

An answer is the defendant's official response to the plaintiff's complaint. *How does this answer respond to the complaint in Figure 2.3 on page 37?*

Figure 2.4

COMMONWEALTH OF MASSACHUSETTS
DISTRICT COURTS OF MASSACHUSETTS

ESSEX, SS   FIRST DISTRICT COURT OF ESSEX
                                       Civil Action No. 87-316

STEVEN GRAZIO, a minor by
MATTHEW GRAZIO, his father
and next friend,   Plaintiff
                  V.   } DEFENDANT'S ANSWER
WAYNE WILLIAMSON,   Defendant

    1. The defendant has no knowledge or information sufficient to form a belief regarding the truth of the allegation of paragraph one of the complaint.

    2. The defendant denies the allegations of paragraph two of the complaint.

    3. Further answering, the defendant says that at the time of alleged accident, the plaintiff's motor vehicle was parked next to a fire hydrant. This violated the law and caused or contributed to the causing of the damages complained of.

                         By his attorney,

December 10, 20--   _____
                                       George Rodriguez
                                       792 Washington Street
                                       Peabody, MA 01960

Steps in a Jury Trial

The trial begins by selecting the jury and continues through opening statements, introduction of evidence, closing arguments, instructions to the jury, the jury's verdict, and the judgment (see Figure 2.5).

Selecting the Jury   The judge calls the court to order and has a jury drawn from a pool of citizens who have been called to serve. The jury must determine the facts of the case and apply the law to those facts. The lawyers question each juror selected from the pool, trying to

Figure 2.5

The Litigation Process

In a civil case, the steps in a lawsuit appear straightforward. However, there are many points at which the process can be delayed.

1 Avoiding Litigation

Litigation may be avoided by compromise, mediation, or arbitration.

2 Commencing an Action

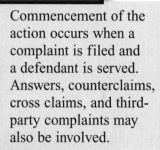

Commencement of the action occurs when a complaint is filed and a defendant is served. Answers, counterclaims, cross claims, and third-party complaints may also be involved.

3 Preparing for Trial

Pretrial procedures include discovery[1], pretrial motions[2], and pretrial conferences.

4 Trying the Case

Cases that are tried may involve jury selection and proceed to a trial, verdict, and judgment. Appeals must involve a legal error made at trial.

5 Executing a Judgment

The judgment is executed after it's delivered. A writ of execution may be needed.

(1) Discovery may involve depositions, interrogations, and request for real evidence.
(2) Motions, if granted, may end the case; the losing party may appeal.

predict whether a juror will be fair or prejudiced. Attorneys consider the juror's background, education, experience, relationships, attitudes, and employment.

Opening Statements   After jurors are selected, attorneys for each side make opening statements, explaining what they intend to prove. The plaintiff's attorney goes first. In some states, the defendant's attorney may decide to postpone an opening statement until after the plaintiff's evidence has been presented.

Introduction of Evidence   The plaintiff's attorney presents all of the plaintiff's evidence. Types of evidence include the following: documentary items, such as written contracts, sales slips, letters, or affidavits (sworn statements); physical objects, such as weapons, photographs, and items from the crime scene; and witness testimony.

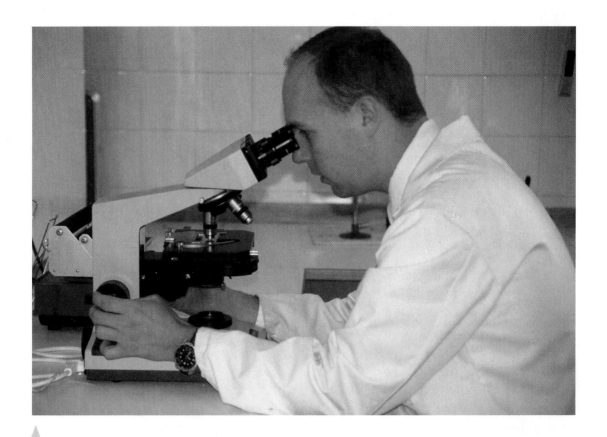

INTRODUCTION OF EVIDENCE
Physical objects are one type of admissible evidence. *Is DNA information from blood or hair samples admissible evidence?*

Witnesses respond to a subpoena, or order to appear, to testify. Some attorneys present expert witnesses who give authoritative opinions for the case.

The defense attorney has the chance to cross-examine the plaintiff's witnesses, asking questions to test the truth of statements and bring out evidence that was not developed on direct examination. When the plaintiff's attorney rests, the defendant's attorney presents evidence favorable to his or her client. Defense witnesses and any other evidence important to the defendant's case are put forward. The plaintiff's attorney may then cross-examine the defendant's witnesses. When the attorneys have introduced all of their evidence, they rest their cases.

Closing Arguments The plaintiff's attorney is the first to present closing arguments, followed by the defense attorney. Each attorney summarizes the evidence and suggests reasons why the judge or jury should find in favor of his or her client.

Instructions to the Jury The judge must explain the law to the jury in a process called jury instruction. Attorneys from both sides may suggest instructions.

Verdict and Judgment Members of the jury go to the jury room to deliberate upon their **verdict**, or decision. In a civil case, the jury, influenced by the evidence that carries the most weight, finds "in favor of" one of the parties. There are variations from state to state as to the number of jurors who must agree to reach a verdict. In Massachusetts, for example, five-sixths of the jury members must agree on verdicts in a civil case.

Following the jury's verdict, the court issues a **judgment**, the court's determination or decision in the case.

Remedies

When a defendant is found liable in a civil trial, the plaintiff is entitled to a remedy. American courts generally provide two categories of remedies: the payment of damages or an equitable remedy (which asks the court to do what is fair and just). The plaintiff may want the defendant to do what he or she promised in a contract, which is known as **specific performance**. Sometimes the plaintiff wants to prevent the defendant from doing something that he or she is planning to do or has already begun doing. In this case, the plaintiff seeks an **injunction**, an order to stop the defendant from performing an action.

Execution of Judgment

After a trial determines a winning party and a losing party, the judgment of the court must be carried out. The defendant may have to pay the plaintiff in settlement or may retain property claimed by the plaintiff. Sometimes the winning party must return to court to seek enforcement of a judgment. A judgment is enforced by the issuance of an execution by the court. The judge, for example, might order the sheriff to take property belonging to the person who lost the case. The sheriff must sell the property at an auction and use the proceeds to pay the amount of the judgment to the person who won the case. The execution may also be an order to the sheriff to remove a person or property to another location.

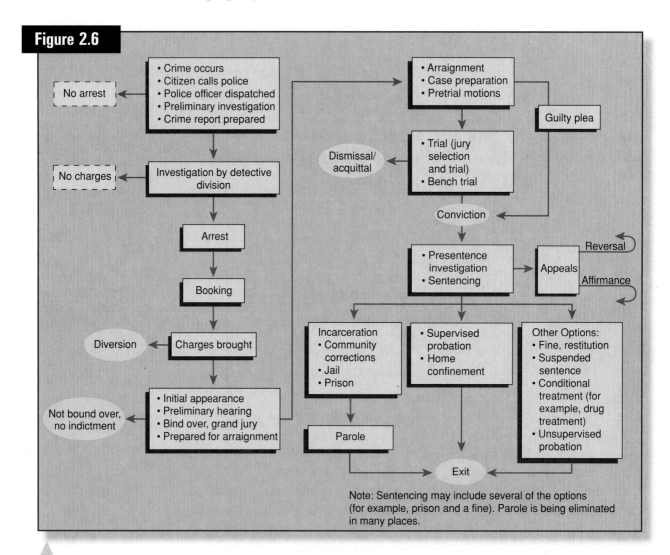

Figure 2.6

THE STEPS IN A CRIMINAL PROSECUTION

In a criminal prosecution, the defendant's rights must be guarded at every step. *What are some of the points at which the defendant's rights must be especially protected?*

Criminal Trial Procedure

Criminal cases often start with the arrest of the defendant (see Figure 2.6). The law requires an immediate court hearing to protect the defendant's rights. The trial is scheduled later to give the prosecuting attorney and the defendant's attorney time to prepare their cases.

Arrest of the Defendant

An **arrest** occurs when a person is deprived of his or her freedom. A police officer may arrest a person at any time if the officer has a warrant. An officer may arrest a person without a warrant if he or she believes the person has committed or is committing a felony, or if the person has committed a misdemeanor involving a breach of the peace in the officer's presence. Various state statutes also allow officers to arrest people for specific misdemeanors done in their presence, even if there is no breach of peace.

Rights of the Defendant Arrested people must be informed of their constitutional rights as set forth in the case of *Miranda v. Arizona*. The Miranda warnings require that people be told what crimes they are being arrested for and the names of the police officers making the arrest. Arrested people also have the right to make a telephone call. A person who has been arrested can sometimes be released on bail. **Bail** is money or other property that is left with the court to assure that a person who has been arrested, but released, will return to trial.

People who are arrested have the right to remain silent. If they answer questions, they have the right to talk to an attorney first and may have an attorney present during the questioning. If a defendant cannot afford an attorney, the court must appoint one at no cost. Under the Constitution, accused individuals also have a right to a fair trial and are presumed innocent until proven guilty.

Search and Seizure A police officer may search a person, car, house, or other building only if permission is given or if the officer has a search warrant. The search must be limited to the area mentioned in the warrant. An officer may conduct a limited search, called a frisk, if he or she believes that a person is carrying a weapon. When the search is over, the person must be released or arrested.

Persons who have been arrested may be searched without a warrant. When police arrest someone in a house or building, they may conduct a limited search of the area in which the arrest takes place without a search warrant. They need a warrant, however, to search the entire building. When an arrest takes place in a car, police may conduct a limited search of the vehicle without a warrant. A more complete search may be made if there is good reason to believe the car

Legal Briefs

In 1995, 12 percent of students ages 12 through 18 reported that they were sometimes or most of the time fearful at school. This percentage dropped to 7 percent in 1999 and 6 percent in 2001.

SEARCH WARRANT
The scope of a search warrant is determined by the object that is being searched for. *How might the search areas differ for a large television versus a small handgun?*

contains something illegal. In addition, the police may impound (take possession of) a car until a search warrant is obtained from the court.

Example 3. In 1976, police impounded a car in South Dakota for a number of parking violations. While making a list of the car's contents, police found a bag of marijuana and charged the owner with possession. The Supreme Court of the United States held that the search without a warrant was constitutional because standard procedure called for police to list the contents of every car they impounded.

Police may seize items (such as illegal drugs or weapons) that are in plain view without obtaining a warrant. This rule is known as the plain-view exception. In 1981, the Supreme Court said police may search the entire passenger area of a car without a search warrant once the occupants are placed under arrest. A year later the Court modified that position. Police officers who have legitimately stopped an automobile and have probable cause to believe that contraband (illegal goods or substances) is hidden inside may search the vehicle without a warrant, including compartments and containers within the vehicle whose contents are not in plain view.

In 1991, the U.S. Supreme Court held that once police have probable cause to believe a crime is being committed, they do not need a warrant to seize a vehicle and search it, as well as any closed container inside. In that same year, the Court said that once a motorist gives police permission to search a car, officers may open bags or containers within the car.

The Supreme Court has also held that school officials may search students without a warrant. However, the officials must have reasonable grounds to believe the search will turn up evidence that the student has violated school rules.

The Arraignment

The suspect is brought before the court as soon as possible after an arrest, informed of the nature of the complaint, and made aware of his or her rights. At this time, the judge may find cause to dismiss the complaint or decide if there is probable cause that a crime was committed.

Depending upon the jurisdiction, the prosecuting attorney either prepares an information or presents the case to the grand jury. An information is a set of formal charges drawn up by the prosecuting attorney. A grand jury is a jury of inquiry made up of citizens who must decide whether there is enough evidence to justify accusing certain persons of certain crimes.

A grand jury conducts a preliminary hearing in secret to determine whether someone must stand trial. A petit jury decides on the guilt or innocence of the person tried. A trial jury is a petit jury because it has fewer members than a grand jury.

The grand jury hears evidence and testimony of witnesses. If jurors decide a crime has been committed, they issue an **indictment**, or written accusation charging the individual. This issuance does not mean that the named person is guilty but that the grand jury believes there is a possibility he or she is guilty.

Following the indictment or information, the accused is brought to court for **arraignment**. The suspect is read the indictment or

Community Works

Guns in School
According to a recent report on state implementation of the Gun-Free Schools Act, 55 percent of expulsions for bringing firearms to school involved high school students, 33 percent involved middle school students, and 10 percent involved elementary school students. *How can you make your school safer?*

Get Involved
Locate local, state, and national children's advocacy groups to determine what programs in your area help educate teens about gun violence. Find out how you and your friends can form a group at school that promotes nonviolent solutions and encourages mediation.

Forensic Scientist

If you're a fan of mysteries, you might wonder how homicide detectives really discover "whodunit." Chances are, they've received some help along the way from a forensic scientist.

"Forensics just means something relating to law," says Midori Albert, professor of anthropology and forensics consultant at the University of North Carolina, Wilmington. "People in many different fields—chemistry, engineering, botany, even bug scientists—can help to solve a crime."

Although most of Albert's time is spent teaching anthropology, she is also part of a team of crime sleuths who tackle about 30 cases per year in North Carolina. Simply by studying bones, she can reconstruct many characteristics of victims, including their age, gender, ethnic background, previous disease and bone injury, and sometimes the cause of death. This information is useful in reconstructing the scene and circumstances of a crime and ultimately help to solve cases.

"A lot of people think forensic scientists are into gore," Albert says. "That's not true. This is a science based on observation and logic. We're dealing with people's lives, and we care about the victims of these crimes. Our work often helps a victim's surviving family and friends to come to some resolution."

Skills	Photography and videography, computer, statistical analysis, organization, communication, archaeological field techniques
Personality	Patient, discreet, sociable, detail oriented
Education	Academic forensic scientists are usually required to have a Ph.D. People interested in the technical aspects of forensics will need a bachelor's degree in general forensic science.

For more information on forensic science, visit the American Academy of Forensic Sciences Web site at www.aafs.org, **ubpl.glencoe.com**, or your local library.

information and is asked to plead guilty or not guilty. The accused is informed of his or her rights. If the person pleads guilty, the judge may then impose the sentence. If the person pleads not guilty, the case proceeds to trial.

The Trial

If the defendant requests a jury trial, selection of jurors proceeds and attorneys make opening statements and introduce evidence. Otherwise, the case is tried before the judge, who decides the verdict. The trial ends with the attorney's closing statements and the judge's instructions to the jury.

In a criminal case with a jury, the verdict must be unanimous— either guilty beyond a reasonable doubt, or not guilty. A mistrial is called if the jury cannot agree, and a new trial may be held at the option of the prosecution. If the defendant is not guilty, he or she is released. If the defendant is found guilty, the judge imposes a sentence in the form of a fine, imprisonment, or both.

Sentencing

After a person has been convicted of a crime, he or she is sentenced by the court, which means the judge decides the punishment. The law provides certain sentencing guidelines and penalties, including fines, imprisonment, and even death.

Fines   A fine is the payment of money as a penalty for committing a crime, generally a minor one. Fines are also attached to more serious crimes and may be levied by the judge along with imprisonment.

Imprisonment   States deal with imprisonment in different ways. In some states, the judge may hand down an indefinite or indeterminate sentence, ordering a minimum and maximum amount of time the convicted criminal may spend in prison. A prisoner might be sentenced to five to ten years; however, good behavior might shorten his or her time behind bars.

Other states insist on compelling the judge to use a definite sentence. The judge must state the exact period of time a criminal will spend in prison. Some states have created mandatory sentences for certain crimes, which cannot be altered for any reason.

The Death Penalty   Our Constitution says death penalty laws must include guidelines to ensure fair treatment. Death penalty laws require three phases:
- The jury determines whether the defendant is guilty.
- The judge or jury listens to attorneys' arguments and determines the punishment under state laws that clearly set forth factors to be considered in a presentencing hearing.
- An appeal is taken to the state's highest court.

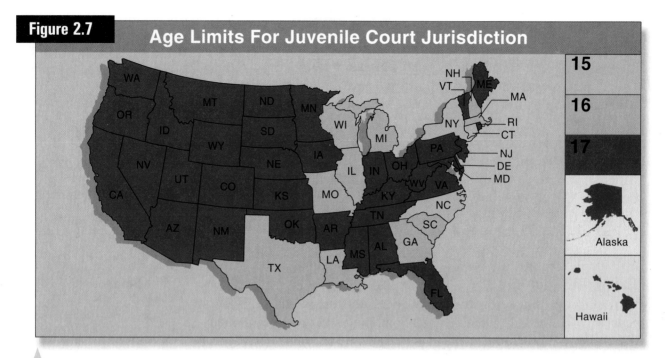

Figure 2.7

Age Limits For Juvenile Court Jurisdiction

15

16

17

Alaska

Hawaii

THE AGE LIMITS FOR JUVENILE
COURT JURISDICTION
Most states hold 17 as the oldest age for
juvenile court jurisdiction. *What is the age
limit in your state?*

Disposition of Juvenile Cases

Cases involving juvenile offenders are handled by the juvenile court, which has limited jurisdiction (see Figure 2.7). The juvenile court system is designed so that each case and special circumstances are considered individually.

As a first step, the judge usually holds a **detention hearing** to learn whether there are good reasons to keep the accused in custody. The court's probation department or a child welfare agency begins an investigation into the minor's background and home life. The judge might dismiss the charges upon hearing the investigation findings. There may be special circumstances; the matter may be deemed not serious enough to pursue further; or the judge may feel the youth was wrongly accused.

If the charges are not dismissed, the judge conducts an adjudicatory hearing. This is the informal, actual hearing of the case by the court. The judge may question the youth and his or her parents, listen to witnesses, and seek advice from the probation officer. Some courts decide what action to take at this point. Other courts hold a third hearing, called a dispositional hearing. After one of these hearings, the judge decides the outcome of the case. The matter is generally settled in one of three ways:

- The judge may allow the offender to return home on probation for a period of time, under the supervision of a probation officer. Failure to meet probation requirements may result in more severe punishment.
- The judge may place the offender in an agency or foster home. The natural parents will then be required to pay what they can toward the offender's support.
- The judge may commit the offender to a training or reform school. This option is usually a last resort, employed when both probation and foster care have already been tried and have failed, or when those options seem unlikely to work.

The judge can also order the juvenile offender to pay for the damages with money, work, or both. The parents of the offender may have to repay the victim in some cases. Sentences for youthful offenders are set with rehabilitation in mind. They are generally limited to probation under court supervision, confinement for not more than three years in a reformative institution, or another course of action designed to help, rather than to punish.

Section 2.2 Assessment

Reviewing What You Learned

1. What are some alternatives to litigation?
2. What is the difference between a civil case and a criminal case?
3. Specify the steps in a civil lawsuit.
4. What rights do people have when they are arrested?
5. Specify the steps in a criminal lawsuit.
6. How do the courts treat juvenile cases?

Critical Thinking Activity

Resolution Proceeding Using the newspaper, Internet, or your school library, research how consumers might use dispute resolution to resolve conflicts with businesses. Then make an oral presentation on an actual resolution proceeding.

Legal Skills in Action

Dispute Resolution Centers In this chapter, you learned about alternative dispute resolution, an increasingly popular approach to resolving disputes out of court and avoiding the time and cost of trial. Contact the office of the district court administrator to locate dispute resolution centers.

Chapter Summary

Section 2.1 Dual Court System

- Jurisdiction is the power and authority given a court to hear a case and to make a judgment. A court with original jurisdiction hears a case tried for the first time in its court. A court with appellate jurisdiction reviews a case on appeal from a lower court. Courts with limited jurisdiction handle minor matters, such as misdemeanors. General jurisdiction means that a court has the power to hear most types of cases.

- Federal courts are arranged in three levels: U.S. district courts located throughout the United States, U.S. courts of appeals, and the Supreme Court of the United States.

- The U.S. Supreme Court has original jurisdiction on certain types of cases involving ambassadors, consuls, and cases in which a state is a party. The Supreme Court hears the majority of its cases in its appellate capacity. It considers cases that have been tried in lower courts and cases that have been selected for review by four of nine Supreme Court Justices.

- State court systems generally consist of local trial courts, courts of general jurisdiction, and appellate courts. At the highest level, each state has its own supreme court.

- A delinquent juvenile is a child who commits an adult crime. An unruly child is generally a minor who has done something that wouldn't be a crime if committed by an adult, such as violating curfew, skipping school, or using tobacco. A neglected or abused child is one who is without adequate parental care or one who is homeless. Such a child will become a ward of the state.

Section 2.2: Trial Procedures

- There are several different alternatives to traditional litigation. Mediation and arbitration, med-arb, early neutral evaluation (ENE), summary jury trial, and private civil trial are some reactive examples of Alternate Dispute Resolution (ADR). Reactive methods of ADR are used after a dispute has arisen. Proactive ADR methods, such as partnering and settlement week, are used before a dispute arises.

- A criminal case often starts with an arrest. To protect the defendant's constitutional right to a speedy trial, the criminal trial is scheduled more quickly than a civil trial. A plaintiff in a civil case may wait years before having her day in court. In civil court, the plaintiff sues the defendant for a remedy. In a criminal proceeding, the district attorney prosecutes on behalf of the government against the defendant for a different type of price—his or her freedom.

- The steps in a civil trial are: (1) jury selection, (2) presentation of opening statements, (3) introduction of the evidence, (4) presentation of closing arguments, (5) instructions to the jury, (6) the jury verdict, and (7) the court's judgment.

- People placed under arrest may exercise their rights in several ways: (1) they may remain silent; (2) they may call an attorney; and (3) if they choose to answer questions, they may have an attorney present.

- After a defendant is arrested, evidence of the crime is presented to a grand jury. If the grand jury decides there is enough evidence to go to trial, it issues an indictment. The defendant is arraigned. At the time of arraignment, the defendant pleads guilty or not guilty. Defendants pleading not guilty proceed to trial, and those pleading guilty are sentenced by the judge.

- In a juvenile case, the judge may: (1) place the offender on probation and allow him or her to return home, (2) place the offender in an agency or foster home, or (3) commit the offender to a training or reform school.

Using Legal Language

Consider the key terms in the list below. Then use these terms to complete the following exercises.

jurisdiction

original jurisdiction

appellate court

limited jurisdiction

delinquent child

abused child

mediation

med-arb

private civil trial

answer

judgment

bail

arraignment

diversity of citizenship

intermediate court

appellate jurisdiction

general jurisdiction

unruly child

alternative resolution

arbitration

summary jury trial

ADR contract clause

verdict

arrest

indictment

Understanding Business and Personal Law

Online

Self-Check Quiz Visit the *Understanding Business and Personal Law* Web site at **ubpl.glencoe.com** and click on Chapter 2: The Court System— Self-Check Quizzes to prepare for the chapter exam.

1. Your business law professor has asked you to create a reference manual for new students. Provide a definition for each key term.
2. The reference manual will be organized according to groups of related terms. Place each key term into one of three to five categories that you create.

The Law Review

Answer the following questions. Refer to the chapter for additional reinforcement.

3. What are the two court systems in the United States?
4. What is the source of the federal court system's authority?
5. In what kind of case does a federal district court have original jurisdiction?
6. When are the police allowed to search a vehicle without a warrant?
7. How does a verdict differ from a judgment?
8. Describe the rights of an arrested person.
9. There are likely dispute resolution centers in your area. Contact the office of the district court administrator to define the scope of their jurisdiction.
10. What happens if a jury cannot agree on a verdict?
11. Under what circumstances might a judge commit a juvenile offender to a reform school?

Linking School to Work

Connect with Language Arts

Jeremy is a 15-year-old student. One night, after his parents thought he was asleep, he and two friends went to the golf course. As a prank, they drove five golf carts into a nearby lake. All the carts were destroyed, and Jeremy and his friends were arrested. In juvenile court, Jeremy and his friends were fined and placed on probation for two years, and their parents were required to reimburse the owner of the golf course for the golf carts. Analyze the following issues:

12. Is this result fair to the juveniles' parents?
13. Is this result fair to the golf course?

Write a paragraph explaining your opinion. Next, write another paragraph defending the perspective of the golf course. Finally, write a paragraph as if you were representing Jeremy.

Let's Debate

Privacy and Drug Testing

Your school has decided that it will require random drug testing for students who are involved in extracurricular activities. Many students in the school feel this is illegal. Others believe that all students, including those who do not participate in extracurricular activities, should face the same rules.

Debate

14. Do you think school districts should impose this type of policy?
15. Do you think random drug testing of high school students involved in extracurricular activities is legal?
16. If you were the principal, would you require random drug testing? Why or why not?

Grasping Case Issues

For the following cases, give your decision and state a legal principle that applies.

17. Kepano brought a lawsuit in his home state involving a contract claim against another resident of that state. When Kepano lost, he decided to take the case directly to the United States Supreme Court. Is the Supreme Court required to hear the case? Why or why not?
18. Shahnaz and Vasu Harinath decide to get a divorce. Because they want to keep the matter as quiet as possible in their community, they elected to have their divorce heard by a federal district court. Do federal courts have jurisdiction over divorce cases? Why or why not?
19. When Ivan Gagarin was at the mall, he was served with a copy of a complaint and a summons in a lawsuit. Certain that he has done nothing wrong, Ivan decides to do nothing about the lawsuit. What will happen to him?
20. Speculate on which of the following cases the U.S. Supreme Court might decide to review: (1) a libel case involving a local high school football coach; (2) a case involving a student who has been denied admission to a college program because of her religion; (3) a case involving whether the American flag can be burned in protest over new taxes. Explain your answer.
21. Abel Agapois was given a speeding ticket for going 65 miles per hour in a zone that only permitted the speed of 25 miles per hour. His case was heard in mayor's court, and the mayor fined him $275. Abel believes the fine constitutes cruel and unusual punishment, and he intends to appeal to the federal district court. Will he be permitted to do so? Why or why not?

In each case that follows, you be the judge.

22. Search and Seizure

The police received a tip that marijuana was being grown in Michael Riley's greenhouse. Police could not see inside the greenhouse from the road, but the investigating officer did see marijuana plants in the greenhouse from a helicopter circling the property. Riley argued the helicopter search was an unconstitutional violation of the Fourth Amendment. *Could this case be appealed to the United States Supreme Court? Why or why not?*

Florida v. Riley, 102 L.Ed. 2d 835 (U.S. Sup. Ct.).

23. Equal Protection

The city council of Richmond adopted a minority business utilization plan. Primary contractors of any city construction project were required to subcontract a minimum of 30 percent of their work to at least one minority business enterprise. However, any contractor that was owned by minority group members was not bound by this rule. The plan was challenged in federal district court. *What is the jurisdictional basis for bringing the case to federal court? Is this the type of case that could be brought to the United States Supreme Court? Why or why not?*

Richmond v. Croson Co., 488 U.S. 469 (U.S. Sup. Ct.).

Legal Link

Who's Who on the U.S. Supreme Court
After studying the justices of the Supreme Court in your American History class, you decide you want to know more.

Connect
Select one of the current U.S. Supreme Court justices. Using a variety of Internet search engines, conduct research to find out more about that justice. Answer the following questions:

24. Where and when was he/she born?

25. Where did he/she go to law school?

26. Which president nominated the justice to the U.S. Supreme Court?

27. Where is he/she seated on the bench?

28. What is the significance of the quill pen?

29. Describe the conference handshake.

POWER READING STRATEGIES

30. Predict What do you think would happen if we didn't have the 51 court systems in the United States?

31. Connect Under what circumstances, if any, do you think a minor should be treated as an adult in a murder case?

32. Question What do you think would happen if there were juries in the appeals court?

33. Respond How do you think lawyers determine whether a juror will be biased or prejudiced?

Criminal Law

**Understanding Business
and Personal Law** *Online*

Chapter Overview Visit the *Understanding Business and Personal Law* Web
site at ubpl.glencoe.com and click on
Chapter 3: Criminal Law—Chapter Overviews to preview the chapter information.

The Opening Scene

During lunch in the cafeteria, Jamila, Trai, Peggy, and Daniel discuss their plans for the Friday night football game in a neighboring town.

Crime and Punishment

JAMILA: Hey Trai, I need a ride to the football game tonight. I figured that I could catch one with you. What time can you pick me up?

TRAI: *(Looking in Daniel's direction.)* I'm always the driver. In fact, I drove last week. I was hoping to catch a ride with Daniel.

DANIEL: *(Sheepishly.)* I know that it's my turn, but it's not going to happen. My dad said it's too dangerous to go to a game at Danville High. He read the newspaper article about what happened in the chemistry lab last month. I tried to beg him, but he wouldn't change his mind. You know how he is.

PEGGY: Are you kidding? Your father is so overprotective! Danville isn't dangerous. Does your dad know what really happened over there?

TRAI: Yeah, it's just a case of a small fire that one kid started. It doesn't mean the whole school is dangerous. You can't judge an entire school based on the behavior of one person. Plus, they caught the guy who did it, and he's been charged with arson.

JAMILA: Arson! Wow! I'm not sure, but I think that may be a federal offense. I bet the penalty for that is tough—students there are going to be on their best behavior for a long time.

PEGGY: I think the guy who did it got in trouble for something he was doing on the Internet, too. He sounds like he has some big problems. What's going to happen to him, anyway?

TRAI: I read in the paper that his lawyer is going to plead insanity.

DANIEL: *(Throwing his hands up in the air.)* Great! He'll end up getting off with nothing. It's not fair. He deserves to be punished.

PEGGY: *(Frowning.)* I'm not sure that I consider a lengthy stay at a state mental institution a good time. Mental institutions are not luxury hotels, you know.

JAMILA: I don't think it's fair for him to be able to plead insanity. Can't anybody claim insanity just to get out of going to jail?

TRAI: *(Crumpling up his lunch bag.)* How should I know? Maybe you'd better check with Mrs. Martinez. Right now, let's worry about getting to the football game tonight. That kid will get what he deserves, whatever that may be. Daniel, my mom's car is in the shop, and my dad is out of town on a business trip. You've got to drive tonight, or we won't be able to go.

PEGGY: Tell your dad what we just talked about. You can convince him. Better yet, I'll help you talk to him. Your dad likes me.

DANIEL: *(Reluctantly.)* I guess we can talk him into it. How about if I pick everybody up around six o'clock?

What Are the Legal Issues?

1. What is the difference between federal and state law?
2. What are some specific crimes that are part of our legal system?
3. What statutes have been passed to address computer crimes?
4. What defenses are available for criminal defendants?

What Is a Crime?

Classifications of Crimes

Crime is considered an act against the public good. Our laws in the United States detail crimes and provide punishment by fine, imprisonment, or both. In a criminal proceeding, the state or federal government, representing the public at large, is the **plaintiff**, or the party that accuses a person of a crime. The **prosecutor** is the government attorney who presents the case in court against the person accused, called the **defendant**.

Felonies

A **felony** is a major crime punishable by imprisonment or death. The punishment set for a particular crime determines whether it is a felony. Murder, manslaughter, burglary, robbery, and arson are examples of felonies. Some states, such as New Jersey, do not use the word *felony*. New Jersey labels its most serious crimes "high misdemeanors." See Figure 3.1 to view statistics on crime in the United States.

Misdemeanors

A less serious crime with a less severe penalty is a **misdemeanor**. Misdemeanors are penalized by a fine or brief imprisonment in a county or city jail. Driving an automobile without a license, lying about one's age to purchase alcohol, and leaving the scene of an automobile accident are examples of misdemeanors. Some states also classify lesser crimes as minor misdemeanors or petty offenses. Typical examples of these types of offenses include some traffic and parking violations.

Criminal Law in the American System

The American legal system actually consists of two systems: the federal system and the state system. Both systems make and enforce criminal law, but the source of their power for making criminal law differs.

State Criminal Law

Each state government has inherent police power, allowing it to make statutes to protect the public health, safety, welfare, and morals.

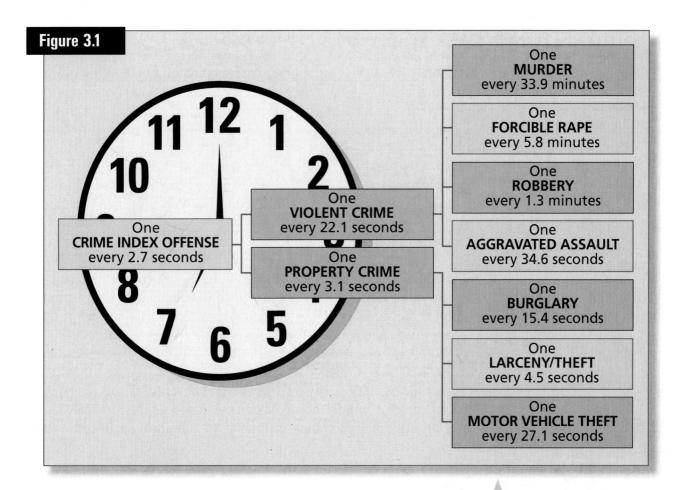

Figure 3.1

One
CRIME INDEX OFFENSE
every 2.7 seconds

One
VIOLENT CRIME
every 22.1 seconds

One
PROPERTY CRIME
every 3.1 seconds

One
MURDER
every 33.9 minutes

One
FORCIBLE RAPE
every 5.8 minutes

One
ROBBERY
every 1.3 minutes

One
AGGRAVATED ASSAULT
every 34.6 seconds

One
BURGLARY
every 15.4 seconds

One
LARCENY/THEFT
every 4.5 seconds

One
MOTOR VEHICLE THEFT
every 27.1 seconds

Although state laws closely resemble each other, the exact definitions and penalties for crimes may differ from state to state. For instance, a crime that is called assault in one state may be called battery in another.

Federal Criminal Law

Unlike state governments, the federal government has no police power. When the Constitution was written in 1787, its authors imposed limits on the powers granted to the national government. One limitation was the act of withholding the general police power enjoyed by the states. Consequently, the federal government is able to create criminal statutes only in areas over which it has jurisdiction. For example, the federal government has created laws against counterfeiting because it has the power to coin money.

Today, however, the federal government does have a criminal code and several national police agencies, including the Federal Bureau of Investigation (FBI) and the Drug Enforcement Agency (DEA). The federal government's power to establish these agencies comes primarily from the commerce clause of the U.S. Constitution, which requires

A CRIME INDEX
As this crime index indicates, the rate at which crimes are committed in this country is quite consistent. *Why does the crime rate remain so steady despite the efforts of our law enforcement officials and the criminal court system?*

Congress to regulate commerce among the states. As a result, federal criminal law statutes must involve some sort of interstate activity.

Treason   Treason is one crime named and defined in the U.S. Constitution. A confession in open court or the testimony of two witnesses verifying the same overt act of treason is required to convict someone of treason.

Double Jeopardy   The federal and state systems of justice sometimes overlap. For example, both federal laws and state laws address the manufacture, sale, and use of illicit drugs. This overlap can create a problem for a person who has been accused of a crime that could be construed as both a federal and a state crime. The Fifth Amendment of the Constitution guarantees that no person can be tried twice for the same crime, a principle known as double jeopardy. In practice, however, the courts have held that although an individual may not be tried twice for the same crime in the same court, he or she may be tried twice for the same actions in two different courts.

Elements of a Crime

A crime is defined by two elements: the criminal act and the required state of mind. The two elements may be defined somewhat differently by the states, but definitions are similar enough to allow certain generalizations.

Criminal Act

Most criminal statutes specifically explain conduct that is forbidden. For example, a statute that makes stealing a crime specifically prohibits the wrongful taking of another person's personal property. Some criminal law statutes, however, make failure to act a crime. For instance, a young man who fails to register for the draft after reaching his eighteenth birthday has committed a crime.

A criminal act must also involve voluntary conduct. Similarly, a person cannot be accused of a crime if that accusation is based on one's physical or mental status or condition. For example, the government could not make it a crime to be an alcoholic because alcoholism is a physical condition. However, the government can have laws regarding at what age a person can consume alcohol.

Required State of Mind

The second element establishing a crime is the required state of mind. A statute defining murder forbids the *intentional* taking of a person's life; the required mental state is intent. In contrast, a statute defining involuntary manslaughter outlaws the *accidental* taking of a person's life. In both statutes the criminal act involves taking a life, but the crime changes according to the state of mind of the person committing the act.

Motive

When television and movie detectives hunt for a criminal, they always seem to make the motive for a crime a crucial part of their case. This is misleading because motive actually plays no part in proving criminal liability. If a person has committed a forbidden act with the required state of mind, then he or she is criminally liable, regardless of motive.

Defenses to Crimes

If you were a defense attorney, your job would be to try to show that the prosecution failed to prove the required elements for the crime charged to your client. The most common defenses include insanity, entrapment, self-defense, and defense of family members.

LAWS in Your Life

Teen Courts

Authorities have long sought ways to reduce teen crime. One approach that many communities have adopted is to establish teen courts. In teen courts, teenagers serve as jurors, defense attorneys, and prosecutors. The courts hear the cases of teens who have committed a minor, first-time offense. These offenders get a chance to avoid the record that would result from a juvenile court proceeding. They also learn a valuable lesson in how the law works.

Teen courts began in Texas in the 1970s and have since spread to more than 30 states. They often are supported by funds from school districts, traditional courts, or by civic groups that hope to reach young offenders before they become hardened criminals. Statistics show that teen crime is generally down in communities where such programs exist.

Conduct Research Call or write the municipal governments in your area to determine whether they have teen courts and how these courts work.

Insanity

American law recognizes that people cannot be held responsible for their actions if they do not know what they are doing. This recognition makes insanity a valid defense to criminal conduct.

The oldest legal test of insanity is the *M'Naughten Rule*, developed in England in 1843. To be deemed legally insane under this rule, a defendant must be proven to suffer from a mental disease so serious that he or she did not know the nature or moral inappropriateness of an illegal action at the time it was committed. This test is still used in about two-fifths of U.S. states.

The American Law Institute (ALI) has developed a more modern test for insanity. A person is not considered responsible if "as a result of mental disease or defect he or she lacks substantial capacity either to appreciate the criminality of his conduct or to conform his conduct to the requirements of law." About three-fifths of U.S. states follow the ALI test.

People who are found not guilty by reason of insanity do not automatically go free. Rather, they are committed to institutions and must undergo periodic psychiatric examinations. These people are released only when they are found to be sane.

Entrapment

If a law enforcement officer induces a law-abiding citizen to commit a crime, the person can use a defense known as entrapment. The defense must show that the crime would not have been committed without the involvement of the officer.

> *Example 1.* Several students told Mrs. Martinez that Grant offered to sell them drugs. When she reported this to the police, an undercover officer was sent to the school. Grant tried to sell the officer some drugs, and the officer arrested Grant. The defense of entrapment could not apply because Grant would have sold the drugs regardless of the officer's intervention.

Self-Defense

When people have good reason to believe they are in danger of serious injury or death, they can use force to protect themselves. This defense is known as self-defense. A person claiming self-defense must have tried to retreat before resorting to force. If an attack occurs in one's own home, however, a person does not need to retreat. Defendants must also show that they did not start the altercation and that they did not use excessive force to stop the attack.

Defense of Family Members

Most states will not punish someone for using force to rescue a family member from attack. As in self-defense, the rescuer must have good reason to believe the victim was in danger of severe bodily injury or death. Figure 3.2 displays the criminal defenses available to defendants.

Example 2. Mark returned home one evening to find his sister being attacked in their living room. He struck and injured his sister's assailant. Most states would allow Mark to use defense of family members to explain his actions.

Figure 3.2 — Criminal Liability and Defenses

Criminal Liability	Criminal Defenses
The act:	Defenses to the act:
Criminal behavior specifically outlined by statute	Act as defined is "status" only
	Act as defined is ambiguous
The mental state:	Act as defined is overbroad
Mental state specifically outlined by statute	Defenses to the mental state:
Purpose	Insanity
Knowledge	Entrapment
Recklessness	Justifiable force
Negligence	Mistake

CRIMINAL LIABILITY AND DEFENSES
A proper understanding of the relationship between the elements of criminal liability and the chief criminal defenses is at the heart of criminal law. *Which of the two elements of criminal liability does the insanity defense seek to eliminate?*

Section 3.1 Assessment

Reviewing What You Learned

1. What determines the difference between a felony and a misdemeanor?
2. How do state and federal criminal law differ?
3. What are the elements of a crime?
4. What are the major criminal law defenses?

Critical Thinking Activity

Legal Defenses Why is it crucial to understand the different defenses to criminal liability?

Legal Skills in Action

The Insanity Defense Many people have misconceptions about the insanity defense in the American legal system. They often see it as a way for criminals to go free without serving time for their offenses. Imagine that you are a legal columnist for a newsletter intended for people who support civil liberties. Write a column in which you defend the insanity defense as a necessary part of the American legal system.

Particular Crimes

Why It's Important

Learning how to distinguish among various crimes will help you understand criminal liability.

Legal Terms

- murder
- manslaughter
- battery
- assault
- kidnapping
- burglary
- larceny
- embezzlement
- robbery
- arson
- vandalism
- shoplifting

Crimes Against People

Generally, crimes can be grouped under three headlines: crimes against people, crimes against property, and crimes against business interests. The killing of one human being by another is known as homicide. Justifiable homicide takes place when a police officer kills a criminal in the line of duty or in self-defense. This type of homicide also takes place when a soldier kills the enemy in battle. When someone is killed by accident, the death is an excusable homicide.

Murder

Under the law, **murder** is the unlawful killing of another human being with malice aforethought, which means the killer had evil intent. In many states, murder is divided into first-degree murder and second-degree murder.

The definition of first-degree murder, also called aggravated murder, differs from state to state. However, first-degree murder generally involves one or more of the following circumstances: killing with premeditation (thinking about or planning the crime in advance); killing in a cruel way, such as with torture; and killing while committing a felony, such as rape or robbery. If none of these conditions apply, the crime is considered second-degree murder. The distinction between first- and second-degree murder is important because in some states those found guilty of first-degree murder are subject to the death penalty.

Manslaughter

The unlawful killing of another human being without malice aforethought is known as **manslaughter**, which can be divided into two categories: voluntary and involuntary. Voluntary manslaughter occurs when one person intends to kill another but does so suddenly and as the result of great personal distress. The wrongdoer must have become very upset before the killing.

Example 3. Alex Fielder's son was kidnapped and murdered. When the police caught the kidnapper, he immediately confessed. The next day, while being interviewed at the police station, Alex saw the kidnapper being transported to another part of the jail. In a sudden rage, Alex grabbed a nearby officer's service revolver and shot the kidnapper dead. Alex was charged with voluntary manslaughter.

Involuntary manslaughter occurs when one person, while committing an unlawful or reckless act, unintentionally kills another.

Example 4. Rosco McMurphy and Max Cavendish live in a state in which drag racing is a misdemeanor. They challenged each other to a drag race on the outskirts of town. Both cars hit a top speed of 95 miles per hour in an area where the speed limit was 45 miles per hour. Rosco lost control of his car and crashed into a crowd of spectators, killing two of them. Consequently, he was charged with involuntary manslaughter.

If drag racing were a felony in the state in which the race occurred, then Rosco, Max, and anyone else who had taken part in the drag race could be charged with murder. A killing that takes place during a felony is murder.

Assault and Battery

The unlawful touching of another person is known as **battery**, and it usually involves the forceful use of a person's hand, knife, or gun against another. Battery may also be committed by giving poison or drugs to an unsuspecting victim, spitting in someone's face, commanding a dog to attack someone, or even kissing someone who does not want to be kissed. Accidentally bumping someone in the cafeteria line at school would not be battery, because the crime requires criminal intent or at least reckless behavior.

An **assault** is an attempt to commit a battery. Pointing or shooting a gun at someone is the assault; the bullet striking the person is the battery. Some states no longer follow the common law distinction between assault and battery. Ohio, for example, has eliminated the term *battery* from its criminal code and substituted *assault* by itself.

Simple assault and battery are generally misdemeanors. Aggravated assault and aggravated battery, however, are felonies in most states. To qualify as an aggravated offense, the assault or battery would have to be committed with a deadly weapon, or with the intent to murder, commit rape, or commit robbery. Some states call aggravated assault felonious assault.

Kidnapping

The unlawful removal or restraint of a person against his or her will is called **kidnapping**. Often, a kidnapping victim is forced to be

It's a Question of Ethics

Ethical Crime?
Is there such a thing as an ethical crime? In other words, if an act is a crime, is it automatically unethical as well? Consider the story of Robin Hood, who stole from the rich and gave to the poor. Imagine a clerk employed at a multibillion dollar corporation who embezzles money and donates it to a homeless shelter. *Would you consider the clerk's behavior ethical or unethical?*

a captive. Kidnapping usually includes unlawful imprisonment for ransom, terrorism, torture, rape, or to commit a felony.

Sex Offenses

In the past, the crime of rape included only two types of situations: a male forcing a female to have sexual intercourse and a male having sexual intercourse with an underage female. Today laws have expanded the crime to include other types of sexual misconduct. The crime of statutory rape applies to situations in which the victim is underage. The consent of the underage person does not make the sexual encounter legal. Furthermore, a minor can also be prosecuted for having sex with another minor. Statutes defining rape do not specify the age of the offender.

Sexual assault by a friend or date has been recently recognized as a sex offense. Such crimes are usually labeled date rape or acquaintance rape.

Sexual assault is a very serious crime. Victims are hurt not only physically but also emotionally and psychologically. For these reasons, sex offenses carry very serious penalties. In one state, for example, the rape of a child under the age of 13 carries the penalty of life in prison.

Domestic Violence

Many children, spouses, and elderly people suffer harm from members of their own families. Any reckless form of physical or mental abuse within a family or household is known as domestic violence. Children are protected by child endangering or child abuse statutes, which prohibit neglect, ill treatment, and abuse. These laws provide for the relocation of mistreated children from abusive homes to places where they will be treated properly. The laws also provide for punishment of the abusers.

The law also protects a married individual from being abused by his or her spouse. Many communities have shelters where abused and battered spouses can seek safety. Abused spouses may also seek legal protection from the courts. They may request a protective order, which bars the abusing spouse from maintaining any contact with the victim. Such orders are enforced by the local police.

Hate Crimes

Many states have tried in recent years to make it a crime to use certain symbols, writings, pictures, or spoken words to cause fear or anger in people because of their race, religion, color, or gender. Such actions are sometimes referred to as *hate crimes* and *hate speech*.

The courts have held that hate crime statutes must be drafted very narrowly, which means the statutes must not specify the content of the hate speech. A legislature can pass a statute that outlaws language or symbols that are designed to rouse fear or outrage regardless of the content of that speech. However, a statute making it illegal to use speech designed to incite outrage or fear based only on race, religion, color, gender, or any similar category would not be correct.

Crimes Against Property

The most common crimes against property include burglary, robbery, arson, larceny, and embezzlement. Crimes against property can be classified as felonies or misdemeanors, depending on the severity of the crimes. See Figure 3.3 and Figure 3.4 for statistical data on violent crime in the United States.

VIOLENT CRIME RATES BY AGE OF VICTIM
The crimes represented by the statistics in this table include murder, sexual offenses, robbery, and assault. *Which age groups of victims have the highest crime rates for the two most recent years in the table?*

Figure 3.3	Violent Crime Rates by Age of Victim						
Year	**Age of Victim (Adjusted victimization rate in percent per 1,000 persons age 12 and over)**						
	12–15	**16–19**	**20–24**	**25–34**	**35–49**	**50–64**	**65 +**
1979	78.5	93.4	98.4	66.3	38.2	13.6	6.2
1980	72.5	91.3	94.1	60.0	37.4	15.6	7.2
1981	86.0	90.7	93.7	65.8	41.6	17.3	8.3
1982	75.6	94.4	93.8	69.6	38.6	13.8	6.1
1983	75.4	86.3	82.0	62.2	36.5	11.9	5.9
1984	78.2	90.0	87.5	56.6	37.9	13.2	5.2
1985	79.6	89.4	82.0	56.5	35.6	13.0	4.8
1986	77.1	80.8	80.1	52.0	36.0	10.8	4.8
1987	87.2	92.4	85.5	51.9	34.7	11.4	5.2
1988	83.7	95.9	80.2	53.2	39.1	13.4	4.4
1989	92.5	98.2	78.8	52.8	37.3	10.5	4.2
1990	101.1	99.1	86.1	55.2	34.4	9.9	3.7
1991	94.5	122.6	103.6	54.3	37.2	12.5	4.0
1992	111.0	103.7	95.2	56.8	38.1	13.2	5.2
1993	115.5	114.2	91.6	56.9	42.5	15.2	5.9
1994	118.6	123.9	100.4	59.1	41.3	17.6	4.6
1995	113.1	106.6	85.8	58.5	35.7	12.9	6.4
1996	95.0	102.8	74.5	51.2	32.9	15.7	4.9
1997	87.9	96.3	68.0	47.0	32.3	14.6	4.4
1998	82.5	91.3	67.5	41.6	29.9	15.4	2.8
1999	74.4	77.5	68.7	36.4	25.3	14.4	3.8
2000	60.1	64.4	49.5	34.9	21.9	13.7	3.7
2001	55.1	55.9	44.9	29.4	23.0	9.5	3.2
2002	44.4	58.3	47.6	26.4	18.2	10.7	3.4

SOURCE: Rape, robbery, and assault data are from the *National Crime Victimization Survey (NCVS)*. The homicide data are collected by the *FBI's Uniform Crime Reports (UCR)* from reports from law enforcement agencies.

Figure 3.4	Violent Crime Rates by Race of Victim	
Year	**White**	**Black**
1979	19.6	33.2
1980	18.7	34.0
1981	19.7	40.4
1982	19.0	36.9
1983	16.3	33.1
1984	17.1	32.7
1985	15.6	28.9
1986	15.6	25.2
1987	15.0	33.8
1988	16.0	31.4
1989	16.1	29.5
1990	15.4	31.8
1991	16.2	31.3
1992	16.9	33.0
1993	17.8	34.3
1994	17.1	33.5
1995	13.5	26.4
1996	13.3	26.3
1997	12.9	20.7
1998	11.6	19.2
1999	10.2	19.5
2000	8.7	16.2
2001	8.4	12.7
2002	6.6	13.0

NOTE:

Serious violent crime victimization rates by race.

Rates per 1,000 persons age 12 +.

Serious violent crime includes homicide, rape, robbery, and aggravated assault.

SOURCE: Rape, robbery, and assault data are from the *National Crime Victimization Survey (NCVS)*. The homicide data are collected by the *FBI's Uniform Crime Reports (UCR)* from reports from law enforcement agencies.

VIOLENT CRIME RATES BY RACE OF VICTIM

The crimes represented by the statistics in this table include murder, sexual offenses, robbery, and assault. *What trend is evident over time in the data on crime victimization by racial group?*

Burglary

Common law defines **burglary** as the breaking and entering of a dwelling house at night with the intent to commit a felony. Today, state laws have expanded the definition of the crime to include breaking and entering in the daytime, breaking and entering places other than homes, and breaking and entering with the intent to commit a misdemeanor. If any part of the definition of burglary cannot be proven, the defendant cannot be found guilty.

A Global Perspective: Laws Around the World

Native American Groups

The people we have come to know as American Indians or Native Americans came to the North American continent from Northeast Asia by way of the Bering Strait. Most historians and scientists agree these people began their migration before 30,000 BC and were the Americas first inhabitants. Yet it took less than 200 years for European settlers to decimate these natives. In time, however, organizations like the American Indian Movement (AIM) pressured the federal government to take action. Finally, a series of laws were passed in the 1970s to promote the welfare of the Native Americans. These acts encourage tribes to set up and govern their own communities, health care, housing, law enforcement, and schools. They also provide funding for teachers, counselors, and educational materials, like computers.

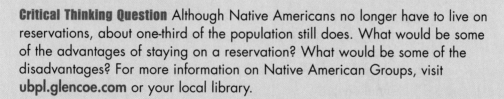

Native Americans still face many hardships, but one statistic in particular may reflect a hopeful future. The 1890 U.S. census recorded just over 200,000 Native Americans. The 1990 census shows a Native American population of close to two million. Many experts believe these to be the highest figures since European colonization.

Critical Thinking Question Although Native Americans no longer have to live on reservations, about one-third of the population still does. What would be some of the advantages of staying on a reservation? What would be some of the disadvantages? For more information on Native American Groups, visit **ubpl.glencoe.com** or your local library.

Example 5. Todd was jogging after dark and noticed a house with a partly opened window. He raised the window farther, climbed inside, and stole expensive shoes. A neighbor saw Todd leaving and called the police, who arrested him nearby and charged him with burglary. Applying the common law definition, a court could not find Todd guilty because there was no breaking—the window of entry was open. However, most state statutes now say that a breaking has occurred even when someone raises a partially opened window.

Larceny

The unlawful taking and carrying away of the personal property of another with the intent to deprive the owner of the property is called **larceny**, the legal term for stealing. In many states, larceny is classified as petty or grand, depending on the value of the property taken. Petty larceny is a misdemeanor; grand larceny is a felony. In some states, stealing property with a value of $300 or less is a misdemeanor; stealing property valued at more than $300 is a felony. Shoplifting is a form of larceny.

Embezzlement

The crime of **embezzlement** is the wrongful taking of another's property by a person who has been entrusted with that property.

> *Example 6.* Virginia Waddell worked as a supermarket cashier to help pay for college. A customer bought groceries and paid with cash. Virginia put the money directly into her pocket instead of the cash register. This act was embezzlement because Virginia was entrusted with the money before she stole it.

Robbery

The wrongful taking and carrying away of the personal property of another through violence or threats is the crime of **robbery**. Robbery involves taking "from the person"; that is, from the body or close to the body of the victim, by using force, violence, or threats. Naturally, the penalty for robbery is greater than the penalty for larceny.

> *Example 7.* Suppose, in Example 6, that someone came into the store, pointed a gun at Virginia, and demanded money from the register. This act would be armed robbery because the robber used a weapon to forcefully take the money from Virginia's personal custody.

Arson

Under common law, **arson** was defined as the willful and malicious burning of the dwelling house of another. Most states have added arson statutes to cover the burning of buildings other than dwelling houses. The scorching or blackening of a part of a building is not enough to be considered arson. Some portion of the building must actually have been on fire so that the wood or other building material is charred.

Vandalism

Vandalism is a serious problem in many communities today. The crime of **vandalism** involves willful or malicious damage to property and may also be called malicious mischief or criminal damaging. To be guilty of vandalism, a person does not have to be the one who actually does the damage; anyone who supports the crime of vandalism by acting as a "lookout" can also be charged.

Shoplifting

The act of stealing goods from a store, called **shoplifting**, is a form of theft that costs American consumers billions of dollars each year. Shoplifting losses and the cost of extra security increase retail prices considerably. The severity of a shoplifting charge depends on the value of the goods stolen. In some cases, a person can be charged with stealing before the act is completed. Many states have laws that regard the concealment on one's person of an article of merchandise to be persuasive evidence of the intent to steal.

PRIMA FACIE EVIDENCE
Shoplifting has become one of the most widespread crimes in America today. *Why would the law permit the mere concealment of merchandise on your person to be prima facie evidence of shoplifting?*

Law & Academics

Science
Do you like solving problems? Do you find science fascinating? If so, forensic science might be a career possibility for you. Forensic scientists use highly technical skills and procedures to uncover evidence from a crime scene. They can find clues in blood, hair, and skin that often lead to the arrest and conviction of criminals.

Research Activity
Investigate forensic science. Research its history and the tools and equipment used by forensic scientists. Then find out what education is needed to become a forensic scientist. *Is forensic science for you?*

▲ DRAG RACING AND LIABILITY
Many states have statutes that specifically outlaw drag racing. *Who would be criminally
liable if these students decided to engage in
an illegal drag race?*

Motor Vehicle Violations

A license to drive a motor vehicle is a privilege and may be suspended temporarily or permanently if abused. Young drivers who
break traffic laws are not offered special protection as juveniles in
most states. They may be tried in traffic court and can be fined or have
their licenses suspended or revoked.

Many states have statutes that specifically outlaw drag racing and
joyriding. Drag racing generally includes the unauthorized racing of
two vehicles side by side and the timing of vehicles that separately run
a prearranged course. Joyriding occurs when someone temporarily
takes a motor vehicle without the owner's permission. It is important
to remember that in both drag racing and joyriding, all those who participate can be held liable, not just the driver(s).

Crimes Involving Controlled Substances

Another serious problem facing society today is drug abuse. Alcohol and tobacco may be considered drugs because they are not legal for teenagers or children.

Alcohol

Alcohol is the major chemical found in beer, wine, whiskey, and other distilled beverages. It is the most commonly used drug in the United States. A merchant or bartender convicted of selling an alcoholic beverage to someone under the legal drinking age may be imprisoned, fined, or both, and may lose the license that is required to sell such beverages. The underage individual also may be prosecuted for making the illegal purchase, for lying about his or her age, or for both.

Drugs

Drugs are chemicals that alter the functions of the mind or body. Possession, distribution, or sale of certain drugs may violate a federal

Virtual Law

Investigating Cyber Crime

The federal Computer Fraud and Abuse Act makes it a felony for anyone to "knowingly cause the transmission of a program, information, code or command, and as a result of such conduct, intentionally cause damage without authorization to a protected computer." A protected computer is one used in interstate commerce or communication.

John Michael Sullivan was convicted under this law. In retaliation for receiving a poor performance review, Sullivan inserted a "code bomb," including a date trigger for noon on September 23, 1998, to cause his company's computers to become inoperative. The company's operations were disrupted for several days, and its direct loss as a result of Sullivan's conduct was more than $100,000. (Source: U. S. Department of Justice, www.cybercrime.gov)

Connect Visit the U.S. Department of Justice Web site at www.usdoj.gov. Research what efforts are being taken in the criminal division toward investigating Internet crime. (Source: U.S. Department of Justice, www.cybercrime.gov)

▲COMPUTER CRIME
Both the state and the federal governments
have used innovative tactics to deal with the
increased incidence of computer crime. *What
are some examples of tactics used by the
states and the federal government?*

law, a state law, or both. Each state sets its own penalties in relation to
drug offenses. The sale of drugs is always considered a more serious
crime than the mere possession or use of drugs. It is also a crime to
give drugs away.

Computer Crimes

Although computers and network devices have helped make our
lives easier, they have also introduced new ways to commit crimes.
Both state and federal government statutes address this new legal
problem in a variety of ways.

Federal Crimes and Laws

The federal government has extended the interpretation of many
criminal statutes already on the books so that these statutes will also
apply to computers. For instance, statutes prohibiting mail fraud and

wire fraud have been used to apprehend computer criminals. However, these attempts were not always successful, so the federal government has now passed statutes that are directly related to computer crime. These statutes include the Computer Fraud and Abuse Act and the National Information Infrastructure Act of 1996.

The Computer Fraud and Abuse Act is specifically aimed at computer hackers. Hackers gain unauthorized entry to a computer system, generally to do some sort of mischief. The National Information Infrastructure Act is designed to outlaw the practice of extorting money or other favors in exchange for not causing a computer system to crash.

State Crimes and Computers

Some states have created the crime of computer trespass, which simply outlaws using a computer to commit any crime. Other states have passed computer fraud statutes, which make it an offense to use a computer to acquire property, services, or money by fraud. Some states have a detailed list of computer-related crimes, including theft of computer services, destruction of equipment, and misuse of computer information.

Section 3.2 Assessment

Reviewing What You Learned
1. What are the major crimes committed against people?
2. What are the major crimes committed against property?
3. What are the major crimes that involve controlled substances?
4. Identify federal legislation pertaining to computer crime, fraud, and abuse.

Critical Thinking Activity
Computer Crime Using the Internet, library, or other resource, identify state legislation pertaining to computer crime, fraud, and abuse. List and describe some of the laws in your state, and then compare them with the laws of another state. How are they the same? How are they different?

Legal Skills in Action
Hate Speech Many states have made it a crime to use certain symbols, writings, pictures, or spoken words to cause fear or anger in people because of their race, religion, color, or gender. The courts have held that hate crime or hate speech statutes must be drafted very narrowly. Imagine that you are a television newscaster for a cable news network. Write an opinion piece in which you argue that the courts are wrong in their rulings regarding hate speech.

Chapter Summary

Section 3.1 What Is a Crime?

- Crime is considered an act against the public good. Crimes can be classified as felonies or misdemeanors. A felony is a major crime punishable by imprisonment or death. Murder, manslaughter, burglary, robbery, and arson are examples of felonies. A less serious crime is called a misdemeanor. Driving an automobile without a license, lying about one's age to purchase alcohol, and leaving the scene of an automobile accident are examples of misdemeanors. To determine felonies from misdemeanors, one can examine the severity of punishment for any given crime.

- Each state government has inherent police power, and enacting criminal statues is a part of this power. In contrast, the federal government was created with no general police power. The federal government is able to create criminal statutes only in areas over which it has jurisdiction. However, the federal government has interpreted its power under the commerce clause rather expansively to legislate a body of criminal law. The commerce clause requires Congress to regulate commerce among the states.

- A crime is defined by two elements: the criminal act and the required state of mind. A criminal act must involve voluntary conduct. A person cannot be accused of a crime if that accusation is based on the one's physical or mental state.

- Criminal defendants can argue the following defenses: insanity, entrapment, self-defense, and defense of family members. In many states, a person is considered legally insane if "as a result of mental disease or defect he or she lacks substantial capacity to appreciate the criminality of his conduct or to conform his conduct to the requirements of the law." A person can use the defense of entrapment if a law enforcement officer induces him or her to commit a crime.

The defense of self-defense can be used if a person uses force to protect himself or herself from attack. Similarly, most states will not punish people who can prove that they used force to rescue a family member from attack.

Section 3.2 Particular Crimes

- Crimes against people include murder, manslaughter, assault, battery, kidnapping, sex offenses, domestic violence, and hate crimes. Murder is the unlawful killing of anther human being with malice aforethought. Manslaughter is the unlawful killing of another person without malice aforethought. Battery is the unlawful touching of another person, and assault is an attempt to commit battery. The unlawful removal or restraint of a person against his or her will is called kidnapping. Sex offenses include various forms of rape. Reckless physical or mental abuse within a family constitutes domestic violence. Hate crimes occur when a perpetrator uses specific symbols, writings, or speech to cause fear or anger in people because of their race, religion, color, or gender.

- Crimes against property include burglary, larceny, embezzlement, robbery, arson, vandalism, and shoplifting.

- Selling an alcoholic beverage to an underage person is a crime. It is also a crime for the underage individual to purchase alcohol or even to lie about his or her age to attempt to purchase it. The sale, possession, or free distribution of drugs is considered a criminal offense.

- States have enacted different laws to deal with computer crimes. Some states have created the crime of computer trespass; others have passed computer fraud statutes. Some states have legislated a list of computer-related crimes, including theft of computer services, destruction of equipment, and misuse of computer information.

Using Legal Language

Consider the key terms in the list below. Then use these terms to complete the following exercises.

crime   murder
prosecutor   assault
defendant   kidnapping
felony   burglary
misdemeanor   robbery

1. Imagine that you are a rookie police officer. You are assigned to work with a veteran who is helping you understand the criminal justice system. Create a script of a conversation with your partner. Use the key terms in the script.
2. Carry out the conversation in front of the class, using gestures, voice inflections, and props to emphasize your key points.
3. Discuss with your partner ways in which you could have improved your conversation.
4. As a class, vote to select the best presentation. If possible, winners should arrange to videotape their presentation.

Understanding Business and Personal Law Online

Self-Check Quiz Visit the *Understanding Business and Personal Law* Web site at **ubpl.glencoe.com** and click on Chapter 3: Criminal Law— Self-Check Quizzes to prepare for the chapter exam.

The Law Review

Answer the following questions. Refer to the chapter for additional reinforcement.
5. Who is always the plaintiff in a criminal case? Who is the prosecutor? Who is the defendant?
6. What is the one crime named and defined in the U.S. Constitution?
7. Explain the difference among first-degree murder, second-degree murder, and manslaughter.
8. Why does the crime of rape carry very serious penalties?
9. Why is the penalty for robbery greater than the penalty for larceny?
10. What is double jeopardy?
11. What is embezzlement?
12. How does burglary differ from robbery?
13. What are some examples of motor vehicle violations?

Linking School to Work

Acquiring and Evaluating Information

Dalia dated Alfonso, a coworker, a few times and decided that he was not for her. Alfonso, however, had other ideas. He began to send Dalia flowers regularly and followed her home from work most days. On the weekends, Alfonso would show up at the restaurants where Dalia was eating. Dalia became frightened, and on several occasions, she asked Alfonso to stop following her because she believed she was being stalked. Today, all U.S. states have an anti-stalking law.

14. Find out when your state enacted an anti-stalking law and the circumstances surrounding why it became law.

15. Research if there are federal laws against stalking. Write a 250-word paper about your findings.

Let's Debate

Vigilante Justice

Ennis Gonzales works as a computer programmer for a large corporation. He is considered an expert in his field. Recently, he embarked on a campaign against child pornography. Ennis has been able to hack into Web sites that feature child pornography and disable them. So far, he has destroyed about 50 sites.

Debate

16. Is destroying someone else's Web site illegal?

17. Do you think a court of law would find Ennis guilty if he were arrested?

18. What is your opinion of Ennis's actions?

Grasping Case Issues

For the following cases, give your decision and state a legal principle that applies.

19. Several years ago, four Los Angeles police officers were tried in the state court of California for assaulting Rodney King while attempting to arrest him after a lengthy car chase. The jury found the defendants not guilty. Despite this state court decision, the defendants were put on trial again in federal court. Did the second trial violate the Fifth Amendment prohibition against double jeopardy? Why or why not?

20. Julius Davidson is arrested for shoplifting. He asks his attorney to plead not guilty by reason of insanity. Davidson believes that he will be free if he is found not guilty by reason of insanity. Is he correct? Why or why not?

21. Shane and Kira were riding through town one Saturday evening when two classmates challenged them to a drag race. Shane, who was driving, agreed. When they were picked up by the police, Kira believed she would not be criminally liable because she was just a passenger. Is she correct? Why or why not?

22. Pyrrah is part of a group of students who decide to break into the high school and spray paint the hallways. Pyrrah agrees to act as lookout, believing that she will not be criminally liable if they are picked up by the police. Is she correct? Why or why not?

23. Ben Feeney runs a pawn shop. He often accepts stolen merchandise, sells it, and splits the profits with the thief. Lt. Jose Urena sends several undercover police officers to the shop, and they catch Ben in the act of fencing stolen goods. At trial, Ben's attorney tries to use the defense of entrapment. Will this defense work? Why or why not?

In each case that follows, you be the judge.

24. Property Crimes

Reese entered a fast food restaurant through a rear door, having arranged for an accomplice who worked there to leave the door unlocked. Reese pushed one employee against a soda machine, and while holding a gun on the manager, forced the manager to open the safe. Reese then locked the employees in a cooler and left with more than $5,000. *Has Reese committed burglary, robbery, or larceny? Explain your answer.*

State v. Reese, 113 Ohio App. 3d. 642 (OH).

25. Hate Crimes

Several teenagers burned a cross on the lawn of a black family in their neighborhood. One of the youths, a minor, was charged under a city ordinance that stated it was a crime to place on private property "any symbol, object, appellation, characterization or graffiti. . . which one knows or has reasonable grounds to know arouses anger, alarm, or resentment in others on the basis of race, color, creed, religion, or gender." The defendant argued that the ordinance was unconstitutional. *Was it? Why or why not?*

R.A.V. v. St. Paul, 505 U.S. 1992 (U.S. Sup. Ct.).

Legal Link

Teen Criminals

Although most teenagers do not commit crimes, some do. Perhaps with additional education, at-risk teenagers would think twice about committing crimes. Create a pamphlet that highlights those crimes that are most often committed by teenagers in your state. Share the pamphlet with other members of your class.

Connect

Use a variety of search engines to complete the following exercises.

26. Locate information about crimes committed by teens.

27. Find statistics that show the numbers of teens who commit crimes.

28. Determine the usual punishments imposed.

29. Discuss the impact on the teenager's record now and when he or she is an adult.

POWER READING STRATEGIES

30. **Predict** Most people are honest and hard working. Are all the laws we have in this country really necessary?

31. **Connect** Do you watch any television show about the police, criminal investigations, lawyers, or court cases? Which ones seem most realistic? Explain your answer.

32. **Question** Discuss why driving a car is a privilege, not a right.

33. **Respond** Many of the people in jail are drug addicts who were arrested for possession of controlled substances. Do you believe they should be incarcerated? Can you think of any other options for them?

The Law of Torts

Understanding Business and Personal Law *Online*

Chapter Overview Visit the *Understanding Business and Personal Law* Web site at ubpl.glencoe.com and click on Chapter 4: The Law of Torts—Chapter Overviews to preview the chapter information.

The Opening Scene

After the football game, some New Hope High students arrive at The Corner Café, a local hangout popular with students.

The Corner Café

JAMILA: You drive like a fool, Trai! The way you took that last corner could have caused an accident! It's too bad that Daniel's dad wouldn't let him drive. I'm never getting in a car with you again!

TRAI: You're not exactly a great driver either, Jamila. I don't know why you have to make such a big deal out of everything. If you don't like my driving, you can feel free to walk home tonight—I don't care!

JAMILA: Walk five miles? I don't think so. I guess I'll just have to deal with your driving for tonight.

TRAI: Well, then I guess you've assumed the risk, as Mrs. Martinez would say.

DANIEL: Yeah, just like that kid who was attacked by those tigers.

TRAI: Tigers? As usual, Daniel is miles away! What are you talking about?

DANIEL: I'm talking about the Tiger Zoo. Maybe you should try reading the paper sometime, Trai.

TRAI: The what?

DANIEL: The Tiger Zoo! It's located out on Route 229.

PEGGY: Danny's right, Trai. I took my little sisters there last month. The zoo has six or seven baby tigers, and you can pet them and everything. They're really cute!

DANIEL: You can't pet the tigers anymore. One of them bit a kid, and they shut the place down. It was all over the papers last week.

(A waiter arrives and takes everyone's orders. Trai, Peggy, and Jamila order burgers and fries. Daniel orders only a soda.)

JAMILA: Aren't you going to order some food, Danny? If you're short on money, I can lend you some.

DANIEL: A girl who ate here last week got really sick. There's no way I'm going to allow that to happen to me.

TRAI: You're full of good news tonight.

PEGGY: Once again, he's right. This girl ate some bad fish and got really sick. Now she's suing this place.

TRAI: Why? It was an accident. You can't sue somebody for an accident. Besides, what are the odds that it'll happen again? Order up, Danny boy.

DANIEL: No way. I don't believe in taking unnecessary risks.

JAMILA: Then you'd better not ride in a car that Trai's driving. He's the most negligent driver on earth.

PEGGY: You can't be negligent until you actually hurt somebody.

TRAI: Thanks, Peg.

PEGGY: Stupid, yes. Negligent, no.

What Are the Legal Issues?

1. What is the difference between a crime and a tort?
2. What are some specific intentional torts in our legal system?
3. What is involved in the tort of negligence?
4. What defenses exist for negligence?
5. What is involved in the tort of strict liability?

Intentional Torts

The Difference between Criminal Law and Tort Law

When people commit a **crime**, they harm not only specific individuals but also the general welfare. The role of government is to preserve the safety and well-being of the entire social structure. A crime is considered an offense against the public at large and is therefore punishable by the government.

In contrast, a **tort** is a private wrong committed by one person against another. It involves one person's interference with another person's rights. A tort will lead the wronged party to try and recover money as compensation for the loss or injury suffered. However, such an offense does not call upon the government to punish wrongdoers and to protect society.

In some situations, however, a single action can be both a tort and a crime.

Example 1. Dr. John Boyle was prosecuted, tried, and convicted of strangling his wife, Noreen. After being criminally prosecuted for aggravated murder, a wrongful death suit was brought under tort law on behalf of Noreen's two minor children. The single act of killing his wife involved Dr. Boyle in two court actions: one brought by the state for a crime and the other filed on behalf of the children for a tort offense. The law punished the defendant with a sentence of life imprisonment and also gave the children the right to recover money as compensation for the death of their mother.

The law of torts is grounded in the concept of rights. Under tort law, all people are entitled to certain rights simply because they are members of our society. These rights include, among others: the right to be free from bodily harm, the right to enjoy a good reputation, the right to conduct business without unwarranted interference, and the right to own property free from damage or trespass.

Other rights arise under special circumstances. For example, patients who enter a hospital have the right to expect competent care from the healthcare providers assigned to their cases.

The law imposes a duty on all of us to respect the rights of others. Tort law governs this interplay between rights and duties. The word *tort*, from the Latin word *tortus*, meaning "twisted," is used to refer to a wrong against an individual.

Intentional Torts

Torts are classified as intentional or unintentional. An **intentional tort** occurs when a person knows and desires the consequences of his or her act. Conversely, the person who commits an unintentional tort does not have this mental determination. The most common intentional torts are listed and defined in Figure 4.1. Let's take a closer look at some intentional torts and selected situations to which they apply.

Assault and Battery

Assault and battery are two separate torts, which may or may not be committed together. The tort of assault occurs when one person deliberately leads another person to believe that he or she is about to be harmed. Rushing toward someone with a raised knife while shouting threats would constitute an assault, even if the victim is not touched. The assault occurs because the victim fears immediate bodily harm. The tort of

Figure 4.1	Intentional Torts
Tort	**Description**
Assault	Threatening to strike or harm with a weapon or physical movement, resulting in fear.
Battery	Unlawful, unprivileged touching of another person.
Trespass	Wrongful injury or interference with the property of another.
Nuisance	Anything that intereferes with the enjoyment of life or property.
Interference with contractual relations	Intentionally causing one person to break or refrain from entering a contract with another.
Deceit	False statement or deceptive practice done with intent to injure another.
Conversion	Unauthorized taking or borrowing of personal property of another for the use of the taker.
False imprisonment (false arrest)	Unlawful restraint of a person, whether in prison or otherwise.
Defamation	Wrongful act of injuring another's reputation by making false statements.
Invasion of privacy	Interference with a person's right to be left alone.
Misuse of legal procedure	Bringing of legal action with malice and without probable cause.
Infliction of emotional distress	Intentionally or recklessly causing emotional or mental suffering to others.

INTENTIONAL TORTS

In criminal law when someone commits a wrong, the action is called a crime. In civil law when someone commits a wrong, the action is called a tort. *Which of the torts listed do you think is the most serious?*

battery involves the unlawful, unprivileged touching of another person, even if the physical contact is not harmful. The essence of battery is the unwanted touch, regardless of the intent of the wrongdoer.

The tort of assault is different from the crime of assault, which you learned about in Chapter 3. The essential difference between the two lies in the fact that the victim of a tort assault must know that the **tortfeasor**, or person who committed the tort, meant to commit harm. Otherwise, the victim has not been frightened, and no harm has resulted. In criminal law, however, an assault is an attempted battery, and the intended victim need not be aware of the attempt at all. For example, a criminal assault can be carried out against an unconscious victim. Trying an individual for the crime of assault is done on behalf of society as a whole. On the other hand, a person is tried for the tort of assault to compensate a victim for personal anguish or stress suffered.

Trespass

A **trespass** is the wrongful damage to or interference with the property of another. Property refers to anything you may own, including movable items (cars, VCRs, CD players, purses, wallets) and nonmovable items (real property). Real property includes land and things built on the land, growing on the land, or located within the land. The tort of trespass refers most commonly to real property.

> *Example 2.* Sorensen and some friends went hunting on Lashutka's private ranch without her permission. This constituted the tort of trespass, and the landowner could bring a lawsuit against Sorensen and the others. Notice that Sorensen and his

ASSAULT
Physical touching is not necessary for a person to commit an assault. *Which of the two people in this photograph would you consider to be in the process of committing an assault?*

friends did not actually harm Lashutka's property. This makes no difference because the law of torts presumes injury merely from someone's unwelcome presence on the property of another.

Under common law, ownership of real property extended from the center of the earth to the highest point in the sky. A person owned not only a portion of the earth's crust but also the ground below and the airspace above. Today, however, most states have rewritten laws to limit a property owner's claim to the airspace far above his or her land. Doing so ensures that private ownership will not interfere with air travel.

Nuisance

The tort of **nuisance** is anything that interferes with the enjoyment of life or property. Loud noises at night, noxious odors, or smoke or fumes coming from a nearby house are examples of nuisances. A public nuisance is one that affects many people. In contrast, a private nuisance affects only one person. A complaint by local residents about the noise at The Corner Café in The Opening Scene could make its owner the target of a lawsuit for creating a public nuisance.

False Imprisonment

Law enforcement officers must have probable cause or a warrant to arrest someone. Consequently, they can be sued for **false imprisonment**, or false arrest, if they make an arrest without meeting

Virtual Law

Privacy in Cyberspace

Many companies that rely on the Internet are paying more attention to their privacy policies. Supporters of privacy rights say that some e-commerce companies violate consumer privacy. Laws are being considered to require companies to reveal how they gather and use information about consumers. As a result, many companies are hiring Chief Privacy Officers. These executives set up information-gathering policies and create programs that inform and educate employees on privacy policies. Chief Privacy Officers would also review privacy policies as they relate to new products and services. (Source: *New York Times*, p. A7, Feb. 12, 2001)

Connect Search several Web sites of corporations that do business online. Compare their privacy policies on sharing consumer information with other companies.

You're going to be late for soccer practice again! As you hurry through the produce department of the grocery store where you work, you notice some smashed grapes on the floor. Cleaning the floors is your job, but you've already clocked out and if you're late for soccer practice again, you'll get benched. You don't see anyone around immediately that you can tell. What do you do? *Are you ethically responsible for cleaning up the grapes? for taking time to notify someone? for being on time for soccer practice?*

these requirements. However, because of the prevalence of shoplifting in our society, most states now have laws that allow store managers and detectives to detain suspected shoplifters. Store personnel must have reasonable grounds to suspect that shoplifting has occurred, and they must detain the suspect in a reasonable manner for only a reasonable length of time. Determining what is "reasonable" can be difficult.

Example 3. Betty Brandon, a store detective for the Brennan Department Store, thought she saw customer Gwen Forsythe place lipstick in her purse. The detective apprehended the woman and locked her in a storeroom for questioning. However, Betty and the store manager became satisfied that Gwen was innocent and released her. Gwen sued for false imprisonment, and the court ruled that the store employees had acted unreasonably. Gwen won a large sum of money as compensation for her humiliation and emotional suffering.

Defamation

The wrongful act of injuring another's reputation by making false statements is called **defamation**. Defamation is divided into two categories: libel and slander. Libel is a false statement in written or printed form that injures another's reputation or reflects negatively on that person's character. Radio and television broadcasts, newspaper stories, video and audio recordings, movies, photographs, signs, and even

DEFAMATION
Freedom of the press and the right of individuals to bring a defamation suit often clash in this country. *How has the United States Supreme Court created safeguards to help preserve freedom of the press and the right to sue for defamation?*

paintings and statues may be subject to charges of libel. All such forms of communication reduce a false statement to a permanent form. In contrast, slander is a false statement that is made orally to a third party.

You can usually sue for libel if the permanent statement in question damages your reputation, is false, and is communicated to at least one other person. People are allowed to speak the truth, however, as long as it is done without spite or ill will. In addition, statements made by senators and representatives on the floor of Congress and statements made in a court of law are privileged. This means they are not vulnerable to a defamation lawsuit. The concept of privileged speech is intended to protect the open debate of legislative and judicial matters.

People in the public limelight also have more difficulty than the average person in proving damage to their reputations in defamation lawsuits. Public officials such as politicians and judges, as well as a variety of other public personalities including movie stars, pop singers,

LAWS in Your Life

Privacy on the Phone

Innovations in telephone technology have made communication much more convenient. Cordless, cellular, and digital phones allow varying degrees of mobility while talking on the telephone. When you use such phones, however, you are transmitting signals through the air that are similar to a radio broadcast. Anyone with a receiver tuned to the right frequency can overhear your conversation. Digital phones offer the most protection against eavesdropping, but special decoders can convert even digital transmissions into voice audio.

Federal laws offer some protection of telephone privacy. Although it is not unlawful to overhear a phone call, it is against the law to divulge the conversation or to use it for someone's benefit. The manufacture or sale of scanning devices that can intercept cellular or digital calls is also illegal. With some exceptions, the recording of telephone conversations without the knowledge or consent of both parties is a violation of federal and state law.

Survey Your Class How many people in your class use a cordless, cellular, or digital phone regularly? How many of your classmates are concerned that their conversations may not be private? Contact the Federal Communications Commission to obtain more information about laws protecting telephone use.

sports figures, and other entertainers, are considered people in the public limelight. Under guidelines established by the U.S. Supreme Court, these public figures must prove that false statements about them were made with actual malice. In other words, it must be proven that the offending statement was made with the knowledge that it was false or with a reckless disregard for whether it was true.

Public figures are held to a more difficult standard because they have voluntarily chosen a lifestyle that naturally exposes them to close scrutiny by the press. They can respond to damaging statements in a way the average person can't, such as by calling a news conference, appearing on a television talk show, buying newspaper space, buying air time on radio and television, or issuing a press release.

Invasion of Privacy

Invasion of privacy is interfering with a person's right to be left alone, which includes the right to be free from unwanted publicity and interference with private matters. In most states, the invasion of privacy is a tort. Some states, such as New York, have established this right by statute. The state of California, on the other hand, has established the right of privacy by amending the state constitution.

The Federal Privacy Act of 1974 provides safeguards for individuals against the invasion of privacy by agencies of the federal government. With some exceptions, the act requires federal agencies to let you determine what personal records will be kept by any agency. You also have the right to know what records are being kept about you, to receive copies of any records, and to correct any errors. Agencies must get permission to use records for purposes other than those for which

INVASION OF PRIVACY
Keeping personal records private is important to many people. The right to privacy may be invaded by people or businesses with access to computer records. *How can people protect themselves against an invasion of their privacy by computer?*

they were gathered. People in business who are entrusted with confidential records must make great efforts to ensure that the records are not made public. Failure to protect such confidential matters could result in an invasion of privacy lawsuit.

Your right to privacy does not merely involve written records. It is also considered an invasion of privacy for any group or agency to use your photograph, likeness, or name without your permission for advertising, publicity, or publication purposes.

New privacy concerns have arisen with increased use of computers because computers store a great deal of information about an enormous number of people. For instance, the right to privacy is violated when unauthorized people use the computer to gain access to confidential information. Other invasions of privacy occur when unnecessary data is recorded and stored by an organization or business, inaccurate information is kept on file, and private information is revealed to the public without appropriate authorization.

Two important federal statutes designed to protect privacy include the Fair Credit Reporting Act and the Right to Financial Privacy Act. Under the Fair Credit Reporting Act, credit bureaus must, on request, inform you about information they have on file about you. The Right to Financial Privacy Act forbids financial institutions from opening your records, most of which are kept in computer files, to the government without appropriate authorization from you or without an official court order.

Section 4.1 Assessment

Reviewing What You Learned

1. What is the difference between a crime and a tort?
2. What concept is at the heart of tort law?
3. How can a tort be committed?
4. What are the most common intentional torts?

Critical Thinking Activity

Tort Law If criminal law is responsible for dealing with individuals who commit wrongful acts, what purpose does tort law serve? Why do you need to understand the different intentional torts?

Legal Skills in Action

Computer Privacy Many people, businesses, and government agencies today have increased access to computers. Although this access may be a great convenience, it is also a source of danger, especially to privacy. Write a research paper in which you trace the development of the computer along with the increased threat to privacy represented by its development.

Negligence and Strict Liability

What You'll Learn

- How to define negligence
- How to explain the elements of negligence
- How to define the major defenses to negligence
- How to define strict liability

Why It's Important

Because any person is a potential victim and a perpetrator of negligence, understanding this vital area of tort law will help you protect yourself legally.

Legal Terms

- negligence
- strict liability
- breach of duty
- proximate cause
- contributory negligence
- comparative negligence
- assumption of risk

Unintentional Torts

A person can breach his or her duty in our society through other ways than by committing an intentional tort. For example, you may act in a careless manner and, as a result, cause injury to a person, damage to property, or both. Your participation in an activity that is considered very dangerous, such as keeping a tiger in your backyard, may also cause harm to others. Injury that is caused by a person's mere carelessness is known as **negligence**; injury caused by an individual's participation in ultrahazardous activity is known as **strict liability**.

Negligence

Negligence is an accidental or unintentional tort and is the tort that occurs most often in society today. Negligence is the failure to exercise the degree of care that a reasonable person would have exercised in the same circumstances. Negligence may be present, for example, in an automobile accident or when someone trips on a broken floorboard.

Elements of Negligence

The law has established specific standards to prevent people from suing innocent parties for negligence. To succeed in a tort suit for negligence, the plaintiff must prove all of the following elements:

- The defendant owed the plaintiff a duty of care. In other words, the defendant failed to act as a reasonable person would have acted.
- This failure to use the degree of care required under the circumstances is called a **breach of duty**.
- The breach of duty by the defendant was the proximate cause of the injury to the plaintiff.
- The plaintiff suffered some actual harm or injury.

Duty of Care

As noted earlier, the law of torts is grounded in the concept of rights. Because every person has certain rights in our society, all of us have a duty to not violate those rights. This concept of duty of care is especially crucial in negligence lawsuits. If the plaintiff cannot demonstrate that the defendant owed him or her a duty of care, then there is no need to look at any other elements.

Careers in Law

Corporate Attorney

Kendall Meyer is a corporate and business law attorney for one of Chicago's oldest law firms. He's worked on his share of "big" cases, but nothing quite as big as Sue. "Sue" is the nickname of the largest Tyrannosaurus Rex skeleton ever found. Two years after Sue's 1990 discovery in South Dakota, a dispute arose about who actually owned the fossil. After a series of court cases, the landowner was allowed to sell the bones at auction. When Chicago's world-renowned Field Museum of Natural History decided it wanted to bid on the bones, museum directors asked for help from the museum's outside counsel, Kendall Meyer. Meyer first determined who owned legal title to the bones—much like an attorney would when a client wants to buy a house. "I just asked classic legal questions in a unique context," Meyer says.

As the museum's legal representative, Meyer was also involved in securing funds for the new acquisition. Corporations such as Walt Disney World Resorts and McDonald's offered financial assistance to the museum to buy the 65-million-year-old fossil skeleton. In the end, Sue was auctioned off in an eight-minute war of nerves between nine bidders. The winner—with an offer of $8.36 million—was Meyer's client, the Field Museum of Natural History.

Skills	An understanding of basic business principles, research, negotiation
Personality	Sociable, outgoing, likable, enjoys working with business people
Education	Business, accounting, finance, contracts

For more information on corporate and business attorneys, visit **ubpl.glencoe.com** or your public library.

Example 4. While using the diving board at a public pool, Julia fell and was injured. The injury could have been avoided if the diving board had a guardrail. Julia later sued her state's Department of Health, arguing that the department had inspected the pool but did not do anything about the missing guardrail. The state supreme court ruled against Julia. The court said that the state's sanitary code gave the Department of Health the duty to inspect water-related facilities for health problems, but not a duty to inspect for safety problems. Because there was no need to examine the other elements, the Department of Health had no duty to Julia.

Breach of Duty   You may commit breach of duty to another person by not exercising the degree of care that a reasonable person would exercise in that same situation. This "reasonable person" test is an objective test. As a result, the judge in a tort case must be careful when giving instructions to the jury. The use of the descriptive term *reasonable* is of particular importance. The judge cannot alter the test by telling jurors to determine what they would have done in this situation, nor can the judge substitute such words as "average person," "normal person," or even "logical person." The jury must be told to determine what a "reasonable person" would have done in this situation.

Proximate Cause   The third element of negligence is **proximate cause**, which is the legal connection between unreasonable conduct and the resulting harm. Without proximate cause, the result would not have occurred. Proximate cause is not the same as actual cause. An action by the defendant may actually cause the plaintiff's injury but still not be the proximate cause. Courts apply the foreseeability test to determine proximate cause by asking: "Was the injury to the plaintiff foreseeable at the time that the defendant engaged in the unreasonable conduct?"

> *Example 5.* Mrs. Palsgraf was waiting for a train on the platform of the Long Island Railroad Company. As another train was pulling out of the station, a man carrying a package ran to catch it. A railroad attendant on the platform helped push the man forward, and an attendant on the train pulled the man upward. In the process, the man's plainly wrapped package fell to the ground. It contained fireworks, and the resulting explosion shook the platform and knocked over some scales, which hit Mrs. Palsgraf and caused extensive injuries. To seek compensation for her injuries, Mrs. Palsgraf decided to sue the railroad for negligence. The court ruled that the railroad employees could not reasonably foresee that pushing and pulling a man onto a train would injure a woman standing many feet away.

Actual Harm   Because the essence of any tort suit is a violation of a duty that results in injury to the plaintiff, a successful case must establish proof of actual harm. That is, did the plaintiff suffer physical injuries, property damage, or financial loss? Without actual harm, even the dumbest mistake or the most careless conduct will not result in liability for negligence.

> *Example 6.* In The Opening Scene, Jamila says that Trai's foolish driving amounts to negligence. Peggy reminds her that actual harm must result before Trai's conduct would be negligent. She is

Figure 4.2 — The Elements of Negligence

Element	Definition
Legal duty	A determination that legal duty exists between parties must be made to establish liability through negligence. This is solely a question of whether the tortfeasor should have reasonably foreseen a risk of harm to the injured party.
Breach of duty	The judge or the jury must determine whether the person accused of negligence has breached the duty owed to the victim. To determine if the alleged tortfeasor has met the appropriate standard of care, the court uses the reasonable person test.
Proximate cause	For the tortfeasor to be held liable, the unreasonable conduct must be the proximate cause of the victim's injuries. Proximate cause is the legal connection between the unreasonable conduct and the resulting harm.
Actual harm	The injured party in a lawsuit for negligence must show that actual harm was suffered.

NEGLIGENCE Negligence is the failure to exercise the degree of care that a reasonable person would have exercised in the same circumstances. A suit for negligence must prove four elements: duty of care, breach of duty, proximate cause, and actual harm. *Which of the elements do you believe would be the most difficult to prove in a lawsuit?*

correct. However, she is also correct in pointing out that Trai's reckless driving is very stupid.

Defenses to Negligence

People can defend themselves in a negligence suit by eliminating one of the four elements (see Figure 4.2). Specifically, they can argue that they owed no duty to the plaintiff; their conduct conformed to the reasonable person standard; their conduct was not the proximate cause of the plaintiff's injuries; or that the plaintiff suffered no injuries. In cases in which the defendants cannot attack one of these elements, they may try to use one of the following defenses: contributory negligence, comparative negligence, or assumption of risk.

DEFENSES TO NEGLIGENCE Many individuals engage in very risky sports as a matter of routine. *What defense might the defendant in such a negligence case have if one of the participants in a dangerous sport were injured?*

Contributory Negligence Behavior by the plaintiff that helps cause his or her injuries may fall under the doctrine of **contributory negligence**. If the defendant can prove that the plaintiff's own negligence helped cause the injuries, then the plaintiff loses the lawsuit. It does not matter how slight his or her negligence was. Many states no longer follow this doctrine, however, because it is unfair to plaintiffs who may have been only slightly negligent. These states have adopted another standard called comparative negligence.

Comparative Negligence

The negligence of each party is compared under the doctrine of **comparative negligence**, and the amount of the plaintiff's recovery is reduced by the percent of his or her negligence. Comparative negligence protects plaintiffs from realizing huge losses for comparatively minor acts of negligence.

> *Example 7.* Jason Cohen sued Mark Goodhue for damages suffered in an automobile accident. The jury found the damages to be $100,000, and also found that Jason was 10 percent negligent and Mark was 90 percent negligent. As a result, Jason recovered $90,000 instead of the full amount of damages.

Most states that use comparative negligence follow the 50 percent rule. The plaintiff is allowed to recover part of the award as long as his or her negligence was not greater than that of the defendant. If the plaintiff's negligence exceeds 50 percent, he or she recovers nothing.

Assumption of Risk

If the defendant can show the plaintiff knew of the risk involved and still took the chance of being injured, he or she may claim

STRICT LIABILITY
Strict liability involves the performance of an ultrahazardous activity. *What activities might you classify as ultra-hazardous?*

assumption of risk as a defense. Baseball clubs have successfully used this defense when sued by spectators injured by baseballs hit into the stands. People who are injured while participating in extreme sports may also be unable to bring lawsuits for negligence because of the defense of assumption of risk.

Strict Liability

Some activities are so dangerous that the law will apply neither the principles of negligence nor the rules of intentional torts to them. According to strict liability, if these activities injure someone or damage property, the people engaged in the activities will be held liable, regardless of how careful they were and regardless of their intent. This rule applies only to ultrahazardous activities that involve a great risk to people and property. The risk must be of such a nature that no amount of care will eliminate it. Using explosives, keeping wild animals, and storing highly flammable liquids in densely populated areas have all been labeled as ultrahazardous.

In recent years, the doctrine of strict liability has also been applied in product liability cases. When people are injured from defects in products that they bought in the marketplace, the firm that manufactures the products is liable for injuries, regardless of fault.

Product liability does have its limits. Most courts have held that product liability does not apply if the seller of the defective product does not usually engage in the sale of such items. For example, a corporation that auctions off some machinery after one of its plants closes would be labeled an occasional seller. The corporation would not be liable for an injury caused by a defect in one of the machines.

Law & Academics

Social Studies
In the United States, a tort can be defined as a private wrong committed by one person against another. The legal systems in other countries use different terms. For example, Germans speak of *unlawful acts*, and the French use the expression *civil responsibility*. Since World War II, tort law has expanded everywhere, but especially in Europe.

Research Activity
Choose England, Germany, or France and research the tort law in that country. Then compare it to U.S. tort law.

Section 4.2 Assessment

Reviewing What You Learned
1. What is negligence?
2. What are the elements of negligence?
3. What are the major defenses to negligence?
4. What is strict liability?

Critical Thinking Activity
Defenses to Negligence Which defense to negligence do you feel is the most effective?

Legal Skills in Action
Strict Liability Historically, some activities that we take for granted today were originally considered ultrahazardous. One such activity is the flying of an airplane. Imagine you are a lawyer who wants to change the law in relation to strict liability. Research and write a report on strict liability in relation to airplanes, and demonstrate how the doctrine became obsolete in regard to that activity.

Chapter Summary

Section 4.1 Intentional Torts

- A crime is an offense against the public at large. The role of the government is to preserve the safety and well-being of the entire social structure. As such, the government can punish the perpetrator of a crime. In contrast, a tort is a private wrong committed by one person against another. Such an offense does not call upon the government to punish wrongdoers and protect society. A tort, therefore, involves one person's interference with another person's rights. In some situations, a single action can be both a tort and a crime.

- The law of torts is grounded in rights. Under tort law, all people are entitled to certain rights simply because they are members of our society. The law imposes a duty on all of us to respect the rights of others. Some of the rights of members of our society include: the right to be free from bodily harm, the right to enjoy a good reputation, the right to conduct business without unwarranted interference, and the right to own property free from damage or trespass. Anyone who violates such rights has committed a wrongful act, and often this wrongful act can be classified as a tort.

- Torts can be committed intentionally and unintentionally. Unintentional torts can be further classified as negligence or strict liability.

- The major intentional torts are assault, battery, trespass, nuisance, false imprisonment, defamation, and invasion of privacy. Assault involves threatening to strike or harm another person with a weapon or physical movement. Battery is the unlawful, unprivileged touching of another person. Wrongful injury or interference with the property of another is known as trespass. Nuisance refers to anything, such as noise or unpleasant odors, that interferes with the enjoyment of life or property. False imprisonment occurs when a person is unlawfully restrained, whether in prison or otherwise. Defamation is the act of injuring another's reputation by making false statements, and invasion of privacy is interference with a person's right to be left alone.

Section 4.2 Negligence and Strict Liability

- Negligence is an accidental or unintentional tort and is the tort that occurs most often in society today. Negligence is the failure to exercise the degree of care that a reasonable person would have exercised under the same set of circumstances.

- A suit for negligence must prove four elements: duty of care, breach of duty, proximate cause, and actual harm. To prove duty of care, the plaintiff must show that the defendant owed him or her a duty of care. The failure to use the degree of care required under the circumstances is breach of duty. Proximate cause requires that the plaintiff prove that the defendant's breach of duty caused the injury. The plaintiff must also prove that he or she suffered some actual harm or injury to succeed in a suit for negligence.

- People can defend themselves by finding flaws in one of the previously mentioned elements. If the defendant cannot find a flaw in one of the elements of negligence, he or she can still argue affirmative defenses to negligence, which include contributory negligence, comparative negligence, and assumption of risk.

- According to the doctrine of strict liability, those who engage in ultrahazardous activities will be held liable for any injury or damage that occurs because of that activity, regardless of intent or care. The doctrine of strict liability has also been applied in product liability cases. When people are injured from defects in products that they bought in the marketplace, the firm that manufactures the products is liable for injuries, regardless of fault.

Using Legal Language

Consider the key terms in the list below. Then use these terms to complete the following exercises.

tort

intentional tort

assault

battery

trespass

nuisance

false imprisonment

defamation

invasion of privacy

negligence

breach of duty

proximate cause

strict liability

contributory negligence

comparative negligence

assumption of risk

Understanding Business and Personal Law Online

Self-Check Quiz Visit the *Understanding Business and Personal Law* Web site at **ubpl.glencoe.com** and click on Chapter 4: The Law of Torts—Self-Check Quizzes to prepare for the chapter exam.

1. In groups of two, define each term in the vocabulary.
2. Create an infomercial, in which one student has completed Chapter 4 and is trying to convince another student to study the chapter material. The first student will explain what he has learned using the terms above.
3. Present your infomercials to the class.
4. As a class, vote to choose the best infomercial.
5. In a paragraph, explain the strengths of the infomercial that you chose. How could you have improved your infomercial?

The Law Review

Answer the following questions. Refer to the chapter for additional reinforcement.

6. How is an intentional tort different from an unintentional tort?
7. Under today's laws, to what extent do property owners own the airspace above their land?
8. What does the Federal Privacy Act of 1974 require federal agencies to do?
9. What defenses can you use if you are faced with a negligence suit?
10. Explain the difference between contributory negligence and comparative negligence.
11. Explain how the tort of assault differs from the crime of assault.
12. What types of people have a difficult time proving damage to their reputation as part of defamation lawsuits?
13. Why have some states started using the standard of comparative negligence?
14. Under what circumstances may a defendant to a negligence suit claim the assumption of risk defense?

Linking School to Work

Working with Technology

Eric Rolfe Greenberg of the American Management Association estimates that 45 percent of large U.S. companies monitor electronic communications, including e-mail, voicemail, and fax machines.

15. If you are employed, find out whether your employer monitors the electronic communications at your place of business.
16. If you are not employed, find out whether the teachers' and students' e-mail is monitored at your school.
17. Share your findings with the class.

As a class, debate the issue of whether electronic monitoring is an invasion of privacy.

Let's Debate

Trespassing and Conversion

Friends often have an understanding that they can borrow each other's things. One day, Becky's lawnmower wouldn't start, so she took the lawnmower from Alice's garage. Alice had planned to mow her lawn at the same time and became angry with Becky for taking the lawnmower without asking. She accused Becky of trespassing (entering her garage) and conversion (unauthorized removal of another's property).

Debate

18. Was this a crime or a tort?
19. How could this fight have been prevented?
20. What could Becky and Alice do to improve their communication skills?

Grasping Case Issues

For the following cases, give your decision and state a legal principle that applies.

21. Jake Richards decided to play a practical joke on Ursula Brakestone. As Ursula prepared to sit down at her table in the cafeteria, Jake pulled the chair out from under her. Ursula fell to the hardwood floor and fractured her hip. Jake says he committed neither assault nor battery. Is Jake correct on either count? Why or why not?
22. A photographer took a photo of Maria Lao without permission while Maria was sun-bathing by the pool in her own backyard. Maria later discovered that the photo had been used in an advertisement for suntan lotion. What tort, if any, has been committed?
23. Al asks to borrow Juanita's videocassette library. He likes several of the video-cassettes so much that he decides to keep them. Despite repeated requests from Juanita, Al refuses to return the cassettes he borrowed. What tort, if any, has been committed?
24. Philip Carstairs kept a poisonous spider in his locker at school. He was very careful to keep it locked up so that it would not harm anyone. One day, while Philip was in class, two students got the spider out of Philip's locker and let the spider loose in the girl's gymnasium. Judy Norton was bitten by the spider. Is Philip legally responsible for Judy's injuries? Explain your answer.
25. An elderly woman was beaten and robbed by an unknown person. Emily Simpson told several people that Max Newmark was guilty of the crime. This was a false statement. Has Emily committed a tort for which Max can recover damages?

Analyzing Real Cases

In each case that follows, you be the judge.

26. Duty of Care

Ramona Booker entered a drugstore by pushing her way through one door and then through a second. She had to use two hands to push the heavy doors open. As a result, she dropped her cane, which caught on the exposed coil of a security device and caused her to fall and hurt herself. Ramona brought suit against Revco DS, Inc. to recover for her injuries. *Did the drugstore owe a duty to its customers to provide an establishment that was safe? Why or why not? Is this lawsuit based on an intentional tort or negligence? What test would be used to judge whether the drugstore owners should be held liable for Ramona's injuries? Explain your answer.*
Booker v. Revco DS, Inc. 681 N.E.2d. 499 (OH).

27. Negligence

Myers slipped and fell and was injured on ice on the front walkway of the Canton Centre Mall. The mall was owned and run by Forest City Enterprises. Certain employees from Forest City were supposed to keep the walkways clear of ice. They had cleared the ice from the walkway a short time before Myers fell. One of the employees guessed that after they had cleaned the walk, passing cars may have splashed water on it, which froze. *Was Forest City negligent in failing to keep the walk clear of ice at all times? Why or why not? What test would be used to judge Forest City's conduct? Explain your answer.*
Myers v. Forest City Enterprises, Inc. 635 N. E. 2d 1268 (OH).

Legal Link

State Laws and Computer Crime

State governments are creating legislation to address the problems of computer crime, fraud, and abuse. States are also adopting existing laws and passing new legislation to protect consumer privacy, particularly when it involves online business transactions and other private issues.

Connect

Using a variety of search engines, research the current Internet-related legislation under discussion by some of the state governments. Report on the following:

28. Current and pending legislation surrounding computer crime, fraud, and abuse.
29. Steps taken by state governments to protect computer users' privacy.

POWER READING STRATEGIES

30. **Predict** Why do you think we have tort law? Would life be less complicated if we only had criminal law?

31. **Connect** Can you think of a case that has been both a tort and a crime? If not, create an example.

32. **Question** Do you think it is fair that people in the public limelight must prove more damage to their reputations than the average person when involved in a defamation lawsuit? Explain your answer.

33. **Respond** Why do you think the doctrine of strict liability exists?

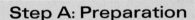

UNIT ① Law Workshop:
Using Legal Tools

How Would You Conduct a Jury Trial?

You have learned about the court system, trial procedures, and how criminal law differs from civil law. By completing this workshop, you will have the opportunity to put your knowledge into action.

Step A: Preparation

Problem: *How would you organize and conduct a jury trial?*

Objectives: In this workshop, you will work with a team to perform a mock jury trial for your class.

- **Research** legal issues that you find interesting.
- **Analyze** data associated with the trial, and organize the data meaningfully.
- **Research** court procedures.
- **Conduct** a trial that mimics how a real court case might be handled.
- **Evaluate** the classroom verdict.

Step B: Procedure

1. Form a team of five or six students.
2. Research interesting or controversial legal issues that have been covered recently in local or national publications.

3. As a team, choose a legal topic around which to build a court case. Read as much as you can about your topic, and organize the information so that both sides of the issue can be presented to the class as a trial.
4. Assign each team member a role in the trial. Your team should include a defending attorney, prosecuting attorney, judge, and several witnesses, including a plaintiff and a defendant. (Witnesses can play several parts.)
5. Write a script for a mock trial based on the steps for a jury trial presented in Chapter 2. (Create imaginary evidence if necessary.) Your script should not include a verdict; a jury will determine the verdict. The rest of the class will serve as the jury. The judge should direct the jury to select a foreman to act as a spokesperson. Follow your state's law regarding the minimum number of jurors who must agree for a jury verdict to be considered valid.
6. Perform your mock trial for the class. Have the foreman deliver the jury's verdict and explain its decision.

Step C: Create a Model to Analyze the Verdict

7. After hearing the jury's verdict and its reasons for the decision, prepare a chart that organizes this information. You should categorize the jury's reasons. For example, if the jury votes in favor of the plaintiff, you might use a two-column table with the labels "For the Plaintiff" and "Against the Defendant." List several reasons in each column.

Step D: Workshop Analysis Report

Consider the chart your team created and answer the questions below.

8. What was the verdict?
9. How did the jury reach this verdict?
10. Do you agree with the jury's verdict? Why or why not?
11. How might the mock trial have been conducted differently to reach a different verdict?

Cipollone v. Liggett Group, Inc.

United States Supreme Court

505 U.S. 504 (1992)

Issue Does a federal law requiring warning labels on cigarette packages preempt a smoker's state law tort claims against cigarette manufacturers?

Facts After 42 years of smoking, Rose Cipollone died of lung cancer. During the last 15 years of her life, cigarette packages contained the following label: "WARNING: THE SURGEON GENERAL HAS DETERMINED THAT CIGARETTE SMOKING IS DANGEROUS TO YOUR HEALTH."[1]

Rose and her husband brought suit in federal court against three cigarette manufacturers. They blamed the cigarette makers for Rose's cancer and sought compensation based upon New Jersey tort law.

The manufacturers held they were not liable for state law tort claims arising before 1966. They further argued that the Federal Cigarette Labeling and Advertising Act of 1965 and the Public Health Cigarette Smoking Act of 1969 preempted such claims.

Rose died before trial. The jury ruled in favor of the manufacturers, stating that Rose had voluntarily assumed the risks of smoking. However, the jury did award Rose's husband $400,000 as compensation for his losses, holding that Liggett, a cigarette manufacturer, had breached its express warranties that smoking was not hazardous. Both sides appealed.

Opinion In 1965, Congress passed the Federal Cigarette Labeling and Advertising Act, which required cigarette packages to contain the following label: "CAUTION: CIGARETTE SMOKING MAY BE HAZARDOUS TO YOUR HEALTH." Congress later passed the Public Health Cigarette Smoking Act of 1969, which required a stronger label to be placed on cigarette packages: "WARNING: THE SURGEON GENERAL HAS DETERMINED THAT CIGARETTE SMOKING IS DANGEROUS TO YOUR HEALTH."

The Petitioner's Complaint

The petitioner's complaint alleged that the cigarette makers were responsible for Rose's illness on the following grounds:

- **Design Defect** The cigarette manufacturers didn't use a safer alternative design, and the dangers created by cigarettes outweighed their social value.
- **Failure to Warn** There was no adequate warning about the health dangers of cigarettes, and manufacturers were negligent when "they tested, researched, sold, promoted and advertised" cigarette products.
- **Express Warranty** The cigarette makers expressly warranted that their cigarettes did not pose serious health dangers.

- **Fraudulent Misrepresentation** The cigarette manufacturers tried to negate federal health warning labels and ignored scientific evidence demonstrating the hazards of smoking.
- **Conspiracy to Defraud** The cigarette makers tried to deny scientific evidence about the hazards of smoking.

The Defendant's Reply

The cigarette manufacturers replied that federal laws preempt New Jersey's tort laws. According to the supremacy clause of the U.S. Constitution, if a state law conflicts with a federal law, the federal law overrules the state law. The petitioner claimed that state tort law should apply in this case because, unlike the 1969 Act, state tort claims for damages do not impose "requirement[s] or prohibition[s]" by statutes or regulations. Instead, the petitioner seeks compensation based upon prior court decisions (common law).

The Relationship of Federal and State Law

In its opinion, the Court rejected the petitioner's argument. It held that state common law tort actions are based on the existence of a legal duty, which imposes "requirements and prohibitions." The Court also cited an earlier case in which it said that "[state] regulation can be effectively exerted through an award of damages as through some form of preventive relief. The obligation to pay compensation can be, indeed is designed to be, a potent method of governing conduct and controlling policy." Consequently, the Court rejected the petitioner's claim that common law tort

claims brought by individuals do not constitute matters of state law, and therefore ruled that they could be overruled by federal law.

After clarifying the applicable law, the Court examined each of the petitioner's claims to determine if it was preempted by the federal law. To determine whether a state law is preempted, the Court said that it must look to the intent of Congress. It ruled that federal law does not preempt state law unless it is "the clear and manifest purpose of Congress" that a federal law supersede a state law.

Holding The Court held that the 1965 Act did not preempt state tort claims because Congress did not intend that result. The Court further held that, although the 1969 Act preempted state claims based on failure to warn, it did not preempt claims based upon express warranty, intentional fraud and misrepresentation, or conspiracy.

---

[1] In 1984, Congress amended the law to require four different warning labels to appear on cigarette packages on a rotating basis.

Questions for Analysis

1. On what New Jersey tort law theories did the Cipollones base their claims against the cigarette manufactures?
2. What five specific grounds for recovery were stated in the Cipollones' complaint?
3. Why did the jury deny Rose Cipollone's claim for compensation?
4. What defense did the cigarette manufacturers raise in this case?
5. Describe the general provisions of the Public Health Cigarette Smoking Act of 1969.
6. What is the effect of the supremacy clause in the U.S. Constitution?
7. When does federal law preempt state law?

Web Resources

Go to the *Understanding Business and Personal Law* Web site at ubpl.glencoe.com for information about how to access online resources for the Landmark Cases.

UNIT 2

UNIT OVERVIEW

You regularly take part in a wide variety of contracts. Whether it's cutting your neighbor's grass or buying a cell phone, contract law is intended to protect the interests of buyers and sellers, facilitate trade, and promote fairness and efficiency. In this unit, you will learn about:

- Contracts and their elements
- Genuine agreement, capacity to contract, and consideration
- Legality and the form of a contract
- The end of contracts, transfer of contracts, and remedies for breach of contract

Entering into Contracts

YOUR *Justice Journal*

Web Work Imagine you have your own Web site design company. You have several contracts with small businesses in your community. In addition to doing design work, you host Web sites, keep the information updated, and troubleshoot problems for these companies.

In your Justice Journal, write about the importance of having a contract, what type of information is included in your contract, and how to bring your contract to an end.

POWER READING STRATEGIES

To get the most out of your reading:
PREDICT what the section will be about.
CONNECT what you read with your own life.
QUESTION as you read to make sure you understand the content.
RESPOND to what you've read.

How Contracts Arise

Understanding Business and Personal Law *Online*

Chapter Overview Visit the *Understanding Business and Personal Law* Web site at ubpl.glencoe.com and click on Chapter 5: How Contracts Arise—Chapter Overviews to preview the chapter information.

The Opening Scene

Starting in this chapter, we meet the Benes family. Mr. Benes is a widower with four teenage children: Alena, 18; Viktor, 16; Hana, 15; and Emil, 13. The children attend Euclid High School, a large public school in a major urban area in the Midwest. Mr. Benes owns a concession business and has just returned home from work.

Contractual Chaos

MR. BENES: Vik, you promised to have the garbage at the curb before I got home. I wish that I didn't have to get on your case about the same things over and over again.

VIKTOR: You're home early.

MR. BENES: I left work early to go to the newspaper and renew that ad about my lost laptop.

VIKTOR: Your ad's been running for three weeks, and you haven't received a single response. I don't think you're going to get your laptop back.

MR. BENES: Don't change the subject, Vik. Why do you always insist on waiting until the last minute to do your chores?

HANA: That's not true. Vik doesn't do his chores most of the time. He pays Emil to do them.

VIKTOR: Hana! Would you mind your own business for once? Nobody asked for your input on this!

MR. BENES: Since when has Viktor been paying Emil to do his chores?

HANA: Since he found a job. Vik's been working after school lately.

MR. BENES: You found a job?

VIKTOR: It's just for some extra spending money, Dad.

MR. BENES: What's the job?

HANA: He works for Mrs. Garcia.

VIKTOR: There you go again, Hana! Stay out of this!

MR. BENES: You're working at a gun shop?

VIKTOR: My job has nothing to do with the guns. I just sweep out the back room and stock the shelves and stuff.

MR. BENES: I don't care what you do there. You can just quit.

VIKTOR: I can't quit. I have a contract.

(Alena arrives at home.)

ALENA: Hey, Vik. Get your skateboard out of my car, will you?

VIKTOR: Shut up, Allie.

MR. BENES: You bought a skateboard?

VIKTOR: Not exactly.

MR. BENES: How am I supposed to interpret that statement?

(Emil enters the house.)

EMIL: It means that he offered Jake 50 bucks for it, but he didn't pay him yet. Vik still owes me for five weeks of chores.

VIKTOR: Shut up, Emil.

MR. BENES: Well, I guess that I need to come home early more often. It's the only way I can find out what's going on with my family!

What Are the Legal Issues?

1. Does the promise to do a favor create a binding contract?
2. What characteristics do contracts share?
3. When does a contract legally come into existence?
4. What constitutes a legal offer?
5. What constitutes a legal acceptance?

Contracts

What You'll Learn

- Explain the elements of legal contracts
- How to identify valid, void, voidable, and unenforceable contracts
- How to distinguish between express and implied contracts
- How to identify unilateral and bilateral contracts
- How to distinguish between oral and written contracts

Why It's Important

Identifying a contract's elements will help you manage your affairs in an intelligent and effective manner.

Legal Terms

- contract
- offer/acceptance
- genuine agreement
- capacity
- consideration
- legality
- void/voidable contract
- unenforceable contract
- express/implied contract
- bilateral/unilateral contract

Understanding Contract Law

When was the last time you made a contract? If you bought your first car last year or sold your old skis at a flea market, you probably know that these activities involve contracts. Many common daily activities may also involve contracts, from buying a fast food meal to filling your car with gas. Most people think a "contract" is a long, preprinted, formal document that they sign when buying a vehicle, selling their house, or purchasing insurance. Such formal documents represent only a small fraction of the contracts that you will make in your lifetime. The truth is that you create a contract any time you agree to exchange things of value.

Because contracts pervade your life, you need to know about their nature, purpose, and effect. Further, contract law forms the foundation for all other areas of the law that we will explore in this text. Understanding contract law is necessary to grasp the law of sales, consumer law, agency law, property law, employment law, partnership law, corporate law, and computer law. We will begin with the most basic concepts: what contracts are and how they come into existence.

The Nature of a Contract

A **contract** is any agreement enforceable by law. You should never enter into a contract without understanding the legal responsibilities involved. Not all agreements are contracts, however. In The Opening Scene, Vik's promise to take the garbage to the curb before his father returned home is probably not a contract. In contrast, Mr. Benes's agreement to run an ad in the newspaper is undoubtedly a contract. Similarly, if someone answers Mr. Benes's advertisement and returns his lost laptop, he will owe that person what he promised as a reward in the ad. Whether Vik's deal with Jake about the skateboard is a contract depends on the circumstances of the agreement.

The Three Theories of Contract Law

The legal responsibilities associated with contracts are based on what the involved parties do and say to one another. In the past, courts asked whether the parties to a contract exchanged things of equal value. This approach was called the equity theory of contract law. However, the advent of industrial capitalism and the need to support a

A Global Perspective: Laws Around the World

Antarctica

In 1959, officials of 12 nations (Argentina, Australia, Belgium, Chile, France, Great Britain, Japan, New Zealand, Norway, the Soviet Union, South Africa, and the United States) signed the Antarctica Treaty. This treaty is designed to protect one of earth's most pristine and cold environments, and it states that Antarctica can be used only for peaceful purposes, such as scientific exploration. It prohibits military troops, except those assisting research efforts, and outlaws using nuclear weapons or dumping nuclear waste on Antarctica. The treaty also asks scientists to freely share their research. Today more than 30 scientific stations have been set up to study the icy continent. Scientists describe Antarctica as a natural laboratory. It is ideal for examining weather data, collecting rock and mineral samples, and observing animal behavior. Antarctica is also ideal for studying something that affects the entire world—the "ozone hole" that lies directly overhead. Here's a snapshot of Antarctica.

- About 98 percent of Antarctica is covered year round in ice up to 15,000 feet thick.
- Winter temperatures can drop below −114° Fahrenheit.
- Geologists have found copper, gold, silver, and zinc on the Antarctic Peninsula.
- Traveling by dogsleds and skis, Roald Amundsen and four other Norwegians were the first people to reach the geographic South Pole on December 14, 1911. The 1,860-mile trip lasted 99 days.

Critical Thinking Question Some tourists pay huge sums to visit Antarctica. They come by ship, dinghy, or helicopter. Can you think of reasons why allowing sightseers to visit Antarctica might be both a good and bad idea? For more information on Antarctica, visit **ubpl.glencoe.com** or your local library.

profit-making system forced the courts to shift their focus. When asked to settle a contract dispute, the courts would ask whether the parties had agreed to the terms set forth in the agreement. This new theory was called the will theory of contract law because it focused on the exercise of each party's free will. The courts no longer asked if the contract was fair; instead they pondered, "Did the parties really agree to these terms?"

One problem with the will theory is that it was difficult to know what the parties were actually thinking when they entered into an agreement. Consequently, the courts studied actions and words to determine if the parties reached a "meeting of the minds." Gradually, this approach led to a search for certain fixed elements to contracts. If these elements existed, the courts would hold that a contract existed. This approach became known as the formalist theory because it relied on the form of the agreement.

ELEMENTS OF A CONTRACT

An agreement is not a contract unless it contains the six elements of contracts: offer, acceptance, genuine agreement, capacity, consideration, and legality. *Of the six elements, which is the most crucial to setting up a valid contract?*

The Elements of a Contract

The six elements of a contract, as shown in Figure 5.1, are offer, acceptance, genuine agreement, consideration, capacity, and legality. To be legally complete, a contract must include all six elements. Notice that the list does not include anything written. Not all contracts have to be in writing to be enforceable.

An **offer** is a proposal by one party to another intended to create a legally binding agreement. An **acceptance** is the second party's

Figure 5.1	Elements of a Contract
Element	**Description**
Offer	A proposal made by one party (the offeror) to another party (the offeree) indicating a willingness to enter a contract.
Acceptance	The agreement of the offeree to be bound by the terms of the offer.
Genuine Agreement	Offer and acceptance go together to create genuine agreement, or a meeting of the minds. Agreement can be destroyed by fraud, misrepresentation, mistake, duress, or undue influence.
Consideration	Consideration is the thing of value promised to one party in a contract in exchange for something else of value promised by the other party. The mutual exchange binds the parties together.
Capacity	The law presumes that anyone entering a contract has the legal capacity to do so. Minors are generally excused from contractual responsibility, as are mentally incompetent and drugged or drunk individuals.
Legality	Parties are not allowed to enforce contracts that involve illegal acts. Some illegal contracts involve agreements to commit a crime or a tort. Others involve activities made illegal by statutory law.

Take It or Leave It

Contracts come in many forms. One form is the contract printed on the back of tickets. On airline tickets, for instance, you'll find several important legal notices. These notices include "Conditions of Contract," "Notice of Incorporated Terms," "Notice of Baggage Liability Limitations," "Notice of Overbooking," or the specific terms and conditions related to nonair transportation or services.

On the back of a concert ticket, you're likely to find language stating that the ticket you bought is a "revocable license." Terms typical of such licenses include conditions stating that you may not resell the ticket at a price greater than its face value. Such language often includes a term stating that the ticket may be taken and admission refused upon refunding the ticket price.

Many courts have held that these so-called "take it or leave it" contracts are binding. In many states, the small print is just as binding as the large print, except where it is found to be grossly unfair or unreasonable.

Critical Thinking Next time you fly on an airplane or attend a concert, check the fine print on the back of your ticket. What are the terms of the contract you just entered? Would you agree with these terms if you had a choice?

unqualified willingness to go along with the first party's proposal. If a valid offer is met by a valid acceptance, a **genuine agreement** exists. Some circumstances, such as fraud, misrepresentation, mistake, undue influence, and economic duress, can destroy the genuineness of an agreement.

The fourth element, **capacity**, is the legal ability to enter a contract. The law generally assumes that anyone entering a contract has the capacity, but this assumption can be disputed.

The fifth element, **consideration**, is the exchange of things of value. In The Opening Scene, Mr. Benes gave nothing to Vik in exchange for his promise to deliver the garbage to the curb, so there was no consideration in that agreement.

People cannot enter into contracts to commit illegal acts. Consequently, **legality** is the final element of a contract.

Characteristics of a Contract

Contracts can be created in different ways and can assume diverse forms. A contract can be described by any of the following characteristics:

- Valid, void, voidable, or unenforceable
- Express or implied
- Bilateral or unilateral
- Oral or written

Any contract can have characteristics from one or more of these four groups. That is, a contract can be valid, express, bilateral, and written. Let's take a closer look at what these characteristics indicate about a contract.

Valid, Void, Voidable, or Unenforceable

The word *valid* means legally good, meaning that a valid contract is one that is legally binding. On the other hand, a contract that is **void** has no legal effect. An agreement that is missing one of the previously

Virtual Law

Online High School

One of the many advantages of the Internet is its potential to provide an immense amount of information to anyone anywhere with an online connection. This amazing capability has intrigued many educators, who are increasingly drawn to the Internet as a way of communicating ideas, exposing students to technology, and reaching students who may not otherwise have access to the information that the Internet can provide. Many states have even started experimenting with state-run online high schools. These schools can deliver courses to hundreds of students, including those who are taught at home by their parents. This trend has caught the attention of commercial companies that want to enter contracts with school districts to offer online programs.

Not everyone supports virtual high schools. Some teachers and parents have expressed concern about the quality of education received online. They are also worried that students might not be getting a well-rounded education without peer contact. (Source: *New York Times*, February 15, 2001, p. D1)

Connect Visit the Web sites of your state or local school board to see whether online classes are being offered, and explore how such courses are being handled.

discussed elements would be void, such as any agreement to do something illegal.

When a party to a contract is able to void or cancel a contract for some legal reason, it is a **voidable contract**. It is not void in itself but may be voided by one or more of the parties. A contract between two minors, for example, could be voidable by either of them.

An **unenforceable contract** is one the court will not uphold, generally because of some rule of law, such as the statute of limitations. If you wait too long to bring a lawsuit for breach of contract, the statute of limitations may have run its course, making the contract unenforceable.

Express or Implied

An **express contract** is stated in words and may be either oral or written. An **implied contract** comes about from the actions of the parties. People often enter into implied contracts without exchanging a single word.

Example 1. Herb Schneider went to a self-service gas station that requires payment before the attendant will turn on the pumps. He handed the attendant $10, returned to his car, pumped $10 worth of gas into his tank, and drove off. Neither party spoke a single word, yet an implied contract arose from their actions.

Bilateral or Unilateral

The word *bilateral* means two-sided. Thus, a **bilateral contract** contains two promises. One party promises to do something in exchange

IMPLIED CONTRACTS
An implied contract can be created by the action of the parties. When you pump gas at a self-service gas station, your actions indicate a willingness to pay for the gas. *What actions are displayed by the gas company?*

for the other's promise to do something else. If a friend says, "I'll sell you my DVD player for $150," and you say, "I'll buy it," a bilateral contract comes into existence. Each of you has made a promise—you have promised to buy, and your friend has agreed to sell. Most contracts are created in this way.

In contrast, the word *unilateral* means one-sided. A **unilateral contract** contains a promise by only one person to do something, if and when the other party performs some act. If your friend says, "I'll sell you my DVD player for $150 if you give me the cash before noon tomorrow," he or she will not be required to keep the promise unless you hand over the cash before noon on the following day. See Figure 5.2 for a visual representation of bilateral and unilateral contracts.

A reward offer is one of the most common instances of a unilateral contract. The acceptance of the reward offer must precisely comply with the offer.

> *Example 2.* In The Opening Scene, Mr. Benes placed an advertisement in the local newspaper offering a reward for the return of his lost laptop. However, Mr. Benes's offer of a reward alone did not create a contract. The contract would come into existence only when someone returns the laptop. Mr. Benes would then owe the finder the reward.

Oral or Written

An oral contract is created by word of mouth and comes into existence when two or more people form a contract by speaking to each other. One person usually offers to do something, and the other party agrees to do something else in return. Most contracts are oral contracts of this nature.

HOW PARTIES REACH AGREEMENT
A contract may be unilateral or bilateral. *In which type of contract do both parties, the offeror and the offeree, make promises?*

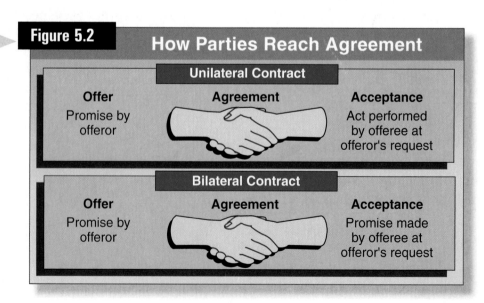

Figure 5.2

How Parties Reach Agreement

Unilateral Contract

Offer	Agreement	Acceptance
Promise by offeror		Act performed by offeree at offeror's request

Bilateral Contract

Offer	Agreement	Acceptance
Promise by offeror		Promise made by offeree at offeror's request

UNILATERAL CONTRACTS

A classic example of the unilateral contract principle is a reward advertisement placed on a bulletin board or in a newspaper. When you read an advertisement offering a reward for a lost item, a contract does not yet exist. *When does the contract come into existence? What would happen if someone who had never read the ad found and returned the lost item?*

Sometimes, however, it is desirable to put contracts in writing. A written contract assures that both parties know the exact terms of the contract and also provides proof that the agreement was made. A law, the Statute of Frauds, requires that certain contracts must be in writing to be enforceable. We will learn more about this law in Chapter 10.

Section 5.1   Assessment

Reviewing What You Learned

1. Explain the elements of legal contracts.
2. What are the differences among valid, void, voidable, and unenforceable contracts?
3. What are the differences between express and implied contracts?
4. What are the differences between unilateral and bilateral contracts?
5. What are the differences between oral and written contracts?

Critical Thinking Activity

History How did the Industrial Revolution change the court's attitude toward interpreting contract law?

Legal Skills in Action

Elements of a Contract Your friend, Arkadi, has begun teaching contract law classes at a local senior citizens' center. Write a paragraph in which you explain the six elements of a contract in a way that will help Arkadi create his course outline. Remember to include information on the historical development of the will theory, which led to the need to develop the six elements included within the formalist theory of contract law.

Offer and Acceptance

What You'll Learn

- How to recognize the requirements of an offer
- How to distinguish between an offer and an invitation to negotiate
- How to recognize the requirements of an acceptance
- How to distinguish between an acceptance and a counteroffer
- How to recognize when an offer has terminated

Why It's Important

You need to know when an offer has been made and when an acceptance goes into effect to make sound contracts.

Legal Terms

- invitations to negotiate
- mirror image rule
- counteroffer
- revocation
- rejection

Requirements of an Offer

Because the six elements of a contract form the heart of contract law, we will build our study of contracts around them. Understanding the elements of offer and acceptance is necessary before moving on to other matters, such as which contracts must be in writing, how contract rights are transferred, how contracts end, and what happens when one party breaches a contract.

As noted earlier, an offer is a proposal by one party to another party to enter a contract. The person making the offer is the offeror, and the person who receives the offer is the offeree. An offer has three basic requirements. It must be:

- Made seriously.
- Definite and certain.
- Communicated to the offeree.

Serious Intent

An offer must be made with the intention of entering into a legal obligation. An offer made in the heat of anger or as a joke would not meet this requirement. For example, a friend complaining about her unreliable car might say, "Give me five bucks and it's yours." This statement may sound like an offer, but your friend cannot be forced to sell her car for five dollars.

Often an invitation to negotiate is confused with an offer. Sellers usually have limited merchandise to sell and cannot possibly sell an advertised product to everyone who sees an ad. For this reason, most advertisements in newspapers, magazines, and catalogs are treated as **invitations to negotiate** rather than as offers. They are also called invitations to deal, invitations to trade, and invitations to make an offer.

Example 3. An advertisement in the newspaper read, "Lava Lamps, $49.98." Carole Lauretig went to the store the next day and said, "I would like to buy a Lava Lamp." A clerk apologized, saying the lamps had sold out within an hour after the store opened.

INVITATION TO NEGOTIATE
Very often invitations to negotiate are confused with genuine offers. *Is a price tag on a sale item an offer or an invitation to negotiate?*

The advertisement in Example 3 was merely an invitation to the public to come in, see the lamps, and make an offer. When Carole said, "I would like to buy a Lava Lamp," she was actually making an offer to buy at the advertised price of $49.98. The storeowner is free to accept or reject the offer.

There are exceptions to this rule. The courts consider some advertisements as offers when they contain specific promises, use phrases such as "first come, first served," or limit the number of items that will be sold. In such cases, under the terms of the advertisement, the number of people who can buy the product becomes limited, making the advertisement an offer rather than an invitation to negotiate.

Price tags, signs in store windows and on counters, and prices marked on merchandise are treated as invitations to negotiate rather than as offers. This rule of law probably stems from days when people negotiated for products more than they do today.

Definiteness and Certainty

An offer must be definite and certain to be enforceable. A landlord of an apartment with faulty plumbing might agree to pay "a share" of the cost if the tenant fixes the plumbing, but the court would not enforce the contract because it was not possible to determine what the parties meant by "a share."

Example 4. Joe Vasquez was offered a position as an account executive with the International Corporation at a salary of

$2,400 a month plus a "reasonable" commission on total sales. Is this a definite and certain offer? No, because it would be difficult to determine exactly what a "reasonable" commission is. The court, however, could fix a commission based upon general practices of the trade.

Communication to the Offeree

Offers may be made by telephone, letter, telegram, fax machine, e-mail, or by any other method that communicates the offer to the offeree.

Example 5. Jean Lefevre found a wallet. A driver's license identified the owner, and Jean returned the wallet. The owner thanked her but did nothing more. Later in the evening, while reading the newspaper, Lefevre discovered that the owner had offered a reward for return of the wallet. However, she cannot claim the reward because the offer was not communicated to her. She did not know about the reward when she returned the wallet.

Requirements of an Acceptance

The second element of a legally binding contract is acceptance of the offer by the offeree. As in the case of an offer, certain basic

THE MIRROR IMAGE RULE
In real estate and service contracts, the acceptance must repeat the exact terms that are used in the offer. *What can a couple do if they want to purchase a house but cannot afford the price at which the house is listed?*

requirements must be met: the acceptance must be unconditional and must follow the rules regarding the method of acceptance.

Unconditional Acceptance

The acceptance must not change the terms of the original offer in any way. This principle is called **the mirror image rule**. Any change in the terms of the offer means the offeree has not really accepted the offer but has made a **counteroffer**. In that case, the original offeror is not obligated to go along, and no contract results. Instead, the offeror becomes an offeree and may accept or reject the counteroffer.

> *Example 6.* Art Clifford sent a letter to Marge and Norm Grayson, offering to buy their home for $80,000. The Graysons, who had advertised their house at $85,000, wrote a reply stating, "We accept your offer. However, we would like the price set at $83,000."

The Graysons didn't really accept Clifford's offer, as their letter claimed. Instead, they made a counteroffer, which Art is free to accept or reject. He may choose to make a counteroffer of his own, agreeing to buy the home for an amount somewhere between $80,000 and $83,000. Then the initiative to accept or reject would shift back to the Graysons. This process could continue until the terms of the offer and the acceptance "mirror" each other. The parties could also decide they will never agree on a mutually satisfactory price.

Contracts for the sale of goods are exceptions to the mirror image rule. These exceptions include contracts for personal property such as clothing, furniture, food, motor vehicles, appliances, and other items. The primary exceptions are created by the Uniform Commercial Code (UCC), which is a set of statutes that covers the law of sales as well as other areas of commercial law. It was drafted to make trade among the states easier and has been adopted with minor variations by 49 states. Only Louisiana has not adopted all of its provisions.

One UCC exception involves nonmerchants. Nonmerchants are people who do not regularly buy or sell goods and do not claim to be experts on the goods. In nonmerchant situations, the offeree may make minor changes, and a contract will still be created. For example, if someone says to you, "I'll sell you my camera for $150," and you answer, "I'll buy it and pay you next week," a contract is created. The added term, "I'll pay you next week," may be accepted or rejected by the offeror. Remember that this rule applies only to goods.

A second exception involves sale-of-goods contracts between merchants. When both parties are merchants, the additional or different

terms become a part of the contract. This exception applies only if the following conditions are met:

- The new or different terms do not make a material or crucial difference to the nature of the contract
- The offeror does not object to the new or different terms within a reasonable time
- The original offer did not expressly limit acceptance to the terms in that original offer

Methods of Acceptance

The time at which an acceptance takes place is important because that is when the contract comes into existence. When the parties are dealing face-to-face or on the telephone, no special problem exists. One party speaks, and the other listens and communicates the offer or the acceptance.

Special rules, however, govern acceptances that take place when the parties are separated by a distance and must communicate by letters, telegrams, or fax. According to common law, an acceptance that must be sent over long distances is effective when it is sent. Any method of communication that has been expressly or impliedly endorsed by the offeror would qualify. Common law also says that an acceptance is implied when the offeree accepts by the same or a faster means than that used by the offeror.

The authorization of an acceptance can also be implied by any reasonable means, including past practices between the parties, the usual method in the trade, or the customary means in comparable transactions. Naturally, the offeree must correctly address the acceptance so that it is delivered to the right place. If the address is faulty, the acceptance is not complete until delivery has been made to the offeror. It is also possible for the offeror to specify the time by which the acceptance must be received to be effective.

This rule applies to contracts for real estate and services. For sale-of-goods contracts under the UCC, the acceptance takes place when it is sent, as long as the method of communication is reasonable. Consequently, the acceptance of a mailed offer for goods would be effective when it is sent electronically, via fax, or through an overnight carrier. If the offeror states in the offer what method the offeree must use to accept, that method must be followed.

Sometimes an offer specifies that it must be accepted by an action. In these cases, the action must take place before there is an acceptance. For example, Larry McNulty promised to pay Floyd Little $50 to don a gorilla suit and march with the band at a football game's halftime. Floyd would have to perform the action to accept the offer.

The offeror cannot impose silence on the offeree as the means of acceptance unless he or she has previously agreed to this condition or

LONG DISTANCE ACCEPTANCE
Problems arise when the acceptance of a contract must travel over long distances. *How can people make certain that an acceptance is valid and effective when it must travel to a distant location?*

has allowed silence to signal acceptance in the past. In contrast, if the offeror has established silence as the means of acceptance, then he or she will have to live by that condition if the offeree accepts by remaining silent.

> *Example 7.* Bradley wrote a letter to Franz offering to sell his motorcycle. "If I do not hear from you, I shall assume that you have accepted my offer," he said. However, Franz's silence after receiving the offer would not bind him to pay. A person cannot be forced to respond to avoid a binding agreement. On the other hand, if Franz intended to accept the offer and complied with Bradley's directions to remain silent, then Bradley must honor that silence as his acceptance.

Termination of an Offer

Even though an offer has been properly communicated to the offeree, it may be terminated. This termination may occur in any of the following five ways.

Revocation

Revocation is the taking back of an offer by the offeror. The offeror has a change of mind or circumstances and decides to withdraw the offer before it has been accepted. Two important rules govern revocation: an offer can be revoked any time before it is accepted, and a revocation becomes effective when it is received by or communicated to the offeree.

Example 8. Rob Garceau offered to sell his CD burner to Jodi Costa for $250. Jodi examined the CD burner and found that it was in good condition. However, Jodi couldn't decide if she wanted to spend so much money for a used piece of equipment. She told Rob that she would consider his offer. In the meantime, Rob decided that he didn't want to sell his CD burner after all. He telephoned Jodi and informed her of his decision. Rob could revoke his offer because Jodi had not yet accepted it.

Rejection

Rejection, or refusal, of an offer by the offeree brings the offer to an end. For example, if someone says to you, "I'll sell you my camera for $150," and you say, "I don't want it," then the offer has come to an end.

Example 9. Diane Amato decided that she wanted to make some extra money by selling some dried floral arrangements that she had made using flowers from her own garden. Diane spoke to her neighbor, Shawna Washington, about the flower arrangements and offered to sell them for $40 each. Shawna liked the descriptions and decided to take a look at Diane's work. When Diane showed the arrangements to her, however, Shawna realized that they were not what she had expected. Shawna decided to reject Diane's offer.

Counteroffer

A counteroffer ends the first offer. If someone says to you, "I'll sell you my camera for $50," and you say, "I'll give you $35 for it," no contract comes into existence unless the original offeror accepts your new offer. If you later say, "Okay, I'll give you $50 for the camera," you will be making a new offer, which the original offeror may accept or reject.

Expiration of Time

If the offeror sets a time limit for the acceptance of the offer, it must be honored. Assume that Bradley has offered to sell Franz his motorcycle for $1,745. Bradley tells Franz the offer will remain open until noon of the following day. To create the contract, Franz must accept within that time.

If no time for acceptance is stated in the offer, it must be accepted within a reasonable time. Otherwise, no contract exists. What is a reasonable time depends on the circumstances. For example, a reasonable time to accept an offer for purchasing a truckload of ripe tomatoes would be different from a reasonable time to accept an offer for purchase of a house.

When an offeree pays money or other consideration to an offeror to hold an offer open for an agreed period of time, an option contract comes into existence. An option is a binding promise to hold an offer open for a specified period of time. It offers to the holder of the option the exclusive right to accept the offer within the agreed time, subject to the terms of the option. For example, you might offer a seller $50 to hold an offer open for two days. Such a contract is legally binding. For an entire contract to be completed, the option must be exercised by the person holding the option. This requires an absolute, unconditional, unqualified acceptance exactly according to the terms of the option.

Death or Insanity

If the offeror dies or becomes insane before the offer is accepted, the offer comes to an end. Although death ends an offer, it does not end a contract, except for contracts related to personal services.

It's a Question of Ethics

Seller's Choice
You are selling your car. You offer to sell it to Martin for $800 if he pays you by Saturday. On Friday Maria offers you $1,000 for it. *Ethically, should you wait to see if Martin brings the $800 on Saturday? Is it okay to sell the car to Maria on Friday? What is your ethical responsibility?*

Section 5.2 Assessment

Reviewing What You Learned
1. What are the requirements of an offer?
2. What is the difference between an offer and an invitation to negotiate?
3. What are the requirements of an acceptance?
4. What is the difference between an acceptance and a counteroffer?
5. When is an offer terminated?

Critical Thinking Activity
Identifying an Offer Why is it important to be able to distinguish between an offer and an invitation to negotiate?

Legal Skills in Action
Invitations to Negotiate Tina believes that she can compel a used car dealership to sell her a car that was advertised in the newspaper. She tells you that she believes the advertisement is an offer that she intends to accept tomorrow. Write a short letter to Tina that explains why advertisements in a newspaper are considered invitations to negotiate rather than offers.

Chapter Summary

Section 5.1 Contracts

- A contract is any agreement enforceable by law. There are six elements of a contract: offer, acceptance, genuine agreement, consideration, capacity, and legality. An offer is a proposal by one party to another intended to create a contract. An acceptance is the second party's unqualified willingness to go along with the first party's proposal. Genuine agreement occurs when a valid offer is met by a valid acceptance. Capacity is the legal ability to enter a contract. Consideration is the exchange of things of value. Legality refers to the fact that a legally binding contract must not require people to commit illegal acts.

- Valid contracts are legally binding. A void contract has no legal effect because one of the elements of a contract is missing. A voidable contract is not void, but it may be voided by one of the parties because of some defect. For instance, a contract between two minors could be voidable by either of the parties. An unenforceable contract cannot be enforced because there is some rule of law, such as the statute of limitations, that makes it unenforceable.

- An express contract is stated in words. It may be written or oral. An implied contract is implied from the actions of the parties.

- Bilateral contracts are formed by promises that each party makes to the other. A unilateral contract contains one party's promise that it will fulfill if and when the other party performs an act.

- Oral contracts are created when a party promises something by speaking that promise and the other party responds with a spoken promise. In contrast, a written contract is one in which the promises are in writing.

Section 5.2 Offer and Acceptance

- An offer is a proposal by one party to another party to enter a contract. An offer must be (1) seriously intended, (2) definite and certain, and (3) communicated to the offeree. An offer made in the heat of anger or as a joke would not be seriously intended. An offer must include clear, specific terms to be considered definite and certain. When communicating an offer, the offeror may use a telephone, letter, telegram, fax machine, e-mail message, or any other method of communication.

- An invitation to negotiate may look like an offer, but it is not. Moreover, any such invitation cannot be made into an offer by agreeing to the terms of the invitation. For example, an advertisement is not an offer, but rather an invitation to negotiate. It means that a merchant does not have to sell to a buyer who says, "I'll take it" in response to an ad in the paper. The customer's statement that he or she will buy acts as the offer in this case, and the merchant may then choose to accept or reject this offer to buy.

- An acceptance must meet two requirements: (1) it must be unconditional; and (2) it must follow the rules regarding the method of acceptance. Unconditional acceptances do not seek to change the terms of the original offer in any way. When parties are dealing face-to-face or on the telephone, no special problems exist with regard to method of acceptances. One party speaks, and the other listens and communicates the offer or acceptance. However, special rules govern acceptances that take place when parties are separated by a distance and must communicate by letters, telegrams, or fax.

- An offer must be accepted without changing its terms. As a result, when an offeree changes the terms of an offer, the offeree cannot be said to have accepted. Instead, he or she is deemed to have made a counteroffer, which the original offeree then may choose to accept or reject.

- An offer is terminated by revocation, rejection, counteroffer, expiration of time, death, or insanity.

Using Legal Language

Consider the key terms in the list below. Then use these terms to complete the following exercises.

contract

mirror image rule

counteroffer

consideration

capacity

legality

acceptance

invitation to negotiate

genuine agreement

revocation

rejection

offer

1. Write a poem or short play about two people who are planning to enter into a contract, using all of the terms listed above. Be creative and humorous.
2. Share your poem or play with the rest of the class, using various other forms of expression (music, silent modern dance, mime, etc.) to communicate important details.
3. As a class, vote to select the best performance.
4. Encourage the winner to present his or her poem or play to other classes that are studying business law.

The Law Review

Answer the following questions. Refer to the chapter for additional reinforcement.
5. Describe the formalist theory of contract law.
6. Explain the elements of legal contracts.
7. Why are most advertisements in the newspaper treated as invitations to negotiate? Are there exceptions? What are they?
8. What are the exceptions to the mirror image rule?
9. When an acceptance is sent over a long distance, when does it become effective?
10. How can genuine agreement be disrupted or destroyed?
11. Under what circumstances might contract be voidable?
12. Why is it desirable to put some contracts in writing?
13. What two rules govern the revocation of contracts?

Linking School to Work

Interpret and Communicate Ideas

Interview the manager of a business or government agency located in your community. Find out when and why contracts are being used in the course of doing business. Share your findings with your class. Then as a class, determine:

14. How contracts are used across your community.
15. The similarities or differences among businesses/government agencies and how these similarities or differences are manifested in their business contracts.

Let's Debate

Is There a Contract?

Tara and Victor had a deal. Each week, Victor cleans Tara's house. In return, Tara pays Victor $50. For the past few weeks, however, Victor missed a few things. One week he forgot to clean the oven; the next week he forgot to dust the living room. Tara wasn't happy and deducted $10 from his fee. Victor argued that Tara should not have deducted $10 because they had a contract and his forgetfulness concerned minor things, but Tara disagreed.

Debate

16. Do Tara and Victor have a valid contract?
17. Is it voidable?
18. What should happen if Victor "forgets" a few things while cleaning?
19. If you were Tara, what would you do?

Grasping Case Issues

For the following cases, give your decision and state a legal principle that applies.

20. The Galaxy Research Center e-mailed an offer to the owners of Twin Pines, a farm in rural Arkansas. The e-mail message stated: "Please consider this our offer to purchase between 9,000 and 11,000 acres of your 15,000-acre tract of farmland land near Twin Pines, Arkansas. Our offering price is between $15,000 and $19,000 per acre. Please respond soon." Is this e-mail message a legally effective offer? Why or why not?

21. Connie Adler agreed to go to the home-coming dance with Fred Wolfe. Later, Steve McNamara, the captain of the football team, asked Connie to be his date for home-coming. Connie broke her date with Fred to go to the dance with Steve. Does Fred have a legal claim against Connie? Explain your answer.

22. Bob Goodman made a verbal agreement to buy a pocket calculator from Howard Hermann for $35. When Hermann delivered the calculator, Goodman refused to accept it, stating that he was not bound by his verbal agreement. Was he correct? Explain your answer.

23. Home Furniture Company advertised its waterbeds in a local newspaper. The newspaper mistakenly advertised the beds for $49 instead of $249. Must Home Furniture sell the beds at the advertised price? Explain your answer.

24. Victor Archer mailed an offer to Sally Miles. Sally mailed a properly addressed and stamped letter of acceptance 10 minutes before she received a revocation from Victor. Was the revocation effective? Explain your answer.

In each case that follows, you be the judge.

25. Terms of Advertisement

The following advertisement was placed in a Minneapolis newspaper by the Great Minneapolis Surplus Store: "Saturday 9 A.M. 2 Brand-new Pastel Mink 3-Skin Scarves selling for $89.50— Out they go Saturday. Each...$1.00. 1 Black Lapin Stole. Beautiful, Worth $139.50...$1.00. First Come, First Served." Lefkowitz was the first customer admitted to the store on Saturday, and he attempted to purchase the Lapin stole. The store said it would not sell him the stole because the offer was intended only for women. Lefkowitz sued. *Was the offer definite enough to allow Lefkowitz to tender a valid acceptance, or was it an invitation to negotiate? Lefkowitz v. Great Minneapolis Surplus Store,* 86 N.W.2dd 689 (MN).

26. Terms of Acceptance

Tockstein wrote, signed, and delivered an offer to Rothenbeucher stating that he wished to purchase Rothenbeucher's house. The offer included a statement that acceptance must be made within 24 hours. After 24 hours, the offer would be revoked unless Rothenbeucher had accepted. Rothenbeucher signed the agreement within 24 hours but did not deliver it to Tockstein personally, as Tockstein had done with the offer. Instead, Rothenbeucher gave it to his real estate agent, who delivered it to Tockstein after the 24-hour period had expired. Tockstein claimed the offer was revoked when Rothenbeucher did not deliver it within the specified time period. *Was he correct? Why or why not? Rothenbeucher v. Tockstein,* 411 N.E.2d 92 (IL).

Legal Link

Automobile Accidents

The greatest risk facing teens today is not drugs, alcohol, school violence, or suicide—it's motor vehicle crashes.

Connect

Using a variety of search engines, research teen motor vehicle crashes.

27. Locate statistics, major causes, and ways to help teens become safer drivers.

28. Create a contract between you and your parent or guardian that will help you manage the use of your vehicle.

POWER READING STRATEGIES

29. Predict Contracts seem to be a part of everything we do. Why are they so important?

30. Connect Have you ever faced a situation where you wished you had a contract in place?

31. Question Can you think of a situation where an oral contract would be better than a written contract? Explain your answer.

32. Respond Why do you think that although death ends an offer, it does not end a contract? Is that fair?

Genuine Agreement

Understanding Business and Personal Law *Online*

Chapter Overview Visit the *Understanding Business and Personal Law Web* site at ubpl.glencoe.com and click on Chapter 6: Genuine Agreement—Chapter Overviews to preview the chapter information.

The Opening Scene

Viktor and his friend Jake are pushing Jake's "new" car six blocks to the Benes' home. Mr. Benes, Alena, and Hana are sitting out in front of the house.

Transmission Troubles

ALENA: Look, Hana, a horse-drawn chariot—without the horse.

HANA: Having trouble, guys? Is there anything I can do to help?

VIKTOR: No.

ALENA: I guess, you're just pushing that thing around to impress people. Where on earth did you get that piece of junk?

VIKTOR: Shut up, Allie. We don't need to hear any of your smart comments right now. We're not in the mood.

JAKE: I've been cheated!

ALENA: Do you actually mean that someone got the best of Jake? Now there's a shocker!

MR. BENES: Take it easy please, Allie. What happened, guys?

JAKE: The stupid transmission gave out. I've only had the car for three days. I can't believe I'm having car problems already.

MR. BENES: Don't get too excited—we don't know what's wrong yet. Maybe it's not that serious. Let me take a look.

HANA: I like the color. It's so . . . red. Where'd you get it?

JAKE: Nowhere.

ALENA: Sure, Hana. See, Jake woke up this morning and, "boom," the car was on his front lawn, just like that.

JAKE: All right, all right. I bought it at that Buy-a-Heap used car place in Shelby. I got it for a pretty good price.

ALENA: Didn't you see this coming? Anyone who buys something at a place called Buy-a-Heap deserves what he gets.

VIKTOR: Shut up, Allie. The sales guys said that the car was just fine. He seemed like a nice guy.

MR. BENES: Here's your problem, Jake. Looks like somebody put sawdust in the transmission to make it run smoothly for a while. It's an old trick.

JAKE: What?

MR. BENES: I said, somebody put sawdust. . . .

JAKE: I heard you the first time, Mr. B. I've been cheated, haven't I? Great, what am I going to do now?

ALENA: Duh! You should have known better!

HANA: Maybe it was a mistake.

ALENA: I doubt that.

VIKTOR: Oh, yeah. The guy reached for the transmission fluid and got the sawdust by mistake. What are the odds?

HANA: It could happen, I guess.

MR. BENES: C'mon, Jake. I'll drive you and Vik back to . . . what was the name of the place?

ALENA: Buy-a-Heap.

MR. BENES: Right. Buy-a-Heap.

What Are the Legal Issues?

1. Do customers have the right to expect salespeople to tell the truth about important facts in a contract?
2. Can fraud be committed by words?
3. Can fraud be committed by actions?
4. Will a mistake void a contract?

Fraud and Misrepresentation

What You'll Learn

- How to identify the elements of fraud
- How to distinguish between fraud and concealment
- How to distinguish between fraud and innocent misrepresentation
- How to distinguish between the remedy available for fraud and the remedy available for misrepresentation

Why It's Important

Learning the elements of fraud may prevent you from being victimized or help you claim your rights if you are defrauded.

Legal Terms

- fraud
- rescind
- material fact
- concealment
- misrepresentation

Defective Agreements

If the offeror makes a valid offer, and the offeree has made a valid acceptance, then a genuine agreement has been reached. The courts describe this type of agreement as a "meeting of the minds." Assuming the other three elements—consideration, capacity, and legality—are also present, a valid contract exists between the parties.

Sometimes, however, something goes wrong and what seems like a valid contract turns out to be nothing of the kind. In these cases, we say that the agreement is defective. Several circumstances might create a defective agreement: fraud, misrepresentation, mistake, duress, and undue influence.

Fraud

Fraud is a deliberate deception intended to secure an unfair or unlawful gain. If you have been induced to enter into a contract by fraud, you have a choice: You may **rescind**, or cancel, the contract, or you may sue for money damages. Because of the deliberate deception involved in fraud, you may also try to collect punitive damages. Damages are designed to punish the wrongdoer for his or her conduct and can greatly exceed the amount of money needed to pay back the victim.

Figure 6.1 — The Elements of Fraud

1. A false representation of fact.
2. Knowledge of the falsity by the party making the false representation.
3. Intent to deceive by the party making the false representation.
4. Reasonable reliance by the innocent party.
5. Actual loss suffered by the innocent party.

ELEMENTS OF FRAUD
Genuine agreement can be disrupted by fraudulent representation made by one party to another. *Why does the law use the expression, "false representation" instead of just using "lie"?*

To succeed in a lawsuit for fraud, the following five elements must be demonstrated (see Figure 6.1):

- There must be a false representation of fact.
- The party making the representation must know it is false.
- The false representation must be made with the intent that it be relied upon.
- The innocent party must reasonably rely upon the false representation.
- The innocent party must actually suffer some monetary loss.

False Representation of Fact

Fraud requires a false representation of a material, existing fact. A **material fact** is a fact that is important; it matters to one of the parties. It cannot be a promise of something that will happen in the future, nor can it be someone's opinion.

The law does allow salespeople to use a certain amount of "sales talk," sometimes called "sales puffing" or "sales puffery." A statement such as, "This car is really flashy," is an example of sales puffery. Another example of sales puffery is, "You'll get plenty of dates with this car," which is not only the seller's opinion, but also a promise of something to happen in the future.

Material false representations are not confined to oral or written statements. Actions intended to deceive are considered to be false representations. See Figure 6.2 for a listing of false representations.

Under some circumstances, individuals can make false representation by choosing not to reveal important information. This is known as **concealment**, also called passive fraud or nondisclosure, and it may be just as fraudulent as actively deceiving an innocent party. For example, if the seller of a house knows about some hidden problem that cannot be easily discovered by the potential buyer—a problem with the heating system or leaky pipes in the bathroom—that knowledge

Legal Briefs

Copyright is a form of protection provided by the laws of the United States (Title 17, U.S. Code) to the creators of "original works of authorship," including literary, dramatic, musical, artistic, and other intellectual works. When material is copyrighted, the work of authorship immediately becomes the property of the author who created the work.

AGREEMENTS MADE DEFECTIVE BY FALSEHOOD
Genuine agreement can be disrupted by fraud, concealment, and misrepresentation. *Which of the three agreements made defective by falsehood is the least serious?*

Figure 6.2	Agreements Made Defective by Falsehood
Element	**Description**
Fraud	Fraud is a deliberate deception to secure an unfair or unlawful gain in a contractual situation.
Concealment	Concealment, also called nondisclosure and passive fraud, occurs when one party does not say something that he or she is obligated to reveal. Obligations arise in situations involving hidden problems and in special relationships.
Misrepresentation	Misrepresentation occurs when a false statement is made innocently with no intent to deceive.

creates a duty to reveal the hidden problem. Put another way, if one party has special knowledge about the subject, and the other party relies on that party's expertise, the knowledgeable party is obligated to reveal any facts.

Representation Known to Be False

To be held accountable for fraud, the party making the false representation must be aware that the representation is false. This may be shown by proving actual knowledge, or by showing that the statement was made recklessly, without regard for the truth.

Example 1. Jeff Banner purchased a used car from Al Reed's Quality Used Autos. The salesperson at the lot assured Jeff that his car had never been involved in an accident. While looking through his car's glove box a week after purchasing it, Jeff discovered repair receipts that indicated the car had been in a major accident. As a result, Jeff is able to pursue a claim of false representation.

LAWS in Your Life

Choosing a Lawyer

Having to sign a document you do not completely understand is just one reason that you might need a lawyer. Some lawyers are general practitioners. Others specialize in certain areas, such as personal injury, divorce, or criminal law. When in need of a lawyer, look for an attorney who specializes in handling the type of situation that confronts you.

The best way to find a lawyer is to talk with relatives and friends who have used lawyers. If their legal problems were similar to yours, ask if they would recommend their lawyer. Another good source is the *Martindale-Hubbell Law Directory*, found in every courthouse library. This book lists nearly every lawyer in the United States by specialty. Your county bar association can also refer you to a competent attorney. The attorney referral services listed in the Yellow Pages are usually businesses that some attorneys pay for referrals.

If possible, talk with two or more candidates before hiring your attorney. Many attorneys offer a first meeting for free.

Make a List Create an imaginary situation that would require you to hire a lawyer. Prepare a list of topics and questions that you would ask an attorney.

False Representation Intended to Be Relied Upon

To prove fraud, one must show that the false representation was made with the intent that it be relied upon. That is, the person making the misrepresentation must intend that the other party rely upon the information as part of the contract negotiations.

Example 2. Suppose that Eduardo met Mr. Johnson, a man whose car he admired. He asked Mr. Johnson, "Is this car a 1964 Mustang?" Mr. Johnson, with no intention of selling his car but with knowledge that it was really a 1965 model said, "Yes, it's a 1964." If Eduardo then went out and purchased a car like Mr. Johnson's, believing it was really a 1964 Mustang, he could not win a lawsuit against Johnson for fraud. Johnson did not make the statement with the intent that Eduardo rely on it.

False Representation Actually Relied Upon

If fraud is to be proven, the false representation must be reasonably relied upon by the other party when the agreement is made. Sometimes people make misrepresentations to others who pay no attention to those misrepresentations. In these cases, the party cannot bring suit for fraud.

Example 3. Suppose that Johnson wants to sell his car and tells Eduardo that it is a 1964 Mustang. However, Eduardo is accompanied by George Timmer, an antique car expert. Timmer takes Eduardo aside and tells him that the car is actually a 1965 and is worth far less money than a 1964. If Eduardo still insisted on buying Johnson's car at an inflated price, he could not later win a lawsuit for fraud because he did not actually rely on Johnson's false statement.

FALSE REPRESENTATION
Fraud involves false representations made to entice an innocent party into a contract. In The Opening Scene, assume that not everything the salesperson told Jake about the car was true. *If this is the case, how has Jake been a victim of fraud?*

Resulting Loss

You may choose to enter into a contract as the result of false statements made by the other party. Unless you suffer loss as a result, however, you cannot win a lawsuit for fraud. For instance, if you paid a friend $75 for a CD player that was said to be "in perfect working order" and then discovered the track selection feature did not work, you have lost $75 and may make a claim for fraud. If, however, you agreed to accept the CD player in exchange for a favor, such as helping your friend perform a community project, you suffered no monetary loss. In such a situation, you would not be legally entitled to make a claim for fraud.

Innocent Misrepresentation

Sometimes a person will make an innocent statement that turns out to be false. However, that person honestly believed the statement was true at the time it was made. Such an act is a **misrepresentation**, or an untrue statement of facts, and the law gives you the right to rescind the contract. You may not win damages if the false representation is innocently made.

Example 4. Fred bought a mountain bike from Matt, an acquaintance at school. Matt said he believed the bike did not need any repairs. After a weekend ride at a local reservoir, Fred discovered the back wheel was severely misaligned. Fred could cancel the deal and ask for his money back. He is not entitled to damages because Mike genuinely believed the bike was in good shape.

Section 6.1 Assessment

Reviewing What You Learned

1. What are the elements of fraud?
2. What is the difference between fraud and concealment?
3. What is the difference between fraud and innocent misrepresentation?
4. What is the difference between the remedy available for fraud and the remedy available for misrepresentation?

Critical Thinking Activity

Fraud Why do courts permit fraud to disrupt genuine agreement in a contractual setting?

Legal Skills in Action

Too Good to Be True? You recently received a phone call from a travel agency offering a vacation package to Europe for less than $200. To take advantage of the offer, you were told to send $200 in cash within 24 hours or to supply a credit card number on the spot. Working in a small group with your classmates, discuss whether this sounds like a case of potential fraud. Begin by listing the elements of fraud.

Mistake, Duress, and Undue Influence

Mistake

The purpose of contract law is to fulfill the reasonable expectations of the parties to a contract. People sometimes enter into contracts believing that certain information is true when it is actually not, or that information is not true when it really is. When the truth is learned, one or both of the parties may wish to avoid the contract. Canceling the contract may or may not be possible. See Figure 6.3 for the types of mistake that can disrupt an agreement.

Unilateral Mistake

A **unilateral mistake** is an error on the part of one of the parties to the contract. A person usually cannot avoid a contract because of such a mistake. Through words or actions, one party has created reasonable expectations on the part of the other party to the contract. Those expectations should not be blocked because one of the parties has made an error.

> *Example 5.* The town of Sharonville received four bids for construction of a new city hall. Angelini Construction won the contract because its bid was the lowest. A few days later, Angelini's general manager discovered the bid should have been $2 million, not $1.5 million. The error was discovered too late. The company is bound by the bid it made to build the city hall for $1.5 million.

Mistake as to the Nature of the Agreement A mistake as to the nature of the agreement is one type of unilateral mistake. It cannot be an excuse to avoid a contract. Let's say you sign a contract to mow your neighbor's lawn through the summer, and the written agreement says this means mowing every week. You would be obligated to fulfill that schedule—even if you believe that you agreed orally to mow the lawn only every other week.

People who sign an agreement are bound to it, even if they have not read it or are mistaken about what it says. Your signature shows that you agree that the contract sets forth the terms of the agreement. This rule even applies to those who cannot read English. People who don't understand English are expected to have the agreement read and explained to them by someone they trust.

What You'll Learn

- How to distinguish between unilateral and bilateral mistake
- How to recognize the types of mistake that will allow rescission of a contract
- How to recognize the requirements of economic duress
- How to recognize the requirements of undue influence

Why It's Important

Recognizing how mistake, duress, and undue influence can affect agreements will help you make better decisions in such situations.

Legal Terms

- unilateral mistake
- bilateral mistake
- duress
- economic duress
- undue influence

Figure 6.3 — Agreements Made Defective by Mistake

Unilateral Mistake	Bilateral Mistake
1. Mistake as to the nature of the agreement. Rescission will not be granted.	1. Mistake as to possibility of performance. Rescission will be granted.
2. Mistake as to the identity of a party. Rescission may be granted.	2. Mistake as to the subject matter. Rescission will be granted.

AGREEMENTS MADE DEFECTIVE BY MISTAKE Genuine agreements can be disrupted by unilateral and bilateral mistake. *Which of the two types of mistakes will grant rescission most often?*

Mistake as to the Identity of a Party Another type of unilateral mistake involves the identity of a party to a contract. Unlike the previous cases, however, this mistake may be cause to void a contract.

Example 6. Genevieve Sands sent a letter offering baby-sitting services at a certain rate to Jill Gomez, a mother of toddlers in the neighborhood. The letter carrier mistakenly delivered the letter to another Jill Gomez, who happened to live across town and also had children. This other Jill Gomez liked Genevieve's offer and accepted it. However, the contract was voidable because this Jill Gomez was not the person Genevieve had in mind.

If Genevieve had made a baby-sitting offer face-to-face with a woman she thought was Jill Gomez, but who really was not, the mistaken identity would not prevent a binding contract. Genevieve would have made an offer facing the person who could accept it.

UNILATERAL MISTAKE Unilateral mistake usually will not allow rescission of a contract. *What type of mistake was made by Angelini Construction when their representatives promised to build the Sharonville city hall for $1.5 million?*

Careers in Law

District Court Judge

At age 12, Annette Scieszinski knew that she wanted to be part of the legal system. "I thought that lawyers should do the right thing and serve the public," she says from her office in Ottumwa, Iowa. "I still think that."

Today, Scieszinski is a district court judge who presides over a wide range of civil and criminal cases. She spends about half of her time handling trials and the proceedings leading up to them. One day she may be in her chambers, helping lawyers resolve issues in a contract dispute. The next day she may be in court, instructing a jury about a murder case.

The other half of Scieszinski's time is spent researching the law, updating judicial forms, and deciding what documents she needs to help settle a case. In nonjury trials, she also devotes at least one afternoon to "ruling time."

"'Ruling time' is kind of like study hall," she says. "When I preside over a nonjury trial, I'm the one who decides the verdict. So after I've taken evidence and heard testimony, I use ruling time to study the law and write my opinion."

Scieszinski says that judges can make a difference in peoples' lives. "This is a great job," she says. "It gives you an opportunity to creatively help people solve their problems and understand that even if they lose their case, justice is done."

Skills	Oral and written communication, logic, library and database research, interpersonal
Personality	Even-tempered, self-motivated, conscientious
Education	Many undergraduate majors, but English and economics are particularly useful; law degree; broad practice (not just trial work)

For more information on district court judges, visit **ubpl.glencoe.com** or your public library.

Bilateral Mistake

Sometimes both parties to a contract are mistaken about an important fact. This is usually known as a **bilateral mistake**, but is sometimes called a mutual mistake. When this mistake occurs, either party may avoid the contract.

Mistake as to the Possibility of Performance A bilateral mistake can be a mistake as to the possibility of performance. Suppose both parties entering into a contract believe that the duties described in the agreement can be performed when, in fact, they cannot. In this type of situation, either party may get out of the contract because of the bilateral mistake.

> *Example 7.* Robert Houlihan agreed to sell his car to Cynthia Stamatopoulos for $1,000. Unknown to both of them, however, was the fact that overnight the car had been sideswiped and severely damaged by a hit-and-run driver as it sat in front of Robert's house. Either party may now avoid the contract on the grounds of bilateral mistake as to the possibility of performance.

Mistake as to the Subject Matter   Both parties can be mistaken as to the identity of the subject matter when they enter into a contract. In this type of bilateral mistake, the contract may be avoided by either one of the parties.

> *Example 8.* Ellery Weimer agreed to sell Alvin McCormick five vacant lots on Indiana Avenue in Parkersburg. McCormick refused to go through with the agreement when he discovered that the land he thought he was buying was on another Indiana Avenue, also in Parkersburg. Weimer sued McCormick for breach of contract. However, because there was a bilateral mistake as to the location of the land in the contract, Weimer lost the case.

DURESS
An individual's free will may be disrupted by violence, threats of violence, or by economic threats. *Which type of duress is the most serious?*

Figure 6.4

Agreements Made Defective by Duress

Element	Description
Physical Duress	Actual physical violence is used to force a person to enter a contract.
Emotional Duress	Threat of physical force is used to force a person to enter a contract.
Economic Duress	Threats to a person's business or professional reputation are used to force a party to enter a contract.

AGREEMENTS MADE DEFECTIVE BY DURESS
Genuine agreement can be disrupted by duress. *Which of the types of duress is used most often to gain commercial advantage?*

Duress

Parties to an agreement must enter into it voluntarily, not under duress. **Duress** is overcoming a person's will by use of force or by threat of force or bodily harm. Agreements made under duress are either void or voidable. Figure 6.4 explains the specific types of duress recognized by the law. Criminal figures who threaten to hurt merchants if they do not pay fees for "protection" are using duress to secure an agreement.

When actual physical force is used to cause another to enter a contract, the contract is void. When a threat of physical force is used, the contract is voidable. Such a threat may be made against the party to a contract or against a member of that person's family. The innocent party may avoid the contract if he or she chooses to do so.

Another type of duress is **economic duress**. It consists of threats to a person's business or income that cause him or her to enter a contract without real consent.

Example 9. Baby-sitter Genevieve Sands sat with the children of one mother several times for an agreed price. One day the mother said that she wished to now pay 50 cents less per hour. The woman threatened to spread rumors around the neighborhood that Genevieve was a careless baby-sitter if Genevieve refused to agree to the pay cut. This was an attempt to reach an agreement by threatening economic harm to the baby-sitter's future business.

Note, however, that a threat to exercise one's legal rights is not duress. For example, to enforce an agreement, a party with grounds to sue may threaten to do so or demand satisfaction.

Community Works

Voidable Contracts
The contracts of mentally impaired persons are voidable, and guardians are often appointed to help protect these individuals. The elderly are particularly vulnerable because they may suffer from dementia-related illnesses such as Alzheimer's disease, which slowly destroys the brain. *How do these victims manage their day-to-day affairs and avoid becoming victims?*

Get Involved
Inquire about volunteering at the geriatric department of a local hospital. Become a volunteer reader at a local nursing home or hospice. Offer to help elderly family members.

UNDUE INFLUENCE
Genuine agreements can be disrupted by undue influence. *What type of relationships might lead to the temptation to use undue influence?*

Figure 6.5 — Elements of Undue Influence

Element	Description
A Dependency Relationship	One party in a relationship is dependent on the other party because of ill health, old age, or mental immaturity.
Unfair or Improper Pressure	The independent person uses excessive pressure to force the dependent person to enter a contract.
A Beneficial Contract	The contract that results benefits the independent party at the expense of the dependent party.

Undue Influence

The exercise of undue influence is another factor that can cause a contract to be voidable. **Undue influence** occurs when a person uses unfair and improper persuasive pressure to force another person to enter into an agreement. (See Figure 6.5 for the elements of undue influence.) Circumstances such as ill health, old age, or mental immaturity may put a person in a weaker position. The stronger person substitutes his or her will for the will of the weaker person.

Virtual Law

E-Book Publishing Rights

Until recently, few book contracts specified who owned the rights to publish electronic versions of printed books. This issue has become increasingly important because income from the sale of electronic books has grown as this format has become more popular. Publishers argue that they own the right to sell digital editions of printed books, even when their contract with an author might not address the issue. Publishers compare their industry to the film industry, where studios have the right to sell videotapes of movies. Publishers have started to change their contract language over the past several years to refer specifically to electronic books. Most authors argue that there is no genuine agreement on this issue until such language is included. (Source: *New York Times*, February 28, 2001, p. C5)

Connect Go to the Web site for Text and Academic Authors (TAA) and see what this group has to say about electronic rights.

Example 10. Paulding, an elderly woman, lived with her son, Emory, her only child and sole caretaker. Emory persuaded his mother to sell him some land that was worth $150,000 for only $50,000. Shortly before the transfer of title, Paulding discovered her son planned to resell the property for $175,000 to Visconti, a developer who planned to build an apartment complex. Paulding had thought her son planned to use the property as a lot for building a vacation home. She did not expect her son to deceive her. The mother refused to go through with the sale. In the breach of contract suit that followed, the court ruled that Emory had taken advantage of his mother's trust in him to persuade her to sell the land. Paulding could avoid the contract.

UNDUE INFLUENCE
An individual's free will may be disrupted by the undue influence of someone upon whom they depend. *Why is undue influence difficult to prove?*

Section 6.2   Assessment

Reviewing What You Learned

1. What is the difference between unilateral and bilateral mistakes?
2. What types of mistake will allow rescission of a contract?
3. What are the requirements of economic duress?
4. What are the requirements of undue influence?

Critical Thinking Activity

Types of Mistakes Why is it important to be able to distinguish between a unilateral and bilateral mistake?

Legal Skills in Action

Undue Influence Suppose that a close friend has sent you an e-mail message saying that she believes her grandfather was tricked into signing over all of his property to his live-in caretaker. Your friend asks for your advice on how to proceed with the problem. Write an e-mail reply to your friend in which you explain the elements she would have to prove to demonstrate that her grandfather signed over his property because of undue influence.

Chapter Summary

Section 6.1 Fraud and Misrepresentation

- Fraud is deliberate deception to secure an unfair or unlawful gain. To succeed in a lawsuit for fraud, the party bringing suit must prove five elements: (1) false representation of fact, (2) representation known to be false, (3) false representation intended to be relied upon, (4) false representation reasonably relied upon, and (5) resulting loss. Fraud requires a false representation of a material, existing fact. It cannot be a promise of something that will happen in the future, nor can it be someone's opinion. Material false representations are not confined to oral or written statements. Actions intended to deceive are considered to be false representations.

- Concealment, also called nondisclosure and passive fraud, is a type of fraud. This type of fraud is employed when a party keeps silent about a material fact of which the other party has no knowledge. The other person relies on the first person's special knowledge and gets hurt. Concealment can occur when a seller keeps quiet about a hidden defect that cannot be easily discovered by the buyer. Concealment can be just as fraudulent as actively deceiving an innocent party.

- An innocent statement of supposed fact that turns out to be false is a misrepresentation. The law gives an injured party the right to rescind a contract because of misrepresentation. You may not win damages if a false representation is innocently made.

- If you have been induced to enter a contract by fraud, you have several remedies available. You may cancel, or rescind, the contract. You may also sue for damages. Damages are designed to punish the wrongdoer for his or her conduct and can greatly exceed the amount of money needed to repay the victim. If a person has merely made a misrepresentation, remember that, although you can rescind the contract, you cannot win damages.

Section 6.2 Mistake, Duress, and Undue Influence

- Unilateral mistake is an error on the part of one of the parties to the contract. A person usually cannot avoid a contract because of such a mistake. A unilateral mistake may be a mistake as to the nature of the agreement or a mistake as to the identity of a party. When both parties to a contract are mistaken about some important fact, a bilateral mistake has been made. A bilateral mistake may be a mistake as to the possibility of performance or a mistake as to the subject matter.

- When you make a unilateral mistake, you are bound to the contract, except when you make a mistake as to the identity of the party. When there has been a bilateral mistake, either party may rescind the contract.

- Duress is defined as overcoming a person's will by using force or by threat of force or bodily harm. Economic duress occurs when a person threatens another person's business or income to cause someone to enter a contract without true consent.

- Unfair and improper persuasive pressure used by a person to force a close friend, family member, or otherwise vulnerable person into entering into a contract is called undue influence.

Using Legal Language

Consider the key terms in the list below. Then use these terms to complete the following exercises.

fraud	unilateral mistake
rescind	bilateral mistake
material fact	duress
concealment	economic duress
misrepresentation	undue influence

1. Imagine one of your friends is facing a defective agreement with a recent contract. Write a story about the situation using as many of the key terms in the story as possible.
2. Exchange stories with a classmate and review the terms that you each used in your stories.
3. Present your story to the class.
4. As a class, vote to choose the best story.
5. Post the winning story somewhere in the classroom.

Understanding Business and Personal Law *Online*

Self-Check Quiz Visit the *Understanding Business and Personal Law* Web site at **ubpl.glencoe.com** and click on Chapter 6: Genuine Agreement— Self-Check Quizzes to prepare for the chapter exam.

The Law Review

Answer the following questions. Refer to the chapter for additional reinforcement.

6. Name five circumstances that might create a defective agreement.
7. What are the two options for seeking recovery if you are induced to enter a fraudulent contract?
8. Describe a situation in which one party might be tempted to conceal information that would discourage the other party from entering into a contract.
9. What are two kinds of bilateral mistakes? Who may avoid a contract that contains a bilateral mistake?
10. What is the essential difference between duress and undue influence?
11. What is a material fact?
12. How does emotional duress differ from physical duress?

Linking School to Work

Interpreting and Communicating Ideas

Using the newspaper, news magazines, or the Internet, locate an article about a contract case in which punitive damages were awarded.

13. Review the facts of the case from the plaintiff's and the defendant's viewpoints.

14. Write a one-page paper explaining whether you would have awarded similar damages.

15. Present your case and decision to the class.

Let's Debate

Fraud

Serina called Erik to inquire about a washer and dryer that he is selling. Erik told Serina that the washer and dryer are in top-notch condition and haven't been used much. He told her that he is selling the appliances because he dislikes their color. You know for a fact, however, that Erik is not being totally honest with Serina. The washer doesn't rinse well, and the dryer cannot run for more than 20 minutes.

Debate

16. Is Erik misrepresenting his offer?

17. Is this a fraudulent situation?

18. Is nondisclosure involved?

19. What should Erik do?

Grasping Case Issues

For the following cases, give your decision and state a legal principle that applies.

20. The Oxford Art Gallery, operated by Allen Oxford, owned two 1907 photographs that depicted immigrants arriving in America. One of the photographs, taken by the famous photographer Alfred Stieglitz, was worth a substantial sum of money. The other photo, taken by a relatively unknown photographer named Alexander Sergent, was worth about $50. Ginny Thomas arranged to buy one of the photos, thinking the agreement was for the photo by Sergent. Oxford understood that the sale was for the Stieglitz. Was there a true meeting of the minds in this case? Would the circumstances support an action for rescission of this agreement? Why or why not?

21. Akeo Shimazu signed a form without reading it. He assumed the form was a request for a sample copy of an expensive book. When his order arrived, he found that he had actually signed an order form for the book itself. Shimazu refused the book, claiming he was not bound by the agreement because of his mistake. Is Shimazu legally bound by the agreement? Explain your answer.

22. The basement of Rodney Wiseman's house flooded every time it rained. Nevertheless, when Phelps, a potential buyer, asked about water in the basement, Wiseman said that the basement was dry. Phelps had an expert check the basement for dryness before he purchased the home. After a heavy rain, Phelps's new home's basement flooded. Can Phelps recover damages from Wiseman for fraud? Explain your answer.

23. Estelle Petkins put her summer cottage up for sale. Edith Ong, who was interested in buying the cottage, asked if it had termites. Petkins was not aware of a termite problem, so her answer was no. Ong bought the cottage and later found termites. Does Ong have any recourse against Petkins for fraud? Explain your answer.

In each case that follows, you be the judge.

24. Intentional Misrepresentation

Walker and Cousineau were in the gravel business. Walker wanted to sell a tract of land. He claimed that he had an engineer's report showing the land held 80,000 cubic yards of gravel. However, Walker knew the land held substantially less gravel. Cousineau bought the land and quickly discovered that the land held only about 6,000 cubic yards of gravel. He sued Walker, asking the court to rescind the contract. *Will Cousineau win the case? Why or why not?*
Cousineau v. Walker, 613 P.2d 608 (AL).

25. Forced Promises

During a riot at the Iowa State Penitentiary, prisoners held staff members hostage. The hostages were released after the warden agreed in writing that the prisoners would experience no reprisals. Afterward, however, some of the prisoners were punished. One prisoner, Wagner, was placed in solitary confinement for 30 days and received 180 days of administrative segregation. He also lost 1,283 days of good time earned. *On what legal grounds can the warden refuse to keep his promise to the inmates, and why?*
Wagner v. State, 364 N.W.2d 246 (IA).

Legal Link

Last-Minute Changes

Seig hired "Deiter's Delights" to cater his daughter's wedding reception. Deiter, the owner of the service, told Seig that his company would provide all of the serving dishes, plates, and cups. On the day of the wedding, Deiter told Seig that there would be an extra charge for the dishes. Although Seig paid the bill in full, he has decided to hire a lawyer to determine whether this is a case of misrepresentation or fraud.

Connect

Using a variety of search engines:

26. Help Seig find a lawyer online.
27. Create a short checklist of criteria that you would use when locating a lawyer.

POWER READING STRATEGIES

28. **Predict** How will understanding the elements of fraud help you avoid being a victim of fraud in the future?

29. **Connect** Create sample statements of "sales puffery" that border on being fraudulent.

30. **Question** In Example 5, given that Angelini Construction made an honest mistake when bidding the project to rebuild city hall, is it fair to bind them to the unreasonably low price they submitted? Explain. (Locate the text that corresponds with this item near the example under unilateral mistake.)

31. **Respond** In negotiating a contract, is the use of duress and undue influence unethical as well as illegal? Explain your answer.

Contractual Capacity

Understanding Business and Personal Law *Online*

Chapter Overview Visit the *Understanding Business and Personal Law* Web site at **ubpl.glencoe.com** and click on Chapter 7: Contractual Capacity—Chapter Overviews to preview the chapter information.

The Opening Scene

It's Saturday morning, a few days after Jake bought his "new" car. Alena, Viktor, Jake, and their college friend, Arkadi, are at the used car lot.

A Minor's Major Return

ALENA: You've dreamed up a crazy plan, Arkadi. I don't think this is going to work. The dealership is not going to return Jake's money. Maybe he doesn't even deserve to get it back. His decision was pretty stupid.

JAKE: Thanks a lot, Alena. Why do you always have to act like such a know-it-all?

ARKADI: Trust me. When I was a kid like Jake, a similar thing happened to me. We'll get Jake's money.

JAKE: Who are you calling a kid? I'm not in elementary school.

ALENA: *(Ignoring Jake.)* But you were 14 when you bought that defective stereo system, Arkadi. Jake is 16 right now.

ARKADI: It doesn't matter. Jake's still a kid. *(Turning to Jake.)* Are you ready? Do you have the paper we talked about?

JAKE: I'm prepared. Here it is. And stop calling me a kid. I'm not a kid.

(A salesperson in a cheap suit approaches the group. He grins broadly and greets the group with excessive enthusiasm.)

MR. BARENBLATT: Hello there, boys and girls. Barenblatt's the name. Cars are my game. We have a lot of good deals today—plenty of used cars and trucks that are perfect for first-time buyers. How'd you like to take this little beauty for a spin?

JAKE: I know who you are. You sold me a bogus vehicle the other day.

(Mr. Barenblatt takes a closer look at Jake, recognizes him, and smiles.)

MR. BARENBLATT: Oh yeah. I thought that I knew you from somewhere. I sell a lot of cars. Sometimes it's hard to remember everyone. Hi there, kid. How's your car running?

JAKE: It's not.

MR. BARENBLATT: What are you trying to say? It's not running?

JAKE: No. It's not my car anymore. Here you go— I guess you'll want to read this.

(Jake hands him the paper. Mr. Barenblatt reads it quickly.)

MR. BARENBLATT: What is this, some kind of stupid joke?

ALENA: It's no joke, friend. He's a minor, and he wants out of the bogus deal that you forced him into. Next time, you'll think twice before you try to hustle a minor.

MR. BARENBLATT: You can't do that! We had an agreement, and you can't just change your mind and pull out of it now. You signed a contract!

JAKE: *(Smiling.)* It makes no difference. After all, I'm just a kid.

What Are the Legal Issues?

1. When is a person considered a minor?
2. Why does the law permit minors to void their contracts?
3. Are there any exceptions to the rule that says that minors can void their contracts?
4. What individuals, besides minors, can void their contracts?

Contractual Capacity

What You'll Learn

- How to explain the legal concept of minority
- How to identify the rights of minors in relation to contracts
- How to identify contracts that are voidable by a minor
- How a person can ratify a contract made in minority
- How to identify others, besides minors, who can rescind contracts

Why It's Important

Understanding the rights afforded to minors in contract law will enable you to exercise your rights and help others.

Legal Terms

- capacity
- rebuttable presumption
- majority
- minor/minority
- emancipated
- abandoned
- ratify
- necessaries
- guardian
- aliens

The Requirement of Capacity

The last two chapters established that a legally binding contract requires six elements. The first two elements, offer and acceptance, combine to make the third, which is genuine acceptance. Remember that if genuine agreement is disrupted by fraud, misrepresentation, mistake, duress, or undue influence, a contract may not be considered binding. Three other elements are also required of legally valid contracts. These final elements are capacity, consideration, and legality. Capacity relates directly to the involvement of minors in contracts.

CONTRACTUAL CAPACITY
The law permits minors to rescind their contracts. This law is intended to protect minors from unscrupulous adults who might try to take advantage of their inexperience. *If the idea behind granting minors the ability to withdraw from contracts is to protect minors from adults, why does the court permit minors to rescind contracts with one another?*

A Global Perspective: Laws Around the World

China

Do you have brothers or sisters? Can you imagine your life without them? In China, many children grow up as only children by order of the Chinese government. In 1979, the government introduced the one-child policy to make sure the country—the world's most populous—could feed and support all of its people. The policy, with a few exceptions, permits couples to have only one child per family. Failure to obey the policy results in a heavy fine to cover the additional child's "cost to society." Sanctions against parents might also include loss of employment or benefits, or even sterilization. Officials say that 250 million births have already been prevented since 1980. China's goal is zero population growth by the middle of the twenty-first century. In 2050, China's population is expected to top 1.5 billion. Here's a snapshot of China.

Geographical area	**3,705,820 sq. mi.**
Population	**1,284,303,705**
Capital	**Beijing**
Legal System	**Complex mix of custom and statute**
Language	**Chinese, Mandarin, many dialects**
Religion	**Many, but officially atheist**
Life expectancy	**70 years**

Critical Thinking Question If you were a Chinese citizen and could decide the fate of the one-child policy, would you vote to abolish or preserve it? Explain your answer. For more information on China, visit **ubpl.glencoe.com** or your local library.

Minor's Rights and Obligations

Capacity is the legal ability to enter a contract. When individuals enter into contracts, they are permitted by law to presume that the other party or parties have the capacity to contract. This presumption, known as a **rebuttable presumption**, can be challenged in a court of law. The presumption of capacity plays a key role in contracts made by minors because the law permits minors, within certain limits, to rescind or void their contracts. The court has established specific standards regarding who is considered a minor and what is meant by the term *minority*.

Definition of Minority

A person who has not yet reached the age of legal adulthood, known as the age of **majority**, is considered a **minor**. Sometimes we say that a person below the age of majority is still in his or her **minority**.

Legal Age In 1972, when the voting age was lowered from 21 to 18, most states also lowered the age of majority from 21 to 18. For many years following this change, the age of majority and the age at which young people could purchase alcoholic beverages were the same. Now, however, most states have revised this policy. The age of majority remains 18 nationwide, but most states have raised the legal drinking age to 21.

For legal purposes, people reach a particular age at the beginning of the day before their birthday. The reason is that the date of a person's birth is counted as the first day of his or her life; the law does not consider fractions of a day. As a result, on a person's eighteenth birthday, that person is considered 18 years and 1 day old.

Emancipation and Abandonment Some states have declared that minors who are no longer under the control of their parents are **emancipated**. This means that they are responsible for their contracts. A minor who marries or leaves home, giving up all rights to parental support, is considered emancipated. Such individuals are said to have **abandoned** the protection afforded them as minors. Although emancipated minors are fully responsible for their own contracts, many

EMANCIPATION
Minors who are no longer under parental control are emancipated. *Why does the law withdraw the right to disaffirm contracts from emancipated minors?*

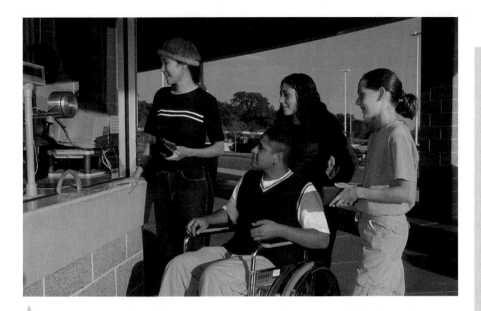

MISREPRESENTING AGE
Minors who lie about their age or use phony identification to misrepresent their age are in violation of the law.
Should an adult who permits minors to use their IDs to misrepresent their age also be held liable?

Social Studies
The laws affecting children under age 18 vary from country to country. Some countries allow children as young as five years old to work. Other countries allow children to drink alcohol when they turn 14. Still others won't allow children to apply for a driver's license until they are over 21.

Research Activity
Choose a country and find out how old a child in that country must be to do the following:
● **Enter into a legal contract**
● **Work and earn money**
● **Apply for a driver's license**
● **Get married**

merchants are still reluctant to deal with such minors because the merchants assume that the shield of minority still protects them.

Misrepresentation of Age

If a minor claims to be over the age of majority, then he or she has committed fraud. Fraud is a wrongful act, and minors are responsible for their wrongful acts. In some states, when a minor lies about his or her age and then disaffirms a contract, the other party may sue the minor for fraud. Such a suit would be successful only if all of the five elements of fraud were present and could be proven by the adult party, including the element of actual loss. Consequently, if the adult party to a contract cannot prove that the minor's lie caused financial loss, a fraud case would not succeed.

Some states still follow an older law stating that minors cannot be sued for fraud, even when they lie about their age. However, most states still consider it a criminal offense for a minor to lie about his or her age to buy age-restricted products. Some states require people whose ages are in question to fill out a form similar to the one shown in Figure 7.1 when purchasing alcohol. The New York Alcoholic Beverage Control Law has made it illegal to misrepresent one's age to buy alcohol. This restriction prohibits giving any written evidence of age, such as a driver's license or other photo identification, that is false, fraudulent, or not truly

PROVING MAJORITY
Some states require people whose ages are in question to fill out a form before they are permitted to purchase alcohol. *What procedure is used in your state?*

Figure 7.1

_______________, 20___

I, _______________, hereby represent to _______________, a permittee of the Connecticut Department of Liquor Control, that I am over the age of 21 years, having been born on _______________, 19___, at _______________. This statement is made to induce said permittee to sell or otherwise furnish alcoholic beverages to the undersigned. I UNDERSTAND THAT TITLE 30 OF THE GENERAL STATUTES PROHIBITS THE SALE OF ALCOHOLIC LIQUOR TO ANY PERSON WHO IS NOT TWENTY-ONE YEARS OF AGE.

I understand that I am subject to a fine of one hundred dollars for the first offense and not more than two hundred fifty dollars for each subsequent offense for willfully misrepresenting my age for the purposes set forth in this statement.

_______________________ (Name)

_______________________ (Address)

____

owned by the person presenting it. The law prohibits minors from purchasing alcohol as a protective measure. Many minors lack the maturity and judgment required to successfully regulate alcohol consumption.

Contracts of Minors

The law shields minors in making contracts as a protective measure. Immaturity, inexperience, lack of education, or naïveté could allow an unscrupulous adult to take advantage of a minor. The law does not intend, however, to give a minor the right to take advantage of other people.

EXCEPTIONS TO THE RULE

As is the case with most rules, the rule that holds that minors can rescind their contracts has exceptions. *Why does the law not permit minors to disaffirm military enlistment agreements?*

Voidable Contracts

Contracts made by minors are voidable by the minor. As a result, minors may disaffirm, or avoid, their contracts if they so choose. To disaffirm a contract means to show the intent not to live up to the contract by a statement or some other act.

> *Example 1.* In The Opening Scene, Jake, who is 16, attempts to disaffirm his contract with the Buy-a-Heap used car lot. He gives a letter that states his intent to Mr. Barenblatt. Jake is a minor, and as a result, Buy-a-Heap will have to comply with his request.

In essence, by permitting minors to have the privilege of disaffirming contacts, the law provides young people with a second chance when they use poor judgment. Young people may disaffirm contracts even if they damage or destroy an item purchased as part of a contractual agreement. In a few states, however, an amount can be deducted for damaged or soiled items returned by a minor. Young people also have a reasonable amount of time after reaching majority to disaffirm their contracts.

Returning the Merchandise   If a minor still has the merchandise he or she received upon entering a contract, that merchandise should be returned when the contract is disaffirmed. This requirement can be fulfilled by a tender, or offer to return the item. In fact, most states will permit a minor to disaffirm a contract and still get back the full amount paid for an item, even if the minor no longer has the item.

Disaffirming the Whole Contract   A minor may not affirm parts of a contract that are favorable and disaffirm the unfavorable parts. Rather, a minor must disaffirm all or none. A minor may, however, disaffirm one (or both) of two separate contracts. A letter written by a minor to disaffirm a contract is shown in Figure 7.2.

Disaffirming Contracts Made With Other Minors   When two minors enter into a contract with each other, both parties have the right to disaffirm the contract. Consequently, both enter the contract with the risk that the other may attempt to get out of that contract. When only one

LAWS in Your Life

Let's Rock

Suppose you decide to form a band with your friends, all of whom are minors. A few questions arise: Can you enter a legally binding contract with the other band members? Can the band enter a legally binding contract with outside parties who may want to do business? As your textbook explains, minors lack the capacity to enter into a binding contract unless it is a contract for necessaries. This is true whether the contract is between minors and adults or all minors. If a minor signs a contract but decides later to get out of it, often he or she can legally do so.

One way to enter into a binding contract with fellow band members is to have each member's parent or guardian sign the agreement on behalf of the minor. By the same token, any agreement signed by members of the band with a manager, concert promoter, or record company must also be cosigned by a parent or guardian for it to be enforceable.

Research Some states give limited capacity to minors who are engaged in business in their own name to make contracts that are essential to running their businesses. What is the law in your state? How might the law apply to forming a band and entering contracts with outside parties?

Figure 7.2

17810 Windward Road
Chicago, IL 31485
September 9, 20--

Attn: Buy-A-Heap Used Cars
Mr. Fred Barenblatt
660 Lexington Avenue
Chicago, IL 31480

Dear Mr. Barenblatt,

Please take notice that I, Jake Novak, of 17810 Windward
Road, Chicago, Illinois, hereby disaffirm the contract entered
into between you and me on September 8, 20--, at your
place of business (Buy-A-Heap Used Cars) at 660 Lexington
Avenue, Chicago, Illinois, for the purchase of a Ford Mustang,
serial number LTR 4565293433 xa.

On the date of the contract, I was 16 years of age and a
minor under the laws of this state. Demand is hereby made of
you for a return of all money paid to you by me under the
contract, which was $500.00.

I will return the Ford Mustang to your auto lot at 10:00 A.M.
on September 10. I am sorry to tell you that the
transmission is no longer operating properly.

Cordially yours,

Jake Novak

Jake Novak

DISAFFIRMING CONTRACTS
It is generally best to make sure any attempt to disaffirm a contract is in writing. *Would it also be necessary to use a writing to ratify a contract?*

Seller's name and address

Minor's name and address

Date and place of contracting

Time and place to return consideration

of the parties to a contract is a minor, that person is the only one who can avoid the contract. If the minor chooses to enforce the contract, he or she may do so.

Example 2. Rob, who is 15, offered to sell his mountain bike to Corey, who is 16. Corey initially agreed to buy the bike but then changed his mind. Because Corey is a minor, he has the right to avoid the contract. The fact that Rob is also a minor makes no difference.

Ratification of Minors' Contracts

After reaching the age of majority, a person can **ratify**, or approve, contracts made during minority (see Figure 7.3). Ratification ends the privileges that a person had while still a legal "child." Ratification can only be done upon reaching majority, and it may be accomplished orally, in writing, or by one's actions. Ratification need not consist of a formal process in which one writes a letter or takes deliberate action to renew a contract. In fact, a number of actions or behaviors constitute ratification of a contract made in minority. Using or selling items obtained by contract after reaching the age of majority has the effect of ratifying the contract. Making an installment payment on an item or keeping an item for a reasonable period of time after reaching majority is also considered ratification.

Example 2. Colleen Gregory bought a car when she was 17 years old. She made a down payment and promised to pay the balance in installments over the next two years. After she reached 18, she continued to make her installment payments. Gregory's act of making payments after reaching majority was a ratification. She could no longer return the car and demand the return of her money. Even if she had made no payments, she would be bound to the contract if she had kept the car for a reasonable time after reaching the age of majority.

Virtual Law

H1-B Worker Status

Technology companies face a thinning pool of qualified workers from which to hire. These companies are looking overseas for skilled programmers. At the same time, they are lobbying the government to loosen current restrictions on H1-B visas. H1-B is a category under the U.S. Immigration and Naturalization Act. It allows foreign nationals to enter the United States and work for a limited time. The work the foreign nationals do must fall within a specialized field. Programmers and other technicians in the computer field can enter the United States under this law. Technology workers who do not have H1-B visas lack the legal capacity to contract with employers to work in the United States. (Source: *Bureau of Citizenship and Immigration Services*)
Connect Search the Internet to find out more about H1-B restrictions.

Figure 7.3

RATIFICATION

Contracts made by a minor are generally voidable contracts. However, these contracts can be ratified after the minor reaches the age of majority.

1 Offer

A business advertisement in a newspaper can constitute an offer of sale, even if the advertisement is aimed toward minors.

2 Acceptance

If a minor agrees to the terms of an offer, then a voidable contract is created.

3 Reaching Majority

When a minor reaches the age of majority, his or her contracts can be ratified.

4 Ratification

Using or selling an item obtained by contract for a reasonable time after reaching the age of majority has the effect of ratifying the contract. Ratification can also be accomplished orally or in writing.

"Reasonable time" has no exact definition. It varies under different circumstances, and is determined by a judge or a jury acting on a judge's instructions. A reasonable time for a person to return a perishable item such as a birthday cake, for example, would be less than a reasonable time for returning a nonperishable item, such as an automobile or a CD player.

Contracts for Necessaries

A minor is held responsible for the fair value of necessaries. **Necessaries**, sometimes called necessities, include food, clothing, shelter, and medical care. Under common law, one's "station in life" has a bearing on whether an item is a necessary. A $150 pair of custom-made shoes may be a necessary for someone who has a foot injury. In contrast, a pair of designer shoes could be considered a luxury for someone else. If a minor pays more than the fair value for a necessary, he or she is entitled to the difference between the fair value and the price actually paid.

Example 3. Suppose that Eddie DeFino purchased a sweater, hat, jacket, and pair of boots from a retail store. If these items were things he actually needed, Eddie would be bound to keep them and pay the fair value for them. However, Eddie must actually *need* the clothing. In addition, it must be shown that he was not being adequately provided for by his parents or guardian. If he already had plenty of winter clothing or if his parents were willing and able to support him, then the items would not be considered necessaries, and he could disaffirm the contract in the regular way.

Special Statutory Rules

Many states have made changes in their statutes that control the capacity of minors to enter into contracts. For example, many states give minors the capacity to enter into contracts for car insurance and life insurance. Some states give limited capacity to minors who are engaged in businesses in their own names to make contracts that are essential to running that business. Other states treat married minors as adults. Still others consider the renting of an apartment as a necessary, regardless of whether the minor actually needs it. These are just a few of the many differences in state statutes regarding minors. Minors should check the statutes of their own states to find out about special contractual capacities that they may be allowed.

Minors are protected by the special rights given to them, but their rights are limited at the same time. In effect, the law warns adults against contracting with minors, except for necessaries. Consequently, minors may be required to have their parents make major purchases for them. Parents may also need to guarantee contracts made by their children.

Other Contractual Capacity Rules

As you have seen, parties to a contract must have the capacity to enter into the contract. Under certain conditions, a minor may disaffirm a contract into which he or she has entered. Other classes of persons are also able to avoid contracts.

Mentally Impaired Persons

The right given to minors to disaffirm contracts is also given to the mentally impaired, and for the same reason. They are considered unable to make sound judgments. Before a **guardian** is appointed, a mentally impaired person's contracts are voidable. A mentally impaired person is responsible for the fair value of necessaries. If a mentally impaired person has been declared insane or incompetent by a court action, and a guardian has been appointed to look after his or her affairs, the mentally impaired person's contracts are absolutely valid.

Intoxicated Persons

Persons who are intoxicated by alcohol or drugs at the time they enter a contract are sometimes able to disaffirm those contracts. Their contracts are treated in much the same way as the contracts of minors and the mentally impaired. To disaffirm a contract for this reason, a person must have been so intoxicated at the time of the contracting that he or she did not understand the purpose, nature, or effect of the transaction. The judge or the jury must decide that question. Intoxicated persons, like minors and the mentally impaired, are responsible for the fair value of necessaries.

Other Capacity Limitations

Other classes of persons lack the capacity to enter into certain types of contracts. In a few states, convicts have certain limitations placed on their powers to contract. **Aliens** —people who are living in this country but owe their allegiance to another country—may also have limitations placed on their capacity to contract. In times of war, foreign-born persons who are designated as enemy aliens are denied certain legal capacities. Even in peacetime, some states prevent aliens from entering into certain types of contracts.

When an international crisis calls for severe measures, the government may freeze most or all of the assets belonging to a foreign nation on deposit in this country's financial institutions. This drastic action limits the ability of the country owning the frozen assets to make contracts. Following the terrorist attacks of September 11, 2001, and the wars in Afghanistan and Iraq, many foreign assets in this country were frozen. Some foreign nationals who remained in this country became enemy aliens, and their capacity to contract was limited.

It's a Question of Ethics

Eat, Drink, and Be Merry?
Pang Woo is a sales representative for a carpet retailer. She is responsible for corporate accounts and selling to large office buildings. When finalizing contracts with clients, she likes to take them out for lunch or dinner and a few drinks. She insists that they eat, drink, and be merry before discussing business. While she, herself, drinks very little alcohol, she sees to it that everyone else has plenty. Only after her clients have had a few drinks will she finalize a contract. *Are Ms. Woo's actions ethical? Do the clients have an ethical responsibility to avoid drinking before signing a contract?*

Chapter Summary

Section 7.1 Contractual Capacity

- A person who has not yet reached the age of legal adulthood, known as the age of majority, is considered a minor. A person under the age of 18 years is considered a minor. In most states, however, the age of majority does not entitle a person to legally purchase alcohol. A person's minority ends when he or she reaches the day before his or her 18th birthday. The reason for this policy is that the law does not consider fractions of a day. As a result, on a person's 18th birthday, that person is considered 18 years and 1 day old.

- The law gives minors the right to disaffirm their contracts. To disaffirm a contract means to show the intent not to live up to the contract by a statement or some act. This rule protects minors from unscrupulous adults who might try to induce minors to enter unfair agreements by preying on the lack of experience and knowledge that often accompanies youth. The legal policy also frees minors from the consequences of poor decisions. The law is not intended, however, to give minors the right to take advantage of people by using this privilege. Emancipated minors, or minors who are no longer under the control of their parents, are fully responsible for their contracts. However, many merchants are still reluctant to deal with such minors because the merchants assume the shield of minority still protects them.

- Minors have broad rights to disaffirm contracts, and they may do so even if they damage or destroy the item they purchased under the contract. However, there are some limitations. After the contract is disaffirmed, the minor must return the purchased item. The contract also must be disaffirmed in its entirety. A minor may not affirm parts of a contract that are favorable and disaffirm the unfavorable parts. Minors are also responsible for the fair value of necessaries, which include food, clothing, shelter, and medical care. A minor who claims to be over the age of majority has committed fraud, and he or she can be sued in some states.

- A person may ratify or approve contracts that he or she made as a minor when he or she reaches the age of majority. Ratification may be accomplished orally, in writing, or by actions. Many different types of actions can ratify a contract made in minority. For example, using or selling items obtained by contract after reaching the age of majority has the effect of ratifying the contract. Making an installment payment on an item or keeping an item for a reasonable period of time after reaching majority is also considered ratification. "Reasonable time" has no exact definition and varies under different circumstances.

- The right to disaffirm contracts is also given to mentally impaired people and to people who are intoxicated at the time they enter a contract. Intoxicated persons can disaffirm contracts if they can prove that their state of mind impaired them to the extent that they were not able to understand the purpose, nature, or effect of the transaction. Moreover, certain limits are also placed on an alien's ability to contract. An alien is a person who lives in this country but owes his or her allegiance to another country. In times of war, foreign-born persons who are designated as enemy aliens are denied certain legal capacities. Even in peacetime, some states prevent aliens from entering into certain types of contracts.

Using Legal Language

Consider the key terms in the list below. Then use these terms to complete the following exercises.

capacity

ratify

majority

minor

minority

abandoned

emancipated

necessaries

guardian

aliens

Understanding Business and Personal Law Online

Self-Check Quiz Visit the *Understanding Business and Personal Law* Web site at **ubpl.glencoe.com** and click on Chapter 7: Contractual Capacity— Self-Check Quizzes to prepare for the chapter exam.

1. Write a one- to two-page report explaining contractual capacity to another classmate. Use the key terms listed above in your report.
2. Ask a classmate to critique your report, making sure it was easy to read and understand.
3. Use your classmate's suggestions to improve your report.
4. Share your revised report with your classmates.
5. As a class, vote to select the best report.
6. Post the winning report somewhere in the class.

The Law Review

Answer the following questions. Refer to the chapter for additional reinforcement.

7. What are the two age-related milestones that many states have?
8. Why does the law shield minors in the making of their contracts?
9. May a minor affirm and disaffirm parts of the same contract? Explain your answer.
10. May a minor avoid a contract with another minor? Why or why not?
11. Are intoxicated persons always able to disaffirm their contracts? Explain your answer.
12. What is an emancipated minor?
13. What are necessaries?
14. What is capacity?
15. When are the contracts of a mentally impaired person considered valid?

CHAPTER 7 ASSESSMENT

Linking School to Work

Acquiring and Evaluating Information
Research the special statutory rules in your state regarding the capacity of minors to enter into contracts. Find out whether a minor can enter into a contract:
16. For car and/or life insurance.
17. When it involves his or her own business.
18. If married.
19. To rent an apartment.

Let's Debate

Money Matters
It seems parents have many more responsibilities than rights when it comes to their minor children. According to the law, parents are obligated to provide their minor children with all of the necessities of life. However, parents have the legal right to the money their children earn.

Debate
20. Why do you think parents have this right? Do you think it's fair? Explain your answer.

Grasping Case Issues

For the following cases, give your decision and state a legal principle that applies.
21. Tom Molinero, 17, buys a car from Clyde Tait for $1,500. Two weeks later, while still a minor, Molinero is involved in an accident that occurs because Tait neglected to replace a faulty wire. The car is damaged beyond repair. Molinero wants Tait to return the $1,500. Is Molinero entitled to the money? Explain your answer.

22. Max Fisher, 16, bought a used personal computer from an electronics store. The box the computer came in indicated that it carried a 90-day manufacturer's limited warranty. The computer stopped working two months later. The clerk in the electronics store tells Fisher that the warranty applied only when the machine was new and suggests that Fisher return it to the factory for repair. Is another remedy available to Fisher?

23. Dana Niebuhr, 17, buys an electric guitar. She tells the owner of the shop that she is 19. Two months later she returns the guitar and demands the return of her money. The owner refuses to comply. Can Niebuhr avoid the contract? Explain your answer.

24. Joel Petro, 17, operates a VCR repair business. He finds that he has ordered more supplies for his business than he needs, so he contacts one of his suppliers to cancel his contract. The supplier refuses to cancel the contract. What might Petro do?

25. Two months before reaching the age of majority, Helen Smythe buys a motorcycle for $3,000. Three years later, she seeks to void the contract, claiming that she was a minor at the time of the purchase. Is she legally bound by the contract? Explain your answer.

26. Tina Kepler makes an agreement to purchase certain clothes from a local department store. Kepler has been declared legally insane, and a guardian has been appointed to take care of her. Is the agreement binding on Kepler? Why or why not?

27. Marty Eng, 16, sells his car to Joseph Lutz, 19, for $1,500. Two days later, Marty changes his mind. He asks Joseph to return his car and offers to refund the $1,500. Joseph refuses. Does Joseph have the legal right to do so? Explain your answer.

In each case that follows, you be the judge.

28. Legal Age

Leo's left hand was seriously injured in a job-related accident at 12:45 P.M. on August 3, 1977. Under the Workers' Compensation law, minors are entitled to triple damages. Leo was born on August 3, 1959, at 3:56 P.M. The age of majority is 18. *Is Leo entitled to triple damages? Explain your answer.*

Leo v. Maro Display, 412 A.2d 221 (RI).

29. Rescinding a Sale

Before reaching the age of 18, Brenda Sanchez sold property to Norman and Mary Ann Sanchez for $3,000. Upon reaching the age of 21, Brenda signed an official acknowledgment that she had sold the property to Norman and Mary Ann. Brenda then attempted to rescind the sale on the grounds that she was a minor at the time of the sale. *May she do so? Why or why not?*

Sanchez v. Sanchez, 464 So.2d 1009 (LA).

Legal Link

Doing Business Online

Freda, a student in your business law class, wonders if minors can legally enter into contracts over the Internet. She is interested in purchasing items such as books, CDs, and plane tickets, and has also considered bidding for some items available on a popular online auction site. She asks for your help.

Connect

Using a variety of search engines:

30. Help Freda answer her question.
31. Explain the issues that surround minors, e-commerce, and the Internet.

POWER READING STRATEGIES

32. **Predict** Why do you think minors are allowed to rescind or void the contracts they make?

33. **Connect** Have you, as a minor, entered into a contract? Did you void it or carry out the terms of the contract?

34. **Question** Why do you think minors, the mentally impaired, and intoxicated persons are held responsible for necessaries in a contract situation?

35. **Respond** Do you think it is fair that enemy aliens are prevented from entering certain types of contracts?

Consideration

Understanding Business and Personal Law *Online*

Chapter Overview Visit the *Understanding Business and Personal Law* Web site at **ubpl.glencoe.com** and click on Chapter 8: Consideration—Chapter Overviews to preview the chapter information.

The Opening Scene

It's Saturday afternoon, the same day Jake returned his "new" car and disaffirmed his contract with Buy-a-Heap. Alena, Viktor, Jake, and Arkadi are having lunch at a local restaurant.

To Pay or Not to Pay?

JAKE: Well, I sure showed Barenblatt. I am so glad that I got out of that mess. I saved myself a lot of money.

ALENA: You showed him? If it weren't for Arkadi, you'd be stuck with that heap of junk. You would never have thought to disaffirm your contract with Buy-a-Heap. In fact, I think that you should pay Arkadi for helping you.

JAKE: What Arkadi did was a favor. You must be joking.

ALENA: Why do you think I'm joking? You know that I never joke.

JAKE: No, that's true. You don't have a sense of humor, do you?

ALENA: You are so funny. So, are you going to pay Arkadi or not? You need to decide soon.

ARKADI: Hey, Allie, it's okay. I don't want any money. I just wanted to help Jake.

JAKE: See! Some people actually feel good when they help others.

ALENA: *(Ignoring Jake.)* But if it weren't for you, Arkadi, Jake wouldn't have known that trick about being a minor and being able to disaffirm his contracts. You saved Jake a lot of money.

ARKADI: Thanks, Alena, but it wasn't some secret trick. It's the law.

ALENA: Well, sure it's the law and all, but it's also a pretty good trick. You deserve to make some money for your knowledge. You didn't have to help.

JAKE: Okay. Okay. I'll pay him something on Monday.

(Jessica, the waitress, approaches the group and places the check on the table. Viktor picks up the check and reaches for his wallet. His facial expression changes as he looks at the bill.)

VIKTOR: Hey! This bill is too much! You added a tip on our bill. You can't just add a tip on your own. That's not fair!

JESSICA: Sure I can. Read the menu next time. It says parties of four or more get the tip added in, automatically. You're a group of four, so I get to add the tip. *(She turns and leaves.)*

VIKTOR: That's stupid. We should be able to decide our tip. I'm not paying this.

ALENA: You better pay, kid, if you want to go the ball game with Jake tomorrow.

JAKE: Hey, you can't do that. You promised to take both of us!

VIKTOR: Yeah! Jake and I have been looking forward to going all week.

ALENA: Promises to little brothers aren't binding, right Arkadi?

ARKADI: Right, Alena.

What Are the Legal Issues?

1. When is a contract sealed with consideration?
2. Does the law permit past actions to serve as consideration in a new contract?
3. Is there any recourse in the law when people disagree on the amount owed in a contractual situation?
4. Are promises to fulfill social engagements supported by consideration?

Consideration

What You'll Learn

- How to explain the legal concept of consideration
- How to explain the types of consideration
- How to identify certain problems regarding consideration
- How to identify the principles that apply to consideration in everyday life

Why It's Important

By understanding the concept of consideration, you will be able to avoid problems that frequently result when agreements lack this important contractual element.

Legal Terms

- gratuitous
- consideration
- benefit
- detriment
- forbearance
- bargained-for exchange
- unconscionable
- release
- accord and satisfaction

Requirements of Consideration

The law has always refused to enforce most **gratuitous**, or free, agreements. The terms of an agreement must be bargained for if they are to be binding on the parties. An agreement is bargained for when each side is compelled to surrender something of value in exchange for something else of value. This exchange, or the promise to exchange things of value, is what binds the parties to each other in a contractual relationship. This binding element is known as consideration.

Consideration distinguishes a legally binding agreement from other types of agreements. Many agreements are not legally binding because they lack consideration. For instance, social agreements that contain an offer and an acceptance, such as an agreement to accompany someone to the homecoming dance, are not contracts. Because of the central importance of consideration to all contractual relationships, it is crucial to understand the nature of consideration.

The Legal Concept of Consideration

Consideration is the exchange of benefits and detriments by parties to an agreement. A **benefit** is something that a party was not previously entitled to receive. A **detriment** is any loss suffered. There are three types of consideration. The first type of consideration involves giving up or promising to give up something that you have the legal right to keep. The second type involves doing something or promising to do something that you have the legal right not to do. The final type of consideration, which is known as **forbearance**, is not doing something that you have the legal right to do.

The Characteristics of Consideration

When we began our study of contracts, we noted that all contracts have certain characteristics. The same is true of consideration. Consideration has three key characteristics:

- Promises must involve the concept of a **bargained-for exchange**.
- Something of value must be involved.
- The benefits and detriments promised must be legal.

Bargained-for Exchange The law supports agreements that have been bargained for. An agreement involves a bargained-for exchange when a promise is made in return for another promise, an act, or a promise not to act. Bargaining requires that a party will be injured if the other party does not keep his or her promise. Of course, the opposite is also true. Both parties gain something when the promises are kept and the exchange is made. Figure 8.1 illustrates an example of a common type of agreement that involves consideration.

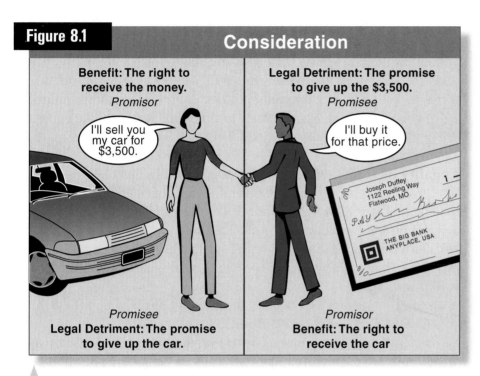

Figure 8.1

Consideration

Benefit: The right to receive the money.
Promisor

I'll sell you my car for $3,500.

Legal Detriment: The promise to give up the $3,500.
Promisee

I'll buy it for that price.

Joseph Duffey
1122 Reeling Way
Flatwood, MO

PAY

THE BIG BANK
ANYPLACE, USA

Promisee
Legal Detriment: The promise to give up the car.

Promisor
Benefit: The right to receive the car

CONSIDERATION
Consideration is an exchange of benefits and detriments by the parties to an agreement. *Is consideration necessary to make a contract legally binding?*

It's a Question of Ethics

Gestures of Kindness
Michael Baird's car would not start. He was stuck in the parking lot of Turner Field at 11:00 P.M. with a dead battery. As Rich and Marg Spratling drove by, they offered to help by jump-starting Michael's car. The jump-start worked, and the engine of Michael's car came to life. As Rich was disconnecting the jumper cables, Michael asked for their address. He wanted to send them $25 for their trouble. *Is Michael legally or ethically obligated to send the money?*

Example 1. Abha agreed to let Ulick use her snowboard for the weekend. There was no understanding that Ulick would pay Abha for using the snowboard. On Friday afternoon, Abha told Ulick that she would not lend her snowboard to him. Although it is unfair for Abha to change her mind, the agreement contained no bargained-for promise from Ulick in exchange for using the snowboard. As a result, there was no contract.

Something of Value   The law has no specific value requirements on consideration. Consequently, a promise to help a friend clean her room can be considered *something of value* promised. In addition, the value of the goods or services involved in a contract do not have to be the

same as the market value of those goods or services. All that matters is that the parties agreed freely on the value and the price. Most of the time, the courts will not even consider whether the value of the consideration is adequate. The reason is that the courts permit individuals to devise their own agreements. The courts are merely concerned with enforcing these agreements. However, there is one exception to this rule.

There are times when the courts believe that the consideration in a contract is completely out of line. In such a situation, a contract is deemed **unconscionable**. This situation usually occurs when a great inequality in bargaining power exists between the parties, and the party with all or most of the power takes advantage of the other party. The court may do one of three things to rectify an unconscionable contract. It may refuse to enforce the contract. It may enforce the contract minus the unconscionable clause, or it may limit the application of the unconscionable clause.

Legality of Consideration   The courts require that the consideration involved in an agreement be legal. If the consideration is illegal, the contract is invalid. As a result of this requirement, a party cannot agree to do something that he or she does not have the legal right to do. Nor can a party agree to give up something that he or she does not legally own. In addition, a party cannot promise to stop doing something that is illegal.

Types of Consideration

Generally speaking, money, property, and services all qualify as valid consideration. Other special types of consideration include promises not to sue and charitable pledges.

TYPES OF CONSIDERATION
Most of the time, consideration takes the form of money or credit. *What other forms of consideration can you identify?*

Promising Not to Compete

Employers in businesses that involve specialized skills will sometimes ask employees to sign contracts not to compete. A non-compete contract relies on a promise by the employee to refrain from working for a direct competitor for a certain period of time after the employee leaves the company. Non-compete contracts have obvious advantages for the employer. However, they can also present severe disadvantages for an employee, especially if an employee works in an area with limited work opportunities.

Courts will not uphold non-compete contracts if they place unreasonable burdens on a person's right to earn a living. Such clauses may be found unreasonable if they last for too long or cover too wide a geographic area. Nor will a non-compete contract be upheld if the type of business activity that it covers is too broad.

When asked to sign to a contract not to compete, it is wise to negotiate the terms so that finding employment after leaving the company is not too difficult.

Negotiate Can you think of some negotiating strategies that an employee could use to lessen the burden of a non-compete contract?

Money as Consideration

Usually, one party will offer money in exchange for another party's promise or performance. Unless price limits have been placed on certain transactions by administrative regulations, legislative fiat, or executive ruling, the parties are free to exchange any amount of money that they negotiate. In the past, the price of such things as rent, fuel, oil, and natural gas have been controlled by the government. Similarly, employers must follow certain pricing regulations set by the government, such as the minimum wage rate established by the federal Fair Labor Standards Act.

Property and Services as Consideration

Before money was accepted as a medium of exchange, it was common to use property and services as consideration. Some parties still prefer to engage in barter agreements that involve goods and services rather than money. For example, a promise by one comic book collector to another collector to exchange an issue of *The Uncanny X-Men*® for an issue of *The Fantastic Four*® would represent a valid agreement.

A Promise Not to Sue

If one party has the right to sue another party but gives up that right in exchange for something of value, the court will generally uphold the exchange as valid consideration. A promise by one party not to sue another party is a clear example of forbearance. Pending lawsuits are frequently settled in this manner.

Example 2. Abigail was eating a tuna steak for lunch at Martini's Eatery when she began to suffer terrible stomach pains. She was rushed to a local hospital. In the emergency room, she was diagnosed with food poisoning. The type of food poisoning that she had could only have resulted from the improper refrigeration of the tuna that she had for lunch. Abigail elected to sue Martini's, alleging the restaurant was negligent in not properly refrigerating the tuna. Martini's offered her $5,000 if she would drop her lawsuit. Abigail agreed. The thing of value that Abigail transferred to Martini's was her right to complete her lawsuit.

In Example 2, after Abigail accepted the offer and agreed not to sue Martini's, her right to sue was terminated, at least on the grounds described in the agreement. The agreement she would be asked to sign is called a **release**. Often, agreements not to sue are negotiated even after a lawsuit has started. In fact, such agreements can even be negotiated in the middle of a trial.

PROMISES NOT TO SUE Often an insurance company will want an individual to sign a release promising not to sue the company in exchange for a monetary settlement. *Is a promise not to sue valid if the parties later discover that the party promising not to sue really had no legal grounds to sue in the first place?*

CHARITABLE PLEDGES
Pledges to charities for specific projects are enforceable when the project begins. *Why does the law enforce charitable pledges, even when a specific project is not involved?*

Charitable Pledges

Charitable organizations and nonprofit institutions often depend upon contributions. This dependency has led the court to enforce charitable pledges just as if they were contracts. If a specific project is involved with a pledge, the charity must carry out its side of the deal by completing the project. In such a situation, the pledges would be considered unilateral agreements.

> *Example 3.* Father Olaf Laubacher, pastor of St. Carmela's Catholic Church, announced that the parish was beginning a campaign to raise funds for an addition to the church's parking lot. Parishioners at St. Carmela's pledged more than $12,000. Relying on these pledges, St. Carmela's began work on the parking lot. Each pledge became an enforceable agreement at that point, no matter how small.

Some charities use pledges for their general operation and maintenance, not for a specific project.

Problems With Consideration

When parties disagree about the amount of money that the debtor owes the creditor, a problem has arisen over the consideration involved in the contract. The resolution of this kind of problem depends upon whether the transaction involves a genuine dispute as to the amount of money owed.

Disputed Amounts

If the parties to a contract cannot agree as to the actual amount owed, that amount is said to be in dispute. A dispute can be settled by **accord and satisfaction** if the creditor accepts a payment that is less than the amount due as full payment. The acceptance by the creditor of less than what has been billed to the debtor is **accord**. The agreed-to settlement as contained in the accord is the **satisfaction**. The dispute must be real, must occur in good faith, and must not be trivial.

Example 4. Claudette and Ludwig Cerny contracted with Roberta Stoner for installation of a roof on their cottage. Stoner charged the Cernys $50 per hour for a job that lasted 200 hours. The Cernys received a bill for $11,250. When they examined the bill, they saw that Stoner had charged them one extra hour each day for lunch. The Cernys felt that it was unfair to have to pay Stoner to eat lunch. They subtracted $1,250 (25 lunch hours at $50 per hour) and sent Stoner a check for $10,000. On the check they wrote, "In full payment for the installation of the roof at 280 Kenton Row, Lakeside, Ohio." When Stoner cashed the check, she accepted the lesser amount that the Cernys offered in good faith and as full payment of the amount in dispute.

DISPUTED AMOUNTS
Customers and business people sometimes disagree over the exact price of a service after the service has been performed. *In what ways can such disputes be resolved?*

Undisputed Amounts

If the parties have mutually agreed to a set amount of money in the contract, then the amount cannot be disputed. The debtor might have remorse over the amount that he or she has agreed to pay in the contract, but he or she would still owe that amount. This would be true even if the debtor later discovered that another party was offering the same contractual arrangements at a lesser amount.

> *Example 5.* Irene Georgetown paid the Fairchild Paving Company $9,876 to pave her driveway with concrete. She felt that Fairchild's rate was a reasonable fee for such a job. Two days later, Georgetown saw a booth at the Delaware County Fair and learned that Greenbrier Cement, Ltd. would do the same job for $7,810. Georgetown sent a check to Fairchild for $7,810, adding the notation, "In full payment of the asphalt driveway laid at 2300 Hamilton Avenue, Marburg, Montana." Fairchild deposited the check and demanded payment of the balance. Georgetown would still be obligated to pay that balance.

In Example 5, no good faith dispute over what Georgetown owed to Fairchild existed. Georgetown was just trying to pay less than the fee to which she had already agreed.

Consideration in Your Everyday Life

As an essential element of any valid contract, consideration is something that you will encounter regularly. Remembering the following principles will help you in the agreements that you make in your daily life.

- Consideration is the contractual element that distinguishes a legally binding agreement from all other types of agreements.
- For something to amount to consideration, the act performed or promised must be legal.
- To constitute consideration, an act or a promise must be bargained for.
- If a person pays a debt in advance, it is something that he or she is not legally bound to do. Paying in advance would be consideration for settling the debt for a lesser amount.
- The courts enforce charitable pledges as if they were contracts.
- A promise by one party not to sue another party is generally proven by evidence of a release.
- Usually, a party will offer money in exchange for another party's promise or performance.
- Some people prefer barter agreements that involve goods and services rather than money.
- Generally, the courts do not get involved in determining how much consideration is enough.
- Forbearance is a type of consideration that involves promising not to do something that you are legally entitled to do.

Section 8.1 Assessment

Reviewing What You Learned

1. What is consideration?
2. What are the types of consideration?
3. What problems can arise regarding consideration?
4. What are the principles that apply to consideration in everyday life?

Critical Thinking Activity

Is Enough Really Enough? Why do the courts usually refuse to get involved in disputes over the adequacy of consideration?

Legal Skills in Action

Accord and Satisfaction Your older sister is about to be married. She purchased her wedding dress at the Duquesne Department Store. Later, she had the dress altered and added a special lace trim. Today she saw the same dress at another store for $245 less than the price she paid. When she pays Duquesne, she intends to subtract $245 from the bill. In a small team setting, discuss whether your sister is entitled to use accord and satisfaction in this case.

Agreements Without Consideration

Enforceable Agreements Without Consideration

In most situations, a contract is invalid if it does not include consideration. However, there are some agreements in which the requirement of consideration is eliminated. This is true despite the fact that these agreements may appear to offer the necessary element of consideration.

Some courts have chosen to eliminate the requirement of consideration in certain kinds of agreements. As is often the case, it is difficult to generalize about such things because states differ in the rules they apply to promises made in such agreements. Nevertheless, we can discuss some of the most common agreements that fall into this category: promises under seal, promises after discharge in bankruptcy, debts barred by the statute of limitations, promises enforced by promissory estoppel, and options.

Promises Under Seal

A **seal** is a mark or an impression placed on a written contract indicating that the instrument was executed and accepted in a formal manner. Today, most of the states that still require a seal will permit the seal to be indicated by the addition of the word "seal" or the letters L.S. (*locus sigilli*, which translates to "place of the seal") after the signature of a party.

Using a seal in sale of goods contracts is not required by the UCC. However, some states still require the use of a seal in contracts involving real property and in certain other contracts specified by law. Because the law varies so much from state to state, it's a good idea to research individual state requirements.

Promises After Discharge in Bankruptcy

It is possible for a person who has had his or her debts discharged in bankruptcy to decide to pay such debts voluntarily. To prevent abuse by creditors who might pressure debtors into making such promises, Congress reformed the law governing bankruptcy. Court hearings must now be held when the reaffirmation of a debt is intended. In these

What You'll Learn

- How to identify agreements that are enforceable without consideration
- How to explain the legal concept of promissory estoppel
- How to identify agreements that are not enforceable without consideration
- How to distinguish between past consideration and preexisting duties

Why It's Important

Understanding the difference between contracts that require consideration and those that do not will enable you to avoid common problems associated with consideration or the lack thereof.

Legal Terms

- seal
- promissory estoppel
- option
- firm offer
- illusory promise
- past consideration
- preexisting duty

Careers in Law

Court Reporter

Sally Harmon provides a vital legal service, and she does it by using a machine invented more than a century ago. Harmon owns Bredeman & Associates, Inc. and is a freelance court reporter in Jefferson City, Missouri. Court reporters record what is said during legal proceedings, including depositions and trial. Harmon's record of depositions and courtroom proceedings can be used as evidence in a trial.

Although court reporters appear to be typing, they are actually using a stenotype machine, which uses a specialized form of shorthand developed just for recording legal proceedings.

"Stenotype is a fascinating invention," Harmon says. "It's phonetic, not alphabetical, so it records speech according to how it sounds. And stenotype uses its own system for those sounds. So, for instance, the word *as* is written *az*. The sound made by the letter *D* actually is written in stenotype as *tk*."

Court reporters are highly skilled professionals. "People sometimes say that court reporters will be replaced by computers," Harmon says. "But even in courtrooms, people can interrupt or talk over each other. Our brains are able to sort these things out and tune out extraneous noise in a way that computers can't."

In addition to recording court proceedings, court reporters must also proofread their work. Harmon says that for every hour of recording, she performs four hours of proofing and document preparation.

Skills	Listening, reading, punctuation, language skills
Personality	Must like to work alone, detail-oriented, excellent listener
Education	More than 150 reporter-training programs are offered across the country in schools, community colleges, and universities.

For more information on court reporters, visit **ubpl.glencoe.com** or your public library.

hearings, the debtor must be informed of the legal consequences of assuming the debt. The debtor must also be reminded that reaffirmation of the debt is optional. Under most state laws, no new consideration needs to be provided in support of this reaffirmation. Instead, the reaffirmation must be supported by contractual intent. A writing is also required by some states.

BANKRUPTCY COURT
Hearings are now needed when someone who has declared bankruptcy reaffirms debts that were discharged under the bankruptcy proceeding. *Why does the law now require such hearings?*

Debts Barred by Statutes of Limitations

A statute of limitations establishes the time frame within which a party is allowed to bring suit. Different states set different time limits for the collection of a debt. Such variations can run from three to ten years. When the document of indebtedness is under seal, some states allow more time for collection. No new consideration is needed for a debtor to reaffirm a debt barred by the statute of limitations. The partial payment of the debt will result in affirmation. After the debtor affirms the debt, the creditor is permitted the full term as provided by the statute of limitations.

Promises Enforced by Promissory Estoppel

Under the doctrine of **promissory estoppel**, a promise may be enforceable without consideration. The word *promissory* means "containing or consisting of a promise." The word *estoppel* means "restraint on a person to prevent him or her from contradicting a previous act." The doctrine is used to prevent injustice when a person changes his or her position significantly in reliance on another person's promise, and the promise is not fulfilled. The court will "estop" the person who made the promise from claiming that there was no consideration.

Figure 8.2 shows that certain conditions must be met before a court will apply the principle of promissory estoppel:

- The promise must be made to bring about action or forbearance by another person who gave no consideration.
- The party that gave no consideration must have relied upon the promise and changed his or her position in a significant way.
- Injustice can be avoided only by enforcing the promise.

| Figure 8.2 | The Elements of Promissory Estoppel |

1. The promise must be made to bring about action or forbearance by another person who gave no consideration.

2. The one who gave no consideration must have relied on the promise and changed his or her position in a significant way.

3. Injustice can be avoided only by enforcing the agreement.

THE ELEMENTS OF PROMISSORY ESTOPPEL
Promissory estoppel was created to prevent injustice.
Which of the three elements of promissory estoppel would be the most difficult to prove?

Example 6. Zeke knows that his niece, Chalese, wants to go to art school but has little money to do so. When she gets into the school of her choice, he promises to give her $50,000 to help her pay off her loans after she graduates. Chalese is very excited about her Uncle's promise and takes action immediately. She quits her job, borrows money, accumulates a great deal of debt, and eventually graduates from art school. Zeke then notifies Chalese that he has changed his mind. Chalese is devastated. To prevent injustice, the court may stop Zeke from claiming that Chalese gave no consideration for his promise.

Option

Sometimes an offeree will give consideration to an offeror in exchange for a promise from the offeror to keep an offer open for a specified period of time. This is known as an **option** . Under the UCC, an exception exists to the rule requiring consideration for an option. When a merchant makes a written offer stating the period of time during which an offer will remain open, consideration is not needed. The offer, which is called a **firm offer** , or an irrevocable offer, must be signed by the offeror. The time permitted for acceptance cannot exceed three months.

Unenforceable Agreements Without Consideration

The promises previously described are exceptions to the general rule that consideration must support an enforceable contract. The exceptions are allowed by state statute or because the courts, in the interest of fairness or justice, find it inappropriate to require consideration.

There are certain promises, however, that the courts will not enforce because they lack even the most basic qualities of valid consideration. Included in this category are illusory promises, promises of future gifts, promises of legacies, promises based on past consideration, promises based on preexisting duties, and agreements to attend social engagements.

Illusory Promises

For a binding contract to be formed, both parties must be under an obligation to do something. If this is not the case, then neither party is bound to do anything. Some contracts are illusory, meaning they appear at first glance to be contracts but on further scrutiny are revealed to be hollow. Such agreements are said to involve **illusory promises**.

> *Example 7.* Sun-Hi and Badr reached an agreement. Sun-Hi agreed to sell Bahr any apples that he might need over a three-month period. Sun-Hi and Badr developed a fixed price for all apples that might be sold during this time frame. However, because Badr might not order any apples within the next three months, he is not bound to do anything. The contract is illusory.

Future Gifts

If a person promises to bestow a gift at some future time or in a will, that promise is not enforceable if no consideration is given for the promise. This rule would also include promises to provide free services or to lend something without asking or expecting any benefit in return.

Past Consideration

The act of giving or exchanging benefits and detriments must occur when a contract is made. **Past consideration**, or consideration that took place in the past or that is given for something that has already been done, is not regarded as legal by the courts.

> *Example 8.* In The Opening Scene, Jake promises to give Arkadi a sum of money for his legal advice. However, Arkadi has already advised Jake that he does not expect payment. As a result, Jake would have no legal obligation to pay Arkadi. Jake's promise is the result of Arkadi's past performance. No consideration passed from Arkadi to Jake for the money. In addition, note that Jake has actually offered to give Arkadi a gift. A promise of a gift cannot be enforced.

Preexisting Duties

If a person is already under a legal obligation to do something, a promise to do that same thing is not consideration. These obligations are called **preexisting duties**.

PREEXISTING DUTIES ▶
Preexisting duties cannot be made consideration in a new contract. *Why does the law prevent preexisting duties from being consideration in a new contract?*

Example 9. A county commissioner offered a reward to anyone who gave information that led to the arrest and conviction of a person who had been vandalizing subway stations in the county. The commissioner also hired extra security officers to guard subway stations in the evenings. The night security guard at one of the stations caught the person who had been vandalizing the stations. She then sought the reward. The court held that she was not entitled to the reward because she was under a legal duty to capture the alleged vandal. Consequently, she had not furnished consideration to the county for the promise to pay the reward.

Police officers, fire fighters, and other public officials, who might promise special services in exchange for monetary or other rewards for doing what is actually their job, would also be affected by this rule. Suppose, for example, that a police officer promises to provide a homeowner with added protection against crime by making additional rounds of the neighborhood in return for some money. This arrangement cannot be enforced by either party because it is an empty promise. An officer is already required by law to provide these services.

Promise to Attend a Social Engagement

All contracts consist of agreements, but not all agreements consist of contracts. An agreement to meet a friend for lunch or another social engagement would not be a legally binding agreement because the friend has given nothing in exchange for the promise. As a result, that agreement lacks consideration. See Figure 8.3 for a listing of the legal status of various agreements without consideration.

Figure 8.3

Agreements without Consideration

Agreement	Legal Status
Promises under seal	Enforceable in some states for contracts not involving goods; unenforceable under the UCC for contracts involving goods
Promises after discharge in bankruptcy	Enforceable in most states
Promise to pay debts barred by statute of limitations	Enforceable
Promises enforced by promissory estoppel	Enforceable only if offeror knew that offeree would rely on the promise and offeree places himself or herself in a different and difficult position as a result of that promise
Option	Enforceable under the UCC if made by a merchant, in writing, and stating the time period over which the offer would remain open
Illusory promises	Unenforceable
Promise of a gift	Unenforceable
Past considerations	Unenforceable
Preexisting duties	Unenforceable as a consideration in a new contract

AGREEMENTS WITHOUT CONSIDERATION
The law recognizes many agreements without consideration.
However, few of these agreements are enforceable.
Which of the unenforceable agreements do you believe should be enforceable?

Section 8.2 Assessment

Reviewing What You Learned

1. What agreements are enforceable without consideration?
2. What is the legal doctrine of promissory estoppel?
3. What agreements are not enforceable without consideration?
4. What is the difference between past consideration and preexisting duties?

Critical Thinking Activity

Public Policy Why does the law support the doctrine of promissory estoppel?

Legal Skills in Action

Promissory Estoppel Your cousin, Geri, has just called you from California. She recently quit her job, broke the lease on her apartment, emptied her bank account to buy a used car, and moved to California because a movie producer promised her a job. Now in California, she realizes that the job offer was an empty promise. Write a letter to the producer in which you explain how the doctrine of promissory estoppel applies in this situation.

Chapter Summary

Section 8.1 Consideration

- Consideration is the exchange of benefits and detriments between parties to an agreement. A benefit is something that a party was not previously entitled to receive; a detriment is a loss suffered. Consideration has three key characteristics: (1) promises must involve the concept of a bargained-for exchange; (2) something of value must be involved; and (3) the benefits and detriments promised must be legal. An agreement involves a bargained-for exchange when a promise is made in return for another promise, an act, or a promise not to act. The law has no specific value requirements on consideration. Therefore, a promise to help a friend clean her room can be considered something of value promised. In regard to legality, a party cannot agree to give up something that he or she does not legally own. Nor can a party promise to stop doing something that is illegal as consideration.

- There are three types of consideration: (1) you give something that you have the legal right to keep; (2) you do something that you have the legal right not to do; and (3) you refrain from doing something that you have the legal right to do. Money, property, services, promises not to sue, and charitable pledges are some common forms of consideration.

- There are instances in which a problem occurs regarding consideration. A genuine dispute over the amount of money owed could occur. Additionally, a party with all of the power might take advantage of the other party, in which case the resultant contract is deemed void.

- The following are some principles pertaining to consideration: (1) a party will offer money, goods, or services in exchange for another party's promise or performance; (2) generally, the courts do not get involved in determining how much consideration is enough; (3) for something to amount to consideration, the act performed or promised must be legal; (4) if a person pays a debt in advance, it is deemed to be consideration; and (5) because many charities depend upon contributions, the courts enforce charitable pledges as if they were contracts.

Section 8.2 Agreements without Consideration

- Agreements enforceable without consideration include promises under seal, promises after discharge in bankruptcy, debts barred by the statute of limitations, promises enforced by promissory estoppel, and options.

- The doctrine of promissory estoppel involves a person promising to do something in exchange for your action or forebearance, and your relying on that promise and changing your position in a significant way to your detriment. In these cases, a sense of fairness will compel a court to enforce the promise, although there is no consideration. This enforcement is based on the doctrine of promissory estoppel.

- Agreements that are unenforceable without consideration include illusory promises, promises of future gifts, promises of legacies, promises based on past consideration, promises based on preexisting duties, and social engagements.

- Past consideration is consideration given for a promise or an act that took place in the past, and is not regarded as sufficient by the courts. If a person is already under a legal obligation to do something, a promise to do that same thing is called a preexisting duty and is also not deemed sufficient consideration.

Using Legal Language

Consider the key terms in the list below. Then use these terms to complete the following exercises.

gratuitous

consideration

benefit

detriment

firm offer

accord and satisfaction

past consideration

seal

promissory estoppel

forbearance

unconscionable

release

1. Write a brief play in which two or more of the characters are involved in a contract negotiation. Make sure that the dialogue you create uses each of the key terms.
2. Select members of your class to play each of the character roles in your play. Practice your lines together, and make sure that you use each of the key terms correctly.
3. Present your play to the class. When you are finished, have class members in the audience critique your performance. Next, have your classmates provide definitions of each of the key terms based on the play that you present.

Understanding Business and Personal Law Online

Self-Check Quiz Visit the *Understanding Business and Personal Law* Web site at **ubpl.glencoe.com** and click on Chapter 8: Consideration— Self-Check Quizzes to prepare for the chapter exam.

The Law Review

Answer the following questions. Refer to the chapter for additional reinforcement.

4. Name the three promises that, when made, constitute a bargained-for exchange.
5. What does the term *unconscionable* mean as it pertains to consideration? Describe the circumstances that frequently exist when an unconscionable agreement arises.
6. How does the court view charitable pledges? Explain your answer.
7. What is an illusory promise? Provide an example.
8. Can a preexisting duty be consideration? Why or why not?
9. What is a release?
10. What is an option?
11. What is accord and satisfaction?

Linking School to Work

Acquiring and Evaluating Information
Contact a local attorney or use the Internet to determine if your state requires the use of a seal. If so, write a paragraph about the following:

12. What type of contracts require a seal.
13. What a seal looks like, and how it must be applied.

If your state does not require the use of a seal, research a state that does to determine the answers.

Let's Debate

Repaying a Debt
Seven years ago, Abdul borrowed $10,000 from his friend Tony to open a business. After only one year, Abdul sold his business and fled to another state. Although Tony tried several times to collect his $10,000 from Abdul, he has not been successful.

Debate
14. Do you believe that Abdul owes Tony the $10,000 he borrowed to start his business? Under what circumstances might your answer change?
15. What factors do you consider most important in evaluating this scenario?
16. What steps can Tony take to ensure the return of his money?
17. What are some of the advantages and disadvantages to borrowing money from family or friends?

Grasping Case Issues

For the following cases, give your decision and state a legal principle that applies.

18. Carrie Johnson agreed to let Richard Frank use her truck for a move from Bellville to Centerberg. There was no understanding that Frank would pay Johnson for using the truck. Johnson later refused to let Frank use the truck. Is there a breach of contract in this case? Why or why not?
19. Horace Kushner was injured in an accident with Vic Ling. Kushner promises not to sue if Ling promises to pay $1,000. Ling agrees. Is Ling legally bound to his promise?
20. Tammy Carson's car runs out of gas. Ned Grover, driving by, sees Carson and offers to tow her car to the next service station. Carson accepts the offer. After they reach the service station, Carson tells Grover she will send him a check for $25 for his kindness. Is she legally bound to do so? Why or why not?
21. Lisa Lowe takes her car to the Browning Garage and agrees to pay $75 for a tune-up. Before the job is completed, Lowe tells the owner, "I'll pay you $10 extra if you do a good job." Is Lowe bound to her promise? Explain your answer.
22. Carmen Sanchez's debt to Bernie Martin is due on June 1. On May 20, Martin signs a written promise to give Sanchez an additional two months to pay the debt. Is this promise binding? Why or why not?
23. Demi Grayson works for Viorst Caterers. Grayson's doctor has recommended that she have surgery. If she has the surgery, she will be unable to work for a month. The owner and president of Viorst says, "Don't worry, your job here is safe. When you're well enough, come back." When Grayson returns one month later, she is fired for taking so much time off. Explain the legal theory that might give Grayson a cause of action against Viorst.

In each case that follows, you be the judge.

24. A Promise Not to Sue

Koedding engaged N.B. West Contracting Co. to repave his parking lot. After the job was completed, Koedding was not satisfied with the quality of the work and threatened to sue. West agreed to reseal the lot and to guarantee the job for two years if Koedding agreed not to sue. Koedding was still not satisfied after the second paving was completed. *Will the agreement not to sue stop Koedding's lawsuit? Why or why not?*
Koedding v. N.B. West Contracting Co., Inc., 596 S.W.2d 744 (MO).

25. Preexisting Duty

Vignola Furniture Company sold Trisko a loveseat. Unfortunately, the loveseat was damaged when it arrived at Trisko's home. The furniture company agreed to repair the loveseat in exchange for Trisko's promise not to sue. Trisko agreed but later sued anyway, arguing that Vignola had a preexisting duty to deliver an undamaged loveseat. This preexisting duty could not be consideration in the new agreement. *Is Trisko correct? Why or why not?*
Trisko v. Vignola Furniture Company, 299 N.E.2d 421 (IL).

Legal Link

Cyber Contract?
Tara uses the Internet all the time. She makes purchases, downloads music and software, and uses it for finding information at a moment's notice. Recently, Tara has been wondering if she has been entering into a contract every time she clicks "I Accept."

Connect
Using a variety of search engines:

26. Locate a Web site that has an online agreement where the user must click "I Accept" to validate the transaction.
27. Print the agreement, and bring it to class.
28. Generate a discussion about whether the agreements downloaded would be considered valid contracts.

POWER READING STRATEGIES

29. **Predict** Why is consideration the central focus of most contractual relationships?

30. **Connect** Can you think of an example of consideration that pertains to your everyday life?

31. **Question** Why do you think the Uniform Commercial Code eliminated the use of the seal? In what ways might using a seal be impractical?

32. **Respond** Do you think a police officer should receive the reward money for locating a missing person? Why or why not? Does your answer depend on whether the officer is on or off duty?

Legality

Understanding Business and Personal Law *Online*

Chapter Overview Visit the *Under-standing Business and Personal Law* Web site at ubpl.glencoe.com and click on Chapter 9: Legality—Chapter Overviews to preview the chapter information.

The Opening Scene

It's Sunday afternoon. Viktor, Alena, Hana, and Emil are at the local shopping mall.

A Trip to the Mall

JAKE: I'm so glad that I got my money back from Buy-a-Heap. I just saw the best stereo system. I think I'm going to buy it. This time, though, I'm going to do a little research before I make a major purchase. I don't want to make another big mistake.

ALENA: We're so happy that we won't have to bail you out of another disaster, Jake. Then again, I guess I shouldn't count on that yet. I'm sure you'll find a way to mess up.

JAKE: Thanks for the vote of confidence, Alena. I knew you wouldn't miss out on an opportunity to cut on me.

VIKTOR: Would you guys stop arguing. It's getting really boring—just like this mall. I'm ready to move on. I'm sick of shopping. I don't know how you guys can stand to waste your day at the mall. It's gorgeous outside.

ALENA: You don't have any money, Viktor. That's why you have no interest in shopping. If you'd save for a little bit, you'd actually be able to make a purchase.

VIKTOR: I do need to start saving my money. Dad's going to be really mad at me if I ask to borrow money again.

JAKE: I'm ready to do something else, too. Let's head down to the food court. I could go for a burger.

ALENA: You can't. It's Sunday.

JAKE: What does Sunday have to do with anything?

ALENA: The food court is closed on Sunday.

JAKE: That's stupid. Why would the food court be closed on Sunday?

ALENA: It's the law.

JAKE: You're making that up. See you later.

EMIL: Is the food court really closed on Sunday?

ALENA: Don't be dumb. Of course not. It used to be, back when it was illegal to have any stores open on Sunday. But if that were true now, then the whole mall would be closed.

EMIL: Why were stores closed on Sunday?

ALENA: How should I know?

HANA: The stores were closed on Sunday so that people could stay home and watch football.

EMIL: You don't know what you're talking about.

HANA: Wanna bet?

ALENA: Betting is illegal.

HANA: No it's not! You're lying.

ALENA: Lying is also illegal.

EMIL: That wouldn't stop you.

ALENA: Sure it would. I'd never lie, and I'd never do anything illegal.

EMIL: Oh, yes you would.

ALENA: Wanna bet?

What Are the Legal Issues?

1. What makes a contract illegal?
2. Why were Sunday contracts made illegal?
3. Is a gambling contract valid and enforceable?
4. What consequences are associated with making illegal contracts?

Agreements that Violate Statutes

What You'll Learn

- How to explain what makes a contract illegal
- How to identify the consequences of illegality in relation to contract law
- How to identify contracts that are illegal by statutory law
- How to identify different types of licenses

Why It's Important

By understanding the concept of illegality in contract law, you will be able to avoid problems that might arise when you consider entering a contract.

Legal Terms

- conspiracy
- interest
- usury
- lottery
- license

The Nature and Consequences of Illegality

The last of the six elements that make up a valid contract is the element of legality. As we've seen, a contract must involve many elements: a valid offer, an effective acceptance, genuine agreement, competent parties, and valid consideration. Even if a contract contains all of these elements, however, it may still be invalid if it lacks a legal purpose.

A contract can be made illegal in several ways. For example, a contract may involve an agreement to do something that violates statutory law. In such a situation, the illegality of the action would render the contract void. Moreover, if the agreement were carried out, it would also subject the parties to whatever penalty is specified in the statute. In fact, even making the agreement itself may be illegal. For example, individuals who agree to commit crimes for a promised consideration are involved in what criminal law calls **conspiracy**.

Illegality in Entire Agreement

If it's impossible to separate a contract into isolated promises and acts, each of which can be performed independently of the others, then the entire contract is rendered illegal. If any part of an agreement is contaminated by illegality, a valid contract cannot result. This would be true even if specific sections of the agreement would have been legally enforceable.

In Pari Delicto and Divisible Contracts

If certain promises and actions in a contract can be successfully performed by themselves, then the contract is said to be divisible. In such a case, the courts may enforce those parts of the agreement that are legal and revoke the parts that are not.

Example 1. Fraser Connery, a truck driver, agreed to drive nonstop from Maine to Nevada to deliver a shipment. Regulations established by the Interstate Commerce Commission prohibit drivers from driving more than eight hours without layover and rest. Fraser's nonstop trip would take longer than that eight-hour limit.

A Global Perspective:
Laws Around the World

Greece

The Greek culture is extremely proud of its ancient cultural achievements in the arts. In April of 1990, 285 objects of "immense archaeological value" were stolen from the Museum of Corinth. These 2,500-year-old artifacts included terra cotta heads and figurines, finely crafted glass vessels, exquisite vases, and bronze statues. The heist, carried out by a gang of four, was the largest theft of Greek antiquities in modern times. The Greek authorities acted quickly, informing border stations, airports, the international police force, embassies and consulates, the International Council of Museums (ICOM), and the United Nations Educational, Scientific, and Cultural Organization (UNESCO). Under Greek law, such action prevents stolen treasure from being exhibited anywhere else and makes an immediate claim for repatriation. Descriptions and photographs of the artifacts also appeared in a special Interpol publication, ensuring that the artifacts could not be easily sold. Eager to tighten security, the country's Cultural Minister plans to submit a landmark bill to parliament, asking for strict measures for crimes "against the state, the Greek people, and historical memory." The bill calls for stiff punishment for those who steal, damage, or illegally transfer antiquities. Thieves will get up to fifteen years in prison. Vandals will receive sentences of up to one year. Unlike other countries, Greece also condemns any sale of artifacts.

Geographical area	**50,962 sq. mi.**
Population	**10,645,343**
Capital	**Athens**
Legal system	**Based on codified Roman law**
Language	**Greek, English, French**
Religion	**Greek Orthodox**
Life expectancy	**78 years**

Critical Thinking Question Greece isn't the only country that has had trouble protecting its precious cultural possessions. In the United States, we are also familiar with antiquity theft. In particular, we have problems with people we call pot hunters—individuals who loot historical or archaeological sites. Laws aside, why is it so important for artifacts to be left *in situ* (in place)?

The main purpose of the agreement, to deliver goods, is legal and can be separated from the illegal part. Consequently, that part of the contract is valid, and Fraser must be paid for delivering the goods.

Parties to a contract are said to be *in pari delicto* (in equal fault) if they both know that the agreement is illegal. In such cases, the court will aid neither party. On the other hand, if one of the parties is innocent or unaware of wrongdoing, then the parties are not *in pari delicto*. In that situation, the courts may grant relief to the innocent party. This principle may be applied when one party does not know that a law is being broken and has no intent to break the law.

Example 2. Leonard Graham agreed to remodel a cottage owned by Harriet Gavin so that it could be used as a bed and breakfast. Gavin paid Graham $18,000 in advance with a promise to pay the balance after the job was completed. Graham accepted the money, even though he knew that zoning laws would prohibit the placement of a bed and breakfast within the village limits. Gavin knew nothing about the zoning prohibition. The court would rule that Gavin might recover her money because the parties were not *in pari delicto*.

Agreements that Violate Statutes

State legislatures pass laws declaring that certain types of agreements are illegal and void. These agreements are illegal and void because they violate the state's civil or criminal statutes, usury statutes, gambling statutes, licensing statutes, or Sunday statutes.

Civil and Criminal Statutes

Agreements that require one party to commit a tort or a crime are illegal. Common torts are slander, libel, and fraud. Crimes include burglary, larceny, murder, and arson. An agreement is illegal if it is made to interfere with or violate the rights of another person.

Example 3. Sanger, a candidate for mayor, agreed to pay McLaughlin, a newspaper reporter, $1,000 to write an article containing false statements that would damage the reputation of Bonney, Sanger's opponent. Because this agreement required McLaughlin to commit libel, it was illegal. A court would not enforce the agreement if Sanger refused to pay McLaughlin.

Agreements to protect one party from the consequences of torts or crimes committed are also illegal.

Example 4. The mayor persuaded one of her campaign workers to break into the home of an opponent in the upcoming election.

The worker was told to remove papers that would be helpful in the mayor's reelection campaign. The mayor agreed to pay the campaign worker a large sum of money and to protect the worker from criminal charges if he were caught. The agreement was illegal and void. The mayor and the campaign worker would both be criminally liable for their illegal acts.

Usury Statutes

Each state sets a maximum interest rate that lenders can charge for loans by statute. **Interest** is the fee the borrower pays to the lender for using the money. The interest rate the lender and borrower agree upon must not exceed the maximum rate allowed by state law. Charging more than the maximum legal interest rate is **usury**.

Example 5. Linda Chavez wants to buy a car when she turns 18. To make the down payment, Linda borrows $600 from Robert Lightner. Linda promises to pay Lightner $100 per month for 12 months—a total payout of $1,200 for the use of $600. The law would not require Linda to pay the full $1,200. She has promised to pay a higher rate of interest than the law permits. The bargain is illegal, and the courts would not enforce it.

The Truth in Lending Act is one step the federal government has taken to make consumers aware of the cost of borrowing money. Under such legislation, the lender must clearly convey the annual percentage rate (APR) on each loan to the borrower. Before you sign any loan agreement, be sure to look for a statement of the true rate of interest.

Gambling Statutes

State statutes also prohibit gambling agreements. Gambling agreements are those in which one party wins and another party loses, even if some skill may be involved. Gambling agreements may include playing cards for money, money wagers or bets on elections or sports events, or buying tickets in a sports pool. Giveaway games by stores or businesses for promotion are legal as long as you are not required to buy a ticket or product to participate. Casual gamblers may not enforce their gambling agreements in court because they are performing an illegal act.

Example 6. Emil and Rita live in a state where gambling agreements are illegal. They made a $200 bet on the World Series. When Emil won the bet, Rita refused to pay the $200. Emil then threatened to sue Rita in small claims court. Because the bet was illegal, Emil could not collect from Rita.

Community Works

Politically Correct
Volunteering to work on a political campaign is one way to become involved in politics. Ideally, a political campaign should be organized, enthusiastic, and ethical. Unfortunately, some campaigns use unethical and illegal tactics to gain voter support. Libel is one of the most common unethical tactics used by politicians. *Do you think it is ever justified to spread false or misleading rumors about a political opponent?*

Get Involved
Become politically involved at school by joining your student council or by running for class president. Volunteer to work on a local, state, or national political campaign in your area.

At one time, most states prohibited gambling. In recent years, however, many states have changed their laws to allow some types of regulated gambling. For example, betting at racetracks is allowed in New York, Illinois, California, Massachusetts, Ohio, and some other states. However, even in these states, certain forms of off-track betting are unlawful. Lotteries, other than those run by the state government, are also considered illegal in many states. A **lottery** is a game that consists of drawing lots, typically tickets with different combinations of numbers printed on them, in which prizes are distributed to the winners among persons buying a chance. A state-run lottery must be approved by the state legislature and administered by an agency of the state government. Legalized lotteries are sources of additional money for state governments and are popular in some states.

Although a state may legalize one form of gambling, a person cannot assume that other types of gambling are legal in that state. Only regulated types of gambling are legal, and these types of gambling are legal only when conducted strictly in accordance with state law.

SUNDAY AGREEMENTS
Formerly, most states outlawed the making of contracts on Sunday. This practice has gradually changed over the last 100 years. *What considerations motivated lawmakers to relax the ban on Sunday agreements?*

Sunday Statutes

Under common law, contracts could be made on Sunday. However, today it is illegal in some states to make or perform contracts on Sunday. Many states chose to pass special Sunday statutes, also called blue laws, making Sunday contracts illegal. These statutes vary greatly from state to state. Since the 1960s, some states have begun to do away with Sunday laws altogether. In those states that still hold Sunday contracts illegal, the following rules apply: an agreement made on a Sunday is void; an offer made on a day other than Sunday but accepted on a Sunday is void; and an agreement made on a Sunday with a date other than a Sunday placed on the paper is void. Furthermore, states that still observe Sunday laws often apply the same restrictions to legal holidays.

Licensing Statutes

All states have statutes that require persons to have a license to practice certain trades or professions (see Figure 9.1). A **license** is a legal document stating that the holder has permission from the proper authorities to carry on a certain trade or profession. Engaging in such a trade or profession without a license is illegal. Licensing laws are

Figure 9.1

COLLIER COUNTY OCCUPATIONAL LICENSE TAX

LOCATION: DISPLAY AT PLACE OF BUSINESS FOR PUBLIC INSPECTION
FAILURE TO DO IS CONTRARY TO LOCAL LAWS

3033 50TH ST SW

LIC. FEE	18.00 20--/--	
PENALTY	.00	
TR. FEE	.00	
COLL. FEE	.00	
PREV. FEE	.00	
PREV. PEN	.00	
TOTAL	18.00	

COLLIER COUNTY TAX COLLECTOR
2800 NORTH HORSESHOE DRIVE
NAPLES, FLORIDA 33942
813/643-8477

THIS LICENSE EXPIRES SEPTEMBER 30, 20 - -
CLASSIFICATION
CABINET &
MILLWORK CONTRACTOR

NAME & ADDRESS
GERBEC, ANTHONY E
3033 65TH ST SW
NAPLES
FL 33999

CODE   02107501
SEATING CAPACITY
ROOM COUNT
NUMBER OF EMPLOYEES

1-10 EMPLOYEES
NUMBER OF VENDING MACHINES
PHONE COUNT

11/25/-- 12 12 SMY T 8282 R 80
LIC OC 911316
$18.00 CA   P-A-I-D
Guy L. Carlton

LICENSE NUMBER   911316

LICENSING AGREEMENTS The absence of a license in some agreements will not render a contract void. *Why do local governments require trade or occupational licenses?*

designed to protect people from dealing with unqualified persons. In most states, trade and professional workers such as nurses, surveyors, funeral directors, barbers, and plumbers must be licensed. An agreement made with an unlicensed person working in such capacities is illegal.

Some state statutes require licenses simply to raise revenue (see Figure 9.2). Any person paying the fee gets the license; there is no need to show competence. A law requiring a seller to have a vendor's license is designed to raise revenue for the local government that issues the license. Because the purpose of such licenses is merely to raise revenue, agreements made with unlicensed vendors are valid. However, the unlicensed person is subject to a penalty for violating the licensing statute.

Example 7. For $250, Ardner hired Wheeler, an auctioneer, to sell his household goods at a public auction. The state's only requirement for an auctioneer's license, which Wheeler did not

VENDORS LICENSE
Local governments can require sellers to obtain and display a vendor's license. *How would you obtain a vendor's license in your area?*

Figure 9.2

STATE OF OHIO
DEPARTMENT OF TAXATION
P.O. BOX 530, COLUMBUS, OHIO 43266-0030
VENDOR'S LICENSE

PRESCRIBED
SALES TAX FORM
NO. ST 3 (REV. 5-86)

LICENSE NUMBER ASSIGNED
BY COUNTY AUDITOR

THIS LICENSE MUST BE RENEWED ANNUALLY AT A FEE OF $10.00

COUNTY OF _____   DATE_____

THIS IS TO CERTIFY, that the vendor herein named, having complied with the provisions of Sec. 5739.17 of the Revised Code of Ohio, is hereby authorized to make taxable sales, at the location specified below. THIS LICENSE SHALL TERMINATE AND BE NULL AND VOID: IF THE BUSINESS IS MOVED TO A NEW LOCATION; IF THE BUSINESS IS SOLD; IF AN INDIVIDUAL OR PARTNERSHIP INCORPORATES HIS OR THEIR BUSINESS; IF A PARTNERSHIP IS DISSOLVED; IF A CORPORATION DISSOLVES, OR IS CANCELLED, FOR CAUSE, BY THE TAX COMMISSIONER.

_____ # _____
NAME   CORPORATION CHARTER

_____
TRADE NAME OR DBA, IF OTHER THAN ABOVE

_____
BUSINESS ADDRESS

_____
CITY   ZIP CODE   TELEPHONE NO.

_____
KIND OF BUSINESS   CODE NUMBER
_____, County Auditor   By _____Deputy

The Ohio Sales Tax Law provides that no vendor shall fail to collect the full and exact tax as required by Sections 5739.01 to 5739.31, inclusive, of the Revised Code, or fail to comply with such sections and the rules and regulations of the tax commissioner.

Whoever violates this provision shall be fined not less than twenty-five nor more than one hundred dollars for a first offense; for each subsequent offense such person shall, if a corporation, be fined not less than one hundred nor more than five hundred dollars, or if an individual or a member of a partnership, firm, or association, be fined not less than twenty-five nor more than one hundred dollars, or imprisoned not more than sixty days, or both.

honor, was the payment of a $35 fee. After the auction, Ardner learned that Wheeler was not licensed. As a result, Ardner refused to pay Wheeler the $250. Because the statute was for revenue purposes only, Ardner must pay Wheeler the $250. Wheeler, however, is guilty of violating the licensing law.

▲ OCCUPATIONAL LICENSING
Many mechanical, technical, and trade professions require licensing to practice. *What considerations might have motivated lawmakers to require licenses for some activities?*

Section 9.1   Assessment

Reviewing What You Learned
1. What makes a contract illegal?
2. What are the consequences of illegality in relation to contract law?
3. What contracts are illegal by statutory law?
4. What are the different types of licenses?

Critical Thinking Activity
Illegal Contracts Why does the law usually refuse to uphold illegal contracts?

Legal Skills in Action
Discouraging Illegal Contracts Inez and Chris have been in business together for three years. Their business is doing badly, so Chris comes up with a plan that involves making contractual arrangements with illegal aliens who are willing to work for low pay. How would you help Inez talk Chris out of implementing this scheme?

Agreements Contrary to Public Policy

What You'll Learn

- How to explain the legal doctrine of public policy
- How to identify agreements that are contrary to public policy
- How to identify contracts that involve an unreasonable restraint of trade
- How to explain the nature of a restrictive covenant

Why It's Important

By understanding public policy and contracts that are contrary to public policy, you will be able to avoid common problems associated with violations of this important legal doctrine.

Legal Terms

- restraint of trade
- restrictive covenant
- price fixing
- competitive bidding

The Nature of Public Policy

Not all illegal agreements directly violate statutory law. Some agreements are illegal because they violate a time-honored legal doctrine known as public policy.

The ability to regulate the health, safety, welfare, and morals of the public is a power that belongs to the government. The states have this power because they possess legitimate governmental authority. The federal government has this ability because of various interpretations of the U.S. Constitution. The underlying principle that nobody should get

AGREEMENTS TO DEFEAT COMPETITIVE BIDDING
The principle of public policy makes agreements to defeat competitive bidding unenforceable. *What considerations might have motivated lawmakers to outlaw agreements to defeat competitive bidding?*

How to Find a Supreme Court Decision

A law library, or even the library in your local courthouse, may have more than a thousand volumes containing legal cases. How can you find information about a particular Supreme Court case? If you know the parties in a case, you can look in a "Digest" of cases. If you look up "Olmstead," for example, you will find *"Olmstead v. United States, 277 U.S. 438."* This citation means that the report of the Olmstead decision begins on page 438 of volume 277 of the *United States Reports.*

Reports discussing Supreme Court legal cases are published by the Government Printing Office several times each year and date back to the very first year of the Court's history. Possibly an easier way to locate a case is by using the Internet. A federal government home page will allow you to choose the Supreme Court's Web site. From there it is simple to locate cases if you know the parties or even the approximate year the case was decided.

Research a Case Choose an interesting Supreme Court case from the past ten years, and research it. Take notes, and prepare to share your findings with the class.

away with doing something that harms the public at large is the basis for every public policy decision made.

Violations of Public Policy

If an activity harms the health, safety, welfare, or morals of the public, that activity violates public policy. The most common agreements that violate public policy include the following:

- Agreements that involve an unreasonable **restraint of trade**, or a limitation on the full exercise of doing business with others
  —Contracts not to compete
  —Price-fixing agreements, or competitors' agreements on certain price ranges within which to set their own prices
  —Agreements to defeat competitive bidding, or the process in which rivals submit bids for a project
- Agreements to obstruct justice

- Agreements inducing fraud or a breach of duty
- Contracts interfering with marriage

Agreements that Unreasonably Restrain Trade

The law protects the rights of persons to make a living and do business in a market economy. If a contract takes away these rights, the law will restore them by declaring such a contract void. A restraint of trade is a limitation on the full exercise of doing business with others. Three types of contracts are generally considered to violate this rule: agreements not to compete, price fixing, and agreements to defeat competitive bidding.

Outright Contracts Not to Compete   When a person buys a business, such as a deli, print shop, or specialty clothes store, that person is also buying the seller's goodwill. This is the continued public approval and patronage of the business. In some sales contracts, the seller agrees not to open a competing business within a certain area for a period of time after the sale. This agreement is called a **restrictive covenant**, or a promise not to compete, and will be upheld by a court if it is reasonable in time and geographic location (see Figure 9.3).

For instance, an agreement by the seller of a barbershop not to open another shop anywhere in the United States for the next 99 years would not be reasonable. It would not be reasonable in either time or geographic area. If the restraint is unreasonable considering the nature of the business sold, then the restraint is illegal and unenforceable.

Promises not to compete also are sometimes found in employment contracts. Employees agree not to work at similar jobs for a period of time after they leave the company. Such contracts are enforced only as necessary to protect the former employer from unfair competition.

Price Fixing   The law views competition in the marketplace as an efficient way of determining prices. Producers compete to provide better products at attractive prices. **Price fixing** occurs when competitors agree on certain price ranges within which to set their prices. Sometimes, competitors agree to sell a particular product or service at an agreed price. Other times, manufacturers dictate the price at which retailers must sell a product. Price fixing discourages competition and raises prices. Because they are contrary to public policy, price-fixing agreements will not be enforced by courts. In fact, competitors who seek to fix prices may be prosecuted by state or federal agencies.

Agreements to Defeat Competitive Bidding   A bid is an offer to buy or sell goods or services at a stated price. Laws often require governments to construct public works or buy goods and services through **competitive bidding**. In this process, rivals submit bids for a project. The firm with the lowest qualified bid wins the contract. If, before bids are made, the bidders get together and agree not to bid lower than a certain price, then they are not bidding fairly. The agreements and contracts are not enforceable.

Example 8. Central City planned to build three new parks. Only three contractors were available to bid on the projects. Local law required the city government to open the contracts to competitive bidding and to accept the lowest bid for each park project. Before the bidding began, however, the contractors met secretly. They fixed the bids so that each of them would be awarded one of the park projects. This agreement among the contractors is void.

Figure 9.3

RESTRICTIVE EMPLOYMENT COVENANT

In consideration of my being employed by Hawthorne Savings and Loan, I, Vytataus Angelitus, the undersigned, hereby agree that when I leave the employment of Hawthorne, regardless of the reason I leave, I will not compete with Hawthorne, or its assigns or successors.

The phrase "NOT COMPETE" stated above means that I will not directly or indirectly work as a loan officer for a savings and loan association or any other financial institution that is in competition with Hawthorne.

This restrictive employment covenant will extend for a radius of five miles from the present location of Hawthorne at 6802 East 185th Street, Cleveland, Ohio. This covenant will be in effect for six months, beginning on the date of the termination of employment.

Signed this second of March, 20--.

Vytataus Angelitus

Employee

RESTRICTIVE EMPLOYMENT COVENANTS
Some restrictive employment covenants are upheld by the courts. *Would this restrictive employment covenant be upheld by the court?*

Agreements to Obstruct Justice

Any contract that interferes with the administration of justice is illegal. Such agreements include protecting someone from arrest, encouraging lawsuits, giving false testimony, or bribing a juror. This category also includes an agreement to pay a nonexpert to testify at a trial, or an agreement not to prosecute a person who has committed a crime in return for money.

> *Example 9.* Kelly, an employee at Van City, stole $5,000 from the company safe. Kelly returned the stolen money, and Van City promised not to prosecute if Kelly paid them $1,000. Kelly agreed, but then refused to pay Van City the money. The company could not enforce this illegal agreement in a court of law.

Agreements Inducing Breach of Duty or Fraud

Many persons hold positions of trust. They have a responsibility for the well-being of other people. Your representative in Congress, your state senator, and all other public officials fall within this class. These officials owe a duty to work for the best interest of the public. Any

Virtual Law

Uniform Computer Information Transaction Act

In March of 2000, Virginia was the first state in the country to pass a law covering Internet contracts. This act, the Uniform Computer Information Transactions Act, creates uniform provisions for contracts made over the Internet. Software licenses, such as the one that appears when downloading Acrobat Reader, are an example of such contracts. The law would allow software companies to send binding legal notices about software restrictions by e-mail to software users. Because contract law varies by state, many software companies support some uniformity. However, many consumer groups oppose the law, arguing that it turns a simple buying decision into a binding agreement. Virginia lawmakers will study the impact of the new law within the state. Similar bills are also being debated in Hawaii, Illinois, Maryland, and Oklahoma. (Source: *EE Times*, March 15, 2000)

Connect Visit the state of Virginia's Web site. Search for the text of the Uniform Computer Information Transactions Act and see what is says about sending binding legal notices to customers.

contract that tries to influence these representatives to use their positions for private gain is unenforceable. This rule also applies to private persons who are in positions of trust.

Agreements Interfering with Marriage

The law encourages marriages and protects family relationships. Contracts that discourage, harm, or interfere with good family relationships are illegal, and as a result, are unenforceable in the courts. For instance, if Mr. Novak promises to give his daughter, Juleanne, $1,000 if she never gets married, the contract would be void. The same would be true if, once Juleanne were married, Mr. Novak promised her $1,000 to leave her husband.

Effect of Illegality

In general, a court will not aid either party to an illegal contract. Instead, it will leave the parties where they placed themselves. Neither party can enforce the agreement, nor can they receive aid from the court. However, an exception occurs when the parties are not equally at fault. In such cases the court may aid people who are less at fault in recovering any money or property they may have lost.

Occasionally there may be a case in which only part of the contract is illegal. If the legal part can be separated from the illegal part, the legal part can be enforced. If the legal part cannot be separated from the illegal part, however, the entire agreement will be void.

Legal Briefs

On April 14, 1912, the RMS Titanic struck an iceberg off Newfoundland, Canada, and sunk. At the time, the Titanic was the largest and most luxurious ship ever built, and many deemed it unsinkable. As a result of the Titanic disaster, ships around the world were required to carry enough lifeboats for everyone on board. The U.S. Coastguard also established the International Ice Patrol, which continues to this day.

Section 9.2   Assessment

Reviewing What You Learned
1. What is the legal doctrine of public policy?
2. What contracts are considered to be contrary to public policy?
3. What types of contracts involve an unreasonable restraint of trade?
4. What is a restrictive covenant?

Critical Thinking Activity
Philosophy of Law What is the legal philosophy behind public policy as a grounds for law?

Legal Skills in Action
Restrictive Employment Covenant Your Uncle Larry has just been offered a job at a computer software company. His employer has asked him to sign a restrictive covenant that would not permit him to work for another software company located anywhere in the United States for the next seven years. Write a letter to your uncle telling him whether this restrictive employment covenant would be upheld by the court.

Chapter Summary

Section 9.1 Legality

- A contract may be illegal if it involves an agreement to do something that violates statutory law. In addition, a contract may be illegal if it violates public policy.
- If a contract is tainted by illegality and it is impossible to separate the contract into isolated promises and acts, the entire contract is rendered illegal and is void. In contrast, if certain promises and actions in a contract can be successfully performed by themselves, the contract is said to be divisible, and the court may enforce those parts of the agreement that are legal and rescind the parts that are not. If both parties to a contract know that the agreement is illegal, neither party will be aided by the court in enforcing the illegal agreement. On the other hand, if one of the parties is innocent of wrongdoing, then the courts may grant relief to the innocent party.
- Some state statutes make some of the following contracts illegal: gambling agreements, contracts made on Sunday, agreements involving licensing requirements, and usury.
- A license is a legal document stating that the holder has permission from the proper authorities to carry on a certain trade or profession. Engaging in such a trade or profession without a license is illegal. Licensing laws are designed to protect people from dealing with unqualified persons. In most states, trade and professional workers such as nurses, surveyors, funeral directors, barbers, and plumbers must be licensed. Some state statutes require licenses simply to raise revenue. Any person paying the fee gets the license; there is no need to show competence. Because the purpose of such licenses is merely to raise revenue, agreements made with unlicensed vendors are valid. However, the unlicensed person is subject to a penalty for violating the licensing statute.

Section 9.2 Agreements Contrary to Public Policy

- Governmental bodies regulate the health, safety, welfare, and public to prevent harm to the public at large. Public policy considerations are a significant part of the legislative process. The underlying principle that nobody should get away with doing something that harms the public at large is the basis for every public policy decision made.
- Contracts that are contrary to public policy include: (1) agreements involving unreasonable restraint of trade, (2) contracts not to compete, (3) price-fixing agreements, (4) agreements to defeat competitive bidding, (5) agreements to obstruct justice, (6) agreements inducing fraud or a breach of duty, and (7) contracts interfering with marriage.
- A restraint of trade is a limitation on the full exercise of doing business with others. If a contract takes away a person's right to make a living, a court will restore that right by declaring such a contract to be void. Three types of contracts are generally considered to violate this rule: agreements not to compete, price-fixing agreements, and agreements to defeat competitive bidding. Agreements not to compete could restrict employees from working at similar jobs for a certain period of time after they leave a company. Price-fixing agreements occur when competitors agree on certain price ranges within which to set their prices. Agreements to defeat competitive bidding occur when bidders get together and agree not to bid lower than a certain price, thereby artificially raising overall prices.
- A restrictive covenant is a promise not to compete, which is commonly included in the sale of a business. This covenant limits the seller of the business from opening a competing business within a geographic location for a specified amount of time.

Using Legal Language

Consider the key terms in the list below. Then use these terms to complete the following exercises.

conspiracy

interest

usury

lottery

restraint of trade

license

restrictive covenant

price fixing

competitive bidding

1. Using all of the key terms listed above, create a crossword puzzle. Make sure to provide definitions for each term.
2. Exchange crossword puzzles with a partner and complete your classmate's puzzle.
3. Check your classmate's performance on your crossword puzzle, and have him or her check your performance. Make sure that each of you fully understand each term by verifying that the definitions provided are accurate and the puzzles are completed correctly.

Understanding Business and Personal Law Online

Self-Check Quiz Visit the *Understanding Business and Personal Law* Web site at **ubpl.glencoe.com** and click on Chapter 9: Legality—Self-Check Quizzes to prepare for the chapter exam.

The Law Review

Answer the following questions. Refer to the chapter for additional reinforcement.

4. What makes a contract divisible? How does the court treat a divisible contract?
5. What is a gambling agreement? Is gambling legal? Explain your answer.
6. What agreements are void under Sunday statutes?
7. Why do states have statutes that require people in certain trades or professions to have licenses?
8. Do all illegal agreements violate statutory law? Why or why not?
9. What is usury?
10. Why do some states choose to run legal lotteries?
11. What duty related to public policy do elected officials have?
12. What are some examples of agreements to obstruct justice?

Linking School to Work

Participate as a Member of a Team
In a group of two or three, research the licensing laws in your state. Select one profession or trade that requires a license and answer the following questions:

13. What are the requirements of the license?

14. How much does the license cost?

15. What is the penalty for violating the licensing statute?

16. Why do you think your state requires a member of this profession to have a license?

Let's Debate

Gambling Pools
You work in an office where there are gambling pools for almost every sporting event. Although gambling is illegal in your state, your co-workers tell you that office gambling is just a friendly game and there is nothing wrong with it.

Debate
17. Is office gambling just a friendly game?

18. Is it ethical?

19. Would you participate in office gambling? Why or why not?

Grasping Case Issues

For the following cases, give your decision and state a legal principle that applies.

20. Phil Jackson agreed to drive a truck transporting a shipment of illegally manufactured slot machines from New York to Atlanta. When Jackson arrived in Atlanta, he and the person who had hired him were arrested by federal agents. Both men were charged with transporting illegal cargo across state lines. Jackson still demands to be paid for his trip, arguing that the contract is divisible. He claims that the driving portion of the contract is legal and can be separated from the illegal part, which involves loading and unloading the shipment. Is Jackson correct? Why or why not?

21. A state statute requires real estate brokers to obtain a license. Burke, without getting a license, buys and sells real estate for others. He sues one of his clients to collect a fee. Is he entitled to judgment? Explain your answer.

22. Jose Hope sells Suzie Tanaka a camera repair shop located in Rochester, New York. Hope signs a contract agreeing never to engage in a similar business in New York State. Five years later, Hope opens a camera repair shop in New York City. Is Hope liable for breach of contract? Why or why not?

23. Olive Mower, a defendant, promises to pay $300 to Sue Dorsey if she will testify falsely for Mower at her trial. Dorsey testifies as agreed. Is she legally entitled to the $300? Explain your answer.

24. Ann Perkins promises her daughter, Sue, $10,000 if she never marries. Is Sue entitled to collect this amount from her mother's estate if she is not married when her mother dies? Why or why not?

For the following cases, you be the judge.

25. Gambling

The members of the "last man's club" purchased a lodge in upstate New York to serve as their headquarters. As a part of their arrangement, the members agreed that the last surviving member of the club would assume ownership of the lodge. The last surviving member turned out to be Crawford. According to the agreement, Crawford claimed exclusive title to the land. Quinn, the daughter of a deceased club member, contested Crawford's ownership. She argued that the contract was actually a wagering agreement and was therefore illegal. *Is Quinn correct? Why or why not?*

Quinn v. Stuart Lakes Club, Inc., 439 N.Y.S.2d 30 (NY).

26. Market Competition

The Major League Baseball Players Association and the Topps Chewing Gum company entered exclusive contracts for the services of baseball players. Under the agreement, Topps would have the exclusive right to use photographs of major league baseball players on baseball cards distributed for five years. A rival company, the Fleer Corporation, sued for $16 million. Fleer argued that the contracts were an effort to eliminate competition and therefore constituted "an illegal restraint on trade." Topps said that Fleer could still compete by making contracts with players in the minor leagues. Topps concluded that their competitive efforts were not unreasonable. *Is Topps correct? Why or why not?*

Fleer Corporation v. Topps Chewing Gum, Inc. 501 F. Supp. 485 (E.D. PA).

Legal Link

Legal Lotteries

Many states currently run lottery games as a source of additional money for the government.

Connect

Using a variety of search engines, research the lottery games available in your state. Find out:

27. When the lottery was first established.
28. What type of games are available.
29. What the state uses the money for.
30. Whether you can purchase lottery tickets online.

If your state does not have a lottery game, choose a state that does.

POWER READING STRATEGIES

31. **Predict** Do you think it's possible for a contract to be invalid, even if it contains all six of the proper elements? Explain your answer.

32. **Connect** Have you ever participated in a giveaway game that a store or business was conducting for promotional purposes? Explain your answer.

33. **Question** Do you think we should still have strict Sunday laws? Why or why not?

34. **Respond** Do you think the government should be responsible for the health, safety, welfare, and morals of the public? Why or why not?

Form of the Contract

Understanding Business and Personal Law *Online*

Chapter Overview Visit the *Understanding Business and Personal Law* Web site at ubpl.glencoe.com and click on Chapter 10: Form of the Contract—Chapter Overviews to preview the chapter information.

The Opening Scene

Viktor, Alena, Hana, and Emil are spending a Sunday evening at home with their father.

The Ever-Elusive Car

VIKTOR: I'm not going to make the same mistake Jake made when he bought his car.

ALENA: You mean you've decided that Buy-a-Heap isn't good enough for you?

VIKTOR: Exactly. I'm buying a car from someone I know. Keith from school has agreed to sell me his old convertible for $1,500.

ALENA: Wow! That sounds like a good deal. That's a nice car—I've seen Keith driving it. Did you get the deal in writing?

VIKTOR: Well, sort of. I wrote on my deposit check how much the total cost would be.

EMIL: Did you win the lottery? Since when do you have that kind of money?

ALENA: I know! How much did Keith want you to put down on the car?

VIKTOR: Just $500. I told you that Keith would give me a better deal than some sneaky used car salesperson.

ALENA: You're forgetting something that's very important. Where do you plan on getting the remaining $1,000?

VIKTOR: Relax, will you? I've already thought about that. I'll take out a loan from the bank and get Dad to co-sign for me.

MR. BENES: Excuse me? Did I just hear you say that you expect me to co-sign for a car loan?

ALENA: *(Snickering.)* Yep. You heard right. Vik has a plan, and you're definitely involved.

MR. BENES: I hate to disappoint you, Viktor, but there's absolutely no way that I'll co-sign a loan for you. I hope you didn't do anything foolish.

VIKTOR: But Dad. . . .

MR. BENES: It's completely out of the question, Viktor. I'll never co-sign for another loan, ever. I've learned my lesson when it comes to that.

ALENA: What are you talking about? What happened?

MR. BENES: Have you ever heard of an acceleration clause before?

VIKTOR: No.

ALENA: Me neither.

MR. BENES: Well, neither did I until I co-signed the papers for your Aunt Agatha's home improvement loan.

EMIL: What happened?

MR. BENES: Aunt Agatha didn't pay, and I ended up having to give $2,000 to the contractor right then and there.

(The phone rings and Viktor answers. He becomes increasingly upset as the conversation progresses.)

VIKTOR: Come on, Keith, we had a deal! You can't do that! You took my check. I thought that I could trust you. *(Viktor hangs up the phone in disgust.)*

MR. BENES: That doesn't sound good.

VIKTOR: Keith says he was thinking about it and now wants $2,000 for the car. Now I have to borrow $1,500. Can he do that?

MR. BENES: Sounds like a breach of contract to me. I think there are laws against that.

What Are the Legal Issues?

1. What is the purpose of the Statute of Frauds?
2. What is the legal status of a contract that is not in formal writing?
3. Which contracts must be in writing?
4. What elements must be included in a written contract?

The Statute of Frauds

Why It's Important

Understanding which contracts must be in writing, as well as the elements of a writing, will help you avoid pitfalls associated with the Statute of Frauds.

Legal Terms

- breach of contract
- perjury
- Statute of Frauds
- memorandum
- goods
- real property

Purpose of a Writing

In early England contracts did not necessarily have to be written to be fully enforceable. Persons could be brought to trial for breach of written or oral contracts. A **breach of contract** is a wrongful failure to perform one or more promises of a contract. The accused could not testify on his or her behalf, however. Only persons who were not parties to the contract could be witnesses in court. To protect their friends or their own interests, witnesses often made false statements under oath in court. Making such false statements is called **perjury** and is a crime.

To discourage such practices, the English Parliament passed a special statute in 1677. It required certain contracts to be evidenced by a writing to be enforceable. This statute, entitled an "Act for the Prevention of Frauds and Perjuries," became known as the Statute of Frauds. A better name might be the Statute of Writings, however, because the statute states that certain contracts must be in writing.

Most states in the United States now have a **Statute of Frauds**, which are state laws requiring that certain contracts be evidenced by a writing. We commonly say such contracts must be "in writing." Putting a contract in writing can help to clarify an agreement for both parties and for the courts, if necessary.

Elements of a Writing

A writing need not be formal to satisfy the Statute of Frauds. The written evidence of an agreement is known as a **memorandum**. It may consist of such things as a letter, a sales slip, an invoice, a telegram, or words written on a check. The writing should typically identify the place, date, involved parties, subject matter, price and terms, and intent of the parties. It should also contain the signature of the party who may be charged on the agreement. See Figure 10.1 for a sample memorandum.

Example 1. In The Opening Scene, Viktor agreed to buy Keith's car for $1,500. On his deposit check for $500, Viktor wrote, "Down payment on 1987 convertible. Total price $1,500." Keith signed the back of the check and put it in his bank account. Although Keith later told Viktor he wanted $2,000 for the car, a court would hold that the oral contract for $1,500 was enforceable because the words on the check satisfied the requirements of a written agreement.

Figure 10.1

Elmsford, New York
September 1, 20--

ELMSFORD LANDSCAPING AND JEANNINE MASON hereby agree as follows:

ELMSFORD LANDSCAPING agrees to build a flagstone terrace for JEANNINE MASON at her residence, 52 Locust Drive, Elmsford, New York, for the sum of $2,750. The dimensions of the terrace are to be 20 feet in length by 15 feet in width and 4 inches in thickness. All material used is to be of good quality, conforming with standard specifications of the American Society for Testing Materials.

ELMSFORD LANDSCAPING

By _Joseph Vontana_
President
Jeannine Mason
Jeannine Mason

THE REQUIREMENTS OF A WRITING
The Statute of Frauds is designed to prevent fraud and perjury by requiring a written memorandum as evidence of the agreement and its terms. *Does this written memorandum satisfy the Statute of Frauds?*

Evaluating Contradictory Terms

Sometimes parties to an agreement will make handwritten changes on a typewritten or printed contract. When the handwritten terms contradict the typed or printed terms, the handwritten terms will prevail because the court will presume that these terms were placed in the writing after the contract was typed or printed. For that reason, the handwritten changes likely represent the final intent of the parties. Generally, handwriting prevails over typewriting or printing, and typewriting prevails over printing. When there is a discrepancy in an amount written in both words and figures, as in a check, the amount written in words will prevail over the amount written in figures (see Figure 10.2).

Figure 10.2

FIRST NATIONAL BANK   0000

Nov 10 20 -- -- 56-292
213

PAY TO THE ORDER OF _Doug Williams_ $ _500.00_

Five and 00/100 ————————————————— DOLLARS

Harriet DeLuca

FOR _____

"·002130"· ı:0292000001: "·0240 0688"·

CONTRADICTORY TERMS
Sometimes the terms of a written memorandum will contradict one another. *Which amount will the bank pay in this case?*

Evaluating Ambiguous Clauses

Sometimes written contracts can be understood in different ways. When such ambiguous language exists, the court will lean in favor of the party who did not draft the contract and against the one who drafted it.

Example 2. Katharine Black was involved in an automobile accident. The insurance company refused to pay Black, interpreting an ambiguous clause in her policy against her. When Black sued, the court interpreted the clause in her favor because the company had drafted the ambiguous policy.

Contracts That Must Be in Writing

Every state has a law requiring that certain kinds of contracts be in writing to be enforceable. However, this Statute of Frauds does not pertain to all contracts. The law does not eliminate the essential elements of a valid contract: offer, acceptance, genuine agreement, capacity, consideration, and legality. Instead, it merely adds the requirement of written evidence that a contract exists. The following types of contracts must be in writing:

- Contracts to pay the debts of others
- Contracts in which executors and administrators of estates agree to pay the debts of deceased persons
- Contracts requiring more than a year to perform

Virtual Law

Legal Guidance Without a Lawyer

Asking lawyers to draft contracts can be very costly. Instead of paying lawyers to draft contracts, some companies are turning to the Internet to buy generic contracts. Such contracts can be found for a variety of business uses. Companies can use these contracts simply by filling in the blanks, or they can ask a lawyer to customize the contracts at a savings of several hundred dollars apiece. Businesses that sell generic contracts on the Internet have helped consumers by providing them with information that until now has only been available from lawyers. Web sites now offer generic contracts and other legal documents for under $50. Chat sessions with lawyers are also available at very reasonable rates. (Source: *New York Times*, February 22, 2001, p. D1)

Connect Go to the Web site of your state bar association and see whether the site refers to any online resources for consumers.

- Contracts in consideration of marriage
- Contracts for the sale of goods valued at $500 or more
- Contracts to sell an interest in real property

In addition to these contracts, some states require that other kinds of contracts be in writing. Also be aware that the Statute of Frauds applies only to executory contracts; that is, to contracts that have not been fully performed. If two parties perform an oral contract that should have been in writing, then neither party can try to have it set aside later because it was not in writing (see Figure 10.3).

Contracts to Pay Debts of Others

A contract that one person makes with another to pay the debts of someone else must be in writing to be enforceable. Under this type of agreement, the debtor still owes the money; the person promising to cover his or her debt does so only if the debtor fails to pay.

It's a Question of Ethics

Green Acres
At a family picnic, Jesus Perez discussed selling 10 acres of pasture with his brother-in-law, Eduardo. Jesus was asking $6,000 per acre—$1,000 per acre less than the market price. Eduardo knew a good deal when he heard it and quickly accepted the offer. After taking six weeks to organize financing, Eduardo called Jesus to arrange payment. Jesus said the land had already been sold. He apologized and explained that someone had offered him $7,500 an acre, a total of $15,000 more than Eduardo was going to pay. *Did Jesus have an ethical obligation to sell the land to Eduardo? Does Jesus, who wants to send his children to college, have an ethical obligation to earn the greatest possible profit?*

Figure 10.3

THIS AGREEMENT, made the 12th day of May, 20--, by and between CRESTWOOD REALTY CORPORATION of Crestwood, Texas, and hereinafter called the OWNER, and JAMES M. LEW, hereinafter called the ARCHITECT, WITNESSETH, that whereas the Owner intends to build a one-family dwelling in Crestwood, Texas, of approximately 16,500 cubic feet in volume, and will furnish a survey of the property to the Architect, NOW, THEREFORE, the Owner and the Architect, for the considerations hereinafter named, agree as follows:

The Architect agrees to perform for the above-named work the following professional services:

Prepare plans and specifications suitable for the construction of said dwelling and for obtaining the approval of local building authorities having legal jurisdiction. Architect will furnish three sets of plans and specifications to Owner. Additional sets will be furnished to Owner at cost.

The Owner agrees to pay the Architect the sum of Six-Thousand Dollars ($6,000), payable as follows:

As a retainer upon signing of this agreement	$2,000
When preliminary designs and plans are approved	$2,000
When plans and specifications are completed and three sets are furnished to Owner	$2,000

The Owner and the Architect further agree that the Standard Conditions of Agreement between Owner and Architect as now published by the American Institute of Architects shall be part of this Agreement insofar as they are applicable hereto.

The Owner and the Architect hereby agree to the full performance of the covenants contained herein.

IN WITNESS WHEREOF, the said parties have executed this Agreement on the day and year first above written.

CRESTWOOD REALTY CORPORATION

Martin D Welch

Clara Barlow Witness

Witness

Barbara M. Bono President

James M. Lew Architect

FORMAL CONTRACT
To satisfy the Statute of Frauds, a writing need not be as formal as this one. *Why can this contract be considered executory?*

Civil Process Server

It's a good thing Harry McKenney likes people because, as a civil process server, he encounters a lot of them—and not always in ideal situations. Under the American legal system, citizens have the right to be informed that legal action is being taken against them. As a result, the courts or agencies involved in the legal action must tell people they are involved. The person who informs defendants or witnesses that they have been summoned to appear in a legal proceeding is called a "process server." Being a process server can be stressful.

"I know sometimes I'm entering a difficult moment in someone's life," McKenney says, "and I try not to embarrass them or make them feel like they're being harassed."

Civil process servers let people know they are defendants or witnesses in cases involving divorces, evictions, foreclosures, landlord-tenant disputes, unpaid bills, or other noncriminal cases. McKenney is deputized and gets paid for each successful service of process. Unlike process servers shown on television shows, McKenney does not hide in bushes to surprise people with official papers. Instead, he usually serves people with the documents at their front doors.

"Usually they understand that I'm just like a mailman," he says. "People don't get mad at the mailman for bringing bills, and they usually don't get mad at me."

However, when people do purposely avoid him, McKenney is sometimes forced to serve process in other settings, even while defendants and witnesses attend weddings and funerals.

"I mostly love this job," says the former Xerox sales representative. "It's really exciting and is a bridge between being a cop and being a lawyer. I get to read all the legal documents, and have learned a lot of law in the process."

Skills	Communication, mediation techniques
Personality	Assertive, confident, patient, appreciative of many different kinds of people
Education	In Maine, civil process servers must complete 100 hours of training in the police academy as a sheriff's reserve; must undergo retraining with weapons twice yearly; and must pass 40 hours of continuing education within two years of certification.

For more information on process servers, visit **ubpl.glencoe.com** or your public library.

Contracts to Pay Debts of Deceased Persons

Executors and administrators handle the estates of deceased persons. They gather the property of the deceased, pay all debts, and divide the remaining property according to the terms of a will. The executor is not personally responsible for the deceased person's debts; these are paid out of the estate. If the estate lacks the money to pay all debts, the executor may promise to pay the debts with his or her own money. Such an agreement must be in writing to be enforceable.

> *Example 3.* When Morgan died, he had an estate worth $10,000 but owed creditors $12,000. Morgan's son, who was the executor of the estate, wanted to clear his father's name. He made an oral agreement with the creditors to pay the additional $2,000 owed by his father out of his own pocket. This oral agreement, however, would not be legally enforceable by the creditors.

Contracts Requiring More Than a Year to Perform

All contracts must be written if they cannot be performed within one year of the date they are made. The year legally begins when the contract is made, not when the performance is to start.

> *Example 4.* Jake and Mr. Lucas enter an agreement in which Jake promises to help paint the offices of the new Lucas Company building on Michigan Avenue. Because the job is estimated to take 14 months, the contract must be in writing to be enforceable.

In Example 4, if Jake had contracted to work for "as long as Mr. Lucas continues to be president of the Lucas Company," then the agreement would not have to be in writing because the time involved would be uncertain. Lucas might continue to be president of the company for many years. On the other hand, he might be president for only a short time, and the contract could be completed in less than a year.

Contracts in Consideration of Marriage

When two persons agree to marry, they enter into a valid, binding contract. The promises they make to each other serve as the consideration for the contract. Agreements to marry have never required a written contract. Under present-day law, an agreement between two people to marry is generally not enforceable. Consequently, either party can break the agreement without being liable to the other.

Community Works

Debt
Easy credit and the high cost of living lead far too many of us into debt. Many people who are in serious financial trouble file for bankruptcy to wipe out their debt. *Did you know that a bankruptcy filing can stay on your record for 10 years and can affect your ability to get a loan, acquire a credit card, and rent an apartment?*

Get involved
Take a money management course at your local community college to learn how to budget, save, and invest your money. Research differences among employer-sponsored savings plans, IRAs, and Roth IRAs.

▲ MARRIAGE CONTRACTS
Although the law does not require that the marriage
agreement itself be in writing, certain contracts that
are associated with marriage must be in writing. *Why
would two people enter into a prenuptial agreement?*

Example 5. Paul Vincenti proposed to his girlfriend, Joanna
Panos, after six years of dating. Joanna accepted the proposal
and immediately sent an announcement to the local newspaper.
Three weeks after his marriage proposal, Paul changed his mind
and informed Joanna that he didn't want to get married after all.
Paul is not liable to Joanna for backing out of the wedding, and
Joanna will have to accept his decision.

If one person agrees to marry another person in return for a third
person's promise of money or property, the agreement must be in writing.
A promise to adopt a child from a former marriage or to care for another
relative in return for a promise of marriage also must be in writing to
be enforceable.

Contracts for Sale of Goods of $500 or More

A contract for the sale of goods for the price of $500 or more must be in writing to be enforceable. **Goods** consist of movable items, including specially manufactured items. Furniture, books, livestock, cultivated crops, clothing, automobiles, and personal effects of any kind are considered goods.

Example 6. Al Jaworski agreed to buy a motorcycle from his friend, Evan Allard, for $950. This agreement was not in writing. A short time later, Al changed his mind and told Evan he didn't want to buy the motorcycle. The agreement was not enforceable because there was no written contract. There are four exceptions to this rule, which will be explained in Chapter 13.

According to the UCC, a writing is sufficient if it indicates that a contract for sale has been made between the parties and it is signed by the party (or his or her representative) against whom enforcement is sought. The UCC does not require that all the terms of the contract be in writing (or even that they be stated accurately).

Contracts to Sell Real Property

Contracts for the sale of **real property** must be in writing to be enforceable. Real property is land and anything permanently attached to it. One important contract for real property that you may enter into is the contract to buy or sell a home. The contract of sale, sometimes called a purchase and sale agreement, consists of an offer by the buyer and an acceptance by the seller. The purchase and sale agreement must also contain the other elements of a contract.

CONTRACTS IN WRITING
Contracts for the sale of goods costing $500 or more must be in writing to be enforceable. *Would the purchase of a bike on sale for $499 require a written contract if the bike's original price was $550?*

An exception to the requirement that a contract for the sale of real property must be in writing is known as equitable estoppel. According to this doctrine, a party is prevented or "estopped" from claiming the Statute of Frauds when the other party changes his or her position based on an oral promise. Sometimes this exception is called part performance. It applies to an oral contract to sell real property when either the buyer or the seller makes improvements on the property or changes his or her position in an important way, based on the other's representations.

Example 7. Gladys Green orally agreed to sell a lot to Thomas and Patricia Hickey for $15,000. The Hickeys told Green they intended to sell their present home and build a new house on the lot. They immediately advertised their house for sale. Within 10 days, the Hickeys found a buyer and signed a written contract to sell their house. Green then decided to sell her lot to someone else for $16,000. The court held, however, that Green's oral contract with the Hickeys was enforceable because the Hickeys had changed their position in reliance upon the agreement by selling their house. For that reason, Green could not cancel the oral contract.

Section 10.1 Assessment

Reviewing What You Learned

1. What is the purpose of the Statute of Frauds?
2. What is the legal status of a contract that is not in writing?
3. What are the elements that must be included in a written contract?
4. How are contradictory and ambiguous terms in a written agreement interpreted by a court?
5. What contracts must be in writing?

Critical Thinking Activity

Contract Disputes The legal system impacts business by establishing rules for legal contracts. Research and evaluate the facts of a contract dispute involving a business and one of the laws discussed in this chapter. What were the facts in the case, how did the court rule, and how was business impacted by the court's decision?

Legal Skills in Action

History of the Law Clark and Fiona believe that the Statute of Frauds was originally intended as a criminal provision designed to catch con artists who prey on innocent, unsuspecting victims. Write a report in which you explain the actual historical context in which the Statute of Frauds was first enacted in England.

Special Rules and Formalities

Special Rules for Written Contracts

It is crucial to understand which contracts must be in writing to be enforceable in a court of law. You also must know the essential elements to include within a writing that purports to represent an agreement. However, all of this knowledge would be useless if you do not also understand some special rules that apply to written contracts. These rules include the parol evidence rule and the best evidence rule.

Parol Evidence Rule

It is important to make sure that a written contract contains everything that was agreed upon between the parties. By ensuring that all of the terms are in writing, neither party can go to court and claim a contract is incorrect or fails to show the parties' real intentions. This long-established rule is called the **parol evidence rule**. Parol means word of mouth; evidence, in this instance, means anything presented as proof at a court trial. The rule says that evidence of oral statements made before signing a written agreement cannot be presented in court to change or add to the terms of that written agreement. The court presumes that a written contract contains all of the terms and provisions intended by the parties.

> *Example 8.* Sylvia Cohen needed a car to get to and from her new job. She chose one because the dealer said, "This car has a 90-day guarantee, but if it breaks down during the next year we'll lend you a car for free while it's being repaired." Although Sylvia signed a written agreement to buy the car, the writing did not contain the dealer's promise. Eight months later, when the car broke down, the dealer refused to lend Sylvia a car. The parol evidence rule would prevent Sylvia from relating the dealer's statement in court.

Parol evidence may be introduced in some particular instances. It may be introduced to explain some point that is not clear in a written agreement. Parol evidence may also be used to show that certain terms were agreed to but incorrectly typed in the written contract. In addition, it may be presented to prove that someone was persuaded by the fraud of the other party to make a written contract.

What You'll Learn

- How to explain the parol evidence rule
- How to identify the exceptions to the parol evidence rule
- How to explain the best evidence rule
- How to change a contractual writing

Why It's Important

By understanding the parol evidence and best evidence rules, you will know what business records to keep when you enter a contractual relationship that requires a writing.

Legal Terms

- parol evidence rule
- best evidence rule
- duplicate originals

The Best Evidence Rule

The courts usually require that the original copy of a written agreement be submitted into evidence rather than any sort of copy. This requirement is generally referred to as the **best evidence rule**. The rule means a court would look with disfavor at photocopies or carbon copies of the written agreement, preferring instead to see the original agreement. Copying a contract can make it easier for an unscrupulous party to conceal any misleading alterations to the original agreement. For this reason, when a contract is reduced to writing, each party receives an original version of the contract. Such original versions are generally referred to as **duplicate originals**. When you enter into a contract, do not accept a photocopy or a carbon copy of your agreement because such a contract will not be acceptable to the court if you should need to pursue legal action.

Contracts for Unmarried Couples

When unmarried couples live together, or cohabit, certain legal rules apply. For the most part, these rules have come about as a result of court cases rather than state law. The leading court case to address legal principles involving the rights of cohabiting couples to make contracts was decided in California.

In *Marvin v. Marvin*, the court set forth several principles related to contract formation and cohabiting couples. First, cohabiting couples may make written or oral contracts. If there is no contract, a court may look to the couple's actions to find out whether an implied contract exists. If there is no implied contract, the court may presume that "the parties intend to deal fairly with each other."

The Marvin case was tried in California, but other states have since applied its principles to cohabitation contracts, including contracts between gay and lesbian partners. Many states now recognize contracts between gay and lesbian partners, but some states require such contracts be in writing. A few states prohibit contracts between cohabiting couples on the principle that such contracts foster immorality.

Research What is the law in your state regarding the enforcement of cohabitation contracts? What are some things that can be covered in such contracts?

Changing the Writing

A contract is an agreement between two or more parties. Any writing should be an expression of their mutual consent. Signing a business or legal document starts a chain of events that may be difficult to control. When you are asked to sign an order blank, sales slip, or other printed form, be aware that such documents may contain small print on the front or reverse side. The words are often difficult to read and the language may be difficult to understand. Quite often, the small print is not written in your favor. Follow these guidelines when you are asked to sign your name to any document:

- Read the entire text of the document before you sign it.
- If you don't understand something or don't agree to it, cross it out before you sign. Have the other party initial what you have crossed out.
- Don't be afraid to make changes on a printed form. If any promises are made to you, write them in.
- Refuse to sign if you do not agree with everything contained in the writing. You are sometimes in a better position with an oral agreement than with a written agreement that is not in your favor.
- If a contract contains a lot of complicated or ambiguous language, consider asking a lawyer to review the agreement before you sign it. Although you will probably be obligated to pay for the advice, you may find that the protection and peace of mind afforded by qualified legal counsel is worth the price.

Law & Academics

Social Studies
Did you know the words *jury* and *perjury* are related? One old definition of jury is "a company of persons (originally men) sworn to render a 'verdict' or true answer upon some question(s) officially submitted to them. . . ." When perjury was first used, it meant, ". . . the offense of jurors in giving a willfully false verdict."

Research Activity
Use a comprehensive dictionary and look up the etymology of the words *just* and *judge.* Find out how they are related.

Section 10.2 Assessment

Reviewing What You Learned
1. What is the parol evidence rule?
2. What are the exceptions to the parol evidence rule?
3. What is the best evidence rule?
4. What rules govern the changes in a written contract?

Critical Thinking Activity
Parol Evidence What is the legal philosophy behind the parol evidence rule?

Legal Skills in Action
Parol Evidence Rule Your friend, Pete, is about to lease an apartment. Although he intends to stay in the apartment for an entire year, he thinks he might have to move to another state before that time. Pete tells you the lease he is about to enter has an acceleration clause, which says that if he breaks his lease, the rest of the rent is due at that precise moment. The landlord has told Pete to ignore that particular clause. Write to your friend explaining how the parol evidence rule affects his lease.

Chapter Summary

Section 10.1 **Statute of Frauds**

- The Statute of Frauds is designed to prevent fraud and perjury by requiring written evidence of the terms of a contract. Putting a contract in writing can help to clarify an agreement for both parties and for the courts, if necessary.

- A contract that falls under the Statute of Frauds but is not in writing is deemed unenforceable. Oral contracts that do not fall under the statute of frauds are valid.

- The following elements must be in a written contract: (1) place, (2) date, (3) parties, (4) subject matter, (5) price and terms, (6) the intent of the parties, and (7) signatures of the parties.

- Generally, handwritten terms prevail over typewritten or printed terms. The court will presume that the handwritten terms were placed in the writing after the contract was typed or printed. For that reason, the handwritten changes likely represent the final intent of the parties. Generally, handwriting prevails over typewriting or printing, and typewriting prevails over printing. When there is a discrepancy in an amount written in both words and figures, as in a check, the amount written in words will prevail over the amount written in figures. Sometimes written contracts can be understood in different ways. When such ambiguous language exists, the court will favor the intent of the party who did not draft the contract.

- The following are types of contracts that must be in writing: (1) contracts to pay the debts of another, (2) contracts to pay the debts of a deceased person, (3) contracts requiring more than a year to perform, (4) contracts in consideration of marriage, (5) contracts to sell real property, and (6) contracts for the sale of goods costing $500 or more. Be aware that the Statute of Frauds applies only to executory contracts; that is, contracts that have not been fully performed. If two parties perform an oral contract that should have been in writing, then neither party can try to have it set aside later because it was not in writing.

Section 10.2 **Special Rules and Formalities**

- The parol evidence rule presumes that all the terms of a contract are within the document. No evidence of oral statements made before signing a written agreement can be presented to change or add to the written agreement. *Parol* means word of mouth; evidence, in this instance, means anything presented as proof at a court trial.

- Exceptions to the parol evidence rule permit oral statements to be used to: (1) explain some point that is not clear in a written agreement, (2) show that certain terms were agreed to but incorrectly typed in the written contract, and (3) prove that someone was persuaded by the fraud of the other party to make a written contract.

- The best evidence rule is the preference given by the courts to the original copy of an agreement. The court looks with disfavor at photocopies or carbon copies of a written agreement. Copying a contract can make it easier for an unscrupulous party to conceal any misleading alterations to the original agreement. For this reason, each party receives an original version of the contract.

- Because the parol evidence rule presumes that all the terms of a contract are contained within the document, if you do not agree to the terms of a preprinted contract, you may cross out the offensive terms. You may also write in promises made to you that are not evidenced on the preprinted contract. To insure the validity of the new terms, both parties must initial the changes. If a contract contains a lot of complicated or ambiguous language, ask a lawyer to review the agreement before you sign it.

Using Legal Language

Consider the key terms in the list below. Then use these terms to complete the following exercises.

breach of contract

perjury

Statute of Frauds

memorandum

goods

real property

parol evidence rule

best evidence rule

duplicate originals

1. With a team of three or four, role-play a situation in which a contract must be in writing. Use as many of the terms listed above as possible.
2. Present the role-playing exercise to the class. Be animated and energetic in your presentation.
3. As a class, vote for the best presentation.

Understanding Business and Personal Law Online

Self-Check Quiz Visit the *Understanding Business and Personal Law* Web site at **ubpl.glencoe.com** and click on Chapter 10: Form of a Contract— Self-Check Quizzes to prepare for the chapter exam.

The Law Review

Answer the following questions. Refer to the chapter for additional reinforcement.

4. Why did the English Parliament pass the "Act for the Prevention of Frauds and Perjuries" in 1677?
5. Must a writing be formal to satisfy the Statue of Frauds? Explain your answer.
6. When does the equitable estoppel exception apply to an oral contract to sell real property?
7. When may the parol evidence be introduced?
8. What guidelines should you follow when you are asked to sign your name to any document?

Linking School to Work

Acquiring and Evaluating Information

If you are employed, ask permission to bring to class copies of invoices, sales slips, receipts, letters, etc. from your place of business.

9. As a class, review the documents to see if they meet the requirements of a memorandum.

Let's Debate

Warranty

Sergeant had an irrigation system installed in his yard. The company that did the work told Sergeant the system had a one-year warranty for parts and labor. After six months, the irrigation system no longer worked. The company refused to honor the promise of the warranty. Sergeant discovered the warranty was not in writing anywhere in his signed contract or on the sales receipt.

Debate

10. Would the promise of the warranty hold up in court? Explain your answer.
11. Would the parol evidence rule come into play? Why or why not?
12. What would you do if you were Sergeant?

Grasping Case Issues

For the following cases, give your decision and state a legal principle that applies.

13. Rubenstein hired Mason to audit her chain of 92 art galleries. When they made the agreement, Rubenstein insisted that, as a part of the auditing process, Mason would be required to spend one week at each gallery. Mason demanded a written agreement before he would agree to Rubenstein's terms. Is Mason correct in making such a demand? Why or why not?

14. Frank Larson orally promises to give Gena Little $10,000 if she will marry Larson's nephew, Charles Cohen. Little marries Cohen, but Larson refuses to pay. Can Little have the promise enforced? Why or why not?

15. A.R. Norton orally agrees to sell her farm to E.J. Dillon for $20,000. She gives Dillon the following memorandum: "On this date I hereby agree to sell my farm to E.J. Dillon for $20,000. A.R. Norton." Dillon later refuses to carry out the agreement. May Norton recover from Dillon for breach of contract? Explain your answer.

16. Carlos Beck orally agrees to buy property from the Bitner Realty Company. He writes, signs, and gives to the realty company a memorandum of the agreement. The company does not sign the memorandum. When Beck fails to buy the property, the Bitner Realty Company brings an action for damages. Is the realty company entitled to judgment? Why or why not?

17. David Abrams agrees to buy printing equipment from Aaron Ackerman. A contract to serve as evidence of the agreement is drafted and typed, but before signing, both parties add a handwritten clause. It is later discovered that the handwritten clause contradicts a typewritten clause. Which clause will the court follow in determining the intent of the parties?

In each case that follows, you be the judge.

18. Separate Documents

Wheeler and Butler entered a lease-purchase agreement. Under terms of the agreement, Butler leased and had the option to purchase land that was owned by Wheeler. The agreement was reduced to writing. However, the agreement was written on two separate documents. When a dispute later arose over Butler's right to buy the land, Wheeler argued that the entire agreement was unenforceable because it was contained in two documents. *Is Wheeler correct? Why or why not?*

Butler v. Lovoll, 620 P.2d 1251 (NV).

19. Stock Options

Buzzy and Hall entered an employment agreement. As a part of the agreement, Hall was promised that he would receive an option to buy 1,000 shares of the company stock at $20 per share. Later the company refused to sell Hall the shares. *What legal argument might be used by the company to justify its refusal to sell the shares to Hall?*

Hall v. Horizon House Microwave, Inc. 506 N.E. 2d. 178 (MA).

Legal Link

Common Law in Early England

Bert has chosen the topic of "Early English Common Law" for his history paper that is due next week. He wants to find out more about how the laws in early England influenced the laws in the United States.

Connect

Using a variety of search engines:

20. Help Bert conduct the research he needs for his paper. List 3–4 Web sites that may be useful for conducting the necessary historical research.
21. Find at least five English laws that influenced the U. S. legal system.

POWER READING STRATEGIES

22. **Predict** Are written contracts always preferable to oral contracts? Explain your answer.

23. **Connect** Have you ever signed a contract or other document without reading the fine print? Why is this a good idea?

24. **Question** Why do you think the Statute of Frauds does not pertain to all contracts? Explain your answer.

25. **Respond** Why do the courts prefer the original copy of a written agreement rather than a photocopy?

How Contracts Come to an End

Understanding Business and Personal Law *Online*

Chapter Overview Visit the *Understanding Business and Personal Law* Web site at ubpl.glencoe.com and click on Chapter 11: How Contracts Come to an End—Chapter Overviews to preview the chapter information.

The Opening Scene

Viktor and Alena are outside their high school, chatting with their friends, Trevor and Micha.

The Burning Barn

VIKTOR: I'm not buying Keith's car, after all. We agreed that the deal wouldn't work. I'm really disappointed. I was counting on getting a car before the end of the month. What am I supposed to do now? Dad has already made it clear that he won't co-sign for a car loan.

ALENA: It's not that bad. Look on the bright side of things. At least you got your $500 deposit back. You'd be in much worse shape if that hadn't happened.

VIKTOR: But I still don't have a car. It doesn't look like I'm going to get one anytime soon, either.

MICHA: Did somebody just mention that he needed a car?

ALENA: Just my genius brother.

MICHA: What's the problem? Why do you look so down, Viktor?

VIKTOR: Simple. I need wheels, but I don't have any money.

MICHA: I have a great idea! Maybe you can take my brother's car.

VIKTOR: Your brother has a car for sale? How much does he want for it?

MICHA: His car is not exactly for sale. He owes money on it, but he can't make the payments anymore because he got sick and had to quit his job. Maybe you can work something out with him.

ALENA: He can't just stop paying his bills because he's sick.

VIKTOR: Yes he can!

ALENA: That's stupid. Do you think that's fair? I'd be pretty mad if your brother owed me money and told me he wasn't going to pay me because of an illness.

TREVOR: You need a job, Viktor.

VIKTOR: No thanks. A job means work.

ALENA: Yeah, a job would be a stretch for you. I can't imagine you working for money.

VIKTOR: Hey! I had a job once. Remember when I worked for Mr. Olsen?

ALENA: You can't count that as a job. You helped him paint the Granger barn for one afternoon!

VIKTOR: So?

ALENA: So the barn burned down, and that was the end of your job.

TREVOR: Did you ever get paid?

VIKTOR: No.

TREVOR: Well, there you are.

VIKTOR: Where am I?

TREVOR: Get your money from Mr. Olsen.

MICHA: One day's pay won't buy my brother's car.

TREVOR: Maybe you can sue for damages.

ALENA: The statute of limitations has probably long since passed.

VIKTOR: Maybe, but maybe not. It's worth a try.

TREVOR: Good. Let's meet after school to talk some more.

VIKTOR: Done.

What Are the Legal Issues?

1. What happens if one party to a contract is not satisfied with the other party's performance?
2. Will a slight deviation from the promised performance amount to a breach of the entire contract?
3. Can a contract be ended by mutual agreement?
4. What happens if the subject matter of a contract is destroyed?

Performance and Agreement

What You'll Learn

- **How to identify when time is important in a contract**
- **How to distinguish between satisfactory and substantial performance**
- **How to explain tender of performance**
- **How to explain how contracts can be discharged by agreement**

Why It's Important

Understanding when contracts come to an end will help you determine your legal rights and obligations in such situations.

Legal Terms

- discharged
- performance
- complete performance
- reasonable time
- substantial performance
- tender
- legal tender
- mutual release
- accord and satisfaction

Ending a Contract

When contracts eventually end, they are said to be **discharged**. The parties to the contract may enforce their rights and must perform their duties up to the time of discharge. The law specifies how contracts end so that people will know when their rights and duties expire. In this section, we will see that contracts can be discharged by performance and by agreement.

Discharge by Performance

Most contracts are discharged by **performance**, meaning the parties fulfill the terms of the contract by doing what they promised earlier. As long as all terms have been carried out properly and completely, the contract is discharged by **complete performance**.

Time for Performance

The time for completing a contract may be important to one or both of the parties. If the time for performance is not stated in a contract and there is a question of performance, the court will say that the actions or duties associated with the contract must be completed within a **reasonable time**. A reasonable time will vary with the circumstances of each individual case. However, it is generally defined as the time that is suitable, fair, and proper to the objective in view. For example, the

SUBSTANTIAL PERFORMANCE Sometimes small deviations occur when a long and involved construction contract is entered into by various parties. *What happens if there is a slight deviation from the original terms of the construction contract?*

SATISFACTORY PERFORMANCE
Sometimes one person will agree to perform services for another "to the other's satisfaction." *In such a situation, if a party is dissatisfied with the services performed by the other party, can that party refuse to comply with the payment terms of the contract?*

reasonable time for selling a crate of ripe tomatoes would not be the same as the reasonable time for selling a house.

If the parties specify a time limit for carrying out the terms of the contract, the court will usually allow a longer time for performance unless time is of the essence. Time is of the essence when it is a vital or essential element of the contract.

Example 1. Carol Wolloff contracted Peter Miles to paint her house. As part of the agreement, Peter promised to begin the job on or before June 1. He showed up on June 3 to do the job. A court would probably excuse his tardiness because there was nothing to show that time was of the essence.

However, if the agreement said that Peter was to finish the job by June 10 because Carol was having a party on June 12, a court would likely enforce the time period because the contract implied that time was of the essence.

Example 2. The Seasons Store agreed to buy 5,000 chocolate rabbits from Northern Confectioneries. The contract specified that delivery was to be made three weeks before Easter and stated that time was of the essence. The rabbits arrived just one week before Easter, by which time Seasons had ordered and received substitute products from another supplier. Seasons refused the late delivery of rabbits. The court would probably uphold Seasons Store's refusal.

Satisfactory Performance

When people perform services for others, the law requires that those services be done in a satisfactory manner. Sometimes contracts say nothing about satisfaction; other times, contracts specifically state that work must be done "in a satisfactory manner." In both situations, when one party believes the job is unsatisfactory, the court uses the reasonable person test. The court asks, "Would a reasonable person consider the job to be completed in a satisfactory manner?" The dispute will then be settled based on the answer to this question as determined by a judge or jury.

Occasionally one party will agree to perform services for another "to the other's satisfaction." In such a case, the other party must be satisfied to be bound to the contract.

> *Example 3.* Marc Marcel, an artist, agreed to paint Juleanne's portrait "to her satisfaction" for $500. When the painting was completed, all of Juleanne's friends, relatives, and acquaintances thought that it was a perfect likeness of her. However, Juleanne thought the portrait was hideous, believing the nose was too long and the mouth too big. In many states, if Juleanne honestly did not like the portrait, she would not have to pay for it. Because a portrait is a highly personal matter and subject to one's personal taste, and because Marcel had agreed to paint it "to her satisfaction," Juleanne could reject it. However, Juleanne could not keep the painting if she opted not to pay for it.

Substantial Performance

As previously noted, both parties must fully perform their parts of the bargain to discharge a contract by complete performance. Someone who has not fully performed his or her duties cannot, in most instances, win a lawsuit against the other party for money owed or other damages.

An exception to this rule is known as the doctrine of **substantial performance**. Substantial performance is slightly less than full performance. Someone who has fulfilled the major requirements of a contract in good faith, leaving only minor details incomplete, has substantially performed. The courts will allow the person to recover the amount agreed upon under the contract, minus the cost of completing the job. Courts permit recovery if they can determine that it would be unfair to deny payment. The doctrine of substantial performance is often applied to construction contracts.

> *Example 4.* Mr. Lucas insists that Ziming Enterprises should tear down and completely rebuild the second floor of his new office building on Michigan Avenue because the construction company installed the wrong type of tile in the bathrooms. Lucas's attorney correctly points out that the doctrine of substantial performance

A Global Perspective: Laws Around the World

South Africa

In Afrikaans, one of South Africa's 11 official languages, *apartheid* means "apartness." Apartheid also defines a strict policy of racial segregation mandated by an all-white South African government from the 1940s to the 1990s. Many countries worldwide opposed apartheid, and some countries expressed their disapproval by refusing to trade with South Africa.

By law, apartheid denied the nonwhite majority the right to vote and required the separation of races in housing, school, employment, transportation, and public facilities such as movie theaters, restaurants, and parks. Many South Africans opposed segregation and staged boycotts, demonstrations, and strikes in protest. In response to growing domestic and international pressure to end apartheid, the South African government began repealing the laws in the 1970s. The last of these laws were abolished in 1991. In the spring of 1994, political activist Nelson Mandela triumphed over his white opponent to become South Africa's first black president. On the day of his election, Mandela rejoiced: "To the people of South Africa and the world who are watching: this is a joyous night for the human spirit. This is your victory, too. . . . Free at last!" Here's a snapshot of South Africa.

Geographical area	**471,445 sq. mi.**
Population	**43,647,658**
Capitals	**Pretoria, administrative**
	Cape Town, legislative
	Bloemfontein, judicial
Legal system	**Based on Roman-Dutch law and**
	English common law
Language	**Afrikaans, English, Ndebele, Pedi, Sotho,**
	Swazi, Tsonga, Tswana, Venda, Xhosa, Zulu
Religion	**68% Christian, 2% Muslim, 15% Hindu**
Life expectancy	**45 years**

Critical Thinking Question Nelson Mandela and the South African people made the world a better place by standing up for their beliefs. List some of the things that you might do to make your community a better place. For more information on South Africa, visit **ubpl.glencoe.com** or your local library.

would prevent such a drastic and unfair condition. Lucas would have to pay Ziming Enterprises for the construction of the building. However, Lucas may deduct the cost of replacing the tile or any other damages suffered as a result of Ziming's failure to perform correctly.

Tender of Performance

A party can fulfill the terms of a contract by performing an act or by paying money. A **tender** is an offer to do what you have agreed to do under a contract. If you agree to buy a car, for example, making tender would be offering to pay the money at the agreed time for performance. If you were selling a car, making tender would be offering to give the car to the buyer at the agreed time. It is important to make tender even if you know the other party will not perform his or her part of the contract. In some states, making tender is necessary to test the other party's willingness and ability to perform. If neither party has made tender, then neither party is in a position to bring suit against the other.

LAWS in Your Life

A Contract with Cupid

Matchmaking services are plentiful these days. Many people are looking for love but have no time to find it. Some matchmaking and dating services require an up-front payment of half the total fee upon signing a contract. Contracts usually stipulate a specific number of referrals or dates. The balance of the fee is often due on completion of the service.

Most matchmaking contracts obligate the customer to make full payment, regardless of whether he or she finds true love. Even if the customer never uses or refuses to continue using the service at some point before the agreement has expired, the contact is enforceable once it is signed.

One cannot simply end a contract because he or she becomes bored with a service. However, a few states give customers 30 days to cancel a contract for dating services. If state law offers no relief, other options may be considered. These options include selling the membership to someone else or appealing to the manager's sense of customer relations in refunding all or part of the purchase price.

Research Check to see if your state has a law regulating dating services. If so, is there a refund policy mandated by the state?

An offer to perform a certain act to fulfill a contract is a tender of performance. If a person who must perform an act makes a tender of performance and is rejected, that person is excused from fulfilling the contract. The same principle does not apply to debts. An offer to pay a certain amount to fulfill a contract is a tender of payment. If a person makes a tender of payment and is rejected, that person is not excused from the debt. He or she is only excused from paying further interest on the debt.

Example 5. Kenneth Hanson owed Carla Miller $500, which was due on the first of July. Kenneth did not tender payment until the first of August. Carla refused to take the money at that time, saying, "You didn't pay the money when it was due. Therefore, I'm going to sue you."

Kenneth still owes Carla $500. If Carla did sue, she could collect the $500 plus interest at the legal rate only for the one month between the due date and the actual tender of payment.

The person offering to pay the required amount of money must offer **legal tender**; that is, the person must offer U.S. coins or currency. Offering a check is not a valid tender of payment, even if it is certified. However, the person who offered the check must be given reasonable time to obtain legal tender.

Discharge by Agreement

Contracts are created by mutual agreement and may be terminated by mutual agreement.

Example 6. Jodi Plume has always admired Mark Jackson's red convertible. At school, she hears a rumor that Mark wants to sell his car. Jodi approaches Mark and offers him $6,000 for the car. Although he really had not planned to sell his car, Mark agrees when he hears such a high offer. Later that night, Jodi telephones Mark when she realizes that she can't afford the car. Mark is happy to call off the agreement because he has decided he wants to keep his car, after all.

DAMAGED GOODS
Sometimes purchased goods are damaged after they are sold but before they are delivered. *If the buyer agrees to accept the altered goods, is the original contract discharged?*

Mutual Release

Jodi and Mark mutually agreed to end their agreement. A **mutual release** is an agreement between two parties to end an agreement. By mutual agreement, the contract no longer exists. Whatever parties agree to do in the first place, they may later mutually agree not to do. Otherwise, there would be no consideration for the promised release.

Accord and Satisfaction

A contract also can be discharged when one party to an agreement agrees to accept performance from the other party that is different from what was agreed upon in the original contract. In effect, one contract is substituted for another, which is known as **accord and satisfaction**. Accord and satisfaction is often used to settle an honest disagreement or unforeseen circumstances regarding an amount owed.

Example 7. Lawrence Langham contracted to sell his tractor to Jerry Bodoni for $1,200. Before the sale is completed, Bodoni suffers several financial reversals and no longer has the cash to pay for the tractor. Bodoni explains the situation to Langham and offers to give Langham his DVD player, video camera, and color television instead of the $1,200. If Langham accepts these items, Bodoni's promise to pay the $1,200 is discharged. However, Langham must actually accept the items. The promise to accept the items is the accord. The carrying out of the promise is the satisfaction.

Section 11.1 Assessment

Reviewing What You Learned

1. What is a reasonable time for completing a contract?
2. What is the difference between satisfactory and substantial performance of a contract?
3. What is tender of performance?
4. How can contracts be discharged by agreement?

Critical Thinking Activity

Discharge by Agreement Why does the court permit certain contracts to be discharged by accord and satisfaction?

Legal Skills in Action

Accord and Satisfaction Last week, your friend Cynthia used a credit card to purchase a snowboard for $277.89. This week she saw the same snowboard on sale for $250.43 at another store. Cynthia believes she can use accord and satisfaction to pay the lesser amount when her credit card bill comes in the mail. Send Cynthia an e-mail message explaining why accord and satisfaction will not work in this case.

Impossibility of Performance and Operation of Law

Involuntary Discharge

It is crucial to understand that some contracts come to an end despite what the parties intend or what they actually do. In these situations, the obligations that exist under the contract may also expire. The two primary ways contracts are discharged are by impossibility of performance and by operation of law.

Discharge by Impossibility of Performance

A contract that becomes legally impossible to perform generally may be discharged and both parties released from the obligation. The situations in which the courts will allow a discharge for **impossibility of performance** are death or illness that prevents the performance of a personal service contract; destruction of the exact subject matter or the means for performance; and illegality, or situations in which the performance of a contract becomes illegal.

Death or Illness in a Personal Service Contract

The death or illness of a party to a contract may be an excuse for nonperformance only if the contract requires the personal service of the person who has died or become ill. In Example 3, for instance, if Marcel were to die before completing the portrait for Juleanne, the contract would be discharged. She selected him for his ability to do the work.

Suppose, however, the contract is such that the party who became ill or died had the right to hire someone else to perform the obligation. In this situation, neither death nor illness will discharge the contract. In the case of death, the person appointed to settle the deceased person's affairs would be obligated to hire someone else to carry out the contract.

Destruction of the Exact Subject Matter

If the subject matter that is essential to the performance of the contract is destroyed through no fault of either party, the contract is discharged. The destruction must occur after the contract is entered into, but before it is carried out.

What You'll Learn

- How to explain situations in which the law will permit a discharge by impossibility
- How to identify discharges that occur by operation of law
- How to define the statute of limitations
- How to identify debts that cannot be discharged in bankruptcy

Why It's Important

Understanding when contracts are discharged by impossibility and by operation of law will help you know your legal rights and obligations in such situations.

Legal Terms

- impossibility of performance
- operation of law
- statute of limitations
- bankruptcy laws

Example 8. Harold is negotiating a contract for the purchase of an antique printing press from Mr. Frolock. The price was set, and the printing press was to be delivered the next day. That night, however, the press was destroyed when the delivery truck carrying it was involved in an accident.

This contract would be discharged because of the destruction of the particular subject matter that had been identified in the contract.

However, compare Example 8 with the following example:

Example 9. Broz Kucan went into the Kenney Industrial Supply Shop and selected a particular type of sewing machine for his tailoring business. The salesperson told Kucan that the shop had many of the machines in the warehouse and that one would be delivered to him the next day. That night, a fire destroyed the Kenney Industrial Supply Shop's warehouse and all of its contents. The shop would still be obligated to obtain another sewing machine for Kucan. Although a type of model had been selected, the exact machine had not been chosen.

Sometimes the means for performance of a contract is destroyed so that the contract cannot be completed. For example, suppose a person contracts to reshingle the roof of a house, but the house is destroyed before the job is done. The contract is discharged because the house must exist for the job to be performed.

Illegality

Another type of impossibility of performance arises when performance of the contract becomes illegal. As previous chapters discuss, a contract is considered void if its performance would be illegal at the time the agreement was

 LEGALITY
Some street vendors contract with a business to sell their goods on the street. *If an unlicensed vendor made such an agreement with a business and a law was later passed that required street vendors to be licensed, would the contract between the vendor and the business be legal?*

initiated. The same general rule applies when performance becomes illegal after the contract has been initiated.

Example 10. Mr. Novak has contracted to print the labels and instructional brochures for the Toth-VonMeader Pharmaceutical Company's new wonder drug, biotheramyacin. At the time the agreement was made, the drug was legal. Shortly afterward, however, the Food and Drug Administration made the drug illegal. Because the manufacture, distribution, sale, and use of the drug are now illegal, Mr. Novak and Toth-VonMeader have no choice in the matter. The contract must be terminated. Legal performance has now become impossible.

Discharge by Operation of Law

At times, the best interests of society demand that a contract be terminated. Under these circumstances, the law declares contracts discharged by **operation of law**.

Wrongful Alteration

Sometimes wrongful acts of one of the parties will discharge a contract by operation of law. One of these wrongful acts is altering, or changing, a contract.

Example 11. A written contract provided that Peter Merkle was to buy Bart Little's canoe for $95. Bart secretly inserted the numeral "1" in front of the "95" and then attempted to collect $195 from Peter. The contract was discharged as a result of Bart's wrongful alteration. Not only may Bart not collect $195, but he is no longer entitled to enforce the original contract at all. The contract, however, is not discharged if Peter chooses to enforce it. If Peter still wants the canoe at $95, he can purchase it or collect damages if Bart will not deliver.

Statute of Limitations

If you make a contract that is breached by the other party, you ordinarily have a right to sue that party. Under some circumstances, however, this right may be taken away when the law specifies the time within which a contract may be enforced. All states have a law that specifies in what time a legal action may be brought on a contract, which is called the **statute of limitations**.

Example 12. Suppose that Smart Shoppes, Inc. owed the Gould Corporation $1,000 for a shipment of dresses but did not pay. For more than ten years, Gould did not bring any action against Smart Shoppes to collect. In most states, Gould has waited too

It's a Question of Ethics

Barn or Beach?
Sean agreed to work on his grandfather's farm for the summer for $1,000—a rate of $100 a week for 10 weeks. After eight weeks, Sean feels exhausted. Mucking out stalls is the hardest work he has ever done! He just received a call from his friend Marcus, who wants him to come to the beach for the last two weeks of summer vacation. Sean really wants to go, but he doesn't want to let his grandfather down. *What is Sean's ethical responsibility? What would you do if you were Sean?*

long to seek payment. You may not "sleep on your rights" and then expect the law to help you collect.

The statute of limitations for failure to perform contracts for the sale of goods is four years in most states. For that reason, an action must be begun within four years after the contract is broken. The parties may reduce the period of limitation to not less than one year by the original agreement. They may not, however, extend the period to more than the limit set by their state. The time begins to run the moment that the failure to perform occurs. However, a "time out" is called when a creditor is a minor or is mentally ill. These situations "stop the clock" on the statute of limitations.

Example 13. Suppose Olive Briggs breached her contract and refused to pay $1,000 that she had borrowed from Jill Hamilton. A month later, Jill was declared mentally incompetent and committed to a state mental hospital. Even though she may remain in the hospital for 10 years, Jill could still bring suit for the money due her as soon as she is declared mentally competent and released from the hospital. The time of Jill's mental incapacity would not be counted in the statutory limitation period.

Virtual Law

Termination of Technology Contract

Daw Technologies helps to build computer semiconductor factories. It was awarded a subcontract to install a "clean room" system at a semiconductor plant in Utah. The general contractor notified all subcontractors that the completion date of the project had been delayed by 18 months. This delay caused suspension of all work on the project. The cessation of work required the contractor to terminate all subcontracts. The total amount of the subcontract was $15 million. Daw's contract with the contractor was conditioned on the building project remaining on schedule. Both parties had agreed that the contract would be terminated in the event of a major delay in the project. (Source: *TechWeb News*, February 24, 2001)

Connect Use the Internet to research the law of contract. Can you think of any scenarios under which Daw Technologies might seek a remedy, even though this discharge is by agreement?

Under the law of some states, people who are in prison suffer "civil death." They lose the right to vote, to contract, and to bring and defend against civil lawsuits. In these states, the statute of limitations on contracts often stops running while a person is in prison. Also, in some instances, the debt may be renewed. If a debtor makes a partial payment or admits that the debt exists after the time period has passed, the debt is renewed for another time period set by the state statute. In New York and some other states, such a new promise must be in writing. There are many special statutes of limitations in every state. To protect yourself fully in important business relationships, you should refer to the most recent statutes in your state.

Bankruptcy

Sometimes people and businesses get hopelessly in debt and cannot pay their debts as they become due. Under Old English common law, such people were placed in debtors' prisons and had no hope of recovering. The drafters of the U.S. Constitution opposed such treatment of debtors. They gave Congress the authority to pass **bankruptcy laws**. These laws set procedures for discharging a debtor's obligations. These obligations still exist, but the debtor can no longer be imprisoned for failure to pay.

Certain debts cannot be discharged under bankruptcy laws. Education loans, for example, usually cannot be discharged during the first five years of the repayment period. In addition, debts for taxes, alimony, support, and maintenance are not affected by a general discharge of debts in bankruptcy.

Law & Academics

Computer Technology

Electronic money will become legal tender in Singapore by the year 2008. Every merchant in the country will be required to accept e-money from customers, regardless of the price of the item being purchased. E-money will be loaded in electronic purses stored on smart chips located in devices such as mobile phones or personal digital assistants.

Research Activity

Predict when electronic money will be used in the United States. Explain whether you believe e-money will ever totally replace our paper currency.

Section 11.2 Assessment

Reviewing What You Learned
1. When will the law permit a discharge by impossibility?
2. When will the law permit a discharge by operation of law?
3. What is the statute of limitations?
4. What debts cannot be discharged in bankruptcy?

Critical Thinking Activity
Bankruptcy What is the legal philosophy behind the idea that certain contracts cannot be discharged in bankruptcy?

Legal Skills in Action
Debts after Bankruptcy Your friend Charlotte says her parents are about to go to bankruptcy court. She believes that all of the family's debts will vanish as a result of the bankruptcy proceedings. Write a letter to your friend explaining that some of her family's debts will remain even after declaring bankruptcy. Name some of the kinds of debt that cannot be discharged.

Chapter Summary

Section 11.1 Performance and Agreement

- A reasonable time for completing a contract varies, but it is generally defined as the time that is suitable, fair, and proper to the objective of the contract. For example, the reasonable time for selling perishable food would not be the same as the reasonable time for selling a car or house. If the parties specify a time limit for carrying out the terms of the contract, the court will usually allow a longer time for performance unless time is of the essence. Time is of the essence when it is a vital or essential element of the contract.

- Satisfactory performance is completion of a service that a reasonable person would deem performed to his satisfaction. In determining whether satisfactory performance has been made, the court asks, "Would a reasonable person consider the job to be completed in a satisfactory manner?" A judge or jury would then decide the matter based on the answer to this question. Unlike satisfactory performance, however, substantial performance is not complete performance. Nonetheless, if the major requirements have been fulfilled, the courts will allow the performer to recover the contract amount minus the cost of completing the job.

- A tender of performance is an offer to perform a certain act to fulfill a contract. It is important to make tender even if you know the other party will not perform his or her part of the contract. In some states, making tender is necessary to test the other party's willingness and ability to perform.

- Contracts can be terminated by mutual release and accord and satisfaction. A mutual release is an agreement between two parties to end an agreement. Whatever parties agree to do in the first place, they may later mutually agree not to do. Accord and satisfaction occurs when one party to an agreement agrees to accept performance from the other party that is different from what was agreed upon in the original contract. Accord and satisfaction is often used to settle an honest disagreement or unforeseen circumstances regarding an amount owed.

Section 11.2 Impossibility of Performance and Operation of Law

- Some contracts come to an end despite what the parties intend or what they actually do. A contract becomes legally impossible to perform and becomes discharged in the case of (1) death or illness that prevents the performance of a personal service contract, (2) destruction of the exact subject matter or the means for performance, and (3) illegality. The death or illness of a party may be an excuse for nonperformance only if the contract requires the personal service of the person who has died or become ill.

- A contract may be discharged by operation of law in the following cases: (1) when one of the parties commits a wrongful act, (2) when the statute of limitations has expired, and (3) when the debtor declares bankruptcy.

- The statute of limitations limits the time within which a legal action may be brought. The statute of limitations for failure to perform contracts for the sale of goods is four years in most states.

- Educational loans, debts for taxes, alimony, support, and maintenance are not affected by a general discharge of debts in bankruptcy.

Using Legal Language

Consider the key terms in the list below. Then use these terms to complete the following exercises.

discharged

performance

accord and satisfaction

substantial performance

tender

legal tender

operation of law

statute of limitations

bankruptcy laws

reasonable time

1. With a team of three or four, role-play a situation in which a contract is coming to an end. Use as many of the terms listed above as possible.
2. Present the role-playing exercise to the class. Be animated and energetic in your presentation.
3. Have your classmates critique your team's performance.
4. Read your classmates' comments and briefly discuss with your team how you could improve your role-play.

Understanding Business and Personal Law *Online*

Self-Check Quiz Visit the *Understanding Business and Personal Law* Web site at **ubpl.glencoe.com** and click on Chapter 11: How Contracts Come to an End—Self-Check Quizzes to prepare for the chapter exam.

The Law Review

Answer the following questions. Refer to the chapter for additional reinforcement.

5. Will a court allow a longer time for performance of a contract than the contract specifies? Explain your answer.
6. What is the test called that the courts use to determine satisfactory performance?
7. What is it called when one contract is substituted for another? How often is this procedure used?
8. Can the death or illness of a party be used as an excuse for nonperformance of a contract? Explain your answer.
9. What situations "stop the clock" on the statute of limitations?
10. Why do some states require a party to make tender, even if the other party cannot fulfill the terms of the contract?
11. Why does the law require that some debts be retained after a person declares bankruptcy?
12. What is legal tender?

Linking School to Work

Participate as a Member of a Team

In groups of three or four people, interview a business owner or manager in your community. Find out if he or she has ever ended a contract based on:

13. Satisfactory performance.
14. Substantial performance.
15. Mutual release.
16. Accord and satisfaction.

Ask about the details of the situation, and if possible, share your information with the class.

Let's Debate

Impossibility of Performance

Milka hired Albert Cole, a landscape architect, to design a patio and backyard landscape for her home. It would include a custom designed barbeque grill and fishpond. When he was almost done with the design, Albert became ill and his son, Albert Jr., also a landscape architect, finished the project.

Debate

17. Does Milka have to accept the son's design? Explain your answer.
18. Is the contract discharged by impossibility of performance? Why or why not?
19. Does Milka have to wait until Albert gets well, or can she legally discharge the contract? Explain your answer.

Grasping Case Issues

For the following cases, give your decision and state a legal principle that applies.

20. Ferguson had seriously overextended himself financially until he was faced with filing for bankruptcy. He was especially anxious to file quickly because he had an enormous payment of back taxes due in April. He also had child support payments due, as well as several enormous credit card bills. Which of these debts can be excused in bankruptcy and which cannot? Explain your answer.

21. Earl Kirton agrees to put vinyl siding on Ben Finkel's house for $4,500. After almost completing the job, with only one more row of clapboards to be covered, Kirton cannot stand Finkel's watching his every move any longer. Kirton picks up his tools and leaves; Finkel argues that he does not have to pay Kirton because Kirton did not finish the job. Is Finkel correct? Why or why not?

22. Ruth Collins finds an antique table she likes. She tells the proprietor that she will buy it. She has no money with her, so she agrees to pick it up and pay for it the next day. That night the antique shop and its contents burn to the ground. Is the contract to buy the table discharged? Explain your answer.

23. Otto Mandel enters into a contract with the Hewlett Lumber Company for purchasing 50,000 feet of yellow pine. Mandel intends to use the wood in the manufacture of pinball games. After the contract is made, a state law is passed making the manufacture and sale of pinball games illegal. Does this new law relieve Mandel from liability on the contract? Why or why not?

In each case that follows, you be the judge.

24. Partial Payment

Weaver and Brewer hired Grafio to paint their house for $5,650. After the job was completed, Weaver and Brewer discovered a footprint left on the roof. The damage would require $50 to fix. Weaver and Brewer stopped payment on a check made to Grafio for $1,845, which represented the last installment payment. *Would Grafio be permitted to recover the money owed to him for the paint job? Why or why not?*
Weaver v. Grafio, 595 A.2d 983 (DC).

25. Impossibility of Performance

Parker entered a contract with Arthur Murray, Inc. to learn how to dance. The contract eliminated any possibility of getting a refund. Later, Parker suffered a permanent disability that made it impossible for him to dance. The dance company pointed to the anti-refund provision and refused to give Parker his money back. Parker sued, arguing that the impossibility of performance ended the contract. Arthur Murray argued that the anti-refund provision overruled the impossibility of performance doctrine. *Who is correct? Explain your answer.*
Parker v. Arthur Murray, Inc. 295 N.E.2d 487 (IL).

Legal Link

Felon's Rights

Some states take away some of the civil rights of convicted felons. Felons may lose the right to vote, to contract, and to bring and defend against civil lawsuits. Some states have even considered requiring felons to register their genetic profiles.

Connect

Using a variety of search engines, research:

26. The laws in your state regarding the loss of rights for a convicted felon.

27. Any special statute of limitations that might affect people in prison.

POWER READING STRATEGIES

28. **Predict** Why do you think time is so important in a contract?

29. **Connect** Can you describe a situation in which you have made tender?

30. **Question** Do you think it is fair that felons lose some of their civil rights while in prison? Explain your answer.

31. **Respond** Do you think the drafters of the U.S. Constitution were correct when they gave Congress the right to pass bankruptcy laws? Why or why not?

CHAPTER 12

Transfer of Contracts and Remedies for Breach

Understanding Business and Personal Law *Online*

Chapter Overview Visit the *Understanding Business and Personal Law* Web site at **ubpl.glencoe.com** and click on Chapter 12: Transfer of Contracts and Remedies for Breach—Chapter Overviews to preview the chapter information.

The Opening Scene

After school, Viktor and Alena meet Trevor and Micha on the school's athletic field.

An Imaginary Settlement

VIKTOR: Hey, Micha! Thanks for meeting me. I've been thinking about our conversation a lot today. I think you might have the answer to all of my money problems. So, if I sue Mr. Olsen, what do I get?

MICHA: You'll get money, of course. That's what you want, isn't it?

VIKTOR: Yeah, but how much do you think that I can get?

MICHA: Well, for starters, I'm sure you can get the amount that he was supposed to pay you for the paint job.

VIKTOR: That's not much. It's no more than $20, tops.

TREVOR: I have an idea! Maybe you can get some extra money to compensate you for your pain and suffering.

ALENA: Oh, please! You guys are too much. What pain did Vik suffer, other than having to do some work? If I remember correctly, he was actually happy that the job ended early. He wanted out of the deal before the fire even occurred. It's not fair for you to sue Mr. Olsen.

VIKTOR: Allie's right for once, guys. I didn't suffer much. . . . Well, maybe just a little on the account of having to walk all the way over there. I think that I may have gotten up really early that morning, too.

MICHA: That's something. Now we have something to go on. What about punitive damages?

VIKTOR: I don't know what you mean. What are punitive damages?

MICHA: It's when the court makes you pay so much that it hurts.

ALENA: Come on, Vik. Let's drop this right now and move on. You know that you're not going to sue him.

VIKTOR: No, I don't suppose it would be fair to bring a lawsuit, but it has been fun imagining a big lawsuit settlement. I could really use the money. I'm never going to be able to afford a car.

TREVOR: So maybe that job idea is the best thing after all?

VIKTOR: Yeah, maybe so. I guess I have no other choice than to get a job. I'm going to look for another job on the Internet tonight.

MICHA: Well, I was saving this news for last, so I guess now is the time.

VIKTOR: What news?

MICHA: Mrs. Miniver hired me to mow her lawn every week this summer, but now my dad says I've gotta go with him to Florida. Maybe I can give you my job. Mrs. Miniver pays pretty well, and the job's not that hard. Even you could handle it, Vik. It won't cut into your social life at all. What do you think? The job's yours if you want it.

VIKTOR: That would be great. Sweet! Thanks, Micha!

MICHA: No problem. That's what friends are for.

What Are the Legal Issues?

1. What happens when one party to a contract decides to assign his or her rights under the contract to a third party?
2. How is a novation formed?
3. What remedies are available in a lawsuit for breach of contract?
4. What is the difference between specific performance and an injunction?

The Transfer of Contractual Rights and Duties

What You'll Learn

- How to explain the nature of an assignment
- How to identify contractual rights that can be assigned
- How to explain the nature of a delegation
- How to explain the nature of a novation
- How to identify a situation involving privity of contract

Why It's Important

Understanding when contractual rights and duties can be assigned will prepare you to deal with such situations when they arise.

Legal Terms

- assignment
- delegation
- novation
- privity of contract
- third-party beneficiary

Transfer of Rights

At the beginning of our study of contracts, we learned that when individuals enter contracts, they receive rights (benefits) and incur duties (detriments). In the vast majority of cases, people retain their rights and perform their duties on their own. At times, however, these rights and duties are transferred from the original parties to someone new. There are a variety of reasons why people choose to transfer their contractual rights and duties. Some people transfer their right to receive payments to other parties to pay off debts. Other people take on more work than they can handle and need to transfer some of their duties to other qualified parties. The law permits this sort of transfer, with a few exceptions. When transferring contractual rights and duties, there are many details that you should know.

You may legally transfer your rights under any contract to which you have agreed, as long as the contract does not specifically say you can't. The transfer of a right under a contract is called an **assignment**. The party who transfers the right is called the assignor, and the party to whom the right is transferred is called the assignee. The assignee is a third person who is not a party to the original contract.

Example 1. Anthony Cuomo entered into a contract with Cathy Michaud to rebuild the front steps of her house for $1,800. The carpenter was pleased to get the contract because he owed $1,800 to his landlord, David Brown. Before beginning work, Anthony assigned the right to receive the payment for the work to his landlord. When payment was due, Cathy paid the $1,800 to David Brown directly.

How Rights May Be Assigned

No consideration is necessary for an assignment to be valid. In most cases, the law does not specify how one party may assign a right to another. It's best to put an assignment in writing, however, because an oral assignment can be difficult to prove. Let's consider why it would be important for an assignment to be in writing. Suppose that the party to whom money is owed decides to assign the rights to the money. The party who owes the money is entitled to notice of the assignment. If the party who owes money or duties is notified or shown such a written assignment, then that party is legally bound to pay or render services to the assignee only; payment to the assignor will not discharge the debt.

Example 2. Nathan Ecker, who rents out two rooms of his house, is moving temporarily to another state. To make sure rent is collected during his absence, Nathan assigns one tenant, Richard Taft, the duty to collect the $700 rent from Jerry Golden, the other tenant. He also gives Jerry a note asking him to pay Richard his monthly rent. Richard then has the right to receive the $700 from Jerry. However, if Nathan merely told Richard to collect rent, Jerry would not know this was actually the case.

What Rights May Be Assigned

Most rights may be assigned unless the assignment changes the obligations of the other party to the contract in an important way. In Example 1, when Anthony assigned the right to receive the $1,800 to his landlord, Cathy's obligation to pay the money did not change. The assignment was valid. However, not all assignments are valid.

Example 3. Cathy Michaud decided, after contracting for the step replacement with Anthony Cuomo, that the steps at the home of

Virtual Law

Breach of Contract

A telecommunications company recently cut off service to two Internet service providers and their customers. These providers were under contract to make payments for their telecommunications service. When millions of dollars in bills became past due, the telecommunications company treated the lack of payment as a breach of contract. As a result, they cut off service. One of the Internet service providers accused the telecommunications company of shutting off service in an effort to steal its customers. If true, this would also be a breach of contract. (Source: *New York Times*, February 16, 2001, p. C3)

Connect Find out which Internet service providers are in your area and which telecommunications companies support their service. Research any legal options that you may have if your service were to be cut off prior to the end of your service contract.

her neighbor, Helen Kane, were in worse condition. Helen, an elderly woman, might easily be injured on the dilapidated steps, and Cathy knew that Helen didn't have the money to pay for new steps. Cathy decided that she wanted to change her contract with Anthony. She now wanted Anthony to fix Helen's steps instead. However, this materially changed Anthony's obligation, and such an assignment would likely be void. Rights to receive personal services are usually not assignable.

An assignor can assign nothing more than the rights that he or she possesses. An assignee takes those rights, subject to other people's defenses.

Example 4. In Example 1, suppose that when Anthony Cuomo assigned the right to receive the $1,800 to his landlord, Anthony then did a poor job of fixing the steps. Cathy Michaud could then raise the defense of a poor repair job if she were sued by the assignee, who wanted to collect the $1,800.

AN ASSIGNMENT
Assignments transfer a party's rights in a contract to a third party. *Is it always necessary for an assignment to be in writing?*

Figure 12.1

ASSIGNMENT

KNOW ALL MEN BY THESE PRESENTS:

That I, John P. Beney, residing at 1131 39th Street, New York, in consideration of ($) paid by LYDIA A. BENIQUEZ, residing at 24379 Riverdale Parkway, New York, New York, (herein called "the Assignee"), hereby assign to the Assignee all my rights, title, and interest in the monies due me from JOSEPH ORMOND, for work, labor, and services as a carpenter performed by me, between May 1, 20--, and May 31, 20--, which services were performed at the request of said JOSEPH ORMOND, and were of the agreed value of two thousand, two hundred dollars ($2,200).

IN WITNESS WHEREOF, I have hereunto set my hand and seal this 1st day of June, 20--.

John P. Beney

Rights to the payment of money (wages, money owed on accounts, royalties on books, etc.) and rights to the delivery of goods are the most common types of rights that are assigned. After the assignment, the assignor no longer has an interest in the right that was assigned. This right now belongs exclusively to the assignee.

Generally, no special form is required to make an assignment. Any words that clearly indicate a person's intent are sufficient (see Figure 12.1). This assignment may be made on a separate paper, or it may be written on the back of a written contract containing the rights to be assigned.

Transfer of Duties

Duties may be transferred to someone else. The transfer of a duty is called a **delegation**. A delegation should not be confused with an assignment. An assignment is a transfer of rights; a delegation is a transfer of duties. In a transfer of duties, a party to a contract delegates another person to perform the obligation in his or her place. In The Opening Scene, Micha could make a delegation to Viktor involving his job of mowing lawns at Mrs. Miniver's property.

Legal Briefs

In the "Institutes" of Justinian, the precepts of ancient Roman law were described as "to live honestly, to injure no one, and to give every man his due." In ancient Rome, civil law, or *publici juris*, related to the state or public worship. Private law, or *juris private*, related to the legal interrelations of citizens.

DELEGATION OF DUTIES Sometimes the duties agreed to under a contract cannot be delegated to another party. *When is a party unable to delegate a contractual duty?*

Example 5. Ivan Remec, owner of the Eastern Print Shop, was in financial trouble. He had overextended himself and could not meet all of his printing contracts. When the time came to print the monthly newsletter for the high school's Parent Teacher Association, he transferred his contract obligation to another printer, Stanley Novak of ABC Press, who was not a party to the original contract.

Figure 12.2

Bryant, Inc.
6225 St. Clair Avenue
Cleveland, OH 44103

June 15, 20--

Mr. Carl Newfield:

You are hereby notified that Pendleton Architects Limited of Euclid, Ohio, has assigned to Bryant, Inc. all rights to its claim against you in the amount of $750.

You are further notified to direct all payments to Bryant, Inc. at the above address to ensure credit for payment.

Sincerely yours,

Norbert Bryant

Norbert Bryant
Vice President

NOTIFICATION OF AN ASSIGNMENT
When an assignment is made, the original party should be notified of the assignment. *What ethical reasons could be given for notifying the other party of an assignment?*

Although the performance of an obligation may be delegated, the responsibility for it may not. In Example 5, Eastern Print Shop continues to be liable for the terms of the contract. If both parties understand the situation, it is all right to delegate the duty of doing the work to someone else. This is really a form of subcontracting and occurs often in business contracts. It is quite common, for example, in building contracts. When an assignment is made, however, it is generally considered ethical and courteous to inform the original party (see Figure 12.2).

Delegating duties can make business and personal obligations much easier to fulfill. Duties may not be delegated, however, in any of these scenarios: a party agrees to perform the service personally; the contract calls for the exercise of personal skill and judgment; or the contract itself prohibits delegation.

Example 6. Suppose, in Example 5, that Ivan Remec had told Mrs. Kolenich, the president of the PTA, that he would personally

Lawyer-Client Confidentiality

As members of state bar associations, lawyers are subject to rules of professional conduct. One important rule is the obligation of confidentiality, which requires lawyers to protect the private and confidential information that they receive from their clients. This obligation is preserved even after the termination of the attorney-client relationship. The purpose of this rule is to foster trust, honesty, and openness in the attorney-client relationship, and to make people feel comfortable sharing information with their lawyers.

There are exceptions to a lawyer's obligation of confidentiality. A lawyer may release private information with the client's consent. He or she may also release information if it is necessary to establish a defense in a legal controversy with the client. There are also exceptions when confidentiality is inconsistent with the interests of society. An attorney may alert the proper authorities if he or she reasonably believes that the information will prevent a client from committing a criminal act likely to result in death or substantial bodily or financial harm to others.

Research What other professions have rules about protecting your confidentiality? What, if any, are the exceptions to these rules?

do her printing job. He could not then delegate the job to ABC Press.

Duties that require personal skill and judgment, such as the work of teachers, writers, artists, or entertainers, cannot be delegated to others. Such persons are selected to perform their services because of their particular skills or talents. Another person would not be able to perform the services in same manner.

The offeror and the offeree may include in their contract a statement that the contract may not be assigned or delegated. In this case, both parties are restrained.

Example 7. Herbert Ryan contracted to build a garage for Roberta McGovern. The contract said Herbert would do the work himself and could not assign or delegate the contract to any outside third party. Ordinarily a contract of this type could be assigned or delegated to another competent builder, but the words of this particular contract would prevent any such action.

If you have the right to delegate a contractual obligation and decide to do so, choose your third party carefully. As explained earlier, you retain responsibility for any job duties that you subcontract, or assign to a third party. If you select an unreliable third party, you may end up causing yourself a great deal of anxiety or frustration.

Novation

You don't need the permission of the other party to assign contract rights or to delegate duties to a third person. If you do receive permission to do so, however, and the other party agrees to deal with the assignee, the resulting contract is called a novation. A **novation** is an agreement whereby an original party to a contract is replaced by a new party. The other terms of the new contract generally remain the same as those in the original contract. To be effective, the substitution requires the consent of all of the parties involved.

Example 8. One of the jobs that Ivan Remec delegated to ABC Press was printing a book of poetry for Henrietta Gladstone. ABC Press agreed to do the work, and Ivan assigned the right to receive the money to ABC's owner, Stanley Novak. Henrietta agreed to release Eastern Print Shop from all obligations and deal solely with ABC Press. This substitution of parties was a novation.

Third Parties

A contract is a binding agreement that establishes a relationship between the parties to the contract. This relationship between the parties is termed **privity of contract**. It determines who can sue whom over a question of performance required by a contract. Usually the parties to a contract have standing to sue.

Example 9. In The Opening Scene, Micha does not succeed in convincing Viktor to sue Mr. Olsen for back pay and damages. Could Micha go ahead and sue Mr. Olsen himself? No, because he was not a party to the original contract between Viktor and Mr. Olsen. Micha might argue that he would have received some benefit under contract if his friend were to win a lawsuit against Mr. Olsen, but this would be only an incidental benefit. Micha has no reasonable standing to bring suit.

A third person may sometimes enforce a contract when it is made specifically for that person's benefit. A person who is not a party to a contract but still benefits from the contract is called a **third-party beneficiary**.

Example 10. Uncle Leo bought a life insurance policy that named his nephew, Andrew Wollack, as beneficiary. When Uncle Leo died, the insurance company refused to pay off on the policy, claiming that Uncle Leo had not disclosed to them that he had cancer. Andrew said that his uncle did not know he had the illness when he took out the policy. Because Andrew was an intended third-party beneficiary of the life insurance contract, he has standing to bring suit against the insurance company.

Section 12.1 Assessment

Reviewing What You Learned
1. What is an assignment?
2. What contractual rights can be assigned?
3. What is a delegation?
4. What is a novation?
5. What is privity of contract?

Critical Thinking Activity
Third Parties Why does the law grant third-party beneficiaries standing to bring lawsuits?

Legal Skills in Action
Privity of Contract Your brother is the general manager of a restaurant in Capital City. He has just learned that the Brotherhood of International Electronic Workers (BIEW) has canceled its plans to hold its annual convention in Capital City. This cancellation will cause your brother's restaurant to lose an enormous amount of money. He has decided to bring a lawsuit against the BIEW. Discuss with several of your classmates whether your brother has standing to bring a lawsuit against the BIEW.

Remedies of the Injured Party

What You'll Learn

- How to explain the concept of anticipatory breach
- How to identify remedies available for breach of contract
- How to define specific performance
- Why you must minimize the damages involved in a breach of contract

Why It's Important

Understanding the remedies available when a contract is breached will help you pursue satisfaction if this happens to you.

Legal Terms

- breach of contract
- anticipatory breach
- damages
- actual damages
- incidental damages
- liquidated damages
- mitigation of damages
- specific performance
- injunction

Breach of Contract

A **breach of contract** occurs when one party to a contract fails to perform the duties set out in the terms of the agreement. If you fail to fulfill your obligations by not carrying them out or by performing them in an incomplete or unsatisfactory manner, then you are said to have breached the contract.

Contracts are usually breached after the performance date. Sometimes, however, parties to a contract notify the other party that they will not go through with the contract before the time for performance. They have breached, or violated, the agreement before they were required to act. This is called **anticipatory breach**. Formerly, the injured party had to wait to bring suit until the time for performance had passed. Many states now permit the injured party to bring an action for damages immediately, without waiting for the actual time for performance to arrive.

Example 11. A youth group to which you belong has made a contract with a carpenter to build a teen activity center. The carpenter is supposed to begin work on June 20, but she calls the director of your group on January 9 to explain that she will not be able to fulfill her obligation. Your group can bring an action for damages against the carpenter for an anticipatory breach anytime after January 9.

The principle of anticipatory breach does not apply to promises to pay money at some future date. Someone who refuses to pay money owed on a future date cannot be sued until after the payment is due.

Damages

When a contract is breached, the injured party has a choice of remedies. A remedy is a legal means of enforcing a right or correcting a wrong. If you are the injured party, you have three options. You may: accept the breach; sue for money damages; or, in some cases, ask the court for an equitable remedy.

Acceptance of Breach

If one party breaches a contract, it is an excuse for the other party not to perform. For example, if someone failed to perform under a contract with you, you may simply accept the breach and consider the contract discharged. This is often the best choice, especially if no damages have been suffered. Damages awarded to recognize a breach of contract that did not cause loss often amount to less than one dollar. These damages are intended merely to recognize that a breach of contract has occurred. Your legal fees for pursuing and winning such a suit would likely far outweigh any damages you would receive.

Money Damages

If you suffer a loss as the injured party, however, you may sue for money damages resulting from the breach of contract. **Damages** are payment recovered in court by a person who has suffered an injury (see Figure 12.3). The money damages should, by law, place you in the position you would have been in if the contract had been carried out. Let's take a closer look at some selected categories of damages. To recover damages, the injured party must make tender; that is, the injured party must offer to do what he or she agreed to do under the contract.

Actual and Incidental Damages

In actions for breach of contract, the injured party may recover the actual damages caused by the other party's failure of performance. **Actual damages** are damages directly attributable to another party's breach of contract. For instance, if someone contracts to buy land at a certain price but the contract is breached, he or she can seek damages amounting to the difference between the agreed price of the land and its market value at the time of the breach. If a seller of goods breaches a contract, the measure of damages for the prospective buyer is the difference between the market price at the time of the breach and the contract price, plus incidental damages. **Incidental damages** are any reasonable expenses, resulting from a breach, that have been incurred by the buyer.

> *Example 12.* Yukio Tanaka contracted with a local bookstore to buy a set of encyclopedias at a price of $1,500. The store failed to deliver the books according to the agreement. Tanaka learned that he would have to pay $1,800 to buy the same set of books at another store across town. He is entitled to sue the first store for his actual damage of $300, which is the difference between $1,500 and $1,800, plus any other expenses incurred in getting the books at the other bookstore. These incidental damages might include transportation or delivery costs.

Liquidated Damages

Damages agreed upon by the parties when they first enter into a contract are called **liquidated damages**. The parties agree beforehand

Law & Academics

History
In the book of Exodus in the Old Testament, many of the old Hebrew laws are cited. One states, "Wherever hurt is done, you shall give life for life, eye for eye, tooth for tooth, hand for hand, foot for foot, burn for burn, bruise for bruise, wound for wound." (Exodus 21:23–25, *The New English Bible*)

Research Activity
Today, we award money damages. Research a lawsuit in which a contract has been breached and money damages have been awarded. Make an oral presentation to your class outlining the case and whether you believe the award was sufficient.

Figure 12.3 — Damages

Type	Description
Actual Damages	An amount of money awarded for damages directly attributable to another party's breach of contract or tort; for example, physician's fees when one party wrongly injures another, and financial losses resulting from failure to deliver goods already contracted for.
Compensatory Damages	An award of an amount of money that compensates a plainiff for the injuries suffered and nothing more.
Consequential Damages	Damage, loss, or injury (such as loss of profits) that does not flow directly and immediately from the act of the party but only from some of the consequences or results of the act.
Incidental Damages	Reasonable expenses that indirectly result from a breach of contract. They include expenses such as those incurred in stopping delivery of goods, transporting goods, and caring for goods that have been rightfully rejected by a buyer.
Liquidated Damages	An amount of anticipated damages, agreed to by both parties and contained in a contract, to be the basis of any award in the event of a breach of the contract.
Nominal Damages	Damages awarded by a court when a successful plaintiff has proven a legal injury but no actual resulting damages; six cents by common law, usually $1 today.
Punitive Damages	Damages in excess of losses suffered by the plaintiff awarded to the plaintiff as a measure of punishment for the defendant's wrongful act. Also called exemplary damages because they set an example of punishment awaiting other wrongdoers.
Speculative Damages	Damages not founded on fact but on the expectations that a party may have hoped for from a contract that has been breached; not allowed in any claim for money damages.

DAMAGES
Suing for money damages is one remedy for breach of contract. *What is the objective of awarding damages to the injured party in a contract case?*

what damages may be recovered if either one breaches the contract. The law requires that liquidated damages be reasonable.

Example 13. The Young Supply Company ordered a sorting machine for its new distribution center, which was being built in Sacramento. The machine was a vital link in delivering many products to the firm's customers. The Young Company inserted in its contract with the machine seller the following terms: "The Young Company will be paid $500 each day beyond the date agreed upon for delivery of said machine if the machine is delivered late." Considering the profits that might be lost through delay in delivery, the liquidated damages provision would be considered reasonable and proper.

Minimizing Damages

An injured party must take all reasonable steps to minimize the damages that might result from the other party's failure of performance. At all times, you must protect the other party in a contract from any unnecessary losses. This principle is known as **mitigation of damages**.

Example 14. Peter Lister contracted to deliver 1,000 baskets of tomatoes from his farm to a cannery for a certain price. When he tried to deliver the tomatoes, however, the canner would not accept them. Under the mitigation of damages principle, Lister would be obligated to try to find another buyer for the tomatoes. If he didn't make as much money, he could demand payment from the cannery for the difference between what he was paid for the produce and what the cannery had agreed to pay.

Equitable Remedies

The remedy of money damages is not always enough to repay an injured party for breach of contract. In these cases, the injured party may seek an equitable remedy (see Figure 12.4). Two chief equitable remedies are specific performance and an injunction.

Specific Performance

Sometimes the remedy of money damages is not enough to repay a breach of contract. In that case, one party may sue the other for **specific performance** by asking the court to order the other party to do specifically what he or she originally agreed to do. However, this remedy can only be used when money damages are not sufficient to give relief.

Example 15. Doreen Russell contracted to sell Betsy Keller a valuable original oil painting. Doreen then breached the contract and refused to sell. Money damages would not be adequate in this case because the painting could not be purchased elsewhere. The court would order Doreen to turn the painting over to Betsy for the agreed price.

As Example 15 illustrates, specific performance can be granted when the subject matter of the contract is rare or unique. It would not

Figure 12.4

Equitable Remedies Type

Type	Description
Specific Performance	Specific performance requires the other party to carry out the terms of the contract as originally agreed.
Injunction	An injunction is an official order of the court compelling a party to stop the performance of some action.

EQUITABLE REMEDIES Money damages are not the only remedy that might be available in a contract case. *When might damages be an insufficient remedy in a breach of a contract case?*

Careers in Law

Corporate Lawyer

Richard Negrin is a tough, talented attorney at one of the most prestigious law firms in the country. Prior to joining the firm of Morgan Lewis, Negrin worked five years as a prosecuting attorney. Today he litigates parts liability cases for his clients, which include Fortune 100 companies; but when Negrin was growing up in Elizabeth, New Jersey, no one in his family even knew a lawyer.

"We lived in the poor section of town and my first language was Spanish," says the Philadelphia attorney whose family emigrated from Cuba. "We thought of lawyers as mysterious and inaccessible."

Negrin graduated from Rutgers University Law School, and today—in addition to his role as an attorney—he serves as president of the Hispanic Bar Association of Pennsylvania (HBA). In that role, Negrin raises scholarship money, encourages Hispanic students to pursue careers in law, and helps worthy law students to get noticed by potential employers.

"Hispanic students are often kids from a lower economic background," Negrin says. "Their parents don't socialize in the same circles as local lawyers and judges, and their application might be buried in a pile of resumes. If a Hispanic student has done well in law school, we try to help her resume get the notice it deserves."

In addition to serving as HBA president, Negrin also gives back to the community by serving on the boards of the local Red Cross and Community Legal Services. Negrin also performs pro bono (free) legal work for clients who are too poor to pay for his services.

Each year, the 138 Hispanic Bar Association members raise scholarship funds for about 12 local students.

"It's a good way to network and develop mentors," Negrin says. "And it allows members to use our abilities and experience to help those who follow."

Skills	Research and writing, speaking, organizational, managerial skills.
Personality	Outgoing, hardworking, logical.
Education	Undergraduate degree, law degree. Serving on community service boards usually requires some volunteer experience with the organization.

You can find more information about HBA at www.hba-pa.com.

For more information about corporate attorneys, visit **ubpl.glencoe.com** or visit your public library.

be ordered in the case of contracts involving common goods or easily obtained services.

This particular rule is especially important in real estate contracts. The law considers each parcel (separate piece) of real estate to be unlike any other, if for no other reason than that the locations are different. Consequently, it is usually possible to sue for specific performance of an agreement to buy or sell real estate.

Injunction

An **injunction** is a court order that prevents a party from performing an act of some sort. An injunction is only available in special circumstances, such as when money damages will be inadequate to compensate the injured party.

> *Example 16.* Alicia Swartz owns a house in the countryside only five miles from the nearest airport. The airport needs another runway and contracts with a local firm to build the runway. Planes using the new runway would descend directly over Swartz's house. Swartz decides to sue the airport, seeking an injunction to stop construction of the runway.

An injunction may be temporary or permanent. A temporary injunction is issued as a means of delaying further activity in any contested matter until the court determines whether a permanent injunction should be entered or the injunction should be removed entirely. One who disobeys an injunction does so under penalty of contempt of court.

Section 12.2 Assessment

Reviewing What You Learned

1. What is involved in an anticipatory breach of a contract?
2. What remedies are available to an innocent party when a breach of contract occurs?
3. What is specific performance?
4. Why is it necessary to minimize the damages involved in a breach of contract?

Critical Thinking Activity

Damages What is the principle that forms the basis of the theory of damages in contract law?

Legal Skills in Action

Anticipatory Breach Harriet Iafigliano owes your friend, Andy, $500 that she is supposed to pay to him on May 20. Harriet sent an e-mail to Andy in April indicating that she could not pay him on that date. Andy believes that the doctrine of anticipatory breach applies in this situation. Write a letter to Andy explaining whether anticipatory breach applies in his case.

Chapter Summary

Section 12.1 The Transfer of Contractual Rights and Duties

- The transfer of a right under a contract is an assignment. The party who transfers the right is the assignor. The party to whom the right is transferred is the assignee. No consideration is necessary for an assignment to be valid. It's best to put an assignment in writing, because an oral assignment can be difficult to prove.

- Most rights can be assigned unless the assignment changes the obligations of the other party to the contract in an important way. Rights to the payment of money (e.g., wages, money owed on accounts, or royalties on books) and rights to the delivery of goods are the most common types of rights that are assigned.

- Duties may sometimes be transferred. The transfer of a duty is called a delegation. Duties may not be delegated when a party agrees to perform the service personally, the contract calls for personal skill and judgment, or the contract itself prohibits delegation. Usually, the work of teachers, writers, artists, or entertainers cannot be delegated to others. Such persons are selected to perform their services because of their particular skills or talents. Another person would not be able to perform the services in the same manner.

- A novation is the resulting agreement when an original party to a contract is replaced by a new party and all the involved parties agree to the assignment. The other terms of the contract generally remain the same as those in the original contract.

- A contract establishes a binding relationship between parties. This relationship is called privity of contract. With the exception of third-party beneficiaries, only parties with privity have standing to sue under a contract.

Section 12.2 Remedies of the Injured Party

- Contracts are usually breached after the time of performance has begun. Sometimes, however, one of the parties notifies the other before the time of performance that he will not perform. This breach is called anticipatory breach. Many states now permit the injured party to bring an action for damages immediately, without waiting for the actual time for performance to arrive. The principle of anticipatory breach does not apply to promises to pay money at some future date. Someone who refuses to pay money owed on a future date cannot be sued until after the payment is due.

- When a contract is breached, the injured party has a choice of accepting the breach, suing for damages, or asking the court for an equitable remedy. Accepting the breach is generally the best choice if no damages have been suffered. Damages awarded to recognize a breach that did not cause loss often amount to less than one dollar. Suing for damages allows the injured party to recover compensation that would place him or her in the position that he or she would have been if the contract had been carried out. An injured party may seek an equitable remedy when money does not adequately compensate for the loss suffered by the breach of contract. Two chief equitable remedies are specific performance and an injunction.

- Sometimes no amount of money damages is sufficient to fix a breach of contract. In such cases, courts will order the other party to do specifically what she agreed to do. This remedy is called specific performance, and it will be invoked to satisfy a unique subject matter such as a painting or a parcel of land.

- The principle of mitigation states that even if you are the innocent party, you must try to minimize damages that might result from the other party's failure of performance.

Using Legal Language

Consider the key terms in the list below. Then use these terms to complete the following exercises.

assignment	third-party beneficiary
delegation	anticipatory breach
novation	damages
privity of contract	mitigation of damages

1. Write a short story about a contract that has been transferred and breached, using as many of the terms as possible.
2. Create illustrations to highlight the important points in your story. Include these illustrations in your story.
3. Exchange stories with a classmate. Read your classmate's story, noting interesting perspectives and styles.
4. Offer constructive criticism to help your partner improve his or her story. Point out strengths and weaknesses. Make sure all legal language is used correctly.
5. Reflect on your partner's suggestions regarding your story.

Understanding Business and Personal Law Online

Self-Check Quiz Visit the *Understanding Business and Personal Law* Web site at **ubpl.glencoe.com** and click on Chapter 12: Transfer of Contracts and Remedies for Breach—Self-Check Quizzes to prepare for the chapter exam.

The Law Review

Answer the following questions. Refer to the chapter for additional reinforcement.

6. When rights are transferred, who is the assignor? Who is the assignee?
7. Why is it important for an assignment to be in writing?
8. What duties cannot be delegated to others?
9. Define the principle of mitigation of damages.
10. Describe the two chief equitable remedies.
11. What is an injunction?
12. How do actual damages differ from incidental damages?
13. Why is it usually a bad idea to sue for breach of contract that did not cause actual loss?
14. What is a third-party beneficiary?
15. Why do courts award damages to injured parties?

Linking School to Work

Acquiring and Evaluating Information
Working with contracts is a regular part of most businesses. Companies make contracts with their customers and employees, and often with governments and other businesses.

16. Using newspapers, magazines, or the Internet, locate an article relating to a breach of contract in the workplace. Write a summary of the breach and the remedy. Next, evaluate the ethical nature of the breach. Share your findings with the class.

Let's Debate

Concert Cancellation
Peter purchased a $50 ticket to see his favorite band perform. He waited all week for the concert, only to find out the day before the scheduled event that it had been cancelled.

Debate
17. Do you think that Peter should be refunded the money for his ticket? What are Peter's rights?
18. Has there been a breach of contract?
19. What remedies are available to Peter and the other ticket holders?

Grasping Case Issues

For the following cases, give your decision and state a legal principle that applies.
20. Horton contracted with Findlay to purchase a used computer for $500. When Findlay refused to go along with his part of the agreement, Horton went to the local computer specialty shop and purchased a new computer for $2,500. He then demanded $2,000 from Findlay as damages for Findlay's breach. Is Horton entitled to this much money as the measure of damages? Why or why not?
21. Don Blair contracts to work as a mechanic for Henry Lee for one year. A month later, Lee assigns his right to receive Blair's services to Titus. Must Blair work for Titus? Explain your answer.
22. The Turner Company sells goods to Pierre Moreau on credit. After waiting several months for Moreau to make a payment on his account, the Turner Company informs Moreau that it is assigning its rights to a collection agency. Is this legally possible? Why or why not?
23. Janine Drake owes Duncan Coe $500. Coe assigns the right to receive the money to Abram Burke in payment of a debt. Coe then moves out of town and takes up a new residence. No one notifies Drake of the assignment. She mails the $500 to Coe at his new address. Can Burke sue Drake for failing to honor the assignment? Explain your answer.
24. Dea Duk Sung buys a $100,000 life insurance policy naming Yung Shen Sung as the beneficiary. If the insurance company refuses to pay the proceeds of the policy to Yung Shen when Dea Duk Sung dies, does Yung Shen have standing to sue? Why or why not?

In each case that follows, you be the judge.

25. Assignments in Writing

The terms of the Blackstone divorce decree required that Mr. Blackstone pay child support of $600 per month to his former wife. Payments were to be made via the office of the clerk of courts. The right to receive the payments was transferred to the Department of Human Resources by the clerk's office. *Must the assignment in this case be in writing? Why or why not?*
Blackstone v. State Ex. Rel. Blackstone, 585 So.2d 58 (AL).

26. Assignments after Bankruptcy

The Washington Post Company had a contract with *The Chicago Tribune*, requiring that the *Tribune* supply *The Post* with several comic strips, including *Dick Tracy, Winnie Winkle, Gasoline Alley,* and *The Gumps*. After *The Post's* bankruptcy, the bankruptcy trustees assigned the right to receive the comics to a reorganized company, owned by Meyers. *The Tribune* canceled the contract and entered a new contract with *The Washington Tribune,* giving the *Tribune* the right to receive the comic strips. When Meyers objected, *The Chicago Tribune* argued that the rights to the comic strips could not be assigned. *Is The Chicago Tribune correct? Explain your answer.*
Meyers v. Washington Times Co., 76 F2d. 988 (DC Cir.).

Legal Link

Computer Security

Martin is a lawyer practicing in New York. All of the contracts he creates are saved on the computer in his office. Recently, Martin asked for advice regarding his duties to implement and practice computer security.

Connect

Using a variety of search engines, help Martin find:

27. Information about his legal and ethical responsibilities in this area. What standard of care should Martin observe in protecting the confidentiality and privacy of his clients' records?

POWER READING STRATEGIES

28. **Predict** Why do you think consideration is unnecessary for an assignment of rights to be valid?

29. **Connect** Have any rights or duties ever been transferred to you? Explain your answer.

30. **Question** Why do you think that although a performance of an obligation can be delegated, the responsibility for it may not be?

31. **Respond** Can you think of a time when you might have breached a contract you made with a friend or family member? Explain your answer.

How Would You Write a Contract?

In this unit, you learned many things about contracts, including the elements of a legally enforceable contract, the form of a contract, and how contracts come to an end. In this workshop, you will work with a partner and use what you have learned to prepare a written contract.

Step A: Preparation

Problem: *How would you write a contract with another person?*

Objectives: In this workshop, you will write a contract between yourself and a partner.

- **Research** contract forms.
- **Negotiate** the type and terms of the contract with your partner.
- **Write** the contract, and use technology to prepare it.
- **Compare** your contract with the contracts of other pairs of students.
- **Analyze** the essential elements of the contracts.

Step B: Procedure

1. Choose a partner.
2. Review the text in this unit and make a list of the essential elements of a contract. Use the Internet to locate online contract forms. (Hint: www.morebusiness.com offers sample business agreements online.)

3. With your partner, create a business scenario that would require a written contract between the two of you.
4. Write the contract based on your knowledge and research. Use the Internet to download a form for an agreement, or create a contract by using word processing software. Make copies for everyone in the class.
5. Describe the business scenario that requires a written contract and present your contract to the class.

Step C: Creating a Model to Compare the Contracts

As a class, compare the contracts presented. Create a chart that presents and describes the type of agreement created and the responsibilities involved. Make sure that you have also accounted for each of the elements required for a valid and enforceable contract.

Team: Todd D. and Katya F.	Type of Contract: Todd is selling his stereo to Katya for $800.
Contract Element: Legality	Yes, this contract is legal.

Step D: Workshop Analysis Report

Look at the charts your classmates have created and answer the following questions:
1. How many and what types of contracts were presented?
2. Did all of the contracts presented include all the necessary elements?
3. If not, how does the absence of the element(s) affect the contract(s)?
4. How was your contract similar to and different from the other contracts presented?

Mastrobuono v. Shearson Lehman Hutton, Inc.

United States Supreme Court

514 U.S. 52 (1995)

Issue Does a contract that does not address punitive damages authorize such damages if the parties agreed to arbitrate controversies under rules that allow for such damages, but a conflicting provision in the contract appears to prohibit such damages?

Facts Antonio Mastrobuono and his wife started an investment account at Shearson Lehman Hutton, Inc. When they opened their account, the Mastrobuonos signed a contract provided by Shearson Lehman Hutton. The contract required that the parties arbitrate any disputes that might arise. The contract also contained a provision stating that it would be governed by New York state law. In an arbitration proceeding, the parties present their dispute to an impartial third person or panel and agree to abide by the arbitrator's lawful decision. Because arbitration is considered less time consuming and less costly than litigation, many contracts contain a provision in which the parties agree that disputes be resolved through arbitration.

For a variety of reasons, the Mastrobuonos became dissatisfied with the investment services they received from Shearson Lehman Hutton. They closed their account and sued Shearson Lehman Hutton, alleging that their account had been mismanaged. Because of the contract's arbitration provision, Shearson Lehman Hutton suspended the litigation and forced the Mastrobuonos to go before a three-member panel of arbitrators. The panel awarded the Mastrobuonos compensatory damages

of $159,327 and punitive damages of $400,000. Compensatory damages are awarded to compensate an injured party for actual losses. Punitive damages may be awarded in limited circumstances to punish a person or company for wrongful conduct. Punitive damages are also awarded to prevent other companies from behaving in a similar unlawful or unethical manner. In many cases, the threat of suffering financial loss by way of punitive damages will discourage a company or individual from engaging in unscrupulous behavior.

Shearson Lehman Hutton paid the compensatory damages but obtained a court order vacating the award for punitive damages because New York law permits only courts to award punitive damages.

Opinion The Court observed that contract between the parties in this case contained no express provision about punitive damages. Because the parties agreed to arbitrate a dispute, the Mastrobuonos claimed that the parties were bound by the arbitration panel's decision. Shearson Lehman Hutton argued that the contract limits the matters that may be arbitrated because the parties agreed that the contract would be governed by New York law, which only authorizes courts to award punitive damages. As a result of these differing views, the Court had to interpret the meaning of the contract.

Determining the Intent of the Parties

The Court said that when interpreting a contract, it must determine the intent of the parties at the time that they entered into the agreement. The original intent of the parties would be used to guide the court's decision. In this contract, the parties agreed that arbitration would be conducted in accordance with rules of the National Association of Security Dealers (NASD), which states that arbitrators may award "damages and other relief." The NASD manual further provides that "No agreement [between a member and a customer] shall include any condition which . . . limits the ability of a party to file any claim in arbitration or limits the ability of an arbitrators to make any award." However, the contract also states that it is governed by New York law, which permits only courts to award punitive damages. These conflicting provisions create an ambiguity in the contract.

Ambiguous Terms

Under common law, ambiguous terms in a contract are interpreted against the party that drafted the contract. Ambiguous terms can be understood in different ways. This view of ambiguity protects the party who did not prepare the contract. A party that had no input in drafting a contract cannot be blamed for that contract's ambiguities. As stated in the Restatement (Second) of Contracts § 206, Comment A (1979):

"Where one party chooses the terms of a contract, he is likely to provide more carefully for the protection of his own interests than for those of the other party. He is also more likely than the other party to have reason to know of uncertainties of meaning. Indeed, he may leave meaning deliberately obscure, intending to decide at a later date what meaning to assert. In cases of doubt, therefore, so long as other factors are not decisive, there is substantial reason for preferring the meaning of the other party."

Because Shearson Lehman Hutton prepared the contract for the Mastrobuonos' signatures, any ambiguity must be interpreted in favor of the Mastrobuonos.

Holding The contact between the parties is ambiguous. Under well-established rules of common law, ambiguities in a contract are construed against the party who wrote the contract. As a result, the arbitration panel's award of punitive damages was upheld.

Questions for Analysis

1. What type of contract is involved in this case?
2. Why did Shearson Lehman Hutton force the Mastrobuonos to participate in arbitration?
3. Why didn't Shearson Lehman Hutton agree with the full decision of the arbitration panel, when they were the party who wanted the dispute to be resolved through arbitration?
4. What does a court attempt to determine when it interprets a contract?
5. What common law rule does a court apply when interpreting an ambiguous contract?
6. What is the purpose of the rule addressed in question 5?

Web Resources

Go to the *Understanding Business and Personal Law* Web site at ubpl.glencoe.com for information about how to access online resources for the Landmark Cases.

UNIT 3

UNIT OVERVIEW

Throughout your life, you will take part in transactions involving the sale of goods. Laws intended to promote efficient economic relationships and protect you as a consumer govern these contracts. In this unit, you will learn about these laws by studying the following topics:

- Contracts for selling goods
- The law of warranties
- Consumer protection law
- Purchasing and selling automobiles
- Personal property, intellectual property, and bailments

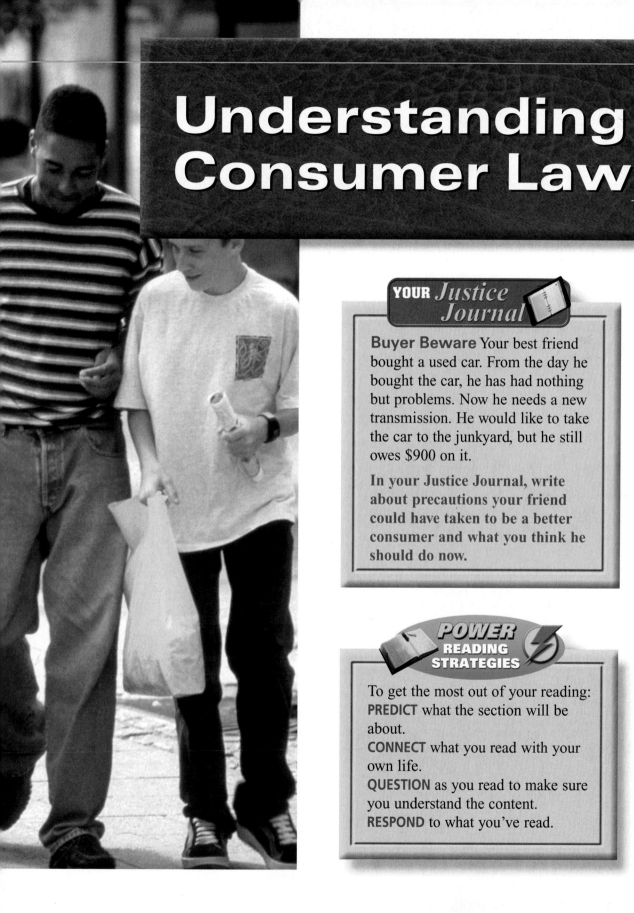

Understanding Consumer Law

Contracts for the Sale of Goods

Understanding Business and Personal Law *Online*

Chapter Overview Visit the *Understanding Business and Personal Law* Web site at ubpl.glencoe.com and click on Chapter 13: Contracts for the Sale of Goods—Chapter Overviews to preview the chapter information.

The Opening Scene

Starting in this chapter, you will see how laws regulating sales affect the lives of the Lee family. Mei Lee, 22, is a senior in college. Her brother, An Lee, 16, is a high school sophomore. They both live with their parents. Mei is trying on wedding gowns at The Blushing Bride, a local bridal shop. Her mother is with her.

The Blushing Bride

Mei: *(Stepping out of the dressing room with a smile.)* How about this one, Mom?

Mrs. Lee: It's stunning!

Proprietor: Gorgeous!

Mei: *(Viewing herself in a mirror.)* I like it, too. Can we afford $869 for this dress, Mom?

Mrs. Lee: *(Frowning.)* I was hoping to pay less, but it is beautiful. Let's go to one more store before we decide.

Mei: *(To the proprietor.)* Can you hold this dress for a week while I think about it?

Proprietor: I'll be glad to. *(The proprietor gives Mei a sales slip stating that the dress will be held for one week, at the price of $869.)*

Mei: *(Five days later, talking with her brother.)* An, have you ordered your tuxedo for the wedding yet?

An: Don't worry. I'm going to look for one tonight on an Internet auction site.

Mei: You don't have much time. I'm supposed to pick up my wedding dress tomorrow. Did you hear? At the last store we visited we found a pretty dress for just $400 if we paid cash.

Mr. Lee: *(That evening, reading the newspaper.)* Mei, didn't you buy your dress from a shop on the corner of 60th Street and 8th Avenue? It says here that the building burned down last night.

Mei: Oh, no! My wedding dress was in there!

Mrs. Lee: We should call that other store, The Blushing Bride, and tell them you'll take that expensive dress.

An: *(Sauntering into the room.)* I just got a tux online. Perfect size, too. They'll mail it to me when they receive the money. Dad, can you spare $50? They want me to send cash. Don't worry about my paying you back. One of Mei's college friends says he will buy the tux from me for $55 when the wedding's over.

Mr. Lee: Are you sure you know what you're doing? Is it safe to send cash?

Mei: *(Next day, on the phone with the proprietor of The Blushing Bride.)* This is Mei Lee. I've decided to buy that wedding dress you're holding for me.

Proprietor: Oh, I'm sorry. You didn't leave any deposit, so we sold it to someone else.

An: *(The day before the wedding.)* My tuxedo just came, but the pant legs are six inches too short!

Mr. Lee: We'll just call you "the blushing usher."

What Are the Legal Issues?

1. Is the proprietor's promise to hold the wedding dress binding without payment of a deposit?
2. When the other store burned, who had title to Mei's dress? Who had the risk of loss? Is Mei entitled to get her money back?
3. What risks did An take when he bought his tux at the Internet auction? Does he have a legal remedy against the seller?
4. Was An's plan to sell the tux to Mei's friend a legal sale? Can the friend get good title from An?

The Sale and Lease of Goods

What You'll Learn

- **When to apply the law of sales in your daily life**
- **How to describe the special rules for sales contracts**
- **How to determine when sales contracts must be in writing**
- **How to explain the rules for auctions and bulk sales**

Why It's Important

As you learn more about the law of sales, you will be better able to protect your legal rights and your money when buying or selling a product.

Legal Terms

- sale
- price
- goods
- Uniform Commercial Code
- contract to sell
- merchant
- usage of trade
- firm offer
- output contract
- requirement contract
- auction with/without reserve
- bulk transfer

Sales

In the previous eight chapters, you studied general contract law, which governs contracts for such things as real estate, employment, and personal services. This chapter explains a different type of law—the law of sales—that governs contracts for the sale and lease of goods. A **sale** is a contract in which ownership of goods is transferred from the seller to the buyer for consideration. The consideration is also known as the **price**, or the money that is paid for goods. **Goods** are all things that are moveable, such as your clothing, books, pens, food, car, and even the gas you put in your car. Money, stocks, and bonds are not considered goods.

The law of sales grew from the practices of business people, merchants, and mariners in early English times. In those days, merchants administered the law in their own courts. As time went on, the early law of sales combined with English common law and eventually was put into a code (a collection of laws) called the English Sale of Goods Act.

In 1906, a code of law called the Uniform Sales Act was introduced in the United States. It was similar to the English Sale of Goods Act, and over a period of years, was enacted by the legislatures of 35 states. However, it proved to be inadequate. As interstate commerce (trade between the states) developed, the need arose to make uniform the many commercial laws in effect among the states. The result was the development of the Uniform Commercial Code (UCC) in 1952. The **Uniform Commerical Code** is a collection of laws that governs various types of business transactions. When you enter a contract involving goods, the UCC will apply.

Example 1. Malika got a summer job at a Smoothie Shop on the same day that her parents bought a new house. To celebrate, her family went out to dinner. The day's activities involved three different contracts. Malika's oral employment contract and her parents' written contract to buy the house are governed by the law of contracts discussed in Unit 2. In contrast, the family's oral contract with the restaurant for dinner is a sale of goods and is governed by the UCC.

One purpose of UCC is to combine the laws relating to commerce into a single uniform code. Another purpose of the UCC is simplify, clarify, and modernize the law governing commercial transactions. A third purpose is to encourage the expansion of commercial practices through custom, usage, and agreement of the parties. Thus, the many rules governing the various phases of a business transaction may be now found in a single code that is uniform throughout the land. The UCC is the law, at least in part, in every state. Louisiana, a former French possession, has developed its legal system after the pattern set by the Roman Code. Its legislature has adopted part, but not all, of the UCC. Louisiana has not adopted Article 2 governing the sale of goods that is discussed in this chapter.

The Sales Contract

A sales contract may involve either a sale or a **contract to sell**. Every time you buy goods and take ownership of them, a sale occurs. On the other hand, if you will take ownership at some future time, the agreement is a contract to sell, not a sale.

Example 2. Darnell mows lawns in his neighborhood to make money in the summer. He went to a store to buy a new power mower, but the model he wanted was out of stock. The store

SPENDING MONEY
Buying and selling is a part of everyday life.
Is the purchase of clothing from a designer outlet store a contract governed by the UCC?

clerk agreed to order the mower for Darnell to pick up in a week. Darnell knew that his friend, Foster, was interested in buying his used mower. He offered to sell the mower to Foster for $25. Foster accepted his offer and paid Darnell.

Darnell's contract with the hardware store is a contract to sell because he will not take ownership of the mower until a week later. In contrast, his deal with Foster is a sale because Foster took immediate ownership of the mower for the agreed price.

Contracts for Both Goods and Services

When a contract includes both goods and services, the dominant element determines the type of contract. For example, if your parents buy a furnace and have it installed, the sale of goods—the furnace—is dominant and the laws of the UCC apply. However, if your parents have their furnace serviced and some new parts are installed, the performance of services is dominant and the common law of contracts applies instead.

Special Rules for Sales Contracts

With some exceptions, the UCC applies to all sellers and buyers of goods. A **merchant** is a business or person who deals regularly in the sale of goods or who has a specialized knowledge of goods. A nonmerchant is a casual or occasional seller. For example, you are a nonmerchant when you sell a used CD to a music store.

> *Example 3.* Farley, owner of a shoe store, bought 100 pairs of sneakers from Best-Ever Sneakers, Inc., a manufacturer. Both Farley and Best-Ever are merchants because selling is their profession.

A sales contract must contain the same elements as other contracts, but the UCC has relaxed some of the strict rules of contract law. The following flexible rules apply in all contracts for the sale of goods.

Good Faith   Parties to a sales contract must treat each other fairly.

Methods of Dealing and Usage of Trade   When parties have previously dealt with each other, those methods of dealing may be used to supplement or qualify the terms of their sales contract. This rule is true with any **usage of trade**, which is the method of dealing that is commonly used in the particular field.

Russia

What if you were forbidden to listen to your favorite music, read a popular book, or attend church? Suppose you weren't even allowed to express your opinions. For much of the twentieth century, Russian citizens were denied these basic rights. In the late 1980s, however, under the leadership of Mikhail S. Gorbachev (1985–1991), the policy of Glasnost (openness) was officially adopted by the former Soviet Union. In an effort to free up many aspects of Soviet life, Glasnost removed bans from books, movies, and plays, and even permitted criticism of the political system. In 1990, the former Soviet Union promised religious freedom. The parliament also passed a new press law banning manipulation of the mass media, including newspapers, radio, and television. For many Russians, freedom of expression still comes at a high price. Nevertheless, says Gorbachev, "tremendous gains allowed Russia to go forward. It will never return to the past." Here's a snapshot of Russia.

Geographical area	6,592,692 sq. mi.
Population	144,978,573
Capital	Moscow
Legal system	Based on civil law system
Language	Russian
Religion	Russian Orthodox
Life expectancy	67 years

Critical Thinking Question Is censorship of public information and restriction of social or political activities ever appropriate? List several examples. For more information on Russia, visit **ubpl.glencoe.com** or your local library.

Formation of a Sales Contract   You may make a contract in any manner that shows that the parties have reached an agreement. It may be oral (with some exceptions) or in writing. A contract may be created even if the time it was made cannot be determined or any terms have been left open.

Acceptance of an Offer   In most situations, you may accept an offer by any means and in any reasonable manner. However, the party

making the offer may request a particular method to be used for the acceptance. A contract comes into existence when the acceptance is sent and the method used is reasonable.

Different or Additional Terms   An acceptance may have different or additional terms added without a complete rejection of the offer. These different or additional terms are treated as proposals for additions to the contract if both parties are not merchants. If both parties are merchants, the revised terms become part of the contract unless they require a major change or the party making the offer objects.

Firm Offer   A **firm offer** is a merchant's written promise to hold an offer open for the sale of goods. It does not require payment to be binding. A merchant cannot revoke a firm offer during the time stated in the offer or for a reasonable time if none is stated. However, no offer can stand for longer than three months.

Open-Price Terms   A sales contract may be made without a settled price. Unless the parties agree on a price prior to delivery, a reasonable price can be settled at the delivery time.

Output and Requirement Terms   Output and requirement contracts are allowed even if they are not definite. For example, a retailer might agree to buy all of a backpack manufacturer's backpacks. An agreement to buy all of a manufacturer's goods is an **output contract**. On the other hand, Tri-State Petroleum Distributors might agree to sell all of the gasoline needed by the Gabriel Trucking Company. This agreement is a **requirement contract**, which occurs when a seller agrees to supply the needs of a buyer.

Modification   No consideration is necessary to change a contract for the sale of goods. The modification may be oral, unless the original agreement is in writing and states that it must be modified in writing. This kind of statement is only effective when signed by the customer.

Leasing Goods

You can apply the sale-of-goods rules to the leasing of goods, with a few modifications. Rentals for items such as a DVD player, tuxedo, computer, or car are governed by the UCC.

Form of Sales Contracts

Many sales contracts are oral rather than written. They are often made by telephone, at a store counter, or face-to-face between private

Figure 13.1

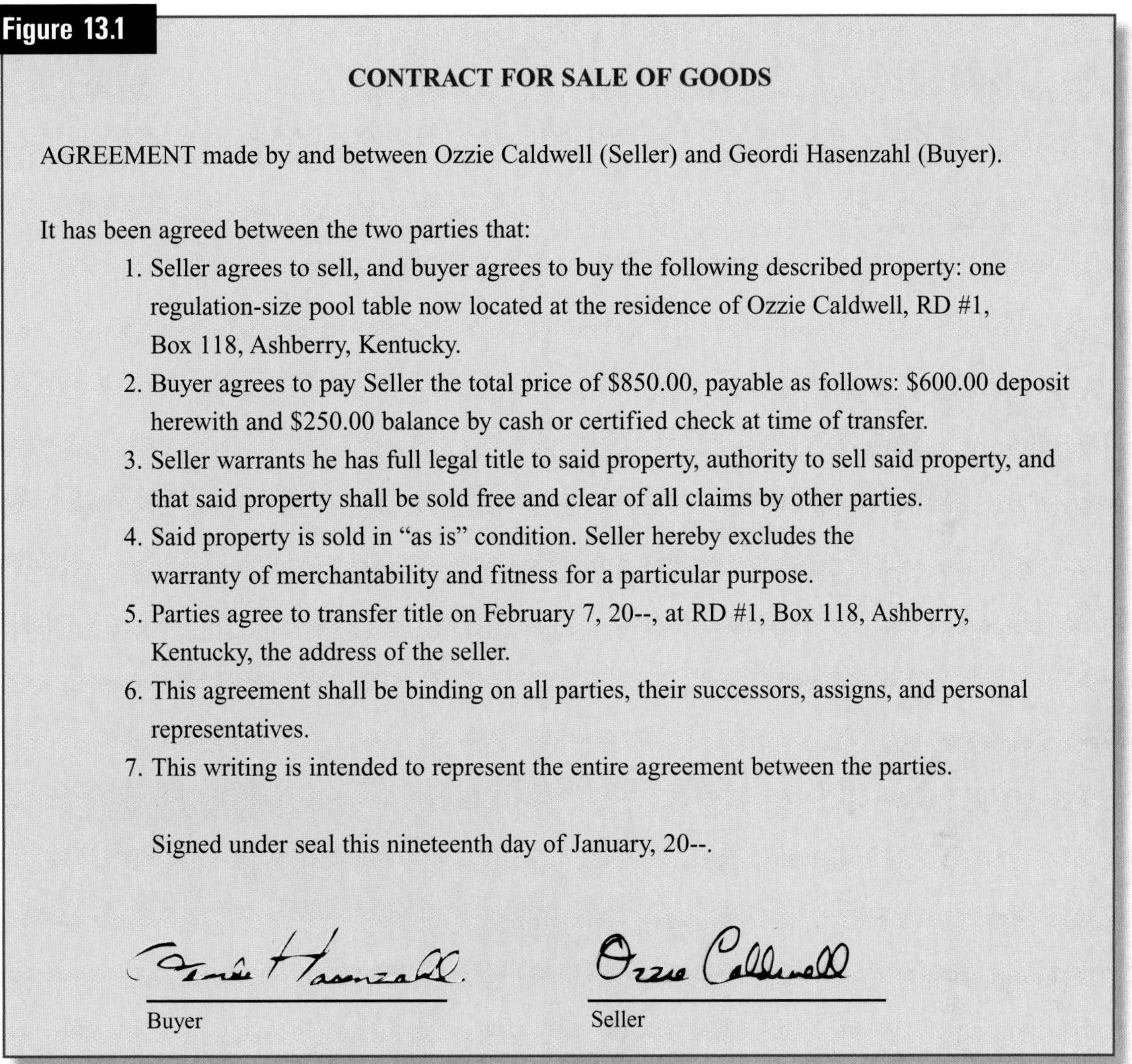

CONTRACT FOR SALE OF GOODS

AGREEMENT made by and between Ozzie Caldwell (Seller) and Geordi Hasenzahl (Buyer).

It has been agreed between the two parties that:

1. Seller agrees to sell, and buyer agrees to buy the following described property: one regulation-size pool table now located at the residence of Ozzie Caldwell, RD #1, Box 118, Ashberry, Kentucky.
2. Buyer agrees to pay Seller the total price of $850.00, payable as follows: $600.00 deposit herewith and $250.00 balance by cash or certified check at time of transfer.
3. Seller warrants he has full legal title to said property, authority to sell said property, and that said property shall be sold free and clear of all claims by other parties.
4. Said property is sold in "as is" condition. Seller hereby excludes the warranty of merchantability and fitness for a particular purpose.
5. Parties agree to transfer title on February 7, 20--, at RD #1, Box 118, Ashberry, Kentucky, the address of the seller.
6. This agreement shall be binding on all parties, their successors, assigns, and personal representatives.
7. This writing is intended to represent the entire agreement between the parties.

Signed under seal this nineteenth day of January, 20--.

_____   _____
Buyer   Seller

---

parties or businesspeople. As long as the price is less than $500, an oral contract for the sale of goods is enforceable. If the price is $500 or more, a sales contract must be in writing to be enforceable (see Figure 13.1). This rule, however, does not apply when:

- A written confirmation of an oral contract between two merchants is sent within a reasonable time, and no objection is made within 10 days.
- The contract involves specially manufactured goods that cannot be resold easily.

FORMAL WRITING UNNECESSARY
Any writing signed by the party against whom enforcement is sought will satisfy the writing requirement. This would include words on a check, a piece of scrap paper, or even a napkin. *Would skywriting by an airplane pilot satisfy the writing requirements of the UCC?*

Buying More Than He Can Afford?

Angelo was promoted to district manager of a chain of music stores. His new job would require him to travel, and he wanted to travel in style. He immediately went to a car dealer to buy a new car. He ordered a custom color, a CD player, leather seats, and a moon roof.

By the time the new car was delivered to the dealer, Angelo realized he had overestimated the raise he received with the promotion and couldn't possibly afford the car. *What are the ethical issues in this case? Should Angelo buy the car even though he can't afford it?*

- The buyer receives and accepts the goods or pays for them.
- The parties admit in court that they entered into an oral contract.

Other Sales Governed By UCC Rules

There are other sales that are governed by UCC rules. These sales include auction sales and bulk transfers.

Auction Sales

Have you ever attended an auction at your school or in your community? In an auction sale, the auctioneer presents goods for sale and invites the audience to make offers, or bids. This process allows people to negotiate, or set their own prices. At a live auction, bidders in the crowd respond with their offers, and the auctioneer accepts the sale. Bids may be withdrawn at any time before the acceptance. If a new bid is made while the gavel is falling, the auctioneer can either reopen the bids or declare the goods sold.

In an **auction with reserve**, the auctioneer doesn't have to sell the goods for the highest bid if it's lower than the reserve amount. The auctioneer may withdraw the goods at any time before a sale is completed. On the other hand, in an **auction without reserve**, the auctioneer

IDENTIFIABLE GOODS Goods must be identified before title to them can be transferred to someone else under a sales contract. *Under what circumstances might identifiable goods, such as fruit, be treated as a future good?*

must sell the goods to the highest bidder. The goods cannot be withdrawn from bidding unless no bid is made. An auction sale is with reserve unless it is expressly stated that it is without reserve.

Have you visited an online auction Web site when searching for a new CD or plane tickets? Internet auctions have become increasingly popular. They offer opportunities to buy and sell goods locally and worldwide. Internet auctions can be person-to-person or business-to-person. In person-to-person auctions, sellers offer items directly to consumers. The highest bidder must deal directly with the seller to arrange for payment and delivery. In contrast, operators of business-to-person auctions have control of the items and handle the payment and delivery of goods.

Internet auction fraud is a concern. Sometimes sellers don't deliver the goods, or they deliver something less valuable than the item they advertised. At other times, sellers fail to deliver an item when they say they will. The Federal Trade Commission (FTC) provides information about Internet auctions in its free brochures and at its Web site.

Bulk Transfers

Sometimes a business transfers all merchandise and supplies at once, known as a **bulk transfer**. The UCC rules require that the buyer of the bulk goods notify all of the seller's creditors at least 10 days before the transfer will take place. The creditors then have the opportunity to take legal steps to get the money that is owed them before the transfer of the goods. Before this rule existed, merchants owing money could sell out their entire stock for less than it was worth.

Law & Academics

Social Studies
Before people exchanged money for goods, people traded goods for goods. This type of sale is called barter. The discovery of nonlocal objects at many archaeological sites suggests that barter existed in prehistoric times.

Research Activity
Anthropologists have found bartered goods throughout the world. Research a country that still uses barter as an important method of exchange. Find out what types of goods are bartered and how a value is placed on those goods. Write a one-page paper that explains your findings.

Section 13.1 Assessment

Reviewing What You Learned
1. When do you use the law of sales?
2. What special rules apply to sales contracts?
3. When must sales contracts be in writing? What are the exceptions?
4. What are some rules for auctions and bulk sales?

Critical Thinking Activity
Law of Sales When you contract for something that includes both goods and services, such as having wall-to-wall carpeting installed in your home, how should you determine whether to apply the law of sales?

Legal Skills in Action
Auctions Conduct a two-part mock auction of music CDs in front of your class. Have your classmates bring in CDs to be auctioned. (Be sure to mention that everything will be returned to the rightful owners after the auction.) Arrange for the first part of the role-play to be an auction without reserve and for the second part an auction with reserve.

Ownership and Risk of Loss in Sales of Goods

What You'll Learn

- How to differentiate between passage of title and risk of loss in sales contracts
- What you can do when someone breaches a sales contract

Why It's Important

Being informed about ownership and risk of loss when you make sales contracts will help you protect your investment when buying or selling products.

Legal Terms

- title
- bill of sale
- voidable title
- risk of loss
- identified goods
- future goods
- carrier
- f.o.b.
- destination contract
- bill of lading
- warehouse receipt

Title

The right of ownership to goods is known as **title**. People who own goods have title to them. A **bill of sale** is formal evidence of ownership (see Figure 13.2). You receive this document when you buy a jacket at a department store or a new stereo system at an electronics store. A bill of sale only proves that you once had title, not that you still own the goods.

Example 4. Steven bought a snowboard from his neighbor Sylvia for $200 and received a bill of sale. He then sold the snowboard to his friend, Mohammed. The day after this sale, Steven wrongfully contracted to sell the same snowboard to Jamie. He presented the bill of sale from Sylvia as proof of his ownership. This meant nothing, however, because Steven no longer had title.

Voidable Title

Anyone who obtains property as a result of another's fraud, mistake, undue influence, or duress holds only voidable title to the goods. **Voidable title** means title that may be voided if the injured party elects to do so. This kind of title is also received when goods are bought from or sold to a minor or a person who is mentally impaired. Anyone with voidable title to goods is able to transfer good title to others.

Example 5. Mariah, 16, bought a used car for $700. Six months later, she sold the car to her 19-year-old cousin, Jason, for $750. Mariah had voidable title because she was a minor, but Jason received good title because he was a good-faith purchaser for value.

Buying from a Merchant

The UCC has a special rule that allows merchants who have no title to goods to pass on good title to their consumers. This occurs when you entrust your own goods to a merchant who sells them in the ordinary course of business.

Figure 13.2

BILL OF SALE

Price

Name and
address of buyer

Receipt

Goods sold

Warranty

Date

Signature
of seller

Name and
address of seller

In consideration of Two Hundred Dollars ($200) paid by

Steven Forman, 7 Maple Ave., Youngstown, OH, the receipt of

which is hereby acknowledged, I, Sylvia Boswell, do hereby

sell and convey to Steven Forman one HomeCraft snowblower

No. F3711.

And hereby covenant that I am a lawful owner of the

goods and agree to warrant and defend their sale against any

lawful claims and demands of all persons.

Witness my hand and seal this 15th day of February 20--.

Sylvia Boswell

Sylvia Boswell
11 Hemlock Drive
Youngstown, OH

Example 6. Mrs. Chin left her watch at a jewelry store to be repaired. The jewelry store sold used watches as part of its regular business. A salesperson at the jewelry store sold Mrs. Chin's watch to a customer by accident. The customer who bought the watch received good title to it and will be able to keep it. Mrs. Chin's claim is against the jewelry store for the tort of conversion.

WHO OWNS THE GOODS?
A seller gives you a bill of sale as formal evidence of ownership. *Does it prove that you own the goods?*

The UCC's law governing merchants gives you confidence you will receive good title when you buy from a merchant. However, UCC laws such as the one described in Example 6 do not apply in the case of stolen goods, because only the rightful owner has title to stolen property.

Passage of Title and Risk of Loss

Sometimes it is necessary to determine who has title to goods—the seller or the buyer. In a bankruptcy case, for example, only goods to which the debtor has title can be taken by the court to satisfy creditors' claims. Some of the goods in the debtor's possession may be owned by someone else; other goods that have left the debtor's possession may still be owned by the debtor; still other goods that have not yet been delivered to the debtor may be owned by the debtor.

Similarly, it is sometimes necessary to determine who must bear the **risk of loss**, or the responsibility for loss or damage to goods. The reason is that goods may be stolen, damaged, or destroyed after the sales contract has been entered but before the transaction is completed. Title to goods cannot be transferred under a sales contract until the goods have been identified. **Identified goods** are goods that presently exist and that have been set aside for a contract.

After the goods are identified, title passes to the buyer when the seller does what is required under the contract to deliver the goods. Goods that are not both existing and selected are known as **future goods**, such as crops that are not yet grown or items that have not yet been manufactured. No one can have title to future goods. They may only be the subject matter of a contract to sell at a later date.

Shipment Contract

A shipment contract is one in which the seller turns the goods over to a carrier for delivery to a buyer. A **carrier** is a transportation company. In a shipment contract, the seller is not responsible for seeing that goods get to their destination. Both title and risk of loss pass to the buyer when the goods are given to the carrier (see Figure 13.3).

Shipment contracts are often designated by the term f.o.b., which designates the place of shipment, such as Boston (see Figure 13.4). The term **f.o.b.**, or *free on board*, means that goods will be delivered free to the designated place. The buyer must pay the freight charges from the shipping point to the destination. Thus, f.o.b. Boston means that the seller will put the goods on freight cars or trucks in Boston, but the buyer will pay all expenses from there.

At the shipping point, the goods become the responsibility of the buyer. Title and risk of loss are transferred when the seller delivers the goods to the carrier for shipment.

TITLE AND
RISK OF LOSS
Usually title and risk of loss pass at the same time. *When do title and risk of loss pass when no delivery is required?*

Figure 13.3	**Passage of Title and Risk of Loss**	
Terms of Contract	**Title Passes**	**Risk of Loss Passes**
Shipment contract	When goods are deliverd to carrier	When goods are delivered to carrier
Destination contract	When goods are tendered at destination	When goods are tendered at destination
No delivery required	When contract is made	*Merchant seller:* When buyer receives goods; *Nonmerchant seller:* When seller tenders goods to buyer
Document of title	When document of title is given to buyer	When document of title is given to buyer
Agreement of the parties	At time and place agreed upon	At time and place agreed upon

Figure 13.4	Abbreviations

Abbreviation	Meaning
f.o.b. New York	Free on board to New York (This would be a *shipment contract* if shipped from New York.)
f.o.b. Los Angeles	Free on board to Los Angeles (This would be a *destination contract* if shipped from New York.)
c.o.d.	Collect on delivery
c.i.f.	Cost of goods shipped, insurance and freight
c.f.	Cost of goods shipped and freight
f.a.s.	Free alongside vessel or at a dock

SHIPPING TERMS In a shipment contract, the seller has no responsibility for seeing that the goods reach their destination. *Who has this responsibility?*

Example 7. A business in New York ships 100 DVD players to Florencia, a customer in Los Angeles. The shipping terms are f.o.b. New York. Title to the DVDs and risk of loss would be transferred to Florencia as soon as the DVD players are delivered and accepted at the freight depot in New York.

Destination Contract

When a contract requires the seller to deliver the goods to a destination, it is a **destination contract**. Both title and risk of loss pass to the buyer when the seller leaves the goods at the place of destination. Destination contracts are often designated by the expression f.o.b. shipping destination. Goods shipped under such terms belong to the seller until they have been delivered to the destination; also, risk of loss remains with the seller until that point.

Example 8. If Florencia, from Example 7, did not wish to accept the responsibility of ownership during shipment of the DVDs, she could have the delivery made f.o.b. Los Angeles. The seller, under such terms, would pay the freight charges from New York to Los Angeles.

When no delivery is required and the contract calls for the buyer to pick up the goods, title passes to the buyer when the contract is made.

Example 9. Aleksei contracted to buy a camcorder from Maria. Neither party to the contract was a merchant. Aleksei gave Maria a $50 deposit at the time of contracting and agreed to pick up the camcorder and pay the balance in two days. Title to the camcorder passed from Maria to Aleksei at the time of contracting because Maria could make delivery without moving the goods.

When goods are not to be shipped by carrier, the passage of risk of loss depends on whether the seller is a merchant or a private party. If the seller is a private party, the risk of loss passes to the buyer when the seller delivers the product. This occurs when the seller offers to turn the goods over to the buyer.

Example 10. Suppose that in Example 9, Maria offered to turn the camcorder over to Aleksei at the agreed time. However, Aleksei refused to take it at that time, saying that he would pick it up in two weeks. Three days later, the camcorder was stolen from Maria's house. Because Maria is a private party, Aleksei must suffer the loss and still pay the contract price to Maria.

If the seller is a merchant, however, the risk of loss is transferred from the seller to the buyer when the buyer receives the goods. Thus, if Aleksei had been in the same situation with a dealer, he would not have suffered the loss. The merchant would have been responsible for the loss. Instead of following these rules, the parties may agree to other times and places regarding the risk of loss.

Documents of Title

Sometimes when you buy goods you receive a document of title, rather than the actual goods. A document of title is a paper giving you the right to receive the goods named in the document. When you give the document of title to the holder of the goods—a warehouse or

Virtual Law

Contracts and the Computer

A university was having problems tracking students who failed to pay financial aid loans. To address this problem, the university took two steps. First, it bought a new mainframe computer. This contract involved only hardware and was a sale-of-goods. Second, it bought software from the same company and had the company write programs to handle its software needs. Because the software purchase was secondary to the computer purchase, this combination of contracts is a sale-of-goods. Software packages that are bought on the open market are considered to be sale-of-goods contracts.

Connect Using the Internet, find a copy of a standard sale-of-goods contract. Then develop a sample contract that may be used in the scenario presented in this feature.

WAREHOUSE RECEIPTS
A warehouse receipt can serve as a document title when goods are stored in a warehouse. *How might a warehouse receipt serve to transfer title?*

carrier—you can receive possession of them. Both title and risk of loss pass to the buyer when the document is delivered to the buyer.

One type of document of title is a bill of lading. A **bill of lading** is a receipt for shipment of goods given by a transportation company (known as a carrier) to a shipper when the carrier accepts goods for shipment. Another type of document of title is a warehouse receipt. A **warehouse receipt** is a document given to a customer by the warehouse that is storing his or her goods.

> *Example 11.* Sanchez stored a large quantity of wheat in a grain elevator, and in return, was given a warehouse receipt. Later, Sanchez sold the wheat to Karen. Upon receipt of the money for the wheat, Sanchez signed and delivered the warehouse receipt to Karen. Karen received title to the wheat when the document was delivered to her.

Remedies for Breach of Sales Contract

There are some remedies that can be used when there is a breach of a sales contract. These specific remedies for both the buyer and the seller are prescribed by the UCC.

Seller's Remedies

Sometimes buyers refuse to accept goods after ordering them. Buyers may do so because they are dissatisfied with products they receive or because their needs have changed since the time when they originally purchased the products. They may also refuse to pay for the goods. In such situations, the seller may:

- Cancel the contract.
- Withhold delivery of goods.
- Stop delivery of any goods that are still in the possession of a carrier.
- Resell any goods that have been rightfully withheld, and bring a claim against the buyer for the difference between the agreed price and the resale price, plus expenses.
- Bring a claim against the buyer for the difference between the agreed price and the market price, plus expenses (only if the goods cannot be resold).
- Bring a claim against the buyer for the price of any goods that were accepted by the buyer.

LAWS in Your Life

Gift Certificates

Transactions for the sale of goods sometimes involve the purchase of a gift certificate. Some merchants place expiration dates on gift certificates, usually requiring that the certificates be used in six months to one year. Frequently, gift certificates expire before recipients have a chance to redeem them.

Only a handful of states have laws dealing with expiration dates on gift certificates. For example, in New Hampshire, gift certificates under $100 are not permitted to have an expiration date. In California and Rhode Island, it's against the law to put an expiration date on any gift certificate. In Hawaii and Massachusetts, sellers must honor gift certificates for a period of at least two years.

In states without laws covering expiration dates on gift certificates, it is still worthwhile to press the merchant to honor a gift certificate even when an expiration date has passed. Most merchants are concerned about their business reputations and can often be persuaded to honor an expired gift certificate or refund the cash value.

Think About It Should gift certificates have expiration dates? Why or why not? Find out if there is a law in your state regulating expiration dates on gift certificates.

Buyer's Remedies

Sometimes the seller fails to make delivery of the goods after agreeing to do so. The seller may also send improper goods, which are goods other than those that were ordered. They may also be damaged or defective goods. In these cases the buyer may:

- Cancel the contract.
- Bring a claim against the seller for the return of any money that has been paid.
- Bring a claim against the seller for the difference between the agreed price and the market price at the time the buyer learned of the breach, plus expenses.
- Refuse to accept the goods if they do not conform to the contract. The buyer must notify the seller of the rejection of the goods, and the seller then has a reasonable time in which to correct the error or defect.
- Cover the sale, or buy similar goods from someone else and bring a claim against the seller for the difference between the agreed price and the cost of the purchase, plus expenses.
- Give notice to the seller that the goods have been accepted but that they do not conform to the contract. If no adjustment is made, the buyer may bring a claim against the seller for breach of contract or warranty.
- Revoke the acceptance and return the goods if a serious defect were undetectable, or if the buyer were led to believe that the seller would fix the defect.

Section 13.2 Assessment

Reviewing What You Learned

1. When does title pass from the seller to the buyer in a sales contract? When does the risk of loss pass?
2. What remedies are available when a seller breaches a sales contract? When a buyer breaches a contract?

Critical Thinking Activity

Fairness Suppose you leave your ring at a jewelry store to be appraised and the store sells it by mistake to an innocent purchaser. Under the UCC, the innocent purchaser receives good title to your ring. Is this rule fair? Support your argument.

Legal Skills in Action

Contracts Involving Minors If you are under the age of 18 when you buy goods, you can return them and get your money back. You lose this right when you become 18. Present a point of view to the class regarding whether this rule is reasonable.

E-Commerce and the Law

Why It's Important

Electronic commerce is on the cutting edge of today's business world. As you learn more about electronic commerce, you will advance further in today's society.

Legal Terms

- electronic commerce
- electronic signature
- online privacy
- Federal Trade Commission (FTC)

Electronic Commerce

Have you ever shopped online? Computers, software, books, wireless phones, DVD players, CDs, clothing, cars, toys, games, sports equipment, and beauty supplies are just a few examples of items that you can purchase online. Because all of these items are goods, the same law of sales applies as when you purchase something from a store.

Technology has allowed many changes to come about quickly, in our personal lives and the business world. **Electronic commerce**, also called e-commerce, is the buying and selling of goods and services, or the transfer of money, over the Internet. As the world moves forward with new technological developments, however, the law sometimes lags behind. This is particularly true in the rapidly developing field of e-commerce.

Shopping Safely on the Internet

Shopping online offers many benefits. You can shop at any time you please, and you can find almost anything you want, often at bargain prices. While shopping on the Internet can be as safe as shopping in a store, there can be some dangers. There are some ways that you can shop safely on the Internet, however, and avoid these dangers (see Figure 13.5).

Shop with Companies You Know Anyone can establish an Internet business. If you're not familiar with a business, ask for a catalog to learn about the company. Find out about return and refund policies before placing your order.

Keep Your Password Private Be creative when you establish a password for purchasing goods online. Avoid using a telephone number, birth date, or a portion of your Social Security number. Instead, use a combination of letters, numbers, and symbols that a stranger would have a hard time figuring out. Most importantly, never give your password to anyone.

Pay by Credit or Charge Card You will be protected by the Fair Credit Billing Act (see Chapter 22) if you pay by credit or charge card. This method of payment gives you the right to dispute certain charges

Figure 13.5

INTERNET AUCTIONS

Internet auctions provide excellent opportunities to find good buys, but they can be risky. Do your homework before buying online.

1 Know the Seller

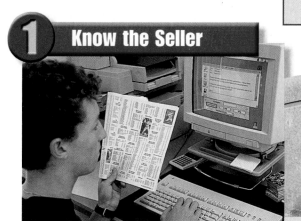

Verify the seller's identity (including telephone number), and find out what form of payment the seller will accept before you bid.

2 Know the Product

Before placing a bid, know exactly what you're buying and try to determine its value.

3 Know the Auction Site

Find out how the auction works and what protections the site offers buyers before bidding.

4 Know How to Bid

Never bid on an item you don't plan to buy. Establish your top price, and stick with it. Protect your privacy by never giving out your Social Security number, driver's license number, or bank account number.

and temporarily withhold payment while a creditor investigates. Verify the online security before giving your credit card number.

Keep a Record Print a copy of your purchase order and confirmation number for your records. Keep in mind that the federal Mail-and-Telephone Order Rule (see Chapter 15) covers orders made over the Internet. Consequently, unless stated otherwise, merchandise must be delivered within 30 days, and the company must notify you of delays.

Worldwide Shopping

Online shopping has opened up a world of available goods. With the click of a mouse, you can order sombreros from Mexico or spices from India. Shopping electronically (especially when dealing with sellers in other countries) raises many questions. Are the prices listed in U.S. dollars or another currency? Does the company ship internationally? How long will delivery take? Will unexpected taxes or duties be added to the price? Who can help you resolve any problems? Answering these questions will help you determine whether a Web site is safe for international online shopping.

SHOP AT HOME There is no limit to the kinds of items that you can buy on the Internet. *How can you safeguard Internet shopping?*

Electronic Signatures

E-Sign (Electronic Signatures in Global and National Commerce Act) is a federal law that permits the use of electronic signatures and records. An **electronic signature** is a method of signing an electronic message. It identifies a particular person as the source of the message. It also indicates that person's approval of the information in the message. Under this law, an electronic signature can be used on a contract if the parties agree. The Uniform Electronic Transactions Act (UETA), adopted by numerous states, is a similar law.

Online Privacy

Do you ever worry about your privacy on the Internet? **Online privacy** is a part of your more general right to privacy. It concerns your identity, movement, and personal and commercial activities on the Internet. Privacy rights can be violated when the wrong people gain access to secret computer records. Many legal safeguards exist to protect your right of privacy.

The common law tort of invasion of privacy is grounded in your right to maintain personal privacy. The U.S. Constitution protects you from unreasonable governmental intrusion into your private life. The Fair Credit Reporting Act (see Chapter 22) protects you against the issuance by credit bureaus of inaccurate personal information. In addition, the Right to Financial Privacy Act forbids financial institutions from opening your records to the government without your permission or a court order.

Because of their lack of worldly experience, children are protected by special statutes. The Children's Online Privacy Protection Act of 1998 requires children's Web site operators to:

- Post comprehensive privacy policies on their sites.
- Notify parents about their information practices.
- Obtain parental consent before collecting personal information from children under the age of 13.

Many state legislatures are beginning to adopt laws regulating Internet privacy. However, one result of this move is that each state's laws could be different. A lack of consistency in legislation can create confusion among consumers. There is a movement for the U.S. Congress to set national standards that override state legislation. Under this plan, the **Federal Trade Commission (FTC)** would investigate violations of the FTC Act. This act states that "unfair or deceptive acts or practices in or affecting commerce are hereby declared unlawful." The FTC Act would also regulate e-commerce privacy.

Section 13.3 Assessment

Reviewing What You Learned

1. What are some tips for safe Internet shopping?
2. How can you determine the consumer friendliness of a Web site when shopping internationally?
3. Describe the law that permits the use of electronic signatures on contracts.
4. Identify legal safeguards that protect your right to computer privacy.

Critical Thinking Activity

Internet Transactions Indicate as true or false whether the UCC law of sales governs the following transactions made over the Internet:

- Buying a used computer
- Hiring lawn care services
- Buying stocks
- Selling a parcel of land
- Buying unborn puppies

Legal Skills in Action

Internet Fraud With your classmates, brainstorm about various types of Internet fraud. Discuss ways to avoid becoming a victim of fraud.

CHAPTER **13** ASSESSMENT

Chapter Summary

Section 1 The Sale and Lease of Goods

- The law of sales applies when ownership of goods is transferred from a seller to a buyer for consideration. When a contract includes both goods and services, the dominant element of the contract determines whether it is a contract for goods or a contract for services.
- Special rules for sales include: (1) contracts may result from the parties' conduct; (2) an offer may be accepted by any reasonable means; (3) an acceptance may include terms that differ from those in the offer; (4) the price need not be settled; (5) output and requirements contracts are allowed; (6) contracts may be modified without consideration; and (7) no consideration is needed for a firm offer.
- Contracts for the sale of goods of $500 or more must be in writing except in: (1) oral contracts between two merchants when a confirmation is sent and no objection is made; (2) oral contracts for specially manufactured goods; (3) admissions in court; and (4) executed oral contracts.
- In an auction sale, people place bids that the auctioneer accepts for a sale. In an auction with reserve, the auctioneer need not accept the highest bid. In an auction without reserve, the auctioneer must accept the highest bid. A bulk transfer occurs when a business transfers all merchandise and supplies at once. The UCC requires that the buyer of bulk goods notify all of the seller's creditors at least 10 days before the transfer will take place.

Section 2 Ownership and Risk of Loss in Sales of Goods

- Title to goods is passed from a seller to a buyer after the goods have been identified and the seller does what is required under the contract to deliver the goods. The risk of loss is born by the party responsible for loss or damage to goods. Usually, title and risk pass at the same time.

- When a buyer breaches a sales contract, the seller may: (1) cancel the contract; (2) withhold delivery; (3) stop delivery of goods in the possession of a carrier; (4) resell goods and bring a claim for the difference between the agreed price and the resale price; (5) bring a claim for the difference between the agreed price and the market price; or (6) bring a claim for any goods that were accepted by the buyer. When a seller breaches a sales contract, the buyer may: (1) cancel the contract; (2) bring a claim for the return of any money paid; (3) bring a claim for the difference between the agreed price and the market price; (4) reject nonconforming goods; (5) cover the sale; (6) accept nonconforming goods and bring a claim if no adjustment is made; and (7) revoke the acceptance.

Section 3 E-Commerce and the Law

- When shopping on the Internet: (1) shop with companies you know; (2) keep your password private; (3) pay by credit or charge card; and (4) keep a record.
- When buying from another country on the Internet, research the currency of prices, shipping policies, delivery time, additional taxes or duties, and customer service policies.
- The federal law that permits using electronic signatures is called E-Sign. Electronic signatures can be used on a contract if the parties agree to do so.
- Legal safeguards that can protect your right to computer privacy include: the common law tort of invasion of privacy, your right against unreasonable government intrusion into your private life, the Fair Credit Reporting Act, the Right to Financial Privacy Act, and the Children's Online Privacy Protection Act.

Consider the key terms in the list below. Then use these terms to complete the following exercises.

auction without reserve

bill of lading

bulk transfer

carrier

contract to sell

destination contract

digital signature

document of title

e-commerce

electronic signature

firm offer

f.o.b.

future goods

goods

identified goods

merchant

output contract

price

requirement contract

risk of loss

sale

shipment contract

title

Uniform Commercial Code

usage of trade

voidable title

warehouse receipt

1. Write 8 to 10 sentences, using as many of these legal terms as possible.
2. Rewrite the sentences, leaving a blank line in place of the legal term.
3. Working with a partner, see how many of each other's sentences you can complete correctly.

The Law Review

Answer the following questions. Refer to the chapter for additional reinforcement.
4. When does the passage of title generally occur?
5. What does it mean to have the risk of loss? Do passage of title and risk of loss occur at the same time?
6. How may an offer for the sale of goods be accepted?
7. Under the law of sales, what does the term *goods* mean?
8. What is an output contract? a requirements contract?
9. When must a contract for the sale of goods be in writing? What are the four exceptions to this requirement?
10. To what does the law of sales apply, as defined by the UCC?
11. What are seven special rules for contracts for the sale of goods?
12. When a contract for the sale of goods is breached, what remedies are available to the seller? to the buyer?
13. When does the risk of loss pass to the buyer?

Linking School to Work

Acquiring and Evaluating Information

During your lifetime, you will sign your name thousands of times—on checks, loan applications, and other business-related documents. Electronic signatures are now legal, but many people are skeptical about them. Conduct research about electronic signatures and answer the following questions:

14. How are they created?
15. What measures are in place to ensure their security?
16. How long will they last?
17. What economic impact will they have on online business?

Let's Debate

Risk of Loss

While reading the newspaper want ads, Marcia discovers a stereo system for sale. When she called the phone number listed in the ad, she realized it was her neighbor Tom who was selling the stereo. Tom was asking $550 for the system, and Marcia agreed to purchase it for that price. Marcia gave Tom a $100 deposit. Because Marcia was leaving the next day to go on vacation, she asked Tom to deliver the stereo to her home when she returned.

A week later, while Tom was transporting the stereo to Marcia's home, he dropped it and it smashed to pieces. Marcia wants her deposit back; Tom wants the other $450. He told Marcia he was just doing her a favor by delivering the stereo to her and she still owed him for the system.

Debate

18. If Tom took Marcia to court for the $450, would he win? Explain your answer.

19. If Marcia took Tom to court, what legal arguments do you think she could make? Explain your answer.

Grasping Case Issues

For the following cases, give your decision and state a legal principle that applies.

20. Brian buys a CD player from Kerri and receives his bill of sale. The next day, Brian gives the CD player to his sister, Heidi, as a birthday present. Six months later, Brian tries to sell the CD player to Jodie, showing her the bill of sale as evidence of his title to the CD player. Can Jodie rely on this evidence? Explain your answer.

21. Renee is hired by a large manufacturing company to work as a computer software engineer. Is her employment contract governed by the UCC? Why or why not?

22. One week after planting tomatoes, Ursula enters into a contract with a canning company, promising to sell the company all of her tomatoes for a particular price. Is this a sale? Explain your answer.

23. Vera agrees to buy a car from Marcus, and Marcus agrees to sell the car to her. They do not, however, agree on the price. Is there a contract? Why or why not?

24. Athena and Yvonne, co-owners of a hair salon in San Jose, California, decide to move to Portland, Oregon. They sell their business to Enrique and Shawn. The hair salon has unpaid debt for equipment installation and beauty supplies. Do Enrique and Shawn have any responsibilities under the bulk transfer section of the UCC? Explain your answer.

In each case that follows, you be the judge.

25. Title and Risk of Loss

Clouser agreed to buy a boat from Roger and Sharon Russell, owners of Performance Marine, for $8,500. Clouser made an initial payment of $1,700 and agreed to pay the balance at delivery. Performance Marine was to replace the boat's engine and drive train before Clouser took delivery. No documents of title were to be delivered by the seller. While Performance Marine was testing the boat, it hit a seawall and was completely destroyed. *Who had title to the boat at the time of the accident? Who had the risk of loss? Explain your answer.*
Russell v. Transamerica Ins. Co., 322 N.W.2d 178 (MI).

26. Auctions

Coleman bid $2,050 for a D-7 tractor at a public auction. It was not stated that the auction was with reserve. The auctioneer yelled, "Sold," accepting Coleman's bid. Later, the owner of the tractor refused to sell it for $2,050, saying that the auction was with reserve and that he could refuse to accept the bid. *Did the owner have to sell the tractor to Coleman for $2,050? Why or why not?*
Coleman v. Duncan, 540 S.W.2d 935 (MO).

Legal Link

Ethics and Technology

Todd's classmates bully him at school. As a result, Todd decides to create a Web site on which he posts the names and addresses of each of the bullies; he also includes derogatory remarks about each of them. When Todd's classmates discover the site, many complain that they have a right not to be mentioned, that their addresses are private, and that his comments constitute defamation.

Connect

27. Research the ethical implications of legislation resulting from the use of current technology. Can you find any legislation that addresses the ethical issues in this case? If yes, what are these laws, and how would they apply?

28. Develop procedural guidelines for implementing appropriate legislation. What are some of the steps that companies, agencies, and others can follow to make sure that they and their employees are obeying the law?

POWER READING STRATEGIES

29. **Predict** What problems might exist if the UCC were not a single uniform code throughout the United States?

30. **Connect** Have you ever ordered anything through a catalog, a television-shopping network, or over the Internet? How were the goods shipped to you?

31. **Question** Do you think it is fair for a buyer to refuse to accept goods after ordering them? Why or why not?

32. **Respond** There are only a few laws in place to protect consumers who buy online. If you were a lawmaker, what laws would you write for the world of e-commerce?

The Importance of Warranties

Understanding Business and Personal Law *Online*

Chapter Overview Visit the *Understanding Business and Personal Law* Web site at ubpl.glencoe.com and click on Chapter 14: The Importance of Warranties—Chapter Overviews to preview the chapter information.

The Opening Scene

An Lee is waiting for the school bus with his friend, Michael.

Wedding Gifts Gone Awry

AN: My sister and her new husband get back from their honeymoon tomorrow, but I haven't gotten them a present yet.

MICHAEL: How about one of those bird clocks that chirps every hour? My neighbor has one. She told me she wants to sell it because the noise bothers her.

AN: Cool! Maybe I'll buy it.

(Next evening, newlyweds Mei and Bruce are opening wedding presents at the home of Mei's parents.)

MEI: Oh, it's beautiful!

BRUCE: It's a lamp shade with feathers.

AN: If you ask me, that thing's for the birds. Why not open my present over there? *(He points to a crudely wrapped box.)*

MRS. LEE: They'll get to your present soon, An.

BRUCE: We'll open yours after this one from Aunt Harriet. *(He reaches for a large, heavy, flat box.)*

MEI: Oh, look! A mirror in a beautiful gold frame.

BRUCE: Look, Mei, the mirror is cracked!

MRS. LEE: Harriet will be so upset. Do you think it's covered by a warranty?

MEI: I hope so! Now for An's gift. *(Opening the present.)* How nice! A bird clock.

AN: It chirps every hour with different birdcalls.

MEI: What a wonderful gift! Thank you.

BRUCE: *(Examining the clock.)* We'll think of you every hour. Uh-oh! The small hand is missing. Did you get it at a local store?

AN: *(Embarrassed.)* I didn't notice that. I'll take it back.

MRS. LEE: One more present, and then we'll have some dessert. I have pie and An's favorite carrot cake in the freezer.

MEI: This gift is from Uncle Max.

MR. LEE: You can bet it'll be good. Max says the salesperson claimed it was the best on the market.

MEI: *(Slightly forlorn, holding up an object to her husband.)* I think it's a feather duster, don't you?

MRS. LEE: *(Screaming from the kitchen.)* Almost everything's melted in the freezer! It must have stopped working. That meat we bought for $100 last week is all ruined. At least the pies and cake are still good!

MR. LEE: Don't worry. The freezer is still under warranty.

AN: I really love this carrot cake. *(He takes a bite and suddenly puts his hand to his mouth.)* Ow! Something cut me!

MRS. LEE: Are you all right, An?

AN: *(Removing something from his mouth.)* A piece of glass! How did that get there?

MR. LEE: Your mouth is bleeding badly. Come on, I'll drive you to the hospital.

MEI: *(To Bruce.)* I guess the honeymoon's over.

What Are the Legal Issues?

1. Does Aunt Harriet have any legal recourse from the store for the damaged mirror? Do Mei and Bruce have recourse from the store, even though they did not purchase the mirror?
2. Does the used clock that An bought from his friend's neighbor have a warranty?
3. What are the legal implications of the statement, "It's the best feather duster on the market"?
4. Does a freezer's warranty cover replacing the food spoiled as a result of a mechanical breakdown?
5. What legal recourse does An have for the injuries to his mouth?

Express and Implied Warranties

What You'll Learn

- **How to describe the three ways an express warranty can be made**
- **How to state the obligations of merchants under the Magnuson-Moss Warranty Act**
- **How to contrast a limited warranty with a full warranty**
- **How to differentiate between the implied warranty of fitness for a particular purpose and the implied warranty of merchantability**
- **How to explain the warranty of title**

Why It's Important

Understanding warranties will keep you from losing money.

Legal Terms

- warranty
- express warranty
- full/limited warranty
- implied warranty
- warranty of fitness for a particular purpose
- warranty of merchantability
- usage of trade
- warranty of title

Law of Warranties

Have you ever bought a radio that wouldn't work when you took it home? Have you found an impurity or a foreign substance in a salad you were served in a restaurant? Have you ever experienced technical problems with a new computer?

The UCC provides protection in these and other situations under its law of warranties. A **warranty** is another name for a guarantee. A breach of warranty is a breach of contract.

Express Warranties

An **express warranty** is an oral or written statement, promise, or other representation about the quality, ability, or performance of a product. Express warranties apply to goods that are sold or leased. These warranties are conveyed in three ways:

- By a statement of fact or a promise made by the seller
- By a description of the goods
- By the use of a sample or model

Statement of Fact or Promise

An express warranty is created when a private party or a merchant sells goods and makes a statement of fact or a promise about the goods to the buyer. The use of formal words, such as *warranty* or *guarantee*, is not necessary, provided the statement relates to the goods and is part of the transaction.

An express warranty may be a statement of fact or a promise of something that may happen in the future. The following example illustrates a statement of an existing fact.

> *Example 1.* Maebelle wanted to sell her car to Waterio. To make her car seem more appealing, she told him the vehicle's engine had been rebuilt. Waterio bought the car but soon discovered the engine had not been rebuilt. Maebelle's statement of fact was an express warranty. Waterio may recover damages from her for breach of express warranty.

The following example illustrates a promise of something that may happen in the future.

Example 2. Nils purchased a car from Robin. As part of the deal, Robin promised the car would pass the next required inspection. When Nils had the car inspected, however, it failed. Robin's promise was an express warranty that was not fulfilled.

Express warranties are often found in sales brochures, circulars, and advertisements.

Example 3. The maker of a liquid drain cleaner advertised the product as "safe" and capable of "fast action." A child was severely injured when she was accidentally splashed with the product. The court held that the advertisement created an express warranty that the product was safe. The child's parents won their case against the company for breach of express warranty.

REBUILT ENGINE?
A statement from a car dealership that an engine is rebuilt creates an express warranty. *Can express warranties be made by private parties?*

To be useful, a warranty must be stated in precise and understandable terms. Suppose that a seller says to you, "This product is warranted," or "This product is guaranteed." These words alone are not enough to give you protection. You need to know exactly what the seller will do for you in the event that a problem arises.

Example 4. Virginia bought a hair-curling iron that was advertised in the newspaper. The ad said simply that the item was guaranteed. She used the curling iron for six months, and then it stopped working. When Virginia returned it to the store, she was told that the guarantee had been for only 90 days.

Always seek written warranties. Although express warranties do not have to be in writing, oral statements are difficult to prove. Also, under the parol evidence rule, a court may refuse to consider oral statements if a written contract exists.

Warranty law allows a certain amount of sales talk, called "puffery," that does not qualify as a warranty. A statement about the value of goods or a seller's opinion is not a warranty. "This car gets great gas mileage," or, "This is the best item on the market," are examples of puffery or opinion, not express warranties. However, a statement like, "This car gets 30 miles per gallon," is an express warranty because it is a statement of fact.

Availability before Sale

Written warranties on consumer products costing more than $15 must be made available before you buy the product. A store must put written warranties close to the product or display a sign stating that warranties can be examined upon request. Manufacturers must provide retailers with materials needed to meet their warranty requirements, such as warranty stickers, tags, signs, or posters. Manufacturers can also print the warranty on the product's package. Similarly, door-to-door salespeople must offer you copies of any written warranties before you buy their products.

Advertising Express Warranties

An advertisement stating that a product is warranted must tell you how to get a copy of the warranty before you buy the product. The following examples of print and broadcast advertisements meet this legal requirement:

- "The Bigwheel bicycle is warranted for five years. Some restrictions may apply. See a copy of our warranty wherever Bigwheel bicycles are sold."
- "See our full two-year warranty at the store nearest you."
- "We offer the best guarantee in the business. Read the details and compare wherever our fine products are sold."

▲
WARRANTY
AVAILABILITY
Written warranties on consumer products costing more than $15 must be available for you to read before you buy the product. *Why do we have this law?*

This rule also applies when you place a mail, telephone, or Internet order. The following are examples of legally sound warranty disclosures:

- "BigSmile digital cameras are backed by our two-year warranty. Write to us for a free copy."
- "Write for a free copy of our full warranty. You'll be impressed at how we stand behind our product."
- "Supersharp knives are guaranteed. Read about our 90-day limited warranty in this catalog."

Advertisers who use expressions such as "Satisfaction Guaranteed," "Money-Back Guarantee," and "Free Trial Offer" must refund the full purchase price of their product at the purchaser's request. Any conditions, such as the return of the product, must be stated in the ad. Here's an example:

- "Money-Back Guarantee! Just return the TellTime watch in its original package, and TellTime will fully refund your money."

Advertisers who warrant products for a lifetime must fully explain the terms of their promises (see Figure 14.1). The following advertisements are correct:

- "Our battery is backed by our lifetime guarantee. Good for as long as you own the car!"

Figure 14.1

Lifetime Guarantee

TACITURN MUFFLERS

WHOSE LIFE? Advertisers who warrant products for a lifetime must disclose the life to which it refers. *Why is this ad illegal?*

- "The lifetime guarantee on the Taciturn Muffler protects you for as long as your car runs—even if you sell it, trade it, or give it away!"

Magnuson-Moss Warranty Act

The Magnuson-Moss Warranty Act is a law affecting only the sale of goods sold in interstate commerce (business activities that touch more than one state). This federal act gives added protection to consumers when written express warranties are made. A consumer is someone who buys or leases goods for personal, family, or household use. When a written warranty is offered on consumer goods costing more than $10 and sold in interstate commerce, the warranty must be labeled as full or limited. A **full warranty** promises to fix or replace a defective product at no charge to the consumer. This promise must be honored by a company within a reasonable amount of time after a complaint is made. A full warranty is good for the period mentioned in the warranty, regardless of who owns the item when it breaks. If the product cannot be fixed,

FULL WARRANTY
A full warranty is one in which a defective product will be fixed or replaced for free. *Why does a manufacturer offer a warranty?*

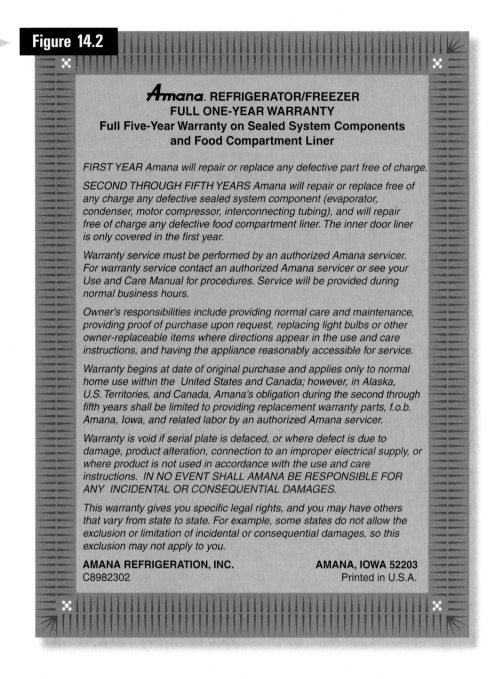

Figure 14.2

***Amana*. REFRIGERATOR/FREEZER**
FULL ONE-YEAR WARRANTY
Full Five-Year Warranty on Sealed System Components
and Food Compartment Liner

FIRST YEAR Amana will repair or replace any defective part free of charge.

SECOND THROUGH FIFTH YEARS Amana will repair or replace free of any charge any defective sealed system component (evaporator, condenser, motor compressor, interconnecting tubing), and will repair free of charge any defective food compartment liner. The inner door liner is only covered in the first year.

Warranty service must be performed by an authorized Amana servicer. For warranty service contact an authorized Amana servicer or see your Use and Care Manual for procedures. Service will be provided during normal business hours.

Owner's responsibilities include providing normal care and maintenance, providing proof of purchase upon request, replacing light bulbs or other owner-replaceable items where directions appear in the use and care instructions, and having the appliance reasonably accessible for service.

Warranty begins at date of original purchase and applies only to normal home use within the United States and Canada; however, in Alaska, U.S. Territories, and Canada, Amana's obligation during the second through fifth years shall be limited to providing replacement warranty parts, f.o.b. Amana, Iowa, and related labor by an authorized Amana servicer.

Warranty is void if serial plate is defaced, or where defect is due to damage, product alteration, connection to an improper electrical supply, or where product is not used in accordance with the use and care instructions. IN NO EVENT SHALL AMANA BE RESPONSIBLE FOR ANY INCIDENTAL OR CONSEQUENTIAL DAMAGES.

This warranty gives you specific legal rights, and you may have others that vary from state to state. For example, some states do not allow the exclusion or limitation of incidental or consequential damages, so this exclusion may not apply to you.

AMANA REFRIGERATION, INC.   **AMANA, IOWA 52203**
C8982302   Printed in U.S.A.

the owner may choose to receive a new product or a full refund. See Figure 14.2 for an example of a manufacturer's full warranty.

A **limited warranty** is any written warranty that does not meet the requirements for a full warranty. It does not promise free repair or replacement. A common limited warranty covers only parts, not labor. Other limited warranties give you only a partial refund when something goes wrong with an item, such as when a tire with a 50,000-mile guarantee fails at 30,000 miles. Some limited warranties require you to pay for shipping a product back for service. Other limited warranties cover a product only as long as it is owned by the original buyer.

Under the Magnuson-Moss Warranty Act, such a warranty must be labeled "limited warranty." When you see these words, read the warranty carefully to learn about its limitations. See Figure 14.3 for an example of a limited warranty.

Figure 14.3

DIGICAM CORPORATION
Limited Warranty

What Does This Warranty Cover? This warranty covers any defects or malfunctions in your new Digicam Camera.

How Long Does the Coverage Last? This warranty lasts as long as you own your Digicam camera. Coverage terminates if you sell or otherwise transfer the camera.

What Will Digicam Do? Digicam will replace any defective or malfunctioning part at no charge. You must pay any labor charges.

What Does This Warranty Not Cover? Batteries, or any problem that is caused by abuse, misuse, or an act of God (such as a flood) are not covered. Also, consequential and incidental damages are not recoverable under this warranty. Some states do not allow the exclusion or limitation of incidental or consequential damages, so the above limitation or exclusion may not apply to you.

How Do You Get Service? To be eligible for service under this warranty you **MUST** return the warranty registration card attached below within 30 days of purchasing the camera.

If something goes wrong with your camera, send it postage paid with a brief written description of the problem to:

Digicam Corp.
Box 10000
Digicam, Ohio

We will inspect your camera and contact you within 72 hours to give the results of our inspection and an estimate of the labor charges required to fix the camera. If you authorize repairs, we will return the repaired camera to you COD within 72 hours. You must pay any labor charges upon receipt of the repaired camera.

If you inform us that you wish us to provide necessary parts to you but you wish to have repairs performed elsewhere, we will return the camera and replacement parts to you within 72 hours.

There is no charge for inspection.

How Does State Law Apply? This warranty gives you specific legal rights, and you may also have other rights that vary from state to state.

LIMITED WARRANTY
A limited warranty gives you something less than a full warranty. *What must you do under this warranty that you would not have to do if it were a full warranty?*

Description of the Goods

Any description of the goods that is part of a transaction also creates an express warranty. The seller warrants that the goods will be the same as the description.

Example 5. Earnest ordered a handheld Global Positioning System (GPS) receiver from a catalog. The catalog described the device and showed a picture of it. When the system arrived, Earnest discovered it was not the same unit that he had seen pictured and described in the catalog. A breach of express warranty had occurred.

Sample or Model

Any sample or model that is part of a transaction creates an express warranty. When displaying a sample or model, the seller warrants that the goods sold will be the same.

Example 6. Suppose Earnest went to a store to buy the GPS receiver. The salesperson showed him several different models, and Earnest selected the one he liked best. At the checkout counter, he was given a sealed carton. At home, however, Earnest found that the carton contained a different model receiver than the one he had been shown. This is a breach of express warranty.

DESCRIPTION OF GOODS
A description of goods that is part of the transaction creates an express warranty. *What does the seller warrant?*

Implied Warranties

An **implied warranty** is a guarantee of quality imposed by law. An implied warranty is not in writing. Under the UCC, implied warranties apply only to goods that are sold; they do not encompass contracts for services. A sale is the passing of ownership of a particular item from a seller to a buyer for a price. There are three types of implied warranties:

- Warranty of fitness for a particular purpose
- Warranty of merchantability
- Warranty that comes from a course of dealing or usage of trade

Warranty of Fitness for a Particular Purpose

A **warranty of fitness for a particular purpose** is created when the seller knows the purpose for which the goods are needed. The seller advises the buyer in making a purchase, and the buyer relies on the seller's knowledge and advice. In this way, the seller warrants by implication that the goods will be fit for the purpose for which they are to be used. This warranty exists whether the seller is a merchant or a private party.

Example 7. Susan Eng went to a paint store and told the proprietor she needed the best paint to use on an outdoor concrete patio. The proprietor selected a gallon of paint from a shelf and told

Susan it would be perfect for that type of job. She bought the paint and resurfaced the patio, following the directions on the can. Two weeks later, during a heavy rainstorm, the paint washed off the patio. The proprietor had breached the implied warranty of fitness for a particular purpose because Susan had relied on the proprietor's knowledge and judgment in selecting the paint.

Warranty of Merchantability

One of the most beneficial warranties to look for when buying something is the implied **warranty of merchantability**. Under this warranty, the merchant warrants that the goods being sold are merchantable. This warranty is given only when the seller regularly sells goods of that kind. Unless disclaimed, retailers, wholesalers, and manufacturers imply such a warranty in every sale, giving assurance that their products are fit for the purpose for which they are purchased. Private parties do not provide the warranty of merchantabililty.

LAWS in Your Life

Extended Warranties

Almost any time you purchase stereo or electronic equipment, the salesperson will encourage you to buy an extended product warranty or service contract. The sale of such warranties represents big profits to the merchant. Profit margins can be up to 50 percent of the price of the extended warranty contract.

The value of buying an extended warranty can be debated. Original product warranties cover any breakdowns that might occur early in the life of the product. Most of the time, major defects will show up within the period covered by the original warranty.

If the item breaks after the original warranty expires, most states offer recourse under certain conditions. If you had repairs made under the original warranty, the seller or manufacturer must extend your warranty to cover the defect if it happens again. This is true even if the original warranty has expired.

Compare and Contrast Visit a local electronics or appliance store. Ask to see an original warranty. Then ask to see an extended warranty contract. Does the cost seem worthwhile in relation to the risk of breakdowns beyond the original warranty period?

Example 8. Norma bought a secondhand VCR from Kenneth. She saw his ad in the classified section of the newspaper. Kenneth was not in the business of selling VCRs. The VCR stopped working on the day after Norma purchased it. Because Kenneth is not a merchant, Norma does not have the benefit of the warranty of merchantability.

Merchantable goods must:
- Pass without objection in the trade under the contract description.
- Be fit for the ordinary purposes for which such goods are used.
- Be adequately contained, packaged, and labeled as the agreement may require.
- Conform to the promises or statements of fact made on the container or label, if any.

Example 9. If Norma had purchased the VCR from a local electronics store, she would have had legal recourse for breach of warranty of merchantability. Even a secondhand VCR is not merchantable if it breaks down the day after someone buys it. It is not fit for the ordinary purpose for which VCRs are used.

Some other examples of items that courts have held to be nonmerchantable include:
- Day-old chickens that had bird cancer.
- Contaminated blood received in a blood transfusion.
- Weed killer that also killed a farmer's squash.
- A boat motor that produced excessive amounts of black smoke.
- A used car that was not reasonably fit for the general purpose for which it was sold.
- Applesauce that was inedible because of poor taste and smell.
- Contaminated cheese.
- Any food containing such impurities as bits of wood, metal, or glass.

Beads and Business

Rashmika and Julia have a business making and selling beaded necklaces, bracelets, and earrings at a flea market on weekends. Some of the necklaces and bracelets are strung on elastic so that they fit snugly. One Saturday Julia found some old elastic thread for $1 a yard. She bought 10 yards of it. Rashmika was concerned that over time the old elastic would stretch or break too easily. Julia thought they could make a lot more money using the less expensive thread. *What are the ethical issues in this case? Do Rashmika and Julia have an ethical responsibility to their customers to provide the strongest, most durable product for the price?*

Usage of Trade

Another implied warranty arises from the customary ways in which the parties have dealt in the past, or **usage of trade**. For example, when a person sells a thoroughbred horse, there is an implied warranty that the seller will provide papers certifying the horse is a thoroughbred. The reason this implied warranty arises is that providing such papers has become a well-established custom among people who trade in horses.

Warranty of Title

When a merchant or a private party sells goods, the seller warrants that the title being conveyed is good and that the transfer is lawful. This is called the **warranty of title**. It includes an implied promise that, to the seller's knowledge, the goods will be delivered free from any lien, or claim by another.

If someone buys goods that turn out to be stolen, the rightful owner is entitled to return of the goods. The innocent purchaser may recover his or her loss from the seller for breach of warranty of title.

Example 10. College student Ted Grossman sold a diamond watch to a friend, Beth Bardley, for $400. A short time later, another student, Jill Lardner, saw the watch on Beth's wrist and claimed ownership. Jill said the watch had been stolen a week earlier from her dorm room, and she was able to produce the original purchase receipt to prove ownership. Although Ted didn't know the watch was stolen, he did not have good title. As a result, he could not transfer good title to Beth. Ted was therefore liable for breach of the warranty of title. Ted could also sue the person who sold the watch to him for breach of the same warranty.

Section 14.1 Assessment

Reviewing What You Learned

1. What are the three ways an express warranty can be made?
2. What are the obligations of merchants under the Magnuson-Moss Warranty Act?
3. What is the difference between a limited warranty and a full warranty?
4. What is the difference between the implied warranty of fitness for a particular purpose and the implied warranty of merchantability?
5. What is the warranty of title?

Critical Thinking Activity

Opinion or Fact A statement of fact by a seller about a product is a warranty; a seller's opinion is not. Talk with another class member and compare the following pairs of statements. Classify each statement as fact or opinion.

1. These goods are 100 percent wool.
   This is the finest wool around.
2. This truck has never been in an accident.
   This truck is solid.
3. This ink will not stain clothes.
   This ink is safe to use.
4. This is an IBM-compatible computer.
   This computer is as good as any IBM.
5. This watch is waterproof.
   This watch is durable.

Legal Skills in Action

Written Guarantees Turner is planning to sell his computer system to Lynne. It is only two years old and has a modem, color monitor, and CD-Rom drive. According to Turner, the system has never had a problem. Lynne is a little nervous about buying a used system and wants a written guarantee. In groups of two, help Turner write a warranty on his computer system.

Exclusion of Warranties, Privity, and Duty to Notify

Exclusion of Warranties

To exclude the warranty of merchantability, the word *merchantability* must be mentioned specifically. If the exclusion is in writing, the word must be written prominently. The warranty of title may not be excluded.

Example 11. Purvis bought a used car from Best Motors. Printed on the sales slip were the following words in large, bold capital letters: "THE SELLER HEREBY EXCLUDES THE WARRANTY OF MERCHANTABILITY AND FITNESS FOR A PARTICULAR PURPOSE." The car broke down two days later, but Purvis had no recourse against the car dealer for breach of either implied warranty.

Implied warranties can also be excluded by the words "as is" and "with all faults." Having buyers examine goods before the sale is another way to exclude warranties. When this is done, there is no implied warranty to cover defects because the examination should have revealed any defects in the goods.

Example 12. Teresa Quigley paid cash for a computer desk she bought from a retail furniture dealer. The sales tag attached to the desk read: "Reduced from $198 to $75, sale final, with all faults." When the desk was delivered to Teresa's home, she found that the drawers stuck and that one side was badly marked and scratched. Despite these flaws, Teresa would have no recourse in many states because of the terms of the sale. The sales tag made clear that Teresa assumed all risk as to quality. She is protected only by an implied warranty of title.

Under the Magnuson-Moss Warranty Act, any clause that excludes or limits consequential damages for breach of warranty must appear conspicuously on the face of the warranty. **Consequential damages** are losses that do not flow directly from an act but only from some of the consequences or results of the act.

Example 13. Souci bought a freezer that was warranted for one year. This sentence appeared in boldfaced type on the written

What You'll Learn

- How to recognize ways that warranties are excluded (not in force)
- How to determine who is covered by warranties made under the laws of your state
- How to explain the buyer's duty to notify the seller of a defect

Why It's Important

Knowing how warranties are excluded, to whom warranties are made, and notification requirements will help you protect your rights and the money you spend.

Legal Terms

- consequential damages
- privity of contract
- duty to notify

warranty: "In no event shall this company be liable for consequential damages." Souci filled the freezer with $1,500 worth of meat. Several days later, the meat spoiled when the freezer broke down. Under the warranty, the company has to repair or replace the freezer. However, it is not responsible for the loss of the meat, which would be considered a consequential damage.

Consumer Protection

The Magnuson-Moss Warranty Act limits the exclusions of implied warranties to consumers. Under this law, if a seller makes a written express warranty to a consumer, the implied warranties cannot be disclaimed or excluded. This law also applies if the seller gives the buyer a service contract. Implied warranties may be limited to the length of time of the express warranty, unless it is too short to be reasonable. If the length of time is limited, however, the agreement becomes a limited warranty rather than a full warranty.

Some states have gone further to protect consumers by saying that implied warranties cannot be excluded when goods are sold. If Theresa Quigley bought the computer desk in Massachusetts, New Hampshire, Oklahoma, or Rhode Island, for example, she would have received additional protection. Those states do not allow sellers to exclude implied warranties when goods are sold to consumers.

Privity of Contract Not Required

People who contract directly with each other are said to be in **privity of contract** . In the past, warranties extended only to the actual buyer of a product.

Example 14. A man purchased a can of salmon from a store. While eating the salmon, the man's young son was injured by bits of metal that were in the fish. Suit was brought on behalf of the son against the store for breach of warranty of merchantability. The case was lost, however, because the son had not purchased the salmon. There was no privity of contract between the store and the son.

The boy would have won the case if the incident had occurred today. The UCC has abolished the requirement of privity of contract. Instead, it provides states with three alternatives. In all of the alternatives, express and implied warranties extend to people who would reasonably be expected to use, consume, or be affected by the goods purchased by the buyer.

- *Alternative A* gives sellers' warranties to any person injured by a breach of warranty who is in the family or household of the buyer. Guests of the buyer are also protected. Sellers cannot exclude this provision. Warranties are not extended to corporations.

Careers in Law

Intellectual Property Attorney

Not many corporate lawyers have collections of board games in their office, but not many corporate lawyers have clients like those of Jennifer Jolley. Jolley is an associate at Stratton Ballew. She specializes in protecting the creative work, or intellectual property, of writers and other artists through patents, copyrights, and trademarks.

"People come to me with sketches for logos or trademarks," she says, "and I conduct a search to find out whether their work is similar to something already out there. I also try to make sure that the creative work of our clients—including logos, trademarks, writing, and new technology—isn't being copied or misused around the world."

One of her clients is Pictionary, Inc., the creator of the popular board game. If, for example, she discovers someone is using the logo or name that most of us associate with Pictionary, she writes a polite but firm letter to that individual or company asking them to stop. If that doesn't work, the company has the option of going to court.

"The law requires us to protect our intellectual property," says Jolley. If a company just lets things go for a few years, the court will eventually say they have no reason to complain."

Jolley especially enjoys meeting the actual inventors and creators behind the work she protects.

"Pictionary was invented by a couple of guys in an apartment," she says. "When they first started, they ran into a manufacturing snag, so they hosted a 'card-sorting party' and asked their friends to come help get everything sorted and boxed up." It worked, and Pictionary has sold more than 30 million copies.

Skills   Organizational, reasoning, and communication skills
Personality   Patient, hardworking, logical
Education   Undergraduate and law degrees. A few upper-level degree programs specialize in intellectual property. It helps to have a background in a technical field.

For more information about intellectual property lawyers, visit www.uspto.gov, www.toc.gov/copyright, **ubpl.glencoe.com**, or your public library.

- *Alternative B* gives sellers' warranties to any person injured by a breach of warranty. Warranties are not extended to corporations. Sellers cannot exclude this provision.

- *Alternative C* gives sellers' warranties to any person or corporation injured by a breach of warranty. Sellers may exclude this provision with respect to injuries to corporations, but not to individuals.

Most states have adopted one of the three alternatives. A few states, however, have written their own versions of the law. See Figure 14.4 for a listing of the alternatives that have been adopted by the states.

Duty to Notify and Remedies for Breach

To succeed in a claim for breach of warranty, the buyer must satisfy his or her **duty to notify**. This duty requires that the buyer notify

Figure 14.4		UCC Alternatives to Privity			
State	Alternative	State	Alternative	State	Alternative
Alabama	B	Kentucky	A	North Dakota	C
Alaska	A	Louisiana	NA	Ohio	A
Arizona	A	Maine	OV	Oklahoma	A
Arkansas	A	Maryland	A	Oregon	A
California	NA	Massachusetts	OV	Pennsylvania	A
Colorado	B	Michigan	A	Rhode Island	OV
Connecticut	A	Minnesota	C	South Carolina	A
Delaware	B	Mississippi	A	South Dakota	B
District of Columbia	A	Missouri	A	Tennessee	A
Florida	A	Montana	A	Texas	OV
Georgia	A	Nebraska	A	Utah	C
Hawaii	C	Nevada	A	Vermont	B
Idaho	A	New Hampshire	OV	Virginia	OV
Illinois	A	New Jersey	A	Washington	A
Indiana	A	New Mexico	A	West Virginia	A
Iowa	C	New York	OV	Wisconsin	A
Kansas	B	North Carolina	A	Wyoming	B

STATE ALTERNATIVES
Most states have adopted one of the three alternatives to privity of contract. *What alternative does your state follow?*

the seller within a reasonable time after the defect is discovered. Failure to do so will prevent the buyer from recovering.

Example 15. Norma Simms, in Example 9, waited for six months before telling the local store about the defective VCR. This wait would probably be considered beyond a reasonable time. Because of the delay in notification, Norma would most likely lose the right to recover from the store for breach of warranty of merchantability.

Often, when sellers are notified that a product is defective or that a warranty has been breached, they will arrange to correct the situation. Sellers usually exchange defective goods for undamaged goods or give the buyer a refund. When sellers do not offer an exchange or refund, the buyer may bring a claim for damages. If the buyer keeps the goods, the buyer is awarded damages that reflect the difference between the value of the goods accepted and the value the goods would have had if they had been as warranted. If the buyer has not yet received the goods, the buyer may refuse to accept them and bring a claim for any losses that were suffered.

When the warranty of title is breached, the buyer has a claim against the seller for damages. This could be the cost of clearing the title, or as with stolen goods, the purchase price of the goods.

Law & Academics

Language Arts
All new cars come with warranties. These warranties usually cover the cost of the parts and labor needed to repair defective items on your car. These warranties are usually for a limited period of time or a limited number of miles.

Research Activity
Contact car dealerships in your area and ask about the warranties they offer. Consider which ones seem most appealing to you, and which offer you the most benefits.

Section 14.2 Assessment

Reviewing What You Learned
1. To whom are warranties made under the laws of your state?
2. How may warranties be excluded under the laws of your state?
3. What is the buyer's duty to notify the seller of a defect?

Critical Thinking Activity
Warranties Clip an advertisement that mentions a warranty from a newspaper or magazine. Is the warranty express or implied? Is it full or limited? Does it offer good protection to the buyer?

Legal Skills in Action
Calculating Warranty Protection Corey paid $600 for new tires for his truck in March 2000. He chose the warranty protection the company offered, which would allow him to pay a reduced price to replace one or more of the tires during a four-year warranty period. When he had to replace a tire in March 2001, Corey paid only 25 percent of the retail cost for a new tire. When he had to replace another tire in March 2003, Corey paid 50 percent of the retail cost for a new tire. Assuming that the price of a new tire did not change during that time, what was the total cost of Corey's replacement tires?

Chapter Summary

Section 14.1 Express and Implied Warranties

- An express warranty is an oral or written statement, promise, or other representation about the quality, ability, or performance of a product. Given by manufacturers or sellers, express warranties can be made in one of three ways: (1) by a statement of fact or a promise made the seller; (2) by a description of the goods; or (3) by the use of a sample or model. The use of formal language, such as warranty or guarantee, is not necessary to convey an express warranty.

- Merchants must label written warranties as either "full" or "limited" for consumer products costing more than $10 under the Magnuson-Moss Warranty Act. The Magnuson-Moss Warranty Act is a federal act that applies only to goods sold in interstate commerce (business activities that touch more than one state).

- A full warranty promises to fix or replace a defective product at no extra charge to the consumer. The promise must be honored by the company issuing the warranty within a reasonable period of time. A full warranty is good for the period of time mentioned in the warranty, regardless of who owns the product at the time it breaks. A limited warranty is any warranty that falls short of a full warranty. Some of the stipulations or terms of a limited warranty may include: (1) the consumer pays for repair or replacement; (2) parts are covered, but labor is not; (3) only a partial refund is given; (4) the consumer pays for shipping a product back for service; or (5) the original buyer must own the product.

- A seller is responsible for an implied warranty of fitness if he or she knows the purpose for which a good is needed and makes a recommendation to the buyer. In offering advice, the seller is suggesting that he or she has expert knowledge on which the buyer should rely. This warranty exists whether the seller is a merchant or a private party. In contrast, sellers who regularly sell goods of a particular kind imply a warranty of merchantability in every sale, assuring that their products are fit for the purpose for which they are purchased. Private parties do not provide the warranty of merchantability.

- A warranty of title is made when sellers warrant that the title on a good being sold is valid and that the transfer is lawful. A warranty of title includes an implied promise that, to the seller's knowledge, the goods will be delivered free from any lien or claim by another. This warranty cannot be excluded.

Section 14.2 Exclusion of Warranties, Privity, and Duty to Notify

- A seller may exclude the warranty of merchantability by expressly mentioning that it be excluded on a warranty document. If the warranty of merchantability is excluded by written notice, the exclusion must be written prominently. Implied warranties can also be excluded by including the words "as is" or "with all faults" on a warranty document. Having a buyer examine and accept goods as being defect-free is another way to exclude warranties.

- Warranties are made to buyers of goods. Warranties also extend to those who would reasonably be expected to use or be affected by goods purchased by the buyer. People affected by a good purchased by a buyer may include people who live in the buyer's household.

- To succeed in a claim for breach of warranty, the buyer must notify the seller of the defect within a reasonable time after the defect is discovered. Failure to do so will prevent the buyer from recovering.

Using Legal Language

Consider the key terms in the list below. Then use these terms to complete the following exercises.

usage of trade	warranty of title
warranty	express warranty
full warranty	consumer
implied warranty	limited warranty
consequential damages	merchantable
warranty of merchantability	duty to notify
warranty of fitness for a particular purpose	
privity of contract	

1. Prepare a speech that explains the importance of the law of warranties to consumers. Be sure to differentiate among the various types of warranties discussed in this chapter. Refer to the chapter when necessary. Use all of the terms listed above in your speech.
2. Practice delivering your speech until you feel confident and comfortable. Then present your speech to the class.

The Law Review

Answer the following questions. Refer to the chapter for additional reinforcement.
3. In what three ways may express warranties be created?
4. Why should you try to obtain written warranties whenever possible?
5. What is the difference between a full warranty and a limited warranty? When must these warranties be mentioned?
6. When does the implied warranty of fitness for a particular purpose arise?
7. When and by whom is the warranty of merchantability given?
8. What does a warranty of title guarantee?
9. In what ways may warranties be excluded?
10. What is a lien?
11. What might happen if you accidentally purchase stolen goods?
12. Explain the significance of usage of trade as it applies to warranties.
13. What are consequential damages?
14. What is privity of contract?

Linking School to Work

Acquiring and Evaluating Information

Consumers face a risk when buying a computer. *Consumer Reports* recently conducted a survey of 54,000 readers who reported that 11 percent of computers they purchased had serious problems within the first month of ownership. Recently, Pennsylvania's state legislature considered the nation's first PC lemon law. The law was based on the automobile lemon law. Computer trade groups believe that consumers already have protection under the Magnuson-Moss Warranty Act. Conduct research on the PC lemon laws and answer the following questions:

15. Has your state passed a PC lemon law?
16. Does the Magnuson-Moss Act have any loopholes? What can you do to protect yourself against a lemon PC?

Report your findings in a one-page paper.

Let's Debate

Warranties

Julia and Franco live in California and recently purchased new furniture for their living room. They ordered it from an outlet located in North Carolina. When the furniture arrived, the fabric on the couch was ripped. Obviously, Julia and Franco were disappointed. However, when they contacted the furniture outlet, they were told that a repairperson would come the next day to fix the furniture. Julia and Franco want it replaced, not fixed.

Debate

17. What are the legal issues involved?
18. Do Julia and Franco have an implied warranty from the furniture outlet?

19. Does the warranty of merchantability cover the furniture?
20. Can the furniture outlet legally repair the furniture instead of replacing it?

Grasping Case Issues

For the following cases, give your decision and state a legal principle that applies.

21. Neal Sanborn buys a used car from a private party. While he is driving to work the next day, the car breaks down. Neal learns that the car needs major repairs. He claims breach of the warranty of merchantability. Is this claim correct?
22. Allison Rantz orders a sports jacket from a store catalog. The jacket she receives is different from the one pictured in the catalog. On what legal grounds may she obtain relief from the store?
23. Ursula Hurkin, who knows little about furnaces, tells the proprietor of the Holland Heating Supply Co. that she wants a furnace to heat her new building. The supply company measures the building and selects a furnace. After installation, Ursula discovers the furnace is too small and does not adequately heat the building. On what legal grounds may she obtain relief?
24. Jennifer Harrington purchases a new television at a discount store. The following is printed on the sales slip: "THE WARRANTY OF MERCHANTABILITY IS HEREBY EXCLUDED." Jennifer takes the television home, unpacks it, and turns it on. It does not work. A written limited warranty from the manufacturer is packed in the box. Does Jennifer have a claim against the manufacturer for breach of warranty of merchantability? Explain your answer.

In each case that follows, you be the judge.

25. Breach of Warranty

Romedy bought a car from Willett Lincoln-Mercury, Inc. He did not inspect it until four or five days after it was delivered to him. Three weeks later, he notified the dealer that the car did not contain the equipment the dealer had said it would contain. However, Romedy did continue to make payments on the car. Later, he brought suit against the dealer for breach of warranty. *Should he be eligible to recover damages? Explain your answer.*
Romedy v. Willett Lincoln-Mercury, Inc., 220 S.E.2d 74 (GA).

26. Liability

David Gentile suffered severe head injuries while playing in a high school football game. His helmet, furnished by the school, was seven years old. Each year the school sent the helmet to a reconditioning company for repair. Gentile brought suit against the manufacturer of the helmet and the reconditioning company for breach of warranty. *Can the reconditioning company be held liable? Why or why not?*
Gentile v. MacGregor Mfg. Co., 493 A.2d 647 (NJ).

Legal Link

Extended Warranties

Blake spent his summer savings on a new DVD player, which he purchased at a local electronics store. The salesperson tried very hard to sell Blake an extended warranty on his new equipment, but Blake wasn't sure what the extended warranty would provide.

Connect

Using a variety of search engines; help Blake learn more about extended warranties. Find out:

27. What extended warranties cover.

28. How much they cost.

29. Where they can be purchased.

30. If there are any laws in your state covering extended warranties.

Create a handout explaining your research that you could share with others.

POWER READING STRATEGIES

31. **Predict** Do you think similar products should have similar warranties? Wouldn't that make it easier to comparison shop?

32. **Connect** When you plan to purchase a product, do you research the warranty and use it as a factor in making the decision to purchase?

33. **Question** Why do you think some companies offer only limited warranties?

34. **Respond** What would you do if you purchased a defective product and the seller from whom you purchased it refused to correct the situation?

Consumer Protection and Product Liability

Understanding Business and Personal Law *Online*

Chapter Overview Visit the *Understanding Business and Personal Law* Web site at ubpl.glencoe.com and click on Chapter 15: Consumer Protection and Product Liability—Chapter Overviews to preview the chapter information.

The Opening Scene

Mrs. Lee is talking with a salesperson in the living room of the family's house.

Trouble with the Mail

SALESPERSON: *(Writing up an order.)* This is the best vacuum cleaner on the market, ma'am. Believe me, you can't go wrong with this model. Sign right here. *(Hands her the order sheet.)*

MRS. LEE: *(Signing.)* When will it be delivered?

SALESPERSON: In about two weeks. Thank you.

(Mrs. Lee lets the salesperson out just as Anita, the neighborhood mail carrier, comes up the walk.)

ANITA: *(Handing her some letters and a small package.)* Good afternoon, Mrs. Lee. I've got a lot for you today.

MRS. LEE: *(Disappointed.)* Oh, I've been expecting a large package.

ANITA: That'll come by truck. I only carry small items.

MRS. LEE: Thanks. Have a nice day.

(As she begins to close the front door behind her, Mrs. Lee hears a noise. She turns to see Anita sprawled on the front sidewalk beside Jason, the young boy who lives next door. A silver scooter lies nearby, and mail is all over the yard.)

ANITA: Ooowww, my back!

JASON: *(Upset.)* I didn't mean to hit her. The wheel of my scooter fell off!

MRS. LEE: Let me help you. *(Assisting Anita to her feet.)* That's a brand-new scooter, isn't it, Jason?

JASON: I got it yesterday.

MRS. LEE: Let's help pick up the mail.

(She and Jason help Anita pick up the mail. The carrier limps off, just as the school bus stops at the corner down the street.)

MRS. LEE: Come inside, Jason. You've scraped your elbow. Let me wash it and put a bandage on it.

AN: *(Bouncing into the house and heading toward the refrigerator.)* What's in the mail, Mom?

MRS. LEE: *(Opening a package.)* Greeting cards? I didn't order these. Look, there's a note asking me to return them if I don't want them. Well, maybe when I get around to it. . . . *(Tossing the package onto a table.)* I was hoping your father's birthday present would come. I ordered it more than six weeks ago.

(Two hours later, Mr. Lee arrives home.)

MRS. LEE: Honey! You're home early!

MR. LEE: I thought I'd surprise you. *(He carries a large box into the kitchen.)*

MRS. LEE: What's that?

MR. LEE: Something for you. Go on, open it.

MRS. LEE: *(Opening the box.)* Oh, my! *(Her face turns red.)* A new vacuum cleaner!

MR. LEE: I got it wholesale through one of our suppliers. He said it's the best one on the market!

What Are the Legal Issues?

1. What is the meaning of the claim, "It's the best vacuum cleaner on the market"?
2. On what legal grounds might Mrs. Lee return the vacuum cleaner she bought from the salesperson?
3. Is Mrs. Lee obligated to return the greeting cards? Must she pay for them if she keeps them?
4. Does Mrs. Lee have any recourse against the catalog company for the lateness of the birthday present she ordered?
5. Does the mail carrier have recourse against anyone for her injuries?

Consumer Protection

Why It's Important

Knowledge of consumer protection laws will prevent you from falling victim to fraud and deception.

Legal Terms

- *caveat emptor*
- *caveat venditor*
- consumer
- unfair and deceptive practice
- fraudulent misrepresentation
- cease and desist orders
- bait and switch
- cooling-off rule
- telemarketers

The Development of Consumer Protection Law

Years ago, smart shoppers understood the Latin phrase, *caveat emptor*, which means, "let the buyer beware." The reason is that consumers who bought faulty merchandise in the past had few ways to seek compensation for damages other than through the contract law discussed in Unit 2. When they were injured by dangerous products, they often had no recourse because they were not in privity of contract with manufacturers.

Society, however, now demands that manufacturers be held responsible for foreseeable injuries to people who use their products. Laws have changed, and the phrase that now guides consumer transactions is *caveat venditor*, which means, "let the seller beware."

Federal and State Consumer Protection Laws

Consumer protection laws apply to transactions between consumers and people conducting business. A **consumer** is someone who buys or leases goods, real estate, or services for personal, family, or household purposes. When you buy a ticket to a concert or rent skis for personal use from a business, consumer protection laws protect you. However, if you acquire the same things from another consumer, then consumer protection laws in most states do not protect you. Nor do consumer protection laws protect you if you buy a product to use in a business.

State consumer protection offices provide information and help enforce state consumer protection laws. Sometimes the offices assist consumers with individual problems. Consumer protection offices are located in state and county offices, and in some cities, in the mayor's office.

Federal consumer protection law applies to businesses that sell real estate, goods, or services in interstate commerce, or business activity that touches more than one state.

Example 1. Levina Yepez grows vegetables on her farm, and she sells them to a local store and at her roadside stand. Because her business is local, federal consumer protection law does not apply.

Instead, the consumer protection laws and other laws of her state regulate her business.

The Federal Trade Commission (FTC) is the agency of the U.S. government that promotes free and fair trade competition. The Bureau of Consumer Protection safeguards consumers against unfair, deceptive, or fraudulent practices. Both organizations investigate violations of federal consumer protection law.

Unfair and Deceptive Practices

An **unfair and deceptive practice** is an act that misleads consumers. Most states have enacted either the Uniform Deceptive Trade Practices Act or their own similar laws. In Texas, for example, the Texas Deceptive Trade Practices Act (DTPA) was enacted to protect consumers against false, misleading, and deceptive business and insurance practices, and unconscionable actions and breach of warranty. Although state laws differ, all are similar to federal law. If you believe you are the victim of an unfair or deceptive practice, you might start by contacting the business with your complaint. Figure 15.1 provides an example of a complaint letter that you might send.

CONSUMER PROTECTION
Federal Consumer Protection law applies to interstate commerce. *Does federal consumer protection law apply to a local farmstand business?*

Virtual Law

Internet Auction Fraud

By far the most reported Internet-related offense is Internet auction fraud. According to the Internet Fraud Complaint Center, Internet auction fraud comprised over 46 percent of referred fraud complaints in 2002, nearly 8 percent more than the previous year. Nondelivery and payment comprised 31 percent of complaints and credit/debit card fraud were nearly 12 percent. (Source: IFCC 2002 Internet Fraud Report)

Connect Visit the Web site for the Federal Trade Commission or related government site and find out what is being done to combat Internet auction fraud.

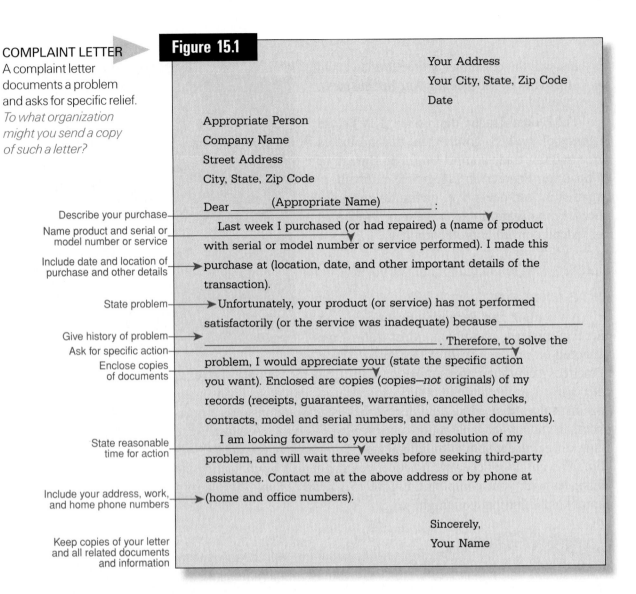

COMPLAINT LETTER
A complaint letter documents a problem and asks for specific relief. *To what organization might you send a copy of such a letter?*

Figure 15.1

Your Address
Your City, State, Zip Code
Date

Appropriate Person
Company Name
Street Address
City, State, Zip Code

Dear _____(Appropriate Name)_____ :

Describe your purchase —
Name product and serial or model number or service —

Last week I purchased (or had repaired) a (name of product with serial or model number or service performed). I made this

Include date and location of purchase and other details —

purchase at (location, date, and other important details of the transaction).

State problem —

Unfortunately, your product (or service) has not performed satisfactorily (or the service was inadequate) because _____

Give history of problem —
Ask for specific action —
Enclose copies of documents —

_____ . Therefore, to solve the problem, I would appreciate your (state the specific action you want). Enclosed are copies (copies—*not* originals) of my records (receipts, guarantees, warranties, cancelled checks, contracts, model and serial numbers, and any other documents).

State reasonable time for action —

I am looking forward to your reply and resolution of my problem, and will wait three weeks before seeking third-party assistance. Contact me at the above address or by phone at

Include your address, work, and home phone numbers —

(home and office numbers).

Sincerely,

Your Name

Keep copies of your letter and all related documents and information

Fraudulent Misrepresentation

A **fraudulent misrepresentation** is any statement that deceives the buyer. A fraudulent misrepresentation usually occurs when a seller misstates the facts about something that is important to the consumer.

Example 2. Worried about the safety of her drinking water, Kristin Holt answered a newspaper ad that read, "free home water testing." A company representative came to her house and added some tablets to a glass of tap water. The representative said the water would change color if it were unsafe. Sure enough, the water quickly turned blue. Believing this "proof," Kristin bought an expensive water-treatment device. She discovered later, however, that the tablet used to test her water caused all water to turn blue. She really didn't need a water purifier.

A Global Perspective: Laws Around the World

Haiti

It is becoming increasingly common for U.S. citizens to adopt children from Latin America, including Haiti. Conservative figures estimate that close to 500,000 children under age 18 live on Haiti's streets. Even so, the adoption laws for would-be American parents are rigorous. Children, for example, are only eligible for adoption if they meet the U. S. immigration law's definition for "orphan"—a child under age 16 whose parents are deceased, have disappeared, or are incapable of providing care. Adoptive parents or a single parent must be over age 35 (compared to age 25 in U.S. adoptions). One parent may be under the age limit, but only if the couple is childless and has been married for 10 years. Furthermore, Haitian law allows children out of the country only after specific requirements have been fulfilled. First, a surviving parent or guardian must sign a release form. The form then must be turned over to the Haitian Ministry of Social Affairs who, before authorizing, investigates the medical and psychological fitness of the parties involved. Finally, the Haitian Civil Court accepts the authorization and issues the official adoption decree—or the "Acte d'Adoption." The entire process may take only a couple of months or more than a year. Here's a snapshot of Haiti.

Geographical area	**10,714 sq. mi.**
Population	**7,063,722**
Capital	**Port-au-Prince**
Legal system	**Based on Roman**
	civil law system
Language	**French, Creole**
Religion	**80% Roman Catholic**
Life expectancy	**50 years**

Critical Thinking Question The Internet advertises children for adoption from all around the world. Do you think this is a good or bad idea? Why? For more information about Haiti, visit **ubpl.glencoe.com** or your local library.

Making false statements about the construction, durability, reliability, safety, strength, condition, or life expectancy of a product is another deceptive practice. It is also deceptive not to disclose any fact that would cause a buyer to avoid entering into a contract. For example, it would be

WORKING AT HOME
Home employment schemes are often examples of fraud. *Why do you think these schemes are one of the oldest kinds of classified advertising fraud?*

unlawful and unethical for a realtor to avoid informing a consumer about major structural problems in a house.

Work-at-Home Schemes

You may see ads in newspapers and magazines that make offers similar to the following: "Would you like to earn hundreds of dollars a week at home in your leisure time? Let us tell you how. . . ."

This offer sounds attractive, especially if you cannot leave your home to work or if you are looking for extra money. Some ads even target students directly. However, you need to be cautious about work-at-home ads, especially if they promise large profits in a short time. Some work-at-home plans are legitimate, but home employment schemes are among the oldest kinds of classified advertising fraud. Many of these ads fail to say, for example, that you may have to work many hours without pay. You may also have to pay for newspaper ads or job supplies. Consumers deceived by these ads have wasted thousands of dollars, not to mention valuable time and energy.

Unordered Merchandise

Have you ever received something you did not request in the mail, as Mrs. Lee did in The Opening Scene? Under federal and state laws, such unordered merchandise may be considered a gift. You can keep it without paying anything.

Only two kinds of products can be sent legally through the mail without the consumer's consent: manufacturers' free samples and merchandise mailed by charities. It is illegal for anyone who sends free samples to include a bill. Similarly, you don't have to contribute to a charity that sends you something free.

False Advertising

The FTC regulates false advertising on the national level and has the power to issue **cease and desist orders**. These orders are legally binding orders to stop a practice that would mislead the public.

Example 3. A company ran an advertisement that said, "Yes, it's true. There is a safe, harmless medicated liquid called Cleerex that dries up pimples overnight. . . . Many users report that they had a red, sore, pimply face one night and were able to surprise their friends the next day with a clear complexion." A doctor testified at a hearing that Cleerex would dry up and remove pimples, but not overnight. The FTC ordered the company to stop advertising that the product would work that quickly.

Bait and Switch Advertising

In **bait and switch** advertising, a store advertises bargains that do not really exist to lure customers in hopes that they will buy more expensive merchandise. This practice is illegal because the advertiser is trying to sell a different product than the one advertised.

Example 4. Irma was looking for a new digital audio player and saw one advertised on sale for $99.98 at The Mayday department store. When Irma went to buy one, the clerk discouraged her by pointing out the player's faults. Instead, he tried to get her to buy a unit that cost $299.95.

BAIT AND SWITCH
Bait and switch is an illegal advertising practice. *In this photograph, what is the bait? What is the switch?*

Bait and switch is a violation of FTC regulations and many state laws. The following sales practices may be signs of a bait and switch:
- Refusing to show, demonstrate, or sell the advertised product
- Attempting to discourage customers by criticizing the advertised product
- Claiming the advertised products are out of stock
- Refusing to promise delivery of the advertised products within a reasonable period of time
- Demonstrating products that are more expensive than the advertised items

FTC Trade Regulation Rules

The FTC has established trade regulation rules for interstate commerce to correct wrongdoing in the marketplace. These rules protect you when you buy goods.

Negative Option Rule

When you subscribe to a magazine, CD club, or other plan that sends products regularly, the negative option rule applies. Under such plans, the seller sends you announcements describing the current selection. If you want the selection, you do nothing; the seller will ship it to you automatically. If you do not want the selection, however, you must tell the seller not to send it, and there is a deadline for notification. Under the negative option rule, sellers must tell you:

- How many selections you must buy, if any.
- How and when you can cancel your membership.
- How to notify the seller when you do not want the selection.
- When to return the "negative option" form to cancel shipment of a selection.
- When you can get credit for the return of a selection.
- How postage and handling costs are charged.
- How often you will receive announcements and forms.

Be sure to read the contract carefully before signing up with any such plan. Consider the overall cost, including any shipping charges. If you do subscribe, keep copies of the seller's promotional materials and any forms that you return to the seller. Also record the dates that you mail these forms.

The Cooling-Off Rule

Have you ever attended a jewelry sale or craft fair at someone's home or a local school? When you buy something at a location that is not the seller's permanent business location, you may be able to cancel the transaction. The **cooling-off rule** gives you three business days to cancel contracts for most purchases made away from the seller's regular place of business. The rule applies to purchases of $25 or more made at the buyer's home, workplace, or dormitory. It also applies to consumer product parties given in private homes and to sales made in rented hotel rooms, fairgrounds, and restaurants.

Under the FTC rule, the salesperson must inform you of your right to cancel at the time that the sale takes place. The salesperson must also give you two copies of a cancellation form (one to keep and one to send) and a copy of your contract or receipt. The contract or receipt must be dated, show the name and address of the seller, and explain your right to cancel. If you decide to cancel, sign and date one copy of the cancellation form. Then mail or deliver it by hand to the address given for cancellation before midnight of the third business day after the contract date. Keep the other copy for your records. Send the cancellation form by certified mail for proof of mailing. You do not have to give a reason for canceling. The seller must do the following within 10 days:

- Cancel and return any papers you signed
- Refund your money
- Tell you whether any product left with you will be picked up
- Return any trade-in

This cooling-off rule does not apply to contracts for real estate, insurance, securities, or emergency home repairs.

Telemarketing Sales Rule

The Telemarketing Sales Rule protects you from abusive **telemarketers**, the people who try to sell you products by telephone. See Figure 15.2 for tips that will help you handle telemarketing calls. The rule gives consumers the power to stop telemarketing calls. It also gives state law enforcement officers the authority to prosecute fraudulent telemarketers. Under the Telemarketing Sales Rule:

- It's illegal for telemarketers to call you if you've asked not to be called. If telemarketers persist in calling, hang up and report them to your state Attorney General's office.

Figure 15.2

When Someone Tries to Sell You Something over the Phone

- Don't give your credit card, checking account, or Social Security number to unknown callers.
- Don't pay for something merely because you'll get a "free gift."
- Get all information in writing *before* you agree to buy.
- Check out a charity before you give. Ask how much of your donation actually goes to the charity. Ask that written information be sent to you so you can make an informed giving decision.
- Don't invest your money with an unknown caller who insists you make up your mind immediately.
- If the offer is an investment, check with your state securities regulator to see if it is properly registered.
- Don't send cash by messenger or overnight mail. If you use cash rather than a credit card in the transaction, you may lose your right to dispute fraudulent charges.
- Make sure you know the per minute charge for any 900 number call you make.
- Be cautious of statements that you've won a prize—particularly if the caller says you must send money to claim it.
- Don't agree to any offer where you have to pay a registration or shipping fee to receive a "prize."
- Check out unsolicited offers with the Better Business Bureau, local consumer protection agency, or state Attorney General's office *before* you agree to send money.
- Beware of offers to "help" you recover money you may have lost previously. Be wary of callers saying they are law enforcement officers who will help you get your money back "for a fee."

If you have been a victim of telemarketing fraud, call 1-877-987-3728; write to P.O. Box 45600, Washington, DC 20026-5600; or visit www.consumer.gov/knowfraud.

You may contact your local law enforcement agency. The Telemarketing Sales Rule gives local law enforcement officers the power to prosecute fraudulent telemarketers who operate across state lines.

You may also wish to contact the Federal Trade Commission about your complaint. Although the FTC cannot represent you directly in a dispute with a company, it can act when it sees a pattern of possible law violation. Contact the Consumer Response Center by phone, toll-free at 1-877-FTC-HELP (382-4357), TDD: 202-326-2502; by mail: Consumer Response Center, Federal Trade Commission, Washington, DC 20580; or use the online complaint form at www.ftc.gov.

TELEMARKETING TIPS These tips can help you avoid trouble when a telemarketer calls. *Why should you not give private information, such as your Social Security number, to unknown callers?*

LAWS in Your Life

Blowing Smoke

There is no doubt that smoking tobacco is harmful to your health. For this reason, cigarette packs display warning labels about the health risks of smoking. Tobacco companies use these labels as the basis for their defense in product liability suits. They point out that smokers are aware of the risks of smoking but choose to smoke anyway. This defense relies on the legal theory that the person assumed the risk of harm when using the product. Beginning in the mid-1990s, documents were discovered showing that tobacco companies were aware that nicotine is addictive. These documents also showed that company officials were aware that smoking poses health risks such as heart disease, lung and mouth cancer, and emphysema. These companies were later found to have deliberately withheld much of this information from the public.

Join the Debate Is it fair to make tobacco companies liable for the harm caused by smoking if smokers are aware of the risks? Can you think of other products that are legal but known to cause great harm? Should the makers of these products be held liable in the same way that the cigarette makers are now being held liable?

- Calling times are restricted to the hours between 8 A.M. and 9 P.M.
- Before beginning their sales pitch, telemarketers must inform you that they are making a sales call and identify the company that they represent.
- It's illegal for telemarketers to make false statements about their goods or services.
- Telemarketers must tell you the total cost of the products or services offered and any restrictions that apply. In a prize promotion, they must tell you the odds of winning and that no purchase or payment is necessary to win. If you're asked to pay for a prize, hang up.
- It's illegal for a telemarketer to withdraw money from your checking account without your permission.
- You do not have to pay for: credit repair (promises to change or erase inaccurate negative information from your credit report); recovery room (promises to recover previously lost money to telemarketing scams); or advance-fee loans (promises to guarantee a loan for a fee paid in advance).

900-Telephone-Number Rules

Many people confuse 900 numbers with 800 numbers. However, if you dial a 900-area-code telephone number, you are charged for the call. Sometimes consumers have been charged excessively for 900-number services or have not received the services advertised after calling. Some 900-number scams may disclose a cost per minute but do not reveal that you must listen for many minutes to hear all of the information. Other services use announcers who speak so quickly that you need to call back to understand the message. You should protect yourself against 900-number scams (see Figure 15.3).

FTC regulations say that when you dial 900 numbers, you must be warned of the cost of the calls. You must also be given a chance to hang up before being charged. Further, telephone companies must block service to 900 numbers at your request. Telephone customers must be sent pay-per-call disclosure statements annually and any prefix other than 900 is prohibited for use as a pay-per-call service. Telephone companies cannot disconnect phone service to customers who refuse to pay for 900-number calls. Rules have also been established to resolve billing disputes.

Shopping by Mail, Telephone, Fax, or Internet

The FTC has established rules to protect you when ordering goods by mail, telephone, fax, and the Internet. Sellers must ship goods within the time they promise in their catalogs or advertisements. If no time is stated, sellers must ship goods within 30 days after receiving an order. You have the right to cancel orders and get your money back if time limits are not met. Sellers must notify you of any delay in shipment and give you a postcard or other free means of responding to the delay.

900-NUMBER SCAMS
There are several ways to protect yourself against 900-number scams. *Why should you not confuse 900 numbers with 800 numbers?*

Figure 15.3

Protect Yourself Against 900-Number Scams

Deal only with reputable companies.
You may see well-known companies or organizations sponsor such 900-number services as opinion surveys or sports information. The costs, usually low, are stated upfront. If you are interested in these services and are willing to pay for them, these are usually legitimate 900-number operations to call.

Think twice before calling a 900 number for a "free" gift.
You may see television ads or receive postcards or phone calls urging you to call 900 numbers for "free" gifts when you make the 900-number call.

Know precisely what the 900 call will cost—before you make the call.
Companies should state costs upfront as flat rates or—if the cost is per minute—the maximum number of minutes for the call. Unfortunately, even with this information, you may still pay to hear sales pitches for bogus products or services.

Don't confuse 900 numbers with toll-free 800 numbers.
You pay for a 900-number call. The company pays for an 800-number call.

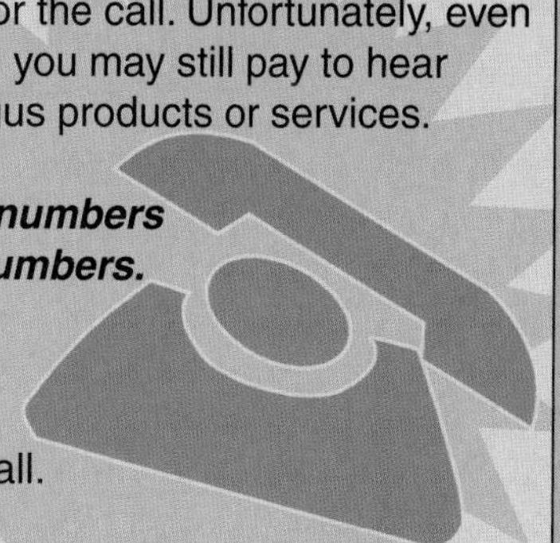

See Figure 15.4 for an example of such a notice. When buyers are notified of a delay in a shipment of goods, they may either cancel the order and get their money back or agree to a new shipping date.

Figure 15.4

Dear Customer:

Thank you for your order. We are sorry to inform you that there will be a delay in shipping the merchandise you ordered. We shall make shipment by the revised shipping date of (date). It is quite possible we could ship earlier.

You have the right to consent to this delay or to cancel your order and receive a prompt refund. Please return the card in the enclosed postpaid envelope with your instructions indicated by checking the appropriate block.

Unless we hear from you prior to shipment or prior to *the revised shipping date,* it will be assumed that you have consented to a delayed shipment on or before the definite revised shipping date stated above.

Sincerely yours,

Name & Title of Signer
Company Name
Address

Enclosure: Envelope

☐ Yes, I will accept a further delay in shipment of my order for this item until _____

(Insert date which is 30 days or less.)

☐ I cannot wait. Please cancel my order for this item and promptly refund my money. _____

Please Sign Here

MAIL ORDER
This letter might be sent by an Internet seller to a buyer when there is a delay in shipment of goods ordered. *What federal agency requires such a notice of delay in shipment?*

Section 15.1 Assessment

Reviewing What You Learned

1. What are the main differences between state and federal consumer law?
2. Describe two unfair and deceptive practices, and using examples, identify given consumer transactions.
3. What is bait and switch advertising?
4. What are four FTC rules designed to protect consumers?

Critical Thinking Activity

Laws of Retail and Commercial Sales Using the Internet, library, or other resource, research consumer protection laws. Distinguish between the laws that apply to retail and commercial sales, for example, the Uniform Commercial Code and Deceptive Trade Practices Act.

Legal Skills in Action

Your Rights as a Consumer Consider one of the ways in which you might purchase goods. Research cases of appropriate consumer protection laws. Present your findings in a brief one-page paper.

Product Liability

What is Product Liability?

Have you ever heard about a car being recalled for the repair of defective parts at no cost to the owner? Did you ever read in the news about a food, drug, or other item being recalled because it was unsafe? Such recalls occur because manufacturers and sellers have product liability.

Example 5. In 2001, Firestone Tire and Rubber Company recalled thousands of tires mounted on sport utility vehicles and gave customers new tires. Defects in the tires may have caused many motor vehicle accidents.

Under **product liability** law, someone who is injured from a product's unsafe or defective condition may recover damages. Manufacturers, sellers, and suppliers of goods can all be held responsible.

Strict Liability

You do not have to prove a negligent act on the part of the manufacturer or seller if you are hurt using a defective product. **Strict liability** makes manufacturers or suppliers responsible for selling goods that are unreasonably dangerous. This is true even when the manufacturer or seller has not been negligent. It is also true when the user of the product is not the one who bought the item. People who are injured or who suffer property damage from a defective product may recover from the manufacturer or seller if they can prove all of the following:

- The manufacturer or seller was engaged in the business of selling the product.
- The product was unreasonably dangerous to the user or consumer.
- The defective condition was the cause of the injury or damage.
- The defective condition existed when the product left the hands of the manufacturer or seller.
- The consumer suffered physical harm or property damage as a result of using the product.

The defective condition may arise through faulty product design or faulty manufacturing. Inadequate warning of danger and improper instructions for the product's use are also considered defects.

What You'll Learn

- How to differentiate between product liability and strict liability
- How to describe the purpose of the Consumer Product Safety Act
- How to identify the prohibitions contained in the Food, Drug, and Cosmetic Act
- How to determine where to get consumer protection assistance

Why It's Important

Learning about product liability law will help you take effective action if you or a family member suffers injury from faulty products.

Legal Terms

- product liability
- strict liability
- adulterated
- intrastate sales

Community Works

Health Hazard
For many people, smoking is a habit that becomes an addiction. They continue to smoke despite the health risks and the warning labels on cigarette packages. Many new government regulations have been imposed on the tobacco industry and the sales of their products to discourage teens from becoming smokers. *Do you think that the tobacco industry should be allowed to direct its advertising toward teens?*

Get Involved
Research the laws governing cigarette sales, and encourage local storeowners to display signs on their counters that warn that the sale of cigarettes to minors is illegal.

Example 6. Jackson leased a truck from Ryder Truck Rental. When he stopped at a traffic light, the brakes failed, and Jackson hit the car in front of him. Martine, the driver of the other car, was injured. The Delaware Supreme Court ruled that Ryder could be held liable, even without proof that the company was negligent. It was only necessary for the injured party to prove the truck had an unreasonably dangerous product design that caused personal injury or property damage.

Not every state has strict liability laws. In some states you must prove that your injuries or damages resulted from the negligent, reckless, or intentional misconduct of the manufacturer.

Federal and State Consumer Protection Laws

Both the federal and state governments pass laws to protect consumers in the marketplace. These laws are necessary because some state laws may apply only to those goods that are produced and purchased within one state. The laws protect consumers from harmful or defective products, foods, drugs, and cosmetic products, as well as from unethical businesses.

RECALL
Manufacturers and sellers can be liable when a product is defective. *Why do manufacturers recall products that are defective instead of taking the risk of being sued?*

Consumer Product Safety Act

The federal Consumer Product Safety Act protects you from unreasonable risk of injury while using consumer products that are sold in interstate commerce. Defects in products are divided into three categories:

- Manufacturing defects (e.g., a ladder with missing rivets)
- Poor design (e.g., a toy with small parts that can be easily removed and swallowed)
- Inadequate instructions and warnings about the safe use of the product (e.g., a chain saw that does not include instructions about using the safety guard)

Manufacturers and sellers who place items on the market must test the quality and reliability (fitness) of all products before shipping. They must prove that the product has been tested and is safe. All manufacturers and sellers have the capability to recall the product if the need arises, and they must act quickly to address any valid complaints made by users of the product.

Food, Drug, and Cosmetic Act

One of the most important federal laws regarding product liability is the Food, Drug, and Cosmetic Act. This law prohibits the manufacture and shipment of faulty products in interstate commerce. Faulty products include any food, drug, cosmetic, or health-related device that is injurious, adulterated, or misbranded.

A food or drug is said to be injurious if it contains any substance that may make it harmful to health. An **adulterated** food or drug is one that contains any substance that will reduce its quality or strength below minimum standards. A food or drug is misbranded if its labeling or packaging is false or misleading.

The Food, Drug, and Cosmetic Act requires that packaged drugs bear the name and address of the manufacturer and a statement of the quantity or weight of the contents. Labels on nonprescription drugs must give the common name of the drug if a trade name is used, and the labels must detail directions for the drug's use. Labels must also caution against any use that may be unsafe for children or harmful to the consumer in general. The label must also indicate if the drug is addictive. The act prescribes criminal penalties for firms or individuals who violate this law.

The federal government has the right to remove from the market any food or food additive shown or believed to cause cancer in humans or animals. The government also uses several other methods to discourage the sale of goods considered harmful to the public health. These methods include the following:

- *Unusually high taxes.* For example, there are special taxes known as excise taxes on liquor and tobacco.

It's a Question of Ethics

Using the Cooling-Off Rule

A door-to-door sales representative for vinyl replacement windows contacted your neighbor, Joseph, at home. Joseph, a salesman himself, was aware of the cooling-off rule and agreed to buy the windows, knowing he had three days to cancel the contract. Joseph knew his windows did not need to be replaced. He just wanted to annoy the salesman because the salesman had bothered him at home. *Is it ethical to buy a product if you know you are going to return it?*

WARNINGS
Warning labels must
be placed on cigarette
packages. *Why does
the federal law require
such warnings?*

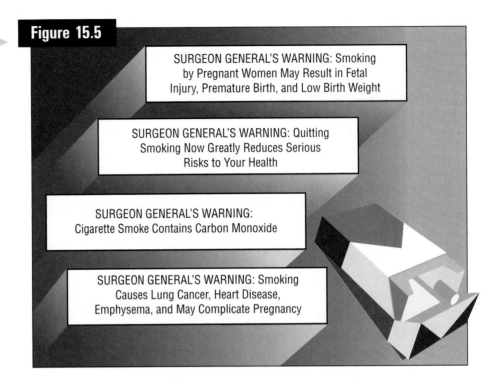

Figure 15.5

SURGEON GENERAL'S WARNING: Smoking
by Pregnant Women May Result in Fetal
Injury, Premature Birth, and Low Birth Weight

SURGEON GENERAL'S WARNING: Quitting
Smoking Now Greatly Reduces Serious
Risks to Your Health

SURGEON GENERAL'S WARNING:
Cigarette Smoke Contains Carbon Monoxide

SURGEON GENERAL'S WARNING: Smoking
Causes Lung Cancer, Heart Disease,
Emphysema, and May Complicate Pregnancy

- *Labeling and packaging.* The Food and Drug Administration requires warning labels and tamper-proof packaging of certain nonprescription drugs and cosmetics. Warning notices must also be placed on cigarettes (see Figure 15.5). Beverage companies must disclose how much fruit juice they put into their drinks.
- *Outright prohibition.* For example, cigarette advertising is banned on television.

State and Local Laws

If goods are manufactured and sold only within the boundaries of a state, the federal government has no control over the goods. For this reason many states have enacted their own product liability laws, which apply to **intrastate sales** (sales within a state). Most states and local governments have their own pure food laws and health laws to protect the public. Nearly all states and localities license and regulate establishments that sell food. Most states also have laws regulating meat and milk, and laws regulating the processing and canning of food.

Consumer Protection Assistance

Many state and local governments have offices of consumer affairs to educate consumers and help protect them against fraud. The business community is also increasingly policing itself, trying to protect consumers from questionable practices.

The federal Consumer Product Safety Commission establishes safety standards for consumer products. It has the power to recall unsafe products and to impose fines on violators. For information or to report unsafe products, you can telephone its hot line at 1-800-638-CPSC.

Better Business Bureau

The Better Business Bureau (BBB) is an example of a nongovernment agency that hears consumer complaints at the local and state levels. It also tries to steer consumers to reliable businesses. The BBB's mission is to promote highly ethical relationships between businesses and the public. It pursues this goal through voluntary self-regulation, consumer and business education, and service excellence. Some services that the BBB provides include the following:

- Providing information on a business's past dealings with people
- Helping resolve complaints by such methods as conciliation, mediation, and arbitration
- Providing information on charitable organizations that solicit donations from the public
- Publishing a wide variety of consumer publications, videos, and Internet advisories
- Alerting businesses, consumers, and law enforcement agencies about current marketplace scams and frauds
- Providing Internet reliability and privacy "Trustmark" seals to inform consumers that a Web site meets specific standards

Law & Academics

Computer Technology
The development of computer technologies has had a tremendous impact on nearly every field of study. It's crucial for lawyers to be aware of how new technologies affect their profession. Many state bar associations offer technology-related resources to attorneys practicing in the state.

Research Activity
Research what the bar association in your state is doing to educate attorneys about computer technology and the law.

Section 15.2 Assessment

Reviewing What You Learned

1. What is the difference between product liability and strict liability?
2. What is the purpose of the Consumer Product Safety Act?
3. What prohibitions are contained in the Food, Drug, and Cosmetic Act?
4. Research cases of appropriate agencies.

Critical Thinking Activity

Consumer Protection Agencies Using the Internet, library, or other resource, research cases involving consumer protection laws and present cases of appropriate consumer agencies.

Legal Skills in Action

Consumer Protection Laws In this section, you learned about several important consumer protection laws. Now imagine situations in which these laws may apply. Next, research three to four actual cases by using the Internet, the library, or other resource. In each case, identify the facts, the issue that the court needs to decide, the basis of the court's decision, and the consumer protection laws involved. Then present cases of appropriate consumer protection laws to the class in a brief oral report.

Chapter Summary

Section 15.1 Consumer Protection

- Federal consumer protection law applies to transactions between businesses and consumers. Consumers are people who buy or lease goods, real estate, or services for personal, family, or household purposes. Federal consumer protection law applies only to interstate commerce, which is business activity that touches more than one state. State consumer law protects consumers who conduct local transactions.

- A false statement about the construction, durability, reliability, safety, strength, condition, or life expectancy of a product is a fraudulent misrepresentation. It is also deceptive to purposely avoid disclosing any fact that would cause a buyer to avoid entering into a contract. Another example of an unfair and deceptive practice is false advertising, which is advertising that misleads the public. Some ads that advertise lucrative work-at-home opportunities are examples of false advertising. Sending unordered merchandise to consumers is another unfair and deceptive practice employed by some unscrupulous businesses. Individuals who receive items in the mail that they did not order are not required to pay for such goods.

- When a store advertises bargains that don't really exist to lure customers to buy more expensive goods, it is engaging in bait and switch advertising. The following sales practices may be signs of a bait and switch: (1) refusing to show, demonstrate, or sell the advertised product; (2) attempting to discourage customers by criticizing the advertised product; (3) claiming that the advertised products are out of stock; (4) refusing to promise delivery of the advertised products within a reasonable period of time; and (5) demonstrating products that are more expensive than the advertised items.

- Some rules designed to protect customers are the negative option rule, the cooling-off rule, the Telemarketing Sales Rule, and the 900-Telephone-Number Rules. The negative option rule applies to plans that send products regularly, such as magazine subscriptions. The cooling-off rule gives you three days to cancel contracts for purchases made away from the seller's usual place of business. The Telemarketing Sales Rule protects you from abusive or unethical telemarketers. The 900-Telephone Number Rules protect you from scams associated with calling 900 numbers.

Section 15.2 Product Liability

- Manufacturers and sellers have product liability when they place defective, unhealthy, or unsafe items on the market. Manufacturers and sellers are strictly liable, without regard to fault, when they sell unreasonably dangerous products to the public.

- The Consumer Product Safety Act was developed to protect consumers from unsafe goods. Under the Consumer Product Safety Act, products must be tested for safety. Manufacturers and sellers must prove the quality and fitness of their products. In the event there is a problem, manufacturers are required to take action, sometimes even recalling unsafe products.

- The Food, Drug, and Cosmetic Act prohibits the manufacture and shipment of faulty products in interstate commerce. A food or drug is said to be injurious if it contains any substance that may be harmful to health.

- Consumer protection can be obtained from state and local consumer protection agencies, such as the Consumer Product Safety Commission and the Better Business Bureau.

Using Legal Language

Consider the key terms in the list below. Then use these terms to complete the following exercises.

bait and switch
caveat emptor
caveat venditor
cooling-off rule
consumer
telemarketers
product liability

strict liability
adulterated
intrastate sales
unfair and deceptive practice
fraudulent misrepresentation
cease and desist orders

Understanding Business and Personal Law *Online*

Self-Check Quiz Visit the *Understanding Business and Personal Law* Web site at **ubpl.glencoe.com** and click on Chapter 15: Consumer Protection— Self-Check Quizzes to prepare for the chapter exam.

1. Write a brief paragraph about consumer protection using at least 10 of the legal terms listed above.
2. Rewrite the paragraph, replacing the terms with blank spaces. Exchange your rewritten paragraph with a partner, and fill in the blanks.
3. Discuss with your partner any inaccuracies in your paragraphs.

The Law Review

Answer the following questions. Refer to the chapter for additional reinforcement.

4. What are your rights if you receive unordered goods in the mail?
5. Analyze the effects of illegal practices on business and on consumers. How do such practices harm each, and what are some of the reasons that businesses should do their best to obey the law?
6. Is it possible to cancel a contract made with a door-to-door salesperson? Explain your answer.
7. What protection do you have when buying goods by mail, telephone, fax, or the Internet? Research cases of appropriate consumer protection laws.
8. If you are hurt by a defective product that you purchased, is a manufacturer or seller responsible? What if you are hurt by a product that someone else purchased? Explain your answer.
9. If you are hurt by a product that you purchased from another consumer, is that consumer liable? Explain your answer.
10. In this chapter, you learned about some of the laws intended to protect consumers and the agencies responsible for enforcing these laws. Using the Internet, the library, or other resource, research cases of appropriate agencies. What were the facts of each case, and how did the court decide the issues?
11. What are three types of defects against which the Consumer Product Safety Act seeks to protect consumers?

Linking School to Work

Acquiring and Evaluating Information

Lois wants to make some extra money. When she read about an opportunity to knit baby booties at home for pay, she jumped at the chance. She paid a $100 fee and received her first shipment of yarn and instructions. She followed the directions, knitted 50 pairs of booties, and sent them to the company. All 50 pairs of booties did not meet the "standards" of the company. Lois felt that she had been ripped off. Research the following topics:

- Ways to prevent falling victim to work-at-home schemes
- Information required to produce a one-page consumer alert document about this type of fraudulent activity
- How to avoid being scammed

Organize and share your document with other students in the class.

Let's Debate

Unethical and Illegal Business Practices

Drugtech Sciences, Inc. designed a drug called SleepPro that was intended to help people who have problems sleeping. After years of costly development, it was approved and marketed to the public. Unfortunately, it was later discovered by the company that using the drug posed serious health risks and it was incorrectly labeled. However, the company decided to hide the risks from consumers, and not to correct the labeling.

Debate

12. Analyze the effects of unethical practices on consumers. If Drugtech continues to market SleepPro, what are some of the ethical consequences?

13. Analyze the effects of illegal practices on consumers. What are some of the risks faced by consumers, who use SleepPro?

14. Analyze the effects of illegal practices on business. If government regulators become aware of the problems with SleepPro, what are some of the consequences?

15. Investigate laws and regulations resulting from unethical practices. What important federal law applies in this case, and how?

Grasping Case Issues

For the following cases, give your decision and state a legal principle that applies.

16. Nick orders a digital camera over the Internet. After 40 days, he still has not received the camera, nor has he heard from the company. Nick asks for his money back. Must the company return his money, even if it is now ready to send the camera?

17. A cosmetics company mails perfume samples to people at random and then bills them for the merchandise. Is the company violating a law? Explain your answer.

18. Trailblazers, Inc. fails to complete all its safety tests before shipping a newly manufactured bike. A defect in the bike's design causes Juan Ramirez, 11, to suffer injury. Does the Ramirez family have any recourse against the company? Explain your answer.

19. Belinda attends a holiday gift party. She buys and pays for several items totaling $88.77. The following day, Belinda realizes she should not have spent so much money. Does Belinda have the right to get her money back? Explain your answer.

20. Bobbi-Lee is awakened at 10:00 P.M. by a telemarketer selling magazine subscriptions. A week earlier, she had told a different person from the company to stop calling her. Has the company violated a law?

In each case that follows, you be the judge.

21. Recovery of Damages

William Everett, Jr. was a member of the New Preparatory School hockey team. During a game, a hockey puck fractured William's skull by penetrating his helmet through a gap between sections of shock foam. *Can William recover damages from the helmet's manufacturer? Why or why not?* *Everett v. Bucky Warren, Inc.,* 380 N.E.2d 653 (MA).

22. Cancelled Transaction

Delores Bierlein paid a $200 deposit to rent a banquet room at Alex's Continental Inn for her daughter's wedding reception. Three months before the wedding, Bierlein notified the inn that the wedding reception had been cancelled. The inn refused to return Delores's deposit, arguing that this was not a consumer transaction. *Does the inn have the right to retain the deposit? Why or why not?* *Bierlein v. Alex's Continental Inn, Inc.,* 475 N.E.2d 1273 (OH).

Legal Link

Can I Trust You?

If you surf the Web, you might find a site with an Internet reliability and privacy "Trustmark" seal set, which was issued by the Better Business Bureau.

Connect

Using a variety of search engines, research the reliability seal program and the privacy seal program. Answer the following questions:

23. What are the standards that companies must meet for both programs?
24. Are there fees that companies must pay to belong to the programs?
25. How are consumer complaints handled through the program?

Locate at least one site with either the reliability seal or the privacy seal.

POWER READING STRATEGIES

26. **Predict** What do you think would happen if there were no laws to protect consumers?

27. **Connect** Do you believe everything you see on TV? Have you ever seen a commercial and wondered if it were really true?

28. **Question** Do you think strict liability laws are fair to manufacturers who have not been negligent?

29. **Respond** Why does the U.S. government provide consumer education to the public? Does it have a responsibility to do so?

Owning a Vehicle

Understanding Business and Personal Law *Online*

Chapter Overview Visit the *Understanding Business and Personal Law* Web site at ubpl.glencoe.com and click on Chapter 16: Owning a Vehicle— Chapter Overviews to preview the chapter information.

The Opening Scene

Newlyweds Mei and Bruce are looking at advertisements for used cars in the newspaper.

The Test Drive

MEI: Here's a good deal. A new car for only $403.93 a month, and with nothing down.

BRUCE: How many months do you have to pay?

MEI: The ad doesn't say.

BRUCE: What's the interest rate?

MEI: I don't see anything about interest. Wait, there's some small print at the bottom. Oh no, this ad is for leasing the car, not buying it.

BRUCE: Let's go over to that used car lot on Broadway and look around. We don't have to buy anything.

(A short time later, Mei and Bruce visit the used car lot.)

BRUCE: This one's real sharp *(Kicking the tire of a car.).* The sign says $5,988. I'll bet they'll take $5,000.

MEI: I wonder if it has a warranty?

BRUCE: The sign doesn't say.

SALES ASSOCIATE: *(Approaching with outstretched hand.)* Hello, my name's Tamara. Can I help you?

MEI: What kind of warranty does this car have?

TAMARA: Thirty days, parts and labor. This one's a honey! It belonged to a retired couple who hardly ever drove it. See the mileage? Only 30,000.

BRUCE: Do you mind if we take it for a spin?

TAMARA: I'll get you the key.

(With Bruce sitting on the passenger side, Mei drives the car out of the lot.)

BRUCE: How does it feel, honey?

MEI: Smooth. Wonder what all these buttons and lights are on the dash?

BRUCE: *(Opening the glove compartment.)* Here's the owner's manual; let's check. Say, look at this. *(He takes a paper out of the manual.)* It's a receipt for work done on this car six months ago. It says it had 97,000 miles on it then!

MEI: What? *(Suddenly, the car in front of them stops, and Mei slams on the brakes.)* The brakes aren't holding! *(CRASH! The cars collide, and the front car's rear bumper and trunk are dented. The car Mei is test-driving is not damaged.)*

MEI: Are you all right, Bruce?

BRUCE: Sure, we weren't going fast.

MOTORIST: *(Approaching Mei's car.)* What's the matter? Didn't you see me stop?

MEI: The brakes are no good! We are just test-driving this car. It belongs to a dealer.

MOTORIST: Look at that! You ruined the back of my car and didn't even scratch yours.

BRUCE: They don't make bumpers like this car's anymore. Don't worry. The dealer's collision insurance will cover it.

MOTORIST: I sure hope so.

What Are the Legal Issues?

1. Does a newspaper ad that states the monthly payment to lease a car have to include information about other costs?
2. Must a dealership display information about warranties on used cars?
3. Does the buyer of an automobile have any legal protection against having the odometer (mileage meter) turned back?
4. Does a consumer have any protection against weak bumpers placed on automobiles by manufacturers?
5. Does collision insurance pay for damages to someone else's car?

Acquiring a Vehicle

What You'll Learn

- How to identify important parts of a loan agreement
- How to trade in a vehicle
- How to identify the pros and cons of leasing a vehicle
- How to compare options for buying a pre-owned vehicle
- How to pursue legal remedies if you buy a defective vehicle
- How to recognize some federal laws designed to protect you when you buy a vehicle
- How to summarize the legal aspects of repairing your vehicle

Why It's Important

Knowing about financing, buying, and leasing a vehicle will enable you to make better purchase decisions.

Legal Terms

- finance charge
- annual percentage rate (APR)
- Used Car Rule
- Buyer's Guide
- repossess
- adhesion contract

Laws of Ownership

You will probably buy many automobiles in your life. The law that applies to these purchases comes from several different sources. Because cars are considered goods, the Uniform Commercial Code (UCC) applies to their sale and lease. If you buy a car for personal, family, or household purposes, both federal and state consumer protection laws may also apply. In addition, if you finance the car, special laws regulate credit.

Financing a Vehicle

One of the first steps in buying a car is to decide how much you can afford to pay. This determination depends on your savings, monthly earnings, living expenses, and any debt that you have.

When buying a car, you will save money by paying cash because car loans require you to pay interest. Offering to pay cash also puts you in a better position to negotiate a lower purchase price. If you decide to borrow money to purchase a car, you may save money by shopping around for credit. Federal law requires lenders to disclose the finance charge and annual percentage rate (APR) to borrowers. The **finance charge** is the cost of the loan in dollars and cents, and the **annual percentage rate (APR)** is the true interest rate of the loan.

Before you sign any documents, you should know the following information:

- The exact price you're paying for the vehicle
- The amount you're financing
- The finance charge
- The APR
- The number and amount of payments
- The total sales price (the sum of the monthly payments plus the down payment)

Dealers sometimes offer very low financing rates for specific models but may not be willing to negotiate. They also may require a large down payment. As a result, it is sometimes better to pay higher financing charges on a car with a lower price or to purchase a car that requires a smaller down payment.

Many people get deeply into debt buying things on credit that they really can't afford. Making monthly payments may seem easy at first,

A BANK LOAN
Regulation Z requires lenders to disclose two important things to you when you borrow money. With this information, you can compare the cost of a loan from different lenders. *What information must lenders disclose to you?*

but before you realize it the total amount of money you owe may be more than you can pay.

Example 1. Antonia found a used truck that she liked, but she couldn't afford the monthly payments under a 24-month payment plan. She bought the truck under a 36-month plan; however, two years later, the vehicle broke down completely and was not worth fixing. Antonia still had to make the monthly payments on the vehicle for a full year after it stopped working.

A Federal Trade Commission (FTC) regulation gives consumers protection when they buy vehicles on credit.

Example 2. Chandra bought a used car from a local dealer. She paid $500 down and signed a contract to pay the balance of $5,500 plus interest in 24 monthly installments. The dealer received the $5,500 the same day by transferring the contract to a finance company under a prearranged agreement. Chandra was then required to pay the finance company the monthly payments, including interest, for the next 24 months.

Under the FTC regulation, Chandra has the same protection against the finance company that she has against the car dealer. If something went wrong with the car and the dealer refused to repair it, she could use the breach of warranty of merchantability defense if sued by the finance company for the debt. This rule does not apply if you borrow money to buy a car from a lending company that has no arrangement with the seller.

Careers in Law

Parole Officer

As a parole officer for the state of Texas, Chu Luu devotes his life to trying to keep 89 people out of trouble. It isn't an easy job. His clients are parolees—convicted murderers, robbers, and drug dealers who have been allowed out of jail after many years.

"Sometimes people have been given sentences of 50 years," Luu says. "But there just isn't room for all the prisoners, so the state might let them out after 25 or 30 years. It's my job to help them reintegrate into society."

Luu tries to increase an ex-convict's chances of success by helping him or her find a job, and if necessary, by arranging for treatment for alcoholism and drug addiction. Ex-convicts are parolees for the rest of their term of sentence, which means they must continue to work and check in with their parole officer. If they fail to do so, they will be returned to prison.

Luu checks up on his clients by visiting their homes or their places of employment. "Of course, sometimes people disappear," he says. "But other times, people get out of prison, get a job, and follow the routine. They've learned a big lesson."

Luu says his job can be high pressure. "We're dealing with criminals," he says, "and when you're supervising criminals, it's not like dealing with other people. You can only trust them 50 percent of the time and when you tell them to do something, they're probably going to do it differently than you or I."

Skills	Listening, creative problem solving, counseling
Personality	Patient, able to take a high-pressure job, sensitive to diversity
Education	College degree plus five weeks at parole academy

For more information on parole officers, visit **ubpl.glencoe.com** or your public library.

Example 3. Kita borrowed $5,500 from her local bank, agreeing to pay the money back in 24 monthly installments at the current interest rate. She used the money to buy a van from a used car dealer; however, the vehicle broke down two days later. The van was not merchantable, and Kita could use breach of warranty of merchantability as grounds to get her money back from the dealer. However, because there was no financing arrangement between the bank and the dealer, Kita still has to pay the bank the full $5,500 plus interest, as agreed.

Buying a New Vehicle

If you prepare before starting to shop for a vehicle, you can make the process easier and save money. Use the library or online resources to research and learn about the cars that you may be interested in buying. Some magazines devote entire issues to rating cars based on their maintenance records, safety, performance, and affordability.

Your research will make you better able to negotiate the price. Dealers are often willing to bargain on their profit margin between 10 and 20 percent, which is generally the difference between the manufacturer's suggested retail price (MSRP) and the invoice price. See Figure 16.1 for more information about buying a new vehicle.

Trade-In

If you are trading in a vehicle, do not discuss it with the dealer until you've negotiated the best price for your new car. You should know the value of your trade-in, which can be found on the Internet or at the library. Some Internet sites will calculate a reasonable price for your trade-in car based on its mileage, condition, options, and the location in which you live. You might get a better price selling a vehicle yourself, rather than trading it in. However, many people opt to trade-in cars because of the convenience it affords them.

Figure 16.1	Car Buying Terms
Invoice Price	The manufacturer's initial charge (including delivery) to the dealer. This is usually higher than the dealer's final cost because dealers receive rebates, allowances, discounts, and incentive awards.
Base Price	The cost of the vehicle with standard equipment and warranty but without optional equipment. This price is printed on the Monroney sticker.
Monroney Sticker Price (MSRP)	The information printed on the Monroney sticker. It shows the base price, the manufacturer's transportation charge, and the fuel economy of the vehicle. The sticker is required by federal law to be affixed to a new vehicle's window. Only the purchaser may remove it.
Dealer Sticker Price	The Monroney sticker price plus the suggested retail price of the dealer-installed options, such as additional dealer markup (ADM) or additional dealer profit (ADP), dealer preparation, and undercoating. This price is usually on a supplemental sticker.

PRICING A VEHICLE The same vehicle can have different prices. *What is the Monroney sticker?*

Leasing a New Vehicle

A popular alternative to buying a vehicle is leasing one, but this method is the most expensive way to acquire a car. A low down payment and smaller monthly payments are the main advantages of leasing (see Figure 16.2). Leasing is also useful for young professional people who have high incomes but little or no savings accumulated. Leasing is not the most desirable way for average consumers to obtain cars, however, because you make a lot of payments and end up with nothing to trade in toward your next vehicle.

When you lease a vehicle, you have the right to:

- Drive it for an agreed-upon number of months and miles.
- Turn it in at the end of the lease, pay any end-of-lease fees and charges, and "walk away."
- Buy the vehicle if you have a purchase option.
- Take advantage of any applicable warranties or recalls.

However, you may be responsible for excess mileage charges, excess wear charges for body damage or worn tires, and charges for ending your lease early.

Consumer Leasing Act

The Consumer Leasing Act is a federal law requiring businesses to tell you about all of the terms of a lease of personal property. This information can be used to compare different leases or to compare the cost of leasing with the cost of buying.

Federal law also regulates advertisements of leases. When certain triggering terms are used in a lease ad, they trigger the need to disclose additional information. These terms include the amount of any payment and a statement of other required payments. If an ad mentions the amount or number of payments, specifies a particular down payment, or states that no down payment is required, it must also disclose the total number of regular payments, the consumer's responsibility at the end of the lease, and whether the consumer may purchase the property.

Buying a Pre-Owned Vehicle

A pre-owned vehicle may be purchased from a new car dealer, a used car dealer, a car rental company, or a private party. Sometimes banks and loan companies sell cars and trucks that have been claimed because someone didn't make payments. You can also search for a pre-owned vehicle online.

Buying from a Dealer

A used car dealer may have a large selection of cars, but often does not maintain facilities to service the car after you buy it. New car dealers,

Figure 16.2

Leasing or Buying a New Vehicle

	Leasing	Buying
Ownership	You must return the vehicle at the end of the lease, unless you choose to buy it.	You own the vehicle and get to keep it at the end of the financing term.
Up-front costs	Up-front costs may include the first month's payment, a refundable security deposit, a capitalized cost reduction (like a down payment), taxes, registration fees, and other charges.	Up-front costs include the cash price or a down payment, taxes, registration fees, and other charges.
Monthly payments	Monthly lease payments are usually lower than monthly loan payments because you are paying for the vehicle's depreciation during the lease term, plus rent charges (like interest), taxes, and fees.	Monthly loan payments are usually higher than monthly lease payments because you are paying for the entire purchase price of the vehicle, plus interest and other finance charges, taxes, and fees.
Early termination	You are responsible for any early termination charges if you end the lease early.	You are responsible for any pay-off amount if you end the loan early.
Vehicle return	You may return the vehicle at lease end, pay any end-of-lease costs, and "walk away."	You may have to sell or trade the vehicle when you decide you want a different vehicle.
Future value	The lessor has the risk of the future market value of the vehicle.	You have the risk of the vehicle's future market value.
Mileage	Most leases limit the number of miles you may drive (often 12,000–15,000 per year). You will likely have to pay charges if you exceed those limits.	You may drive as many miles as you want, but higher mileage will lower the vehicle's trade-in or resale value.
Excess wear	Most leases limit wear to the vehicle. You will likely have to pay extra charges if you exceed those limits.	There are no limits or charges for excessive wear to the vehicle, but excessive wear will lower the vehicle's value.
End of term	At the end of the lease (typically 2–4 years), you may have a new payment to finance the purchase of the existing vehicle or to lease another vehicle.	At the end of the loan term (typically 4–6 years), you have no further loan payments.

LEASE OR BUY?
There are advantages and disadvantages to leasing and buying a vehicle. *Why are monthly payments usually higher when you buy a vehicle than when you lease a vehicle?*

on the other hand, often sell used cars that they have taken in for trade and have service facilities.

Warranties   When selling a vehicle, a dealer gives an implied warranty that the vehicle is merchantable, unless this warranty is excluded. By offering the warranty of merchantability, the dealer warrants that the vehicle is fit for the ordinary purposes for which such vehicles are used. The warranty of fitness for a particular purpose also applies when you buy a vehicle based on the seller's advice that it is suitable for a particular purpose. Be careful to make sure that these warranties are not excluded or disclaimed by the dealer.

> *Example 4.* Ed purchased a used car from a dealer. The dealer wrote "as is" on the sales slip that Ed signed. The car's transmission jammed four days later, but Ed had no legal recourse because the UCC says that all implied warranties are excluded by expressions such as "with all faults" or "as is."

PRE-OWNED VEHICLE
Much information is available to help you make decisions when you are shopping for a pre-owned vehicle. *Where can you find information about buying pre-owned vehicles?*

Another way some dealers exclude implied warranties is by using formal printed language on the front or back of the sales slip. The printing, often in special typeface, may state: "The implied warranties of merchantability and fitness for a particular purpose are hereby disclaimed." Implied warranties cannot be excluded when express warranties are made, according to the Magnuson-Moss Warranty Act. Some states do not allow merchants to disclaim or exclude implied warranties at all when they sell motor vehicles to consumers.

Another advantage of buying a used car from a dealer is that dealers often give you a 30-day, 60-day, or 90-day guarantee. This express warranty can be for parts and labor or for labor only. Sometimes the warranty may be a 50-50 guarantee, in which the buyer pays for half of the parts and labor.

The Used Car Rule   The FTC's **Used Car Rule** requires all used car dealers to place a large sticker, called a **Buyer's Guide**, in the window of each used vehicle they offer for sale (see Figure 16.3). The guide explains any specific warranty protection that is provided. It also states whether there is no warranty, an "as is" warranty, or an implied warranty. The guide also suggests that you have the car inspected by your own mechanic before you buy and that you should get all promises in writing. Finally, the guide lists some of the major problems that may occur in any car. The buyer's guide becomes a part of your sales contract and overrides any contrary provisions that may be in that contract.

Figure 16.3

BUYER'S GUIDE

IMPORTANT: Spoken promises are difficult to enforce. Ask the dealer to put all promises in writing. Keep this form.

VEHICLE MAKE **MODEL** **YEAR** **VIN NUMBER**

DEALER STOCK NUMBER (Optional)

WARRANTIES FOR THIS VEHICLE:

☐ **AS IS - NO WARRANTY**

YOU WILL PAY ALL COSTS FOR ANY REPAIRS. The dealer assumes no responsibility for any repairs regardless of any oral statements about the vehicle.

☐ **WARRANTY**

☐ **FULL** ☐ **LIMITED WARRANTY. The dealer will pay ___% of the labor and ___% of the parts for the covered systems that fail during the warranty period. Ask the dealer for a copy of the warranty document for a full explanation of warranty coverage, exclusions, and the dealer's repair obligations. Under state law, "implied warranties" may give you even more rights.**

SYSTEMS COVERED: **DURATION:**

_____ _____
_____ _____
_____ _____
_____ _____
_____ _____
_____ _____
_____ _____
_____ _____

☐ **SERVICE CONTRACT. A service contract is available at an extra charge on this vehicle. Ask for details as to coverage, deductible, price, and exclusions. If you buy a service contract within 90 days of the time of sale, state law "implied warranties" may give you additional rights.**

PREPURCHASE INSPECTION: ASK THE DEALER IF YOU MAY HAVE THIS VEHICLE INSPECTED BY YOUR MECHANIC EITHER ON OR OFF THE LOT.

SEE THE BACK OF THIS FORM for important additional information, including a list of some major defects that may occur in used motor vehicles.

BUYER'S GUIDE
This form must appear in the window of used vehicles sold by dealers. *Does it become part of the sales contract with the dealer?*

Buying from a Private Party

You might find the lowest price for a car by buying from a private party. Buying from a friend is usually best because he or she can fill you in on the vehicle's history. Buying from a stranger can be risky because private parties do not provide the implied warranty of merchantability. You must buy the car "as is" and will have no recourse if something goes wrong.

An exception occurs if the seller gives you an express warranty. For example, the courts have held that a statement by the seller that a car is in good condition and runs properly amounts to an express warranty. This warranty prevails over a further statement that the car is sold "as is."

Other pitfalls in buying from a private party include the possibility that the car may have been stolen. In this case, a bank or loan company may have the right to **repossess**, or take back the car, regardless of who presently owns it. A repossessed vehicle purchased from a bank or finance company may be a good buy. However, sellers of repossessed vehicles give no warranty, either express or implied.

Before you buy, be sure to:
- Inspect the vehicle carefully or have it inspected by a mechanic.
- Test-drive the vehicle.
- Ask for the vehicle's maintenance record.
- Talk to previous owners.
- Ask to see the certificate of title.

Be sure that the name of the person selling the vehicle appears on the certificate of title. Usually, the names of persons or institutions holding liens on the vehicle (the right to repossess it) are written on the back of the certificate. Lien holders often have possession of the certificate of title. Visit the court clerk's office in the seller's community and ask if there are any liens filed there under the seller's name. Liens, or security interests, are explained in Chapter 22.

PRIVATE PARTIES
Buying a pre-owned vehicle from a private party can be risky. *What can you do to protect yourself before you buy a vehicle from a private party?*

Buying from Rental Companies

Rental companies often buy fleets of new vehicles and sell them when they are a year or two old. These cars can be a good buy, but keep in mind that such vehicles may have had heavy use and will probably have high mileage. On the other hand, rental vehicles usually have had regularly scheduled maintenance and come with warranties.

The Contract to Buy a Vehicle

Under the UCC, a contract for the sale of goods valued at $500 or more must be in writing to be enforceable. When private parties enter into a contract, they can simply write on a piece of paper that one party agrees to sell and the other party agrees to buy the vehicle. The contract must identify the vehicle and must be signed by the party charged—the defendant—in a lawsuit. It is also advisable to include the price of the vehicle, although the UCC does not require it. All of this information can be placed on the check given for a deposit. Law does not require a deposit, but the seller has the right to require it as a condition of the contract.

When a contract is entered into between a private party and a dealer, the private party is usually at a disadvantage. The dealer asks the buyer to sign a printed form. A sentence on the front of the form says that the buyer agrees to the terms on the reverse side. The back of the form contains a full page of small-print terms that favor the seller. Such a standard-form contract is called an **adhesion contract**. Smart buyers read the small print and cross out items with which they disagree.

What to Do If You Buy a Defective Car

Some cars, whether purchased new or used, continually have mechanical problems. If you have bought such a car, you should notify the seller immediately. The seller can be asked to fix the problem, to pay to have it fixed, or to give your money back. The seller, depending on the circumstances, may be liable on any of the following grounds:

- Breach of an express warranty, if a specific guarantee was made and was not kept
- Breach of warranty of merchantability, if the seller was a dealer and the car was not fit
- Fraud or breach of an express warranty, if the seller made any statements of fact about the car that were not true
- Breach of the state consumer protection law, if the buyer purchased the car for nonbusiness use

Revoking the Acceptance   If you buy a car that doesn't conform to the contract, you may be able to revoke your acceptance, even after taking possession of the vehicle. This revocation is allowed under the UCC if the defect is serious and undetectable. It may also be exercised

Community Works

Donating Automobiles
Buying your first car is considered to be a milestone in life. This purchase establishes independence and freedom. Did you know that many people give their cars away? Used cars, running or not, are often donated to organizations that help raise money for community works and services. *What organizations in your community accept automobile donations?*

Get Involved
Look for an organization in your area that accepts donated cars. Organize a donation drive in your area, persuading friends and neighbors to donate automobiles that are not being used.

in cases in which you are led to believe that the seller would fix a defect and the seller does not do so. The revocation must be made within a reasonable time after the defect is discovered.

Notifying the Seller about Defects   Buyers must notify sellers of defects in vehicles within a reasonable time after the purchase. If you fail to do so, you may lose the right to recover. You can also lose the benefits of an express warranty by failing to notify the seller of a defect before the warranty expires. Notification can be made in a number of ways. Doing so by certified mail with return receipt requested is best because it gives you proof that the seller was notified of the defect.

State Lemon Laws   Many states have passed "lemon laws" to protect consumers when they buy defective vehicles, either new or used. In Massachusetts, for example, you can return a vehicle and get back the money paid if the vehicle does not pass the state's required inspection test and it will cost more than 10 percent of the purchase price to repair the vehicle so that it will pass. Dealers in Massachusetts must also give a warranty on used vehicles for 30, 60, or 90 days, depending on the car's mileage. In addition, private parties must disclose defects that they know of when they sell a vehicle to any buyer.

A "lemon" is defined in one state as "a substantially defective new car that has been at a dealer's three times for the repair of the same defect or any combination of defects." The car must be no older than one year and must not have mileage in excess of 15,000 miles to qualify as a lemon. If you purchase such a car, you may write a letter to the dealer and manufacturer demanding the replacement of the defective part or parts or a refund. A refund is based on a formula that takes into account the use of the car. You have 18 months to request arbitration; that is, you can have the complaint heard by a neutral party called an arbiter. If either party is dissatisfied with the arbiter's report, it may be contested in court.

Federal Consumer Protection

The federal Motor Vehicle Information and Cost Savings Act has established bumper standards for passenger vehicles. If you are injured from vehicles not in compliance with the law, you may seek damages from vehicle manufacturers. The act also establishes average fuel economy standards for motor vehicles. Automakers must reach a prescribed average of miles per gallon in the cars they sell or make each year. The law also requires a label (see Figure 16.4) to be placed on each new car when it is sold. The label must show the fuel economy for each vehicle, estimated annual fuel cost of operating the automobile, and range of fuel economy of comparable automobiles.

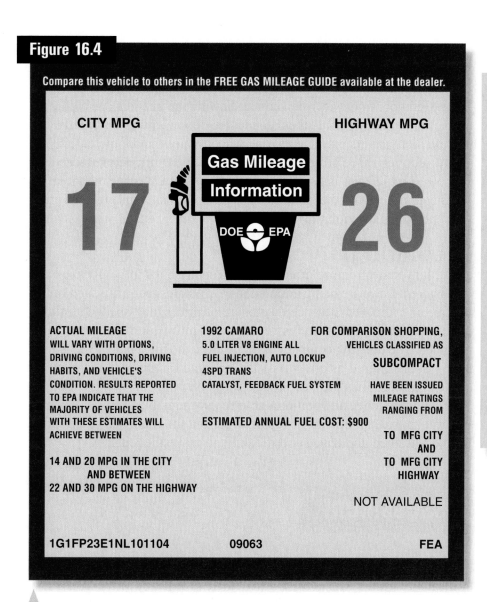

Figure 16.4

Compare this vehicle to others in the FREE GAS MILEAGE GUIDE available at the dealer.

CITY MPG   HIGHWAY MPG

Gas Mileage Information

DOE EPA

17   26

ACTUAL MILEAGE WILL VARY WITH OPTIONS, DRIVING CONDITIONS, DRIVING HABITS, AND VEHICLE'S CONDITION. RESULTS REPORTED TO EPA INDICATE THAT THE MAJORITY OF VEHICLES WITH THESE ESTIMATES WILL ACHIEVE BETWEEN

14 AND 20 MPG IN THE CITY AND BETWEEN 22 AND 30 MPG ON THE HIGHWAY

1992 CAMARO
5.0 LITER V8 ENGINE ALL FUEL INJECTION, AUTO LOCKUP 4SPD TRANS CATALYST, FEEDBACK FUEL SYSTEM

ESTIMATED ANNUAL FUEL COST: $900

FOR COMPARISON SHOPPING, VEHICLES CLASSIFIED AS

SUBCOMPACT

HAVE BEEN ISSUED MILEAGE RATINGS RANGING FROM

TO MFG CITY
AND
TO MFG CITY
HIGHWAY

NOT AVAILABLE

1G1FP23E1NL101104   09063   FEA

USEFUL INFORMATION
A label such as this one must appear on a new car when it is sold. *What federal legislation requires such a label?*

Odometer Protection

It is illegal for a vehicle owner to turn back or disconnect the odometer, or mileage indicator, of a vehicle. The federal odometer law requires everyone who transfers a vehicle, unless it is more than 25 years old, to provide a written mileage disclosure statement. This statement must be provided whether the vehicle is sold or given away. The disclosure statement must show the odometer reading at the time of the transfer. If the seller has reason to believe the mileage reading is incorrect, the statement must indicate that the actual mileage is unknown.

When an odometer is repaired and cannot be adjusted to show the true mileage, it must be set at zero. The owner of the vehicle must also attach to the left door frame a written notice showing the true mileage before the repair or replacement and the date that the odometer was set at zero.

Vehicle buyers may sue anyone who violates the odometer law. You may recover three times the amount of the damages suffered, or $1,500—whichever is greater. To recover, you must prove the violation was committed with the intent to defraud. Some states also impose criminal penalties for violating this law.

Repairing a Vehicle

Many states require motor vehicle repair shops to be licensed and registered. Laws are being adopted in many states requiring such things as repair estimates, advance disclosure of prices, and specific training for mechanics. Some states require automobile repair shops to be bonded. The bonding company is an insurer who must pay the consumer for losses suffered as a result of wrongdoing on the part of the repair shop. Automobiles are becoming more complex each year, requiring special knowledge and equipment to repair them. New car dealers may charge more than others for repair work, but their mechanics are often factory trained and have superior skills to make the repairs.

Section 16.1 Assessment

Reviewing What You Learned

1. What six aspects of the loan agreement should you be sure you understand before you sign the loan documents?
2. What should you do before you buy a new car?
3. Discuss the advantages and disadvantages of leasing a car.
4. Why might it be risky to purchase a pre-owned vehicle from a private party?
5. What should you do if you buy a defective car?
6. What is the purpose of the federal odometer law?
7. Why do some states require auto repair shops to be bonded?

Critical Thinking Activity

Buyer's Guides Visit a used car dealer and read the Buyer's Guides displayed on several of the cars. Decide whether you would be willing to purchase the cars based on the information provided in the Buyer's Guides.

Legal Skills in Action

Automobile Warranties In teams of four, contact three automobile dealerships or car rental companies that sell used cars. Ask about the warranties they provide on the used cars they sell. Make sure you find out if the warranties cover both parts and labor. Next, as a group, come to consensus as to which warranty is best.

Motor Vehicle Insurance

Financial Responsibility

Anyone who owns or drives a car should have protection against personal injury or damage to the property resulting from accidents. You also need protection against loss for injuries to others or damage to the property of others.

Every state has a **financial responsibility law**, which requires vehicle owners to prove they can pay for damages or injury caused by an automobile accident. You may show proof of financial responsibility by depositing money, depositing bonds or other securities, or carrying insurance. As of 2000, more than 40 states had laws requiring people to carry automobile insurance. In the remaining states, most people buy automobile insurance by choice.

Types of Motor Vehicle Insurance

The coverage provided by automobile insurance falls into two categories: protection for bodily injury and protection for property damage (see Figure 16.5).

Figure 16.5

Automobile Insurance Coverage

Bodily Injury Coverages

- Bodily injury liability
- Medical payments coverage
- Uninsured motorist's protection

Property Damage Coverages

- Property damage liability
- Collision
- Comprehensive physical damage

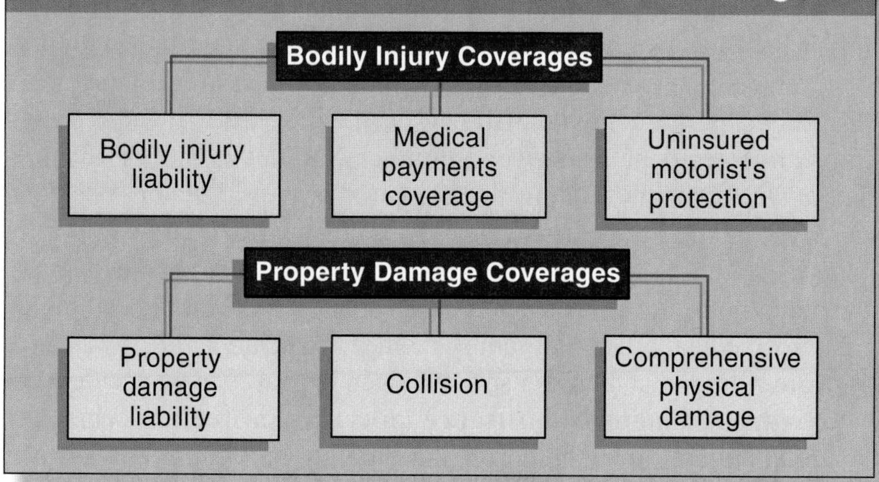

PROTECT YOURSELF
Buying bodily injury and property damage coverage can reduce the financial impact of an accident. *What type of expenses would be paid for by bodily injury liability coverage?*

What You'll Learn

- How to explain the purpose of financial responsibility law
- How to describe the types of automobile insurance

Why It's Important

Knowing about the different types of automobile insurance coverage will help you buy the best policy for your needs.

Legal Terms

- financial responsibility law
- bodily injury liability insurance
- medical payments insurance
- uninsured motorist insurance
- underinsured motorist insurance
- property damage liability insurance
- collision insurance
- comprehensive insurance
- no-fault insurance

The insurance types listed here are often included in a package policy. *Does your state require vehicle owners to carry liability insurance to register a vehicle?*

Figure 16.6	Types of Automobile Insurance
Type of Insurance	**What It Covers**
Bodily Injury Liability	Injuries to other persons if the insured is at fault.
Property Damage Liability	Damage to the car(s) or property of others if the insured is at fault.
Collision	Damage to the insured's car.
Comprehensive	Loss or damage to the insured's car caused by fire, flood, storm, theft, or vandalism.
Medical Payments	Medical expenses incurred by anyone occupying the insured's car.
Uninsured or Underinsured Motorist	Injuries to the insured if another is at fault and has little or no insurance or the insured is involved in a hit-and-run accident.

Bodily Injury Coverage

The main types of bodily injury coverage are bodily injury liability, medical payments, and uninsured motorist's protection (see Figure 16.6).

Bodily injury liability insurance protects the insured against claims or lawsuits for injuries or death caused by negligence. To recover from the insurance company, the injured person must prove that the driver of the motor vehicle was at fault.

Two numbers, such as 100/300, are often used to describe bodily injury liability coverage. These amounts represent thousands of dollars of coverage. In the previous example, $100,000 is the maximum amount that the insurance company will pay for the injuries of any one person in any one accident. The second number, $300,000, is the maximum amount the company will pay for all injured parties in any one accident.

Medical payments insurance pays for medical, and sometimes funeral, expenses resulting from bodily injuries to anyone occupying the policyholder's car in an accident. In some states, this type of policy pays the medical bills of all family members who are struck by a car or who are riding in someone else's car when the car is in an accident.

Uninsured motorist insurance provides protection when the insured is injured in an automobile accident that is caused by a driver who has no insurance. This coverage also protects parties who are injured by a hit-and-run driver. **Underinsured motorist insurance** protects you when another driver has insurance, but not enough to pay for any injuries.

Property Damage Coverage

The main types of property damage coverage are property damage liability, collision, and comprehensive insurance.

Property damage liability insurance applies when you damage the property of others, including such things such as another car, a house, a telephone pole, or a tree. The person bringing the claim must show that the driver of the vehicle was at fault.

Collision insurance covers damage to your vehicle when it is in an accident and pays for vehicle repairs, regardless of who was at fault. The amount you collect is limited to the actual cash value of the vehicle. The cost of collision insurance can be reduced if you carry part of the risk, known as a deductible clause. For example, under a $500-deductible policy, you pay for the first $500 of any loss and the insurance company pays the remainder of any loss more than $500. If you use

LAWS in Your Life

Fighting a Traffic Ticket

Deciding whether to fight a traffic ticket or simply take your lumps should be based on the circumstances surrounding your case. When evaluating your chances of winning, it's a good idea to look at several factors. Determine whether it's worth the fight. If you're a good driver with a clean record, you may want to simply pay the fine and get it over with. Some states offer traffic school as a way to keep your record clean.

If you decide to fight a ticket, develop a proper strategy before going to court. Study the law under which the ticket was issued. Application of the law is usually open to some interpretation. Knowing the exact wording may help you present your case in a way most favorable to you.

Before coming to court, make a diagram or take photographs of the scene to help you explain the situation to the judge. If you have witnesses, ask them to testify on your behalf. Present whatever evidence you can to help the judge understand what happened.

Research Find the traffic laws of your city or state and research U-turns. After reading the law, can you identify any circumstances under which making a U-turn would be legal? Explain your answer.

Maintenance Online

Automakers are beginning to offer car buyers online help for automobile maintenance. Many automakers offer online tips on how to maintain your vehicle, but a few car companies go further than that. Subaru allows customers to create their own MySubaru Web page to track dealer maintenance on their cars. This site links to a database that tracks individual vehicle identification numbers. The dealer is able to update the service records whenever it works on a car. The system is especially useful for tracking warranty work or upkeep performed under maintenance programs purchased by customers. The system also makes it easier for car owners to support a claim under the warranty. (Source: *InternetWeek*, January 2, 2001)

Connect Visit Web sites of other car companies to see if they offer similar systems.

a bank or other lender to finance the purchase of a car, you will probably be required to carry collision insurance.

Comprehensive insurance applies to damage to your vehicle from sources other than collision, including fire, theft, lightning, flood, hail, windstorm, riot, and vandalism. The insurance company's liability is

NEGLIGENCE
Motor vehicle accidents can be caused by negligence. *What type of insurance covers damage to another person's vehicle when you cause an accident? What type of insurance covers your own vehicle?*

limited to the actual cash value of the damaged property at the time of the loss. Carrying a deductible can reduce the cost of comprehensive insurance.

> *Example 5.* Jason's car was covered by a comprehensive insurance policy. When it was stolen and presumed unrecoverable, Jason claimed the insurance company was liable for the replacement cost of the car. Instead, the company offered the actual cash market value of the automobile at the time of the theft. The insurance company was correct in its settlement.

No-Fault Insurance

Until the end of 1970, an automobile accident victim could collect damages for injuries only after proving that the other driver caused the accident. Courts became clogged with lawsuits involving the question of fault. Accident victims sometimes had to wait years before being compensated. In addition, lawsuits resulted in inconsistent decisions. Costs, including insurance premiums, legal fees, and court costs, continued to rise. To solve this problem, no-fault automobile insurance was developed. Under **no-fault insurance**, regardless of who caused the accident, all drivers involved collect money from their own insurance companies. Because no-fault systems vary by state, you should investigate the coverage provided by no-fault insurance in your state.

Section 16.2 Assessment

Reviewing What You Learned
1. Describe bodily injury liability insurance. What does it cover?
2. What type of insurance protects parties who are injured by hit-and-run drivers?

Critical Thinking Activity
Fair Rates Teenage boys pay a much higher rate for automobile insurance than teenage girls do. Is this fair? Explain why or why not. Then take an informal survey of the students in your class who have had tickets or accidents. Are the boys or girls better drivers?

Legal Skills in Action
Motorcycle Helmet Laws Florida recently passed a law allowing people to ride motorcycles without wearing helmets. However, Florida law requires unprotected riders to carry medical insurance in case of injury. With a partner, debate whether people should be allowed to ride motorcycles without helmets. Does the requirement for insurance make a difference?

Chapter Summary

Section 16.1 Owning a Vehicle

- Before you sign any documents to purchase a car, you should know the following facts:(1) the exact price you are paying for the vehicle; (2) the amount you are financing; (3) the finance charge; (4) the APR (the annual percentage rate); (5) the number and amount of payments you will be required to make; and (6) the total sales price (the sum of the monthly payments plus the down payment).

- Before you buy a new car, do some calculations and research. Determine how much you can reasonably afford to pay for a new car. If you decide that you must borrow money, shop around for the best credit terms. If you are planning on trading in a vehicle, do not discuss it with the dealer until you've negotiated the best price for your new car. Consider selling your old vehicle yourself, instead of trading it in.

- Leasing a car is ultimately more expensive than buying the same car. Although leasing has the advantage of a low down payment and smaller monthly payments, you will have to return the car at the end of the lease period and will have nothing to trade in when you need to obtain another vehicle. If you choose to lease a car, you may also be responsible for excess mileage charges, excess wear charges for body damage or worn tires, and charges for ending your lease early.

- If you have bought a defective car, you should notify the seller of any major defect immediately. You may also be able to revoke your acceptance if the seller has sold you a car with serious and initially undetectable defects.

- Buying a car from a dealer usually entitles you to the protection afforded by the warranty of merchantability and the warranty of fitness for a particular purpose. Another advantage of buying a used car from a dealership is that dealers often give you a guarantee. Buying a car from a private party is sometimes cheaper than buying a car from a dealership. However, buying from a private party does not give you the benefit of the implied warranty of merchantability. You must buy the car "as is," and as a result, you will have no recourse if something goes wrong with the car. The car may also be stolen, and it may be repossessed by the rightful owner, even though you have purchased it in good faith. If you choose to buy from a private party, it is generally a good idea to buy from a friend or associate. Buying a rental car might be a good option, but keep in mind that such vehicles may have had heavy use and will probably have high mileage. On the other hand, rental vehicles usually have had regularly scheduled maintenance and come with warranties.

- The federal odometer law requires everyone who transfers a vehicle, unless it is more than 25 years old, to provide a written mileage disclosure statement showing the odometer reading at the time of the transfer. This law is an attempt to prevent odometer fraud.

- If an auto shop is responsible for some wrongdoing with regard to your car, the bonding company is an insurer who must pay you for resulting losses suffered. This requirement protects consumers from unscrupulousness or incompetence of auto repair shops.

Section 16.2 Motor Vehicle Insurance

- The purpose of financial responsibility law is to protect against injury or damage to property resulting from an accident.

- Bodily injury liability insurance protects the insured against claims or lawsuits for injuries or death caused by his or her negligence. The maximum amount of coverage is $100,000 for any person in any one accident, and $300,000 for all injured parties in any one accident. Uninsured motorist insurance protects you from a driver who commits a hit-and-run or a driver who is uninsured.

Using Legal Language

Consider the key terms in the list below. Then use the terms to complete the following exercises.

finance charge

Buyer's Guide

collision insurance

no-fault insurance

financial responsibility law

bodily injury liability insurance

uninsured motorist insurance

property damage liability insurance

Used Car Rule

repossess

comprehensive insurance

adhesion contract

Using as many of the key terms as you can:

1. Create a public service awareness poster on one of the following topics:
   - How to Buy a New Car
   - Car Insurance: Why it is Important
   - How to Buy a Used Car
   - How to Seek Relief if You Purchase a Defective Vehicle
   - How to Decide between Buying and Leasing a Car
2. On a separate sheet of paper, describe your public service awareness poster. Explain why you chose the images you selected.

Understanding Business and Personal Law Online

Self-Check Quiz Visit the *Understanding Business and Personal Law* Web site at **ubpl.glencoe.com** and click on Chapter 16: Owning a Vehicle— Self-Check Quizzes to prepare for the chapter exam.

The Law Review

Answer the following questions. Refer to the chapter for additional reinforcement.

3. What two things must a prospective lender disclose under the requirements issued by Regulation Z?
4. What information should you know before signing any financing documents?
5. Given the financial disadvantages of leasing, why do some people still choose to lease new cars?
6. What does the Used Car Rule require?
7. What are the advantages of buying a used car from a dealership?
8. On what grounds might a seller be liable for damages if a car is defective?
9. Name the principal kinds of automobile insurance. What kind of loss does each cover?
10. Describe no-fault insurance.

Linking School to Work

Acquiring and Evaluating Information

Carlos is a young executive with a phone-based personal digital assistant and Internet-enabled cell phone. He is connected to the World Wide Web no matter where he is, even in his car. He becomes distracted, however, talking to a disgruntled client, checking his stocks, and driving at the same time.

Research

11. What are the current statistics about car accidents that can be attributed to using cell phones while driving?
12. Are there any laws prohibiting the use of cell phones while driving?
13. How does the United States compare with Europe on this issue?

Let's Debate

Leasing a Car

Bena just graduated from law school and needs a new car. She has little savings but has just started a new job at a prestigious law firm. Bena is eager to project the image of a successful attorney by driving a nice car. Bena decides to lease a car because doing so will enable her to afford a more impressive vehicle. The salesperson at the dealership tells Bena she has made a wise decision.

Debate

14. Does Bena have a good reason to lease a car?
15. Under what circumstances is it a good idea to lease a car?
16. What would you do if you were Bena?

Grasping Case Issues

For the following cases, give your decision and state a legal principle that applies.

17. After graduating from high school, Megan got a job as a legal secretary. She needed a car to get to work. The salesperson at a dealership told her that she should lease a new car for three years. Was this good advice? Explain your answer.
18. Hagley buys a used car from a dealer, who arranges financing with a local finance company. The car has a 30-day warranty. Two days after Hagley drives off the lot, the car's engine quits. The next day the dealer goes out of business. Must Hagley still pay the loan? Why or why not?
19. Rosita test drives a truck at a used car dealership. She notices that the truck has no Buyer's Guide attached to it. When she asks about it, the salesperson replies that the Used Car Rule does not cover a truck, which need not have a Buyer's Guide. Is the dealer correct? Why or why not?
20. Millie buys a used SUV from a private party. The seller makes no statements about the quality of the vehicle. That night, Millie discovers the car's engine has a cracked block. Does she have any legal recourse against the seller? Explain your answer.
21. Akira buys insurance for his van, providing for $20,000 property damage and 20/40 bodily injury liability. An accident occurs in which Akira is at fault. He is not hurt, but three people in the other car suffer bodily injuries to the extent of $80,000. The other car is damaged to the extent of $4,000, and Akira's car is damaged to the extent of $6,000. How much and to whom will Akira's insurance company pay as a result of this accident?

In each case that follows, you be the judge.

22. Buyer's Remedy

Kathleen Liarkos purchased a used Jaguar XJS from Pine Grove Auto Sales. After the car experienced various mechanical problems, Liarkos discovered that the vehicle's odometer had been turned back. Liarkos notified the seller that she revoked her acceptance of the vehicle. *When is this remedy available to a buyer?*
Liarkos v. Mello, 639 N.E.2d 716 (MA).

23. Insurance Provisions

Bayer took his car to Whitaker's auto repair shop for repairs. Whitaker took the car for a test drive, with Bayer seated in the passenger seat. During the test drive, a car drove onto the wrong side of the road and collided with Bayer's vehicle, injuring Bayer. The driver who hit Bayer's car was not insured. Bayer also lacked insurance. However, Whitaker carried insurance on his own vehicles, including uninsured motorist insurance. *Could Bayer recover from Whitaker's insurance company under the uninsured-motorist provision of the policy? Why or why not?*
Bayer v. Travelers Indemnity Co., 267 S.E.2d 91 (VA).

Legal Link

Time to Trade

Arun wants to buy a new car and trade in his 1992 Toyota Tercel. Arun's Tercel has 102,000 miles, and he just put new tires on it. Arun knows he needs to research what his Tercel is worth. In addition, he wants to research the new car he might like to buy. Arun has asked for your help.

Connect

Using a variety of search engines:

24. Research the value of Arun's Toyota Tercel.

25. Find three cars that you think Arun would like.

26. Research the prices and options of these vehicles. Then look for consumer information regarding the reliability of the cars. Prepare a chart summarizing your findings.

POWER READING STRATEGIES

27. **Predict** Is it really worth going into debt to buy a new car? Explain your answer.

28. **Connect** If you bought a used car from someone you did not know, what would you do to make sure the car was in good condition?

29. **Question** Teenagers pay high rates for car insurance. Do you think that this is fair to teenagers who are good, responsible drivers? Why or why not?

30. **Respond** Imagine that a truck ran a stoplight and hit your car, causing thousands of dollars worth of damage. Because you live in a no-fault state, your insurance company pays the damage and raises your rates. How do you feel about no-fault insurance? Explain your answer.

CHAPTER 17

Personal Property and Bailments

Understanding Business and Personal Law *Online*

Chapter Overview Visit the *Understanding Business and Personal Law* Web site at ubpl.glencoe.com and click on Chapter 17: Personal Property and Bailments—Chapter Overviews to preview the chapter information.

The Opening Scene

An and his friend, Naomi, are working on a term paper at the library.

Cars and Planes

AN: I told my Dad I'd pick him up at the airport this afternoon. Want to go? The plane gets in at 3:00.

NAOMI: Sure. I'll call my mom and tell her where we're going. *(Naomi uses her cell phone to call home and returns the phone to her book bag.)*

AN: *(Showing Naomi a page in a book.)* This is some really cool stuff for my term paper. I'll use the copier and work on it at home.

NAOMI: I don't think you're supposed to copy from a book like that.

AN: Who's gonna know? We better get going. I don't want to keep my dad waiting.

NAOMI: *(On the way to the airport.)* I love your car, An.

AN: Actually, it's not mine. I'm keeping my friend Michael's car while he's away. I told him I wouldn't drive it out of town, but I'm sure he won't mind a trip to the airport.

NAOMI: The airport's only twenty miles out of town. Uh-oh! I left my book bag with my money and cell phone at the library!

AN: We'll pick it up when we get back. *(He stops in front of a video store.)* I just have to drop off this video I found under my bed. It's a year overdue.

(At the airport parking garage, An takes a parking ticket from a dispenser. The gate opens, and he finds a parking space. In the airport, An sees his father at the luggage carousel.)

AN: Hi, Dad. This is Naomi. How was your flight?

MR. LEE: Hi, Naomi. Actually, my flight was terrible! Someone took my laptop from the overhead bin.

NAOMI: Oh no!

MR. LEE: *(Spotting his luggage on the revolving belt.)* There's my bag, but look. Someone's opened it! *(He pulls the empty, torn-open bag from the luggage carousel.)* I guess this isn't my day.

NAOMI: *(Later, approaching the car in the parking garage.)* I didn't notice that big dent in your friend's car before, An.

AN: That's because it wasn't there! Oh, man, wait until Michael sees this. I've caught your bad luck, Dad.

MR. LEE: I think the parking garage will pay to have that fixed.

AN: I hope so. It wasn't my fault!

(An and Naomi drop Mr. Lee off at his home and drive back to the library. However, Naomi doesn't find her bag where she left it.)

NAOMI: *(To the librarian.)* I left my book bag beside that table. Did anyone find it?

LIBRARIAN: Yes, a girl said she'd look you up and return it.

NAOMI: Do you have her name?

LIBRARIAN: No. I don't know who she was.

What Are the Legal Issues?

1. Can An copy material from a book without violating copyright laws?
2. Did An violate a duty owed to Michael by driving his car out of town?
3. Did An violate a duty owed to the video store by returning the video a year late?
4. Is the parking garage responsible for the damage done to Michael's car? Who has the burden of proving fault?
5. Is an airline responsible for lost goods that were stored in an overhead bin on a plane? For luggage checked at the gate?
6. Does the person who found Naomi's bag in the library have the legal right to hold it?

Personal Property

What You'll Learn

- How to identify tangible and intangible personal property
- How to decide when a gift of personal property is completed
- How to distinguish between lost, misplaced, and abandoned property
- How to explain the law that applies to stolen property
- How to discuss the law of patents, copyrights, and trademarks

Why It's Important

Knowing the law about personal property will help you safeguard your possessions.

Legal Terms

- real property
- personal property
- tangible/intangible personal property
- donor/donee
- abandoned property
- intellectual property
- patent
- copyright
- fair use doctrine
- trademark

Types of Property

Real property is land and anything permanently attached to it; the earth below and the air space above is also included. **Personal property** is everything that can be owned that is not real property. **Tangible personal property** is something that has substance and can be touched, such as CD players, vehicles, and even food on the table. In contrast, **intangible personal property** has no substance and cannot be touched. If someone owes you money, for example, the right to receive the money is intangible personal property.

> *Example 1.* Natalia got a $47 check for baby-sitting. The paper on which the check was written was tangible, yet it had no value. However, the words written on the check were valuable because they ordered the bank to pay Natalia money. Natalia's right to receive the money was intangible personal property.

Gifts of Personal Property

A gift of personal property is completed when three requirements are met:

- The **donor** (the one making the gift) must intend to make the gift
- The gift must be delivered
- The **donee** (the one receiving the gift) must accept the gift

> *Example 2.* Mrs. Nadeau said to Lydia, "I'm giving you this set of china. I'll keep it here in my china cabinet for now, but I want you to consider it yours." The gift was not complete because the china was not delivered to Lydia.

Lost Property

If you find a watch, you have a legal duty to try to find the true owner. If the owner can't be found, you may be able to keep the watch after following the requirements of your local laws.

Local Laws   Some states provide for the special handling of lost articles. Local laws may, for example, require you to advertise for the true owner of the item or to deposit the article at the police station while the owner is being sought. If you find a lost item, check with local authorities to determine the legal policies that apply. Do not keep any items that you may find without researching such policies.

COMPLETED GIFT?
A gift cannot be taken back after three requirements are met. *What are the requirements of a completed gift?*

Rewards and Reimbursement   To be entitled to a reward, you must know about the offer when you return the property. If you learn about the reward after returning the property, you are not entitled to it.

Misplaced Property

If property is found in a public or semi-public place, it is considered misplaced rather than lost. The owner will probably recall where it was left and return for it. If you find an article in such a place, you should leave it with the proprietor or manager. The proprietor must not knowingly allow misplaced property to be taken by anyone other than the rightful owner.

> *Example 3.* While trying on a dress, Alice found a purse in a fitting room of the Fashion Dress Shop. She immediately gave the purse to the owner of the store. Alice was not entitled to keep the purse because she found it in a public area.

Abandoned property is property that has been discarded by the owner without the intent to reclaim ownership. With some exceptions, anyone who finds abandoned property has the right to keep it and obtain good title to it.

Something that is found in a corridor or place where it was probably not placed intentionally would be considered lost rather than misplaced.

Stolen Personal Property

A thief acquires no title to goods that are stolen and cannot give good title to anyone else. An innocent purchaser who acquires a stolen

A Global Perspective: Laws Around the World

Canada

At the University of Montreal in December 1989, tragedy struck. One man with a gun took the lives of 14 young women. Known as the Massacre of Montreal, there is a commemoration each year near the scene of the crime.

- Pass a Canadian Firearms Safety Course test.
- Obtain a renewable firearms license for restricted (handguns) and non-restricted (rifles and shotguns) firearms and ammunition.
- Register for each firearm acquired.
- Obtain permission from the Chief Firearms Officer before selling or giving a firearm to someone else.

These provisions were implemented to decrease criminal offenses, keep firearms away from dangerous people, confiscate dangerous firearms from private ownership and businesses, and regulate the sale, use, transportation, and storage of firearms. "Prevention = Public Safety," reasons one Canadian firearms manual. Here's a snapshot of Canada.

Geographical area	**3,849,670 sq. mi.**
Population	**31,902,268**
Capital	**Ottawa**
Legal system	**Based on English common law, except in Quebec, where civil law system based on French law prevails**
Language	**English, French**
Religion	**46% Roman Catholic, 36% Protestant**
Life expectancy	**80 years**

Critical Thinking Question Gun control is as controversial in the United States as it is in Canada. Many citizens are adamant about defending their right to bear arms, but others feel that strict gun control would greatly reduce the nation's rate of violent crime. The Second Amendment of the United States Constitution states that it's "the right of the people to keep and bear arms." The Constitution was drafted in 1787; do you think that the Second Amendment is still relevant in the twenty-first century? For more information on Canada, visit **ubpl.glencoe.com** or your local library.

item in good faith is obliged to return it to the owner. Title to stolen goods never leaves the owner, who can always regain possession.

Intellectual Property

Intellectual property is an original work fixed in a tangible medium of expression. Patents, copyrights, and trademarks assure that the rightful owners of intellectual property will have exclusive rights to their creations. Figure 17.1 discusses how intellectual property laws protect property rights to software, hardware, and other technologies.

Patents

A **patent** gives an inventor the exclusive right to make, use, or sell an invention for 17 years. To be patented, a device must consist of a new principle or idea. In addition, it must be useful and not obvious to people with ordinary skill in the field. The device may consist of a process, an article of manufacture, or a composition of matter.

To be legally protected, a patented item must be marked with the word "patent" followed by the patent number. If this mark is not made, anyone making the same item without knowledge of the patent cannot be sued for damages. Some inventors put the words "patent pending" or "patent applied for" on their products. This notice informs others that an application for a patent has been filed.

Copyrights

A **copyright** is a right granted to an author, composer, photographer, or artist to exclusively publish and sell an artistic or literary work. Copyrighted works are protected for the life of the author plus 70 years.

A copyright is registered with the U.S. Copyright Office in Washington, D.C. To protect a work in the past, it was necessary to put the notice ©, or the word "copyright," followed by the date and the name of the owner on the work. The use of the copyright notice is now optional. With exceptions, copyrighted material may not be reproduced without the written permission of the holder of the copyright.

Under the **fair use doctrine**, copyrighted material may be reproduced without permission in certain cases. The amount and use of the material must be reasonable and not harmful to the copyright owner. Copying is allowed for literary criticism, news reporting, teaching, school reports, and other research. Downloading and uploading music on the Internet for others' use is a violation of copyright law and subject to civil and criminal penalties.

Trademarks

A **trademark** is a distinctive mark, symbol, or slogan used by a business to identify and distinguish its goods from products sold by others. It may consist of a word, name, symbol, or other device. Owners

It's a Question of Ethics

Leaping Dolphins
Alphonse has found an image on the Internet of three dolphins leaping out of the ocean. It's a photograph that he has seen before in a magazine. He is able to save the image to a disk and create a T-shirt transfer. Then he applies this image to a T-shirt that he wears to school. *Several of Alphonse's friends want similar shirts. Should Alphonse make the T-shirts? What are his ethical responsibilities in this case?*

With the advance of the Internet and other technologies, property owners in software and hardware increasingly rely on copyright and trademark protection in these emerging areas of intellectual property.

Trade Secrets

A trade secret is specialized knowledge associated with a particular firm. These secrets include the business or manufacturing plans, unique technology, customer lists, and other sensitive information that, if known by a competitor, would put the company at a competitive disadvantage. Trade secrets are often protected by restrictive covenants, which are agreements with employees not to work elsewhere in similar employment, or by agreements not to compete, which prohibit a person from operating a similar business in a certain geographical area or for specified period of time.

Computer software makers frequently treat their works as trade secrets. This approach has the advantage of not having set time limits on legal protection. Many software producers have also attempted to use licensing laws to protect their work by requiring users to register their purchased software, often online at the producer's Web site.

Trademark Protection

Trademark law is important to protecting property rights in software and hardware. For example, the law of trademarks applies to domain names. A domain name, such as Amazon.com®, is the Web address that uniquely identifies a firm on the Internet. This domain name is usually part of the larger Universal Resource Locator (URL), such as http://www.amazon.com. Because companies want to protect the goodwill associated with their name and want it to uniquely identify them in customers' minds, they may use trademark law to protect their domain name.

The Anti-Cybersquatting Consumer Protection Act of 1999 makes it illegal for someone to buy a domain name and then resell it to a company that owns the trademark. To win a case under this law, a company needs to demonstrate that it owns the trademark and that the cybersquatter acted in bad faith in buying the domain name.

Copyright Protection

The Computer Software Copyright Act of 1980 protects software makers. This act defines a computer program as a "set of statements or instructions to be used directly in a computer in order to bring about a certain act." Purchasers may make copies for themselves, but the law protects owners from the kinds of widespread copying that result in loss of revenue.

PROTECTING RIGHTS TO TECHNOLOGY
The laws are evolving to protect intellectual property rights in technology. *If someone creates a Web site aimed at disparaging a business, should the business be able to sue for damages?*

of trademarks have the exclusive right to use the particular word, name, or symbol that they have adopted as their trademark.

Trademarks may be established by usage, state trademark laws, and registration with the U.S. Patent and Trademark Office. A registered trademark continues for 10 years and may be renewed for additional 10-year periods. The ® symbol indicates that a trademark is registered.

CORPORATE TRADEMARKS
Many companies spend large amounts of money to develop and protect their trademarks. *How are trademarks established?*

Section 17.1 Assessment

Reviewing What You Learned
1. Give two examples of tangible personal property and one example of intangible personal property.
2. What are the three requirements of a completed gift?
3. Explain the differences between lost, misplaced, and abandoned property.
4. Cite methods of acquiring ownership of personal property.
5. Describe the difference between a patent, copyright, and trademark.
6. Differentiate between personal and really property.

Critical Thinking Activity
Intellectual Property Using the Internet, library, or other resource, research and identify federal and state trademark or copyright laws pertaining to hardware and software. In a one- to two-page paper, briefly describe each law and the protections it provides.

Legal Skills in Action
Personal Property Myra found a diamond and ruby necklace on the sidewalk near her home. She was very excited because rubies are her birthstone and she loves diamonds. Is the necklace considered lost, misplaced, or abandoned property? What should Myra do with the necklace? What laws apply to this situation? Write a letter to Myra offering your advice.

Bailments

What You'll Learn

- How to define a bailment
- How to describe kinds of bailments
- How to explain who has the burden of proof in bailment lawsuits
- How to explain hotel keepers' duties
- How to identify the rights and duties of common carriers
- How to discuss the obligations of common carriers toward passengers

Why It's Important

Understanding the law of bailments can help you avoid difficulties.

Legal Terms

- bailment
- bailor/bailee
- mutuum
- gratuitous bailments
- gross negligence
- slight negligence
- reasonable care
- ordinary negligence
- tortious bailee
- carrier
- common carrier

Bailments of Personal Property

You may have rented movies at a video store, left your car at a shop to be repaired, or dropped clothes off at the cleaners. In these situations, you entered into a relationship called a bailment. Bailments give rise to specific rights and duties.

A **bailment** is the transfer of possession and control of personal property to another with the intent that the same property will be returned later. The person who transfers the property is the **bailor** . The person to whom the property is transferred is the **bailee** .

Example 4. Eric's English teacher assigned a lengthy term paper. Eric had to type his paper but did not own a computer. He borrowed a laptop from his friend, Quanna. This situation illustrates a bailment. Eric was the bailee, and Quanna was the bailor. Even in this simple transaction, basic legal rights and duties exist.

In a bailment, neither the bailor nor the bailee intends that title to the property should pass. The bailee has an obligation to return the same property to the bailor at a later time. A bailment does not occur when the person in possession of the property has no right of control over it.

Example 5. Sewall parked his car in a commercial parking lot and took the keys with him. An attendant was on duty in the morning and left the lot unattended for the rest of the day. In the afternoon, Sewall's car was stolen. This was not a bailment because the attendant had no right of control over Sewall's car. Instead, Sewall had simply rented a parking space.

In contrast, a bailment exists when someone parks a car in a garage or lot that has an attendant present at all times to check cars going in and out. Similarly, the courts have held that a bailment takes place when a car owner surrenders his or her car keys to a parking lot attendant.

When you loan goods to someone with the understanding that they will be used and later replaced with different identical goods, a **mutuum** has occurred.

Example 6. Liang borrowed a cup of sugar from her neighbor to make cookies. She returned a cup of sugar to her neighbor the

BORROWING FROM NEIGHBORS
It's common for neighbors to borrow sugar, milk, flour, or similar goods from each other. These situations illustrate a mutuum. *Why is a mutuum different from a bailment?*

next day after grocery shopping. The loan of the sugar was a mutuum because the parties did not intend that the identical granules of sugar that were borrowed would be returned.

Main Types of Bailments

There are three types of bailments: bailments for the sole benefit of the bailor; bailments for the sole benefit of the bailee; and mutual-benefit bailments. In the first two types, called **gratuitous bailments**, property is transferred to another person without either party giving or asking for payment. Gratuitous bailments are usually considered favors. In reality, however, definite legal responsibilities are placed upon both the bailor and bailee.

Bailments for Sole Benefit of Bailor

When a personal possession is transferred to another person for purposes that will benefit only the bailor, a bailment for the sole benefit of the bailor results.

Example 7. Your friend asks you to look after her car while she is away for a week. You agree to keep your friend's car in your garage. This bailment will be a bailment for the sole benefit of the bailor. Your friend is the only person benefiting from the arrangement.

In a bailment for the sole benefit of the bailor, the bailee owes a duty to use only slight care, as the bailee is receiving no benefit from

the arrangement. The bailee is required only to refrain from **gross negligence** (very great negligence).

The bailor has a duty to reimburse the bailee for expenses involved in the care of the property. However, the bailee has no implied right to use the bailor's property. Suppose that, in Example 7, your friend does not give you permission to use her car, but you drive it anyway. If you were involved in an accident, you would be liable for damages.

Bailments for Sole Benefit of Bailee

When personal property is transferred for purposes that will benefit only the bailee, a bailment for the sole benefit of the bailee occurs.

Example 8. George offered his truck to his friend, Trina, who was moving to a new apartment. This offer was a friendly gesture on George's part; he had no expectation of payment. Trina accepted the offer and used George's truck for her move. This bailment was a bailment for the sole benefit of the bailee. George was the bailor; Trina was the bailee.

In this type of bailment, the bailee is required to use great care because possession of the goods is intended solely for the bailee's benefit. The bailee is responsible for even **slight negligence**, which is the failure to use the care that persons of extraordinary prudence and foresight use. The bailee has the right to use the property only for the purpose for which the bailment was created. Use for another purpose or for a longer time than agreed upon makes the bailee liable for any resulting damage.

Mutual-Benefit Bailments

A mutual-benefit bailment (see Figure 17.2) is one in which both the bailor and the bailee receive some benefit. Leaving a car at a garage to be repaired is an example of a mutual-benefit bailment. Other examples are placing one's property in storage, and leaving a diamond ring at a pawnshop as security for a loan. In a mutual-benefit bailment, the bailee owes a duty to use **reasonable care**, or the degree of care that a reasonably prudent person would use in the situation. The bailee is responsible for **ordinary negligence**, or failing to use the care that a reasonable person would use under the same circumstances.

Example 9. Champine paid to store his boat in Field's building for the winter. Champine expressed some doubts about the soundness of the building, particularly the roof, but Field assured him it was safe. The roof collapsed after a winter snowstorm, damaging Champine's boat. In allowing Champine to recover from Field, the court said the relationship imposed a duty on the bailee to use ordinary care, which he failed to do.

MUTUAL-BENEFIT BAILMENTS
In a mutual-benefit bailment, the bailor and the bailee receive some benefit. *What are some examples of mutual-benefit bailments?*

Figure 17.2	Mutual-Benefit Bailments	
Bailment	**Bailor**	**Bailee**
Service or repair	Owns the item to be serviced or repaired	Performs the repair or service work
Storage or parking	Owns the item to be stored or parked	Is responsible for the storing or parking
Security for a loan	Pledgor, debtor—borrows money	Pledgee, creditor—lends money
Renting or leasing	Rents an item to someone	Pays to use an item
Bailments by necessity	Gives up possession of property	Accepts or protects the property

Many courts today apply the reasonable care standard to all types of bailments, including bailments for the sole benefit of the bailor and bailments for the sole benefit of the bailee.

Short-term storage may also create a bailment. For example, when a customer delivers a coat to the checkroom attendant of a hotel or restaurant, a bailment takes place. In contrast, when a customer hangs a coat on a hook in a shop or restaurant, a bailment does not usually exist because the shop or restaurant owner has no control over the property.

Sometimes a bailment is coupled with the loan of money. Property of the borrower, such as a stock certificate, may be turned over to the lender to hold as security for the loan. The property left as security is called the pledge, or pawn.

Tortious Bailees

A **tortious bailee** refers to a person who wrongfully keeps the lost property of another or knowingly possesses stolen property. One who uses a bailed article for a purpose other than agreed upon or who refuses to return property at the termination of the bailment may also be considered a tortious bailee. If you found a watch and knew who the owner was and refused to return it, you would be considered a tortious

Virtual Law

The Napster Case

Napster was created by a college student who wanted to share music online with friends. He used software that allows anyone to download copies of music from the Internet. This software made it possible for people to log on to Napster for free music downloads. Many of the songs are copyrighted.

At trial, the court said that Napster must prevent users from downloading copyrighted music. The court found that Napster knew the downloading of free music from its system violated copyright law and harmed copyright holders.

Nevertheless, the type of song trading system used by Napster is not going to go away. Eventually the music companies will use similar technology to create subscriber-based services that will allow musicians to receive payment. (Source: *Associated Press*, 2/12/01; *Cox News Service*, 3/3/01)

Connect Check the Web sites of major recording companies. See which, if any, have agreements covering the sharing of downloaded music. Create a contract that would address important legal issues.

bailee. Tortious bailees are responsible for all damage to property in their possession, regardless of the degree of care exercised and the cause of the damage.

Burden of Proof

Sometimes items are damaged, lost, or stolen when they are in the possession of a bailee. The bailor is not in a position to know what caused the loss. If a bailor brings suit for damages, most courts shift the burden of proof to the one who is in the best position to know what happened: the bailee. As a result, the burden is on the bailee to prove a lack of negligence.

Special Bailments

Certain types of bailees have special obligations in addition to the duties imposed on all bailees. These include hotel keepers and common carriers.

Hotel Keepers

Hotel keepers are special bailees because of the special nature of their business. A hotel keeper, also called an innkeeper, is the operator of a hotel, motel, or inn that regularly offers rooms to the public for a price. The common law imposed the duty upon innkeepers to accept all people who requested lodging if rooms were available. In addition, innkeepers were considered to be insurers of their guests' property. With exceptions, this is still the law today.

The relationship between a guest and a hotel keeper begins when the hotel keeper accepts a person as a guest. This usually occurs when that person checks into the hotel. However, a person may become a guest by giving his or her luggage to a hotel porter or to a person operating the hotel's limousine service. Once established, the relationship of hotel keeper and guest continues until the bill is paid and the guest departs.

A transient is a person whose stay at a hotel is uncertain in length. Transients want temporary lodging and may leave at any time. In contrast, a lodger, also called a roomer, is a person staying at a hotel, motel, or rooming house for a definite period of time. Thus the arrangement between a rooming housekeeper and a roomer is of a more permanent character than the relationship between a hotel or motel and a guest.

Example 10. Rhoda Quezada was able to secure a comfortable room at the Mainliner Motel. After three days' residence, she decided that the Mainliner was ideally located for her business. She made arrangements to rent the room for six months at a special rate. Although Quezada was originally a transient guest, the new arrangement changed her status to that of a roomer, or lodger.

RIGHT OF PRIVACY
Hotel keepers must respect their guests' right of privacy. *For what tort are hotels liable for breach of this duty?*

Duty to Accept All Guests   Assuming that rooms are available, a hotel keeper must accept all people who are not dangerous to the health, welfare, or safety of others and who are able to pay for their lodging. The Civil Rights Act of 1964 makes it a crime for hotel keepers to refuse a room to anyone on the grounds of race, creed, color, sex, or national origin.

The requirement to provide lodging for those willing to pay has been the rule for hundreds of years. It dates back to a time in history when travel was not safe. Robbers and highwaymen abounded, and it was not safe to stay on the road overnight. Hotels, or inns, were places of refuge; to refuse guests lodging was to leave them at the mercy of those who would rob them. Travel is comparatively safe today, but the genuine need for convenient overnight accommodations remains.

Example 11. Bob Freytag sought lodging at the Mainliner Motel but was refused. The clerk could give no reason for his refusal other than her personal dislike for Freytag's political affiliation. Freytag was a member of a minority political group that was holding a convention in the town at the time. Freytag could hold the motel liable for any damages that had resulted from the motel's failure to accept him as a guest.

Duty of Reasonable Care Hotels and motels must provide a minimum standard of comfort, safety, and sanitation. Minimum standards include reasonable heat and ventilation, clean beds, reasonably quiet surroundings, and freedom from disturbances by hoodlums, criminals, and persons of immoral character. Hotel keepers must use reasonable care in protecting their guests from harm. They are responsible for injuries to guests caused by the negligence of the hotel or its employees.

> *Example 12.* A section of carpeting in the hall outside Susan's room at the Main Street Motel had torn loose, and the motel housekeeper had neglected to repair it. Susan tripped over the carpeting, suffering painful injuries. She may hold the motel responsible for damages resulting from the injury.

Hotel keepers must respect their guests' right of privacy. Guests are guaranteed exclusive and undisturbed privacy of rooms assigned by the hotel. Interruption of the guests' privacy through uninvited entry by hotel employees or other guests creates a liability in tort for invasion of privacy.

> *Example 13.* Eliza stopped at the Ocean Breeze Motel for the night. After taking a shower, she opened the bathroom door and discovered a couple bringing suitcases into her room. The motel clerk had assigned the room to the couple by mistake. Eliza may seek damages against the motel for invasion of privacy.

Hotel keepers have a greater duty of care toward their guests' property than is imposed in the usual mutual-benefit bailment. With exceptions, hotel keepers are held by law to be insurers of their guests' property. The insured property includes all personal property brought into the hotel for the convenience and purpose of the guests' stay. In the event of loss, the hotel keeper may be held liable, regardless of the amount of care exercised in the protection of the guests' property.

Most state statutes require hotel keepers to provide a secure place, such as a hotel safe, for guests to store valuables. If guests do not use the hotel safe, the hotel keeper is not liable as an insurer for any loss.

> *Example 14.* Isabel rented a room at the Evergreen Hotel. She had in her possession a valuable diamond necklace, which disappeared during the night. The hotel proved that there was a good lock on the door and that all reasonable precautions had been made to protect the hotel against theft. The hotel escaped liability because Isabel should have put her necklace in the hotel safe.

Community Works

Gift of Life
Blood is one of the human body's most precious assets. Around the world there is an ongoing need for blood donors. In the United States, the Red Cross collects about 50 percent of the blood for the nation's blood banks. Licensed by the Food and Drug Administration, blood banks screen blood and donors for infectious diseases, such as hepatitis, AIDS, and malaria. *How do you feel about donating blood?*

Get Involved
Check with your local Red Cross about volunteering with their Blood Drive campaigns. Find out if there are laws that prevent some people from being donors, and write a report.

Guests are permitted to keep in their rooms valuables that they would ordinarily have on their person, such as a watch, jewelry, and a reasonable amount of cash. Hotel keepers are not liable as insurers in the following cases:

- Losses caused by a guest's own negligence
- Losses to the guest's property due to acts of God (events such as earthquakes, floods, or cyclones) or due to acts of the public enemy (people such as terrorists or wartime enemies)
- Loss of property because of accidental fire in which no negligence may be attributed to the hotel keeper

Hotel Keeper's Lien and Credit Card Blocking Hotel keepers have a lien on their guests' property. If a guest cannot pay the bill, the hotel keeper is permitted to take possession of the guest's property as security for payment at some later time.

Credit card blocking is a common method used by hotels to secure payment for a room. Under this system, guests are asked for a credit card number when they register. The hotel then contacts the card company with the estimated cost of the bill. If the card issuer approves the transaction, the guest's available line of credit is reduced by the estimated amount. This procedure is known as a block (or authorization). The final actual charge for the room will replace the block within a day or two after the guest checks out.

Common Carriers

A **carrier** is a business that transports persons, goods, or both. A **common carrier** is a carrier that is compensated for providing transportation to the general public. As with hotels, common carriers cannot turn away people who ask for their services.

Common Carriers of Goods Common carriers of goods are liable for damages to all goods they ship, regardless of whether they are negligent. However, as Figure 17.3 shows, carriers are not liable when damages occur as a result of the following:

- Acts of God
- Acts of a public enemy
- Acts of public authorities
- Acts of the shipper
- The inherent nature of the goods (such as perishable goods, evaporating and fermenting liquids, and diseased animals)

In addition, common carriers must accept without discrimination all goods offered to them for shipment. Discrimination either through the selection of customers or through the use of preferential rates is illegal.

Figure 17.3 — Exceptions to Carrier Liability

1. Act of God	Loss or damage as a result of natural causes such as floods, earthquakes, tornados, and lightning.
2. Act of a Public Enemy	Loss caused by the seizure or destruction of goods by military forces of an opposing government or pirates at sea.
3. Act of Public Authority	Loss as a result of seizure by public authorities.
4. Fault of the Shipper	Loss due to (1) improper packing by the shipper, (2) fraudulent labeling of the contents or concealment of the true value of the goods, and/or (3) improper addressing so that goods are lost.
5. Nature of the Goods	Loss due to damage particular to the good being shipped, such as decay (fruits and vegetables), evaporation or fermentation (liquid), or injury (animals).

An Act of God	A Public Enemy	An Act of a Public Authority	Fault of the Shipper	Inherent Nature of the Goods

INSURERS OF GOODS Common carriers are insurers of all goods they carry with the exceptions listed here. *How are the obligations of common carriers similar to the obligations of hotel keepers?*

Nevertheless, common carriers:

- Are not required to accept goods they are not equipped to carry.
- May refuse goods that are inherently dangerous.
- May refuse goods that they do not haul.
- May refuse goods that are improperly packaged.
- May refuse goods that are not delivered at the proper place and time.

Common carriers will not be excused from liability for losses because of strikes, mob violence, fire, and similar causes. Labor unions are required to give notice of impending strikes weeks in advance of the strike dates to allow carriers to reject shipments that might be damaged by delays during a strike. The carrier is required to ship goods to the proper destination, protect them during shipment, and deliver them to the proper person.

A common carrier has the right to payment of fees agreed upon for the shipment of goods. It also has a lien on all goods shipped for the amount of the shipping charges due. Should the shipper and the party receiving the goods fail to pay the charges, the carrier may sell the goods at public sale.

Common Carriers of Passengers A passenger is a person who enters the premises of a carrier with the intention of buying a ticket for a trip. A carrier must use reasonable care in protecting passengers. The carrier is not responsible, however, if injuries are not foreseeable or preventable.

A carrier's duty of care to its passengers ends, in most cases, when the passenger leaves the carrier's premises. An exception exists when a carrier has a continuing obligation for the care of its passengers, as in the case of a cruise ship. In that instance, the carrier has a duty to warn passengers of known dangers in places where they may reasonably be expected to visit while on the cruise.

Example 15. Mildred and Michael Kushner took a cruise ship to an island in the Caribbean. The members of the ship's crew knew that there were areas on the island where tourists were sometimes robbed but did not warn the passengers of this danger. The Kushners were robbed while visiting one of these areas. The cruise ship had violated its duty to warn passengers of danger and was susceptible to a lawsuit for the Kushner's injuries.

A common carrier must accept all persons who seek passage over its lines, with two exceptions. They may reject passengers when all available space is occupied or reserved, and when passengers are disorderly, intoxicated, insane, or infected with a contagious disease.

Example 16. Howard Anderson, while in a railway coach, started a disturbance that was displeasing to all and possibly dangerous to some. As the train slowed to about five miles per hour through a small town, Anderson was forcibly put off. He suffered an injury and collected damages from the railroad company. The court held that although the carrier was justified in removing Anderson, the train should have come to a full stop before he was removed.

Bumped Airline Passengers When an airline flight is overbooked, the airline must ask for volunteers to give up their seats for seats on the next available flight. If there are not enough volunteers, other passengers may be denied a seat. Airlines are required to establish and publish priority rules for determining which passengers holding confirmed reservation space may be denied boarding on an oversold flight.

Passengers who are denied boarding involuntarily, or "bumped," may be entitled to compensation plus the money back for their tickets. If the airline can arrange alternative transportation that is scheduled to arrive at the passenger's destination within one hour of the original arrival time, there is no compensation. However, if the alternate flight gets to the destination between one and two hours late, the passenger is entitled to a cash payment of up to $200. This amount is doubled if the passenger is more than two hours late. Instead of cash payment, airlines may offer free or reduced-rate air transportation, as long as this rate equals or exceeds the cash payment requirement. Passengers may refuse all compensation and bring private legal action instead.

Passengers' Baggage   Carriers are obligated to accept a reasonable amount of passengers' baggage. Luggage carried aboard an airliner and kept at one's seat does not generally count toward the weight limits permitted each passenger, and you may ship excess baggage by paying additional fees.

A carrier is an insurer of all luggage that is checked through the baggage desk. However, a carrier is not responsible for items that you keep at your seat or in overhead compartments.

Federal rules place limits on the liability of airlines for lost luggage. For travel within the U.S., the maximum liability is $2,500 per passenger. Excess valuation may be declared on certain types of articles. However, some carriers assume no liability for fragile, valuable, or perishable articles.

Section 17.2   Assessment

Reviewing What You Learned
1. What is a bailment? Who is the bailor, and who is the bailee?
2. Name the three main types of bailments.
3. Who has the burden of proof in a bailment lawsuit?
4. What are the hotel keepers' duties of care to their guests?
5. Common carriers are liable for damages to goods unless the damage comes within one of five exceptions. Name the exceptions.
6. When does a carrier's duty of care to its passengers end?

Critical Thinking Activity
Living Bailments The agricultural class at your school raises small animals such as hamsters, rabbits, and guinea pigs. Every weekend several students take the animals home to feed them. Is this a bailment? What is the extent of care that applies? Explain your answer.

Legal Skills in Action
Airline Responsibilities Airlines face a public relations nightmare almost every day. Planes take off late, flights are cancelled, and luggage is lost. Most people don't realize that common carriers have rules they follow regarding the transportation of passengers. Using publishing software, create a brochure that outlines the airline's responsibilities and exceptions. Include information about bumping and baggage.

Chapter Summary

Section 17.1 Personal Property

- Personal property is divided into two categories: tangible, which can be touched; and intangible, which cannot be touched. Examples of tangible property include CD players, vehicles, and food. The right to receive money owed to you is an example of intangible property.

- A gift is completed after three requirements are met: (1) the donor must intend to make a gift; (2) the gift must be delivered; and (3) the donee must accept the gift. After a gift is completed, the original owner cannot take it back.

- Lost property must be returned to the owner if the owner can be found. Misplaced property is property unintentionally left in a public or semi-public area, which must be turned over to the proprietor of the place where it is found. Abandoned property is property that has been intentionally discarded by the owner and may be kept by a finder.

- A thief does not acquire good title to items that are stolen and consequently cannot convey good title to others. Even if a person innocently purchases stolen goods from a thief or other party, the rightful owner still retains title to the goods.

- A patent gives an inventor the exclusive right to make, use, or sell an invention for 17 years. A copyright is a right granted to an artist to exclusively publish and sell an artistic or literary work for the life of the artist plus 70 years. Copyrighted material may be reproduced without permission in some instances. The amount and use of the material must be reasonable and not harmful to the copyright owner. Copying is allowed for literary criticism, news reporting, teaching, school reports, and other research. Trademarks are distinctive marks, names, slogans, and symbols that identify and distinguish a product from other products. A trademark owner has the exclusive right to use the trademark for 10 years. A trademark registration may also be renewed for additional 10-year periods.

Section 17.2 Bailments

- A bailment occurs when someone transfers possession and control of personal property to another with the intent that the same property will be returned later.

- The main types of bailments are: (1) bailments for the sole benefit of the bailor; (2) bailments for the sole benefit of the bailee; and (3) mutual-benefit bailments. The first two types of bailments, bailments for the sole benefit of the bailor and bailments for the sole benefit of the bailee, are called gratuitous bailments.

- If an item that was in the possession of a bailee becomes damaged, lost, or stolen, most courts shift the burden of proof to the bailee, the one who is in the best position to know what happened, to prove lack of negligence.

- Hotel keepers are required to accept all guests unless there are no vacancies. They must use reasonable care in protecting guests from harm, and they must respect their guests' rights of privacy. With some exceptions, hotel keepers are liable as insurers of guests' property, up to an amount set by state statute.

- Common carriers of goods must accept without discrimination all goods offered to them for shipment. Common carriers are liable as insurers of the goods they ship, regardless of whether they have been negligent. They are not responsible, however, for damages caused by certain circumstances beyond their control.

- Common carriers of passengers must accept all persons who seek passage, and they must use reasonable care in protecting their passengers. In addition, a carrier is an insurer of checked luggage, but not carry-on items.

Using Legal Language

Consider the key terms in the list below. Then use these terms to complete the following exercises.

donor
donee
patent
copyright
trademark
bailment
bailor
mutuum
reasonable care
tortious bailee

personal property
tangible personal property
intangible personal property
abandoned property
intellectual property
gross negligence
gratuitous bailments
slight negligence
ordinary negligence

Understanding Business and Personal Law Online

Visit the *Understanding Business and Personal Law* Web site at **ubpl.glencoe.com** and click on Chapter 17: Personal Property and Bailments— Self-Check Quizzes to prepare for the chapter exam.

1. Prepare a two-minute speech about personal property and bailment. Use at least 12 of the key terms listed above in your speech.
2. Give your speech in front of a classmate, and listen carefully while your classmate does the same.
3. Compare and contrast your speeches. What terms were used by your classmate? What are the differences between your speeches? What are the similarities?

The Law Review

Answer the following questions. Refer to the chapter for additional reinforcement.
4. Who may obtain: (1) patents, (2) copyrights, and (3) trademarks?
5. What rights does each of the items listed in question 4 grant, and for how long are these rights granted?
6. In what way does a mutual-benefit bailment differ from a gratuitous bailment?
7. Cite methods of acquiring ownership of personal property.
8. What is the difference between a transient and a lodger?
9. What is credit card blocking, and why is it used?
10. Under what circumstances may common carriers refuse goods?

Linking School to Work

Acquiring and Evaluating Information
Invite a local hotel keeper to make a presentation to your class. Find out how the hotel keeper interprets the special obligations that are imposed on him or her as a bailee. Ask about the following topics:

- The duty to accept all guests
- The duty of reasonable care
- The guests' rights of privacy
- Credit card blocking

11. As a class, prepare your questions ahead of time. After the presentation, write a one-page report about what you learned.

Let's Debate

Damaged Jacket
Your friend Emily lends you her school jacket. While you are walking home, a passing car goes through a puddle and splashes mud on Emily's jacket. You want to take good care of the jacket, so you wash it. Unfortunately, the jacket shrinks. You neglected to read the tag that says the jacket is "dry clean only." Now Emily's jacket is ruined.

Debate
12. This situation represents what type of bailment?
13. Were you required to use slight care or great care during the time you had possession of the jacket?
14. What can Emily do if you refuse to buy her a new jacket?

Grasping Case Issues

For the following cases, give your decision and state a legal principle that applies.

15. Leigh finds a lady's purse under her chair at a restaurant. She shows the hostess the purse, and the hostess tells Leigh to keep it. Is the hostess correct? Why or why not?
16. Evita copies several pages from some books while doing research for a term paper at the library. She takes the copies home so that she can continue working on the paper. Her brother tells her she violated the copyright law when she copied the pages at the library. Is he correct? Explain your answer.
17. A shipment of grain is lost when the lake steamer on which it was shipped collides with another boat and sinks. Will the carrier's claim, that the loss was caused by an act of God, excuse the carrier from liability? Why or why not?
18. Lan purchases an airline ticket, complying with all of the carrier's ticketing, check-in, and confirmation requirements. At the boarding gate, however, she is told that the flight is overbooked, but the carrier will arrange alternate transportation. Must the carrier do anything else for Lan in this situation? Explain your answer.
19. Mr. and Mrs. Kirby are registered guests at the Region Hotel. They keep a large sum of cash in their room, even though the hotel provides a safe for guests' use. If the money were stolen, would the hotel be held liable for the loss under most present-day state statutes? Explain your answer.

In each case that follows, you be the judge.

20. Title

Pollard found a valuable first edition book that someone dropped on the street. She took the book home and placed it with others in her personal collection of first editions. The owner's name could not be found in the lost book, and Pollard made no effort to locate the owner. *Did she have title to the book? Why or why not?*
Doe v. Oceola, 270 N.W.2d 254 (MI).

21. Negligence

Joe Scott left his automobile to be repaired at Purser Truck Sales. The business took the automobile to Lonz Radford to make the repairs, but the car was demolished while in the mechanic's possession. In a suit brought by Scott against Purser Truck Sales, the trial court held in favor of Purser because Scott presented no evidence indicating that Purser was negligent. *Was the trial court correct? Why or why not?*
Scott v. Purser Truck Sales, Inc., 402 S.E.2d 354 (GA).

Legal Link

Technology and Intellectual Property

Imagine that you and your technologically savvy friends have designed a unique computer, and that you have written software for the new machines. Things turned out so well that you are thinking of starting your own company. You have even created a logo for your company and a Web site with a catchy domain name.

Connect

Using a variety of search engines, research and identify federal and state copyright and trademark laws. Then complete the following activities.

22. What federal or state laws might protect your right to the unique design of your computer?

23. What federal or state laws might protect your right to the software you have written for the computers?

24. What federal or state laws might protect your company's logo and the domain name of the Web site you've created?

POWER READING STRATEGIES

25. **Predict** What would you do if you found a watch in the cafeteria at school?

26. **Connect** Look around your classroom. Can you find at least five trademarks?

27. **Question** Do you think credit-card blocking is the best way to ensure that hotel keepers will get the money that is due to them? Is it fair to the consumer? Explain your answer.

28. **Respond** Have you ever been bumped from an airline flight? If so, explain the situation. What type of compensation, if any, did you receive?

UNIT 3 Law Workshop: *Using Legal Tools*

Do You Know How to Shop for a Car?

In Chapter 16, you learned about the laws involved in acquiring a vehicle, including the application of contract law, applicable consumer protection laws, and the law of warranties. Automobiles are generally very expensive; as such, purchasing a vehicle is an important decision, and you should be familiar with the process.

Step A: Preparation

Problem: *What is the smartest way to shop for a car?*

Objectives: In this workshop, you will work with a partner to describe the process of shopping for a car.

- **Research** the shopping strategies needed to compile prices, features, and warranties of a car that you wish to purchase.
- **Investigate** different automobile insurance plans for the car that you wish to purchase.
- **Compare** the product information you have gathered.
- **Describe** your final choice and how you came to your decision.

1. Choose a partner. Imagine that the two of you have received $15,000 to buy a car to share.
2. Locate a copy of the *Consumer Reports* that rates the features and performance of different cars. Look for cars in your price range.

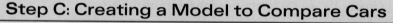

3. Use newspaper ads and the Internet to find prices and features on cars in your price range. Based on your research thus far, narrow your choice of cars to two.
4. Use the Internet or interview an automobile insurance agent to find out about the cost of coverage for automobile insurance for the cars of your choice.

5. Contact the seller to find out about the warranty available with the cars of your choice. Are they express or implied warranties?
6. Create a role-play in which one partner is a car dealer and the other is a car buyer. Using what you learned about contracts and warranties, make a list of questions for the car buyer to ask. Present your role-play to the class.
7. Write a summary comparing the two cars you have been researching.

Step C: Creating a Model to Compare Cars

As a class, create a chart that shows the information gathered about different types of cars. Create your chart using the categories listed below. Interpret and compare the data, and rank the cars based on prices, features, performance, and warranties.

- **Make/Model**
- **Price**
- ***Consumer Reports* Rating**
- **Features**
- **Insurance Cost and Coverage**
- **Warranties Available**

Step D: Workshop Analysis Report

Look at the chart and answer the following questions.
1. Which car would be the smartest purchase? Why do you think so?
2. Would you buy this car? Why or why not?

Denny v. Ford Motor Co.

New York Court of Appeals

662 N.E.2d 730 (NY)

Issue Is a claim of strict product liability identical to a claim of breach of implied warranty liability, making it inconsistent to find a defendant liable under one cause of action but not the other?

Facts Nancy Denny was injured when her Ford Bronco II rolled over after she slammed her brakes to avoid hitting a deer. She sued Ford Motor Company, asserting claims for negligence, strict product liability, and breach of implied warranty of merchantability. Denny introduced evidence showing that the vehicle was more dangerous than ordinary passenger automobiles, but Ford argued that the design features were necessary for the vehicle's off-road capabilities and that the vehicle was not intended to be sold as a conventional passenger vehicle. The jury found that the Bronco II was not "defective" for purposes of strict product liability theory, but that the defendant was still liable for breach of warranty of merchantability. On appeal, Ford argued that the two claims are the same and that the jury's verdict was inconsistent.

Opinion The New York Court of Appeals focused on the development of product liability law as the courts tried to keep pace with a radically changing economic landscape. It pointed out that traditionally the judiciary had relied on contractual warranty theories as the only way of awarding economic recovery for injuries that people suffer as a result of defective goods. This approach made good sense in an economic world in which most transactions occurred in a marketplace in which buyers and sellers interacted on a personal basis. In such cases, it was relatively easy to establish the requirement of a relationship of privity and to recover compensation for injuries.

However, the court recognized that as the fundamentals of the economy changed, courts had to change with them if injured parties were to recover damages: "Eventually, the contractually based implied warranty theory came to be perceived as inadequate in an economic universe that was dominated by mass-produced products and an impersonal marketplace." As a result, courts began to realize the need for a new, more flexible tort cause of action.

Development of Strict Product Liability

The new cause of action was called the strict product liability. This cause of action "significantly diminished the need to rely on the contractually based breach-of-implied warranty remedy as a means of compensating individuals injured because of defective products." While the applicable principles and available defenses differ, the court reasoned that there is a great deal of overlap between the substantive aspects of the two causes of action. The court even admitted that it had earlier observed, in dictum, that "strict liability in tort and implied warranty in the absence of privity are different ways of describing the very same cause of action."

Nevertheless, the court explained that the tort cause of action did not completely replace the older breach-of-implied warranty cause of action and that they were not identical in every respect. In ruling against Ford, the court emphasized two points:

- The warranty approach is still alive, and its vitality is evidenced by its "retention and expansion in New York's version of the Uniform Commercial Code."
- The core element of "defect" in each cause of action is subtly different given its different historical and doctrinal origins.

Distinguishing the Causes of Action

In distinguishing the two causes of action, the court pointed out that under New York law, injury due to a design defect was actionable under strict product liability "if the product is not reasonably safe." The existence of a design defect is determined under New York law by asking whether "if the design defect were known at the time of manufacture, a reasonable person would conclude that the utility of the product did not outweigh the risk inherent in marketing a product designed in that manner." This analysis requires a weighing of the product's dangers against its overall advantages.

In contrast, the UCC-based concept of a "defective" product requires an inquiry only into whether the product at issue is "fit for the ordinary purposes for which such goods are used" (UCC 2-314[2][c]). This analysis focuses on the expectations of a product when used in "the

customary, usual, and reasonably foreseeable manners." Under this cause of action, an injured party can recover by showing that the product was not minimally safe for its expected use "without regard to the feasibility of alternative designs or the manufacturer's 'reasonableness' in marketing it in that unsafe condition."

As a result of these differences, the court explained that "defect" analysis in strict product liability actions are more concerned with social policy and risk allocation. In contrast, "defect" analysis in breach-of-implied-warranty actions originates in contract law and focuses upon a purchaser's disappointed expectations.

Holding Given the historical and doctrinal differences between the two causes of action, the court ruled against Ford and held that "under the circumstances presented here, it is possible to be liable for breach of implied warranty even though a claim of strict product liability has not been satisfactorily established."

Questions for Analysis

1. Why was Ford's argument flawed?
2. What was the primary weakness of the breach of warranty theory in product liability cases?
3. When may a design defect be actionable under a strict product liability theory?
4. What is the New York standard for determining the existence of a design defect?
5. What inquiry must be made to determine whether a product is defective under the UCC?
6. How do the origins of breach of implied warranty actions and strict product liability actions differ?

Web Resources

Go to the *Understanding Business and Personal Law* Web Site at **ubpl.glencoe.com** for information about how to access online resources for the Landmark Cases.

UNIT 4

UNIT OVERVIEW

Most of us must play an active, productive role in the workplace to make a living and support ourselves or our families. Agency relationship laws and employment laws help protect individual's rights in the workplace. In this unit, you will learn about these laws by studying the following topics:

- Creating an agency
- Agency relationships and their termination
- Employment law and employment protection
- Equal opportunity

Being an Agent and Getting a Job

YOUR *Justice Journal*

Working the Night Shift You are a 17-year-old waiter at a small diner. Recently, your manager asked you to start working the night shift, from 6:00 P.M. to 2:00 A.M. The child labor laws in your state do not allow students under the age of 18 to work past 11:00 P.M.

In your Justice Journal, write about what you would do in this situation.

POWER READING STRATEGIES

To get the most out of your reading:
Predict what the section will be about.
Connect what you read with your own life.
Question as you read to make sure you understand the content.
Respond to what you've read.

Creation of an Agency

Understanding Business and Personal Law *Online*

Chapter Overview Visit the *Understanding Business and Personal Law* Web site at ubpl.glencoe.com and click on Chapter 18: Creation of an Agency—Chapter Overviews to preview the chapter information.

The Opening Scene

Starting in this chapter, we meet the Gant family. Broderick and Keeley Gant own a farm in rural Pennsylvania. They have four children: Caterina, 17, who wants to be a reporter for the local newspaper; Lazzaro, 16, who wants to work on the farm; Matilda, 14, who wants to be a surgeon; and Betina, 12, who just wants to be a kid. The scene opens at the storefront office of *The Greensburg Gazette*. Mack Pellis, editor of the paper, is talking to Caterina.

Hook, Line, and Sinker

MR. PELLIS: So why do you want to be a reporter?

CATERINA: I guess because I like to write and I like talking to people.

MR. PELLIS: That's a good start, but it takes a lot more to be a reporter.

CATERINA: Like what?

MR. PELLIS: Well, like having a nose for news and being able to find the "hook" in a story.

CATERINA: The hook?

MR. PELLIS: A hook pulls the reader into the story.

CATERINA: You mean, like something different or unusual?

MR. PELLIS: That's the idea.

CATERINA: That doesn't sound too hard.

MR. PELLIS: Sometimes it's not, but sometimes it is.

CATERINA: If you give me a chance, I bet I can find a hook in just about anything.

MR. PELLIS: Okay, we'll see. I'll hire you on a trial basis for one month.

CATERINA: Great!

MR. PELLIS: Your first assignment is to watch the office while I go over to the courthouse.

CATERINA: What should I do?

MR. PELLIS: Just watch the office. Nothing else.

CATERINA: Right, chief.

MR. PELLIS: And don't call me chief!

(After Mr. Pellis leaves, Mrs. Tui comes onto the office.)

MRS. TUI: Where's Mr. Pellis?

CATERINA: At the courthouse.

MRS. TUI: Can you take this ad copy and my payment?

CATERINA: I'm not supposed to.

MRS. TUI: Well, I can always go to *The Tribune*.

CATERINA: Okay, I'll do it.

(Mr. Pellis returns, and Caterina tells him she accepted the ad.)

MR. PELLIS: I told you not to do anything!

CATERINA: But she was going to go to *The Tribune*. Plus, she paid cash.

MR. PELLIS: Really? I guess you're forgiven.

(Just then the phone rings. Mr. Pellis answers. When he hangs up, he is clearly distressed.)

CATERINA: What's wrong?

MR. PELLIS: That was my lawyer. The delivery service that handles my out-of-state edition had an accident, and I'm being sued.

CATERINA: Now there's a hook for a story!

What Are the Legal Issues?

1. How is an agent appointed?
2. Can a nonagent bind a principal to a contract?
3. Can a principal validate a contract made by a nonagent?
4. Can a person injured by an employee sue the employee's employer?

Agency Relationships

Agency and Similar Relationships

None of us have the ability, education, training, experience, and background to do everything that must be done in our personal and professional lives. We frequently need to accomplish things that require expertise beyond our own abilities. An **agency** relationship lets us act through other people to accomplish tasks that might be difficult or impossible to do on our own. The law governs these relationships.

The term *agency* describes a relationship in which one person, called an **agent**, represents another person, called a **principal**, in some sort of business transaction with a third party (see Figure 18.1). An agent can negotiate business deals, enter into contracts, and perform a variety of other business tasks for the principal, who is normally legally bound by those agreements.

The terms *agent* and *principal*, however, are used freely in the business world to describe different types of relationships, and not all of the relationships described using these terms are true agency relationships. However, the name given to a relationship has little legal effect. The essence or true nature of the relationship is what matters to a court.

Principal-Agent Relationship

The principal-agent relationship is a true agency relationship. The party who needs a representative is the principal, or the client; the party who becomes that representative is the agent. The relationship is

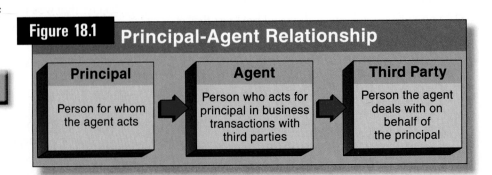

Figure 18.1   Principal-Agent Relationship

Principal	Agent	Third Party
Person for whom the agent acts	Person who acts for principal in business transactions with third parties	Person the agent deals with on behalf of the principal

PRINCIPAL-AGENT RELATIONSHIP
Agents have the right to make independent decisions just as if they were making transactions on their own behalf. *Are agents employees?*

USING AN AGENT

Most people deal with merchants directly when buying goods and services, especially important items like houses, or expensive goods like boats. *When might someone want to deal with merchant indirectly through an agent?*

consensual because both parties agree to it. However, the relationship is not always contractual. An agent can represent a principal without receiving consideration for his or her efforts. An agent who receives no consideration is called a gratuitous agent. The relationship between the agent and the principal is also fiduciary in nature, which means that it is based on trust between the agent and the principal.

An agency relationship is very powerful. Legally, we distinguish an agent from other types of representatives by noting that the agent has the power to transact business for the principal. When someone acts for a principal, the legal effect is the same as if the principal had acted. Some agents, but not all, are employees.

Example 1. Patricia Thompson asked Al Albrecht to sell her car while she was on vacation. When he agreed to become her agent, Al gained the power to legally bind Patricia to a sales contract for her car. This agreement formed a consensual relationship voluntarily agreed upon by both parties. It also is a fiduciary relationship because Patricia has placed her trust in Al to negotiate a deal for her. Finally, because Al is not being paid for representing Patricia, he is a gratuitous agent.

Master-Servant Relationship

The terms *master* and *servant* are no longer used in our everyday language. Nevertheless, these terms identify a specific type of relationship in the law. A **master** is a person who has the right to control the conduct of another who is performing a task for the benefit of the master. A **servant** is a person whose conduct in the performance of a task is subject to the control of another. If a servant has the power to conduct business transactions for the master, he or she is also an agent.

> *Example 2.* Mary Torino, an elderly widow, lives alone. Sally Sexton, Mary's neighbor, cleans house for Mary once a week. Sally knows that Mary is very fussy about her house, so she cleans exactly as directed. Sally also knows that Mary cannot afford to pay her, so she never asks for nor receives any money from her neighbor. Sally is a servant without being an employee.

Proprietor-Independent Contractor Relationship

In the proprietor-independent contractor relationship, an **independent contractor** works for but is not under the control of a proprietor. Thus we may say that the proprietor is a person who chooses to have someone perform a task on his or her behalf but has no control over the way that task is carried out. The only control over the activity of the independent contractor is the right to specify a particular outcome.

> *Example 3.* Ronnie Hampton purchased a home with a three-acre lot. Because Ronnie's job required him to travel, he had little free time to maintain his property. He hired Mike Crawford, a professional gardener, to care for his lawn. Ronnie's only order to Mike was to make his lawn the best-looking lawn in town. Mike did his own work with his own tools at his own pace and at a time of his own choosing. He is an independent contractor.

Independent contractors carry out many kinds of tasks. Some contractors, such as plumbers, delivery truck drivers, and electricians, perform physical labor. Other contractors, such as writers, musicians, computer programmers, and healthcare professionals, provide services. Independent contractors are typically not agents, but there are some exceptions.

Law Librarian

Leah Sandwell-Weiss has lived two lives in the law. Several years ago, she retired as a major in the Air Force after serving 14 years as a military judge advocate. Today, she is a law librarian at the University of Arizona in Tucson.

"The Air Force sent me to law school after I had been working as a librarian," Sandwell-Weiss says. "It was fascinating work, and I was stationed at very interesting places."

When Sandwell-Weiss was ready for a new career, working in a law library seemed to be the perfect fit. Today, she serves University of Arizona Law Library patrons as a reference librarian.

"I help people find specific answers to their questions or direct them to sources about their more general research," she says. "One thing I can't do is offer legal advice."

Sandwell-Weiss says that sometimes people who are not lawyers don't understand that she can't answer questions such as, "What does this mean?"

"That's something a lawyer should answer for his or her client," she says. "I do, however, point patrons in the right direction so they can continue to research and understand the law better."

In addition to serving the public, Sandwell-Weiss assists students, faculty members, and lawyers who are researching legal points. She also invests considerable time educating herself about the latest Internet legal resources.

Skills	Interpersonal, research, computer
Personality	Likes solving mysteries, visionary but practical, likes technical aspects of work
Education	Law librarians at universities usually need a law degree and a master's degree in library science. Law librarians who work in private firms or county law libraries need one degree or the other.

For more information about law librarians, visit **ubpl.glencoe.com** or your public library.

Example 4. Pittsburgh Petroleum spent more than six months trying to collect a fuel bill owed by Transunion Transport before hiring a collection agency, Andrews Intercontinental Collections (AIC). Pittsburgh Petroleum gave AIC only one order: to collect the money due. Because AIC is to conduct a business transaction for Pittsburgh, the collection agency is an agent. However, because AIC may decide on its own how to make that collection, AIC is also an independent contractor.

Why Are These Distinctions Important?

Finding out the true nature of a relationship can be crucial in determining liability. Recall that the labels themselves—principal-agent, master-servant, and proprietor-independent—are not controlling. Calling a servant an independent contractor does not change the relationship if the master still controls the servant's conduct. Figuring out the true nature of the relationship can be crucial in determining liability.

Contractual Liability

A principal is generally bound to the terms of a contract made by an agent unless the agent has no authority to enter the contract. Furthermore, unless a servant is also an agent, he or she does not have the authority to negotiate contracts for the master. Also, an independent contractor would have no power to bind the proprietor to a contract, unless expressly permitted to do so. This rule applies even if the contract benefits the proprietor or is needed to carry out the independent contractor's assigned task.

Example 5. In Example 3, Ronnie Hampton hired Mike Crawford to care for his lawn. Mike decides he should reseed a portion of the lawn. He negotiates a deal with Taylor's Treehouse to purchase several bags of grass seed on credit. He includes the cost of the seed in his bill when Ronnie pays him. Later, however, Mike fails to pay the money he owes to Taylor's. The supply store cannot seek payment from Ronnie, even though Mike purchased the seed for Ronnie's lawn. The contract did not involve the homeowner.

Keep in mind, however, that it is possible for an independent contractor to also be an agent. This situation is illustrated in Example 4, where Pittsburgh Petroleum hired AIC to collect the overdue debt from Transunion. Another example of an independent contractor who works as an agent is a real estate broker.

Example 6. Penelope Petrovsky, who lived in San Diego, found a new job at an advertising agency in Sacramento and had to start immediately. Because she needed to sell her San Diego condominium quickly, Penelope hired the Intra-California Agency (ICA) to negotiate the sale. The only direction she gave was to

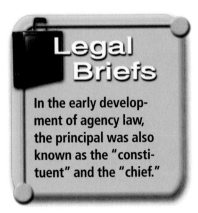

Legal Briefs

In the early development of agency law, the principal was also known as the "constituent" and the "chief."

find a buyer who would pay $250,000. ICA negotiated a deal with Ted Martineau, who agreed to that price. In this situation, ICA is both an independent contractor and an agent.

Tort Liability

The distinction between the master-servant relationship and the proprietor-independent contractor relationship is also important in determining tort liability (see Figure 18.2). All people are responsible for their own tortious conduct. Sometimes, however, the person who hired the tortfeasor may also be held liable. This situation is known as vicarious liability, and it is founded on the principle of ***respondeat superior***, or let the master respond. Typically, *respondeat superior* applies to master-servant relationships because the master has the right to control the physical conduct of the servant. In contrast, a proprietor usually doesn't have that right with an independent contractor.

The right to control the physical conduct of the servant is not the only distinction between these relationships. The court may consider several other factors by asking any of the following specific questions:

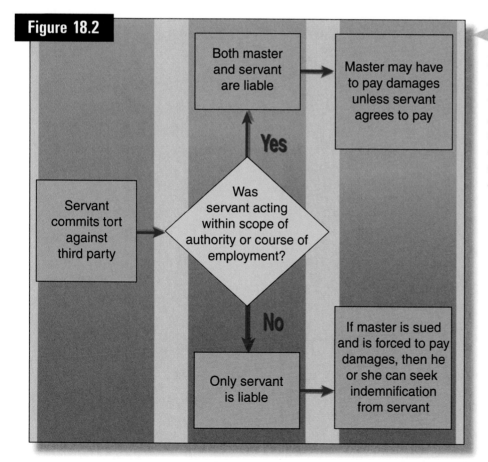

Figure 18.2

RESPONDEAT SUPERIOR
This chart shows the flow of master/servant tort liability under the *respondeat superior* doctrine. *How do the courts defend the use of respondeat superior in tort cases?*

- Does the hiring person supply the tools for the worker?
- Is the worker paid by the hour?
- Does the hiring person set the worker's hours?
- Is the worker employed only by the person responsible for hiring?
- Is the business of the worker the same as the business of the hiring person?
- Does the worker lack authority to hire or fire other workers?
- Does the worker perform his or her tasks in a highly supervised environment?
- Is very little skill required to perform the worker's job?

The more questions that require "yes" answers, the more likely it is that a master-servant relationship exists. If a master-servant relationship is determined to exist, the master could be liable for the servant's tortious conduct. Conversely, the more "no" answers, the more likely it is that a proprietor-independent contractor relationship exists.

Example 7. In The Opening Scene, Mr. Pellis hired a delivery service to transport his out-of-state edition. The truck collided with a car en route. The driver of the car wants to sue Mr. Pellis,

INDEPENDENT CONTRACTORS

Home owners frequently hire workers to make repairs or improvements to their homes. *Are such workers considered independent contractors?*

"Pay Up"

Being an independent contractor has its advantages. Independence is certainly among these advantages. Independent contractors have full control over the way an activity is carried out, as long as the particular outcome is achieved. An independent cotractor may choose his or her own hours. Most independent contractors also play a critical role in determining how much they will be paid for their services. However, getting paid by the proprietor isn't always easy for independent contractors, even when they have satisfactorily completed the work.

Unlike regular employees, independent contractors do not enjoy a full range of government protection. They are generally at the mercy of the proprietor when it comes to getting paid. Some proprietors are deliberately slow to pay, and others simply refuse to pay.

Informal methods that an independent contractor may use to attain payment from an unethical proprietor include being a "squeaky wheel." Letters, phone calls, e-mail messages, and personal meetings are just a few ways to get your point across. More formal ways of proceeding include suing the proprietor in small claims court or municipal court. The type of court depends on the amount of money involved. Sometimes an independent contractor agreement will contain an arbitration clause, which takes the place of a court proceeding and is binding on the parties.

Evaluate What factors might you consider in determining how much to charge for your work as an independent contractor?

who has a contract with the delivery service. Is the delivery service an independent contractor or a servant?

In Example 7, Mr. Pellis does not have the right to control the physical conduct of the delivery service drivers. As a result, the service is an independent contractor. However, Mr. Pellis's lack of control over the physical conduct of the service is not the only factor that proves this relationship is not a master-servant arrangement. By applying the questions listed previously, you can gain a more complete picture of the relationship between Mr. Pellis and the delivery service. Remember, the

more of these questions that the court can answer "no," the more likely it is a relationship between a proprietor and an independent contractor.

- Does Mr. Pellis supply the tools for the worker? No. The delivery service supplies drivers with the "tools of their trade" (the delivery trucks).
- Are the drivers paid by the hour? No. In this situation, Mr. Pellis pays by the delivery rather than by the hour.
- Does Mr. Pellis set the drivers' hours? No. This issue is determined by the delivery service.
- Are the drivers hired to work for Mr. Pellis only? No. The drivers work for a number of different customers.
- Is the business of the driver the same as the business of Mr. Pellis? No. The driver is in the delivery business; Mr. Pellis is in the newspaper business.
- Do the drivers have any authority to hire or fire other workers? Unclear. This determination would depend on the authority of a particular driver. Clearly, however, the delivery service has the authority to hire and fire its workers; Mr. Pellis does not.
- Are the drivers closely supervised? No. The drivers are relatively independent.

A close examination of the relationship between the delivery service and Mr. Pellis reveals that the delivery service is an independent contractor. Mr. Pellis is not liable for any injuries or property damage in the accident involving the delivery truck. However, if the same questions about the relationship between the delivery service and its drivers were asked, it would be discovered that the delivery service is a master and the driver is a servant.

A master may escape vicarious liability, however, if the servant was not acting within the scope of employment. When the tort was committed, the worker must have been performing the task for which he or she was hired. Suppose the driver had taken a side trip to a store to run an errand without the permission or knowledge of the supervisor. While backing out of a parking space at the store, the driver knocked over a large sign that fell onto a parked car, shattering the car's windshield and injuring a family pet waiting in the vehicle. The driver's employer could escape liability because the side trip is not within the scope of the driver's employment.

Vicarious liability is usually limited to negligence rather than intentional torts. There are exceptions, however. For example, a department store may be liable if a security guard injures a suspected shoplifter who is resisting capture.

Just as a master can sometimes be liable for the torts of a servant, a proprietor can also be liable for the torts of an independent contractor.

For example, a proprietor is liable if he or she is negligent when checking qualifications and hires someone who is incompetent. In this situation, called negligent hiring, the proprietor will be held liable should an innocent third party be injured by the negligence of the incompetent independent contractor.

A newly emerging doctrine, similar to negligent hiring, is negligent retention. This situation arises when a proprietor fails to fire a contractor after learning that he or she is incompetent. If the contractor injures someone, the proprietor may be liable.

Another situation that can open a proprietor to liability arises when an independent contractor has been hired to perform a task that involves a nondelegable duty. A nondelegable duty is one that the proprietor cannot pass off to another party.

> *Example 8.* To cut down on expenses, Rochester Railway decided to hire an independent maintenance firm, Ilium Company (IC), to service its railway system. IC made several serious errors that caused a train wreck injuring several people. The injured parties sued both IC and Rochester. Even though Rochester could show that IC was an independent contractor, it could not escape legal liability for the crash. A common carrier, such as a railroad, cannot delegate its duty to maintain a system that protects the safety of its passengers.

Section 18.1 Assessment

Reviewing What You Learned
1. What is an agency relationship?
2. What is the difference between a servant and an independent contractor?
3. What is the nature of contract liability?
4. What is the legal doctrine of *respondeat superior*?

Critical Thinking Activity
Tort Law Why does the law permit an injured party to bring a tort law case against both an employee and his or her employer?

Legal Skills in Action
Agency Your friend, Louis, has just hired Franco as his delivery driver. One afternoon while he is supposed to be making a delivery on the west side of town, Franco decides to take a 15-mile detour to the east side to pick up his dry cleaning. While entering the parking lot of the dry cleaners, Franco makes an illegal turn and collides with a police car. Louis fears he will be liable not only for Franco's traffic ticket but also for all damages to the police cruiser. Write a letter to Louis in which you explain why you think he won't be liable for the traffic ticket or the damage to the police cruiser.

Creation and Types of Agents

What You'll Learn

- How to recognize the creation of an agency relationship by agreement
- How to recognize the creation of an agency relationship by operation of law
- How to distinguish between a general agent and a special agent
- How to distinguish among a subagent, a coagent, and an agent's agent

Why It's Important

Knowing when an agency relationship has been created will help you make sound judgments in business activities.

Legal Terms

- general agent
- special agent
- agency by estoppel
- ratification

Types of Agents

Like most relationships in the law, there are several ways to create an agency relationship. Similarly, there are several types of agents. The type of agent with whom a third party deals depends on the agent's authority and his or her relationship with other similarly situated agents.

We can distinguish between types of agents in two ways. We examine (1) the extent of the agents' authority, and (2) how the agents relate to one another.

Extent of Authority

The two types of agents are distinguished on the basis of extent of authority. General agents have more authority than special agents.

General Agent   A person who has been given authority to perform any act within the scope of a business is a **general agent**. The manager of a department store, for instance, would be a general agent. General agents are sometimes called discretionary agents because they have the right to use their judgment or discretion in all matters pertaining to the agency. General agents may decide to hire or fire employees according to the needs of the business.

Example 9. Allen Ambrose was the managing editor of the *Tiro Telegraph*. When the Gulf War began, he hired several new printers so the newspaper could put out an extra edition. When one of the presses broke down, Ambrose called a mechanic to repair the damage. As managing editor of the paper, he had the authority to make decisions such as these and to bind his employer Paul Winfield, the publisher, to the contracts that resulted from those decisions.

Special Agent   A person who is employed to accomplish a specific purpose or to do a particular job is a **special agent**. Sales representatives are special agents. They can sell and pass title to specific goods sold, but that is the extent of their authority. They can't make purchases in the principal's name, and they usually aren't authorized to collect payment unless they actually deliver the goods to the buyer. Other special agents are hired for other purposes. The real estate broker mentioned in Example 6 is a special agent.

How Agents Relate to One Another

Agents may be classified according to the nature of their relationships with other agents.

Subagents   A subagent is an agent lawfully appointed by another agent. A limited number of situations permit an agent to legally appoint a subagent:

- A principal may give an agent express power to appoint subagents.
- Agents can usually appoint subagents to perform routine or simple clerical tasks.
- An agent faced with an emergency can generally appoint a subagent to act in his or her place.
- An agent's authority to appoint subagents is often recognized in the business world as part of the power that goes with being an agent.

> *Example 10.* Andy Porter is hired to be general manager of the Monarch Hotel. The day after he starts the job, the hotel workers go on strike and Andy can't get in touch with Patricia Arden, the owner of the hotel. Andy is nervous about what lies ahead for the hotel and has little legal expertise. Uncertain of the hotel's legal responsibilities, Porter hires Oscar Spencer, an attorney, to negotiate a contract with the union.

The new manager can argue he has legal authority to hire Spencer on two grounds. First, the emergency nature of the strike made it absolutely necessary to hire the attorney. Second, hiring an attorney to protect the hotel's legal rights is a power that all hotel managers have because of their position as general agents.

Agent's Agent   If an agent has no power to appoint a subagent but does so anyway, he or she has appointed an agent's agent. Suppose in Example 10 that there had been no strike and Patricia Arden had expressly forbidden Andy Porter to hire anyone. The hiring of Oscar Spencer to negotiate the union contract would not then have been authorized. Andy would have hired an agent's agent. The difference is significant. If the lawyer were merely an agent's agent, he could not bind the owner of the hotel to any deal he might negotiate with the union. If Patricia did not want to honor the agreement, she would not have to. Furthermore, she would not have to pay the attorney. That responsibility would fall on Andy's shoulders.

It's a Question of Ethics

An Undisclosed Third Party

Not all agency relationships must be disclosed to third parties. Imagine that a "famous" writer, George Bowlegs, was looking for a new home in a small suburb of Tucson, Arizona. Bowlegs hired a real estate agent, Janelle McCain, to find and negotiate a price for a house meeting certain criteria. George asked Janelle not to reveal that she was representing him. George was afraid that if the seller knew the agent represented someone famous, the prices of the real estate would go way up. *Are George's actions ethical? What would you do if you were George?*

Coagents   If the principal hires two or more agents, he or she has created a coagent situation. Coagents are subject to the authority of the principal but are not subject to one another unless the principal so authorizes. All authority in this case flows from the principal to the agents.

How Agency Relationships Are Created

Generally, any business you can transact personally can also be transacted through an agent. Because agents act not for themselves but for their principals, anyone can be appointed as an agent. A principal-agent relationship can develop in a number of ways.

By Agreement

Most agency relationships are created by agreement. These agreements are usually, but not always, contracts. No contract exists if an agreement does not involve consideration. As noted earlier, an agency agreement that does not involve a contract is called a gratuitous agency.

Example 11. Perry Chaney was getting married on Saturday and had several errands to run. He asked his best man, Arnie Alvarez, to pick up his rented tuxedo and to buy the flowers for the wedding. Arnie agreed to do these things, and no consideration was given. No binding contract was created, but an agency

Virtual Law

From Employee-Agent to Independent Contractor on the Net

Insurance companies, like many other businesses, seek to cut costs while maintaining a level of quality. One way that insurance companies reduce costs is by using the Internet to sell policies. Insurance companies are also encouraging employee-agents to become independent contractors. In this way, insurance companies reduce their work force and avoid the expenses normally associated with having an employee on the payroll. At the same time, policies sold over the Internet or through an independent contractor are just as binding as policies sold by an employee-agent. (Source: *InternetWeek*, January 26, 2001)

Connect Visit the Web site of the U.S. Department of Labor. Find out how many high-tech and Internet workers are independent contractors.

relationship existed because Arnie was authorized to carry out transactions for Perry.

Many agreements are express, but others are implied. An express agreement is one that involves clearly stated terms of agreement. If the parties draw up some sort of written contract, they have created a power of attorney. At other times, however, the parties may imply by words or actions an agreement to the agency relationship.

Example 12. Stan Williams is Paula Paxton's chauffeur. A written agreement says his only duty is to drive Paula and her family around town. One morning, Paula tells Stan to take care of her car while she vacations in Europe for a few weeks. Stan agrees to do so. Stan is now an agent. His original agreement was simply to act as a chauffeur, which made him a servant but not an agent. However, Paula's orders have changed his status. The orders imply that Stan now has the power to make certain types of contracts in Paula's absence, such as arranging for maintenance, hiring mechanics, and buying gas.

The agency agreement does not have to be in any particular form and can be oral or written. However, the equal dignities rule presents an exception to this standard. If the Statute of Frauds requires that a contract negotiated by an agent be in writing, then the contract creating the agency relationship must be given "equal dignity" by also being made in writing. When a formal writing is used to confer authority on an agent, it is known as a power of attorney.

By Operation of Law

Agency relationships may be created automatically by operation of law. Sometimes the law creates an agency relationship by circumstance; at other times agency relationships arise through enactment of specific laws.

Agency by Estoppel   When the law creates an agency relationship by circumstance, it is called **agency by estoppel**, also known as apparent authority. The circumstances usually involve some sort of communication between the principal and a third party, which leads the third party to reasonably believe that a nonagent is an agent.

Example 13. In The Opening Scene, Mr. Pellis had told Mrs. Tui that someone would be in the newspaper office to accept her ad. Because Caterina was there when she walked in, Mrs. Tui could reasonably assume Caterina was Mr. Pellis's agent. As a result, the newspaper publisher could not deny Caterina's authority to take the advertising copy and the money from Mrs. Tui.

Law and Academics
A power of attorney is a written instrument by which one person, a principal, appoints another as agent and confers the authority to perform certain specified acts on behalf of the principal. This power may include the authority to enter into transactions on behalf of the principal.

Research Activity
Power of attorney can be granted in numerous circumstances and give the appointed agent a variety of methods for conducting transactions. Using the Internet, library, or other resource, research some of the circumstances in which the power of attorney might be granted and the methods in which I might be used to conduct transactions.

AGENCY BY ESTOPPEL

Often agency relationships are created by circumstance. *When is it reasonable to assume that someone in a store has agency authority? When might making this assumption be unwise or unreasonable?*

Mr. Pellis told Mrs. Tui that someone would be in the office at noon. He said something that led her to wrongly conclude that Caterina was an agent. Agency by estoppel can also arise by actions or appearances alone. For example, when a retail establishment opens, the owners are communicating to the public that salespeople will be present to help them. If an impostor enters and pretends to be a salesperson, the store will be liable for any loss incurred by an innocent third party duped by the phony salesperson.

By Statute   Sometimes a state legislature decides that certain situations justify automatic creation of agency relationships by statute. Usually, the state has some special interest to protect. For example, in many states the law requires corporations to appoint an agent who can be served with a complaint and summons in case the corporation is sued.

If a corporation's appointed agent leaves the state, the secretary of state automatically becomes its statutory agent for service of process. The state has a special interest to protect in these cases: It wants to make certain that its citizens have a way to sue a corporation that has injured them.

By Ratification

At times a person may act as an agent without the authority, or an agent who has the authority to negotiate one type of contract oversteps that authority and negotiates another type of contract. **Ratification** occurs if the principal, with full knowledge of the facts, accepts the benefits of the unauthorized act. The act is thereby approved or ratified. A principal's failure or refusal to ratify the unauthorized act makes the would-be agent or the agent who has overstepped his or her authority liable to the third party.

> *Example 14.* In The Opening Scene, Caterina was not Mr. Pellis's agent nor was she an agent of his newspaper when she took money from Mrs. Tui to pay for advertising. However, Mr. Pellis is bound by this transaction because he ratified the agreement between Caterina and Mrs. Tui when he accepted Mrs. Tui's money from Caterina.

Section 18.2   Assessment

Reviewing What You Learned

1. How are most agency relationships created?
2. How are agency relationships created by operation of law?
3. What is the difference between a general agent and a special agent?
4. What are the differences among a subagent, a coagent, and an agent's agent?

Critical Thinking Activity

Types of Agents Why is it important to be able to distinguish between a general agent and a special agent?

Legal Skills in Action

Apparent Authority Tony believes that Sara is a salesperson working in the appliance department at the Alomar Brothers Department Store. It turns out that she is actually a disgruntled former employee who is now impersonating a salesperson. Tony gives Sara $100 as a down payment for a new DVD player, and she runs off with the money. Write a paragraph that explains whether the Alomar Brothers Department Store will be compelled to return the $100 to Tony.

Chapter Summary

Section 18.1 Agency Relationships

- An agency relationship is one in which a person represents another person in some sort of business transaction with a third party. Agency relationships let us act through other people to accomplish things that might be difficult or impossible to do on our own. The party for whom an agency acts is known as the principal.

- A servant is a person whose conduct in the performance of a task is subject to the control of another person, called the master. In contrast, an independent contractor works for, but is not under the control, of a proprietor. The only control that the proprietor has over the contractor is the right to specify a particular outcome. Determining the distinction between a servant and a contractor is essential to determining liability. When determining if a party is a servant or contractor, the court will ask the following questions: (1) Does the hiring person supply the tools for the worker? (2) Is the worker paid by the hour? (3) Does the hiring person set the worker's hours? (4) Is the worker employed only by the person responsible for hiring? (5) Is the business of the worker the same as the business of the hiring person? (6) Does the worker lack authority to hire or fire other workers (7) Does the worker perform his or her tasks in a highly supervised environment? and (8) Is very little skill required to perform the worker's job? The more questions that require "yes" answers, the more likely it is that a master-servant relationship exists.

- A principal is generally bound to the terms of the contract made by an agent unless the agent has no authority to enter the contract. An independent contractor would have no power to bind the proprietor to a contract unless expressly permitted to do so by the proprietor. This is true even if the contract benefits the proprietor or is needed to carry out the independent contractor's assigned task.

- The doctrine of *respondeat superior*, which means let the master respond, makes a master responsible for the acts of the servant. Because a master has the right to control the physical conduct of a servant, the person who hires the tortfeasor is vicariously liable if he or she is in a master-servant relationship. However, when the tort was committed, the worker must have been performing the task for which he or she was hired.

Section 18.2 Creation and Types of Agents

- Most agency relationships are created by agreement. These agreements are usually, but not always, contracts. As a result, they follow the rules of contracts.

- A agency relationship may be created by operation of law if the circumstances are such that a party is reasonably believed to be an agent by a third party. This situation is known as agency by estoppel, or apparent authority.

- A general agent is a person who has been given the authority to perform any duties within the scope of running a business. General agents have more authority than special agents. A special agent is employed to accomplish a specific purpose or to do a particular job.

- A subagent is an agent lawfully appointed by another agent. If an agent has no power to appoint a subagent but does so anyway, he has appointed an agent's agent. If the principal does not want to honor the agreement made between the agent and agent's agent, the responsibility of honoring the agreement falls upon the agent's shoulders. An unauthorized act is ratified if the principal, with full knowledge of the facts, accepts the benefit of that act. A principal who hires more than two agents creates a coagent situation.

Using Legal Language

Consider the key terms in the list below. Then use these terms to complete the following exercises.

agency
agent
principal
servant
ratification

respondeat superior
general agent
special agent
agency by estoppel
independent contractor

Understanding Business and Personal Law Online

Self-Check Quiz Visit the *Understanding Business and Personal Law* Web site at **ubpl.glencoe.com** and click on Chapter 18: Creation of an Agency— Self-Check Quizzes to prepare for the chapter exam.

1. Caterina Gant wants to be a reporter. Imagine that you would also like to be a reporter. Write an article about the creation of an agency and use the terms listed above in your article.
2. Exchange your article with another student in the class so that you can read and critique each other's articles.
3. Discuss the strong aspects of the article and the aspects that need improvement.
4. Select one of the articles, and present it to the class.
5. As a class, select the best essay and post it somewhere in the classroom.

The Law Review

Answer the following questions. Refer to the chapter for additional reinforcement.

6. Why is the agency relationship considered powerful?
7. Explain vicarious liability.
8. What is negligent hiring and negligent retention?
9. Define the equal dignities rule.
10. How is an agency by estoppel created? What do the circumstances usually involve?
11. What is ratification?
12. What happens if a principal refuses to ratify the unauthorized actions of an agent?
13. How does a general agent differ from a special agent?
14. How does a servant differ from an independent contractor?
15. What are some advantages of working as an independent contractor?

Linking School to Work

Interpreting and Communicating Information

In groups of four, discuss the proprietor-independent contractor relationship.

- Explore the ways in which teens are involved in this type of relationship.
- As a class, create a list of the ways in which teens work as independent contractors.

Discuss the liability issues that might impact teens who work as independent contractors.

Let's Debate

Liability Risk

Anna is the principal of one of the largest high schools in Texas. She hired some former students to take care of the school's landscaping during the year. Anna paid the students cash each week for their services. While mowing, the students lost control of the school's lawnmower and crashed into three cars in the staff parking lot.

Debate

16. Who is liable? Explain your answer.
17. Were the former students working as independent contractors or employees?
18. If your car were damaged in an accident like this, whom would you blame?

Grasping Case Issues

For the following cases, give your decision and state a legal principle that applies.

19. Uniforms, Ltd. hired Styles as their delivery driver. One morning, while he is supposed to be delivering uniforms to O'Riley's Bar and Grill, Styles makes a side trip to the Richland Mall to purchase a watch for his girlfriend. On his way to the mall, he runs a stop sign and collides with a school bus. Is Uniforms Ltd. responsible for the damage to the school bus? Why or why not?

20. Mary Drouhard sells a set of antique dishes to Betty Sloane. Bruce Richards offers to deliver the dishes and collect the money for Drouhard as a favor. Is Richards an agent?

21. Gary Sharp, an agent of the State Ranch Insurance Agency, is involved in an automobile accident and cannot run his office. Sharp has his wife, Mona, run the office for three days while he recuperates. Is Mona an agent? Why or why not?

22. Joanne Neptune hires Raymond's Roofers to reshingle her Roof. Neptune tells Raymond what she wants done but leaves the details to Raymond and his workers. While on Neptune's roof, one of Raymond's roofers drops his tool box onto neighbor Ted Cafferty's new car, smashing the windshield. Is Neptune liable? Why or why not?

23. Shaun Nyquist works as a radiology technician for Dr. Regina Ingram. The doctor is usually present when Nyquist gives a radiation treatment. One day, however, Ingram tells Nyquist he is on his own. While Nyquist is conducting a patient's radiation therapy, the patient falls and breaks his ankle. Would Ingram be liable if Nyquist is found to have been negligent? Why or why not?

24. Phil Nicholson hires Ted McGraw as general manager of the Nicholson Restaurant. In this capacity, McGraw schedules a wedding reception at the restaurant on a Friday night. Nicholson gets upset because Friday night is the restaurant's busiest night. He cancels the reservation, claiming that McGraw had no authority to make such arrangements. Is Nicholson correct? Explain your answer.

In each case that follows, you be the judge.

25. *Respondeat Superior*

Elliot was an inmate at the Chillicothe Correctional Institution. While serving his sentence, he was hit in the face by a corrections officer. Because the institution was run by the state, Elliot sued the officer and the state. He used the doctrine of *respondeat superior*. The state claimed the guard had been reckless in his conduct and that his actions were therefore outside the scope of his employment. *Was the guard acting within the scope of his employment when he injured Elliot? Why or why not?*

Elliot v. Ohio Department of Rehabilitation and Correction, 637 N.E.2d 106 (OH).

26. Liability

Hoddesons was shopping for furniture at the Koos Brothers Department Store. A man dressed in a suit showed her around the furniture floor, pointing out several pieces of furniture. Eventually, Hoddesons picked out several furniture items. Because she believed the man was a salesperson, Hoddesons gave him the correct amount of cash to cover her purchases. The man told her the items would be shipped to her soon. When the furniture never arrived, Hoddesons complained to the store and eventually learned the man in question was an impostor who did not work for the store. *Will the department store be liable to Hoddesons? Why or why not?*

Hoddesons v. Koos Brothers, 135 A.2d 702 (NJ).

Legal Link

Online Agents

There are many types of agents that serve the public—travel agents, real estate agents, talent agents, and even shopping agents.

Connect

Conduct research on the Internet. Use a variety of search engines to complete the following exercises:

27. Research an online agent.
28. Determine the type of agent and how the agency relationship is created.
29. Determine whether hiring an agent via the Internet is different from hiring an agent in a more traditional manner.

POWER READING STRATEGIES

30. **Predict** Why do you think laws governing agency relationships came into being?

31. **Connect** Have you ever needed to be in two places at once? Have you ever been asked to accomplish tasks beyond your expertise? What did you do about it?

32. **Question** What is the difference between an express and implied agreement?

33. **Respond** Can a person act as an agent without the authority to do so? Explain your answer.

Agency Relationships and Their Termination

Understanding Business and Personal Law *Online*

Chapter Overview Visit the *Understanding Business and Personal Law* Web site at ubpl.glencoe.com and click on Chapter 19: Agency Relationships and Their Termination—Chapter Overviews to preview the chapter information.

The Opening Scene

Caterina has found a job as an editorial assistant at *The Greensburg Gazette*. Mack Pellis, the newspaper's editor, is giving her instructions in the publication's storefront office.

Check the Fax

MR. PELLIS: Cathy, I have to go see my lawyer. Take care of the office while I'm gone—and make sure you don't get conned into buying something from a telemarketer or a door-to-door salesperson, okay?

CATERINA: Sure, Mr. Pellis, no problem.

(Immediately after Mr. Pellis disappears out the door, Mr. Bronowski enters the office.)

MR. BRONOWSKI: Hello. I'd like to place an ad in your paper.

CATERINA: No problem. What's the ad for?

MR. BRONOWSKI: I have a fax machine to sell.

CATERINA: A fax machine? Mr. Pellis, my boss, was just saying he needs a new fax machine because somebody stole the last one he had. What are you asking for it?

MR. BRONOWSKI: Well, I don't know if I can sell it to you. You look kind of young.

CATERINA: That has nothing to do with it. I work for Mr. Pellis, so I'd be buying it for him.

MR. BRONOWSKI: Well, I can't take less than $200.

CATERINA: Sold.

MR. BRONOWSKI: Just like that?

CATERINA: Sure.

MR. BRONOWSKI: Well, I guess it's okay.

(Caterina goes to the back room and gets $200 in cash out of Mr. Pellis's desk. Mr. Bronowski fetches the fax machine from his car, takes the money, and leaves. Mr. Pellis returns 30 minutes later.)

MR. PELLIS: Where did this fax machine come from?

CATERINA: I bought it to replace the stolen one.

(With concern on his face, Mr. Pellis examines the machine.)

MR. PELLIS: I don't believe it!

CATERINA: I know. It was only $200. Great deal, right?

MR. PELLIS: That's not what I mean. This fax machine right here, the one you just bought with my hard-earned money . . .

CATERINA: *(Interrupting.)* What about it?

MR. PELLIS: You see this service sticker on the back?

CATERINA: Oh, no, you mean . . .

MR. PELLIS: Yes, Caterina, it says *The Greensburg Gazette*. You just bought back my stolen fax machine!

CATERINA: Oh! I'm awfully sorry, Mr. Pellis.

MR. PELLIS: Well, I can always stop payment on the check.

CATERINA: Uh-oh!

MR. PELLIS: You didn't pay cash, did you?

CATERINA: *(Whispering.)* Well, yes.

MR. PELLIS: You're fired.

What Are the Legal Issues?

1. What is the difference between express and implied agency authority?
2. What is the difference between actual and apparent agency authority?
3. What are the duties of an agent to a principal? What are the duties of a principal to an agent?
4. How do agency relationships terminate?

Authority and Duties

Agents and Principals

Many different factors, including the way an agency relationship starts, can affect an agent's authority. No matter what type of authority is involved, all agents owe certain duties to their principals, and all principals owe certain duties to their agents. Moreover, agents and principals have certain responsibilities in relation to third parties who deal with the agency. It is important to understand the nature of agency authority, the duties and rights that exist between agents and principals, the responsibilities that extend to third parties, and the ways that agency relationships can end.

Types of Agency Authority

Agents act within the scope of their authority and contract with a third party on behalf of the principal. The contract that results is between

AN AGENT'S DUTIES
When a client engages an attorney, that attorney may be empowered to act as the agent of that client. *In such a situation, what duties would the attorney have in relation to his or her client?*

the principal and the third party. The agent's authority in negotiating the contract with the third party may be actual or apparent.

Actual Authority

Actual authority is the real power a principal gives to an agent to act on the principal's behalf. Such actual authority may be expressed in words or implied from the nature of the relationship or the conduct of the parties.

Express Authority

Express authority includes all of the orders, commands, or directions a principal directly states to an agent when the agency relationship is first created. These instructions may be very general or very specific.

> *Example 1.* While vacationing in Europe, Joanna DiBlasi asks Abe Eney to be her agent in selling her motorcycle. In a written document, Joanna specifically instructs Abe to accept no less than $2,000 for the motorcycle. She also includes in the agreement a clause telling Abe to accept cash only. Finally, the agreement expressly forbids selling the motorcycle to a minor. All of these instructions make up Abe's express authority as an agent in the sale of Joanna's motorcycle.

Implied Authority

Mentioning every single act that the agent is allowed to perform in an agreement with a principal is unnecessary. Doing so would make the agreement cumbersome and confusing. The law allows some actual authority to be implied or understood from the express terms that create the agency relationship, which constitutes an agent's **implied authority**.

> *Example 2.* In Example 1, Abe Eney had express authority to sell Joanna DiBlasi's motorcycle for no less than $2,000 in cash to anyone who had reached the age of majority. From these express powers would come the implied authority to allow a prospective buyer to inspect the motorcycle, take it for a test drive, and have an impartial mechanic examine it. All of these powers can be reasonably implied from Abe's authority to sell the motorcycle, even though the agreement does not specifically address these matters.

Implied authority is simply a form of actual authority because it also arises from the instructions that the principal communicates to the agent.

Community Works

Dress Code
If you wear a uniform to school, you don't have to worry about a dress code. Schools without uniforms create dress codes for their students. Sometimes, students are suspended from school for wearing clothing that administrators deem offensive. In some of these cases, students respond with a lawsuit claiming their First Amendment rights were violated. *How do you feel about students wearing T-shirts that feature racial, ethnic, or religious stereotyping?*

Get Involved
Organize a group of students and teachers at your school to discuss issues of cultural sensitivity and stereotyping. Find out how the First Amendment applies to freedom of speech in today's society.

Consequently, the key to determining implied authority is to focus on what took place between the principal and the agent.

Going Beyond Implied Authority

Sometimes a dispute arises over what powers can be implied from the express authority given to the agent. The court draws the line by saying that implied authority must be "reasonably derived from the express power." What is reasonable in a given situation is determined by looking at the actions that are customarily performed by other agents in similar situations.

> *Example 3.* Abe Eney decides that purchasing a new suit will help him sell Joanna DiBlasi's motorcycle. He purchases a suit and sends the bill to Joanna. Joanna would probably not have to pay for Abe's suit because such expenses are not typically part of an agent's authority in this kind of sales situation.

Apparent Authority

Apparent authority exists when the principal has somehow led a third party to believe that a nonagent is an agent, or that an agent has a power that he or she does not truly have. In contrast to implied authority, the key to understanding apparent authority is to focus on what happened between the principal and a third party. As discussed in Chapter 18, apparent authority is sometimes referred to as agency by estoppel because the principal cannot deny that the nonagent acted on his or her behalf.

Example 4. Pierre Trudeau told Theresa Jackson to come to his jewelry store at 9 A.M. on Tuesday. He said that someone would be there to sell her a diamond ring. At 8:30 A.M. on Tuesday, Pierre left the shop to run a few errands and asked his niece, Amy, to keep an eye on the store. Theresa arrived at 9 A.M., and assuming that Amy was a clerk, purchased a unique diamond ring from Amy. When Pierre returned, he was upset because that ring had been promised to another customer. He called Theresa, but she refused to return the ring. Theresa was within her rights because Pierre had created a situation that caused her to assume that Amy had authority to sell the ring.

APPARENT AUTHORITY
Apparent authority exists when the principal has somehow led a third party to believe that a nonagent is an agent. *Is the management of a department store responsible if an impostor poses as a salesperson and absconds with a customer's cash?*

UNDISCLOSED PRINCIPALS
Works of art are often bought at auction by agents acting for undisclosed principals. *In what other types of situations would it be to the principal's advantage to remain undisclosed?*

The apparent authority was created because of something that Pierre, the principal, had said to Theresa.

Agent's Duties to the Principal

An agent owes a principal the following five duties:

- Obedience
- Good faith
- Loyalty
- Accounting for all of the principal's money handled by the agent
- Exercising judgment and skill in the performance of the assigned work

Obedience

An agent owes the principal the duty of **obedience**, which means the agent must obey all reasonable orders and instructions within the scope of the agency agreement. Even a gratuitous agent must follow instructions. If an agent disobeys instructions, he or she becomes liable to the principal for any loss that results.

Example 5. In The Opening Scene, Mr. Pellis gives Caterina instructions to not get conned into buying something while he is gone. Caterina disobeys Mr. Pellis when she gives Mr. Bronowski $200 in cash for the fax machine.

Good Faith

An agency relationship is a fiduciary relationship. Principals often entrust their agents with their business, property, money, and sometimes even their good reputation. This places a duty of good faith on the agent. To have **good faith** simply means to deal honestly with another party with no intent to seek advantage or to defraud. Good faith also requires an agent to notify the principal of all matters pertaining to the agency relationship.

Loyalty

Agents may not work for others who are competing with their principals, nor may they make deals to their own advantage at the expense of their principals. The only exception to these rules is when the principal knows and approves of the agent's role in representing a competing principal, or if the principal knows the agent is working to the agent's advantage.

LAWS in Your Life

Service of Process

When an individual, an organization, or a corporation files a civil lawsuit, the defendant is served with a copy of the complaint and a summons. This is called service of process.

Most states require out-of-state corporations to have an agent for service of process if the corporation does business in that state. It is necessary to complete service of process by serving an officer of the corporation or the corporation's agent within in that state.

Before being permitted to do business in most states, corporations must designate an agent for service of process. This is usually done through the state secretary of state's office. Corporations are generally required to make sure that contact information about their agents is always current.

Sometimes a corporation has a registered agent within the state but has not actually done any business in the state. In that case, service of process must be completed in the corporation's own state.

Conduct Research Contact the office of your state's secretary of state by phone or through its Web site. Find out about the requirements for having an agent to complete service of process on out-of-state corporations. Then contact a corporation with headquarters in another state. Find the contact information for the corporation's designated agent for service of process.

Duty to Account

An agent who handles money for the principal owes a duty to account for every cent of that money. The **duty to account** means the agent must keep a record of all the money collected and paid out and must report this to the principal. The agent must keep the principal's money safe and separate from others' money. The agent must also turn the principal's money over to the principal in keeping with his or her instructions. If the agent mixes the principal's money with his or her own funds to the extent that it is impossible to determine whose money is whose, the agent loses all claim to the money. The entire amount then belongs to the principal.

Judgment and Skill

Agents must use all of the skill and judgment that they have when performing work for principals. However, agents are not perfect. Even the most well-informed agents make mistakes from time to time. For this reason, agents are not held liable for honest mistakes if they have performed to the best of their ability.

> *Example 6.* Peggy Reinhardt entrusted Avery Wilson with $500,000 and told him to invest it in the best possible stocks. Avery decided to invest in the Van Meader Chemical Company, a new corporation that was clearly one of the best investment opportunities at the time. One week later, a chemical gas leak at a Van Meader plant in Brazil destroyed millions of dollars worth of real estate. Van Meader stock fell, and Reinhardt lost her investment in the company. Avery couldn't be held liable for this loss because he had done his best.

Principal's Duties to the Agent

Agents also have rights guaranteed to them by law. The law imposes specific duties on the principal in dealing with the agent. The same duties are found in the employer-employee relationship, which we will discuss in Chapter 20. These duties include compensation, reimbursement, indemnification, and cooperation.

Compensation

An agent who is working on behalf of a principal is entitled to be paid for services rendered, unless he or she is a gratuitous agent. The principal must pay any compensation agreed upon in the contract. If no specific amount has been set, a reasonable sum must be paid for any authorized acts performed by the agent for the principal. Sometimes it is possible to figure out this reasonable sum by checking the customary salaries or wages paid to other agents performing the same kinds of tasks for their principals.

Law & Academics

Social Studies

Since Benjamin Franklin was named the first Postmaster General in 1775, the post office has used technology to deliver the mail. In 1823, navigable waters were used. In 1862, the postal service started using trains. Today, the U.S. Postal Service delivers hundreds of millions of messages and billions of dollars in financial transactions each day to 8 million businesses and 250 million Americans.

Research Activity

Access the U.S. Postal Service Web site and review the institution's history. Determine when significant changes were made in the use of technology, and create a timeline to describe these changes.

Legal Briefs

In seventeenth century Europe, most monarchs appointed a favorite, who acted as an agent in carrying out the monarch's private and public affairs. The favorite was often the monarch's confidant, companion, proxy, and envoy. One famous example is Cardinal Richelieu (1585–1642), who served as the royal favorite of King Louis XIII of France.

Reimbursement and Indemnification

Agents are entitled to **reimbursement**, or repayment, when they spend their own money for the principal's benefit. In addition, if an agent suffers any loss as a result of the principal's instructions, he or she is entitled to **indemnification**; that is, he or she is entitled to repayment of the amount lost.

Cooperation

The duty of **cooperation** means working together toward a common end. The principal, having given the agent the duty to perform certain tasks, must not interfere with the performance of those tasks. If the principal makes the agent's job difficult or impossible, he or she has breached the duty of cooperation.

> *Example 7.* Phoebe Parkes told Justin Alvarez that he would have exclusive rights to sell the Curren-Bartlett line of cosmetics door-to-door in Willowick, a small town with a population of 5,000. She also told him that to keep his job, he would need to make a quarterly profit of $10,000. Later, Justin learned that Phoebe had hired four other agents to sell the same cosmetics line in Willowick. This action made it impossible for Justin to make $10,000 quarterly because there were not enough customers in the town. Justin could argue successfully that Phoebe had violated her duty to cooperate.

Agent's Liability to Third Parties

The agent is a go-between who brings the contracting parties together and "stands in the shoes of the principal" in making the contract. Sometimes individuals and businesses may prefer to keep their connection to a transaction a secret. Other times principals may wish to disclose the relationship. If the agent represents a disclosed principal, one whose existence and identity are known to the third party, the agent assumes no contractual liability for the resulting contract. The principal alone assumes the responsibility. Agents may be held responsible for contracts negotiated for the principal when the agents do not disclose the identity or the existence of the principal, or when agents wrongfully exceed their authority.

When the Principal Is Not Disclosed

A partially disclosed principal is one whose identity is never revealed, even when the third party knows the agent is acting for someone else. If the third party later learns the identity of the principal, then

A Global Perspective:
Laws Around the World

Brazil

Brazil's Amazon is a region of superlatives. It is home to the world's largest rainforest (approximately two million square miles) and the world's mightiest river. It is also a habitat for the greatest variety of animal life known on earth. Brazil's animal life includes giant spiders, piranha, jaguars, howler monkeys, parrots, and 30-foot anacondas. The area's plant life is also impressive. The forest trees grow in distinctive layers. Some trees adorned with a variety of air plants, reach heights of up to 165 feet. Plant and animal species number in the millions—so many that some believe millions remain unidentified and uncounted. For years, this rich environment has been the focal point of two opposing camps: environmentalists and developers. After satellite photos revealed record deforestation in the mid-1990s, Brazil's government used a Presidential Transitory Act to strengthen the 1965 Forest Code. The rainforest's protected area was increased from 50 to 80 percent. The developers, however, including loggers, farmers, and ranchers, want to relax restrictions so more trees can be cut for cropland and pasture.
The conflict may never end, but for now the preservationists have formed a strong coalition and seek to make protective legislation a permanent law. Here's a snapshot of Brazil:

Geographical area	**3,286,488 sq. mi.**
Population	**176,029,560**
Capital	**Brasília**
Legal system	**Based on Roman codes**
Language	**Portuguese, Spanish, English**
Religion	**80% Roman Catholic**
Life expectancy	**64 years**

Critical Thinking Question What are some of the most important reasons for protecting the rainforests? For more information on Brazil, visit **ubpl.glencoe.com** or your local library.

he or she has the option of holding either the agent or the principal liable should the contract not be performed.

> *Example 8.* Janet Moffet, a famous entertainer, hired a real estate agent, Fred Patterson, to search for a home for her. Fred was directed not to reveal the identity of the person he was representing. Imagine that Fred found a house and told the seller, Mary Teicholz, that he represented a buyer who wished to conceal her identity. After a contract was entered, however, Janet defaulted and refused to buy the house. If the seller, Mary Teicholz, were to uncover Janet Moffet's identity, she could sue Moffet for breach of contract. If not, Mary could bring the breach of contract suit against the agent, Fred Patterson. If Fred were to lose the suit and be forced to pay damages out of his own resources, however, Janet Moffet would have to indemnify him for the money paid out to satisfy the award.

Sometimes agents have instructions to not reveal the existence of an agency relationship. They are then said to be working on behalf of an undisclosed principal. If you were a third party, you would have no idea that the person you were dealing with was really acting for someone else. Should there be a breach, you would have a cause of action against the agent. However, as long as the agent has fulfilled his or her responsibilities, the principal is bound to the contract despite your lack of knowledge of the principal's identity.

Virtual Law

Author Agents in a Digital World

Authors' agents have a duty to battle with publishers over the rights to sell digital versions of printed books. Recent lawsuits highlight the struggle authors and agents have with publishers over this issue. One issue involves who owns the electronic rights for books. Authors and their agents argue that digital rights belong to the author, unless the publishing contract says otherwise. Publishers argue that the print publisher automatically owns the digital rights to a book. The other main issue is money. Authors and agents must negotiate with publishers over how much authors are paid for digital sales of their books. (Source: *New York Times*, February 28, 2001, p. C5)

Connect Visit the Web site of an online bookseller. Find out who publishes electronic books. See if a different publisher publishes the print version of any of those books.

Example 9. Ann Prospect managed a produce stand for Phil Armstrong. The business was called "Ann Prospect's Produce," and no one who dealt with Ann knew that she was actually Phil's agent. Acting under Phil's instructions, Ann entered a contract with Terminal Tower Corporation for the purchase of a new storefront. Phil is bound to this contract just as if he had negotiated it himself.

When Agents Wrongfully Exceed Their Authority

Agents may bind a principal to a contract only when they act within the scope of their authority. If agents enter into contracts on behalf of their principals without authority to do so, the agents themselves are liable for the contract.

Example 10. People's Printing Company told Anita Arnett, an employee, to buy a word processor for no more than $1,400. She found one for $1,050 and used the remaining $350 to buy a CD player for the office. Her employer refused to accept the CD player, which Anita had no authority to buy. She would be required to pay People's Printing Company $350.

Section 19.1 Assessment

Reviewing What You Learned

1. What is the difference between express and implied authority?
2. What is the difference between actual and apparent authority?
3. What are the duties owed by an agent to a principal?
4. What are the duties owed by a principal to an agent?

Critical Thinking Activity

Duty Why does the law extend duties to both the principal and the agent?

Legal Skills in Action

Duty to Account Your friend Tammy was recently hired as a salesperson in Harriet's dress shop. One evening when closing the shop, Tammy forgot to place the day's proceeds in the safe. On her way home, she decided to place all of Harriet's money in her own bank account, along with some cash of her own that she had just received for her birthday. The next day, Tammy forgot to retrieve the money. By the time she remembered to get the money out of her account, she couldn't recall how much of Harriet's money she deposited. Write an e-mail message to Tammy in which you explain why you believe she has lost all rights to the money in her bank account.

Termination of Agency Relationships

What You'll Learn

- How to recognize when an agency relationship is terminated by operation of law
- How to recognize when an agency relationship is terminated by an act of the parties
- How to determine when individuals are entitled to actual notice of an agency termination
- How to determine when individuals are entitled to notice by publication of an agency termination

Why It's Important

You need to know when an agency relationship has been terminated so you may determine your liability as an agent or a principal. You also need to know your rights of notification when you are a third party who has dealt with the agent.

Legal Terms

- bankruptcy
- actual notice
- notice by publication

Terminating the Relationship

Even the most cordial and successful agency relationships must eventually end. Because many such relationships involve contractual arrangements, the usual rules that apply to the termination of contracts are applicable. As a result, agency relationships can be terminated either by operation of law or by the acts of the parties involved. Figure 19.1 shows how liability is determined after the termination of a relationship.

By Operation of Law

When a significant change of circumstances alters the original reason for the agency relationship, a court may hold that agency relationship terminated. These changes are sometimes said to terminate agency agreements by operation of law.

Death of the Principal or Agent

The death of an agent will terminate the agency relationship. This makes sense because an agency relationship is based on the personal services of the agent. The death of the principal will also terminate the agency relationship.

Bankruptcy

Bankruptcy of the principal terminates an agency relationship because it cancels all of the principal's ordinary contracts. Bankruptcy also gives a trustee title to the principal's property for the benefit of creditors.

Bankruptcy of the agent will terminate the agency relationship if the agent has used his or her own funds to conduct the principal's business. If not, however, there is no reason to terminate the agency because the agent's bankruptcy will not prevent him or her from doing the job in the regular way.

Impossibility of Performance

An agency relationship is terminated when the essential subject matter is destroyed or the incapacity of the agent makes performance impossible. Suppose you entered into an agreement to sell a friend's boat to a third party. Before the contract was signed, the boat sank through no fault of anyone involved. The agency would be terminated because the essential subject matter of the contract, the boat, has been destroyed.

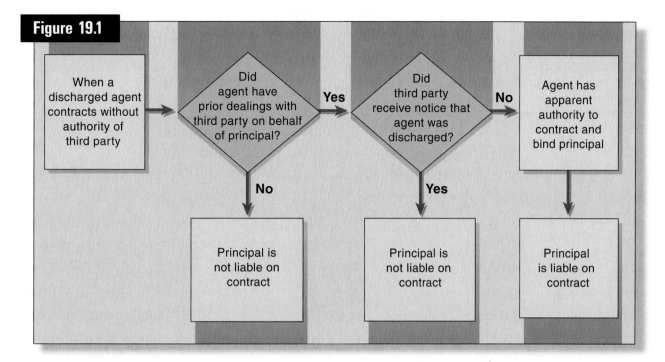

Figure 19.1

When a discharged agent contracts without authority of third party → Did agent have prior dealings with third party on behalf of principal?

Yes → Did third party receive notice that agent was discharged? **No** → Agent has apparent authority to contract and bind principal

No ↓ Principal is not liable on contract

Yes ↓ Principal is not liable on contract

↓ Principal is liable on contract

Agent's Objective Becomes Illegal

If, after an agency agreement has been entered, the purpose of the agency is declared illegal, then the agency is terminated by operation of law. If only part of the agent's required activity becomes illegal, only that part of the authority ends. The remaining authority to perform legal activities remains in effect.

By Acts of the Parties

Most agency relationships are terminated when the parties have fully carried out their duties. The parties may also terminate their relationship by mutual consent before the contract is fully performed. Moreover, certain acts by agents or principals may be enough to terminate a relationship.

Performance

If an agent is appointed to accomplish a certain result, the agency terminates when the result is achieved. In other words, when the job is done, the agency ends.

Mutual Agreement

The principal and the agent may mutually agree to terminate the agency. Termination may result from the passing of a preset time period. However, the principal and the agent may agree to end the relationship at any other time, even if the task is left undone or the time period has not yet elapsed.

TERMINATION OF AN AGENCY RELATIONSHIP This chart indicates how liability is determined after termination of an agency relationship. *Why does the law permit a third party in some cases to hold a principal liable even after the principal has discharged an agent?*

ACTUAL NOTICE OF
TERMINATION
The law gives an extra
degree of responsibility to a
principal when the principal
has permitted an agent to
buy on credit from third
parties. *What is the best
type of mail service to use
when extending actual
notice of the termination
of an agency relationship
to a third party?*

Agent's Withdrawal

An agent may terminate the agency at any time. However, if termination involves a breach of contract, the agent may be liable for any damages suffered by the principal.

Agent's Discharge

The principal may terminate an agency relationship at any time by firing the agent. There are some limits on the authority of the principal to fire an agent, however. When an agent has an interest in the subject matter of the agency, he or she is said to have an irrevocable agency, which cannot be discharged by the principal.

> *Example 11.* Pamona Pratt borrowed money from a financial institution, Associated American, to remodel her office building. To repay the loan, she appointed Associated American as an agent for the collection of rent money from her tenants. The understanding was that the rent money was to be applied to repayment of the loan and that the agency would last until the loan was fully repaid.

Notice to Third Parties

Third parties who have done business with the principal through an agent or who knew of the agency relationship are entitled to notice of its termination. A principal who fails to notify third parties when an agency has ended may be liable for future acts of the agent.

Example 12. Shortly after Vince Arbaugh was discharged by Penrose Products, he visited one of Penrose's customers. While there, he accepted a payment of $125 that the customer expected him to turn over to Penrose. Penrose had given no notice to the customer that Vince had been fired. If Vince does not turn the money in, Penrose will still have to credit its customer for the payment because Penrose failed to give proper notice of the employee's termination.

The type of notice given to a third party depends on how the former business relations were carried out. There are three situations to consider:

- When the third party has given credit to the principal through the agent, the third party is entitled to **actual notice**. Notice by certified mail is perhaps the best way to give actual notice, because receipt of the notice can be obtained from the post office.
- When the third party has never given credit but has done a cash business with the agent, or knows that other persons have dealt with the principal through the agent, **notice by publication** in a newspaper is sufficient.
- When the third party has never heard of the agency relationship, no notice of any kind is required. The third party who is dealing with an agent for the first time has a duty to investigate and determine the exact extent of the agent's authority.

Section 19.2   Assessment

Reviewing What You Learned

1. How can agency relationships be terminated by operation of law?
2. How can agency relationships be terminated by the acts of the parties?
3. Which individuals are entitled to actual notice of an agency termination?
4. Which individuals are entitled to notice by publication of an agency termination?

Critical Thinking Activity

Actual Notice Why is certified mail the best way to give actual notice of the termination of an agency relationship?

Legal Skills in Action

Notice of Termination Ted has just discharged David, who has served as his agent for five years. Morris, who has often extended credit to Ted through David, and Sophie, who has dealt with Ted through David on a cash basis only, have not yet been given notice of this termination. Write a letter to Ted explaining what type of notice he must give to Morris and Sophie. In both cases, recommend a practical course of action for Ted to pursue in giving notice.

Chapter Summary

Section 19.1 Authority and Duties

- Express authority includes all of the orders, commands or directions that a principal directly makes to an agent when the agency relationship is created. These instructions may be general or specific. Mentioning every act that the agent is allowed to perform is cumbersome and unnecessary. The law allows some actual authority to be understood from the express terms that create the agency relationship. The powers that can reasonably be derived from the express terms of an agency agreement constitute an agent's implied authority. Implied authority is a form of actual authority because it also arises from the instructions that the principal communicates to the agent.

- Actual authority is the real power a principal gives to an agent to act on his or her behalf. In contrast, when the principal has led a third party to believe that a nonagent is an agent or that an agent has a power that he or she does not really have, the principal has created apparent authority. Apparent authority is also referred to as agency by estoppel.

- The five duties that an agent owes to a principal are obedience, good faith, loyalty, an accounting of the principal's money handled by the agent, and the exercising of judgment and skill in performing the assigned work. The duty of obedience requires the agent to obey all reasonable orders and instructions within the scope of the agency agreement. To have good faith, an agent must deal honestly with the principal and harbor no intent to seek advantage or defraud. To be loyal, agents must not work for others who are competing with their principals, nor may they make deals to their own advantage at the expense of their principals. The duty to account means that the agent must keep a record of all of the money collected and paid out and must report this to the principal. Agents must also use all of the judgment and skill that they have when performing work for principals.

- The law imposes specific duties on a principal in dealing with an agent. These duties include compensation, reimbursement, indemnification, and cooperation. Compensation is payment given by the principal to the agent in return for the agent's services. Reimbursement is repayment that an agent receives when he or she spends his or her own money for the principal's benefit. Similarly, if an agent suffers any loss as a result of the principal's instruction, he or she is entitled to indemnification, or repayment of the amount lost. Cooperation refers to the principal's duty to refrain from interfering with the agent's duties.

Section 19.2 Termination of Agency Relationships

- An agency relationship may be terminated by operation of law in the case of the death of either party. Other circumstances such as bankruptcy, impossibility of performance, or subsequent declaration of illegality of the act may also terminate the agency relationship.

- Most commonly, agency relationships are terminated when the parties have fully carried out their duties. The parties may also terminate their relationship by mutual consent before the contract is fully performed. An agent may also quit his or her job or give up the agency, or a principal may fire the agent, all of which would result in termination of the agency relationship.

- Actual notice of the termination of an agency relationship must be given to those third parties who have extended credit to the principal through the agent.

- Notice of the termination of an agency relationship may be given by publication to those third parties who have conducted business with the agent without extending credit.

Using Legal Language

Consider the key terms in the list below. Then use these terms to complete the following exercises.

express authority

implied authority

obedience

good faith

duty to account

reimbursement

indemnification

cooperation

bankruptcy

actual notice

notice by publication

1. In a small group, create a bulletin board explaining agency relationships and their termination. Use as many of the terms listed above as possible.
2. As a class, discuss the best qualities of each board, noting legal references, creativity, and use of terms.
3. Display the bulletin boards in the classroom.
4. Write a brief essay explaining how your group could have improved its bulletin board.

Understanding Business and Personal Law Online

Self-Check Quiz Visit the *Understanding Business and Personal Law* Web site at **ubpl.glencoe.com** and click on Chapter 19: Agency Relationships and Their Termination— Self-Check Quizzes to prepare for the chapter exam.

The Law Review

Answer the following questions. Refer to the chapter for additional reinforcement.

5. What is the difference between an agent's actual authority and an agent's apparent authority?
6. What duties does a principal owe to an agent?
7. Explain good faith as it relates to an agency relationship.
8. Is it legal for an agent to keep secret the identity of the principal whom he or she is representing? Explain your answer.
9. What happens if a principal fails to notify third parties that an agency relationship has ended?
10. Under what circumstance may an agent legally represent competing principals?
11. What happens if an agent mingles the principal's funds with his or her personal funds?
12. What is a gratuitous agent?
13. What is indemnification?
14. Under what circumstance might bankruptcy end an agency relationship?

Linking School to Work

Interpreting and Communicating Information

Conduct research to find out more about agents. Use the want ads from the newspaper or the Internet to complete the following exercises.

15. Locate advertisements listing qualifications that would be consistent with those of an agent.
16. As a class, make a list of the duties of the various agents they found in the ads.
17. Choose one job that interests you. Would you be good at this job? Why or why not?

Let's Debate

Conflict of Interest

You and Karl agree that he will act as your agent, promoting your services as a lawn care and gardening specialist. You are planning to use your earnings to pay for technical school. Ms. Vincenza wants some landscaping done, but she likes Karl and insists that he do the work. Karl tells you that he will do the work and give you the money, but you know this isn't fair.

Debate

18. If Karl does the work, has he damaged the agency relationship in any way?
19. Would you terminate your agency relationship with Karl? How? What would you do in this situation?

Grasping Case Issues

For the following cases, give your decision and state a legal principle that applies.

20. Priit Xavier was a European actor who wanted to purchase a home in California. Because it was clear that the price would skyrocket if a seller knew the identity of the buyer, Xavier hired Mattia Doubilet to act as an agent in purchasing the property. Doubilet negotiated a deal with Georges Milan for the purchase of Milan's home. When the deal fell through, Milan wanted to bring a lawsuit against Doubilet. Can Milan bring suit against Doubilet, or must he first uncover the identity of the principal? Explain your answer.

21. Ted Van Dine owes Oliver Wayne $320 for goods shipped to Van Dine's shop. Each month for the past two years Wayne has sent his collection agent, Kent Brewster, to collect on Van Dine's account. Unknown to Van Dine, Wayne fires Brewster. Brewster continues to collect money from Van Dine and keeps it for himself. After Van Dine pays Brewster, does he still owe Wayne? Explain your answer.

22. Leo Anderson hires Shirley Johnson as his literary agent to find a publisher for his books. When Johnson reads Anderson's latest manuscript, she realizes it is a best seller. She tells Anderson the book is so bad that no publisher will want to publish it. She offers to pay him $200 for the manuscript. He agrees. Johnson then sells the manuscript to a publisher for $1 million. What duties has Johnson breached? Explain your answer.

23. Aztron, Inc. hires the Millstern Ad Agency to begin an advertising campaign. This campaign involves placing 30 billboards on 30 highways, each one 10 yards from the road. Before the billboards are placed, the state legislature passes a statute that requires all billboards to be placed at least 50 yards from the road. Millstern wants to continue the campaign, but Aztron says the agency has been terminated by operation of law. Has the agency been terminated? Why or why not?

In each case that follows, you be the judge.

24. Apparent Authority

Stahl brought her car to LePage's service station for repairs. LePage indicated that he could not do the work but would permit his employee, Donley, to use his garage to make the needed repairs. Donley did a bad job, at one point installing the wrong engine in Stahl's car. When Stahl attempted to sue LePage, the garage owner argued that, in this case, Donley had not acted as his agent. Stahl argued that the doctrine of apparent authority could be used to hold LePage liable. *Is Stahl correct? Why or why not?*

Stahl v. LePage, 352 A2d 682 (VT).

25. Commingling

Lloyd was an attorney who acted as the legal guardian of Parker and Hockenberry. He also represented Isaac in the purchase of some land. Lloyd deposited several settlement checks for those clients into his own bank account, commingling the funds with his own. He also used these funds to pay some of his own bills. *What duties has Lloyd violated in relation to his clients? Explain your answer.*

Office of Disciplinary Counsel v. Lloyd, 643 N.E2d 1086 (OH).

Legal Link

Sales Agent

Juan Valdez-Colon runs a chocolate factory in Colorado. He would like to export his candy to buyers in the Middle East. He doesn't know where to begin, but he realizes he might need the help of a foreign sales agent.

Connect

Using a variety of search engines, help Juan find out more about exporting products from the United States to countries overseas.

26. Locate information about foreign sales agents, freight forwarding agents, or export management companies that conduct this type of work.

POWER READING STRATEGIES

27. **Predict** What duties do agents owe to their principals? What duties do principals owe to their agents?

28. **Connect** What is a real-world example of implied authority?

29. **Question** Do you think it is fair for an agent to act for a principal who is never revealed to the third party? Why or why not?

30. **Respond** Why do you think we need laws governing the termination of agency relationships?

Employment Law

Understanding Business and Personal Law *Online*

Chapter Overview Visit the *Understanding Business and Personal Law* Web site at ubpl.glencoe.com and click on Chapter 20: Employment Relationships— Chapter Overviews to preview the chapter information.

The Opening Scene

Caterina has just arrived at home. Her parents are preparing dinner. Her brother, Lazzaro, is also home.

Second Chance

Mr. Gant: Say, you look upset. What's wrong, Caterina?

Caterina: Nothing.

Lazzaro: She got fired.

Caterina: How do you know?

Lazzaro: The rumor's all over school. I heard about it in my English class.

Caterina: Great.

Mrs. Gant: Did Mr. Pellis fire you already? Did you do something to make him angry? What happened, Caterina?

Caterina: Nothing.

Lazzaro: She bought Mr. Pellis's own fax machine back from the guy who stole it last week. No wonder he was angry. Now Mr. Pellis is out $200 because of Caterina's mistake.

Caterina: Shut up.

Mrs. Gant: Is that true, Caterina?

Caterina: No. Well, yes, sort of.

Mrs. Gant: Sort of?

Caterina: Okay, so it's true, but it's not fair that he fired me. I was just trying to help. How could I have known the machine was stolen?

Lazzaro: Sounds fair to me.

Caterina: Shut up.

Mrs. Gant: Why isn't it fair?

Caterina: I don't know.

Mrs. Gant: Then it must be fair.

Caterina: Okay. It's not fair because he promised me that he wouldn't fire me, as long as I did exactly what he asked me to do. Besides, his manual says I should get a second chance.

Mrs. Gant: Manual? What are you talking about, Caterina?

Caterina: He gave me this employment manual to read when he hired me, and it says right on page five that all employees get what he calls progressive discipline. I didn't get progressive discipline. Mr. Pellis fired me for making one mistake.

Lazzaro: All of his employees? You're his only employee.

Caterina: Shut up.

Mr. Gant: Well, it's too bad that you got fired, especially after all that time you spent getting a work permit. I guess you'll just have to look for a new job.

Lazzaro: Oh, she never got a work permit. She said it wasn't important.

Caterina: Shut up.

Mr. Gant: You didn't get your work permit?

Caterina: Not exactly.

Mr. Gant: Caterina.

Caterina: Yes?

Mr. Gant: Not getting a work permit is very irresponsible. Maybe it's better that you got fired after all.

What Are the Legal Issues?

1. What is the doctrine of employment-at-will?
2. What employment situations do not fall within the doctrine of employment-at-will?
3. What are the exceptions to employment-at-will?
4. What are the federal laws that regulate employment relationships?

Employment Relationships

Employment-at-Will

The doctrine known as **employment-at-will** is the general rule governing employment in most states. According to this doctrine, an employer is permitted to discharge an employee at any time, for any or no reason, with or without notice. This doctrine is based on the notion that both parties in an employment relationship must be free to leave the employment arrangement at any time. If employees were not free to leave an employment relationship at any time, then they would actually be slaves. Enslavement, of course, violates the Thirteenth Amendment's prohibition against involuntary servitude.

Unionized Employees

The doctrine of employment-at-will does not apply in certain situations. Employees have the right to organize and participate in a union. A **union** is an organization of employees that is formed to promote the welfare of its members. Employees who belong to labor unions have hiring and firing procedures built into their collective bargaining agreements. A **collective bargaining agreement** is a contract negotiated by the employer and representatives of the labor union, and it covers issues related to employment.

UNION ACTIVITY
A union is an organization of employees that is formed to promote the welfare of its members. Employees who belong to labor unions have hiring and firing procedures built into their collective bargaining agreements. *What procedures are available to union members should an employer violate a collective bargaining agreement?*

Union members select representatives to negotiate a contract with the employer through a series of discussions known as bargaining.

Collective Bargaining Agreements

A collective bargaining session generally concerns issues such as working conditions, wages, benefits, job security, layoffs, and firing policies. For example, a contract might stipulate that an employer must have a legitimate, employment-related reason, or just cause, for disciplining or discharging an employee. Collective bargaining agreements generally include the steps that must be followed in a grievance procedure. A **grievance procedure** establishes a series of steps that an employee must follow to appeal the decision of an employer who may have violated the collective bargaining agreement. Many nonunion companies also include a grievance procedure as part of the employment contract.

> *Example 1.* Edward Ewing worked on the assembly line for Stewart Motors, Inc. He was also a member of the Organization of American Automotive Employees (OAAE). Ewing was discharged because he was late for work on one occasion. The collective bargaining agreement between Stewart Motors and OAAE did not permit the firing of a worker for a single incident of lateness. Also, according to the agreement, all violations for lateness were to be reported in writing, and the employees were to be given a second chance. After going through the grievance procedure, Ewing was restored to his position.

Layoffs and Plant Closings

Despite the many advantages associated with collective bargaining agreements, they do not guarantee that employees will have a job for life. Sometimes, economic conditions force layoffs or plant closings. When such events occur, some or all employees may lose their jobs. Massive layoffs and plant closings can pose great hardships to communities and individual families. Collective bargaining agreements often provide a negotiated procedure under which such layoffs occur. A collective bargaining agreement may also provide for **severance pay**, which is a set amount of money to compensate employees for being discharged and to help them through the time that they remain unemployed. Severance pay is calculated by using a variety of factors, including the position and salary of the person being laid off.

The federal government also endeavors to aid employees who lose their jobs or are laid off. For example, Congress enacted the Worker Adjustment and Retraining Notification Act (WARN). This legislation compels some companies to give employees at least 60 days advance-notice of a factory shut down or massive layoff. Only companies that

Cira Valdez is principal at Morningside Elementary. She is the only daughter of elderly parents. For the past three years, she has missed many days of work to care for her parents. The superintendent of her school district, Adya Perkins, has warned her repeatedly about her absences, and the vice-principal, Don Mattison, has complained about the extra work that Cira's absences have caused him. In March, Mrs. Perkins suspended Ms. Valdez. Parents and teachers were furious. They felt Mrs. Perkins should have taken disciplinary measures in the summer when the students would not be affected. *What are Mrs. Perkin's ethical obligations in the case? Do you agree with her actions? Why or why not?*

employ more than 100 workers are bound by this requirement. Notice of lay off or shut down is not always necessary, especially if it is the result of an emergency situation.

Illegal Discrimination

Even when an employee is not covered by a collective bargaining agreement or a professional employment contract, he or she cannot be discharged for a reason that is discriminatory in nature. According to the Civil Rights Act of 1964, a discharge is discriminatory if it occurs because of a person's race, color, creed, national origin, or gender. Similarly, the Age Discrimination in Employment Act protects people from being discharged because of their age. The Civil Rights Act of 1964 and the Age Discrimination in Employment Act are covered in more detail in Chapter 21.

Rights and Duties of Employers and Employees

Employers and employees have certain mutual expectations in their working relationships. Some of these expectations are determined by the nature of the job, but other expectations are implied or imposed by state and federal statutes. Employers expect their employees to have the experience, education, and skills that they claim to possess. Employers also expect a reasonable amount of work from employees within a reasonable amount of time. They have the right to tell employees what tasks to perform and how to perform them.

Employees are expected to be loyal, honest, and dependable, and they must abide by the employer's rules. Employees can expect their employers to provide regular pay, a safe work environment, appropriate job training, opportunities to earn raises and promotions, and safe tools. They can also expect to be able to make reasonable complaints.

Exceptions to Employment-at-Will

Despite all of the protection afforded to employees, most workers are still subject to the principles outlined in the doctrine of employment-at-will. As explained previously, this doctrine states that an employer is permitted to discharge an employee at any time, for any or no reason, and with or without notice. Terminating an employment contract under the doctrine of employment-at-will has occasionally resulted in injustices. As a result, many courts challenge the employment-at-will doctrine by ruling against the wrongful discharge of employees.

Wrongful Discharge

Wrongful discharge, also called unjust dismissal, provides employees with grounds for legal action against employers who have treated them unfairly. The courts have established five standards it will consider regarding an unjust termination. These five standards include promissory estoppel, implied contract, public policy tort, intentional infliction of emotional distress, and implied covenant.

Promissory Estoppel **Promissory estoppel** has been used by some courts as proper grounds for unjust dismissal lawsuits. However, to build a solid case based on promissory estoppel, four elements must be proven. These elements include the following:

- The employer makes a promise to an employee that the employer can reasonably expect the employee to rely upon.
- The employee actually relies upon that promise, and as a result, does or doesn't do something.
- The employee ordinarily would not have acted or refrained from acting had it not been for the employer's promise.
- The employee is in some way harmed by the employer's failure to honor the promise.

If all of these elements exist, then the court may prevent the employer from denying responsibility for the loss suffered by the employee as a result of that reliance.

Example 2. Nigel Harrington worked as a bookkeeper for Federated Shipping, Inc. In June, he was arrested and charged with embezzlement. Harrington's supervisor told him that he would be suspended pending the results of the case. The supervisor assured Harrington that he would have his job back with full seniority rights if the case were resolved in his favor. In reliance on this promise, Harrington didn't seek another job, and instead concentrated on clearing his name. When the charges were dropped, Harrington attempted to get his old job back only to find that Federated would not employ him.

PROMISSORY ESTOPPEL
If an employer makes a promise to an employee and that employee relies on the promise and suffers a loss as a result, then the employee may be permitted to bring a wrongful discharge lawsuit based on promissory estoppel. *What are the elements of promissory estoppel?*

Harrington's case clearly fits within the guidelines set up by the courts for a case of unjust dismissal based on promissory estoppel. If Harrington were to bring a wrongful discharge suit based on promissory estoppel against Federated Shipping, he would likely succeed.

Implied Contract Another exception to employment-at-will involves implied contract. The **implied contract** exception arises when an employer has said, written, or done something to lead the employee to reasonably believe that he or she is not an at-will employee. When determining whether an employer has created an implied contract, the court can look at all of the facts involving that employment relationship, not just the oral promises made by the employer. The court can examine the nature of the employment relationship, the way that the parties have dealt with one another in the past, the length of the employment arrangement, the customary way that the employer has dealt with other employees, and employment policies and procedures. An employer's polices and procedures are generally outlined in an employee handbook or other company documents. If the handbook contains promises of lifelong employment, fair and just treatment, discipline or discharge

LAWS in Your Life

Organizing and Participating in a Union

Employees have a right to organize into unions if they share common employment interests, do not have supervisory duties, and do not have a confidential role in creating management-labor policies. To establish a union, organizers must have a sufficient number of the prospective bargaining unit members sign authorization cards. A bargaining unit consists of a group of eligible employees whose contract is negotiated as a group. Authorization cards, signed by employees who are eligible for membership in a union, indicate that the workers want their employment to be represented by a particular union. If a certain percentage of workers sign authorization cards, the union may ask management to be recognized as the exclusive bargaining unit for the employees it represents. If management refuses to voluntarily recognize a union, organizers can ask the National Labor Relations Board (NLRB) to conduct hearings and certify the union.

Conduct Research Investigate an employee's right to organize and participate in a union, based on current legislation. What are some of the laws governing management's conduct during the process of establishing a union? What are some of the laws governing the conduct of prospective union members?

only for certain offenses, or progressive discipline, then the employer may have created an implied contract. However, before the plaintiff in a wrongful discharge lawsuit can make such allegations, he or she must convince the court that the employer intended the employment manual to be a part of the employment relationship. This can usually be done if the employer required the employee to read and sign the handbook as a condition of employment.

Most federal and state courts that have recognized that the implied contract exception will still allow employers to maintain an employment-at-will arrangement by using a disclaimer. A **disclaimer** is a statement that holds that, regardless of any provisions, policies, or oral promises to the contrary, an employment-at-will situation still exists between the employer and its employees. To be effective, a disclaimer should include the following statements:

- Neither the employee handbook nor any other communication to employees is intended to create an employment contract between the firm and its employees.
- The employer reserves the right to discharge an employee at any time with or without notice and with or without reason.
- No one other than the president of the firm is empowered to make any oral or written change in this disclaimer.

Example 3. Mary Barnes applied for a job with the Kosar Brothers Department Store. The employee manual contained a disclaimer that preserved employment-at-will. The disclaimer specifically said that employees could be discharged with or without notice at any time for any or no reason. Only the president of the store could alter this provision. Barnes told Jack Gower, the assistant manager, that she would not work under such provisions. Gower told her to ignore the disclaimer and promised Porter a job for life. Gower's oral representation would have no legal effect in light of the ironclad nature of the disclaimer. Barnes realized this and sought employment elsewhere.

Although the disclaimer provides a way for an employer to preserve employment-at-will, many employers are reluctant to include such a statement in their employee handbooks. It may lower morale to remind employees that they can be fired at any time without warning or cause. Some employers qualify the disclaimer by saying that "employees can be dismissed at any time for just cause," or "employees who violate company rules can be terminated at any time." Such qualifying provisions can weaken the disclaimer to the extent that it no longer has the effect of preserving employment-at-will, making it possible for a discharged employee to sue for breach of an implied employment contract.

Law & Academics

Mathematics
In May 2001, the U.S. Department of Labor reported 1,426 mass layoff actions by employers during that month. A mass layoff action means that a single company lays off at least 50 people, regardless of the duration of the layoff.

Research Activity
Look at the chart below.

	Mass Layoff Actions	Total No. of Workers
Jan–May 2001	7,426	878,387
Jan–May 2000	5,873	627,520

What is the percentage increase in the number of mass layoffs and individual workers laid off between January and May of 2000 and between January and May of 2001?

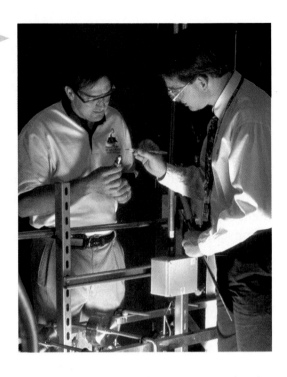

PUBLIC POLICY TORT
If an employee is fired for refusing to violate the law, such a discharge would violate public policy. *Why does punishing someone for obeying the law violate public policy?*

Courts in some states have held that a disclaimer may also be negated if overwhelming evidence suggests that an employer has provided for a detailed dismissal procedure. Providing such detail has established an implied employment contract.

Public Policy Tort   Many states now permit a fired employee to recover compensatory and punitive damages in a **public policy tort** if he or she can prove the firing violated public policy. Public policy holds that no one should be allowed to do anything that tends to hurt the public at large.

> *Example 4.* Allen Kiefer was ordered to appear for jury duty on December 3. The law in his state says that anyone who disobeys such an order can be fined and imprisoned. The same statute also forbids an employer from firing an employee who is ordered to appear for jury duty. Despite this prohibition, Kiefer's employer fired him for being absent from work on December 3. Kiefer can bring a wrongful discharge suit based on public policy tort.

Intentional Infliction of Emotional Distress   Some courts have permitted discharged employees to bring a tort lawsuit against their former employers for intentional infliction of emotional distress. For example, if the conduct of an employer in discharging an employee caused severe mental and emotional trauma, the employee may bring lawsuit based on this provision. However, an employer's conduct must be extremely outrageous to qualify as intentional infliction of emotional distress.

Example 5. Marvin Pardew's employer, Ron Wilson, was having a very bad day. When Wilson discovered several careless errors made by Pardew, he flew into a rage. In the process of firing Pardew, Wilson publicly insulted Pardew using loud, offensive speech. He then grabbed Pardew by the arm and dragged him to the exit of the building. Wilson's behavior caused Pardew to experience feelings of extreme humiliation. Pardew might be able to win a tort lawsuit against his employer.

Legal Briefs

When mediation is used in an attempt to settle cases of sexual harassment in the workplace, 85 percent of the cases are successfully resolved outside of court.

Implied Covenant   Another exception to employment-at-will is the principle of **implied covenant**. This principle holds that any employment relationship is based on an implied promise that the employer and employee will be fair and honest with one another. Unlike implied contract, the existence of an implied covenant exists simply because the employment relationship exists.

Example 6. Ella Ernst was to receive a 25 percent commission on all computer sales she made for her employer, Clarkson Computer Company (CCC). Ernst made a $10 million sale to the federal government, earning a $2.5 million commission. CCC fired her and refused to pay the commission. Ernst sued CCC for unjust dismissal based on the existence of an implied covenant. The court held that CCC had violated an implied covenant of fair dealing and honesty. Ernst was entitled to her commission.

Section 20.1   Assessment

Reviewing What You Learned

1. What is employment-at-will?
2. What situations fall outside of the doctrine of employment-at-will?
3. What are the exceptions to employment-at-will?
4. What is the difference between implied contract and implied covenant?

Critical Thinking Activity

Employment-at-Will Why have the courts begun to carve out exceptions to the employment-at-will doctrine?

Legal Skills In Action

Employment Rights and Duties Your Uncle Ian was recently approached at work by a representative of a union that is attempting to organize the workers at his plant. Uncle Ian believes that as a union member, he will be guaranteed a job for life. Send an e-mail message to your Uncle Ian explaining why the union can't guarantee him lifelong employment.

Legislation Affecting Employment

What You'll Learn

- How to recognize those areas of employment that must be included in any collective bargaining process
- How to identify the objectives of the Taft-Hartley Act
- How to identify the goal of the Landrum-Griffin Act
- How to identify child labor laws

Why It's Important

You need to know the laws that protect union activities because you may be asked to join a union in the future.

Legal Terms

- closed shop
- union shop
- right-to-work laws
- featherbedding
- child labor laws

Regulating Collective Bargaining

As mentioned earlier in the chapter, employment contracts are often negotiated by groups of employees organized into unions. Called collective bargaining, this process is now firmly established as a way of defining working conditions and industrial relations. The government has played an active role in regulating collective bargaining. As we shall see, the government at both the federal and state levels is also very interested in regulating the employment of minors.

In the past, the courts held collective bargaining to be an illegal conspiracy. As attitudes changed, the courts began to accept collective bargaining. Eventually, the government began to encourage collective bargaining, and people felt that the government should regulate the process to some extent.

Wagner Act

The first federal law addressing collective bargaining was the National Labor Relations Act of 1935, also called the Wagner Act. The purpose of this act was to encourage collective bargaining, discourage certain unfair labor practices, and provide federal assistance in obtaining fair bargaining.

The Wagner Act also established guidelines for determining which employment concerns had to be included in the collective bargaining process. The act states that employers must negotiate "wages, hours, and conditions of employment." Subsequent court decisions have helped interpret what "conditions of employment" might include. For example, business decisions that are at the very heart of an executive's ability to control the company, such as decision on how to invest corporate funds, would be outside the scope of collective bargaining.

Example 7. Wilma Durrell, chief executive officer of Collier-Ansen Laboratories, Inc., decides to discontinue a line of over-the-counter medications that had been the object of tampering. Unfortunately, the discontinuation caused the shutdown of one of Collier-Ansen's manufacturing plants. The union incorrectly claimed that the decision to close the plant should have been submitted to collective bargaining. The decision to discontinue that line of medication was clearly within the discretion of corporate management.

Careers in Law

Labor Union President

Every day, thousands of farmworkers who do not own land work long, backbreaking hours to produce the food served at American tables. Many of these farmworkers and their families "follow the crops," migrating from one area of the country to another as the need for farm labor changes with the changing seasons.

Ramon Ramirez is the president of Pineros y Campesinos Unidos del Noroeste (Northwest Treeplanters and Farmworkers United), a labor union that represents 5,000 farmworkers in the Willamette Valley of western Oregon. Ramirez and his PCUN staff of 14 are trying to establish better working conditions, higher wages, and better housing for union members.

"The median annual income for a farmworker in the United States is about $7,500," he says. "They are the lowest-paid work force in the country. After a grueling day working in the fields, some of our members don't even go home to a house. They live in cars, even chicken coops."

The PCUN helps farm workers tackle their employment and housing problems by monitoring enforcement of the state minimum wage and occupational health and safety laws. In addition, Ramirez tries to improve working conditions by negotiating with the growers who hire the farm workers. If all else fails, the PCUN can launch a boycott to encourage consumers not to buy produce from certain farms.

Ramirez believes that the most effective way to improve the lives of farm workers is through education. Ramirez goes into the fields to inform workers about the union and how it can help them. The PCUN helps them understand their legal rights and establish economic development projects.

"Education empowers people," Ramirez says. "We know when we've done our job, because people no longer need our services. They will have learned enough to take control of their own working lives."

Skills	Reading, writing, and multi-lingual, especially Spanish and English.
Personality	Committed to the struggle for social change and justice; interested in helping people live better lives.
Education	Willing to get on-the-job training. Volunteer or propose to perform an unpaid internship with a union.

You can find more information about PCUN at www.pcun.org. For more information about labor activists, visit **ubpl.glencoe.com** or visit your public library.

Using E-Mail at Work

A large company that makes chemical products fired as many as 40 people at a Texas factory for their e-mail use. The employees were sending messages containing sexual and violent images over the company's e-mail system. A similar review of complaints by the company had led to the firing of 50 people some months earlier. Employees should not assume that their e-mail on company computers is private. In fact, just the opposite is true. Action can be taken against employees for inappropriate e-mail use. (Source: *InformationWeek*, August 23, 2000)

Connect Send an e-mail to the human resources department of one or more large companies. Ask if they have a policy on use of e-mail at work.

Taft-Hartley Act

Many people felt that the Wagner Act gave too great an advantage to the union bargaining unit. Consequently, it was amended in 1947 by the Labor-Movement Relations Act, popularly called the Taft-Hartley Act. The purpose of the Taft-Hartley Act was to equalize the power of labor and management. The act provided, among other things, that unions must provide a 60-day notice before calling a strike. If a strike would endanger the nation's health or safety, the president can obtain an injunction to stop the strike for 80 days.

The Taft-Hartley Act also made the closed shop illegal. A **closed shop** is a business or company that requires a person to be a union member before being hired. In contrast, a **union shop**, or a business in which a worker must join the union within 30 days after being employed, is allowed under the act. The act also allows states to pass **right-to-work laws**. State right-to-work laws prohibit union shops. The Taft-Hartley Act prevents a labor union from requiring an employer to retain employees who are no longer needed. **Featherbedding**, or assigning more employees to a job than are actually needed, and pressure exerted by a union to retain unnecessary employees are two more acts prohibited by the Taft-Hartley Act.

Landrum-Griffin Act

The Wagner Act was further amended in 1959 by the Labor Management Reporting and Disclosure Act, usually referred to as the Landrum-Griffin Act. The primary goal of the Landrum-Griffin Act was to stop corruption in the unions. Under provisions of this act, all unions must register their constitutions and bylaws with the Secretary of Labor. Moreover, unions must submit yearly reports on their financial condition. The report must include assets, liabilities, receipts, sources of revenue, loans to union members, and other money paid out of the union treasury. The act also includes the union members' "bill of rights," which ensures that all members of the union have the right to be involved in running the union.

CHILD LABOR LAWS
Both state and federal laws regulate child labor. *Why does the law permit children to work in agriculture as long as the work takes place after school hours?*

Regulating the Employment of Minors

In the industrial revolution, children were often exploited by employers. For example, some mine owners would use children to work deep in mines because they could crawl into small cracks and crevices. Even though this work was dangerous, the children were paid very low wages. Children couldn't refuse to do the work because jobs were scarce. To prevent such abuse, laws were enacted to protect children who enter the labor force.

State Child Labor Laws

Child labor laws, or laws that control the work that children are permitted to do, developed slowly. In 1842, Massachusetts and Connecticut passed laws limiting the amount of hours that a child could work. However, these two states were far ahead of their time. Even as late as 1930, only 44 states had child labor laws dealing with nonmanufacturing occupations. In 1934, the annual Conference on Labor Legislation adopted a set of standards for state child labor legislation, and these standards have had a great influence on child labor laws.

As part of these laws, many states (see Figure 20.1) specify certain types of activities that cannot be performed by minors on the job. Such prohibitions include working on or around dangerous machinery. These laws are designed to protect minors who, because of inexperience, might not understand the dangers involved on a specific job.

Federal Child Labor Laws

A positive step in federal child labor laws was the child labor portion of the Fair Labor Standards Act of 1938, as updated in 1974. This act prohibits the interstate or foreign trade shipment of any goods produced in factories in which "oppressive child labor" had been used within 30 days of the removal of the goods. The act also prohibits the

Figure 20.1

Child Labor Laws

This chart summarizes the state laws (printed in regular type) and the federal Fair Labor Standards Act (FLSA) laws (printed in italics), governing the employment of minors in California. If an employer is covered by both state and federal laws, the higher standard–the provision which gives the most protection to employees–applies. In general, the provisions of FLSA shown in this chart are the higher standard, and therefore prevail.

	All minors under age 18	Minors age 16 –17	Minors age 14 –15	Minors age 12 –13
SPREAD OF HOURS	Work must be performed between 5 A.M. and 10 P.M. Exception: Public messenger service must be performed between 6 A.M.. and 9 P.M.		Work must be performed between 5 A.M. and 10 P.M. Exception: Public messenger service must be performed between 6 A.M. and 9 P.M. (Can be employed as a messenger only in cities having less than 15,000 inhabitants.)	
	Work experience programs up to 12:30 A.M.– see minors ages 16 and 17. Day preceding nonschool day up to 12:30 A.M.–see minors ages 16 and 17. See also Entertainment Industry employment.	If enrolled in a work experience program, may work until 12:30 A.M. on any evening. Minor may work until 12:30 A.M. on any day preceding a nonschool day. *FLSA: No limitations*	*FLSA: Work must be performed between 7 A.M. and 7 P.M. Exceptions: From June 1 to Labor Day can work to 9 P.M.*	*FLSA: Minors under 14 years of age may not be employed in firms subject to the FLSA.*
RESTRICTED OCCUPATIONS	Cannot sell or serve alcoholic beverages. Cannot be employed for the purpose of driving a motor vehicle on the highways or streets. *FLSA–NO MINOR UNDER 18 MAY BE EMPLOYED IN any occupation declared hazardous by the Secretary of Labor, including, but not limited to:*		NO MINOR UNDER 16 MAY BE EMPLOYED:	
	Explosives manufacturing occupations. Motor vehicle occupations. Mining occupations. Logging and sawmilling occupations. Power-driven woodworking machine and power-driven metal forming, punching, and shearing machine operations. Occupations involving exposure to radioactive substances, and to ionizing radiations.	*Occupations in slaughtering, meat packing and rendering plants. Bakery machine operations. Paper products machine operations. Brick, tile, and kindred products manufacturing. Wrecking, demolition, and ship-building operations. Roofing work, including application of weatherproofing materials and substances. Excavation operations.*	In selling or serving alcoholic beverages. In hazardous occupations. In operating an auto or truck. In delivering goods, merchandise, commodities, papers, or packages from a motor vehicle. In the vicinity of moving machinery. In or about any manufacturing or transportation of explosives. In or about the functioning parts of unguarded and dangerous moving equipment, aircraft or vessels, or functioning blades or propellers. In or about a gasoline service station.	In selling to passing motorists newspapers, candy, flowers, or other merchandise or commodities. In door-to-door selling of newspapers or magazine subscriptions, candy, cookies, flowers or other merchandise, or commodities unless the following conditions are met: 1) Minors work in pairs as a team 2) One adult supervisor for 10 or fewer minors 3) Within sight or sound of the supervisor once every 15 minutes 4) Returned to home or rendezvous point daily
	IN ADDITION TO THE ABOVE, FURTHER LIMITATIONS APPLY TO ALL MINORS UNDER AGE 16: (See Child Labor Bulletin 101) Employment is limited to certain occupations not requiring performance of any duties in work places where goods are manufactured, moved, or processed. Some permitted occupations in retail and food services include:		*SEE TEXT OF THIS DIGEST FOR A MORE DETAILED LIST & CONDITIONS* *FLSA: CHILD LABOR PROVISIONS DO NOT APPLY TO: Children under 16 years of age employed by their parents in occupations other than manufacturing, mining, or occupations declared hazardous by the Secretary of Labor; Children employed as actors or performers in motion pictures, theatrical, radio, or television productions. Children engaged in the delivery of newspapers to the consumer.*	
	Office and clerical. Cashiering and selling. Price marking and packaging. Bagging.	*Clean-up maintenance of grounds (cannot use power-driven mowers or cutters). Kitchen work.*		

CHILD LABOR LAWS
Federal and state laws restrict the employment of minors. *What kinds of restrictions does this state impose?*

employment of oppressive child labor in any enterprise engaged in commerce or in the production of goods for commerce. Oppressive child labor is defined as employment of minors under the age of 16 in any of the jobs covered by the act and the employment of minors under 18 in jobs declared especially dangerous by the Secretary of Labor.

Minors between 14 and 16 may be employed in jobs other than those covered by the act, but only if the Secretary of Labor determines that such employment does not interfere with their schooling. There are many exceptions to the minimum wage and maximum hours rules in the Fair Labor Standards Act. They include children working in agriculture after school hours, child actors, children working for their parents in jobs other than manufacturing, and children delivering newspapers.

Industry-Education Cooperation

Effective control of child labor requires the help of industry and schools. Many industries have their own codes that restrict child labor to an even greater extent than do the laws. Other industries, however, conform only if forced by law.

Education and the child labor problem are closely associated. One of the great evils of child labor is its interference with the education of children. Public schools work with the enforcement officers of child labor acts to protect children. Work permits, for example, are often issued by the public school system. A work permit is a document that allows a minor below a certain age to work. Laws regulating work permits vary from state to state.

Section 20.2   Assessment

Reviewing What You Learned

1. What employment areas must be included in any collective bargaining process?
2. What are the objectives of the Taft-Hartley Act?
3. What is the goal of the Landrum-Griffin Act?
4. What are child labor laws?
5. Investigate an employee's right to organize and participate in a union. Explain the legal developments that govern this right.

Critical Thinking Activity

Collective Bargaining Why did the courts once believe that collective bargaining was an illegal conspiracy?

Legal Skills In Action

Child Labor Your friend, Felicia, has threatened to complain to the Secretary of Labor because her parents have put her to work on the family farm after school. Write a letter to Felicia explaining whether her complaint is justified.

Chapter Summary

Section 20.1 Employment Relationships

- Employment-at-will is the general rule governing employment in most states. According to the doctrine of employment-at-will, an employer is permitted to discharge an employee at any time, for any or no reason, with or without notice. This doctrine is based on the notion that both parties in an employment relationship must be free to leave the employment relationship at any time.

- The doctrine of employment-at-will does not apply to employees who are protected by a union. A union is an organization of employees that is formed to promote the welfare of its members. In addition, an employer cannot invoke the doctrine of employment-at-will to discharge an employee for a reason that is discriminatory in nature. It is unlawful to discriminate against employees because of their age, race, color, creed, national origin, or gender.

- Exceptions to employment-at-will include wrongful discharge. Wrongful discharge, also called unjust dismissal, provides employees with grounds for legal action against employers who have treated them unfairly. The courts have established five standards it will consider regarding an unjust termination: promissory estoppel, implied contract, public policy tort, intentional infliction of emotional distress, and implied covenant.

- When an employer does something to lead an employee to reasonably believe that he or she is not an at-will employee, an implied contract is created. All employment relationships are based on an implied covenant that the employer and employee will be fair and honest with one another.

Section 20.2 Legislation Affecting Employment

- The first federal law addressing collective bargaining, the National Labor Relations Act of 1935, also called the Wagner Act, states that employers must include wages, hours, and conditions of employment in the collective bargaining process. Business decisions that are at the very heart of an executive's ability to control a company, such as decisions on how to invest corporate funds, would be outside the scope of collective bargaining.

- The objective of the Taft-Hartley Act was to equalize the power of labor and management. It provides, among other things, for a 60-day "cooling off" period, which the President of the United States could invoke to postpone a strike for up to 60 days under special circumstances. The act also made it illegal to have a closed shop, which requires a person to be a union member to be considered for hiring. In contrast, a union shop, or a business in which a worker must join the union within 30 days after being employed, is allowed under the act. The act also allows states to pass right-to-work laws, and prevents featherbedding.

- The primary goal of the Landrum-Griffin Act was to stop corruption in the unions by mandating, among other things, that all unions must register their constitutions and bylaws with the Secretary of Labor. Under the Landrum-Griffin Act, unions are also required to submit yearly reports on their financial condition. These reports must include assets, liabilities, receipts, sources of revenue, loans to union members, and other money paid out of the union's treasury.

- Child labor laws control the work that children are permitted to do. They specify certain types of activities that cannot be performed by minors on the job. Federal child labor laws prohibit shipment of goods produced in factories in which "oppressive child labor" had been used.

Using Legal Language

Consider the key terms in the list below. Then use these terms to complete the following exercises.

promissory estoppel

union

collective bargaining

grievance procedure

severance pay

public policy tort

implied contract

employment-at-will

disclaimer

implied covenant

union shop

right-to-work laws

child labor laws

1. Imagine you are a friend of Caterina (in "The Opening Scene") and are discussing her recent firing. Write a dialogue between the two of you. Use as many of the terms listed above as possible.
2. With a partner, role-play your dialogues.
3. With your partner, practice your dialogues and present them to the class.
4. As a class, vote to choose the best dialogue.

Understanding Business and Personal Law Online

Self-Check Quiz Visit the *Understanding Business and Personal Law* Web site at **ubpl.glencoe.com** and click on Chapter 20: Employment Relationships— Self-Check Quizzes to prepare for the chapter exam.

The Law Review

Answer the following questions. Refer to the chapter for additional reinforcement.

5. What is the doctrine known as employment-at-will based upon?
6. Do collective bargaining agreements guarantee employees a job for life? Why or why not?
7. Describe an employee's and employer's duties and rights to each other.
8. What must a disclaimer include in order to be effective? Why are many employers reluctant to include a disclaimer in their employee handbooks?
9. Name the first federal law dealing with collective bargaining. What was its purpose?
10 What is a grievance procedure?
11. Why do employee handbooks often play important roles in lawsuits regarding termination of employment?
12. How has the attitude of the court changed regarding collective bargaining?
13. Why is the public school system involved in regulating the number of hours worked by minors?

Linking School to Work

Interpreting and Communicating Information

Research the child labor laws in your state. Locate the answers to the following questions:

14. When and why were the laws were passed?
15. How many hours is a child allowed to work per day and per week?
16. What types of work are children not allowed to perform?
17. What (if any) exceptions are there to the law (e.g., students enrolled in school work-study programs, apprenticeship programs)?
    Write a one-or two-page paper summarizing your findings.

Let's Debate

You learn that your friend Wendy, who is 15, is leaving school early every Tuesday. Her new employer told her she must work on Tuesdays or she will lose her job. You remind Wendy that the child labor laws are being violated and suggest that she ask for a change of schedule.

Debate

18. If Wendy wants to work on Tuesdays and keeps her grades up, is there really a problem? Explain your answer.
19. Whose responsibility is it to comply with the child labor laws? Is it the employer's? Is it Wendy's? Explain your answer.

Grasping Case Issues

For the following cases, give your decision and state a legal principle that applies.

20. Luther McConnell is discharged by Erin Publishing for incompetence. When he passed his probationary period 14 years earlier, McConnell received a copy of Erin's standard letter to employees. The letter welcomed McConnell and said, "Now that you're a permanent employee, you'll always have a home at Erin." All efficiency reports on McConnell rated him very highly. Does McConnell have grounds for a lawsuit based on unjust dismissal? Explain your answer.
21. At the height of a flu epidemic in the United States, workers at several pharmaceutical companies that produce flu vaccines threaten to strike. The flu tends to incapacitate people for a week to 10 days. What options might the President of the United States have in this situation?
22. David Canidy was employed as a server at the Kirkus Tea Room. Canidy was unfairly accused of stealing money. As it turned out, Louis Whittaker, the manager of the restaurant, had simply misplaced some money. However, before discovering his own error, Whittaker fired Canidy in a loud and public display. During the firing, Whittaker accused Canidy of the theft and insulted him. What kind of a wrongful discharge lawsuit might Canidy bring against Whittaker and the Kirkus Tea Room? Explain your answer.
23. Sidi Hassam was hired as a salesperson by the Georgian Plate Glass Company. When hired, he was asked to read and sign the company's employment manual. The manual, which did not include a disclaimer, promised that all employees would be permitted to submit any grievance to a special committee headed by the Director of Human Resources. When Hassam was disciplined for something he did not do, he asked the director to assemble the committee to review his complaint. The director refused, and Hassam was fired. What kind of a wrongful discharge lawsuit might Hassam contemplate bringing against the company? Explain your answer.

In each case that follows, you be the judge.

24. Age Requirements

Neil Bagge, 17, got a job at a construction site where dump trucks were used. State law prevented anyone under 18 from operating a "motor vehicle of any description." Bagge's employer did not hire him to operate a dump truck; however, the employer did assign Bagge to work around and on the trucks. *Would such an assignment violate the state law forbidding the employment of minors to operate motor vehicles? Why or why not?*
Bagge's Case, 363 N.E.2d 1321 (MA).

25. Wrongful Discharge

Juergens worked as a staff accountant at Strang, Klubnik, and Associates, Inc. The employment manual published by the company included an overtime pay provision. Klubnik made a mistake in calculating Juergens's overtime payments. He promised her that it would not happen again when she worked overtime. Later Juergens was asked to assume additional duties. She declined to do so and was discharged. She brought a wrongful discharge suit based on implied contract, arguing that the overtime pay provision and the promise of future overtime pay amounted to an implied promise of continued employment. *Is Juergens correct? Why or why not?*
Juergens v. Stahl, Klubnik, and Associates, Inc., 644 N.E.2d 1006 (OH).

Legal Link

Union Pride

Lawson has been working in the office at the Tennessee Valley Authority for six months. Recently, several of his friends at work have asked him to consider joining the union. Lawson doesn't know enough about unions to make an informed decision, so he looks to you for help.

Connect

Using a variety of search engines, research a union and answer the following questions:

26. What are the benefits of joining?
27. Who is the president of the union?
28. Why and where was the union first started?
29. Who belongs to the union?

POWER READING STRATEGIES

30. **Predict** Why do you think people join unions?

31. **Connect** Have you or has someone you know ever been fired? What were the circumstances?

32. **Question** Why do you think some states have passed right-to-work laws while others have not?

33. **Respond** Do you think the child labor laws are really necessary? Why or why not?

Employment Protection and Equal Opportunity

Understanding Business and Personal Law Online

Chapter Overview Visit the *Understanding Business and Personal Law* Web site at ubpl.glencoe.com and click on Chapter 21: Employment Protection and Equal Opportunity Chapter Overviews— to preview the chapter information.

The Opening Scene

Caterina is sitting on the front steps of the porch, reading a newspaper. Her brother, Lazzaro, and his friend, Dylan, have just arrived at home. They have spent the afternoon at a baseball game.

Paper Chase

CATERINA: It's about time you got home. Where have you been?

LAZZARO: Why should I tell you? It's none of your business.

DYLAN: We were downtown at a ball game. What's in the paper?

LAZZARO: She's looking for another job. She got fired from her last job. I'm sure that you heard about it at school.

CATERINA: Shut up.

DYLAN: Are you getting unemployment compensation?

CATERINA: What's that?

DYLAN: I'm not sure exactly, but every time my Aunt Caitlin gets laid off, she gets unemployment compensation.

CATERINA: She gets money for not working? That sounds too good to be true.

DYLAN: That's right. She gets money for not working, no strings attached.

LAZZARO: That's right up your alley.

CATERINA: Shut up. Where can I find out about that unemployment compensation stuff? I'm definitely interested.

DYLAN: There's an office downtown. You could stop by one day after school.

LAZZARO: Did you find any job prospects in the paper?

CATERINA: Nothing I can do.

LAZZARO: No surprise there.

CATERINA: Shut up.

(Dylan picks up the paper and looks at the want ads. His eyes rest on one ad.)

DYLAN: What about this ad for a Gal Friday? Maybe you could do that.

CATERINA: Gal Friday? What's that?

DYLAN: I have no clue.

CATERINA: Maybe I should just try to get some of that unemployment compensation. Did you say the office is downtown?

DYLAN: On Euclid Avenue where it crosses Ninth Street.

CATERINA: I have one more question. Will I need a social security number?

DYLAN: Probably.

CATERINA: Then I better go to the Social Security Office first.

LAZZARO: You mean you never got a social security card?

CATERINA: That's right. It didn't matter. Mr. Pellis paid me in cash.

LAZZARO: Maybe it's a good thing that you got fired after all.

What Are the Legal Issues?

1. What is the Occupational Safety and Health Administration?
2. What rights do employees have regarding wages, hours, and benefits?
3. What privacy rights do employees have?
4. What classes are protected from unlawful discrimination in employment matters?
5. What rights do employees have in relation to equal employment opportunities?

Laws Relating to Employment Conditions and Benefits

What You'll Learn

- How to recognize the role that OSHA plays in ensuring workplace safety
- How to identify employers' legal requirements with regard to wages and hours
- How to identify the statutes designed to protect employee privacy rights
- How to distinguish between unemployment compensation and workers' compensation

Why It's Important

Understanding the rights that are legally due to employees will help you determine your rights.

Legal Terms

- Occupational Safety and Health Administration (OSHA)
- equal pay rule
- pension plan
- social security
- unemployment compensation
- workers' compensation

Employment Conditions

In the early days of the Industrial Revolution, employers demanded a great deal from workers and often gave little in return. Some employers had little regard for their workers' safety and quality of life. The government eventually passed laws regulating employment conditions. Workers were provided with a variety of benefits and a guarantee that they would have equal employment opportunities. Today there are many federal and state laws that deal with labor conditions and worker benefits.

Employment conditions can be divided into three areas: health and safety, right to fair wages and benefits, and privacy rights. To guarantee these rights, the government has created a variety of laws to protect employees.

Health and Safety

The federal Occupational Safety and Health Act of 1970 was enacted by Congress to ensure that employees are protected in the workplace. The act established the **Occupational Safety and Health Administration (OSHA)**, the agency within the federal government that sets safety and health standards for many companies within the United States. Businesses with 11 or more employees that engage in interstate commerce must meet OSHA's health and safety standards. Figure 21.1 shows the type of safety and health standards that employers must post for all employers to see.

OSHA uses two approaches to accomplish its mission. First, it imposes upon employers the affirmative duty to maintain a safe and healthy work environment. Second, OSHA creates rules that outline the safety steps that businesses must maintain. These rules are enforced by inspections and fines.

Inspections

To make certain that employers adhere to OSHA regulations, the agency randomly inspects workplaces. OSHA also endeavors to inspect

Figure 21.1

SAFETY AND HEALTH PROTECTION ON THE JOB

STATE OF **IOWA**

Chapter 88-Code of Iowa provides job safety and health protection for workers throughout the State of Iowa.

The Iowa Division of Labor Services has the responsibility for administering this Chapter. The Division of Labor adopts federal occupational safety and health standards as State of Iowa standards. Employers and employees are required to comply with these standards.

SAFETY ON THE JOB IS EVERYBODY'S RESPONSIBILITY!

EMPLOYERS: Chapter 88 requires that all employers must furnish to employees employment and a place of employment free from recognized hazards which cause or are likely to cause death or serious physical harm to employees and comply with occupational safety and health standards adopted under this Chapter.

EMPLOYEES: Chapter 88 requires that each employee comply with occupational safety and health standards and all rules, regulations, and orders issued pursuant to this Chapter that are applicable to the employees own actions and conduct.

COMPLIANCE WITH SAFETY AND HEALTH REQUIREMENTS

To ensure compliance with safety and health requirements, the Iowa Division of Labor conducts periodic inspections of places of employment. Inspections are conducted by trained compliance safety and health officers. Chapter 88 requires that an authorized representative employer and a representative authorized by the employees be given an opportunity to accompany the inspector for the purpose of aiding the inspection. Where there is no authorized employee representative, the compliance safety and health officers will consult with a reasonable number of employees concerning safety and health conditions in the workplace.

For assistance and information, including copies of Chapter 88 and of specific safety and health standards, contact:

Iowa Division of Labor
1000 East Grand Avenue
Des Moines, Iowa 50319-0209
Telephone(515) 281-3606

COMPLAINTS ABOUT STATE PROGRAM ADMINISTRATION

Any interested person or representative of such a group of persons or group of persons may submit a complaint to the Federal government concerning the operation or administration of any aspect the Iowa Division of Labor's occupational safety and health activities pursuant to Chapter 88-Code of Iowa.

Complaints may be submitted orally or in writing to:

Assistant Regional Administator
U.S. Department of Labor
Occupational Safety & Health Administation
911 Walnut, Room 496
Kansas City, Missouri 64106
Phone: (816) 426-5861

Any such complaint should describe the grounds for the complaint and specify the aspect or aspects of the administration or operation of Iowa's program that is believed to be inadequate.

If upon receipt of the complaint, the Assistant Regional Administrator (ARA) determines that reasonable grounds exist to believe that an investigation should be made, the ARA shall cause such investigation, including any workplace inspection, to be made as soon as possible.

---

a business when a death or a disaster has occurred, or when an employee files a complaint. Such complaints must be in writing and must be filed at the nearest OSHA office by the employee or someone representing the employee. The law protects employees who file such complaints from being discharged from the job. Employers may be fined for each violation reported by an employee or discovered during an OSHA inspection.

> **STATE REQUIREMENTS**
> In addition to federal OSHA requirements, the states often mandate their own OSHA standards. *To what does this poster alert workers?*

Example 1. Talia L'sar worked on the loading dock for Chamberlain Industries. She discovered that Chamberlain was storing dangerous chemicals in the garage area of the loading dock. When she reported this to her supervisor, her complaint was ignored. Accordingly, she filed a complaint with the local OSHA office, which then scheduled an inspection. Should Chamberlain take retaliatory action against Talia, that action would be illegal.

Wages, Hours, and Benefits

The government's interest in regulating employment extends to the conditions under which employees perform their jobs. In the 1930s, the government responded to many of the hardships suffered by workers during the Great Depression by regulating wages, hours, and benefits of workers by passing several laws that set standards for employment in American businesses.

Fair Labor Standards Act

The federal Fair Labor Standards Act, also known as the Wage and Hour Law, requires certain employers to pay their workers a legal minimum hourly wage rate, plus time-and-a-half for all work over 40 hours per week. The Fair Labor Standards Act also regulates the employment of minors. The act covers employees who produce goods for transport in interstate commerce and workers such as certain hospital, retail, restaurant, and school employees. Professional employees, administrators, and executives are not covered by this act.

Equal Pay Act

In 1963, Congress passed the Equal Pay Act as an amendment to the Fair Labor Standards Act. The amendment established the equal pay rule, which states that employers engaged in interstate commerce must pay women the same rate of pay as men holding the same type of job. The **equal pay rule** covers hourly workers, executives, administrators, professional employees, and outside salespeople who receive salaries and/or commission.

Employment Retirement Income Security Act

A **pension plan** is a program established by an employer or a union that is designed to provide income to employees after they retire. A pension's amount is typically based on an employee's salary and length of service with a company. Previously, funds in some employee pension plans were poorly invested, or the funds deposited in retirement accounts were used for other business expenses. These practices resulted in losses of retirement benefits to workers and severe economic hardship to them and their families.

The Employment Retirement Income Security Act (ERISA) was passed to prevent such abuse. One requirement of the act is that employers must place employee contributions to pension plans in a trust fund that is independent of the employer's control. Another ERISA requirement imposes a duty of good faith on those who manage pension plans. Other ERISA requirements include informing employees of their retirement benefits and submitting reports on the plan to the Secretary of Labor.

A Global Perspective:
Laws Around the World

U.S. Citizens
Working in Other Countries

Today, thousands of Americans and their families live and work abroad. Typically, a U.S. citizen must obtain a work permit and a resident visa before being allowed to work in a foreign country. In most cases, these requirements must be satisfied before entering the country to work. The easiest way to meet these requirements is to have an employment contract with a company that will obtain the necessary permissions and documents for you.

Americans who live in foreign countries retain their U.S. citizenship and continue to pay federal income taxes, even on income earned in a foreign country. A child born to two U.S. citizens while in a foreign country is automatically granted U.S. citizenship. The child may also be granted citizenship in the foreign country, resulting in dual citizenship.

U.S. citizens living in other countries are subject to the laws of the host country, which may differ substantially from those of the United States. Legal procedures in other countries may also provide fewer protections than the Constitutional rights available to persons residing in this country. Americans imprisoned in foreign countries may request aid from the U.S. Department of State, as well as the U.S. Embassies and Consulates in those countries. Although these entities advocate for the fair treatment of Americans, they cannot change the laws of the foreign country or force the country to release an American prisoner.

In a volatile international environment, Americans working abroad may obtain information about different countries from consular information sheets furnished by the U.S. Department of State. If conditions in a particular country threaten the safety of Americans, the U.S. Department issues a travel warning for that country. Consular information sheets and travel warnings may be accessed at the State Department's Web site.

Critical Thinking Question Do you think it's fair for Americans working abroad to be subject to regulations that may be contrary to the laws of the United States? For more information on the rights of Americans working in foreign countries, visit **ubpl.glencoe.com**.

Family and Medical Leave Act

Under the Family and Medical Leave Act, an employee of a company with at least 50 employees is entitled to 12 weeks of leave during any 12-month period because of the birth or adoption of a child, or to care for a spouse, child, or parent who has a serious medical condition. After the leave, the employee is entitled to return to his or her previous position with the same or equivalent pay and benefits. To be eligible for such leave, the employee must work for at least one year and accumulate sufficient service time.

Employee Privacy Rights

In recent years, the subject of employee privacy rights has become of central concern in the workplace. Three areas of primary concern include: privacy for governmental employees, testing employees for drug use, and using polygraph (lie detector) test results in the hiring and firing of employees.

LAWS in Your Life

It's Your Right

Asserting your rights in the workplace can be intimidating. When you feel you have been unlawfully discriminated against at work, you are entitled to take certain steps to remedy the situation, and you should be able to do so without fear of reprisal from your employer.

A talk with your manager or your manager's manager is the first place to start. A frank discussion at this point can often resolve the problem and avoid further legal hassles. Before approaching your employer, try to become familiar with your legal rights. Also try to be as objective as possible, stick to the facts, and avoid being overly emotional in making your point.

Conclude the conversation by asking what steps will be taken next. Your manager might conduct a formal investigation, or he or she might simply want to speak with other employees about the problem. Be sure to schedule a follow-up meeting to monitor progress. It's also a good idea to document your side of the story by taking notes of conversations and gathering information to support your claim.

Research Go to the library or visit the Internet. What is the law in your state regarding the time limit (statute of limitations) for filing a lawsuit for workplace discrimination?

Federal Privacy Act

Because of our general aversion to governmental interference in personal rights, the privacy of government employees is often given greater emphasis than the privacy of employees in the private sector. For instance, the Federal Privacy Act directly addresses the privacy of government employees. Under this act, government employees are given the right to restrict inspection of their employment files, be informed of their employment files, be informed of the contents of those files, and fix any mistake that they might find in those files.

Drug-Free Workplace Act

The Drug-Free Workplace Act, which applies to companies that have contracts with the federal government, aims to create a drug-free work environment. Under the act, firms must initiate a plan to make sure that employees do not use drugs on the job. The statute does not, however, order companies to include drug testing in their plans. If a drug test is performed improperly, it can violate the Fourth Amendment to the United States Constitution, which prohibits unreasonable search and seizure.

The Supreme Court has provided a guideline for such a situation. The Court has held that, when drug tests do not involve criminal activity, the employee's privacy rights must be balanced with the government's duty to protect the public.

> *Example 2.* Rachel Goetz applied for a position as a security guard for the Jackson Biological Product Company. All security officers for Jackson were required to carry firearms. Consequently, Goetz was obligated to undergo a drug test. In this case, Goetz should understand that the public's need to be protected from armed guards who might be under the influence of drugs would outweigh her right to privacy.

Some states have passed statutes that regulate drug testing in the private sector. The guidelines often include making certain that employees or applicants are notified of the testing procedures. Companies are also required to keep the results of such tests confidential. They must communicate the results to the employees or applicants and initiate a backup test when the initial test proves positive. Finally, they must give the applicant or employee a chance to challenge the test results.

Employee Polygraph Protection Act

As with drug testing, polygraph or lie detector testing can violate the privacy rights of employees. Congress passed the Employee Polygraph Protection Act to regulate such testing procedures. The act prohibits

It's a Question of Ethics

Affirmative Action

Employers that have discriminated in the past are often required by the courts to submit an affirmative action plan. Such plans are also frequently required of firms that contract with the government, and many private companies and institutions also implement affirmative action plans. *What are the goals of these plans, and how do they address the problem of unlawful discrimination?*

employers from using lie detector tests either for screening of employment applicants or for random testing of employees.

There are several exceptions to the rules prohibiting such tests. For example, the statute does not apply to businesses involved in security or the handling of controlled substances. Thus, drug firms and private investigation companies would be permitted to use polygraph tests.

Laws Providing Worker Benefits

As industrial society developed, people recognized an increasing need to protect workers and their families. Hitherto, workers who relied on the common law, such as negligence suits against employers in case of injury, were not often successful. As a result, legislatures began to pass laws that protect workers who have left their job because of retirement, injury, disability, or layoffs. Social security, unemployment insurance, unemployment compensation, and workers' compensation are all government initiatives to protect workers.

Social Security Act

Social security is a government program that provides continuing but limited income to workers and their dependents. It provides benefits to employees and their families when their earnings stop or are reduced because of retirement, disability, or death. The Social Security Act of 1935 and its amendments set up a social insurance program funded by contributions from both employers and employees. Employers must automatically deduct a certain amount from employees' paychecks, contribute an equal amount, and send both contributions to the Internal Revenue Service. Congress sets the amount of the employee's contribution as a percentage of annual wages.

People become eligible to receive social security benefits by working for a certain time period in a job or jobs covered by the program or by being a dependent of a person who meets that requirement. When earnings stop or are reduced because the worker retires, dies, or becomes disabled, monthly cash benefits are paid from these funds to replace part of the lost income.

You have one social security number to use throughout your life. The Social Security Administration, the Internal Revenue Service, and certain other federal organizations use social security numbers in their programs. Social security records, which contain a lifetime account of a person's earnings, are confidential.

Unemployment Compensation Laws

When people are out of work, they cannot buy goods. When goods go unsold, the factories that make the goods and the retail stores that sell the goods lay off workers. These workers cannot buy goods, so more workers are laid off, and the cycle continues. To lessen the effects of unemployment, and to provide for the families of out-of-work workers, the government has set up a means of protecting unemployed workers. **Unemployment compensation** is a system of government payments to people who are out of work and looking for a job. Payments are made from an unemployment insurance fund financed by payroll taxes on employers or unemployment insurance premiums paid by employers.

A section of the Social Security Act provides for a joint federal-state system of unemployment compensation. According to the Federal Unemployment Tax Act, each state operates its own unemployment compensation system, subject to certain conditions imposed by the federal government. The states determine the tax rate each employer must pay to fund the unemployment benefits.

Benefits vary among the states, as do minimum and maximum payments, length of work requirements for coverage, and maximum benefit periods. Generally, unemployed workers apply at state employment offices for benefits and for suitable work. Workers may be disqualified for benefits for a limited period if their unemployment arises out of a strike or a lockout. Each state determines the period of the worker's disqualification. Workers are also disqualified if they refuse suitable work without cause, have been discharged for misconduct, or have quit their jobs without "good cause."

WORKERS' BENEFITS
The federal and state governments have passed laws that benefit workers. *How do workers qualify for such benefits?*

Example 3. In The Opening Scene, Dylan tells Caterina that unemployment compensation is paid by the government "with no strings attached" to workers who have been fired or who have quit their jobs. This interpretation is not accurate. Workers are not eligible for benefits if they have been discharged for misconduct or have quit their jobs without "good cause."

Employees who believe they have been denied unemployment compensation for an unjust reason may appeal the decision. Most appeals are resolved at the local level.

Workers' Compensation Laws

Loss of income due to accidents, illness, or death on the job became a serious problem with the introduction of machines to industry. Faced with this situation, several state legislatures passed laws in the early 1900s creating workers' compensation programs. By 1959, all 50 states had programs in place. **Workers' compensation** is an insurance program that provides income for workers who are injured or develop a disability or disease as a result of their job (see Figure 21.2). In Texas, workers' compensation law was first enacted in 1913 and the Texas Workers' Compensation Program evolved over time to address a variety of workplace needs. The Texas Workers' Compensation Act of 1989 was adopted to consolidate and strengthen workplace health and safety programs, improve benefits and benefits delivery, assist in resolving claim disputes, ensure compliance with workers' compensation laws, and develop medical fee and treatment guidelines to help control medical costs. Texas has also established the Texas Workforce Commission (TWC), the state agency that provides workforce development services to employers and job seekers in Texas. Employers are offered recruiting, retention, training, and outplacement services, as well as labor market statistics. Job seekers are provided with access to job search tools, training programs, and career development information, among other job-related resources.

Employers bear the cost of workers' compensation. In most states, employers must pay a tax on their payrolls to fund the state's workers' compensation insurance fund. In some states, employers have the option of contributing to a state fund or purchasing such insurance from a private insurer. In other states, all employers must purchase workers' compensation insurance from private insurers. As a result, state workers' compensation laws vary.

Work Opportunity Laws

In 1996, Congress responded to problems within the government system for providing assistance to poor Americans with dependent

Virtual Law

Bias in the Workplace

Recently, Microsoft Corporation was hit with a $5 billion lawsuit for discrimination. Several present and former African-American employees claimed the company discriminated against them in employee evaluations and pay. These workers also claimed wrongful termination in some cases. The suit asserts that the company does little to hire and promote African Americans and that there is a "glass ceiling" at Microsoft for African Americans. The company denied these claims, but the lawsuit underscores the importance of encouraging diversity in the workplace. (Source: *TechWeb News*, January 3, 2001)

Connect Read more about bias claims by visiting the Web site of the U.S. Department of Justice, Office of Civil Rights.

Figure 21.2

WORKERS' COMPENSATION ACT
State of New Mexico
WORKERS' COMPENSATION ADMINISTRATION

Each employer who is subject to the Workers' Compensation Act must conspicuously display this poster wherever notices to employees and applicants for employment are customarily posted, pursuant to Chapter 52, NMSA 1978, Section 52-1-29.

Each employer and employee enjoys certain rights under the provisions of the New Mexico Workers' Compensation Act. Generally, each employer of three or more workers is required to provide workers' compensation insurance. However, certain categories of employers and employees are exempt under the act; farm and ranch laborers, private domestic servants, and real estate salespersons are not required to be covered by Workers' Compensation insurance. Employers of these categories may file with the Director an election to be subject to the Workers' Compensation Act.

A worker injured on the job is entitled to medical care. Either the worker or the employer may choose the health-care provider for the initial sixty (60) day period. The party who did not choose the initial healthcare provider may select the healthcare provider for the remaining medical benefit period. Either may challenge the healthcare choice of the other by notifying the director, in writing. A Workers' Compensation Administration Judge will hear the challenge and render a final decision within seven (7) days.

Wage disability benefits are not paid for an injury that results in seven (7) or less days of disability. If an on-the-job injury results in more than seven (7) days of disability, benefits are paid at the rate of sixty-six and two-thirds (66 & 2/3) percent of the average weekly wage at the time of the accident, not to exceed the maximum specified by law, or $297.19 for 1991. For information about prior-year maximum-wage benefits, contact the Workers' Compensation Administration at the address or phone number listed below. The first wage disability benefit payment or notice of denial is due to the claimant fourteen (14) days after the Employer's First Report of Accident (WCAE1.1) is filed. If you believe a payment is due to you and you have not received it, contact a Workers' Compensation Administration Ombudsman through one of the telephone numbers listed below.

NOTICE OF ACCIDENT

A worker claiming entitlement to workers' compensation benefits must file a NOTICE OF ACCIDENT with their employer. However, this is not necessary.

ACTA DE COMPENSACIÓN DE LOS TRABAJADORES
Estado de Nuevo México
ADMINISTRACIÓN DE COMPENSACIÓN DE LOS TRABAJADORES

Cada empleador que está bajo el Acta de Compensación de los Trabajadores debe mostrar este cartel en forma visible donde que se acostumbra poner las notificaciones para los empleados y las personas que solicitan trabajo, segun el Capítulo 52, NMSA 1978, Sección 52-1-29.

Cada empleador y cada empleado goza de ciertos derechos bajo las disposiciones del Acta de Compensación de los Trabajadores de Nuevo México. En general, cada emple-ador de tres empleados o más debe ofrecer el seguro de compensación de los trabajadores. Sin embargo, ciertas categorías de empleadores y de empleados están exentas bajo el acta: no se exige que los obreros agrícolas, sirvientes domésticos o agentes inmobiliarios recibir el seguro de compensación de los trabajadores. Los empleadores de estas categorias pueden dar notificación al Director que ellos van a proveer seguro bajo el Acta de Compensación de los Trabajadores.

Un trabajador lastimado en el trabajo tiene derecho a cuidado médico. El trabajador o el empleador puede elegir el proveedor de cuidado médico para el periodo inicial de sesenta (60) días. El que no eligió el proveedor de cuidado médico inicial puede elegir el proveedor de cuidado médico para el resto del periodo de beneficios médicos. Cualquiera de los dos puede protestar la elección de cuidado médico del otro notificando al Director por escrito. Un Juez de la Administración de Compensación de los Trabajadores con-siderará la protesta y pronunciará una decisión final dentro de siete (7) días.

No se pagan beneficios sobre el salario debido a inca-pacidad por una lesión que resulta en siete (7) días o menos de incapacidad. Si una lastimadura producida en el trabajo resulta en más de siete (7) días de incapacidad, se pagan los beneficios a razón del sesenta y seis y dos tercios (66 & 2/3) por ciento del salario semanal promedio en el momento del accidente, sin exceder la cifra máxima especificada por ley, o sea $297.19 para 1991. Para información acerca de los beneficios salariales máximos de años anteriores, póngase en contacto con la Administración de Compensación de los Trabajadores en la dirección o número de teléfono abajo mencionado. El primer pago salarial por incapacidad o la notificación de denegación debe llegar al reclamante dentro de los catorce (14) días después de que se presenta el Primer Aviso de Accidente del Empleador (WCA E1.1). Si usted cree que se le debe un pago y no lo ha recibido, póngase en contacto con un.

WORKERS' COMPENSATION

Workers' compensation laws vary widely, and in some states, must be posted in a second language. *Who bears the cost of workers' compensation?*

children. This system, known as welfare, was criticized for many reasons. One criticism was that the welfare system deterred people from looking for employment because the system penalized people who found work by lessening their welfare payments if they made money at a job.

Congress acknowledged this criticism, as well as several others, by enacting the Personal Responsibility and Work Opportunity Act of 1996. This novel act instituted a new program entitled Temporary Assistance to Needy Families (TANF). Under TANF, a majority of all recipients must hold a job, enter career programs, or face a loss of payments. This requirement becomes effective after a recipient has received benefits during a two-year period. The new system also has a fund that provides payments for child care.

The new system includes many restrictions. For instance, to be eligible for benefits, minors who are parents must maintain their education or be enrolled in a career program. Such minors must also reside in a home that is managed by an adult. In addition, TANF does not provide funds for immigrants, regardless of their legal status as residents of the United States. There is a limit of five years to receive benefits under the act.

Section 21.1 Assessment

Reviewing What You Learned

1. Using the Internet, library, or other resource, identify current legislation that insures employee safety in the workplace.
2. What legal requirements are placed upon employers with regard to wages and hours?
3. What federal statutes are designed to protect employee privacy rights?
4. What is the difference between unemployment compensation and workers' compensation?

Critical Thinking Activity

Right to Privacy What justification can be given for the fact that the privacy rights of government workers are often given more attention than the privacy rights of employees in the private sector?

Legal Skills in Action

Workplace Health and Safety While working on a summer job at a local manufacturing firm, you learn that one of your fellow employees has made a complaint to OSHA about certain unsafe practices at the plant. You overhear a discussion in the lunchroom that reveals that the worker who filed the complaint will likely be discharged. Organize a role-playing session in which one participant is the worker who filed the complaint and another person represents a coworker. In the course of the discussion, explain the nature of OSHA and the safeguards given to employees who file complaints. Also explain the consequences that result if a violation of an OSHA regulation is discovered at the plant.

Laws Regulating Employment Discrimination

Discrimination

In the second half of the twentieth century, the federal government took steps to make the law as fair as possible in the area of employment opportunities. Title VII of the Civil Rights Act was an important step in this direction. Other steps include the Age Discrimination in Employment Act, the Americans with Disabilities Act, and the Pregnancy Discrimination Act (see Figure 21.3). Many of these laws and regulations were the result of unethical practices. We will examine how these acts regulate employment opportunities to discourage **discrimination**, which is the unequal treatment of individuals based on sex, age, race, nationality, or religion.

The Civil Rights Act of 1964

Title VII of the Civil Rights Act of 1964 prohibits discrimination in employment based on race, color, religion, sex, or national origin (see Figure 21.4). These five categories, along with age, are often referred to as protected classes. Discrimination occurs when employment related decisions are made based upon any combination of these protected characteristics. Employees who believe they have been

EQUAL EMPLOYMENT OPPORTUNITIES ▶
The federal and state governments have passed laws that attempt to make employment opportunities as open as possible for all people. *What types of employment opportunities have been opened for people because of the Civil Rights Act of 1964?*

What You'll Learn

- How to define discrimination
- How to identify the objective of the Civil Rights Act
- How to identify the goal of the Age Discrimination in Employment Act
- How to explain the mission of the Americans with Disabilities Act

Why It's Important

You need to know the laws that outlaw employment discrimination to be able to identify instances of discrimination.

Legal Terms

- discrimination
- disparate treatment
- *bona fide* occupational qualification (BFOQ)
- disparate impact
- business necessity
- *quid pro quo* harassment
- hostile work environment
- disability

Figure 21.3 — Federal Laws Against Employment Discrimination

Law	Protection
Civil Rights Act (Title VII) 1964 (amended 1972, 1991)*	Forbids discrimination based on sex, race, color, national origin, or religion.
Age Discrimination Employment Act (ADEA) 1967 (amended 1978)*	Forbids discrimination against any person aged 40 or older in hiring, firing, promotion, or other aspects of employment.
Older Workers' Benefit Protection Plan (OWBPA) 1990*	Forbids discrimination against older workers in handling their employee benefit and retirement plans; amended ADEA above.
Americans with Disabilities Act (ADA) 1990*	Forbids discrimination on the basis of a physical or mental disability if disabled individual can perform "essential function of the job despite the disability."
Vietnam Era Veterans Readjustment Act (VEVRA) 1972**	Encourages employment of veterans of armed forces who served in Vietnam between 1965 and 1975; also covers reservists called up for active duty; applies to federal contracts only.
Immigration Reform and Control Act (IRCA) 1986*	Prohibits private employers from recruiting and hiring aliens who are ineligible for employment in the United States; also prohibits employment agencies from referring ineligible aliens.

* Administered by Equal Employment Opportunity Commission
** Administered by Veteran's Employment Service

FEDERAL LAWS AGAINST EMPLOYMENT DISCRIMINATION
Federal laws establish protected groups of people who may not be discriminated against in employment. *What federal agency administers most of these laws?*

discriminated against can file their complaints with the Equal Employment Opportunity Commission (EEOC). The EEOC has the power to stop unfair employment practices by seeking a court injunction or by suing the employer for damages. Should the EEOC elect not to pursue a case, the complaining party may seek a private remedy in court.

Disparate Treatment   Discrimination can take place in a number of ways, most prominently through disparate treatment and disparate impact. The most obvious and direct way to discriminate is through disparate treatment. Under **disparate treatment**, the employer intentionally discriminates against an individual or a group of individuals belonging to one of the protected classes. For instance, an employer who holds a general policy that declares, "We do not hire female engineers" or, "We do not hire male nurses" would be practicing this type of discrimination.

> *Example 4.* Walther Maggitti owns a large auto repair shop in a suburb of a major midwestern city. Having been a mechanic for most of his life, Walther has firm opinions about how to run a business in the automobile industry. When Linda Fitzgerald

Figure 21.4

EQUAL PROTECTION IN EMPLOYMENT

The federal government has taken many steps to make the law as fair as possible in the area of employment opportunities. One of the major laws in this regard is the Civil Rights Act of 1964.

1 Prohibiting Discrimination

The Civil Rights Act of 1964 prohibits discrimination in employment based on race, color, creed, religion, sex, or national origin.

2 Hiring Practices

Employers are not permitted to discriminate in hiring practices either directly through disparate treatment, or indirectly through disparate impact.

3 Fair Treatment

The protection granted to employees under the Civil Rights Act includes not only hiring practices but also treatment on the job.

applied for a position as an auto mechanic at his shop, Walther refused to consider her as a candidate, in spite of her excellent qualifications and experience. He later told an employee that he "didn't believe in hiring female mechanics." Walther chose to hire a young male mechanic who had little experience and formal training. If sued, Walther could be found guilty of practicing discrimination through disparate treatment.

Employers have a defense against the charge of disparate treatment. This defense is termed a ***bona fide* occupational qualification (BFOQ)**. If the employer can show that the qualification in question is a *bona fide* (good faith) employment qualification, then the discrimination may be justified. For example, requiring that all applicants for a job modeling women's bathing suits be female would be a *bona fide* occupational qualification. However, the BFOQ defense can never be used to justify discrimination based on race.

Disparate Impact   Discrimination can also take place via **disparate impact**, which is indirect discrimination. Discrimination through disparate impact occurs when an employer has an employment policy or criteria that appears neutral on the surface but has an unfair impact on the members of one or more of the protected classes. For example, an employer who only hires people who are over six feet tall may be discriminating through disparate impact.

Example 5. Marcus Kachur, the owner of Allied Trucking and Hauling, stipulated that all employees must be able to bench-press 150 pounds. Nearly all women who applied at Kachur's firm were unable to meet this requirement. Kachur justified his policy by stating that employees needed to be able lift heavy objects to perform their daily job duties. However, Kachur's employees were primarily in charge of driving goods to their destinations. Very seldom did Kachur's employees actually load or unload goods. If sued, Kachur could be found guilty of practicing discrimination through disparate impact.

Employers have a defense against a charge of disparate impact, known as **business necessity**. If the employer can show that qualification is required to perform the job, then it may be permitted despite its disparate impact on a protected class. For instance, a requirement that all applicants for a job as a surgeon have a medical degree might have a disparate impact on one of the protected classes. However, because a medical degree is needed to do the job, this qualification is a business necessity.

Civil Rights Act of 1991

The Civil Rights Act of 1991 was enacted by Congress for several reasons. It was intended to strengthen the doctrine of disparate impact, which had been weakened by a 1989 Supreme Court case. The new law makes it clear that in disparate impact cases, the employer has the burden of proving the existence of a business necessity. Moreover, the employer must also prove that the hiring or promotion qualification is directly related to the specific job involved in the case rather than to general business objectives. A second reason for passing the new civil rights act was to allow plaintiffs who believe that they have been discriminated against because of sex, religion, national origin, or disability to recover not only any back pay owed to them, but also compensatory and punitive damages. Before this new act, only people discriminated against because of race had this right.

Sexual Harassment

Sexual harassment can occur either through a quid pro quo activity or through the creation of a hostile working environment. Neither the expression *quid pro quo harassment* nor the expression *hostile work environment* appears in Title VII of the Civil Rights Act of 1964. Nevertheless, the courts have consistently recognized both types of discrimination. ***Quid pro quo* harassment** occurs when one worker demands sexual favors from another worker in exchange for some employment-related decision, such as a raise or a promotion. In contrast, the creation of a **hostile working environment** occurs when a pattern of severe and pervasive sexually demeaning behavior has altered the workplace, making it a distressing, humiliating, or hostile place. Such demeaning behavior could include sexually explicit comments, jokes, photographs, cartoons, posters, gestures, and so on.

An employer may be liable for sexual harassment committed by an employee's supervisor, or someone else in a position of power, if some sort of employment action occurs as a result of that harassment. Employment action has been defined by the courts to include termination, disadvantageous reassignment, or demotion. In the absence of this type of employment action, the employer may escape liability by demonstrating reasonable care was taken to prohibit or eliminate such harassment. This can be shown if the employer has an effective anti-harassment policy in place. Even with such proof, the employer must also show that the complaining party did not take advantage of the procedures outlined in the anti-harassment policy and that the failure to use the procedures in the policy was unreasonable.

Pregnancy Discrimination Act

To ensure the fair and equal treatment of pregnant women, the Pregnancy Discrimination Act was enacted. The law makes it unlawful to

Law & Academics

Social Studies
The Civil Rights Act of 1964 prohibited discrimination in employment based on race, color, religion, sex, or national origin.

Research Activity
Research the events in history that led up to the passing of this act by considering the following questions:
- What major civil rights events took place between 1954 and 1965?
- Who were the leaders in the civil rights movement?
- Which civil rights event do you think was most important? Why?

Write a two-page report based on your findings.

discriminate against a woman because of childbirth or physical problems associated with pregnancy or childbirth. In addition, the law prohibits an employer from creating an employee benefits package that discriminates against women who are pregnant.

Age Discrimination in Employment Act

The Age Discrimination in Employment Act (ADEA) of 1967, amended in 1978, prohibits employment agencies, employers with 20 or more employees, and labor unions of more than 25 members from discriminating on the basis of age. This act forbids discrimination against any person aged 40 or older in hiring, firing, promotion, or other aspects of employment. The law does not apply if age is a true job qualification, as in the modeling of children's fashions.

The ADEA was amended by Congress in 1990 to make it clear that the act forbids discrimination against older employees with regard to their retirement and pension plans. In addition, the amendment that is known as the Older Workers' Benefit Protection Plan Act (OWBPPA) gives workers a legal way to remedy a situation in which they have been cheated or coerced into surrendering their ADEA rights by signing a waiver.

Americans with Disabilities Act

The Americans with Disabilities Act of 1990 forbids discrimination on the basis of a disability if the disabled individual can do the "essential functions" of a job. The act defines **disability** as any "physical or mental impairment that substantially limits one or more of the major life activities." Employers cannot discriminate against those with disabilities when screening or hiring, granting promotions, offering pay raises, or offering on-the-job-training opportunities. Both direct and indirect discrimination are outlawed. Indirect discrimination occurs when an employer makes a hiring decision based on a qualification that is not related to job performance but has the effect of eliminating the disabled individual.

> *Example 6.* Melinda Breakwater, who has a visual disability, applied for a position as an accountant with the Rawlings Department Store. Ross Benteen, the store's Human Resources Director, tested her eyesight by having her read a chart written in extremely fine print. Breakwater failed the test and was rejected solely on that basis. Breakwater can argue that Rawlings has violated the ADA if she can show that she would not have to read such fine print on the job, or that she could have been reasonably accommodated if provided with a magnifier.

In Example 6, if the job Breakwater had applied for involved driving and her eyesight prevented her from driving, she would not have a discrimination case under the ADA. Moreover, employers are not without some protection. For example, if a proposed accommodation would cause "undue hardship," then the employer would be excused. Factors used in determining whether a proposed accommodation will cause hardship include the nature and cost of the accommodation needed as well as the financial ability of the company to provide the necessary accommodation.

Section 21.2 Assessment

Reviewing What You Learned
1. What is discrimination?
2. What is the objective of the Civil Rights Act of 1964?
3. What is the mission of the Americans with Disabilities Act?

Critical Thinking Activity
Ethical and Social Attitudes Select one of the laws discussed in this chapter. Then in one to two paragraphs, relate ethical and social attitudes to changes that occur in the law. How have ethical and social attitudes changed over time, and how are they reflected in changes in the law?

Legal Skills in Action
Sexual Harrassment Your friend, Alison, believes that she has been the victim of sexual harassment. She is apprehensive about reporting the harassment to the Human Resources Director at her place of employment, which is a requirement of the company's anti-harassment policy. Write a letter to Allison explaining whether she should file the complaint.

Chapter Summary

Section 21.1 Laws Relating to Employment Conditions and Benefits

- Businesses with 11 or more employees that engage in interstate commerce must meet the health and safety standards of the Occupational Safety and Health Administration (OSHA). OSHA makes sure the businesses adhere to safety regulations by conducting random inspections and imposing fines for violations.

- The federal Fair Labor Standards Act of 1938, also known as the Wage and Hour Law, requires certain employers to pay their employees a minimum hourly wage rate, plus time-and-a-half for all work in excess of 40 hours per week. In addition, the Equal Pay Act states that employers engaged in interstate commerce must pay women the same rate of pay as men holding the same type of job. Pension plans are protected by the Employment Retirement Income Security Act (ERISA). ERISA requires employers to place employee contributions to pension plans in a trust that is independent of the employer's control. Another ERISA requirement imposes a duty of good faith on those who manage pension plans. Other ERISA requirements include informing employees of their retirement benefits and submitting reports on the plan to the Secretary of Labor.

- The Drug-Free Workplace Act applies to companies that have contracts with the federal government. Under the act, companies must implement a plan to make sure employees do not use drugs on the job, and drug testing may be used under certain circumstances. The Employee Polygraph Protection Act prohibits employers from using lie detector tests for screening of applicants or for random testing of employees.

- Unemployment compensation is a system of government payments to people who are out of work and looking for a job. You may be disqualified for unemployment benefits for a limited period if your unemployment arises out of a strike or lockout. Workers are also disqualified if they refuse suitable work without cause, have been discharged for misconduct, or have quit their jobs without "good cause." Workers' compensation is an insurance program that provides income for workers who are injured or develop a disease as a result of their jobs.

Section 21.2 Laws Regulating Employment Discrimination

- An employer cannot discriminate on the basis of sex, race, color, national origin, religion, age, disability, or pregnancy.

- The Civil Rights Act of 1991 was enacted by Congress to strengthen the doctrine of disparate impact of employment discrimination by requiring that the employer prove the existence of a business necessity that justifies discriminating against an employee. In addition, the Civil Rights Act allows plaintiffs who believe that they have been discriminated against because of sex, religion, national origin, or disability to recover back pay, and compensatory and punitive damages.

- The Age Discrimination Act (ADEA) of 1967, amended in 1978, prohibits some employers and labor unions from discriminating on the basis of age. The act forbids discrimination against any person aged 40 or older in hiring, firing, promotion, or other aspects of employment.

- The Americans with Disabilities Act of 1990 forbids discrimination on the basis of a disability if the disabled individual can do the "essential functions" of a job. Employers cannot discriminate against any "physical or mental impairment that substantially limits one or more of the major life activities" when screening or hiring, granting promotions, offering pay raises, or offering on-the-job-training opportunities.

Using Legal Language

Consider the key terms in the list below. Then use these terms to complete the following exercises.

OSHA

equal pay rule

social security

unemployment compensation

disability

workers' compensation

hostile work environment

bona fide occupational qualification (BFOQ)

quid pro quo harrassment

disparate treatment

pension plan

disparate impact

business necessity

harassment

discrimination

Understanding Business and Personal Law

Online

Self-Check Quiz Visit the *Understanding Business and Personal Law* Web site at **ubpl.glencoe.com** and click on Chapter 21: Employment Protection and Equal Opportunity— Self-Check Quizzes to prepare for the chapter exam.

1. These terms will help you remember important information about your rights as an employee. Write a summary of Chapter 21 for a friend who is not taking this class. In your summary, use and explain each of the terms listed above.
2. Save a copy of your summary for future reference.

The Law Review

Answer the following questions. Refer to the chapter for additional reinforcement.

3. What is OSHA, and what is its purpose?
4. What is the purpose of the Drug Free Workplace Act? Does it require that companies drug test their employees?
5. Describe the Social Security Act. How many workers in the United States participate in the social security system?
6. What defense do employers have against the charge of disparate treatment? Explain your answer.
7. In what situation might an employment qualification that would encourage disparate impact be permitted?
8. Identify an employee's right to continued employment by examining current legislation, for example, unlawful termination, sexual harassment, family leave, Americans with Disabilities Act, and employee privacy. Select four such laws, and write a one- to two-sentence explanation of each.
9. What is *quid pro quo* harassment?

Linking School to Work

Interpreting and Communicating Information

In this chapter, you learned about various laws covering employment protection and equal opportunity, and government agencies responsible for enforcing these laws.

10. Research the findings on a government agency audit, for example, compliance with regulations of wage and hours, safety and health, and equal employment. Write a two-page report on your findings.

11. Select three laws that regulate the workplace and research which government agencies are charged with enforcing the laws. Then interview workers and employees in your community that are affected by this legislation and ask them if and how the laws have affected their lives.

Let's Debate

You hear a coworker telling your employer—for the third time in two months—that the handrail in the stairway to the shop's basement needs to be replaced. A week later, the rail is still broken.

Debate

12. If you know that the handrail is broken, do you have an obligation to be careful on the stairway? Who is responsible for safety in the workplace?

13. Is there anything you can do to prevent an injury?

Grasping Case Issues

For the following cases, give your decision and state a legal principle that applies.

14. Wilma McAtee is CEO of Nortex International. Douglas Sweeney, a Nortex engineer, believes that several operations in the main plant are endangering workers. He files several internal complaints. When he gets nowhere, he files a complaint with OSHA. McAtee learns that Sweeney filed the complaint and fires him for it. Is McAtee within her rights? Explain your answer.

15. In January, Oxotech Petroleum hires Lydia Truell as a research scientist, at a salary of $65,000 per year. In March, Oxotech hires Gary Carr to do essentially the same job at a salary of $72,000. The two scientists have similar education and experience backgrounds, and they work side by side. Does the law have any provision covering this sort of inequity? Explain your answer.

16. Jerry Figliano applies for a job as an armored-car driver. Because armored-car personnel carry firearms, Figliano is required to take a drug test. He refuses, arguing that the test violates his privacy rights. Is he correct? Explain your answer.

17. Franklin Vasquez wants to become a flight attendant. He is discouraged from applying by a supervisor, who tells him that the company only hires people who took home economics in high school or were members of Future Stewardesses of America. If Vasquez files a complaint with the Equal Employment Opportunities Commission, which of the two theories of discrimination would form the basis for his complaint? Explain your answer.

18. Robert Patton works as an accountant. He has never received an unfavorable performance review. At age 55, Patton develops problems with his eyes that require him to use a special lamp and to take frequent breaks to prevent eye strain. Upon learning of the required changes, Patton's supervisor fires him and hires a younger person. What law or laws might protect Patton? Explain your answer.

In each case that follows, you be the judge.

19. Unemployment Benefits

Pamela White was hired by Inside Radio/Radio Only, Inc. as a newsletter editor. The company told her she would occasionally have to work 10 extra hours per week. Several assistants quit, and White was forced to work more than 80 hours per week for four weeks. During that time, White had to do the assistants' work and had to create the newsletter manually. She was forced to skip meals, and eventually suffered from nutritional problems, a mild case of depression, and a more severe case of nervous exhaustion. White quit her job and filed for unemployment compensation. *Should she receive benefits? Why or why not?*

Inside Radio/Radio Only, Inc. v. Board of Review, 498 A.2d 793 (NJ).

20. Employment Extensions

As part of its retirement system, the state of Wyoming required state employees who were 65 years of age to apply for yearly extensions of their employment. Six state workers, Anderson, Bosshardt, Chessborough, Kuatholz, Nelson, and Ventling, filed a complaint with the EEOC. *Do the state workers have a cause of action against Wyoming? Should the state workers win their case? Why or why not?*

EEOC v. The Wyoming Retirement System, 771 F.2d 1425 (10th Circuit).

Legal Link

Payroll Deduction

Now that Harvey is receiving a steady paycheck, he notices that his employer is deducting a small amount for social security taxes (often called FICA) each week. Harvey doesn't know much about social security.

Connect

Using a variety of search engines, help Harvey answer the following questions:

21. Who runs the Social Security Administration?
22. What benefits does social security provide?
23. Can you predict how much money Harvey will receive from social security when he retires?
24. How can Harvey replace his social security card if he loses it?

POWER READING STRATEGIES

25. **Predict** Why do you think the government has created so much legislation to protect employees?

26. **Connect** What safety features are in place in your school to protect students from danger?

27. **Question** Identify legislation and agencies that regulate an employer's obligation to supply a safe and accessible workplace. Interview workers and employees affected by this legislation, and write a one-page report on your findings.

28. **Respond** Are there any new workplace issues that employees face? Do you think the federal government will create a law to deal with the issues? Explain your answer.

UNIT 4 Law Workshop:
Using Legal Tools

What Is a Sports Agent?

In Unit 4, you learned about the authority and duties of an agent to a principal. In this workshop, you will apply this knowledge to better understand the relationship between a professional athlete and a sports agent.

Step A: Preparation

Problem: *What duties does a sports agent perform for a professional athlete?*

Objectives: In this workshop, you will investigate the career of a sports agent, and create an agreement between yourself (as an agent) and a hypothetical professional athlete. You will also create a contract between the athlete and a hypothetical corporate sponsor.

- **Research** the sports agent career.
- **Analyze** a number of agreements and contracts.
- **Create** an agreement between yourself and a hypothetical professional athlete.
- **Use technology** to produce a contract.

Step B: Procedure

1. Use the Internet and library to locate information about sports agents. Two helpful Web sites are www.prosports.com and www.sports-management.com.
2. Write a brief report about being a sports agent.
3. Based on Chapter 18 and your own research, write an agreement between yourself (as a sports agent) and a hypothetical professional athlete.
4. Write a contract between the athlete you represent and a corporate sponsor. (Corporate sponsors are businesses that pay celebrities to endorse their products.)
5. Present your agreement and contract to the rest of your class. Explain how your agreement and contract fulfill your duties as an agent to the principal and how they fulfill the principal's duties to you.

Step C: Creating a Model to Analyze Your Agreements

Create two charts; one should list the agent's duties to the principal, and the other should list the principal's duties to the agent. Check the duties that you believe are addressed in your agreement and contract. Share your checklist with your class.

Agent's Duties to the Principal	Agency Agreement	Sponsorship Contract
Obedience to Instruction		
Good Faith		

Principal's Duties to the Agent	Agency Agreement	Sponsorship Contract
Compensation		
Reimbursement		

Step D: Workshop Analysis Report

Analyze the charts you created, and answer the following questions:
1. How are the agent's duties to the principal expressed?
2. How are the principal's duties to the agent expressed?
3. Are any duties implied, rather than expressed, in these agreements? If so, what are they?

Automobile Workers v. Johnson Controls, Inc.

United States Supreme Court

499 U.S. 187 (1991)

Issue Can an employer exclude a female employee from certain employment positions to protect the health of a fetus if the woman should become pregnant?

Facts Johnson Controls, Inc. manufactures batteries containing lead. Concerned about the safety of its employees, Johnson Controls adopted safety measures directed at its female workers. Because exposure to lead can pose serious health risks to a fetus, Johnson Controls encouraged women who expected to give birth to choose positions that would not expose them to lead. The company required any woman who wished to work in such a position to sign a statement advising her "that women exposed to lead have a higher rate of abortion." After eight female employees with high levels of lead became pregnant, Johnson Controls excluded nearly all women from positions that exposed them to lead.

. . . [I]t is [Johnson Controls'] policy that women who are pregnant or who are capable of bearing children will not be placed into jobs involving lead exposure or which could expose them to lead through the exercise of job bidding, bumping, transfer, or promotion rights."

Several female employees filed a class action suit against Johnson Controls, alleging that the company's "fetal protection policy" constituted unlawful discrimination on the basis of gender.

Opinion Congress has adopted legislation prohibiting discriminatory practices in employment based on gender. The Civil Rights Act of 1964, as amended, prohibits gender-based classifications as a term or condition of employment and prohibits such classifications in other matters affecting an employee's status in a company. The Civil Rights Act was amended by the Pregnancy Discrimination Act of 1978, which provides that gender discrimination includes discrimination "because of or on the basis of pregnancy, childbirth, or related medical conditions."

Is the Policy Discriminatory?

The Court determined that Johnson Controls' fetal protection policy is discriminatory because it excludes only women with the ability to become pregnant from certain positions. Although evidence exists about the adverse effects of lead on the male reproductive system, Johnson Controls' policy excludes only females from the designated positions. An employer's good intentions for such discrimination do not cure the discriminatory practice.

A *Bona Fide* Occupational Qualification?

Although the Court determined that Johnson Controls' policy was discriminatory, it examined whether the policy fell within the exception in the Civil Rights Act that allows an employer to discriminate on the basis of "religion, sex, or national origin in those certain instances where religion, sex, or national origin is a *bona fide* occupational qualification reasonably necessary to the normal operation of that particular business or enterprise." Johnson Controls argued that its policy fits within the BFOQ exclusions for safety reasons. The Court concluded such an exception is limited to those situations in which gender or pregnancy interferes with the employee's ability to perform the job. The Court noted that fertile women can manufacture batteries as well as other employees.

The above-cited Pregnancy Discrimination Act of 1978 provides that unless pregnant employees differ from other employees "in their ability or inability to work," they must be "treated the same" as other employees. The Court further stated that "[w]omen as capable of doing their jobs as their male counterparts may not be forced to choose between having a child and having a job." The Court observed that "[d]ecisions about the welfare of future children must be left to the parents who conceive, bear, support, and raise them, rather than to the employers who hire those parents."

Holding

The Court held that an employer may not exclude a female employee from certain employment positions to protect the health of a fetus if the woman should become pregnant. Such a policy constitutes sexual discrimination prohibited by the Civil Rights Act of 1964, as amended by the Pregnancy Discrimination Act of 1978.

The Court also explained that Johnson Controls would not likely be held liable for potential fetal injuries or defects of the children of its female employees. As long as an employer informs employees of a potential risk, it has not acted negligently. Any actions on the part of Johnson Controls to avoid hiring women because of fear of liability, therefore, would not be justified.

Questions for Analysis

1. What was the purpose of Johnson Controls' policy of excluding women from employment positions that would expose them to lead?
2. On what two federal acts did the Supreme Court base its decision that Johnson Controls' fetal protection policy constituted unlawful sexual discrimination?
3. Did it matter that Johnson Controls possessed good intentions when it implemented its fetal protection policy?
4. In what instances is an employer permitted to discriminate against employees based on gender?
5. Give an example of a situation wherein an employer may discriminate based on gender.

Web Resources

Go to the *Understanding Business and Personal Law* Web site at ubpl.glencoe.com for information about how to access online resources for the Landmark Cases.

UNIT 5

UNIT OVERVIEW

Most people use some form of currency to purchase goods, but they do not always use cash. As a consumer, you need to be aware of your rights and obligations when you write checks, borrow money, use credit to make purchases, and manage your debts. In this unit, you will study:

- Borrowing money and buying on credit
- Negotiable instruments
- Writing checks
- Transferring and collecting negotiable instruments

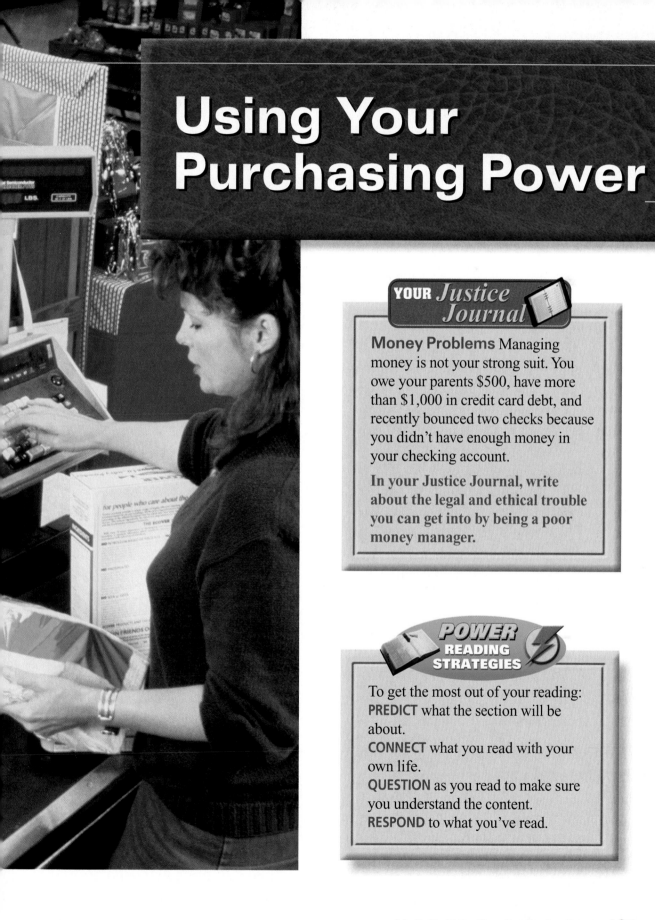

Using Your Purchasing Power

YOUR *Justice Journal*

Money Problems Managing money is not your strong suit. You owe your parents $500, have more than $1,000 in credit card debt, and recently bounced two checks because you didn't have enough money in your checking account.

In your Justice Journal, write about the legal and ethical trouble you can get into by being a poor money manager.

POWER READING STRATEGIES

To get the most out of your reading:
PREDICT what the section will be about.
CONNECT what you read with your own life.
QUESTION as you read to make sure you understand the content.
RESPOND to what you've read.

Borrowing Money and Buying on Credit

Understanding Business and Personal Law *Online*

Chapter Overview Visit the *Understanding Business and Personal Law* Web site at **ubpl.glencoe.com** and click on Chapter 22: Borrowing Money and Buying on Credit—Chapter Overviews to preview the chapter information.

The Opening Scene

Starting in this chapter, you will meet David and Melanie Mueller, a newly married couple. David is tinkering with a laptop computer in the couple's small third-floor apartment when the telephone rings.

Careless Cash

DAVID: Hello?

MELANIE: *(From her cell phone.)* Hi, honey. I'm almost home. Did you miss me?

DAVID: Of course I did! How was work?

MELANIE: Super, but I missed you. Any luck finding a job?

DAVID: Not yet. I was looking for leads on the Web when my laptop stopped working.

MELANIE: Your laptop?

DAVID: I bought it on sale today, but it's defective. I have to take it back. Get a pizza on your way home, will you?

MELANIE: Okay, we'll celebrate our anniversary—it's been six months, you know. See you soon.

(Later, Melanie enters the apartment, and David greets her with a gift-wrapped box.)

DAVID: Happy anniversary, Sweetie!

MELANIE: *(Opening the box and finding a paper shredder.)* Oh, David! You're so romantic.

DAVID: I got it when I bought my new laptop. The sign said, "No Refunds."

MELANIE: Where did you get the money?

DAVID: I charged it.

MELANIE: Oh, did you find your credit card?

DAVID: No, it still hasn't turned up. I used the other one.

MELANIE: David, the APR on that card is 19.8 percent!

DAVID: No problem. Did you get the mail on your way in?

MELANIE: Yes, you got a letter from your aunt and a bill.

DAVID: *(Opening the letter.)* Aunt Mae heard I got laid off and sent us a check for $500.

MELANIE: What a wonderful aunt.

DAVID: This bill is for the credit card I lost. But, hey! I didn't make any of these charges. The bill says we owe $1,697!

MELANIE: Oh, no! Didn't you notify them when you lost the card? *(The telephone rings.)* I'll get it. *(She listens a moment, becoming agitated.)* You can't do that, can you?

DAVID: What is it?

MELANIE: *(Hanging up the phone and going to the window.)* The bank says they just repossessed our car for lack of payments. Yes, it's gone from the parking lot!

DAVID: Can they do that?

MELANIE: *(That evening.)* David, where is the check from Aunt Mae?

DAVID: On the table next to the laptop.

MELANIE: I looked there. I can't find it anywhere.

DAVID: No problem. It's around somewhere.

What Are the Legal Issues?

1. What can you do if you buy something defective using a credit card?
2. What is the meaning and purpose of APR?
3. To what extent is a cardholder liable when a credit card is lost?
4. How must repossession of a vehicle be conducted?

What Is Credit?

What You'll Learn

- How to distinguish between the different types of credit
- How to explain the Truth and Lending Act
- How to describe secured loans
- How to guard against credit card problems

Why It's Important

Knowing the laws that apply and the difficulties that can arise in using credit will help you avoid problems in your personal finances.

Legal Terms

- credit
- interest
- creditor
- debtor
- open-end credit
- line of credit
- closed-end credit
- secured loan
- collateral
- security interest
- secured party
- repossess
- smart card

The Meaning of Credit

Credit is an arrangement through which you may receive cash, goods, or services now and pay for them in the future. The cost of using someone else's money is called **interest**. The party who sells the goods on credit or lends the money is called the **creditor**, and the party who buys the goods on credit or borrows the money is called the **debtor**.

Types of Credit

There are different kinds of credit that you can use. The two main kinds are open-end credit and closed-end credit.

Open-End Credit

Open-end credit is credit that can be increased by the debtor by continuing to purchase goods or services on credit, up to a certain limit. You are given a **line of credit**, or a maximum amount of money made available to you. Charge accounts and credit cards are examples of open-end credit. Your first bank credit card, for example, may have a credit limit of $2,000. You can buy whatever you want until the total of your purchases reaches that level.

Closed-End Credit

Closed-end credit is credit given for a specific amount of money and cannot be increased by making additional purchases. Buying a

LOOK BEFORE YOU LEAP
Before taking out a loan, you should sit down and figure out your finances. *What is perhaps the most important point you should consider?*

vehicle and paying for it in monthly installments is an example of closed-end credit. Many bank loans are also closed-end credit arrangements.

Borrowing Money

You will be asked many questions when you apply for a loan from an institution. Lenders want to make sure that you are a reliable candidate before they issue you a loan. Figure 22.1 shows some sample application questions. You should shop around before borrowing money or buying on credit because lenders charge different rates of interest. Finding a competitive interest rate can save you a lot of money in the long run.

Truth in Lending

The Truth in Lending Act requires that lenders tell you both the finance charge and the annual percentage rate (APR) of the loan. With this information you can compare the cost of a loan from different lenders.

Example 1. When shopping for a truck, Jill asked each dealer she visited what the APR would be to finance the purchase. The first dealer said 7.9 percent, another dealer quoted 8.2 percent, and her bank said that it would be 12 percent. Jill went back to the first dealer, confident that she had found the best deal when shopping around for credit.

Secured Loans

A **secured loan** is one in which creditors obtain an interest in something of value, called **collateral**, from which they can secure payment if you do not pay. The interest that is given to creditors is known as a **security interest**. The lender or seller who holds the security interest is known as the **secured party**.

WHO ARE YOU?
A potential lender will require you to answer a number of specific questions on a credit application. *Why do you think that a creditor would want to know the names and addresses of your present and previous employers?*

Figure 22.1	Sample Credit Application Questions
• Amount of loan requested	• Other income and sources of other income
• Proposed use of the loan	• Have you ever received credit from us?
• Your name and birth date	• If so, when and at which office?
• Social security and driver's license numbers	• Checking account number, institution, and branch
• Present and previous street addresses	• Savings account number, institution, and branch
• Present and previous employers and their addresses	• Name of nearest relative not living with you
• Present salary	• Relative's address and telephone number
• Number and ages of dependents	• Your marital status

Example 2. When Jill bought the truck in Example 1, the dealer took a security interest in the vehicle. To protect the seller's rights in the vehicle, notice of the security interest would be written on the back of Jill's certificate of title to the truck.

Sometimes, creditors file a financing statement in a public office to give notice of their security interest. Anyone can check the records there to see if title is clear on items of personal property.

Repossession   If the debtor does not pay back the loan, the secured party has the right to **repossess**, or take back, the goods. Repossession must be done without breaching the peace (i.e., without causing a disturbance). If the debtor refuses to surrender the goods, legal process must be used to obtain them.

After repossessing goods, a secured party may keep them (with exceptions) or sell them. The sale may be a public auction or private sale. If the goods are consumer goods for which the debtor has paid 60 percent or more of the price, the secured party cannot keep them—they must be sold. The debtor must be notified and is entitled to receive any surplus of the sale after debts and expenses have been paid.

SECURITY INTEREST
When you buy a motor vehicle on credit, the seller will take a security interest in the vehicle.
Why is notice of the security interest written on the back of the certificate of title?

Careers in Law

Nonprofit Attorney

Although Yvonne Knight is an attorney, she works for a special kind of law firm that focuses on a particular area of law. Knight works for the Native American Rights Fund (NARF), a non-profit organization that provides legal representation and technical assistance to Indian tribes, organizations, and individuals. She is a specialist in "Indian Law," which consists of hundreds of treaties and court decisions, and thousands of statutes, regulations, and administrative rulings that determine and protect the rights of Native American tribes and individuals.

"Because of the historical development of the relationship between the United States and Indians, the federal government maintains a special trust relationship with Indian tribes," says Knight, who is a member of the Ponca Tribe of Oklahoma. "That means that as an attorney, I deal mostly with federal law."

Shortly after joining NARF in 1971, Knight was assigned to help the Menomonee Tribe of Wisconsin restore its status as a tribe and reservation.

"The Menomonee had been terminated as a tribe in the 1950s," Knight says. "By the mid-70s, they sought to restore the rights and protections that tribal and reservation status would provide. That meant convincing Congress that those rights needed to be restored."

The effort succeeded, and Knight then worked for three years helping the Menomonee Tribe draft a constitution. That tribal constitution, which had to be approved by members and the Secretary of the Interior, effectively governs the tribe today.

Since then, Knight has continued to fight for Native American rights in trial and appeals courts and around negotiating tables. One of her recent cases involved securing water rights for the Chippewa Cree Tribe of Montana. The case required years of negotiation, but the state of Montana and tribal representative recently reached an agreement. In addition to dividing on-reservation water rights between tribal and non-tribal users, the compact between the tribe and the state also allows the tribe to use water from a federal reservoir.

Skills	Reading, persuasive writing, and articulate speaking.
Personality	Hardworking, detail-oriented, persuasive.
Education	Undergraduate degree and law degree. Although Knight's undergraduate degree was in education and English, she also recommends political science and debate.

You can find more information about NARF at www.narf.com. For more information about nonprofit attorneys, visit **ubpl.glencoe.com** or visit your public library.

Legal Briefs

According to a recent study, the average teen spends $104 a week. In 2001, teens collectively spent $172 billion. Unfortunately, teens do not always spend wisely. The fastest growing age group of people filing for bankruptcy is 25 and under. These statistics point to the importance of solid financial planning.

Cosignature   Loans can also be secured by having a second person, called a cosigner or surety, sign the contract, agreeing to pay the loan if necessary. Often, young people buy their first automobile by having their parents act as cosigners to the loan.

Credit Cards

Credit cards have become an important part of our culture. The amount of credit card debt in the U.S. mushroomed to $680 billion in 2001, with the average family holding 13 different credit cards. The problem was that the average credit card holder had $8,000 in outstanding credit card debt and was paying 17 percent interest on that amount. Figure 22.2 can help you choose a credit card.

Example 3. John charged many items on his credit card, up to its $2,000 limit. Each month he pays $40 on the account, the minimum required by the card issuer. The interest rate is 19 percent. If John maintains the same payment rate, it will take him 33 years

LAWS in Your Life

Your Credit Report

Before credit card companies will give you credit, they will check your credit report. Credit reports contain information about your financial status, including your job history, how much you earn, and how much you owe. Credit reports also contain information about how long you have lived at your current address and whether you pay your bills on time. Credit card companies also want to know whether you own property such as a car or house that can be sold to pay what you owe. Companies that are authorized to gather and report this type of personal information will generate credit reports upon request.

The law requires credit card companies to treat all applicants fairly. Their conduct is regulated by the federal Equal Credit Opportunity Act. This law states that a credit card company may not refuse you credit if you qualify. In determining whether applicants qualify, this law requires credit card companies to follow the same rules for everyone with similar income, bills, and credit histories.

Check It Out Contact a credit reporting agency in your area. Does a credit report exist for you? How can you obtain a copy?

Figure 22.2 — Choosing a Credit Card

When you choose a credit card, it pays to shop around. Follow these suggestions to find the card that best meets your needs and to use it wisely:

1. Department stores and gasoline companies are good places to obtain your first credit card.

2. Bank credit cards are offered through banks and savings and loan associations. Annual fees and finance charges vary widely, so shop around. Shopping around can save you a lot of money.

3. If you plan on paying off your balance every month, look for a card that has a grace period and carries no annual fee or a low annual fee. You might have a higher interest rate, but you plan to pay little or no interest anyway.

4. Watch out for creditors that offer low or no annual fees but instead charge a transaction fee every time you use the card. Such charges can add up quickly.

5. If you plan to carry a balance, look for a card with a low monthly finance charge. Be sure that you understand how the finance charge is calculated.

6. Watch out for cards with variable interest rates. Your interest rate may rise and fall unpredictably.

7. Not all cards offer a grace period. When you use such a card, the bank begins charging you interest on the day you make the purchase or the day the purchase is recorded on your account.

8. If your card offers a grace period, take advantage of it by paying off your balance in full each month. With a grace period of 25 days, you actually get a free loan when you pay bills in full each month.

9. If you have a bad credit history and have trouble getting a credit card, look for a savings institution that will give you a secured credit card. With this type of card, your line of credit depends on how much money you keep in a savings account that you open at the same time.

10. Travel and entertainment cards often charge higher annual fees than most credit cards. Usually, you must make payment in full within 30 days of receiving your bill, or no further purchases will be approved on the account.

11. Many banks and credit card issuers may charge hidden fees, such as service charges. Make sure that you know what they are.

12. Think twice before you make a telephone call to a 900 number to request a credit card. You will pay from $2 to $50 for the 900 call and may never receive a credit card.

Sources: American Bankers Association, *Understanding Credit Card Costs* (San Francisco: Consumer Action), March 1994. *Choosing and Using Credit Cards* (Washington, DC: Federal Trade Commission), January 1999. American Institute of Certified Public Accountants. U.S. Office of Consumer Affairs. Federal Trade Commission.

USING CREDIT RESPONSIBLY
Before you enter the world of credit, you need to understand the various options that are available to you. *Which of these factors would be most important in your choice of a credit card?*

to erase the debt! He will pay $7,000 in interest on the $2,000 that he borrowed to make his purchases. John could save a lot of money by doubling his monthly payments and making every effort to bring the account balance down to zero as soon as possible.

Smart Cards

A **smart card** is a new kind of card with a computer chip that can store a large amount of data. Smart cards can hold debit and credit card balances, identification information, and much more. New data and applications can be downloaded without a new card having to be issued. Smart cards can provide more security for online purchases, especially those made by cell phones. In addition, with new electronic signature laws (see Chapter 13), you will be able to sign online with your private digital signature stored in your smart card. Figure 22.3 offers some tips for buying online with a credit card.

Disputed Purchases

If you have a dispute with a credit card purchase, do not pay the bill for the disputed item. Instead, notify the credit card issuer by telephone immediately. The company or bank that issued the card must put the disputed amount on hold and send you a form to fill out explaining the dispute. The card issuer will attempt to resolve the dispute and inform you of the results. If the problem is not corrected and the credit card issuer brings suit, you may use as a defense the fact that unsatisfactory goods or services were received.

For this law to apply, the initial transaction must have taken place in your state or within 100 miles of your mailing address. Creditors cannot give you a poor credit rating for exercising your rights under this act.

Lost or Stolen Credit Cards

You are responsible for only $50 of any unauthorized charges made before you notify the credit card issuer of the loss, theft, or unauthorized use of your card. You are not responsible for any unauthorized charges made after the company has been notified.

Example 4. Tipper lost her credit card but did not notify the card issuer for a week. Meanwhile, someone who found the card had charged a purchase of $175 with it. Tipper will have to pay $50 toward this unauthorized purchase. If she had notified the card issuer before the illegal purchase happened, however, she would not have had to pay anything.

Credit Card Blocking

When you use a credit card to rent a car or to check into a hotel, the clerk usually gives an estimated bill to the credit card issuer. If the

Figure 22.3 — Online Credit Card Tips

- **Don't give out your credit card number online** unless the latest security protocols are in place and you know and trust the company in question. To ensure the security of your account, your credit card information should be encrypted using the latest technology.

- **Don't trust a site just because it claims to be secure.** Before using a secured transaction site, check out the encrytion software it uses. Some sites may claim to be encrypted when they actually are not. If you are not sure, ask for an alternate method of payment.

- **Read the fine print.** If you receive an offer for a pre-approved credit card or if someone says they'll help you get a credit card, find out the details first. You need to know what interest rate you will be paying and for how long. Some credit cards offer low rates that are raised after a certain period of time or special rates that apply only to balances transferred from other cards. You also need to know about any annual fees, late charges or other fees, and whether there are grace periods for payment before interest is applied. If the terms of the offer aren't provided or aren't clear, look for a credit card somewhere else.

- **Shop around.** Interest rates and other terms vary widely. There are also different types of cards, such as secured cards that require a deposit to cover any charges that are made, cards that can also be used as telephone calling cards, cards that allow you to charge something and pay later or deduct the charge from your bank account immediately, and cards that can only be used to charge merchandise from a catalog.

- **Don't pay fees up front to get a credit card.** Legitimate credit card issuers don't ask for money up front, unless you're applying for a secured card. If you are applying for a secured card, make sure you understand how your deposit will be used. Don't pay someone to help you get a credit card; if you have good enough credit, you can get one yourself.

- **Use your credit wisely.** Many Americans are in debt because they have taken on more credit than they can handle. Don't apply for more cards than you absolutely need, and don't charge more than you can afford. To maintain a good credit rating, pay bills promptly. Avoid interest charges by choosing a card that offers a grace period and paying the entire balance due each month. If you cannot afford to pay your entire balance, pay as much as you possibly can.

- **Get help if you feel you're in over your head.** Consumer Credit Counseling Service, a nonprofit organization, provides low or no cost services to consumers who need a plan to repay debts and improve their credit. To find the nearest CCCS office, call toll-free, 1-800-388-2227.

If you need advice about an Internet or online solicitation, or you want to report a possible scam, use the Online Reporting Form or Online Question & Suggestion Form features on the CCCS Web site, or call the NFIC hotline at 1-800-876-7060.

ONLINE CREDIT CARD TIPS People are defrauded sometimes when they use their credit cards online. *How do you think this occurs?*

CREDIT CARD BLOCK
To be sure you don't exceed your credit card limit, a hotel puts a block on your funds. *How can this cause a problem?*

transaction is approved, your available credit is reduced by this amount immediately. This procedure is called a block. It is used to make sure you don't exceed your credit.

If you pay your bill with the same card you used when you checked in, the final charge should replace the block in a day or two. If you pay your bill with a different card, or with cash or a check, the issuer of the card you presented first might hold the block for up to 15 days. To prevent problems, have the clerk tell the card issuer that you paid another way so that the block is removed.

Section 22.1 Assessment

Reviewing What You Learned

1. What is the difference between open-end credit and closed-end credit? Give an example of each.
2. What does the Truth-in-Lending Act require lenders to tell you?
3. Describe a secured loan.
4. How much does the average credit card holder have in outstanding credit card debt? What is the average interest rate he or she is paying?

Critical Thinking Activity

Economics React to this statement: "America's economic strength is in part due to the ability of people to borrow money and make purchases on credit." Do you agree or disagree? Explain your answer.

Legal Skills in Action

Responsible Use of Credit Many teenagers use credit cards—either their parents' or their own. Some teenagers use credit cards for emergencies only; others use them for everyday purchases and activities. With a partner, debate the role of credit in society today. Explain your philosophy on using credit. Describe how you think credit problems could be prevented.

Credit Protection Laws

Credit Protection Laws

The government has established laws to protect not only your rights as a consumer, but also your credit. You should be familiar with these laws to ensure that you are being treated fairly.

Equal Credit Opportunity Act

The **Equal Credit Opportunity Act** ensures that both businesses and consumers are given an equal chance to obtain credit. The law protects you when you deal with any creditor who regularly gives credit. The law makes it illegal for banks and businesses to discriminate against credit applicants because of their sex, race, marital status, national origin, religion, age, or because they get public assistance income. The details of this law are set forth in Figure 22.4.

Fair Credit Reporting Act

The **Fair Credit Reporting Act** prohibits the abuse of a valuable consumer asset—credit. The act deals with unfavorable reports issued by credit bureaus. These reports, which often contain much personal data, character studies, and so on, are frequently issued to banks, insurance companies, businesses, and prospective employers.

You have the right to know all personal information that is in a consumer reporting agency's files and the sources of the information. Credit reports can be ordered on the Internet or from the following sources:

- Equifax, P. O. Box 740256, Atlanta, GA 30374, (800) 685-1111
- Trans Union, P. O. Box 1000, Chester, PA 19022, (800) 916-8800
- Experian, P. O. Box 949, Allen, TX, 75013, (888) 322-5583

You may be charged a fee of up to $9.00 for the request. You also have the right to be told the name of anyone who received a copy of your credit report in the past year (and in the past two years if the credit report relates to a job application). You may correct errors in the report. If the credit reporting agency retains information that you believe is inaccurate, your version of the facts must be inserted in the file.

Fair Credit Billing Act

When errors are made in bills sent by credit card companies and businesses that give credit, the **Fair Credit Billing Act** can help you. If you believe an error has been made on a bill, notify the creditor in

What You'll Learn

- How to identify and describe credit protection laws
- How to explain your rights and duties under credit protection laws

Why It's Important

Knowing about credit protection laws will help you be a smarter consumer.

Legal Terms

- Equal Credit Opportunity Act
- Fair Credit Reporting Act
- Fair Credit Billing Act
- Fair Debt Collection Practices Act

EQUAL CREDIT
OPPORTUNITY ACT
The Equal Credit
Opportunity Act ensures
that you are given an
equal chance to obtain
credit. *If your credit
application is rejected,
do you have the right to
know why?*

Figure 22.4 | **Equal Credit Opportunity Act**

The Equal Credit Opportunity Act ensures that you are given an equal chance to obtain credit. Here are some of your rights:

- When you apply for credit, you may not be asked to reveal your sex, race, national origin, or religion; whether you're widowed or divorced; your marital status unless you're applying for a joint or a secured loan (marital status may be asked in the states of Arizona, California, Idaho, Louisiana, Nevada, New Mexico, Texas, and Washington—all of which are community property states); your plans for having or raising children; or whether you receive alimony, child support, or separate maintenance payments.

- When deciding to give you credit, a creditor may not consider your sex, marital status, race, national origin or religion; whether you have a telephone listing in your name; the race of people in the neighborhood where you want to buy, refinance, or improve a house; and your age, unless you're a minor or are considered favorably for being over 62.

- You have a right to: have credit in your birth name, your first and your spouse's last name, or your first name and a combined last name; get credit without a cosigner, if you meet the creditor's standards; have a cosigner other than your husband or wife, if one is necessary; keep your own accounts after you change your name, marital status, reach a certain age, or retire, unless the creditor has evidence that you're not willing or able to pay; know whether your application was accepted or rejected within 30 days of filing a complete application; and know why your application was rejected or why you were offered less favorable terms than those you applied for.

writing within 60 days of the date of the statement. State your name, account number, the charge in question, and why you believe there is an error. Figure 22.5 shows a form you can follow to write your letter. The creditor must acknowledge your letter within 30 days. Also, the creditor must investigate and explain why the charge is correct or fix the mistake within 90 days. You do not have to pay the amount in dispute while waiting for an answer from the creditor, but you must pay all charges not in dispute. Creditors may not report you as being delinquent because of the disputed charge.

Fair Debt Collection Practices Act

Under the **Fair Debt Collection Practices Act**, it is illegal for debt collectors to threaten consumers with violence, use obscene language, or contact consumers by telephone at inconvenient times or places. Debt collectors are not allowed to impersonate government officials or attorneys, obtain information under false pretenses, or collect more than is legally owed.

Figure 22.5

Sample Dispute Letter

Date
Your Name

Your Address
Your City, State, Zip Code
Your Account Number

Name of Creditor
Billing Inquiries
Address
City, State, Zip Code

Dear Sir or Madam:
I am writing to dispute a billing error in the amount of $_____
on my account. The amount is inaccurate because (describe
the problem). I am requesting that the error be corrected, that
any finance and other charges related to the disputed amount
be credited as well, and that I receive an accurate statement.

Enclosed are copies of (use this sentence to describe any
enclosed information, such as sales slips, payment records)
supporting my position. Please investigate this matter and
correct the billing error as soon as possible.

Sincerely,

Your name
Enclosures: (List what you are enclosing.)

BILLING DISPUTE
If you believe an error has
been made on a bill, you
should send a letter like this
within 60 days of the date
of the statement. Send
your letter by certified mail,
return receipt requested.
*How soon must the
creditor acknowledge
your letter?*

Section 22.2 Assessment

Reviewing What You Learned
1. What is the purpose of the Equal Credit
   Opportunity Act?
2. What does the Fair Debt Collection Practices
   Act make it illegal for debt collectors to do?

Critical Thinking Activity
Credit Protection Laws Do you think credit
protection laws are necessary? Why or why not?

Legal Skills in Action
Credit Protection Careful use of credit cards
and maintaining good credit are important
financial objectives. Choose one of the credit
protection laws discussed in this section and
research when and why it was made into a law.
Write a one-page report about your findings.

Managing Your Debts

Why It's Important

Most people have financial problems of some kind. Recognizing them and knowing what to do will improve your life.

Legal Terms

- bankruptcy
- family farmer
- homestead exemption

Warning Signs of Debt Problems

It is important to manage your money in a fiscally responsible manner. Here are some warning signs that you may be in financial trouble:

- You make only the minimum monthly payment on credit cards or have trouble paying even that much. The total balance on your credit cards increases every month.
- You miss loan payments or often pay late.
- You receive second or third payment due notices from creditors.
- You borrow money to pay off old debts.
- You exceed the credit limits on your credit cards.
- You've been denied credit because of a bad credit report.

If you experience two or more of these warning signs, it's time to rethink your priorities.

Financial Counseling Services

If you're having trouble paying your bills, you have several options. You can contact your creditors and work out an adjusted repayment plan, or you can contact a nonprofit financial counseling program.

Consumer Credit Counseling Service

The Consumer Credit Counseling Service is a nonprofit organization affiliated with the National Foundation for Consumer Credit. Local branches of the CCCS provide debt-counseling services. Check the white pages of your telephone directory, the Internet, or call 1-800-388-2227. All information is kept confidential.

Declaring Bankruptcy

Sometimes people and businesses get hopelessly mired in debt—so hopelessly that they cannot meet the demands of their creditors. Under old English law, such debtors were put in debtors' prisons. The drafters of the U.S. Constitution opposed this treatment of debtors and gave Congress the authority to help people in this dilemma.

Bankruptcy is the legal process by which a debtor can make a fresh start through the sale of assets to pay off creditors. Bankruptcy laws are named after the chapters where they may be found in the federal bankruptcy code. The bankruptcy and dissolution options for different types of business organizations are explained in Figure 22.6.

Figure 22.6 — Types of Bankruptcy Procedures

Chapter	Who Can File?	When Used?	Special Features
Chapter 7: Ordinary Bankruptcy	Everyone is eligible, except banks, railroads, and insurance companies; filing can be voluntary or involuntary	Used when debtor wants to discharge most debts and begin with a clean slate	Debtor's property is liquidated; some property is exempt; some debts cannot be discharged
Chapter 11: Reorganization	Individuals, partnerships, and corporations can file; railroads can file; only commodity brokers and stockbrokers cannot file; filing can be voluntary or involuntary	Used when debtor, usually a business, wants to continue operating, but needs to reorganize and liquidate debts	Debtor-in-possession feature; debtor files plan within 120 days; plan must be fair, equitable, and feasible; creditors can also file plans; confirmation needed
Chapter 12: Family Farmer Debt Adjustment	Family farmers can file, including partnerships and corporations; debt ceiling of $1.5 million	Used when a debtor is a family farmer who needs a debt adjustment plan to keep the farm running	Debtor-in-possession feature; debtor files plan within 90 days; plan lasts three years (with two-year extension possible); plan must be confirmed
Chapter 13: Individual Debt Adjustment	Individuals only; no corporations or partnerships; no involuntary filings allowed; debt ceiling of $450,000.	Used when an individual debtor with a steady income voluntarily decides to adopt a debt adjustment plan	Only the debtor can file a plan; payments must start 30 days after plan submitted, a few debts cannot be discharged; plan lasts three years (with two-year extension possible)

Chapter 7 bankruptcy may be brought either voluntarily by the debtor or involuntarily by creditors. Three creditors must file the petition for bankruptcy if the debtor has 12 or more creditors. The combined debt owed to the three must exceed $11,625. A single creditor who is owed a debt of more than $11,625 can also file if the debtor has fewer than 12 creditors.

Chapter 11 bankruptcy offers a method for businesses to reorganize their financial affairs and still remain in business. When a petition for reorganization under Chapter 11 is filed, a reorganization plan for the business is developed. Once the plan is approved by a certain number of creditors and the court, it will go into operation. If the plan is successful, the business will continue. If not, it will be forced to close.

Chapter 12 bankruptcy helps family farmers create a plan for debt repayment that allows them to keep their farms running. A **family farmer** is defined as one who receives more than one-half of his or her total income from the farm. To file Chapter 12 bankruptcy, 80 percent of the debt must result from farm expenses.

BANKRUPTCY LAWS Bankruptcy rules apply differently to individuals and businesses. After examining Figure 22.6, compare personal with business bankruptcy law. *What options are available to individuals? How are they different than the options for businesses?*

Chapter 13 bankruptcy permits an individual debtor to develop a repayment plan. During the period of repayment—usually three years—creditors may not continue collection activities.

Exemptions As part of the "fresh start" policy of the Bankruptcy Act, some assets can be kept by the debtor. These so-called exemptions can be doubled for married couples filing jointly. Debtors can elect to use either their own state exemptions or the federal ones. The following federal exemption amounts were in effect in 2004, but they are subject to adjustment in the future.

Virtual Law

Credit Card Security

Cases of theft and fraud on the Internet are on the rise. As a result, credit card companies are working with online merchants to improve security. These companies have Web sites that help merchants review and improve their security policies. With this help from credit card companies, merchants are able to meet industry standards for protecting against online fraud and theft. Making payment methods more private is one way credit card companies are trying to improve security. Improved security can be achieved by requiring additional forms of user identification. Ideally, a user fingerprint will protect a customer's identity. (Source: *InternetWeek*, October 13, 2000)

Connect Visit the Web sites of several major credit card companies, and check their online security policies.

Debtors can keep a maximum of $17,425 in equity in a personal residence—the **homestead exemption**. They can also keep a maximum of $925 for any individual item of furniture, household goods, clothes, appliances, books, crops, animals, or musical instruments. The total of all exemptions taken in this category cannot exceed $9,300. Debtors are also allowed to exempt $1,150 in jewelry beyond the $9,300 mentioned previously. In addition, they may keep any other property not exceeding the value of $925, plus up to $8,725 of any unused amount of the $17,425 homestead exemption.

Debtors may also keep certain necessary items. They include a maximum of $1,750 in professional tools, instruments, and books; up to $2,775 in a motor vehicle; and any medical supplies that have been prescribed for the health of the debtor. Alimony and child support payments can also be excluded. Social security and benefits received under a disability program and certain life insurance policies are also exempt.

The bankruptcy act has modified the common law so that a person who is hopelessly in debt may be relieved of further obligation on contracts if the court grants that person relief. However, debts associated with fraud or wrongdoing are revived even after the debts have been discharged in bankruptcy.

Exceptions to Discharge Some debts cannot be discharged. These include debts caused by the debtor's fraud, back taxes, and student loans that do not impose a hardship on the debtor.

Law & Academics

Science
Research and Development (R&D) is the department within most businesses that is responsible for developing new products and reformulating old ones. Many companies must borrow money for their R&D. Using the Internet, locate the annual report of a pharmaceutical, biotechnology, or other scientific business.

Research Activity
Find out how much the company spent on R&D last year. *Do you think that the company borrowed money to pay for its R&D? Explain your answer.*

Section 22.3   Assessment

Reviewing What You Learned
1. What are the nine warning signs that you might be in financial trouble?
2. What service is provided by the Consumer Credit Counseling Service?
3. Discuss the differences between declaring Chapter 7 and Chapter 13 bankruptcy.

Critical Thinking Activity
Debt Problems Do you recognize any of the warning signs of debt problems? Do they apply to you or someone you know? How might you correct these debt problems or advise someone else to do so? Why is it important to address debt problems as soon as possible?

Legal Skills in Action
Credit Counseling Unfortunately, many people realize they are in financial trouble when it is too late to correct the problem. Create a skit between a young adult who has too much debt and a credit counselor. Have the credit counselor offer advice. Next, act out the skit with a partner.

Chapter Summary

Section 22.1 What is Credit?

- There are two main types of credit. Open-end credit is credit that can be increased by the debtor by continuing to purchase goods or services on credit, up to a limit set by the creditor. Closed-end credit is extended only for a specific amount of money.
- The Truth in Lending Act requires that lenders tell you both the finance charge and the annual percentage rate (APR) of the loan. The purpose of this act is to assist consumers in making informed decisions when shopping for credit.
- A secured loan is one in which you give a creditor a right to something of value, called collateral, in exchange for money it lends you. You have possession and use of your collateral, but the creditor has a security interest and the legal right to repossess your property if you do not pay.
- If there is a problem with a good or service charged on your credit card, and the initial transaction took place in your state or within 100 miles of your mailing address, you may dispute the charge with your credit card issuer. If your credit card is lost or stolen, credit card protection will cover unauthorized charges, except for the initial $50, which you are required to pay. However, you should notify your credit card company immediately if you lose your credit card.

Section 22.2 Credit Protection Laws

- The federal government has passed several credit protection laws to protect consumers. The Equal Credit Opportunity Act prevents credit issuers from discriminating against applicants because of gender, marital status, age, religion, race, national origin, or because they get public assistance income. The Fair Credit Reporting Act helps you know the source of a credit report and to correct any wrong information in it. The Fair Credit Billing Act establishes a procedure for the prompt handling of billing disputes. The Fair Debt Collection Practices Act makes it illegal for debt collectors to threaten consumers with violence, to use obscene language, or to contact consumers at inconvenient times or places to collect debts.

Section 22.3 Managing Your Debts

- If you experience two or more of the following warning signs, you may be in financial trouble: (1) you make only the minimum monthly payment on credit cards or have trouble paying even that much; (2) the total balance on your credit cards increases every month; (3) you miss loan payments or often pay late; (4) you use savings to pay for necessities such as food and utilities; (5) you receive second or third payment due notices from creditors; (6) you borrow money to pay off old debts; (7) you exceed the credit limits on your credit cards; or (8) you have been denied credit because of a bad credit report.
- If you're having trouble paying your bills and need help, you can contact your creditors and try to work out an adjusted repayment plan, or you can contact a nonprofit financial counseling program. The Consumer Credit Counseling Service is an organization that can offer help.
- Chapter 7 bankruptcy permits debtors to liquidate their assets and pay off creditors. Chapter 11 bankruptcy allows businesses to reorganize their financial affairs while remaining open for business. Chapter 12 bankruptcy is reorganization for family farmers. Chapter 13 bankruptcy permits an individual debtor to develop a repayment plan during which period of repayment creditors may not continue collection activities.

Using Legal Language

Consider the key terms in the list below. Then use these terms to complete the following exercises.

annual percentage rate (APR)	line of credit
credit	secured party
creditor	closed-end credit
secured loan	repossess
debtor	finance charge
collateral	bankruptcy
open-end credit	interest
security interest	

1. With a partner, create a script that highlights the duties between a lender and a credit applicant. Use all of the terms listed above.
2. Act out the scenario with your partner.
3. Present your scenario to the class.
4. As a class, vote to select the best scenario. Ensure that the winning script correctly uses each of the key terms.

Understanding Business and Personal Law Online

Self-Check Quiz Visit the *Understanding Business and Personal Law* Web site at **ubpl.glencoe.com** and click on Chapter 22: Borrowing Money and Buying on Credit— Self-Check Quizzes to prepare for the chapter exam.

The Law Review

Answer the following questions. Refer to the chapter for additional reinforcement.

5. Why should you shop around before borrowing money?
6. What should you do if you have a dispute with a credit card purchase?
7. What is credit card blocking, and why is it used?
8. Describe the purpose of the Fair Credit Reporting Act and the Fair Credit Billing Act. How do these acts protect consumers?
9. Which debts can't be discharged when someone declares bankruptcy?
10. How must a creditor go about repossessing a debtor's property?
11. When extending credit, why do lenders sometimes require cosigners?
12. Compare personal with business bankruptcy.

Linking School to Work

Participating Effectively as a Member of a Team

In groups of four or five, contact a consumer credit counseling service in your area. Arrange a brief interview with a counselor. Pose the following questions:

13. What services are offered?
14. What fees are charged for the services?
15. What educational materials are available about the wise use of credit?

If possible, invite someone from one of the services to your class to provide additional information about the best way to handle credit.

Let's Debate

Bankruptcy

Margarita graduated from college and found a job that paid $2,000 per month. She immediately rented an apartment for $800 per month, bought furniture that she paid for on credit, and invested in a new wardrobe. In addition, she has student loans to repay and a $350 monthly car payment. Margarita is drowning in debt and figures she should just declare bankruptcy and start over.

Debate

16. Should Margarita declare bankruptcy?
17. What other options does she have?
18. How can she prevent a problem like this in the future?

Grasping Case Issues

For the following cases, give your decision and state a legal principle that applies.

19. Shirlene lost her job. She was unable to find work for several months and fell behind in paying her bills. A debt collector telephoned her at 11:45 P.M., used profanity, and threatened to "take care of her" if she didn't pay the amount owed. Were Shirlene's rights violated? Explain your answer.
20. Mary and Frank are four months behind on the payments for their living room furniture. Two bill collectors come to their house and attempt to break in to repossess the furniture. Mary becomes quite angry and orders the bill collectors to leave her furniture alone. Is the finance company within its rights? Why or why not?
21. David's wallet, which contained his credit card, is stolen. David does not notify the card issuer of the loss. The next month, he receives a $510 bill for an unauthorized purchase. Will he have to pay? If so, how much?
22. Mary was recently married and goes to a bank to request a loan. The loan officer asks if she plans to have a child in the next few years. Mary refuses to answer and is denied the loan. Did the bank officer break the law? Explain your answer.
23. Ellen always pays her bills on time. Because of a computer error, however, she is given a poor credit rating. Several firms refuse to give her credit, citing her poor rating with the credit reporting agencies. Does Ellen have any legal recourse? Explain your answer.

In each case that follows, you be the judge.

24. Discharging Loans

Lisa and William Leeper filed a Chapter 13 bankruptcy petition. One of the debts they listed was an amount owed to attend college under a guaranteed student loan program. *Will the loan to attend college be discharged by the court? Why or why not?*
Leeper v. Pennsylvania Higher Education Assistance Agency, 94-3372 & 94-3373, U.S. Court of Appeals (3rd Cir.).

25. Truth in Lending

Stewart and Marjory Selmans applied to the Manor Mortgage Company for a loan of $23,000 to be used for personal purposes. They were told that if they incorporated, they would be given a loan. Under Michigan law, money could be loaned to corporations at a higher rate of interest. The Selmans formed a corporation, received the loan, and then dissolved the corporation. *Does the transaction fall within the Truth in Lending Act? Why or why not?*
Selman v. Manor Mortgage Co., 551 F.Supp. 345 (MI).

Legal Link

Teach Others

You and a group of friends have decided to create a program that could be offered to high school students. This program would help students learn about the issues and laws surrounding the use of credit.

Connect

Using a variety of search engines, locate information that could be used in your program. Be sure to include the following information:
26. How to use credit wisely
27. How to recognize potential credit problems
28. How the credit protection laws work
29. Why bankruptcy is a last resort measure

POWER READING STRATEGIES

30. Predict How would life in the United States be different if there were no credit?

31. Connect Do you have a credit card? If so, what do you use it for? If not, when do you think you will get one, and what will you use it for?

32. Question How does knowing about the credit protection laws make you a smarter consumer?

33. Respond Why are bankruptcy laws necessary? Why do you believe that the bankruptcy laws in the United States do not include the possibility of incarceration in a debtor's prison?

Negotiable Instruments

Understanding Business and Personal Law *Online*

Chapter Overview Visit the *Understanding Business and Personal Law* Web site at ubpl.glencoe.com and click on Chapter 23: Negotiable Instruments—Chapter Overviews to preview the chapter information.

The Opening Scene

David Mueller arrives home from work and greets his wife, Melanie.

Checks and Balances

DAVID: *(Handing his wife an envelope.)* Here it is, Melanie, my first paycheck since I got the new job. I can't wait to cash it.

MELANIE: We've waited a long time. *(She reads aloud the words on the check.)* Pay to the order of David Mueller. That's odd—the words say four hundred twelve dollars, but the figures say $422. I wonder which amount is right?

DAVID: *(Taking the check.)* Oh, you're right. Look! There's no date on the check, either. I hope it's still good.

MELANIE: It better be, after all your hard work. We really need the money. We have a lot of bills. I guess that you could always ask your boss for another check, though.

DAVID: I wish we could pay the furniture company, but we have so many other bills. We've got to make a payment on the credit card, too. What should we do?

MELANIE: It would be great if Julio would pay you the money he owes you. It should be almost due, right? I remember that we were making our wedding plans when you loaned him the money. That was about a year ago.

DAVID: You're right. Let's look at the promissory note he gave me. *(David leaves the room and returns with a piece of paper.)* The whole thing is in his handwriting. It says, "One year from date, I, Julio Rueda, promise to pay to the order of David Mueller the sum of $1,000 with interest at the rate of 8 percent per annum." It's not due for another month. Say, I just noticed he never signed on the bottom. Maybe this is no good! Now I'm really worried!

MELANIE: Don't worry. He wrote his name at the beginning, right? Anyway, I'd trust him even if he didn't put it in writing. Julio is our friend, and he wouldn't let us down. Maybe we should call him and remind him of the debt.

DAVID: I think I might give him a call. This amount is the same amount that we owe the furniture company. Wouldn't it be great if Julio could sign a paper to pay the money directly to the furniture company? That way, I wouldn't have the chance to blow the money.

MELANIE: Maybe he can. I'm going to ask him to do it. The furniture company shouldn't care where the money comes from. We should really look into that.

DAVID: I think I'll write out a few checks right now. I can mail them on the way to work early tomorrow morning.

MELANIE: I think you're being hasty. Shouldn't you deposit your paycheck first? We don't want to bounce any checks!

DAVID: I'll just postdate the checks a few days. That way they won't be able to cash them until my paycheck clears.

What Are the Legal Issues?

1. What sum controls on a check when the amount written in words is different from the amount written in figures?
2. Is an undated check valid and negotiable?
3. What is the legal effect of a signature written at the beginning of an instrument instead of at the end?
4. Is there a type of negotiable instrument that can be used to transfer debts?
5. Is it legal to postdate a check?

Purpose and Types of Negotiable Instruments

What You'll Learn

- How to state the purpose of negotiable instruments
- How to identify the types of negotiable instruments
- How to name the parties to each type of negotiable instrument

Why It's Important

Knowing the purpose and types of negotiable instruments will help you manage your financial affairs throughout life.

Legal Terms

- negotiable instrument
- note
- maker
- payee
- certificate of deposit (CD)
- draft
- drawer
- drawee
- acceptor
- sight draft
- time draft
- check

Purpose of Negotiable Instruments

Throughout history, people have found it necessary to transact business without carrying around large sums of money. People have also devised arrangements to purchase items that they will pay for at a later date. The law of negotiable instruments was developed to meet these needs.

The use of checks, notes, drafts, electronic banking, and credit cards has increased dramatically in recent years. More people are opening checking accounts and signing drafts and promissory notes than ever before. These instruments are used conveniently and safely as a substitute for money and to obtain credit.

A **negotiable instrument** is a written document giving special legal rights to the transferee that may be transferred by indorsement or delivery. There are two basic kinds of negotiable instruments: notes (including certificates of deposits) and drafts (including checks).

Notes

A **note** (often called a promissory note) is a written promise by one person, called the **maker**, to pay money to another person, called the

Figure 23.1

No. _381_   _Boston, Massachusetts, October 1_, 20 __
On demand, the undersigned, for value received, promise(s) to pay to the order of
CAMBRIDGE TRUST COMPANY
Two thousand four hundred and 00/100 ——— Dollars,
at its offices in Boston, Massachusetts, together with interest thereon from the
date thereof until paid at the rate of _11_ percent per annum.

Address _100 Bedford Street_   _Victor Powell_
Waltham, Massachusetts

DEMAND NOTE
A demand note is payable whenever the payee demands payment. *Who is the maker of this note? the payee?*

"Neither a Borrower Nor a Lender Be"

If you disregard this time-honored advice, as almost everyone does, use a well-drafted promissory note. When borrowing money from a bank, you will be required to sign a promissory note. Banks typically use a standard form. If you borrow from a friend or relative, then you'll need to come up with your own form. You can obtain fill-in-the-blank promissory note forms at most office supply stores.

It is well worth the effort to sign a promissory note when dealing with family members or friends, especially if you want to keep those relationships intact. Using a promissory note will help avoid misunderstandings about such basic things as how much is owed and when repayment is to occur. It is always wise to use a promissory note, even if the family member or friend insists on keeping things informal.

If you're operating a business and you borrow money on its behalf, then it is important to know that partners and sole proprietors are always personally obligated to repay a business loan. If your business is a corporation, then the business is obligated unless you personally guarantee the loan.

Research and Evaluation Visit a local bank or office supply store. Review the various promissory note forms. Which would you use to keep initial payments as low as possible?

---

payee . When two persons sign a note, they are known as comakers. Creditors who loan money or extend credit ask debtors to sign notes as evidence of debt. An advantage of using a note is that it can be negotiated (transferred) to other people without much difficulty.

There are various types of notes. A demand note is a note that is payable when the payee demands payment (see Figure 23.1). In contrast, a time note is a note that is payable at a future date, which is written on the face of the note. An installment note is a note that is paid in a series of payments. People often sign this type of note when they borrow money to buy a car or a house.

Example 1. Keith bought a car from Laura's Used-Car Exchange for $4,900. He paid $1,000 down and signed a note promising to pay the balance, along with interest at the rate of 18 percent

per year, to the dealer in monthly installments over a two-year period. To get the money immediately, Laura's Used-Car Exchange negotiated the note to the Ace Finance Company, which accepted it for a small service charge. Now Keith will have to make monthly payments to the holder of the note—the Ace Finance Company.

Certificates of Deposit

A **certificate of deposit (CD)** is a note provided by a bank. A CD is a bank's written receipt of money and its promise to pay the money back, usually with interest, on the due date (see Figure 23.2). CDs are written for a specific time period, such as six months, one year, two years, or five years. Banks pay higher interest for longer-term CDs. The interest paid on a CD is higher than the amount paid on a regular savings or checking account because the depositor cannot withdraw the money before the due date without penalty. In certain circumstances, people who have certificates of deposit can obtain money by negotiating the certificates to other people or by pledging them as security for a loan.

Drafts

In contrast to a note, which is a promise to pay money, a **draft** is an order to pay money. Drafts are more complicated than notes because they involve three parties instead of two. Also called a bill of exchange,

CERTIFICATE OF DEPOSIT
A certificate of deposit is basically a promissory note issued by a bank. *Why do people buy CDs?*

Figure 23.2

CSB Columbia Savings Bank
1200 North Street
Columbia, South Carolina

CERTIFICATE OF DEPOSIT

Date: July 1, 20 --

This acknowledges that there has been deposited with the undersigned, the sum of $ 1,000.00

one thousand and 00/100-- Dollars

which is payable to the order of ____Alana Donley____ on the

__1st__ day of ____July____ , 20____ , upon presentation and surrender of this certificate, and bears interest at the rate of __4%__ per annum calculated and credited at maturity. No payment may be made prior to, and no interest runs after, that date.

COLUMBIA SAVINGS BANK
By _Timothy Gorman_
Vice President

a draft is an instrument in which one party (the **drawer**) orders another party (the **drawee**) to pay money to a third party (the payee).

Drawees, although ordered to pay money, are not required to do so unless they have agreed to the arrangement. They agree to a draft by writing the word *accepted* on the document (usually on the front) and signing their name. A drawee who has done this is called an **acceptor** and can be required to pay the draft.

Businesses and private parties frequently use drafts to transfer debts from one party to another. In The Opening Scene, for example, we discover that the $1,000 that Julio owes to David is exactly the amount that David and Melanie owe to the furniture store. This situation can be easily resolved by using a draft. David can draw a draft ordering Julio to pay the $1,000 to the store. If Julio agrees by writing *accepted* and signing the face of the draft, he will then be obligated to pay $1,000 to the furniture dealer, thus paying David and Melanie's debt.

A **sight draft** is a draft that is payable as soon as it is presented to the drawee for payment. A **time draft** is a draft that is not payable until the lapse of the particular time period stated on the draft (see Figure 23.3).

Checks

A **check** is a draft drawn on a bank and payable on demand. It is the most common kind of draft in use today. When issuing a check, you

WHOM DO I PAY?
In Example 1, Keith signed a note promising to pay the money back to Laura's Used-Car Exchange. *Why must he pay the money to the finance company?*

Figure 23.3

$ 500.00	Wilmington Delaware, May 26, **20--**
In or within 60 days--------------------------------	**Pay to**
the order of David Connors----------------------	
Five hundred and 00/100-----------------------------	----Dollars

Accepted Walter Ahearn June 5, 20--

Value received and charge the same to account of

To Walter Ahearn

No. 412   Oxford, Maryland   }   *David Bickum*

TIME DRAFT
A time draft is not payable until the lapse of the particular time period stated on the draft. *What is the legal effect of the words "Accepted, Walter Ahearn, June 5, 20--" on the front of this draft?*

put money in the bank and then order the bank to pay your money to others by writing out checks.

You can write out a check to be paid at a later date by postdating it; that is, you put a date on the check that is later than the date on which the check is written. Failing to put a date on a check does not affect its negotiability. A more detailed discussion about writing checks appears in the next chapter.

NO CHECKS
Some merchants do not accept personal checks. *Why do you think this is so?*

Section 23.1 Assessment

Reviewing What You Learned

1. What is the purpose of a negotiable instrument?
2. Name the two basic kinds of negotiable instruments.
3. Define the parties to each kind of negotiable interest.

Critical Thinking Activity

Certificates of Deposit What do you think the bank does with the money you deposit into a CD?

Legal Skills in Action

Analyze Earned Interest Ed's grandmother gave him $1,000 for his 16th birthday. He decided to deposit it into a savings account until he turns 18. LaToya's aunt gave her $1,000 for her 16th birthday. LaToya decided to deposit her money in a CD until she turns 18. Explain why LaToya will be earning more interest than Ed.

Requirements of Negotiability

Drafting Instruments

To be negotiable, an instrument must satisfy specific criteria (see Figure 23.4). It must:

- Explain the elements of negotiable instruments.
- Bear the signature of the maker or drawer.
- Be an unconditional promise or order to pay.
- Be made out for a fixed amount of money.
- Be payable on demand or at a definite time.
- Be payable to order or to bearer.

What You'll Learn

- How to state the requirements of negotiability
- How to describe the importance of dates on negotiable instruments
- How to identify the controlling words on negotiable instruments

Why It's Important

Recognizing the negotiability and controlling words of instruments will help you make meaningful business and financial decisions.

Legal Terms

- demand paper
- definite-time paper
- words of negotiability

Figure 23.4

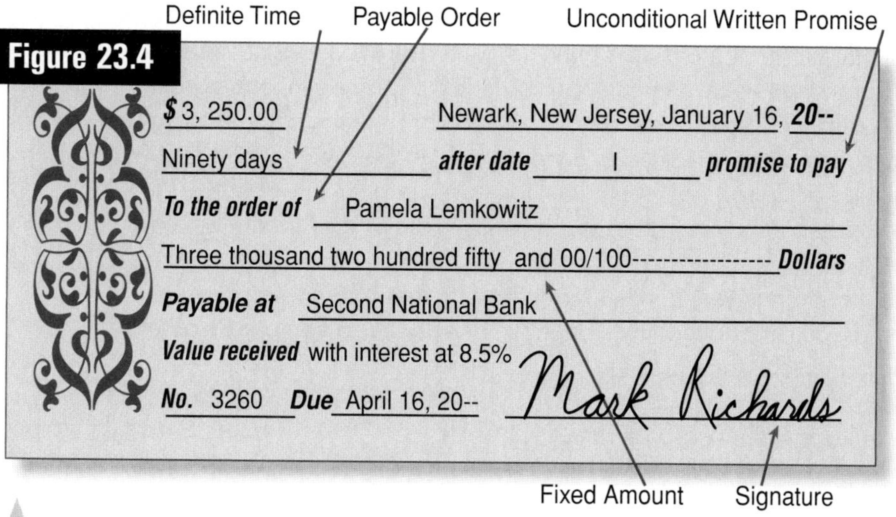

Definite Time   Payable Order   Unconditional Written Promise

$ 3,250.00   Newark, New Jersey, January 16, **20--**

Ninety days _____ **after date** _____ I _____ **promise to pay**

To the order of   Pamela Lemkowitz

Three thousand two hundred fifty and 00/100----------------- **Dollars**

Payable at   Second National Bank

Value received with interest at 8.5%

No. 3260   **Due** April 16, 20--   *Mark Richards*

Fixed Amount   Signature

REQUIREMENTS OF NEGOTIABILITY
The requirements of negotiability are indicated on this 90-day note. *Would the instrument be negotiable if it were for pesos instead of dollars?*

Written Instrument

The promise, or order, to pay must be in writing. It can be printed, typed, handwritten in pen or pencil, or expressed by using any other tangible form of writing. A negotiable instrument written in pencil is, however, an invitation for forgery. The person who drew the instrument would be responsible for any loss caused by the negligent drawing of the instrument.

A Global Perspective: Laws Around the World

U.S. Companies Operating in Other Countries

Many U.S. companies operate facilities in other countries. Like individual citizens, the activities of U.S. companies are regulated by the laws of the host country. Foreign governments require companies to comply with local rules and regulations and may prohibit companies from participating in specific activities, such as providing utilities and entering into defense contracts, which are reserved for domestic companies. Laws governing contracts, employment practices, property rights, and environmental liability may be more or less favorable to a company than corresponding laws in the United States. Although operating in a foreign country, U.S. companies are still subject to many U.S. laws, including the Foreign Corrupt Practices Act (FCPA), which prohibits U.S. companies and their employees from bribing foreign officials.

The creation and form of a business entity (*e.g.*, corporation, partnership, etc.) must conform to the laws of the country in which the business operates. The advantages and disadvantages of any particular form of business depend upon the laws of the host country. Many resources are available to assist companies that wish to do business in particular foreign countries. You can find out more about international business by conducting research on the topic in your library or by using the Internet.

Companies that do business in other countries may risk *expropriation*, which occurs when a host country nationalizes an industry or seizes a company's assets without just compensation. To reduce the losses suffered by expropriation, U.S. companies may purchase insurance for certain types of activities through the Overseas Private Investment Corporation (OPIC)

Critical Thinking Question Many countries protect native businesses by imposing strict laws on foreign companies doing business within their borders. Do you think this kind of protection is fair? For more information on U.S. companies operating in other countries, visit **ubpl.glencoe.com**.

Signature of Maker or Drawer

The maker must sign a note, and the drawer must sign a draft. A signature may be any mark, such as one's initials, that is placed on the instrument with the intention of serving as a signature. Of course, the signature on a check should match the signature card on file with the bank. The signature may appear in the body of the instrument as well as at the end.

Unconditional Promise or Order

The promise in the note, or the order in the draft, must be unconditional. If either is qualified in any way, the instrument is not negotiable.

Example 2. Jasmine's uncle gave her a promissory note for $3,000. The note was complete and regular in every way, except that it bore the statement, "Payable only on Jasmine Sullivan's graduation from high school."

This note is a valid promise to pay. When Jasmine graduates from high school, her uncle will owe her $3,000. The note, however, is not negotiable because it is conditional on its face. Statements requiring that certain things be done or that specific events take place make the instrument a simple contract rather than a negotiable instrument.

Fixed Sum of Money

A negotiable instrument must be payable in a fixed sum of money. Usually it can be payable in any money that has a known or established value. An instrument payable in a foreign currency or any medium of exchange accepted by a foreign government is negotiable.

Payable on Demand or at a Definite Time

Negotiable instruments must be payable on demand or at a definite time. This requirement makes it possible to determine when the debtor or promisor can be compelled to pay.

Community Works

Rubber Checks
Managing a checking account can be done in two easy steps. The first step is to balance your checkbook regularly to minimize the risk of bouncing a check. Most banks and retailers charge a fee for bounced checks. The fee is usually taken from your account when funds are available. The second step is to resist the temptation to spend more money than you have in your account. *What do you think is a fair fee for bouncing a check?*

Get Involved
Read the returned check policy displays of the stores you shop in. Call different banks in your area and ask them how much they charge their customers for bounced checks.

CONDITIONAL PROMISE
A promissory note with a condition (such as graduating from high school) is not negotiable. *Is this true even when the condition is met?*

Virtual Law

Electronic Checks

A group of banks have signed up with TeleCheck Services, a check acceptance company, to use an electronic payment service. The service is called Electronic Check Acceptance. It converts paper checks presented at retail stores into electronic transactions. The system delivers funds directly into the merchant's account. It also eliminates having to chase down bad checks. Consumers sign a receipt for the electronic transaction. They then receive the cancelled check along with a copy of the receipt. Electronic check returns become TeleCheck's responsibility. (Source: *TechFocus*, December 1, 2000, Issue #3712, p. 26)

Connect Visit the Web site of one or more of your area banks. See if they offer similar electronic check acceptance services.

Demand Paper An instrument is payable on demand when it so states, or when it is payable "on sight" or "on presentation." These instruments are called **demand paper**. The key feature of demand instruments is that the holder can require payment at any time by making the demand upon the person obligated to pay.

Definite-Time Paper Instruments meet the definite-time requirement when they are payable on or before a stated date. Instruments payable "one year after date" and "thirty days after sight" also meet the requirement. These instruments are called **definite-time paper**.

In contrast, an instrument payable only upon an act or event, the time of whose occurrence is uncertain, is not payable at a definite time. For instance, an instrument payable when a person marries or reaches a certain age would not be negotiable.

> *Example 3.* If Jasmine's uncle had given him a note that said "payable 30 days after my death," the note would not be negotiable because it is not payable at a definite time. No one can be certain when Jasmine's uncle will die.

Payable to Order or Bearer

Negotiable instruments, except for checks, must be payable to order or to bearer. The words *to the order of* and *to bearer* are called the **words of negotiability**. The maker or drawer may stipulate "Pay to the order of Jane Doe," "Pay to Jane Doe or order," or "Pay to Jane Doe or her assigns." If such words are omitted in instruments other than checks, the instruments are not negotiable.

> *Example 4.* Suppose that the note given to Jasmine in Example 3 read, "I promise to pay Jasmine three hundred dollars." The implication is that the uncle would pay Jasmine but no one else. Thus the instrument would not be negotiable.

In the case of a draft, the drawee must be indicated with reasonable certainty. If an instrument named the drawee as "Global Bank, New York," and there were several Global Banks in New York, the draft would be nonnegotiable.

Dates and Controlling Words

The omission of the date does not affect the negotiability of an instrument. When the date is omitted, the date on which the instrument is received is considered to be the date of issue.

Handwritten terms control typed and printed terms, and typed terms control printed terms. Words control figures, except when the words are unclear.

> *Example 5.* Kayleen received a check from Roni. The check was made out for "Seventy-seven Dollars" in words and $87 in figures. The bank would most likely honor the check for the amount that was written in words.

It's a Question of Ethics

Negotiating with IOUs

D'Marco borrowed $20 from you on Friday and gave you a written IOU. On Monday, you need your $20 back, but D'Marco can't repay you until this weekend. *Would it be ethical to offer the IOU to Jermaine to borrow $20 from him? What would you do if D'Marco refused to pay the $20 to Jermaine?*

Section 23.2 Assessment

Reviewing What You Learned
1. Explain the elements of negotiable instruments.
2. Explain why it is important to have a date on a negotiable instrument.
3. When do words control figures, and what is the exception?

Critical Thinking Activity
Negotiable Instruments Why do you think a person who writes a negotiable instrument in pencil would be responsible for any loss caused by negligence? Explain your answer.

Legal Skills in Action
Requirements of Negotiability You are a clerk for a negotiable instrument attorney. It is important that you remember the six requirements of negotiability. In groups of four or five, write a skit, rap song, poem, or silly story that will help you remember the requirements. Present your creative work to the entire class.

Chapter Summary

Section 23.1 Purpose and Types of Negotiable Instruments

- Popular negotiable instruments include checks, notes, and drafts. Negotiable instruments were developed because people wanted to transact business without carrying around large sums of money and to purchase items that they could pay for at a later date. The use of checks, notes, drafts, electronic banking, and credit cards has increased dramatically in recent years. More people are opening checking accounts and signing drafts and promissory notes than ever before. These instruments are used conveniently and safely as a substitute for money and to obtain credit.

- A negotiable instrument is a written document giving special legal rights to the transferee that may be transferred by endorsement or delivery. There are two basic kinds of negotiable instruments: notes and drafts. When two persons sign a note, they are known as comakers. Creditors who loan money or extend credit ask debtors to sign notes as evidence of debt. An advantage of using a note is that it can be negotiated (transferred) to other people without much difficulty. There are various types of notes. A demand note is a note that is payable when the payee demands payment. In contrast, a time note is a note that is payable at a future date, which is written on the face of the note. An installment note is a note that is paid in a series of payments. People often sign installment notes whey they borrow money to purchase a car or house. A certificate of deposit is a note provided by a bank. A CD is a bank's written receipt of money and its promise to pay the money back, usually with interest, on the due date. Most CDs are written for a specific period of time, such as six months, one year, two years, or five years. Banks pay higher interest for longer-term CDs. Sometime people who hold certificates of deposit can obtain money by negotiating them to other people or by pledging them as security for a loan. A check is a draft drawn on a bank and payable on demand. Checks are the most common type of draft in use today. When you write a check, you order the bank to pay the money in your checking account to others.

- A note is a written promise by one person, called the maker, to pay money to another person, called the payee. A draft is an order to pay money. A draft is an instrument in which one party (the drawer) orders another party (the drawee) to pay money to a third party (the payee). A sight draft is a draft that is payable as soon as it is presented to the drawee for payment. A time draft is a draft that is not payable until the lapse of the particular time period stated on the draft. Businesses and private parties frequently use drafts to transfer debts from one party to another.

Section 23.2 Requirements of Negotiability

- To be negotiable, an instrument must be in writing, must be signed by the maker or drawer, and must contain an unconditional promise or order to pay. In addition, the instrument must be made out for a fixed amount of money, payable on demand or at a definite time, and be payable to order or to bearer.

- The omission of the date does not affect the negotiability of an instrument, but the omission allows the presumption that the date on which the instrument is received is the date of issue.

- Handwritten terms control typed or printed terms, and words control figures. Handwritten terms control typed and printed terms because the court assumes that they represent the final intent of the parties to the contract. Words control figures because it is much harder to make a mistake when writing in words the amount of the negotiable instrument.

Using Legal Language

Consider the key terms in the list below. Then use these terms to complete the following exercises.

negotiable instrument	drawer
note	drawee
maker	acceptor
payee	sight draft
check	time draft
certificate of deposit (CD)	words of negotiability

1. With a partner, create a script in which you discuss negotiability with a banker. Use all of the terms listed above in your role-play.
2. Act out the scenario.
3. Perform your skit in front of the class.
4. Have your classmates critique your performance.
5. Read your classmates' comments and reflect on how you could improve your performance.

Understanding Business and Personal Law Online

Self-Check Quiz Visit the *Understanding Business and Personal Law* Web site at **ubpl.glencoe.com** and click on Chapter 23: Negotiable Instruments— Self-Check Quizzes to prepare for the chapter exam.

The Law Review

Answer the following questions. Refer to the text for additional reinforcement.

6. What is a certificate of deposit?
7. What is an acceptor?
8. Explain the elements of negotiable instruments.
9. Explain the definite-time contract.
10. What are the words of negotiability?
11. Why do some people feel that it is safer to use negotiable instruments than cash?
12. Why do CDs pay higher interest than regular savings accounts?
13. What does it mean to postdate a check?
14. Why do businesses and private parties opt to use drafts?
15. How would a drawee indicate that he or she agrees to the draft?
16. Why is it a bad idea to write a written instrument in pencil?
17. Where should a signature appear on an instrument?

Linking School to Work

Interpreting and Communicating Information

18. Rewrite the following passage from a certificate of deposit in words that a young teen can understand. Test it on several students in your school.

> "Except as otherwise provided herein, in the event of any withdrawal of principal from this account prior to a maturity date, the account holder shall forfeit an amount equal to the lesser of all of the interest earned for the term or renewal term or one half the term in months of interest whether earned or not, on the amount withdrawn at the nominal (simple) interest rate being paid on the account, regardless of the length of time the funds withdrawn have remained in the account."

Let's Debate

Negotiable Check

Carlos works at a local video store called Video Fun. Yesterday, he accepted a check for $22.34 payable to Video Fun. The customer had purchased a new movie release. After the customer left, Carlos took a second look at the check. The check was postdated; there was an "x" instead of a signature; and the figures and the words for the amount of the check did not match. To top it off, the check was written in pencil.

Debate

19. Is the check negotiable? Why or why not?
20. Debate whether each flaw causes non-negotiability in and of itself.
21. If you were Carlos, what would you do now? Explain your answer.

Grasping Case Issues

For the following cases, give your decision and state a legal principle that applies.

22. Percy owns the Country Collectibles Shop, which specializes in buying and selling rare coins, stamps, comic books, gold and silver bars, and other collectors' items. In exchange for a loan of $10,000, Percy gives Kimberly a signed promissory note that reads, "In 60 days, I promise to pay to the order of Kimberly Tate $10,000 worth of silver bars." Is the note negotiable? Why or why not?

23. John writes a check to Donna for $75 and, by mistake, omits the date. As a result of John's error, Donna's friend Linda claims that the check is not negotiable. Is Linda correct? Explain your answer.

24. Cynthia gave Glen a signed note that read, "On May 20, 2004, I promise to pay Glen Fife one hundred dollars." Is this a negotiable instrument? Why or why not?

25. After agreeing to the terms of their contract, Judd gave Henry a signed note that read, "I promise to pay to the order of Henry Lloyd two hundred dollars when he completes the painting of my house." Is this a negotiable instrument? Why or why not?

26. Pierre gave his attorney a promissory note in exchange for legal services. The note read, "I promise to pay to the order of Charles E. Jones, in or within 60 days, the sum of five hundred French francs." Is the instrument negotiable? Why or why not?

In each case that follows, you be the judge.

27. Borrowed Money

In a suit against Dominic Loweth, Philip Fazio introduced into evidence the following written instrument, dated November 15: "This is to certify that I borrowed $15,000 from Philip N. Fazio on this day, to be returned within 10 days." This was followed by what appeared to be the signature of Loweth. Fazio claimed that the instrument was negotiable. *Do you agree? Why or why not?*

Fazio v. Loweth, 490 N.Y.S.2d 859 (NY).

28. Promise to Pay

Sandra McGuire signed the following note as part of a business transaction: "For value received, Thomas J. McGuire and Sandra A. McGuire, husband and wife, do promise to pay to the order of Pascal L. Tursi and Rebecca L. Tursi of 110 Curtis Lane, Moorestown, NJ, and of The Green Mountain Inn, Stowe, VT, the sum of sixty-five thousand dollars ($65,000)." *Is the note a negotiable instrument? Why or why not?*

P.P. Inc. v. McGuire, 509 F.Supp. 1079 (NJ).

Legal Link

Bert has heard of banking online, but he doesn't really understand how it works. How is money deposited? Can you write checks electronically? Is it safe? Bert has asked you to help him find more information.

Connect

Using a variety of search engines:

29. Research online banking.
30. Find out what services are offered online.
31. Explain how to apply for a checking account.
32. Discuss privacy issues that surround banking online.
33. Find out how digital signatures are used.

POWER READING STRATEGIES

34. **Predict** How do you think Americans would transact business if there were no negotiable instruments?

35. **Connect** Why might CDs be a good investment for someone saving to go to college?

36. **Question** Why do you think it is important that the maker sign a negotiable note?

37. **Respond** Scott's uncle signed a promissory note in the top left corner of the document. Is the note still negotiable? Why or why not?

Writing Checks

Understanding Business and Personal Law *Online*

Chapter Overview Visit the *Understanding Business and Personal Law* Web site at ubpl.glencoe.com and click on Chapter 24: Writing Checks—Chapter Overviews to preview the chapter information.

The Opening Scene

David and Melanie Mueller are relaxing in their apartment when they hear an unexpected knock on the door.

Lucky Day?

Melanie: *(Opening the door.)* Julio! How are you?

Julio: Hi, Melanie! Today's your lucky day!

David: *(Walking into the room from the kitchen.)* Julio! It's good to see you.

Julio: *(Entering.)* I have what you've been waiting for. Here's a check for the amount I borrowed from you, plus interest.

Melanie: *(Taking the check.)* Great, we can sure use it! I'll put this in a safe place. *(She opens the desk drawer and lifts up some papers.)* David! Look what I found! It's the check from Aunt Mae we lost. It was under these papers all this time. What a lucky break!

David: Am I glad to hear that! That check must be about seven months old. I thought for sure it had been stolen.

Julio: I told you this was your lucky day!

David: Will you have time to go to the bank tomorrow, Melanie?

Melanie: Yes. I'll deposit both checks.

David: While you're at it, you can cash the paycheck I got today. I'll indorse it right now.

Julio: Well, I have to go. I'm meeting a friend for dinner.

David and Melanie: Thanks, Julio!

Julio: No problem. See you later.

Melanie: I'll write a check for the last payment to the furniture company. It'll be good to have that taken care of. We only owe $125.

(The next evening, David and Melanie discuss their finances after dinner.)

David: Did you cash my paycheck today?

Melanie: The bank said I'd have to wait a few days for it to clear, so I just deposited it.

David: We should sue that bank! I think they have to cash it.

Melanie: They wouldn't take Aunt Mae's check, either. They called it a stale check. I was pretty disappointed.

(Two weeks later, Melanie is trying to reconcile the bank statement.)

Melanie: There's something wrong somewhere! This thing won't balance.

David: What a month! First the bank wouldn't cash my paycheck; then Julio's check bounced. What else could go wrong?

Melanie: *(Looking through the cancelled checks.)* This is funny, David. According to the check stub, that check you wrote to the furniture company was for $125.

David: That's right.

Melanie: But look at the cancelled check. It's written for $425!

David: *(Looking at the check.)* You're right! Somebody changed it. The furniture company must have raised the amount on the check I wrote!

What Are the Legal Issues?

1. Can you sue a bank for not cashing your paycheck?
2. Must a bank honor a check that is seven months old?
3. What are the possible legal consequences of writing a bad check?
4. When a bank pays an altered check, who suffers the loss?

Checking Accounts

What You'll Learn

- How to describe the process of opening a checking account and some of the depositor's rights
- How to explain the proper way to write a check and discuss problems associated with checking accounts
- How to summarize the procedure for balancing a checkbook

Why It's Important

Knowing about checking accounts and writing checks will help you use your money wisely.

Legal Terms

- stale check
- outstanding checks
- bad check
- forgery
- uttering

Using a Checking Account

The check is the most common kind of negotiable instrument in use today. Checks are a safe method for sending funds through the mail, and they provide convenient receipts for the people who write them.

Opening a Checking Account

You open a checking account by depositing money in a bank and signing a signature card. The bank agrees to pay money out, up to the amount you have deposited when you write a check.

If your bank refused to cash your check when sufficient funds were on deposit, this would be a breach of the bank's contract. You could bring a claim against the bank for any damages suffered as a result. Only the depositor has the right to bring a claim against the bank for failing to pay a check. The bank's agreement to cash checks is with the depositor only. An exception to this rule occurs with certified checks, which are discussed later in this chapter.

A bank may refuse to pay a check that is more than six months old without incurring liability. Such a check is known as a **stale check**. A bank also has the right to refuse to pay a check if it is submitted 10 days after the death of the drawer. The bank is not liable, however, for paying a check of a deceased person if it does not have notice of the drawer's death or incompetence.

PAYING BILLS
Many people pay monthly bills by check. Others prefer that automatic payments be made electronically by their banks. *Which method would you choose? Why?*

Balancing Your Checkbook

You should balance, or reconcile, your bank statement as soon as possible after receiving it. Carefully compare the check register balance with the bank statement balance to make sure that they agree (see Figure 24.1). Don't forget to take into consideration **outstanding checks**, or checks you have written that have not yet been returned to the bank for

Figure 24.1

Bank Account Reconciliation Using a Form

American National Bank
WESTOVER, OREGON

Kenneth Buckley
7828 Carl Drive
Westover, OR 98123

Account Number: 303079
Statement Date: 7/15/--

FDIC

Balance Last Statement	Deposits & Other Credits		Checks & Other Debits		Balance This Statement
	No.	Amount	No.	Amount	
00.00	2	700.00	5	482.00	218.00

Description	Checks & Other Debits	Deposits & Other Credits	Date	Balance
Balance Forward				00.00
Deposit		500.00	7/01	500.00
Check 101	273.00		7/04	227.00
Check 102	27.00		7/07	200.00
Check 103	50.00		7/08	150.00
Deposit		200.00	7/10	350.00
Check 104	100.00		7/14	250.00
Check 105	32.00		7/14	218.00

PLEASE EXAMINE YOUR STATEMENT AT ONCE. IF NO ERROR IS REPORTED IN 10 DAYS, THE ACCOUNT WILL BE CONSIDERED CORRECT AND VOUCHERS GENUINE. ALL ITEMS ARE CREDITED SUBJECT TO FINAL PAYMENT.

BANK RECONCILIATION FORM

PLEASE EXAMINE YOUR STATEMENT AT ONCE. ANY DISCREPANCY SHOULD BE REPORTED TO THE BANK IMMEDIATELY.

1. Record any transaction appearing on this statement but not listed in your checkbook.

2. List any checks still outstanding in the space provided to the right.

3. Enter the balance shown on this statement here. → 218 00

4. Enter deposits recorded in your checkbook but not shown on this statement here. → — —

5. Total lines 1 and 2 and enter here. → 218 00

6. Enter total checks outstanding here. → 69 00

7. Subtract line 4 from line 3. This adjusted bank balance should agree with your checkbook balance. → 149 00

CHECKS OUTSTANDING		
Number	Amount	
106	25	00
107	14	00
108	30	00
TOTAL	69	00

BANK RECONCILIATION
The adjusted bank balance should agree with your checkbook register. *Why should you reconcile your checking account with each new statement?*

PERSONAL CHECK
Never write a check in
pencil, and always write
legibly. *Why do you have
to write the amount both
in words and in numerals?*

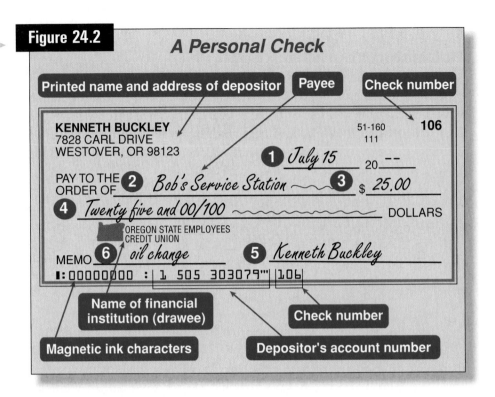

Figure 24.2

A Personal Check

Printed name and address of depositor — Payee — Check number

KENNETH BUCKLEY
7828 CARL DRIVE
WESTOVER, OR 98123

51-160
111   **106**

1 *July 15*   20 --

PAY TO THE ORDER OF **2** *Bob's Service Station* ~~~ **3** $ *25.00*

4 *Twenty five and 00/100* ~~~~~~~~ DOLLARS

OREGON STATE EMPLOYEES
CREDIT UNION

MEMO **6** *oil change*   **5** *Kenneth Buckley*

⑆00000000⑈ 1 505 303079''' 106

Name of financial institution (drawee)   Check number

Magnetic ink characters   Depositor's account number

payment. The bank statement shows only checks that have already been paid from the account.

Writing Checks

Banks provide regular and special printed check forms. These checks display a series of numbers printed in magnetic ink that make it possible for computers to process the checks quickly and accurately (see Figure 24.2).

Parties to a Check   A check is a draft drawn on a bank and payable on demand. The person who writes the check is called the drawer. The bank that is ordered to pay the money is called the drawee. The person to whom the check is made payable is called the payee. As you can see, the parties to a check are the same as the parties to a draft, except that the drawee is always a bank.

Avoiding Negligence   You should take care to write checks that cannot be changed easily or signed by a forger. You are responsible for altered or forged checks only if your negligence contributed to the alteration or forgery. It would be negligent to write a check in a way that would make it easy for a forger to change the amount.

When writing a check, print the figures very close to the dollar sign and keep all of the figures close together. Always start at the extreme left when writing amounts of money in words, and draw a line through any

Figure 24.3

Check Register

NUMBER	DATE	DESCRIPTION OF TRANSACTION	PAYMENT/DEBIT (-)	FEE (IF ANY) (-)	DEPOSIT/CREDIT (+)	BALANCE $	
106	7/15	Bob's Service Station	$ 25 00	$	$	-25	00
		oil change				193	00
107	7/15	Cutler Enterprises	14 00			-14	00
		magazine subscription				179	00
108	7/16	Motor Vehicles Dept.	30 00			-30	00
		driver's license				149	00

KEEPING TRACK
This sample check register shows how to keep track of checks as you write them. *What else would you record in your check register?*

extra space that remains after you've written the amount. This prevents someone from adding words and figures that alter the value of the check. Be sure that the figures are the same as the written amount. If there is a difference between the figures and the words on a check, the bank will honor the written amount. Write the name of the payee close to the words "Pay to the order of," and fill in all unused space with a line. Make a note of the reason for the check.

Sign your name so that it looks as much as possible like the one on the bank signature card. Never sign a blank check, and never cross out or change a check once it has been written. If you make a mistake when writing a check, write a new check and print *VOID* across the incorrect one. Don't forget to write the word *VOID* in the check register, too, to keep your

NEGLIGENCE?
Writing a check with a pencil makes alteration of the check by a dishonest person much easier. *When are you responsible if someone else alters a check you wrote?*

records accurate. Fill out the check register before you write the check so you won't forget to do it later.

Bad Checks A **bad check** is a check drawn on an account in which you have insufficient funds. Writing a check on an account with insufficient funds is larceny or attempted larceny, unless it is accidental.

> *Example 1.* The Lotus Loan Company received Renee Cronyn's check for $125, due on an installment note. After it was deposited, the check was returned to Lotus with the notation "Insufficient Funds." The financial institution sent Renee a certified letter notifying her of the bad check. If she fails to make the check good, a criminal complaint can be filed against her.

Bad-check laws are used as an effective means of debt collection. When notified that they are subject to prosecution, most people make every effort to pay the creditor the amount of the check. Banks and stores generally charge a penalty fee for bad checks.

LAWS in Your Life

Flee Fees

Checking accounts incur fees, and these days banks may charge a fee for almost any service related to your account. Almost all banks charge for such things as printing checks, stopping payment, and bounced checks, but many banks have gone even further in recent years. Many banks now charge a fee for using an ATM, using a teller, keeping a low balance, and receiving cancelled checks. These fees are legal and within the bounds of regulatory practice.

If you want to avoid paying excessive fees for having a checking account, you might want to shop around for a bank that charges less for its services. Start by examining your banking habits and needs. In doing so, you might want to answer the following questions. Do you often use the ATM? Do you have trouble maintaining a minimum balance? Do you write many checks each month? Do you like to receive your cancelled checks with your monthly statement? Do you transact business at the bank often?

Make a List Make a list of your banking habits as suggested above. Ask your bank for a list of fees related to its banking services.

Many banks offer overdraft protection service as a safeguard against any mistakes that you might make in balancing your checkbook. If you have overdraft service, the bank will honor small overdrafts, saving you the inconvenience and embarrassment of having a check bounce.

Forged Checks   **Forgery** is the false making or material alteration of a writing where the writing has the apparent ability to defraud and is of apparent legal efficacy with the intent to defraud. A forged check is a check that is signed by someone other than the drawer without the drawer's authority. Forgery is a crime, subject to a fine and imprisonment. If a bank pays a forged check and the drawer was not negligent, the bank must bear the loss. It is the bank's duty to know the signatures of its depositors. The bank must also bear the loss of the amount added if a check is changed from its original amount to a higher amount. A check that is altered in this manner is a raised check.

Example 2. Lance Yerkes wrote out a $400 check, in a proper manner, to Robin Anderson. Before taking the check to the bank, however, Robin raised the amount to $4,000. If Lance's bank pays the full $4,000 to Robin, it can deduct only $400 from Lance's account when the fraudulent alteration is discovered. The bank must either get the money back from Robin or suffer the loss.

You are guilty of a crime if you knowingly offer a forged check, even if you did not personally commit the act of forgery. When an offeror deliberately submits a forged instrument to another, the resulting crime is called **uttering** .

If one of your checks is forged, you must notify your bank within a reasonable time. Failure to give timely notice relieves the bank of liability. Although you are granted a "reasonable" amount of time to notify your bank of one forged check, you must notify the bank within 14 days after receiving your statement if you discover multiple forged checks.

Stopping Payment of a Check   You may order your bank to stop payment on a check that has not yet been paid by the bank. If the bank pays the check anyway, it is liable for any loss you suffer as a result. An oral stop-payment order is binding on the bank for 14 calendar days, unless the order is confirmed in writing within that period. A written order is effective for six months, unless it is renewed in writing. If you stop payment on a check given in payment of an amount actually owed, you still owe the amount of the debt. Also, in many situations you cannot avoid liability on a check by stopping payment on it if it has been transferred to a holder in due course. A holder in due course is one who takes the instrument for value, in good faith, and without notice that anything is wrong with it.

Section 24.1   Assessment

Reviewing What You Learned
1. How is a checking account opened?
2. Describe the proper way to write a check.
3. Summarize the process of balancing your checkbook.

Critical Thinking Activity
Banking Fees Why do you think banks charge a fee to process an order to stop payment?

Legal Skills in Action
Calculating Costs You deposit a $100 check from your friend Ted into your checking account and then write a $46.18 check to pay for groceries. Four days later, you receive a notice from the bank that Ted's check was bad and your account was debited $25 for the unpaid deposit. Because the funds from your deposit did not become available, your check was returned to the grocer unpaid. Your account is debited another $25 for the unpaid check. The next day you receive notice from your grocer that you must pay a fee of $25 for the returned check and replace it with a bank check or money order. You pay 75 cents for the money order. Calculate how much you really spent to purchase the $46.18 worth of groceries.

Other Payment Methods

Other Types of Checks

Writing a check is a convenient way to make a payment. However, personal checks are sometimes unavailable or unacceptable. Other kinds of checks have been developed for use in these situations.

Certified Checks

A **certified check** is a check that is guaranteed by the bank (see Figure 24.4). At the request of either the depositor or the holder, the bank guarantees that sufficient funds have been withheld from the drawer's account to pay the amount of the check. A prudent person requests a certified check when involved in a business transaction with a stranger.

The drawer may present a check to a bank for certification before it is put in circulation, or the holder may present the check for certification after it comes into the holder's possession. The bank stamps "certified" on the face of the check and withdraws the money from the drawer's account. If the drawer had the check certified, the drawer and all indorsers remain liable. If, on the other hand, the holder had the check certified, the drawer and all indorsers are discharged because the holder

What You'll Learn

- How to describe five types of checks other than personal checks
- How to explain the federal law regarding availability of funds
- How to describe electronic fund transfers and the rules regulating such transfers

Why It's Important

Understanding and using different checking devices and electronic fund transfers will put you on the cutting edge of modern financial activity.

Legal Terms

- certified check
- cashier's check
- bank draft
- money order
- traveler's check
- electronic fund transfer (EFT)
- debit card

Figure 24.4

CERTIFIED CHECK
A certified check is the same as an accepted draft. *Why would a prudent person request a certified check when doing business with a stranger?*

Careers in Law

Canine Enforcement Officer

Christine Oxendine works in a job where partners can make a big difference. Oxendine describes her partner as a hairy, driven workaholic who scratches a lot and sometimes slobbers. Meet Draden, U.S. Customs Service canine extraordinaire.

Six years ago, Oxendine devoted 16 weeks to training Draden, a black lab mix, to help her find illegal drugs that are brought into Texas. The two partners still train every day and average about three illegal drug seizures each month.

"I really enjoy working with animals," says Oxendine, who served in the Air Force prior to joining Customs. "Every day, even if we don't go out and unearth illegal activity, I'm rewarded just by training Draden and seeing that he's rewarded, too. Besides, he's a partner that doesn't talk back!"

Oxendine trains Draden with a rolled up towel that smells like a narcotic. "His natural instinct is to retrieve," she says, "so I throw the towel or hide it, and then we play tug-of-war after he finds it. On command, Draden looks for the towel that is saturated with a pseudo-narcotic. In a real-life situation, he'll be looking for that smell, which ends up being the illegal narcotic."

Skills	(HUMAN) Communication (with dogs and people), computer, physical fitness. Bilingual agents receive higher pay. (DOG) Able to retrieve and communicate a discovery by scratching and biting appropriate objects.
Personality	(HUMAN) Self-motivated, patient, focused, honest, able to work under various levels of stress. (DOG) Very determined, intelligent, and easy to train; wants to find and retrieve things.
Training	(HUMAN) Must complete a regular tour of military duty or have 60 hours of college with a grade point average of 3.5 or better. Must also complete 16 weeks of training at the U.S. Customs Canine Enforcement Academy. (DOG) 16 weeks of training at the same academy. Most dogs in the program have been rescued from the pound.

For more information on canine enforcement officers, visit **ubpl.glencoe.com** or your public library.

could have cashed the check instead of having it certified. Unless otherwise agreed, a bank is not obligated to certify a check. (Because we are discussing the law of negotiable instruments, we will use the term indorse. In other applications, the term endorse is more commonly used.)

Cashier's Checks

A **cashier's check** is a check drawn by a bank upon itself. It is similar to a certified check. However, the bank issues a cashier's check, and payment on it cannot be stopped. Either the bank transfers the amount of the check from the depositor's account to its own, or the depositor writes a check to the bank for that amount. With the money in its control, the bank then issues a check for the amount. No matter where a cashier's check is sent by the bank or by a customer who purchases it from a bank, it must be returned to that bank for final payment. People who will not accept personal checks will often accept cashier's checks.

Bank Drafts

A **bank draft**, sometimes called a teller's check or treasurer's check, is a check drawn by a bank against funds the bank has on deposit with another bank. People will often take a bank draft when they will not take someone's personal check because they have faith that a bank will honor its own check.

Money Orders

A **money order** is a type of draft that substitutes for a check and may be purchased for a fee from banks, post offices, stores, travel offices, and automobile clubs. Instead of being drawn on an individual's account, a money order is drawn on the funds of the organization that issues it.

When purchasing a money order, you fill in your name and address and the name of the payee on the instrument and then receive a receipt for the money order. If the money order is lost and you have the receipt, it will be replaced if it has not already been cashed. Postal Money Orders can be purchased for amounts up to $1,000.

U.S. International Postal Money Orders are often used to send money to foreign countries. Telegraphic money orders can be used to send money quickly. Under the UCC, a bank money order is a check, even though it is described on its face as a money order. Money orders are not as freely negotiable as other instruments because they may be transferred only once.

Traveler's Checks

A **traveler's check** is similar to a cashier's check in that the issuing financial institution is both the drawer and the drawee. As with money orders, the buyers pay the full amount of the checks, plus a service fee. You are required to sign traveler's checks in the presence of the issuer when they are purchased. To cash a check, you write the name of the payee in the space provided and countersign it in the payee's presence. Only the purchaser can negotiate traveler's checks, and the issuing bank easily replaces them if they are stolen.

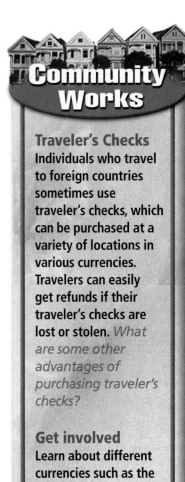

Community Works

Traveler's Checks
Individuals who travel to foreign countries sometimes use traveler's checks, which can be purchased at a variety of locations in various currencies. Travelers can easily get refunds if their traveler's checks are lost or stolen. *What are some other advantages of purchasing traveler's checks?*

Get involved
Learn about different currencies such as the pound, yen, and the Euro. Investigate possible careers that involve international travel.

Availability of Funds

In the past, banks were not uniform in the amount of time they required before they would make funds available on checks deposited in customers' accounts. Some banks held funds longer than others, and many banks did not disclose their holding policy to their customers.

Example 3. Yvette Espinal received a check in the mail from her father, who lived in a distant city. She deposited it in her checking account and was told that she would not be able to draw a check on the funds for 10 days. Yvette's friend inquired at her bank about its holding policy and was told that it would have made the funds available in five days.

To address this issue, Congress passed the Competitive Banking Act. Under the Act, the Federal Reserve Board of Governors issued Regulation CC.

Regulation CC requires banks to make funds available to depositors according to a prescribed schedule (see Figure 24.5). Exceptions are made for new accounts, accounts that are repeatedly overdrawn, and deposits of a suspicious nature. In addition, some state laws require even shorter time periods for banks to make funds available.

Regulation CC also requires banks to disclose in advance their policy for making funds available to depositors. Such disclosures must be made when the account is opened as well as on conspicuous notices at teller stations in the bank.

Electronic Banking

A popular method of banking, called an **electronic fund transfer (EFT)**, uses computers and electronic technology as a substitute for checks and other paper forms of banking. You can go to an automatic

CHECK-HOLDING LIMITS
Banks must make funds available to depositors according to a prescribed schedule. *How long can a bank hold someone's government check before paying it?*

Figure 24.5	Maximum Check-Holding Limits Under Federal Law*
Type of Check	**Holding Limit**
Local	2 business days
Nonlocal	5 business days
Cashier's check	1 business day
Certified check	1 business day
Government check	1 business day
New accounts	Individual bank policy applies
Deposits made at automatic teller machines	5 business days
*Some state banks have shorter holding periods.	

ATM CARD PROTECTION

Consumers are protected against lost or stolen ATM cards provided they notify their bank of the loss or theft within certain time limits. *What is your liability for the unauthorized use of your ATM card when you notify the bank two business days after its theft? three days afterward?*

teller machine (ATM) 24 hours a day to make bank deposits and withdrawals.

A **debit card** (also called a check card or cash card) is used to electronically subtract money from your bank account to pay for goods or services. You insert your debit card into the ATM and enter your secret personal identification number (PIN) to withdraw cash, make deposits, or transfer funds between accounts. You can also use your debit card to buy goods at many retail stores. See Figure 24.6 for tips on managing your EFT card wisely.

Figure 24.6

MANAGE YOUR EFT CARD WISELY

You can incur serious losses if your EFT (debit card) is lost, stolen, or used without authority. If you decide to use EFT, keep these tips in mind.

1 Take Care of Your Card

Know where your EFT (debit) card is at all times; if you lose it, report it as soon as possible.

2 Choosing a PIN

Choose a PIN that is different from personal information (such as the names of friends, family, or pets) or private information (such as your social security number or birthdate). Using a different number will make it more difficult for a thief to use your EFT card.

3 Keep Receipts

Keep and compare your EFT receipts with your periodic statements so that you can find errors or unauthorized transfers and report them.

4 Know the Merchant

Make sure you know and trust the merchant before you provide any bank account information to pre-authorize debits to your account.

Under the Electronic Fund Transfer Act, you are entitled to receive a written receipt when you use an ATM. In addition, the transaction must appear on your periodic statement. You have 60 days to notify the bank of any error on the periodic statement or ATM receipt. After being notified, the bank has 10 business days to investigate the error. If the bank needs more time, it may take up to 45 days to complete the investigation, but only if the money in dispute is returned to your account.

A debit card offers you less legal protection than a credit card. Unlike a credit card, a payment cannot be stopped if your purchase is defective or if your order is not delivered. Your liability for the unauthorized use of an ATM card is limited to $50, as long as notice of the loss or theft of a card is given to the issuer within two business days. Your liability increases to $500, however, if notice is delayed beyond that time, and it becomes unlimited when notice is not given within 60 days. The unauthorized use of an ATM card is a criminal offense punishable by a $10,000 fine and/or 10 years in prison.

Electronic Check Processing

Several large banks are now linking their check processing system to ATM networks. When you give your check to a retailer, for example, the retailer will scan it to verify that there is enough money in your account. If so, the money will be deducted instantly from your checking account. The check itself operates like a debit card, and the time it takes to process a check, called the float, disappears.

Legal Briefs

The debit card has increased in popularity over the years. In the past, debit cards were used simply to withdraw money from a bank account, but now with the imprint of charge card logos, they can be used to make purchases at businesses. When a purchase is made, the money is deducted directly from a bank account.

Section 24.2 Assessment

Reviewing What You Learned

1. Describe the five types of checks other than personal checks.
2. How soon must funds be made available to you when you deposit a local check in your bank? a nonlocal check?
3. What is electronic fund transfer? Under the ETF Act, what are you entitled to receive when you use an ATM?

Critical Thinking Activity

Waiting Periods Why do you think banks require a waiting period before making funds from a check deposit available to the depositor?

How do you think the length of the waiting period specified by Regulation CC was decided?

Legal Skills in Action

Calculating Costs Ginger uses the ATM machine three times per week. It is located in her office building and for that reason it is very convenient. For every transaction, she has to pay a fee of $1.75. How much will Ginger spend in a year on ATM fees?

Chapter Summary

Section 24.1 Checking Accounts

- A checking account is opened by depositing money in the bank and by signing a signature card. The bank agrees to pay money out, up to the amount on deposit, when you write a check. If the bank fails to cash your check despite sufficient funds in the account, you can sue the bank for damages. Only the depositor has the right to bring a claim against the bank for failing to pay a check. The bank's agreement to cash checks is with the depositor only. An exception to this rule occurs with a certified check.

- It is important to write checks so that they cannot be altered or signed by a forger. Print the figures close to the dollar sign and keep all of them close together. Always write from the extreme left and draw a line through any extra space that remains to the right after you've written the amount. Write the name of the payee close to the words "Pay to the order of," and fill in all unused space with a line. Make a note of the reason for the check. Your signature should be consistent with the one on the bank signature card. Never sign a blank check, and never cross out or change a check once it has been written; instead, void the entire check. If you deliberately write a check on an account in which you have insufficient funds, you can be held liable for larceny. Banks and stores generally charge a penalty fee for bad checks. Forging checks is a crime, and you can be fined or imprisoned. A forged check is a check that is signed by someone other than the drawer without the drawer's authority. If the bank pays a forged check and the drawer was not negligent, the bank must bear the loss. The bank must also bear the loss of the amount added if a check is changed from its original amount to a higher amount. A check that is altered in this manner is a raised check.

- You should balance your checkbook as soon as possible after receiving it. Compare the check register balance with the bank statement balance to make sure the two balances agree. Take outstanding checks into consideration, because your statement shows only checks that have already been paid from the account. Also save and compare any receipts that you have from debit card transactions to make sure they agree with the entries posted on your statement.

Section 24.2 Other Payment Methods

- Certified checks are guaranteed by the bank on which they are drawn. A cashier's check is drawn by a bank upon itself. A bank draft is drawn by a bank against funds the bank has on deposit with another bank. Personal money orders may be purchased at banks, post offices, stores, travel offices, and automobile clubs, and they are drawn on the funds of the organization that issues them. Traveler's checks are signed by the purchaser when they are bought and then signed again when cashed. If lost or stolen, they can be replaced.

- Federal Regulation CC requires banks to make funds available to depositors according to a specific schedule.

- Electronic fund transfers (EFTs) are made with the use of computers, ATMs, and debit cards. Under the Electronic Fund Transfer Act, you are entitled to receive a written receipt whenever you use an ATM. In addition, the transaction must appear on your periodic statement. Debit cards offer less legal protection than do credit cards. Your liability for the unauthorized use of an ATM card is limited to $50, as long as notice of the loss or theft of a card is given to the issuer within two business days. Your liability increases to $500, however, if notice is delayed beyond that time; the liability becomes unlimited when notice is not given within 60 days.

Using Legal Language

Consider the key terms in the list below. Then use these terms to complete the following exercises.

stale check	traveler's check
bad check	cashier's check
forgery	bank draft
outstanding checks	uttering
certified check	debit card
electronic fund transfer (EFT)	money order

1. With a partner, practice using the key terms listed above by writing a conversation between a bank officer and a customer. Use all of the terms in your conversation.
2. Present your conversation to the class.
3. Have your classmates critique your performance.
4. Read your classmates' comments and reflect on how you could improve your performance.

Understanding Business and Personal Law *Online*

Self-Check Quiz Visit the *Understanding Business and Personal Law* Web site at **ubpl.glencoe.com** and click on Chapter 24: Writing Checks— Self-Check Quizzes to prepare for the chapter exam.

The Law Review

Answer the following questions. Refer to the chapter for additional reinforcement.

5. What happens when a bank refuses to pay a check and sufficient funds are on deposit?
6. Who are the three parties to a check?
7. Why do most banks offer overdraft protection?
8. What is the difference between a certified check and a cashier's check?
9. Which offers you more legal protection—a credit card or a debit card? Explain.
10. Why do many vacationers opt to use traveler's checks instead of cash?
11. Why might a person stop payment on a check?
12. What type of instrument would you most likely use if you needed to send money to a foreign country? Why?
13. What is a stale check?
14. Why is it important to balance your checkbook?
15. Why should you choose an ATM PIN that is different from your street address, birthdate, or social security number?

CHAPTER 24 ASSESSMENT

Linking School to Work

In groups of two or three, contact banks where several different types of automated teller machines are located. Find out what banking transactions can be made at each machine. Compare the results.

16. What transactions can be made at all the machines?
17. What transactions can be made at some of the machines?
18. Are there banking transactions that cannot be made through an ATM?

Let's Debate

Bank Error?
John Kim paid $655 to have his motorcycle repaired. Two days after the repairs were made, the motorcycle broke down again. John immediately called his bank and put an oral stop payment order on the check. He paid a $20 fee for the order. One month later, John found out that the bank honored the $665 check.

Debate
19. Who is liable for the loss?
20. Can John sue the bank?
21. What would you recommend John do now?

Grasping Case Issues

For the following cases, give your decision and state a legal principle that applies.

22. Nancy Watson receives a check from Harvey Balsam for $500. For no good reason, Harvey's bank refuses to pay it. Can Nancy sue Harvey's bank? Does she have a claim against Harvey? Why or why not?
23. Revisit the previous case. Does Harvey have a claim against his bank?
24. Rita Vicente writes a check for $400 payable to Norma Collins. When Norma receives the check, she has it certified by the bank on which it was drawn. She then gives the certified check to the Sawyer Appliance Company in payment for a television. Is Rita liable if the check is not paid? Why or why not?
25. Revisit the previous case. Would your answer be different if Rita, instead of Norma, had the check certified? Why or why not?
26. While attending college in Massachusetts, Mark Unger receives a check from his father, who lives in Wyoming. When Mark deposits the check in his checking account, the teller informs him that he cannot draw on it for 10 days. Is the teller correct? Why or why not?
27. Colby Sewell wrote a check for $47 to Federal Storage Facilities. Sewell wrote the check using a pencil because she was in a hurry and could not find a pen. When Sewell received her cancelled check and bank statement, she noticed that someone had altered her check by raising the amount to $550. Even though the check had clearly been erased and rewritten, Sewell's bank cashed it. Is the bank liable for this mistake? Why or why not?
28. Paul Bianco's wallet, which contained his ATM card, was stolen while he was at a baseball game. At the end of the game, Bianco telephoned his bank to inform it of the theft of his ATM card. In the meantime, the thief had figured out Paul's PIN and had made a withdrawal of $500. Who is liable for the unauthorized use of Bianco's ATM card? Explain your answer.

In each case that follows, you be the judge.

29. Raised Check

Emmett McDonald, representing an estate, wrote a check to himself as follows: "Pay to the order of Emmett E. McDonald; Ten hundred seventy-five dollars; $10,075.00." The bank paid McDonald $10,075, which was stated in figures on the check, and McDonald left town with the money. The estate sued the bank to recover the $9,000 difference between the amount written in words and the amount written in figures. *For which party would you decide? Explain your answer.*

Yates v. Commercial Bank and Trust Co., 432 So.2d 725 (FL).

30. Postdated Check

On September 14, David Siegel delivered to Peter Peters a check for $20,000, which was postdated for the following November 14. Peter immediately deposited the check in his own bank. David's bank overlooked the date and deducted the money from Peter's account early, on September 17. *Does David have a valid reason to bring suit against his bank? Why or why not?*

Siegel v. New England Merchants National Bank, 437 N.E.2d 218 (MA).

Legal Link

Checkbook Software

Haven wants to use a software program to keep track of the checks she writes and the deposits she makes. She's heard that the programs are easy to use, and she is anxious to give one a try.

Connect

Using a variety of search engines, help Haven research two different checkbook programs and compare the following:

31. Available features.
32. Cost of the software.
33. Required hardware to run the program.

Next, help Haven make a decision as to which program she should buy.

POWER READING STRATEGIES

34. **Predict** Why are checks considered to be a safe method for sending funds through the mail?

35. **Connect** Why do you think it is important to balance your checkbook?

36. **Question** Can you think of a situation that might require you to use a cashier's check?

37. **Respond** Do you have a debit card? What do you use it for?

Transferring Negotiable Instruments

Understanding Business and Personal Law *Online*

Chapter Overview Visit the *Understanding Business and Personal Law* Web site at ubpl.glencoe.com and click on Chapter 25: Transferring Negotiable Instruments—Chapter Overviews to preview the chapter information.

The Opening Scene

Melanie shuffles through a stack of letters and flyers as she opens the door of the apartment.

Pay Day!

MELANIE: David, the mail's here! We got a letter from the furniture company, but these others are all ads. Oh wait; here's a letter from Aunt Mae.

DAVID: What do you think the furniture company wants now? I told them I'd call the police if they didn't make good on that check they raised.

MELANIE: *(Opening an envelope.)* Aunt Mae sent us another $500 check. She says she's sorry the bank wouldn't cash the one we lost and then found later.

DAVID: She's so nice! *(He opens another envelope.)* Well, well! This is a letter from the president of the furniture company apologizing for raising our check. They fired the employee who did it, and there's a $300 check here to cover the amount the bank cashed over our check. It's made out to David and Melanie Mueller.

MELANIE: Wow, two checks in one day! *(There is a knock at the door.)* I'll get it. *(Opening the door.)* Julio! Come in.

JULIO: Hi! Hey, I'm sorry about that bounced check. I thought I had enough to cover it.

MELANIE: No problem. It's easy to make that mistake.

DAVID: How are things, Julio?

JULIO: I just sold my car and the buyer, Maria Reynolds, gave me this check. It's the same amount, so will you take it for the one that bounced? *(He hands the check to David.)*

MELANIE: Are you sure this one's good?

DAVID: I think you have to indorse it, Julio. It's made out to you.

JULIO: I'll sign the back. *(He writes his name on the back of the check.)* Well, I have to run.

DAVID: Thanks, Julio. See you later. *(Julio leaves.)*

MELANIE: Isn't this great? One minute we're broke, and the next minute we have three checks.

DAVID: Let's cash one and put the others in the bank.

MELANIE: I'll cash Aunt Mae's check and deposit the other two at the bank tomorrow. Her check is made out to you. Why don't you indorse it over to me?

DAVID: Okay. *(He writes on the back of the check, "Pay to the order of Melanie Mueller [signed] David Mueller.")* I guess we both have to indorse this furniture company check. *(David writes on the back of that check, "Pay to the order of First Bank and Trust Company for deposit only," and they both sign under the writing.)*

(The next evening, Melanie arrives at home with a troubled expression on her face.)

MELANIE: *(Very upset.)* I'm usually so careful when I go shopping! I can't believe I was robbed!

DAVID: It wasn't your fault.

MELANIE: I'm sure my purse was in the shopping basket. I left it for just a second to get some potato chips. When I came back, it was gone!

DAVID: Don't worry. We'll work it out somehow.

What Are the Legal Issues?

1. Who can cash a check that is indorsed simply with the payee's name?
2. Does a special indorsement, such as "Pay to the order of Melanie Mueller," prevent others from cashing a check?
3. Do both David and Melanie have to indorse the check from the furniture company?
4. Can anyone cash a check indorsed "Pay to the order of First Bank and Trust Company for deposit only"?

Transferring Instruments

What You'll Learn

- How to distinguish between an assignment and a negotiation of an instrument
- How to explain how bearer paper is negotiated
- How to explain how order paper is negotiated

Why It's Important

Knowing how to properly negotiate financial instruments is essential when you open a checking account and begin to spend your money.

Legal Terms

- assignment
- negotiation
- holder
- order paper
- indorsement
- bearer paper

Instruments

When an instrument is signed by the maker or drawer and given to another person, it is issued. When the person to whom it is issued gives it to a third party, the instrument is transferred. Instruments can be transferred by assignment or negotiation.

Assignment

An **assignment** is the transfer of your rights under a contract to someone else. Negotiable instruments are assigned when a person whose indorsement is required on an instrument transfers the instrument without indorsing it. An assignment also occurs when an instrument is transferred to another person and does not meet the requirements of negotiability. In such transfers, the transferee has only the rights of an assignee and is subject to all defenses existing against the assignor (see Chapter 12). An assignment of a negotiable instrument may also occur by operation of law, as well as when the holder of the instrument dies or becomes bankrupt.

Negotiation

Negotiation is the transfer of an agreement in such a way that the transferee becomes a holder. When an instrument is properly negotiated, the one who receives it can legally collect payment on it. A **holder**

BANK DEPOSIT
It is usually a negotiation when you deposit in the bank a check that you have received from someone else. *Why is a negotiation better than an assignment?*

Restrictive Indorsements

Delinquent debtors are sometimes desperate enough to try anything to get out of paying their debts. One trick is writing the restrictive endorsement "paid in full" when paying only a fraction of a debt. The debtor thinks that if the creditor deposits the check, the debtor will be off the hook for the balance owed. In most states this simply will not work.

In many states, a debtor must first inform the creditor in writing that he or she intends to send a check for less than the amount owed as payment in full. The creditor will then have a certain amount of time (usually 15–30 days) in which to object. If the creditor fails to object, the debtor can then send a check with the restrictive endorsement making reference to the written notification. If the creditor cashes the check, then the debtor is relieved of having to pay the balance.

If the debtor sends a check with "paid in full" written on it without prior notification, then the creditor may simply cross out the restriction, cash the check, and collect on the balance owed.

Conduct Research What is the law in your state with regard to using this type of restrictive indorsement?

is a person who possesses a negotiable instrument payable to the order of the person holding it, or to the bearer. You are a holder, for example, when you receive a check made out in your name. You may then transfer the instrument, as David does in The Opening Scene by signing his check from Aunt Mae and writing, "Pay to the order of Melanie Mueller" on the instrument. From this time forward, any transfer in the proper manner to a subsequent holder is a further negotiation of the instrument. A negotiation is better than an assignment because it gives greater rights to a transferee than the transferor possessed.

Negotiation of Order Paper

If an instrument says something like, "Pay to the order of," it is called **order paper**. Nearly all checks feature the printed phrase "Pay to the order of" before the line on which you write the payee's name. To be negotiated, order paper must be indorsed by the payee and delivered to the party to whom it is transferred.

Example 1. Hanako Lin wrote a check to the order of Wireless, Inc. in payment of her cell phone bill. When Wireless indorsed the check and deposited it in its bank, the check was negotiated.

An **indorsement** is the act of placing one's signature on an instrument, usually on the back, to transfer it to another. The person who writes the indorsement is called the *indorser*, and the person to whom the instrument is transferred is the *indorsee*. (As noted in Chapter 24, because we are discussing the law of negotiable instruments, we use the term *indorsement*, rather than the term *endorsement*, which is commonly used in other applications.)

Negotiation of Bearer Paper

If an instrument is payable to bearer or cash, it is called **bearer paper** and may be negotiated by delivery alone, without an indorsement. When order paper is indorsed with a blank indorsement, it is turned into bearer paper and may be further negotiated by delivery alone.

Example 2. Henry Dubrosky bought two soccer game tickets from Molly Prince. Henry handed Molly a check that he had gotten from someone else, which said it was payable to the order of "cash." This delivery constituted a proper negotiation of bearer paper to a holder. Molly would be wise to demand Henry's indorsement as a precaution, even though an indorsement is not required for negotiation. If the bank were to refuse to pay the check when presented with it, Molly would then expect Henry to pay it.

Section 25.1 Assessment

Reviewing What You Learned

1. What is an assignment? How is it different from a negotiation?
2. How is bearer paper negotiated?
3. How is order paper negotiated?

Critical Thinking Activity

Indorsement What problems might occur when you write a check payable to the order of "cash" instead of to a particular person or company?

Legal Skills in Action

Transferring Instruments Your friend Joel agrees to buy your old car stereo for $50 and wants to give you a check that he received from Anita, whom you do not know. He indorses the check to you. Your bank refuses to cash the check but takes it for collection. Later, the check is returned to you due to insufficient funds. Write a letter to Anita explaining what happened and asking her to send a new check, payable to you.

Indorsements

Main Kinds of Indorsements

An instrument is indorsed when you write your name on it, indicating your intent to transfer ownership to another. Indorsements may be written in ink, typed on a typewriter, or even stamped with a rubber stamp. For convenience, the indorsement is usually placed on the back of the instrument. To be acceptable, the indorsement must be written for the entire amount stated on the instrument.

Example 3. Wireless, Inc. receives many checks each day from people making payments on their cell phone bills. To simplify and make the indorsements uniform, the cashier uses a rubber stamp containing Wireless, Inc.'s indorsement.

Regulation CC, issued by the Federal Reserve Board under the Competitive Banking Act, has established standards for check indorsements (see Figure 25.1). Under the regulation, the back of a check is divided into specific sections designed to protect the indorsement of the depository bank (the bank of first deposit). The first $1\frac{1}{2}$ inches from the trailing edge of the check is reserved for the payee's indorsement. Banks that handle the check after the depository bank should limit their indorsements to the three-inch space beginning at the opposite end (leading edge) of the check. The section between the payee's indorsement section and the subsequent bank's indorsement section must be reserved for the depository bank's indorsement. In addition, only depository banks can use purple ink.

BLANK INDORSEMENT
A blank indorsement consists of a signature alone. *Why should a blank indorsement be used only at a teller's window?*

What You'll Learn

- How to describe the four main kinds of indorsements
- How to determine who must indorse an instrument payable to more than one person
- How to state the legal effect of a forged indorsement
- How to discuss the warranties that you make when you indorse negotiable instruments
- How to explain the contract you make when you indorse negotiable instruments

Why It's Important

Understanding the types of indorsements will help you handle your finances wisely.

Legal Terms

- blank indorsement
- special indorsement
- restrictive indorsement
- conditional indorsement
- qualified indorsement

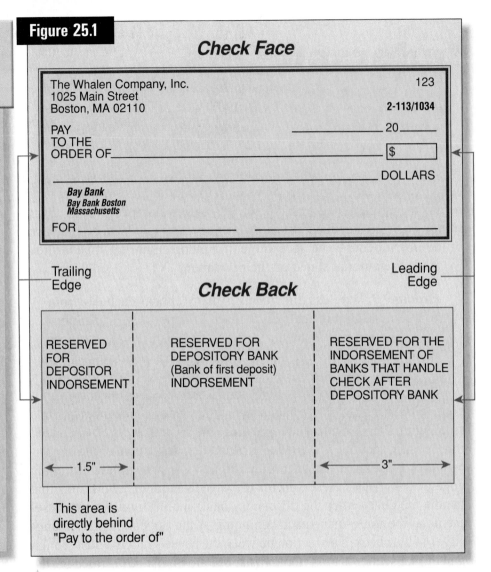

Figure 25.1

Check Face

The Whalen Company, Inc.
1025 Main Street
Boston, MA 02110

123

2-113/1034

PAY
TO THE
ORDER OF_____ $

_____ DOLLARS

Bay Bank
Bay Bank Boston
Massachusetts

FOR _____ _____

Check Back

Trailing Edge

Leading Edge

RESERVED FOR DEPOSITOR INDORSEMENT

RESERVED FOR DEPOSITORY BANK (Bank of first deposit) INDORSEMENT

RESERVED FOR THE INDORSEMENT OF BANKS THAT HANDLE CHECK AFTER DEPOSITORY BANK

← 1.5" →

← 3" →

This area is directly behind "Pay to the order of"

INDORSEMENTS
Regulation CC has issued check indorsement standards. *Where should you indorse a check?*

Each type of indorsement fulfills a special purpose. There are four principal types of indorsements:

- Blank indorsements
- Special indorsements
- Restrictive indorsements
- Qualified indorsements

Blank Indorsement

A **blank indorsement** consists of the signature alone on the instrument. By signing an instrument in this way, you are saying in effect,

Figure 25.2

INDORSE HERE

Carol Barclay

BELOW THIS LINE

February 29 20 ___

Carol Barclay $ 85.00

ty-five 00/100 _____ DOLLARS

Conrad's Restaurant

By *Joseph Conrad*

BLANK INDORSEMENT
A blank indorsement turns order paper into bearer paper and may be transferred by delivery alone. *Why should a blank indorsement be used only in limited situations?*

"This instrument may be paid to anyone." An instrument indorsed in blank becomes bearer paper and may be transferred by delivery alone. It is not safe to carry around this type of indorsement on an instrument or put such an instrument in the mail. If the instrument is lost or stolen and gets into the hands of someone else, that person can cash it by presenting the check for payment. For this reason, a blank indorsement should be used only in limited situations, such as at a bank teller's window. Figure 25.2 shows a blank indorsement.

When an instrument payable to you misspells your name or renders your name incorrectly, you may indorse the back of the instrument with the incorrect name, the correct name, or both. Whoever cashes the check may require signatures in both names.

Special Indorsement

A **special indorsement** (also called an indorsement in full) is made by writing the words *pay to the order of* or *pay to* followed by the name of the person to whom the instrument is to be transferred (the indorsee) and the signature of the indorser. When signed this way, the instrument remains an order instrument and must be indorsed by the indorsee before it can be further negotiated (see Figure 25.3).

Example 4. Frank Cully withdrew $3,500 from his savings account to buy a car from Glendale Motors, Inc. When he made the withdrawal, Cully received a check from the bank payable to him for $3,500. He took the check to Glendale Motors, indorsed it with a special indorsement, and received title to the car. Because the check could not be legally transferred or negotiated further until Glendale Motors indorsed it, all parties were protected.

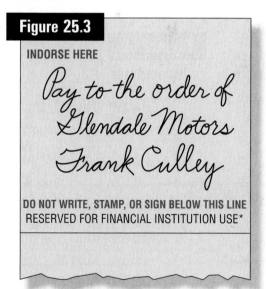

Figure 25.3

INDORSE HERE

Pay to the order of Glendale Motors Frank Culley

DO NOT WRITE, STAMP, OR SIGN BELOW THIS LINE
RESERVED FOR FINANCIAL INSTITUTION USE*

SPECIAL INDORSEMENT
A special indorsement (indorsement in full) creates order paper, which requires the signature of the indorsee. *Whose signature is required to negotiate this instrument further?*

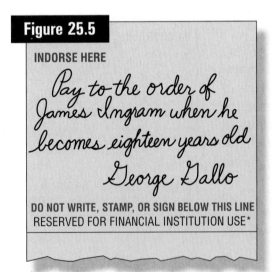

Figure 25.4

INDORSE HERE

For deposit only
Hudson Trust Company
Frederick Herberts

DO NOT WRITE, STAMP, OR SIGN BELOW THIS LINE
RESERVED FOR FINANCIAL INSTITUTION USE*

RESTRICTIVE INDORSEMENT
A restrictive indorsement limits the subsequent use of the instrument. *What must be done before this instrument can be negotiated any further?*

Restrictive Indorsement

A **restrictive indorsement** is one in which words have been added, in addition to the signature of the transferor, to limit its use. A restrictive indorsement does not prevent further transfer or negotiation of the instrument. However, prior to further transfer, it must be used for the purpose stated in the indorsement. For example, when a check is indorsed "for deposit only," as in Figure 25.4, that amount of money must be added to the indorser's bank account before it is negotiated further. Retail stores often stamp checks "for deposit only" when they are received. This provides protection in the event that the checks are stolen.

Example 5. Sharon Clausewitz received her monthly paycheck at the end of the month. Because she knew she could not deposit it for several days, she indorsed it, "For deposit only—Sharon Clausewitz." This is a restrictive indorsement. If the check were to be stolen or lost, the only way that it could be negotiated by someone else would be to deposit it into Sharon's bank account.

Figure 25.5

INDORSE HERE

Pay to the order of
James Ingram when he
becomes eighteen years old
George Gallo

DO NOT WRITE, STAMP, OR SIGN BELOW THIS LINE
RESERVED FOR FINANCIAL INSTITUTION USE*

CONDITIONAL INDORSEMENT
A conditional indorsement makes the rights of the indorsee subject to a certain event or condition. *What event must occur for James Ingram to have the right to cash this check?*

Banks often use restrictive indorsements when they send checks through the collection process. They do this by stamping "Pay any bank" or "For collection only" on the back of each check.

A **conditional indorsement**, a type of restrictive indorsement, makes the rights of the indorsee subject to a specific event or condition (see Figure 25.5).

Example 6. George Gallo wished to transfer a dividend check to his grandson, James Ingram, as a birthday gift. Because George did not want James to cash the check before his 18th birthday, a conditional indorsement was used. Until the condition presented in the indorsement was satisfied, James did not have the right to cash the check.

Figure 25.6

INDORSE HERE

Pay to the order of George Rose without recourse

Samuel Brock

DO NOT WRITE, STAMP, OR SIGN BELOW THIS LINE
RESERVED FOR FINANCIAL INSTITUTION USE*

QUALIFIED INDORSEMENT
A qualified indorsement limits the contractual liability of the indorser. *What is the effect of the words* without recourse *on this indorsement?*

Qualified Indorsement

A **qualified indorsement** is one in which words have been added to the signature to limit the liability of the indorser. The words *without recourse* added to an indorsement, for example, mean the indorser is not liable in the event the maker or drawer does not pay the instrument (see Figure 25.6).

A qualified indorsement transfers title to the instrument. This form of indorsement is frequently used when the instrument is backed by security such as a mortgage or collateral. In case of default by the maker, the indorsee must look to the security for payment of the instrument rather than to the indorser.

> *Example 7.* A $100,000 check was made payable to Attorney Carl Pierce in payment of a client's claim. Pierce indorsed the check to the client, George Anderson, writing "without recourse." By using this indorsement, the attorney would not be responsible for payment if the check failed to clear.

Multiple Payees

If an instrument is payable to either of two payees, only one of the payees needs to indorse it to make it negotiable. On the other hand, if an instrument is payable to both of two payees, as in the case of the check marked "Payable to David and Melanie Mueller" in The Opening Scene, both payees would need to indorse the check for proper negotiation.

A bank that has taken an instrument from a customer to send through the bank collection process may supply any indorsement of the customer that is necessary to title. This rule is designed to speed up bank collections by eliminating the need to return to a depositor any items that were not indorsed. A bank, however, may not supply an indorsement if the instrument contains the phrase "payee's indorsement required."

Forged Indorsements

A forged indorsement is not valid, and anyone who takes a forged instrument does not acquire title and is not a holder. Order paper requires the indorsement of the person to whose order the instrument is made payable. The indorsement may be made by that person or by someone else on that person's behalf (an authorized agent), but not by someone acting without authority. Anyone who pays an instrument on which there is a forged indorsement is liable to the true owner for the amount of the instrument.

Warranties of Indorsers

To encourage people to accept negotiable instruments from others, a system of implied warranties is part of the law of negotiable instruments. An indorser who receives consideration for an instrument makes five warranties to subsequent transferees of the instruments:

1. Indorsers who receive consideration warrant that they have good title to the instrument.

   Example 8. Josephine Enquist gave Wireless, Inc. a check in payment of her cell phone bill. The check contained a blank indorsement by Hannah O'Leary. Later, Wireless, Inc. learned that Josephine had found the check on the street and that the real owner, Hannah O'Leary, had issued a stop-payment order. Josephine, by her indorsement, had warranted that she was the true owner of the instrument. She would be held liable on this warranty for any loss suffered by Wireless, Inc. She also could be vulnerable to criminal prosecution.

2. Indorsers who receive consideration warrant that all signatures are genuine or authorized. If a signature is forged, then the indorser may be held responsible to a subsequent holder for payment of the instrument.
3. Indorsers who receive consideration warrant that the instrument has not been altered.
4. Indorsers who receive consideration warrant that no defense of any party is good against the indorser. If the instrument is dishonored for a valid, legal reason, then the holder can still recover against the indorser.

A Global Perspective: Laws Around the World

Israel

If you're almost 18 in the United States, you might be preparing for college or your first real job. Perhaps you're even thinking about taking some time off to travel. If you were a resident of Israel, you'd be getting ready to serve in the Israel Defense Forces (IDF). Since Israel's birth as a nation in 1948, the IDF has been described as the army of the people—a melting pot of young and old, privileged and poor, native Israelis and immigrants. On the other hand, Israel's regular army is primarily composed of conscripts, or draftees, and a large reserve force.

Required service in the IDF is three years for most Israeli men. After completing this requirement, men generally go on to serve in the reserves until their 40s. Although exempt from combat, women serve in the army for almost two years. Israel is the only country in the world that mandates service for women. Because of a growing population and more specialized defense needs, some Israelis think a volunteer army might better serve the country. Many believe, however, that the IDF's traditions are a common denominator among the people. The IDF "looks forward to the challenges of the future, strengthened by the past," explains a military spokesperson. Here's a snapshot of Israel.

Geographical area	**8,019 sq. miles**
Population	**6,029,529**
Capital	**Jerusalem**
Legal system	**Mix of English common law, British Mandate regulations, and Jewish legal system**
Language	**Hebrew, Arabic, English**
Religion	**80% Jewish**
Life expectancy	**79 years**

Critical Thinking Question List both positive and negative effects of compulsory military service. If the United States reestablished the draft, would you be willing to serve? For more information on Israel, visit **ubpl.glencoe.com** or your local library.

Example 9. Evelyn Siegel, a minor, gave a $350 personal check to Max Horvitz in payment for a second-hand motorbike. She used the vehicle for one day, decided she didn't want it, and stopped payment on her check. Two days after Evelyn had stopped payment on her check, Max indorsed and cashed it at his bank. Evelyn then notified him she was disaffirming her contract to buy the motorbike. When her check was returned to Max's bank because of the stop-payment order, the bank could recover the $350 from Max. By indorsing the check, he warranted to the bank that no defense (including that of minority) was good against him.

A qualified indorsement warrants only that the indorser has no knowledge of any defense.

5. Indorsers who receive consideration warrant that they have no knowledge of any bankruptcy proceeding that would affect the instrument.

Warranties arising from or connected with the transfer of negotiable instruments are transferred to every subsequent holder if the transfer is by indorsement. If the transfer is by delivery alone, the warranty applies to the immediate transferee only.

Example 10. In payment for cleaning services, Harry Adams gave William Bell a $50 check, which was written properly to avoid alteration. However, William altered the check to $500, indorsed the back, and gave it to Mary Carlson in payment for a debt. Mary indorsed the $500 check and deposited it in her bank account. Harry's bank then deducted $500 from his account. Later, when the alteration was discovered, Harry was entitled to a return of the $450 from his bank. His bank could recover the $450 from Mary Carlson's bank, Mary, or William Bell, if they are given proper notice, based on their warranty that the instrument had not been materially altered. Similarly, Mary's bank can recover from either Mary or William to receive the appropriate money. Finally, Mary may recover the money from William for the same reason.

Contract of Indorsers

Unless an indorsement states otherwise (e.g., by such words as *without recourse*), every indorser agrees to pay any subsequent holder the face amount of the instrument if it is dishonored. To enforce this obligation, the holder must do two things:

- He or she must present the instrument for payment to the maker or drawer when it is due. If that person refuses to pay the instrument, it has been dishonored.
- The holder must notify indorsers of the dishonor before midnight of the third full business day after the date of the dishonor. Failure to make presentment and to give timely notice of dishonor to an indorser discharges him or her from liability on the contract to pay subsequent holders of the instrument.

Legal Briefs

Signing the name of a person who cannot write can be considered a forgery. A conviction for forgery can be made solely on proof of intent to commit a fraudulent act. No use of the forged document is required of the offender.

Section 25.2 Assessment

Reviewing What You Learned

1. What are the four main kinds of indorsements?
2. If an instrument is payable to both of two payees, as in the check that is payable to David and Melanie Mueller, who must indorse it?
3. What are the legal effects of a forged instrument?
4. List the five warranties of indorsers.
5. What two things are necessary to enforce the contract of indorsers?

Critical Thinking Activity

Setting Standards Why do you think the Federal Reserve Board has established

standards for check indorsements? What do you think would happen if there were no standards?

Legal Skills in Action

The Impact of Technology With the advent of electronic signatures, digital contracts, and the explosion of e-commerce, are hardcopy negotiable instruments becoming obsolete? Write a paragraph describing the impact of technology on negotiable instruments, such as checks.

Chapter Summary

Section 25.1 Transferring Instruments

- An assignment is the transfer of your rights under a contract to someone else; the transferee has only the rights of an assignee, subject to all defenses existing against you. In contrast, when you negotiate an instrument, you transfer it in such a way that the transferee becomes a holder by way of your indorsement. An indorsement occurs when you write your name on the instrument indicating your intent to transfer ownership to someone else.
- Negotiation of bearer paper occurs upon delivery of the bearer paper.
- Negotiation of order paper occurs when it is indorsed by the payee and delivered to the party to whom it is transferred.

Section 25.2 Indorsements

- A blank indorsement is the simple act of signing an order instrument on the back. By signing an instrument in this way you say, in effect, "This instrument may be paid to anyone." An instrument endorsed in blank becomes bearer paper and may be transferred by delivery alone. If the instrument is lost or stolen and gets into the hands of someone else, that person can cash it by presenting the check for payment. For this reason, a blank indorsement should be used only in limited situations, such as at a bank teller's window. A special indorsement is the act of writing an order to pay a specified party. To create a special indorsement, you simply write the words *pay to the order of* or *pay to* followed by the name of the person to whom the instrument is to be transferred (the indorsee) and the signature of the indorser. When signed in this way, the instrument remains an order instrument and must be indorsed by the indorsee before it can be further negotiated. A restrictive indorsement is one in which words have been added limiting the use of the instrument. A restrictive indorsement does not prevent further transfer or negotiation of the instrument. However, prior to further transfer, it must be used for the purpose stated in the indorsement. Retail stores often stamp checks "for deposit only" when they are received. This provides protection in the event the checks are stolen. A qualified indorsement is one in which words have been added limiting the liability of the indorser. The words indicate that the indorser does not guarantee payment of the instruments. A qualified indorsement transfers title to the instrument. This form of indorsement is frequently used when the instrument is backed by security such as a mortgage or collateral. In case of default by the maker, the indorsee must look to the security for payment of the instrument rather than to the indorser.
- If an instrument is payable to two payees, both payees must indorse the check for proper negotiation.
- A forged indorsement is not valid, and anyone who takes a forged instrument does not acquire title and thus is not considered a holder. Anyone who pays an instrument on which there is a forged indorsement is liable to the true owner for the amount of the instrument.
- Indorsers who receive consideration warrant that: (1) the title is good; (2) all signatures are genuine or authorized; (3) the instrument has not been altered; (4) no defense of any party is good against the indorser; and (5) they have no knowledge of insolvency proceedings that would affect the instrument.
- To enforce the obligation of the indorser, the holder of an instrument must present it to the maker or drawer when it is due. If it is dishonored, the holder must notify the indorser within three business days after the date of dishonor.

Using Legal Language

Consider the key terms in the list below. Then use these terms to complete the following exercises.

instrument	restrictive indorsement
depository bank	order paper
assignment	conditional indorsement
blank indorsement	indorsement
negotiation	qualified indorsement
special indorsement	bearer paper
holder	

1. Imagine that you have just been hired to work as a bank teller and must learn a whole new vocabulary. Create a set of flash cards that define the legal terms listed above.
2. On the flash cards, draw pictures to represent each definition to help you remember the terms.
3. With a partner, review the definitions by using your new flash cards.

The Law Review

Answer the following questions. Refer to the chapter for additional reinforcement:

4. Explain why an order instrument must be indorsed, and why a bearer instrument need not be indorsed.
5. Describe a situation wherein each of the four main types of indorsements would be used. Explain why each type of indorsement would be particularly appropriate for the situations you describe.
6. Describe the standards for check indorsements.
7. What type of indorsement is required when the name of the person to whom the check is made payable is misspelled?
8. What contract does every indorser make if the indorsement does not state otherwise?
9. Why should you only use blank indorsements in limited situations?

Linking School to Work

Participating as a Member of a Team
In groups of three or four, interview a bank teller or other official to find out what kinds of mistakes people make when writing and indorsing checks. Use your notes to prepare a detailed presentation.

10. Report your findings to the class.
11. Structure your presentation so that each group member has a chance to speak in front of the class.
12. Use visual aids or presentation software to enhance your presentation.
13. Compare notes with the other groups.
14. Evaluate your group's presentation. What did you do well? In what areas could you improve?

Let's Debate

Signature Stamp
Antonia sells cosmetics through a catalog. Her customers pay her directly for the products they purchase. Antonia receives hundreds of checks each month, all made payable to her. Instead of indorsing all of the checks by hand, she decided to have a rubber stamp of her signature made. Using a rubber stamp will save Antonia a great deal of time.

Debate
15. If Antonia uses the rubber stamp, are the checks considered indorsed?
16. Is it legal to use a rubber stamp to indorse checks?
17. What are some possible disadvantages of using a rubber stamp?

Grasping Case Issues

For the following cases, give your decision and state a legal principle that applies.

18. A check was payable to Quan and Jie Lee. Can the check be indorsed by either one of them to be negotiated? Why or why not?
19. Michael Reed finds a check payable to Irene Lupi on a downtown street. Is Michael a holder? Why or why not?
20. Suppose the check Michael found in the previous case had been indorsed in blank by Irene Lupi. Would Michael be considered a holder? Why or why not?
21. Suppose the check Michael found in problem 19 was indorsed by Irene Lupi, with a special indorsement to Charles MacLean. Is Michael a holder? Why or why not?
22. Suppose, in problem 20, that Michael also indorses the check and cashes it at a bank. On what two legal grounds does the bank have recourse against him if the check does not clear?
23. Jessica Patton unknowingly lost a blank check that she kept in her wallet for emergency situations. Abby Turner found the check in the restroom of a local mall and made the check out to herself for the sum of $500, forging Patton's signature. Patton's bank did not catch the forged signature and cashed the check. Does Patton have any recourse against her bank? Explain your answer.
24. Ted Wilmot, a landscaper, received a check for $350 from a client. Wilmot was in desperate need of money and planned to cash the check immediately. When he reached the drive-up window at his bank, Wilmot noticed that the check was made out to Theodore Wilmot. Ted's given name was simply Ted. What might Wilmot's bank require him to do?

In each case that follows, you be the judge.

25. Restrictive Indorsement

Holland Farms wrote a check payable to the order of La Sara Grain Company in the amount of $62,000. The check was indorsed by La Sara Grain Company "For deposit only" and taken to the bank by the company's general manager, Harold Jones. The bank deposited $40,000 of the check into Jones's personal account and $22,000 into La Sara Grain Company's account. *Does La Sara Grain Company have recourse against the bank for the loss of the $40,000? Why or why not?*
La Sara Grain v. First National Bank of Mercedes, 673 S.W.2d 558 (TX).

26. Special Indorsement

Humberto Decorators, Inc., a general contracting firm, renovated the Restaurant Argentino Tango, Inc. for an agreed price of $27,415. When the work was completed, a check for the contract price was given to the restaurant by the Plaza National Bank as part of the proceeds of a loan. The check was payable to the order of Humberto Decorators, Inc. Instead of delivering it to the contractor, the restaurant deposited the check in its own bank account at the Plaza National Bank. Humberto Decorators, Inc. never received the money. *May it recover the money from the bank? Why or why not?*
Humberto Decorators, Inc. v. Plaza National Bank, 434 A.2d 618 (NJ).

Legal Link

POWER READING STRATEGIES

A Victim of Theft

Identity theft is the fastest growing crime in America, affecting approximately 900,000 new victims each year. You need to take precautions to protect yourself from this crime.

Connect

Using a variety of search engines:

27. Locate information about identity theft, including how to protect yourself and what to do if you are a victim of this crime.

28. Predict What do you think Melanie should do now that she has lost three checks?

29. Connect Have you ever received a check from someone? If yes, how did you indorse it?

30. Question Must the indorsement be placed on the back of the instrument? Why or why not?

31. Respond Why do you think retail stores stamp checks *for deposit only* when they are received?

Collecting Negotiable Instruments

Understanding Business and Personal Law *Online*

Chapter Overview Visit the *Understanding Business and Personal Law* Web site at **ubpl.glencoe.com** and click on Chapter 26: Collecting Negotiable Instruments—Chapter Overviews to preview the chapter information.

The Opening Scene

Melanie discusses the theft of her purse with an officer at the local police station.

Reality Check

POLICE OFFICER: *(Handing Melanie her purse.)* Whoever stole this must have been scared off. Some children found it in a grocery cart not far from the store where you reported it lost. Look through it to see what's missing.

MELANIE: *(Looking through her purse.)* Everything seems to be here—my driver's license, credit card—oh, oh. There are only two checks here. Aunt Mae's check for $500 is missing.

POLICE OFFICER: You're very fortunate. Most stolen purses that we find are completely empty.

(A week later, Melanie and David discuss their finances over dinner.)

MELANIE: I wasn't the least bit surprised when the check that Julio gave us bounced. He should have gotten cash when he sold his car to a stranger. It was stupid of us to accept that check.

(A sharp knock at the front door interrupts their conversation.)

MELANIE: I'll get it. *(She opens the door.)* Julio! We were just talking about you.

JULIO: *(Entering.)* Hi! How's everything?

DAVID: Not so great. That check from the sale of your car bounced on us.

JULIO: What? Are you kidding?

DAVID: No. The bank returned it with a stop-payment notice attached. I called Maria Reynolds, the girl who made it out, and discovered that she's a minor. Her father won't let her keep that junk car of yours. Thanks a lot for your help!

JULIO: This is the first I've heard of it. When did the bank return it?

DAVID: Yesterday.

MELANIE: I don't think we're ever going to get that money you owe us.

JULIO: Why don't you sue the girl I sold the car to? She's not supposed to stop payment on a check like that!

MELANIE: We should sue you, Julio! You endorsed that check from her before you gave it to us.

JULIO: Don't worry, I'll pay you.

DAVID: Aunt Mae must think we're crazy. We lost the first check she gave us. Then someone stole the second one, forged Melanie's indorsement, and cashed it. She'll never give us a third check. I'd be embarrassed to even ask for another.

MELANIE: It's a good thing Aunt Mae knows my signature. She got her money back from the bank.

JULIO: Really? Do you have to pay the bank back?

MELANIE: I hope not!

JULIO: If you do, you can probably sue Aunt Mae to get your money back.

DAVID: Are you kidding? She gave us those checks out of the goodness of her heart! Is that all you can think about Julio—sue, sue, sue?

What Are the Legal Issues?

1. Was David a holder in due course of the check given to him by Julio in Chapter 25?
2. Would David win the case if he brought suit against Maria Reynolds for the amount of the check on which she stopped payment?
3. What kind of liability would Julio have on the check that he indorsed over to David?
4. Must Melanie pay back the bank for the amount of the check containing her forged indorsement?

Holders of Instruments and Defenses

What You'll Learn

- How to determine if a person is a holder in due course
- How to contrast personal defenses with real defenses

Why It's Important

Recognizing the parties and defenses to negotiable instruments will keep you alert to problems regarding negotiable instruments.

Legal Terms

- holder in due course
- holder
- value
- good faith
- shelter provision
- personal defenses
- real defenses

Holder in Due Course

A **holder in due course** is a holder who takes an instrument for value, in good faith, and without notice. Holders in due course are treated more favorably than mere holders are treated. They receive more rights in negotiable instruments than other parties. For this reason, negotiable instruments are passed almost as freely as money from one person to another.

Holder

To be a holder in due course, you must first be a **holder**. Being a holder means that the instrument must have been issued or indorsed to you, to your order, or to bearer.

When an instrument is properly negotiated, the person to whom it is transferred is a holder. This is important because only a holder can collect the money that is due on an instrument. It is also important because if no defenses are introduced in court, the holder can collect the money simply by proving that the signature on the instrument is authentic.

Example 1. John and Nancy Anderson obtained a commitment for a mortgage loan from a bank to build their house. Periodically, the bank issued checks payable to John, Nancy, and the construction company. The final check was deposited in the construction company's account without Nancy's indorsement. The bank that received the check

HOLDER
You must first be a holder to be a holder in due course. *What are the requirements to be a holder?*

for deposit was not a holder because without Nancy's indorsement, the check was not indorsed to it, to its order, or to bearer.

Even when certain defenses are introduced in court, if a holder has preferred status, the holder may still be able to collect on the instrument.

Value

A person must give value for an instrument to qualify as a holder in due course. You give **value** when you give the consideration that was agreed upon or when you accept an instrument in payment of a debt. If an instrument were negotiated to you as a gift, then you would not qualify as a holder in due course.

Good Faith

To be a holder in due course, the holder must take the instrument in good faith. **Good faith** means honesty in fact and fair dealing. It requires that the taker of a negotiable instrument act honestly. Whether a person took an instrument in good faith is determined at the time of taking the instrument. If a person acted in good faith at the time, but later learned of disturbing facts, he or she is still regarded as having taken the instrument in good faith.

Without Notice

To be a holder in due course, a holder must not have notice of any claim or defense to the instrument, or notice that the instrument is overdue or has been dishonored. A claim is an argument asserted by a person claiming the instrument. A defense, on the other hand, is typically something that is asserted as a reason not to pay it. A holder has notice of a claim or defense if the instrument bears visible evidence of forgery or alteration. The same is true if the instrument is so incomplete or irregular that its legal acceptance is doubtful. Notice of a claim or defense is also given if the holder notices that the obligation of any party is voidable.

Example 2. Eva, 17, borrowed $500 from Krista. She gave Krista a promissory note, promising to pay the money back in 90 days. Krista indorsed the note and sold it at a discount to David, telling David that it came from a minor. David was not a holder in due course because he knew that Eva was a minor and could disaffirm the contract to pay back the money.

Holder Through a Holder in Due Course

A holder who receives an instrument from a holder in due course acquires the rights of the holder in due course, even though he or she

Community Works

Win-Win
Negotiations are usually aimed at the parties eventually reaching an agreement. For example, striking laborers and company management often enter negotiations knowing what they want, but eventually both sides have to compromise to get at least part of what they originally desired. *What kind of negotiations occur in your daily life?*

Get Involved
Learn mediation techniques to become a better negotiator. Related topics are sometimes covered in high school psychology courses, and courses on negotiation are often available through community colleges.

Paying Twice Is Not So Nice

A mechanic's lien, often used in the construction industry, is a claim against property. Contractors and subcontractors might use a mechanic's lien to enforce payment for goods or services they have rendered. For instance, if a contractor fails to pay a subcontractor, the subcontractor can file a mechanic's lien against the property. This is often unfair to property owners because generally the contractor is responsible for paying the subcontractor.

Property owners can protect themselves by taking certain steps to make sure everyone gets paid. Usually, the property owner pays the contractor who in turn pays the subcontractor. However, if the property owner writes a check payable to both the contractor and subcontractor, the subcontractor must sign the check for the contractor to be paid. This type of check helps to ensure that the subcontractor will be paid because the subcontractor can withhold his or her signature until he or she is assured of payment by the contractor. Making the check negotiable only if both parties indorse it will reduce the risk of a mechanic's lien being filed against the owner's property.

Critical Thinking What would happen if the owner wrote a check to both a contractor and subcontractor and the contractor cashed it without the subcontractor's indorsement?

does not qualify as a holder in due course. This provision is called a **shelter provision**. It is designed to permit holders in due course to transfer all of the rights they have in the paper to others. The shelter provision does not apply to a holder who has committed fraud or an illegal act.

Example 3. Alfonso wrote out a check to Brisa. Brisa indorsed the check and gave it to Clara in payment for a debt. Because Clara took the check for value, in good faith, and without notice, she was a holder in due course. Clara indorsed the instrument and gave it to her niece as a gift. Clara's niece wasn't a holder in due course because she didn't give value for the instrument. However, she had the rights of a holder in due course because she received the check from a holder in due course.

Defenses to Negotiable Instruments

Sometimes people charged with paying instruments may try to prevent payment by raising defenses against the holder. Two kinds of defenses are recognized: personal and real. Holders in due course can avoid personal defenses and require payment because of the special position they occupy. Only real defenses may be used against holders in due course.

Personal Defenses

The favorable treatment that holders in due course receive is that they take an instrument free from all claims to it on the part of any person. They also take an instrument free from all personal defenses of any party with whom they have not dealt. **Personal defenses** (also called limited defenses) are defenses that can be used against a holder, although they can't be used against a holder in due course. The most common personal defenses are breach of contract, failure or lack of consideration, fraud in the inducement, lack of delivery, and payment (see Figure 26.1). For example, fraud in the inducement occurs when someone is persuaded to enter into a contract because of a misrepresentation (false statement) of some fact regarding the contract.

It is risky to sign a check or other negotiable instrument without filling it out completely. If such an instrument is lost or stolen, the finder or thief could fill in any amount or other information and negotiate it to someone else. It would have to be paid by the person who signed it,

Figure 26.1

Most Common Personal Defenses

Defense	Description
Breach of contract	One of the parties to a contract has failed to do what he or she has previously agreed to do.
Failure of consideration	One of the parties to a contract has failed to furnish the agreed consideration.
Lack of consideration	No consideration existed in the underlying contract for which the instrument was issued.
Fraud in the inducement	The drawer or maker of an instrument is persuaded to enter into a contract because of a misrepresentation of some fact regarding the item purchased.
Lack of delivery of a negotiable instrument	A payee forcibly, unlawfully, or conditionally takes an instrument from a maker or drawer. The maker or drawer did not intend to deliver the instrument.
Payment of a negotiable instrument	The drawer or maker of an instrument has paid the amount of the instrument.

PERSONAL DEFENSES Holders in due course are not subject to personal defenses. *What defenses are holders in due course subject to?*

FRAUD IN THE INDUCEMENT
When someone uses fraud to persuade another to enter into a contract, it is called fraud in the inducement. *What kind of a defense is fraud in the inducement?*

regardless of the amount that was filled in, if it reached the hands of a holder in due course. This same danger exists when someone signs an instrument, gives it to someone else, and tells that person to fill it out. If an innocent party happens to come into possession of a check that has been fraudulently filled in, the loss must fall upon the party whose conduct in signing the blank paper has made the fraud possible.

Example 4. David sold his sports car to Kristina for $1,200. To make the sale, David told Kristina that the brakes had been relined two weeks earlier; however, this was not true. Kristina gave David a check for $1,200. While driving the car home,

Virtual Law

Selling on Credit to Internet Companies

Internet companies are increasingly in financial trouble. It makes sense that the credit managers of businesses that sell to Internet companies are being more careful when selling to them. As precautionary measures, these vendors are restricting shipments and limiting their financial risks. They are requiring more security from their Internet customers before handing over goods on credit. Some vendors are demanding that Internet companies sign notes with the goods delivered serving as collateral. In this way, if the Internet company goes bankrupt, the vendor will have a better chance of getting some of its money back. (Source: *New York Times*, February 26, 2001, p. C5)

Connect Visit a Web site related to credit management in an e-commerce environment. See if they have any information on this issue.

Careers in Law

Professor of Philosophy

Ron Moore believes that young people in this country "have a real stake in thinking about philosophy. Before they're occupied with making and spending money, young people should be exploring these issues that affect us all."

An associate professor of philosophy at the University of Washington in Seattle, Moore says it's important for people to debate the merits of important concepts such as beauty, justice, and morality.

"The word 'philosophy' means 'love of wisdom,'" Moore says. "Philosophers try to develop strong, clear justifications for their beliefs and then weave those justifications into schemes for understanding the world around them."

While attorneys practice law, philosophers reflect on the nature of law, justice, judicial decision making, punishment, and fairness. These issues have far-reaching effects on who we are and how we function as a society.

Moore notes that good philosophers do more than argue their own point of view—they also can argue the opposite point of view.

"Philosophers are fascinated by ideas," he says, "and are able to weigh several points of view. They take delight in sometimes being found wrong."

He adds that philosophers are concerned with more than just abstract thinking. They also think about the real-world effects of their arguments and beliefs, and ask themselves, "What happens to the world if my ideas are right?"

Moore believes that in the past, many of our finest Supreme Court justices were more than just brilliant lawyers—they were also philosophers of law.

"They were concerned with listening to and weighing all the sides of an argument," he says, "as well as the effects of their decisions. They carefully considered all the issues involved with tough issues such as what constitutes cruel and unusual punishment, what are the boundaries of privacy, and when to abandon segregation."

Skills	Should know something about the content and practice of law; must be able to marshal evidence in support of an argument and draw conclusions; write a clear and convincing argument
Personality	Curious about the world; puzzled and fascinated by "the big questions"; patient, open-minded, and logical
Education	To teach philosophy at the university level, must have a Ph.D. and probably some training in law, art, or another subject specialty

For more information on philosophers of law, visit **ubpl.glencoe.com** or your public library.

Kristina learned that the brakes had not been relined and stopped payment on the check. David, however, had indorsed the check in blank and had given it to Eugene, a holder in due course. Eugene could collect the full $1,200 from Kristina. Even though Kristina was defrauded, she cannot use that defense against a holder in due course because fraud in the inducement is a personal defense.

Real Defenses

Some defenses can be used against holders in due course. These defenses are known as **real defenses** (also called universal defenses). No one is required to pay an instrument when there is a real defense. Real defenses include infancy and mental incompetence, illegality, duress, fraud as to the essential nature of the transaction, bankruptcy, unauthorized signature, and alteration (see Figure 26.2).

Example 5. The Easy Loan Company issued a $5,000 check on an automobile loan. John Bates altered the check to $8,000, indorsed it, and presented it for payment to an out-of-town bank. When the check was returned to Easy's own bank for collection, the bank refused to honor the check, noting the alteration. If the bank that cashed the check sued Easy Loan Co., Easy would have

REAL DEFENSES Everyone, including holders in due course, is subject to real defenses. *What is another name for a real defense?*

Figure 26.2	Most Common Real Defenses
Defense	**Description**
Infancy and mental incompetence	The maker or drawer of the instrument was a minor or mentally incompetent.
Illegality	The underlying contract for which the instrument was issued was illegal.
Duress	The instrument was drawn against the will of the maker or drawer because of threats of force or bodily harm.
Fraud as to the essential nature of the transaction	A false statement was made to the maker or drawer about the nature of the instrument being signed.
Bankruptcy	An order for relief was issued by the federal court that ended all of the debtor's outstanding contractual obligations.
Unauthorized signature	Someone wrongfully signed another's name on an instrument without authority to do so.
Material alteration	The amount of the instrument or the payee's name was changed wrongfully after the instrument was originally drawn by the maker or drawer.

FRAUD AS TO THE ESSENTIAL NATURE Fraud as to the essential nature of a contract is more serious than fraud in the inducement. *What type of defense is this type of fraud?*

an obligation to pay only the amount for which the check was originally drawn, $5,000, because alteration is a real defense.

Another example of a real defense is fraud as to the essential nature of the instrument. This kind of fraud occurs when someone makes a false statement about the nature of the instrument being signed. This real defense can be used against anyone, even a holder in due course.

Example 6. Jerry told Carmen, who could not speak English, that the paper she was signing was a receipt. It was actually a promissory note. Carmen would not have to pay the instrument even if it were transferred to a holder in due course because of the fraud as to the essential nature of the instrument.

Section 26.1 Assessment

Reviewing What You Learned

1. What requirements must a holder in due course meet?
2. What is the difference between a personal defense and a real defense? Provide an example of each.

Critical Thinking Activity

Forgery What recourse, if any, is available to a holder in due course when a real defense such as forgery is used to avoid payment of a negotiable instrument?

Legal Skills in Action

Holder in Due Course Guillermo bought a box of used computer parts from Miguel. He paid for the parts with a check for $50. Miguel indorsed the check and gave it to Roger as payment for a debt. Roger indorsed the check and gave it to his sister as a birthday gift. Make a chart indicating who is (are) the holder(s) in due course and who has the rights of a holder in due course.

Liabilities of Parties

What You'll Learn

- How to explain primary liability and name the parties who are primarily liable on negotiable instruments
- How to explain secondary liability and name the parties who are secondarily liable on negotiable instruments

Why It's Important

Knowing about the liability of parties will make you better able to tackle problems with negotiable instruments.

Legal Terms

- primary liability
- secondary liability
- presentment
- dishonor

Liability of Parties

Liability refers primarily to responsibility for paying the instrument. The UCC divides the liability of the parties into two groups: primary liability and secondary liability.

Primary Liability

Primary liability is an absolute liability to pay. A party with primary liability has promised to pay the instrument without reservations of any kind. Two parties have primary liability: the maker of a note and the acceptor, if any, of a draft. Each of these parties has personally promised to pay the obligation represented by the instrument without reservation. When there are comakers on notes, they have primary liability and are considered makers, regardless of whether they receive any consideration.

Secondary Liability

Secondary liability is a liability to pay only after certain conditions have been met. Two types of parties are secondarily liable on negotiable instruments: the drawer of a draft and the indorsers of either

SECONDARY LIABILITY
The drawer of a draft and indorsers of either a note or a draft are secondarily liable on negotiable instruments. *What does secondary liability mean?*

a note or a draft. Three conditions must be met before the drawer or indorsers have liability to pay:

- The instrument must be properly presented to the primary party or drawee, and payment must be demanded.
- Payment must have been refused by the primary party (this kind of refusal is called dishonor).
- Notice of this refusal must be given to the secondary party within the time and in the manner prescribed by the UCC.

Presentment   A demand made by a holder to pay or accept an instrument is called **presentment**. Presentment may be made by using any commercially reasonable means, including oral, written, or electronic communication. If requested by the person to whom presentment is made, the person making presentment must exhibit the instrument and provide identification. A holder need not make proper presentment to hold secondary parties liable in some situations (see Figure 26.3).

For some instruments, presentment is made twice—once for acceptance and once for payment. To be sure that a secondary party (drawer or indorser) will be liable on an instrument, the holder must make proper presentment for payment unless excused. This means that the holder must present the instrument to the maker or drawee and ask for payment. If such presentment is not made at the proper time, all indorsers are discharged from their obligation. They will not have to pay the holder of the instrument. In addition, if such presentment is not properly made and the drawee cannot pay because of insolvency (inability to pay debts), the drawer is discharged from all obligation.

Time for Presentment   Presentment must be made on the date the instrument is due. If there is no due date stated on the instrument, presentment must be made in a reasonable time after the maker or drawer becomes liable on it. The definition of a reasonable time for instruments other than checks will vary according to the circumstances. A reasonable time for a check is 30 days with respect to the liability of the drawer and 7 days with respect to the liability of an indorser.

> *Example 7.* Joanne Lawler made out a check to Doris Madden for $100. Madden indorsed the check and cashed it at a grocery store near her home. The store kept the check for eight days before taking it to the bank. If the check did not clear, the store could not hold Madden liable on the instrument. She would not have to pay it because the store did not present the check to the bank within a reasonable time to hold the indorser responsible.

It's a Question of Ethics

Financial Difficulties
Dominique does yard work for a dozen homeowners in her neighborhood. One of her clients is Mrs. Belfield, an elderly widow. Some of Dominique's clients pay her when she comes to their homes, but others mail their checks. Mrs. Belfield has requested that she be allowed to mail her check, even though she's home when Dominique is working there. For the past three months, Mrs. Belfield's checks have been late. They have become so late that she is now two payments behind. The last check she sent bounced. Dominique has tried to talk to Mrs. Belfield, but Mrs. Belfield claims she is having financial difficulties. *What should Dominique do?*

Figure 26.3

DIRECT REDUCTION
MORTGAGE NOTE

Account No. R-4814

$ 50,000.00

April 14, 20 --

FOR VALUE RECEIVED we jointly and severally, promise to pay to
Paul J. Kelleher

or order the sum of Fifty Thousand ($50,000)----------- Dollars in or within twenty-five years from this date, with interest thereon at the rate of 12 per cent per annum, payable in monthly installments of $ 526.62 on the first day of each month hereafter, which payments shall first be applied to interest then due and the balance thereof remaining applied to principal; the interest to be computed monthly in advance on the unpaid balance, together with such fines on interest in arrears as are provided.

We reserve the right to make additional payments on account of said principal sum on any payment date.

Failure to pay any of said installments within thirty (30) days from the date when the same becomes due, notwithstanding any license or waiver of any prior breach of conditions, shall make the whole of the balance of said principal sum immediately due and payable at the option of the holder thereof.

The makers, endorsers, and guarantors or other parties to this note, and each of them, severally waive presentment, notice, and protest.

Signed and sealed in the presence of

Charles E. Jones   *Carl Pierce*
Sylvia Pierce

PROPER NOTICE
The holder of this note does not have to make proper presentment or give proper notice to hold secondary parties liable. *Why is this so?*

If payment is made, the instrument must be handed over then and there to the person paying the money. This is important because, if the party paying does not get the instrument back, it might show up later in the hands of a holder in due course, and the holder would have to pay it again.

Dishonor   The party who presents a negotiable instrument is entitled to have the instrument paid or accepted. If the party to whom the instrument is presented refuses to pay or to accept it, the instrument is **dishonored**. The instrument is also considered to be dishonored if the presentment has been excused and the instrument is past due and unpaid. The presenting party then has recourse against the indorsers or other secondary parties.

Example 8. A note was presented to Charro for payment on the due date. Charro refused to honor it, claiming the note was a forgery. The holder would have to proceed against the indorsers to obtain payment. The note is considered dishonored because of Charro's refusal to pay it.

Notice of Dishonor Obligations of indorsers and drawers of instruments cannot be enforced unless the indorsers and drawers are given notice of the dishonor. Notice of dishonor may be given by any reasonable means, including oral, written, or electronic communication, and is sufficient if it identifies the instrument and indicates that the instrument has been dishonored or has not been paid or accepted. The return of an instrument given to a bank for collection is sufficient notice of dishonor.

Holders other than banks must give notice of the dishonor to the drawer and indorsers within 30 days following the day of dishonor. Banks taking instruments for collection must give notice before midnight of the banking day following the day the bank was notified of the dishonor. Delay in giving notice of dishonor is excused when the holder has acted carefully and the delay is due to circumstances beyond the holder's control. Presentment and notice of dishonor are also excused when the party waived the right to presentment or notice of dishonor.

Legal Briefs

A negotiable instrument is an object that can be used to do business. The term *negotiate* comes from the Latin term *negotiari*, which means "to do business."

Section 26.2 Assessment

Reviewing What You Learned

1. What is primary liability? What parties are primarily liable on negotiable instruments?
2. What is secondary liability? What parties are secondarily liable on negotiable instruments?

Critical Thinking Activity

Enforcing Obligations Why do you think that the obligations of indorsers and drawers of instruments may not be enforced unless they are given notice of the dishonor?

Legal Skills in Action

Taking Precautions The local video store accepts checks for renting and purchasing videos and DVDs. Recently, the store has accepted many bad checks. As a team, create a document listing the precautions the store clerks might take to be sure that they will collect the funds.

Chapter Summary

Section 26.1 Holders of Instruments and Defenses

- Even when certain defenses are introduced in court, if a holder has preferred status, the holder may still be able to collect on the instrument. Preferred status is given to a party called a holder in due course. A holder in due course is a holder who takes an instrument for value, in good faith, and without notice. To be a holder, the instrument must have been issued or indorsed to you. You must give value when you accept an instrument; a gift would not allow you to qualify as a holder in due course. You give value when you give the consideration that was agreed upon or when you accept an instrument in payment of a debt. The holder must also act honestly to qualify under the "good faith" requirement. Whether a person took an instrument in good faith is determined at the time of taking the instrument. If a person acted in good faith at the time, but later learned of disturbing facts, he or she is still regarded as having taken the instrument in good faith. A holder must not have notice of any claim or defense to the instrument. A holder has notice of a claim or defense if the instrument bears visible evidence of forgery or alteration. The same is true if the instrument is so incomplete or irregular that its legal acceptance is doubtful. Notice of a claim or defense is also given if the holder notices that the obligation of any party is voidable. Holders in due course are treated more favorably than mere holders are treated. They receive more rights in negotiable instruments than other parties. For this reason, negotiable instruments are passed almost as freely as money from one person to another. To be a holder in due course, you must first be a holder.
- Two kinds of defenses against a holder are recognized: personal and real. Real defenses may be used against holders in due course; personal defenses may not. Personal defenses such as breach of contract, failure or lack of consideration, fraud in the inducement, and lack of delivery and payment may not be used against holders in due course. A real defense is a defense directed against the instrument itself. The contention is that no valid instrument ever came into existence; therefore, the instrument could not be real or genuine. Some examples of real defenses are infancy and mental incompetence, illegality and duress, fraud as to the essential nature of the transaction, bankruptcy, unauthorized signature, and alteration.

Section 26.2 Liabilities of Parties

- Primary liability is an absolute liability to pay. A party with primary liability has promised to pay the instrument without reservation. Makers of promissory notes and acceptors of drafts have primary liability. When there are comakers on notes, they have primary liability and are considered makers regardless of whether they receive any consideration.
- A party with secondary liability has a liability to pay only after certain conditions have been met: (1) the instrument must be properly presented to the primary party or drawee; (2) payment must be demanded; (3) payment must be dishonored (refused by the primary party) or be impossible; and (4) notice of refusal must be given to the secondary party within the time and in the manner prescribed by law. There are two types of parties who may have secondary liability for the payment of an instrument. They are (1) the drawer of a draft (a check is the most common kind of draft) and (2) the indorser or indorsers of either a draft or note.

Using Legal Language

Consider the key terms in the list below. Then use these terms to complete the following exercises.

holder in due course	real defenses
holder	primary liability
value	secondary liability
good faith	presentment
shelter provision	dishonor
personal defenses	

1. Write a letter to a bank explaining recent problems you have had with a negotiable instrument.
2. Role-play with a partner how the banker may respond to your letters. As the banker, make sure to address all the terms used in the letters.
3. Practice your role-play activities until you and your partner feel comfortable.
4. Present your role-play activities to the class. If possible, dress in costumes and use appropriate props.
5. After you have finished delivering your role-play activities, ask your classmates for constructive criticism.
6. Reflect on you could have improved your role-play activities.

Understanding Business and Personal Law Online

Self-Check Quiz Visit the *Understanding Business and Personal Law* Web site at **ubpl.glencoe.com** and click on Chapter 26: Collecting Negotiable Instruments—Self-Check Quizzes to prepare for the chapter exam.

The Law Review

Answer the following questions. Refer to the chapter for additional reinforcement.

7. When is value for an instrument given?
8. Explain what it means to be a "holder through a holder in due course."
9. Can personal defenses be used against holders in due course? Why or why not?
10. What are the three conditions that must be met for secondary liability?
11. Banks that take instruments for collection must give notice of dishonor by when?
12. What is good faith?
13. Describe the shelter provision.
14. What is fraud in the inducement?
15. What might a person be requested to do when making presentment of an instrument?

Linking School to Work

Interpreting and Communicating Information

Interview the managers of two local businesses, either in person or on the phone, about:

16. What their check policies are.
17. The reasons for those policies.

As a class, compare your findings.

Let's Debate

Altered Check

Fatima gave your friend Isabel a check for $4 as payment for a book. Isabel alters the check and endorses it over to a finance company, presenting it as a $400 payment on her car.

Debate

18. Who is the holder in due course?
19. Is there a holder through a holder in due course?
20. Does the shelter provision apply?
21. Explain the primary and/or secondary liability in this situation.

Explain all of your answers.

Grasping Case Issues

For the following cases, give your decision and state a legal principle that applies.

22. Cynthia, a minor, purchased a used truck for $1,500 from a dealer. In payment, she gave $500 in cash and a promissory note for the balance to be paid in three months. The dealer indorsed the note and negotiated it to a bank. A week later, Cynthia was involved in an accident, and the vehicle was damaged beyond repair. Must Cynthia pay the amount of the note to the bank when it is due? Why or why not?

23. Moynihan executed and left on her desk a note made out to Pappas. Moynihan owed Pappas the money specified on the note for the purchase of a lawn tractor. Pappas was admitted to Moynihan's office, saw the note made out to her, picked it up, and departed without seeing Moynihan. Pappas negotiated the note to her bank through indorsement and delivery. When the bank presented the note for payment, Moynihan refused, claiming she had not delivered the note to the indorser. Did Moynihan have a defense against the bank? Why or why not?

24. Daniel, a minor, gives Carmenza a $200 check in payment for a VCR. Daniel uses the VCR over the weekend, decides to return it, and stops payment on the check. Carmenza cashes the check at her bank, which becomes a holder in due course. What defense, if any, may Daniel use against Carmenza's bank if suit is brought for payment of the money?

25. Steve forges the name of Joanne Newman, a well-known merchant, on a $500 note. He then negotiates the note to William Kester, an innocent purchaser, for value. Kester sues Newman when payment is refused at maturity. Is Newman required to pay the note? Why or why not?

26. Louise Torelli presented a note to Duke Fairfax for payment on the due date. Fairfax had become insolvent and could not honor the note. There were four indorsers on the note, and Torelli gave notice of dishonor to the indorser immediately ahead of her. That indorser failed to give notice to the other indorsers. If Torelli cannot collect from the indorser to whom notice was given, may she then proceed against each of the others for payment? Explain your answer.

In each case that follows, you be the judge.

27. Indorsement Authority

Refrigerated Transport Co., Inc. employed a collection agency to collect some of its overdue accounts. The collection agency indorsed, without authority, checks made payable to Refrigerated Transport and deposited them in the agency's own checking account. *Was the bank that accepted the checks for deposit a holder in due course? Why or why not?* *Nat'l Bank v. Refrigerated Transp.,* 248 S.E.2d 496 (GA).

28. Transferring Notes

John and Beverly Girner executed a $5,000 promissory note payable to the order of First Realty Corporation. The note was to be paid in monthly installments. First Realty transferred the note to Imran Bohra in exchange for property. When the note was six months past due, Bohra transferred the note to his attorney in exchange for legal services and told the attorney that the note was past due. *Is the attorney a holder in due course? Why or why not?* *Richardson v. Girner,* 668 S.W.2d 523 (AK).

Legal Link

Legal Lingo

Toyka and Lindsay are taking a business law course together in high school. This week they have been learning about negotiable instruments and the collection of those instruments. Lindsay often struggles with all of the legal vocabulary, so Toyka has decided to help her by locating online legal dictionaries that Lindsay and other classmates could use.

Connect

Using a variety of search engines:

29. Create a list of at least five Web sites that offer legal dictionaries.

As a class, combine the sites to create a comprehensive tool that all the students can use.

POWER READING STRATEGIES

30. Predict Why do you think holders in due course are treated more favorably than holders?

31. Connect What would you do if a friend forged a check to be used as payment for a new DVD player?

32. Question Why are personal defenses sometimes called limited defenses?

33. Respond What are some of the reasons a bank would dishonor a negotiable instrument?

UNIT 5 Law Workshop:

Using Legal Tools

Can You Explain Negotiable Instruments?

The law of negotiable instruments enables businesses to engage in transactions without carrying around excessive amounts of cash. As a result, negotiable instruments are very practical in business contexts. Negotiable instruments include checks, notes, and certificates of deposit.

Step A: Preparation

Problem: *How do negotiable instruments work?*

Objectives: In this workshop, you will work in small groups to analyze negotiable instruments and legal situations in which they are involved.

- **Investigate** what information must appear on notes, certificates of deposit, and checks.
- **Produce** a note, certificate of deposit, or check, and explain the document to the class.
- **Demonstrate** a situation involving a holder in due course.
- **Explain** the legal issues present in the situation you choose to demonstrate.

Step B: Procedure

1. Form a team of three or four students, and create an imaginary name for a bank.
2. Use markers, poster board, and information in Chapter 23 to produce one of the following items:

   - A promissory note received by your bank from a local business owner who wants to borrow $10,000
   - A certificate of deposit issued by your bank
   - A cancelled check from a checking account established at your bank
3. Present your negotiable instrument to the class, and explain why it qualifies as a negotiable instrument.
4. Write and perform two role-playing skits involving a holder in due course. Demonstrate situations in which a party tries to prevent payment. Use a personal defense in one case and a real defense in the other.

Step C: Creating a Model to Compare Defenses

Create a chart that illustrates the different defenses used by your group. Explain the elements that make the defense personal or real. Use the following labels, and display your chart for the class.

	Type of Personal Defense	Type of Real Defense
Description of Defense		
Explanation of Defense		

Step D: Workshop Analysis Report

Review the charts displayed by the class, and answer the following questions:

1. Is there a common element among the explanations of personal defenses? If so, what is it?
2. Is there a common element among the explanations of real defenses? If so, what is it?
3. Explain why a personal defense cannot be used against a holder in due course.

<u>Beach</u> v. <u>Ocwen</u> <u>Federal</u> <u>Bank</u>

U.S. Supreme Court

523 U.S. 410 (1998)

Issue If the lender in a consumer credit transaction did not deliver required forms to the borrower or failed to accurately disclose important terms of the contract, can a borrower rescind a loan agreement that is secured by his or her home more than three years after the date of the loan?

Facts The Truth in Lending Act, an act passed to protect borrowers, seeks to ensure that consumers will not be victimized by unfair or opportunistic lending practices. The act provides that when a loan in a consumer credit transaction is guaranteed by the borrower's principal residence, the borrower has the right to rescind, or cancel, the loan if the lender does not deliver certain forms or render the terms of the loan accurately. However, the act also provides that the borrower's right to rescind expires after three years or after the sale of the property in question, whichever event occurs first.

David and Linda Beach obtained a construction loan for $85,000 from Fidelity Federal Savings Bank, secured by a mortgage on the house built with the loan. A few months later, the Beaches refinanced their loan by using Ocwen Federal Bank. Five years later, the Beaches ceased making their mortgage payments. The bank began foreclosure proceedings against the Beaches. The Beaches admit the default in the payment of their loan, but they allege, as an affirmative defense, that the bank failed to disclose information required by the Truth in Lending Act. They claim that, as authorized by the act, such failure gives

them the right to rescind the mortgage and to reduce their indebtedness to the bank. The Beaches also hold that they are justified in making a claim against their lender, despite the expiration of the three-year period stipulated by the Truth in Lending Act, because they are making their claim as an affirmative defense.

The Circuit Court of the 15th Judicial Circuit of Florida, the state's intermediate appellate court, and the Supreme Court of Florida all found that the Beaches right to rescind the mortgage had expired when the three-year time limit passed.

Opinion Congress passed the Truth in Lending Act "to assure meaningful disclosure of credit terms so that the consumer will be able to compare more readily the various credit terms available to him and to avoid the uninformed use of credit, and to protect the consumer against inaccurate and unfair credit billing and credit card practices." The act requires lenders in consumer credit transactions to accurately inform borrowers of the terms of the contract, such as finance charges, annual percentage rates, and borrower's rights.

Noncompliance

A lender that fails to comply with the act may be subject to criminal liability and may be required to compensate the borrower in a civil action brought by the borrower. The Truth in Lending Act also states that a borrower whose loan is secured by the borrower's principal dwelling may rescind the loan agreement if the lender fails to deliver required forms or accurately disclose important terms of the transaction. Upon such rescission, the borrower "is not liable for any finance or other charges, and any security interest (mortgage) given by [him] . . . becomes void," and the lender must "return to the [borrower] any money or property" paid by the borrower. The right to rescind usually terminates three years after the date of the loan or when the property is sold, whichever is sooner.

Time Limitations

Although more than three years had passed since the date of the loan, the Beaches argued that they could still exercise their right of rescission because it was brought in the form of an affirmative defense to the bank's mortgage foreclosure action. The Court was not persuaded by this argument. After reviewing the act, the Court concluded that Congress intended that the right to rescind expire three years after the date of the loan, regardless of the circumstances.

The Court expressed that "Section 1635(f) [of the Truth in Lending Act], however, takes beyond any question whether it limits more than the time for bringing a suit, by governing the life of the underlying right as well. The subsection says nothing in terms of bringing an action but instead provides that 'the right of rescission [under the Act] shall expire' at the end of the time period. It talks not of a suit's commencement but a right's duration, which it addresses in terms so straightforward as to render any limitation on the time for seeking a remedy superfluous."

Holding The Court concluded that Congress intended that the act permits "no federal right to rescind, defensively or otherwise, after the 3-year period of §1635(f) has run" and affirmed the judgment of the Supreme Court of Florida. As a result of the Court's decision, a borrower in a consumer credit transaction cannot rescind the loan agreement secured by the borrower's home more than three years after the date of the loan, even if the lender failed to deliver required forms to the borrower or failed to accurately disclose important terms of the transaction as governed by the federal truth-in-lending law.

Questions for Analysis

1. What was Congress's purpose in adopting the Truth in Lending Act?
2. To what types of loans does the Truth in Lending Act apply?
3. What information must a lender provide to the borrower in a transaction subject to the Truth in Lending Act?
4. What are the consequences a lender may face if it does not comply with the disclosure requirements of the Truth in Lending Act?
5. During what time period may a borrower usually exercise the right to rescission authorized under the Truth in Lending Act?

Web Resources

Go to the *Understanding Business and Personal Law* Web site at **ubpl.glencoe.com** for information about how to access online resources for the Landmark Cases.

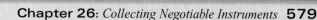

UNIT 6

UNIT OVERVIEW

Most Americans are employed in business, and all Americans purchase goods and services from business people. Businesses come in a variety of forms, from sole proprietorships to large corporations. Each type of business has its own characteristics, advantages and disadvantages, and individual legal rules. In this unit, you will learn about:

- Sole proprietorship and partnership
- Forming, financing, and operating a corporation
- Regulation and expansion

Starting a Business

YOUR *Justice Journal*

Be Your Own Boss Have you ever considered going into business for yourself? If you start your own business, you would be an entrepreneur. Seven out of ten high school students want to start their own businesses, and you could be one of them.

In your Justice Journal, write about a business that you might like to open. Provide as many details as possible about your potential business.

POWER READING STRATEGIES

To get the most out of your reading:
PREDICT what the section will be about.
CONNECT what you read with your own life.
QUESTION as you read to make sure you understand the content.
RESPOND to what you've read.

Sole Proprietorship and Partnership

Understanding Business and Personal Law *Online*

Chapter Overview Visit the *Under-standing Business and Personal Law* Web site at ubpl.glencoe.com and click on Chapter 27: Sole Proprietorship and Partnership—Chapter Overviews to preview the chapter information.

The Opening Scene

Starting in this chapter, you will witness the growth of JAC Industries from a partnership to a corporation. The business is owned and operated by Jakob and Aaron Kowalski and Cecilia Bronislawa. Jakob, Aaron, and Cecilia are touring a warehouse outside the city limits.

Setting Up Shop

CECILIA: I'm not sure that I like it here. Just how much do they want for this place?

JAKOB: About $2,700 per month. I think that's a reasonable rate.

CECILIA: Are you crazy? I disagree. That's too much for only one floor.

AARON: It's for the whole building.

CECILIA: It's still too much. Besides, I don't like the neighborhood.

JAKOB: *(Exasperated.)* What's wrong with the neighborhood?

CECILIA: It's too . . . industrial. I wanted something a little more refined.

AARON: You were expecting green lawns and swimming pools, maybe?

CECILIA: No. I wasn't expecting a palace. But we're not a manufacturing firm, and everything else around here looks like a factory.

JAKOB: That's because everything else around here really is a factory.

CECILIA: See, that's just what I mean. Did you even check with the zoning board? It might not even be legal for us to operate here.

AARON: Yes. We picked this place precisely because the zoning board said this area is okay for our kind of work.

CECILIA: Well, I suppose it will have to do. I guess I can live with it.

AARON: Thank you, Ms. Perfection. Anyway, I thought you were going to be a silent partner. You certainly have raised a lot of fuss for a silent partner. I'm not surprised by your behavior, though.

CECILIA: Secret—a secret partner, not a silent partner.

AARON: What's the difference?

JAKOB: If you're a secret partner, no one knows that you're part of the business. If you're a silent partner, everyone knows you're a partner, but you can't manage anything.

AARON: Well, I don't care what we call her, as long as she signs the partnership papers tomorrow. Are you planning on signing, Cecilia? You'd better not let us down or cause any problems.

CECILIA: Don't worry; I'll sign.

AARON: And you'll have your capital contribution in hand?

CECILIA: Every penny. What about you guys? Can I count on you to have the money?

AARON: Every red cent.

CECILIA: I guess we have a deal.

JAKOB: Agreed.

CECILIA: Then that makes us JAC Industries.

AARON: Absolutely.

CECILIA: I still think we paid too much for this place.

What Are the Legal Issues?

1. What is a sole proprietorship?
2. What are the advantages and disadvantages of a sole proprietorship?
3. What is a general partnership?
4. What is a registered limited liability partnership?
5. What is a limited partnership?

Sole Proprietorship

What You'll Learn

- How to define sole proprietorship
- How to create a sole proprietorship
- How to identify the advantages of a sole proprietorship
- How to identify the disadvantages of a sole proprietorship

Why It's Important

Understanding the nature of a sole proprietorship will help you decide when to form that type of business association rather than the other associations that are available in the market today.

Legal Terms

- sole proprietorship
- fictitious name
- employer identification number
- unlimited liability

Creation and Operation of a Sole Proprietorship

A **sole proprietorship** is a form of business that is owned and operated by one person. However, that owner may have any number of agents or employees. A sole proprietorship is the most common type of business and is the easiest to form. Typical sole proprietorships are repair shops, small retail stores, and service organizations.

A person who goes into business as a sole proprietor can choose to operate under his or her own name or can make up a name. If a sole proprietor uses anything but his or her own name, the law calls the made-up name a **fictitious name**. In selecting a fictitious name, sole proprietors must not choose a company name already in use. In some states, the first user of a fictitious name can get a court order to prevent another sole proprietor from doing business under that name.

SOLE PROPRIETOR
In a sole proprietorship, one person is responsible for running the entire business. *What advantages and disadvantages exist for a sole proprietor?*

There usually are few formal requirements in establishing a sole proprietorship. However, some sole proprietorships, such as restaurants and motels, are required to have licenses to legally operate as businesses. Other sole proprietors, such as barbers or plumbers, must have occupational licenses as well as certain types of liability insurance. Some states require a formal filing when a sole proprietorship begins or if the sole proprietorship chooses to use a fictitious name. Zoning ordinances, which prohibit businesses in certain parts of the community, can also affect sole proprietorships.

Example 1. Jennifer Edwards operated an accounting firm named Accountants International, Inc. Jennifer had some trouble collecting on the account of a local corporate client that owed her several thousand dollars. When Jennifer decided to sue, she discovered that under state law, she could not sue in court because she had not filed her business name with the city clerk's office. She also found out that zoning ordinances prohibited businesses in homes in her neighborhood.

Advantages of a Sole Proprietorship

Sole proprietorships offer specific advantages. These advantages include ease of creation, total control, retention of profits, freedom from excessive governmental control, and one-time taxation of profits.

Ease of Creation   A sole proprietorship is the easiest form of business association to form. To create a sole proprietorship, a person needs only to begin the operation of the business.

Although some government regulations need to be addressed, most applicable regulations have nothing to do with the actual operation of the business. For instance, it may be necessary to check local zoning regulations or to research governmental licensing requirements. Furthermore, when a sole proprietor decides to hire workers, he or she will have to contact the Internal Revenue Service to obtain an **employer identification number**, which is assigned for income tax purposes.

Total Control   Sole proprietorships offer business owners complete control over the operation of the business. All decisions are up to the sole proprietor. However, a sole proprietor is always free to seek the advice of experts such as accountants, attorneys, and financial planners.

Retention of Profits   Another advantage of a sole proprietorship is that the proprietor gets to keep all of the profits that the firm makes. Proprietors must still pay taxes on the profits that they make, however.

It's a Question of Ethics

Becoming a Sole Proprietor Elsie Begay has been working for a local day care center, The ABC Daycare Center, for several years. Last month she attended a meeting in which new ideas for improving service were discussed. Some ideas were innovative and would help The ABC Learning Center stand out from its competition. Elsie had been thinking about starting her own day care center, so she decided to open a center that implemented the ideas discussed at the meeting. *Is Elsie's decision an ethical one? Why or why not?*

Taxing the Sole Proprietor

One advantage of operating a sole proprietorship is that business profits and losses are combined with the sole proprietor's other income for tax purposes, so that the owner is taxed only once. When filing an income tax return, the sole proprietor must keep several factors in mind when reporting business profits. Profits are total sales minus expenses. The more tax deductions a business can take, the lower the taxable profit. As a result, more money stays in the sole proprietor's pocket at the end of the year.

Paying attention to Internal Revenue Service rules is the key to taking advantage of legitimate tax deductions. For instance, auto expenses related to operating the business are deductible. Costs associated with getting started in business are also deductible. Other deductions include legal and professional fees, business travel and moving expenses, and the cost of advertising and promotion. A percentage of business entertaining costs and certain taxes paid by the business are also deductible.

Many business deductions are often overlooked. As a result, it is important for the sole proprietor to learn as much as possible about business tax provisions.

Conduct Research Use the Internet to find IRS form Schedule C and instructions. Identify some other business deductions not previously mentioned.

Freedom from Excessive Governmental Control   As previously noted, a sole proprietorship must follow some government regulations. However, these regulations are not cumbersome when compared to the paperwork associated with limited partnerships, registered limited liability partnerships, corporations, and limited liability companies. A sole proprietorship allows the proprietor to have a great deal of flexibility and leeway.

One-Time Taxation of Profits   Sole proprietorships do not pay taxes as a business. Rather, the individual sole proprietor who owns the business pays taxes based upon his or her income. A full-time sole proprietor will pay income taxes on all profits that are made in the course of a year. If the business is only a part-time venture, then those profits plus all other income made by the sole proprietor will be taxed by the government.

Disadvantages of a Sole Proprietorship

Sole proprietorships have several disadvantages. These disadvantages include limited capital, unlimited liability, limited human resources, and limited lifetime.

Limited Capital   An obvious shortcoming of a sole proprietorship is the fact that the business owner has limited access to capital. All money used to finance the business must come from the proprietor's savings or income, or from loans obtained by the proprietor.

Unlimited Liability   Perhaps the biggest disadvantage of a sole proprietorship is unlimited liability. **Unlimited liability** means that the business owner is responsible for all losses experienced by the business.

Limited Human Resources   As the only person responsible for the decisions that affect the business, a sole proprietor is subject to tremendous stress. This stress is multiplied when the owner must make decisions that are outside his or her areas of expertise. Even if he or she consults an expert in such cases, the decision-making responsibility still falls upon the owner.

Limited Lifetime   Unlike a corporation, which has perpetual existence, a sole proprietorship lasts only as long as the proprietor. When the proprietor dies or chooses to sell or close the business, the company no longer exists.

Section 27.1   Assessment

Reviewing What You Learned
1. What is a sole proprietorship?
2. How does a sole proprietorship begin?
3. What are the advantages of a sole proprietorship?
4. What are the disadvantages of a sole proprietorship?

Critical Thinking Activity
Licensing Requirements Why does the government interfere in the formation and regulation of some sole proprietorships by creating licensing requirements?

Legal Skills in Action
The Responsibilities of a Sole Proprietor
Your Aunt Matilda, a sole proprietor, owns a store called Scrapbook Heaven. She has decided to hire you and your friend Ted to work in the store on the weekends. Aunt Matilda is convinced that hiring you and Ted will not involve any new entanglement with the government. Send Aunt Matilda an e-mail message that explains the responsibilities of a sole proprietor who hires additional workers.

The Partnership

What You'll Learn

- How to define general partnership
- How to identify the ways that a partnership can be created
- How to identify partnership rights in relation to property
- How to explain the effects of the dissolution of a partnership

Why It's Important

Understanding the nature of a partnership will help you decide when to form that type of business association.

Legal Terms

- general partnership
- articles of partnership
- partnership by proof of existence
- partnership by estoppel
- tenancy in partnership
- joint liability
- dissolution
- registered limited liability partnership (RLLP)
- limited partnership

The Nature of Partnership

Partnership law is largely found in the Uniform Partnership Act (UPA). Many states have adopted at least part of the UPA. The UPA defines partnership as "an association of two or more persons to carry on a business for profit." Partnerships have several advantages over sole proprietorships. More capital and credit is usually available to a partnership, and the burden of all the work does not fall on one person. Furthermore, a partner does not have sole responsibility for any losses suffered.

On the other hand, one disadvantage of a partnership is that the partners share in the liabilities. Each partner is responsible for the other partners' actions within the scope of the partnership. Another disadvantage to a partnership is that the partners must share any profits. Because all partners have a voice in running the business, bickering can cause problems. Furthermore, the death of a partner also dissolves the partnership.

Forming a General Partnership

When two or more competent parties combine their money, labor, and skills for the purpose of carrying on a lawful business, they create a **general partnership**. The partners will share in the profits and losses arising from the undertaking. General partnerships can be formed in one of three ways: by agreement, by proof of existence, or by estoppel.

By Agreement Forming a general partnership by agreement requires the valid assent of all parties. Such an agreement is usually express and may be written or oral. However, under the Statute of Frauds, if a partnership is to last more than a year, it must be evidenced in writing. Following the same principle, a partnership formed to sell, buy, or lease real property must also be in writing. The partnership agreement is known as the **articles of partnership**, or as the articles of copartnership (see Figure 27.1).

There are many possible points of difference between partners, so the agreement should be clearly and fully explained. Some important issues that should be covered include the following:
- Parties to the agreement
- Specific nature, scope, and limits of the business

- Planned duration of the business
- Amount of each partner's original investment and procedures for future investments
- Provisions regarding salaries, withdrawal of funds, and the division of profits
- Terms under which a partner may withdraw from the partnership

Figure 27.1

ARTICLES OF PARTNERSHIP

This agreement, made March 17, 20 – –, between Cecilia Bronislawa of 291 Cedar Lane, Jackson, Mississippi, and Jacob Kowalski and Aaron Kowalski of 1892 Mosley Avenue, Jackson, Mississippi.

1. The above named persons have this day formed a partnership that shall operate under the name of JAC Enterprises, located at 1856 Chadwick Drive, Jackson, Mississippi 39204, and shall engage in manufacturing and selling petroleum products.

2. The duration of this agreement will be for a term of five (5) years, beginning on March 17, 20 – –, or for a shorter term if agreed upon in writing by both partners.

3. The initial investment by each partner will be as follows: Cecilia Bronislawa, cash of $100,000; Jacob Kowalski, cash of $50,000; Aaron Kowalski, cash of $50,000. These investments are partnership property.

4. Each partner will give his or her time, skill, and attention to the operation of this partnership and will engage in no other business enterprise unless permission is granted in writing by the other partners.

5. The salary for each partner will be as follows: Cecilia Bronislawa, $50,000 per year; Jacob Kowalski, $40,000 per year; Aaron Kowalski, $40,000 per year. No partner may withdraw cash or other assets from the business without express permission in writing from the other partners. All profits and losses of the business will be shared as follows: Cecilia Bronislawa, 50 percent; Jacob Kowalski, 25 percent; Aaron Kowalski, 25 percent.

6. Upon the dissolution of the partnership due to termination of this agreement, or to written permission by each of the partners, or to the death or incapacitation of one or all partners, a new contract may be entered into by the partners; or the sole continuing partner has the option to purchase the other partner's interest in the business at a price that shall not exceed the balance in the terminating partner's capital account. The payment shall be made in cash in equal quarterly installments from the date of termination.

7. At the conclusion of this contract, unless it is agreed by all partners to continue the operation of the business under a new contract, the assets of the partnership, after the liabilities are paid, will be divided in proportion to the balance in each partner's capital account on that date.

Cecilia Bronislawa	*March 17, 20 – –*
Cecilia Bronislawa	Date
Jacob Kowalski	*March 17, 20 – –*
Jacob Kowalski	Date
Aaron Kowalski	*March 17, 20 – –*
Aaron Kowalski	Date

ARTICLES OF PARTNERSHIP
Partners share profits, losses, and management decisions. *How will the profits and losses be shared in this partnership?*

PARTNERSHIP
FORMATION
A partnership can be
formed in one of three
ways. *What is the most
effective way to form
a general partnership?*

Figure 27.2 | **Partnership Formation**

Form	Definition
Partnership by contract	Express agreement drawn up by partners Articles of partnership
Partnership by proof of existence	Individuals form partnership because of their method of doing business Sharing of profits is *prima facie* evidence
Partnership by estoppel	Third party led to believe a partnership exists No true partnership created

By Proof of Existence   Drawing up the articles of partnership is not the only way to form a partnership (see Figure 27.2). Sometimes a partnership can be formed because of the way that two or more people conduct their business together. Such a partnership, which forms regardless of the label given to the enterprise or the intent of the parties involved, is termed a **partnership by proof of existence**. The UPA provides a list of characteristics to determine whether a partnership actually exists. The sharing of profits is at the top of this list. If two or more people share the profits of a business venture, it will be difficult for them to deny that a partnership exists. However, there are exceptions to the rule. A person may share profits and not be able to claim partnership status if the share that is paid is one of the following:

- Repayment of a debt
- Wages to an employee or rent to a landlord
- An annuity to the widow or the widower of a deceased partner
- Interest on a loan
- Consideration for the sale of a business

> *Example 2.* Patrick Tyler opened Planetary Videos, a video rental store. At first, he worked in the day-to-day operation of the business. However, he gradually became interested in other ventures and hired Molly Petro to take care of the details of the business. Most of the time, Petro was in charge. Tyler showed up on Fridays to collect his 60-percent share of the profits. Each week Petro would draw her 40-percent share of the profits according to the agreement with Tyler. This arrangement went on for five years. Then the state government took the video store by eminent domain for a new highway project. Petro claimed that, as a partner, she was entitled to a share of this money. Tyler disagreed, and Petro sued. The court held that she was a partner because

she had shared in the profits and had contributed a great deal of her time and expertise to the business.

By Estoppel   If someone does or says something that leads a third party to believe that a partnership exists, then a court may treat the arrangement as a **partnership by estoppel**. This type of partnership is not a real partnership. It is a way for the court to prevent injustice because someone has relied on the words or actions of another party and has acted accordingly.

> *Example 3.* Perry Welsh and Paula Porter were partners in a fast-food restaurant. The business needed a loan quickly or it would be forced to close down. Unknown to Welsh, Porter convinced Roscoe Standard to cooperate in a charade to convince the bank's loan officer that Standard was a partner in the restaurant. The loan officer checked Standard's credit record and extended a loan. If the partnership defaulted on the loan, the bank could hold Standard liable along with the partners.

Note, however, that a real partnership was not created here. Standard would not have any partnership rights in relation to the fast-food restaurant.

Types of Partners

There are five types of partners: general, secret, silent, dormant, and limited (see Figure 27.3). Each of these partners is a co-owner of the business and has some liability for the debts of the firm.

Figure 27.3	Types of Partners		
Type of Partner	Participation in the Business	Relationship to the Public	Degree of Liability
General	Active	Known	Unlimited
Secret	Active	Unknown	Unlimited
Silent	Not active	Known	Unlimited
Dormant	Not active	Unknown	Unlimited
Limited	Not active	Known	Limited

TYPES OF PARTNERS
A partnership is more complicated than a sole proprietorship. *Is there a limit on the number of people who may form a general partnership?*

Every partnership must have at least one general partner. In most firms, the partners are general partners. A general partner plays an active role in the management of the partnership and is publicly known as a partner. A general partner has unlimited liability for the firm's debts.

A secret partner is a general partner who has an active role in the management of the partnership, but whose connection with the partnership is kept a secret. A secret partner also has unlimited liability for the firm's debts.

A silent partner is a general partner who takes no active role in the management of the partnership. A silent partner is known publicly as a partner and has unlimited liability for the firm's debts.

Example 4. In The Opening Scene, Aaron describes Cecilia as a silent partner in JAC Industries and tells her that she has no role in managing the business. However, Aaron has incorrectly labeled Cecilia's role. Cecilia will be a secret partner because she will take part in the management of the partnership while her identity remains a secret to the public.

A dormant partner is a general partner who takes no active part in the management of the firm and whose connection with the firm is kept secret. A dormant partner, however, has unlimited liability for the firm's debts. In contrast, a limited partner is one whose liability does not extend beyond his or her investment. This liability arrangement is known as a limited partnership.

Partnership Property

Certain rights and limitations arise regarding partnership property. For this reason, it is important to distinguish between property that belongs to the partnership and property that belongs to individual partners. Property contributed directly to the partnership when the partnership is created is partnership property. The UPA also states that partnership property includes property that is bought with partnership funds. In other circumstances, the question of ownership of a piece of property is difficult to answer. Other indicators can help a court make the determination. For example, a court may ask the following questions:

- Has the partnership consistently used the property?
- Has the partnership listed the property on its account books?
- Has the partnership paid expenses involving the property?
- Has the partnership improved or repaired the property?
- Has the partnership paid taxes on the property?

Each "yes" answer makes it more likely the court will decide that the property belongs to the partnership.

▲
PARTNERSHIP PROPERTY
A partner may not use partnership property for
personal or other nonpartnership purposes.
How can this agreement come about?

Property Rights of the Partners

Certain rights arise regarding property that belongs to the partnership. These rights include the right to use the property, the right to manage the firm, and the right to share in the profits.

Right to Use Property   Partners are co-owners of all the real and personal property included in the partnership. As a result, the partners can use the property for partnership business. The property cannot be used for other business unless the other partners give their permission. This co-ownership, called **tenancy in partnership** by the UPA, gives rise to other limitations. For example, a partner cannot, on his or her own, transfer ownership of the property. Also, the property cannot be taken by a partner's personal creditors. Moreover, when a partner dies, the right to use partnership property passes to the other partners.

Example 5. The articles of partnership for a business called HDJ Enterprises include a tenancy in partnership provision. In a matter not involving HDJ Enterprises, Holden, a partner in HDJ enterprises, is sued by Karen Yeltsin. Yeltsin wins the suit, but finds

that she cannot collect from Holden because his personal assets are insufficient to cover the amount that he owes her. Yeltsin then tries to seize several of HDJ Enterprise's computers to cover Holden's debt to her. The court would prevent such a seizure because the computers are not Holden's individual property. However, if the judgment had been granted against the entire partnership, then the computers could be seized to pay the debt.

Right to Manage the Firm   Unless a partner's rights are limited in the partnership agreement, each partner has an equal voice in managing the partnership's business. As a result, each partner can bind the partnership on any matter within the scope of its business affairs. In a disagreement about ordinary business matters, the decision of the majority is final. If there is an even number of partners and the vote is split, then no decision can be made. If such deadlocks persist, the partners must consider ending the partnership.

The UPA provides that some partnership decisions cannot be made without the consent of all the partners. For example, a new partner cannot be admitted to the firm without unanimous consent. Similarly, it takes a unanimous vote of all partners to change the essential nature of the business or to embark on a new line of business not originally provided for in the articles of partnership. A unanimous vote is needed to amend the original articles of partnership. Also, any agreement to dispose of the partnership's goodwill requires unanimous consent. If the partners are considering an action that would make continuing the partnership impossible, such action would require unanimous approval.

Right to Share in the Profits   Unless there is an agreement to the contrary, partners share equally in the profits, regardless of their initial capital contribution or the time devoted by each partner to the business. This right can be assigned to others and passes to the partner's heirs upon the partner's death. This right also includes the right to an accounting at the end of the partnership.

Duties of the Partners

Partners must trust one another. Each partner is an agent of the other partner and has duties comparable to those of an agent. Partners have the following duties:

- To always act in good faith and in the best interests of the firm
- To always use their best skill and judgment in looking after the firm's affairs
- To be loyal to the firm and put the firm's interests first.

A Global Perspective:
Laws Around the World

Iceland

If you could cure any disease in the world, what would it be? Multiple Sclerosis? Cancer? One day, this question might be outdated. In 1999, Iceland's parliament, in the first legislation of its kind, gave a local biotech company permission to build a database from the health files of all its citizens. Many scientists believe that this collection of medical information can help unravel the genetic, or hereditary, cause of disease.

Iceland makes the perfect laboratory for such an endeavor. Icelanders are a mostly homogenous people whose families have lived in isolation on the island for more than 1,000 years. In such an environment, medical and genealogical data can be matched to pinpoint diseases that run in families. This information enables scientists to search for the genes that cause specific diseases. As one scientist explains, "If you're trying to find a diabetes gene in the American population, it's almost impossible because we all have very different histories and ancestries." In Iceland's "simpler genetic landscape," however, the mutant gene should stand out like a beacon. After the mutation is discovered, a treatment is that much closer. Here's a snapshot of Iceland.

Geographical area	**39,769 sq. mi.**
Population	**279,384**
Capital	**Reykjavik**
Legal system	**Civil law based on Danish law**
Language	**Icelandic**
Religion	**87.1% Evangelical Lutheran**
Life expectancy	**80 years**

Critical Thinking Question A gene is a minute part of a cell that gives us our mother's curly hair, our father's straight nose, and maybe even our grandmother's outgoing personality. What traits or characteristics do you have that are like those of other family members? For more information on Iceland, visit **ubpl.glencoe.com** or your local library.

Because each partner is an agent of the firm, each may bind the firm by any act that is part of the firm's business. Any act of a partner that is not a part of the firm's business is not binding on the firm. Similarly, if the majority of the partners vote not to enter a particular contract, and one of the partners ignores the vote and enters that forbidden contract, then that partner alone is bound to that contract.

Liability of the Partners

Partners have unlimited liability for all of the debts of the partnership incurred while they are partners, even to the extent of their personal assets. Partners are liable to other members of the firm for their share of the firm's debts. Partners share losses in the same proportion that they share profits.

In addition, partners are jointly liable with their partners on contracts entered into by any member of the firm acting within the actual or apparent scope of the firm's business. **Joint liability** means that in the event of a lawsuit, all the partners must be sued together. Partners are jointly and severally (separately) liable for torts committed within the scope of the firm's business. As a result, an injured party has the choice of suing all the partners together or one or more of them separately. This liability is possibly the most significant drawback to the partnership approach to doing business. One result is that an innocent partner can be held responsible for the wrongdoings of other partners.

Virtual Law

Online Legal Advice

Small business owners can get legal forms such as contracts and leases from the Internet. There are Web sites that exist especially for this purpose. The fees for access to these legal documents vary. The amount charged depends on the complexity of the document. For very complex documents, fees can be broken into parts or can be paid by subscription. There are also several Web sites that offer consumer documents such as marriage separation agreements. So far there have not been any widespread efforts to regulate online legal activities. However, some state bar associations have issued strong opinions about offering legal advice on the Internet. (Source: *New York Times*, February 22, 2001)

Connect Search the Internet for online providers of legal advice. Notice the fine line between making information available and offering legal advice.

Example 6. Suppose that one year after the articles of partnership for HDJ Enterprises are signed, Holden (a partner) loses control of a delivery truck and crashes into Thompson Industries' laboratory building. Boris Thompson is severely injured. Thompson could sue Holden's partners even though they were not personally involved in the accident.

Dissolving a Partnership

A **dissolution** is a legal detachment. The dissolution of a partnership is a change in the relationship of the partners that occurs when any partner stops being associated with the business. Dissolution is not the same as the termination of the business. When a partner dies or voluntarily withdraws from the firm, the firm is dissolved. The firm also may be dissolved by court decree. The partners then are no longer carrying on as co-owners of a business for profit. In contrast, dissolution occurs at the moment that one partner ceases to be associated with the firm. The business operations, however, cannot be stopped on a moment's notice. It takes time to close the firm's affairs and formally bring the firm to an end. During this period, the partners are not carrying on business.

Effects of Dissolution

Dissolution does not necessarily bring the business to an end. Other partners may want to continue in business together. If so, there must be an accounting of the old firm's affairs. New financial arrangements must be made regarding the new firm. A new agreement must be drawn up regarding the conduct of the new firm. Public notice must usually be given to relieve retiring partners from liability for any new debts.

Distribution of Assets

Upon dissolution, an accounting of the firm's financial affairs is necessary to determine how the firm's assets will be distributed or divided. The firm's liabilities are paid in the following order:

1. Money owed to creditors other than partners
2. Money lent by partners to the firm
3. The original money paid into the partnership by each partner
4. The surplus, if any, owed to the partners

Example 7. Suppose that one year after forming JAC Industries, Cecilia loans $50,000 to the business. If JAC Industries is dissolved, the firm's creditors would be the first to be paid. Cecilia would be next in line for payment. After Cecilia's loan was repaid, the three partners could then recover their initial contributions to the partnership.

If the business is insolvent, its assets must be sold to pay the creditors. In addition, the partners are individually liable for any unpaid balance that the sale of the assets will not cover. If both the business and one or more of its partners are insolvent, liability for debts is distributed differently. The firm's creditors have the first claim on the partnership's assets; the personal creditors of the individual insolvent partners have first claim on the insolvent partner's personal assets.

The Revised Uniform Partnership Act

Since the UPA was written in 1914, it has undergone extensive revision. The revision process resulted in a new variation of the act, which is referred to as the Revised Uniform Partnership Act (RUPA).

This new act has already been adopted in many states. As a result, it is a good idea to check the current status of the UPA in your home state. Some of the major revisions that are now found in the RUPA include the elimination of the concept of tenancy in partnership and the establishment of a way to file a statement of authority with the state government.

Registered Limited Liability Partnerships

In recent years a new type of partnership, generally referred to as a **registered limited liability partnership (RLLP)**, has been created. A RLLP is designed to eliminate a major disadvantage of the general partnership, namely, joint and several liability. Under terms of a statute permitting the formation of RLLPs, partners can escape joint and several liability for the torts, wrongful acts, negligence, or misconduct of other partners by registering with the appropriate state office. The registration statement usually includes the following information:

- The RLLP's name (Usually, the name must include either the expression *Registered Limited Liability Partnership*, the words *Limited Liability Partnership*, or an abbreviation such as *RLLP* or *LLP*.)
- The purpose of the partnership
- The number of partners in the partnership
- A statement of the intent to form an RLLP
- The address of the partnership's main place of business
- The name and address of a statutory agent for service of process

All the partners, or at least the partners holding a majority interest in the partnership, must file the statement. The registration statement must be updated annually. RLLPs are to be taxed as general partnerships.

Limited Partnerships

A **limited partnership** is quite different from a general partnership. RUPA defines a limited partnership as "a partnership formed by two or more persons . . . having one or more general partners and one or more limited partners." Limited partners are investors who have no control in managing the partnership, and their names may not appear in the partnership name. A limited partner's liability for the partnership's debts does not extend beyond his or her investment in the partnership. Thus, the term *limited* in the title of the partner refers to the partner's liability.

Limited partnerships are often used in real estate ventures and tax shelter investments. Investors want the tax advantages of a partnership, but not the general liability that goes with being a general partner. For instance, if someone sells you a $10,000 limited partnership interest in a $3 million real estate deal and the whole thing goes bankrupt, you will be out only your original $10,000.

Limited partnerships must meet more stringent formalities than general partnerships. The partners must file a certificate of limited partnership with the appropriate state or county office. The business name must also indicate that it is a limited partnership. These requirements are necessary to warn third parties that certain partners possess limited liability. The limited partner could lose limited liability if the limited partnership certificate is not filed or is filed improperly. In terms of liability, the limited partnership falls between the general partnership, in which all owners have unlimited liability, and the corporation, in which all owners have limited liability.

Section 27.2   Assessment

Reviewing What You Learned

1. What is a general partnership?
2. How can a partnership be created?
3. What are a partner's rights in relation to property?
4. What are the effects of the dissolution of a partnership?

Critical Thinking Activity

Limited Liability Partnership Why did some state legislatures decide to create registered limited liability partnerships?

Legal Skills in Action

Partnership Liability Clay, who is a general partner in Harrington Enterprises, believes he will not be liable for a tort committed by Ian, another partner in the firm. Write a letter to Clay explaining whether he will be liable for Ian's tort.

Chapter Summary

Section 27.1 Sole Proprietorship

- A sole proprietorship is a business that is owned by one person. It is the most common kind of business and is the easiest to establish. Typical sole proprietorships are repair shops, small retail stores, and service organizations. Many locally owned businesses in your community are probably sole proprietorships.

- A sole proprietor can choose to operate under his or her own name, or he or she can make up a fictitious name for the business entity. In selecting a fictitious name, sole proprietors must not choose a company name already in use. In some states, the first user of a fictitious name can get a court order to prevent another sole proprietor from doing business under that name. Some requirements may affect sole proprietorships such as licenses, insurance, or zoning requirements for conducting business. Barbers and plumbers are examples of sole proprietors who must have occupational licenses as well as certain types of liability insurance. Zoning ordinances prohibit businesses from operating in certain parts of the community.

- Sole proprietorships are easily created, and the sole proprietor has total control of how the business is run and of the profits. The government does not overly regulate sole proprietorships, and profits are taxed only once.

- Most disadvantages of sole proprietorships are related to limitations of capital and human resources. All money used to finance a sole proprietorship must come from the proprietor's savings or income, or from loans obtained by the proprietor. Human resources are limited in that a sole proprietor is responsible for making all decisions that affect the business. Aside from facing limitations in available capital and human resources, a sole proprietorship also has a limited lifetime. When the proprietor dies or chooses to sell or close the business, the company no longer exists. Another disadvantage to the sole proprietor is that there is no limit to the liability she or he could incur. As a result, the proprietor's personal assets are at risk if the business fails.

Section 27.2 The Partnership

- A general partnership is created when two or more parties combine their money, labor, and skills for the purpose of carrying on a lawful business. The Uniform Partnership Act (UPA) defines partnership as "an association of two or more persons to carry on a business for profit."

- General partnerships can be formed by agreement, proof of existence, or estoppel. A limited partnership is a partnership formed by two or more persons having one or more general partners and one or more limited partners. Limited partners are investors only. They invest in the business and share in profits. They have no management rights, and their liability is limited to their investment.

- In a partnership, a partner has the right to use the partnership property, manage the partnership, and share in the profits.

- The dissolution of a partnership is a change in the relationship of the partners that occurs when any partner stops being associated with the business. The business operations cannot be stopped on a moment's notice. It takes time to close the firm's affairs and formally bring the firm to an end. During this period, the partners are not carrying on business. Upon dissolution, liabilities are paid in the following order: (1) debts to creditors other than partners; (2) money lent by partners to the firm; (3) the original money paid by each partner; and (4) surplus owed to the partners.

Using Legal Language

Consider the key terms in the list below. Then use these terms to complete the following exercises.

sole proprietorship

tenancy in partnership

fictitious name

employer identification number

joint liability

dissolution

unlimited liability

Revised Uniform Partnership
 Act (RUPA)

Uniform Partnership Act (UPA)

general partnership

articles of partnership

partnership by proof of
 existence

limited partnership

partnership by estoppel

Understanding Business and Personal Law Online

Self-Check Quiz Visit the *Understanding Business and Personal Law* Web site at **ubpl.glencoe.com** and click on Chapter 27: Sole Proprietorship and Partnership—Self-Check Quizzes to prepare for the chapter exam.

1. Imagine you are a business attorney and have been hired by a new business owner to discuss the legal forms of business association. With a partner, create a role-play in which you are a business attorney, and your partner, a new business owner, has hired you to discuss the legal forms of business association.
2. Perform your dialogue in front of the class.

The Law Review

Answer the following questions. Refer to the chapter for additional reinforcement.

3. Why is a sole proprietorship the most common type of business and easiest to form?
4. What are the advantages and disadvantages of a partnership?
5. What are the differences among a secret partner, a silent partner, and a dormant partner?
6. What questions might the court ask to determine whether certain property belongs to the partnership?
7. What are the duties of the partners to each other?
8. In some states, what can a sole proprietor do to prevent other companies from adopting his or her fictitious name?
9. What is tenancy in partnership?

Linking School to Work

Acquiring and Evaluating Information
Research the local requirements for starting a business in your state. Find out:
10. What types of businesses require a license
11. What the local requirements are
12. How to select a fictitious name
13. How to acquire an occupational license
14. What type of zoning ordinances might be an issue

Write a two-page paper explaining your findings.

Let's Debate

Tax Evasion
Richard and Emilio own a plumbing supply business. They sell parts and tools to plumbers, irrigation specialists, and homeowners. Richard files the tax return each year and purposely provides inaccurate information so that neither he nor Emilio will have to pay taxes. Emilio is unaware of what Richard is doing.

Debate
15. Is Emilio legally responsible for the tax return Richard filed for their business? Why or why not?
16. If the IRS decides to audit the business, is Emilio financially liable for any back taxes? Why or why not?
17. What would you do if you were Emilio and you discovered what Richard was doing?

Grasping Case Issues

For the following cases, give your decision and state a legal principle that applies.
18. Nancy Myers's law office is in the prestigious Brown & Brown Law Office Building. To help her business, Myers has business cards printed that read, "Nancy Myers of the Brown & Brown Law Office." When Samuel Brown, one of the Brown partners, discovers what Nancy has done, he laughs and tells her she is very clever. Relying on the information on the business card, Bob Wash loans Myers $5,000. When Myers does not pay the money back, Wash sues both Myers and the Brown partnership. Who will be liable to Wash for the money Myers borrowed? Explain your answer.
19. Ruth Drummond, a general partner, purchases all merchandise for the partnership. A manufacturer gives Drummond a 10-percent discount on goods she purchases for the partnership. Drummond never tells the other partners about the discount and keeps the difference for herself. When the other partners learn of the discount, they demand that Drummond turn over the money she pocketed. Are the partners correct in their demand? Explain your answer.
20. Max Massie is a general partner in the construction firm of Massie, Briggs, and Yates. While operating a forklift at a construction site, Massie collides with a limousine owned by the mayor. The mayor sues all three partners. Yates and Briggs argue that because Massie was at fault, the mayor has no cause of action against them. Are they correct? Explain your answer.
21. Alan Gallagher and Norma Kendall each contribute $20,000 to begin their partnership. At one point, the venture is in trouble, so Gallagher lends the partnership an additional $10,000. Eventually, the partnership is dissolved. After the creditors are paid, $50,000 of assets remain. Kendall claims that each of them should receive $25,000. Is Kendall correct? Why or why not?

In each case that follows, you be the judge.

22. Partnership by Proof of Evidence

George and Clarence Simandl, brothers, jointly owned a gas station-delicatessen-magazine stand. All building permits were issued in both names, and both parties signed all of the business contracts. They carried on the business and shared profits and losses for 40 years, until George's death. When George died, his wife, Albina, carried on his part of the business. When Clarence died, his sister claimed that all property was in Clarence's estate. Albina disagreed, contending that a partnership had existed and that she was entitled to a share of the assets. *Is Albina correct? Why or why not?*
Simandl v. Simandl, 445 N.E.2d 734 (OH).

23. Dissolution

As a partner, Hanes contributed $19,875 to a new partnership as his capital contribution. The other partners, Giambrone, Hayes, and Medley, made no capital contribution, although they had agreed to do so. Medley withdrew some of the money contributed by Hanes without the unanimous consent of the partners, although such consent was required by the articles. Medley also failed to make mortgage payments which caused the firm to default on the loan. Hanes asked a court for a dissolution. *Is Hanes entitled to a dissolution? Why or why not?*
Hanes v. Giambrone, 471 N. E. 2d 801 (OH).

Legal Link

Find Resources for Entrepreneurs

Taquita is ready to become a sole proprietor. She just finished a business degree at the local community college and has saved over $25,000 by working while she was going to school.

Connect

Using a variety of search engines, help Taquita:
24. Research 10 Web sites that provide resources to entrepreneurs and small business owners.
25. Prioritize the sites according to the importance of the information they might be able to provide.

POWER READING STRATEGIES

26. **Predict** Why would a small business owner choose to use a fictitious name instead of his or her own?
27. **Connect** Would you like to own a business one day? Why or why not?
28. **Question** Do you think it is fair that the law holds each partner responsible for the other partners' actions within the partnership? Why or why not?
29. **Respond** How is a business partnership like a marriage? How is it different?

Forming and Financing a Corporation

Understanding Business and Personal Law *Online*

Chapter Overview Visit the *Understanding Business and Personal Law* Web site at ubpl.glencoe.com and click on Chapter 28: Forming and Financing a Corporation—Chapter Overviews to preview the chapter information.

The Opening Scene

Jakob and Aaron Kowalski and Cecilia Bronislawa have decided to change their business from a partnership to a corporation. In this scene, they are holding a lunch meeting at an expensive restaurant to discuss some of the details associated with the incorporation process.

Free Lunch, Inc.

Jakob: This is a pretty expensive place.

Cecilia: We can afford it.

Jakob: You can afford it. You were taking 50 percent of the profits from the partnership.

Cecilia: I wasn't taking anything. That's what we agreed to. But if it makes you happy, I'll pick up the check.

Jakob: It makes me very happy.

Aaron: If you two are through bickering, let's get down to business.

Cecilia: Sure thing, chief.

Aaron: Okay, the main thing we have to deal with today is getting this incorporation process started.

Cecilia: So what do we need to do first?

Aaron: Well, first of all, we need to get our hands on those incorporation forms as soon as possible.

Cecilia: Don't worry. After lunch, I'm going to the capitol to buy some equipment for us. I can pick up the incorporation papers at the attorney general's office.

Jakob: Oh no, you can't.

Cecilia: What's wrong? Are you getting cold feet again?

Jakob: No. You're talking about the wrong office. You're supposed to go to the secretary of state's office.

Cecilia: That's right. Sorry.

Aaron: Maybe we should use a promoter.

Cecilia: We don't need a promoter.

Aaron: I know we don't need one. I just thought that maybe we could use one to handle the complicated stuff.

Cecilia: There's nothing complicated about this.

Aaron: I hope you're right.

Jakob: Don't forget the forms for the statutory agent.

Cecilia: The what?

Jakob: The statutory agent.

Cecilia: I heard what you said. I just don't know what it is.

Jakob: The statutory agent is for when we get sued.

Aaron: Once again, my brother, the optimist.

Jakob: Once again, your brother, the realist.

Cecilia: Once again, I'm leaving. I'll see you later.

(Cecilia exits quickly.)

Jakob: Well what do you know? She did it again.

Aaron: Did what?

Jakob: Stuck us with the check!

Aaron: *(Aaron jumps up.)* Cecilia!

What Are the Legal Issues?

1. What is a corporation?
2. What are the advantages and disadvantages of a corporation?
3. What state office regulates the incorporation process?
4. Are promoters necessary during the incorporation process?
5. Why are statutory agents required for all corporations?

Corporations

What You'll Learn

- How to define corporation
- How to distinguish among various types of corporations
- How to create a corporation
- How to finance a corporation
- How to distinguish between a corporation and a limited liability company

Why It's Important

Understanding the nature of a corporation will help you decide when to form one rather than the other associations that are available.

Legal Terms

- corporation
- shareholder
- share
- promoter
- articles of incorporation
- certificate of incorporation
- common stock
- dividends
- preferred stock
- limited liability company (LLC)

The Nature of a Corporation

Although partnerships and sole proprietorships are excellent forms of organization for some kinds of businesses, about 90 percent of all business in the United States is done by corporations. A **corporation** is a body formed and authorized by law to act as a single person, distinct from its members or owners. The word "corporation" generally brings to mind large businesses such as McDonald's and AOL Time Warner. Not all corporations are large, however. In fact, approximately 40 percent of all corporations employ fewer than five employees. Regardless of their size, all corporations have the same basic form.

An individual who owns shares of a corporation is called a **shareholder** or a stockholder. A **share** is a single unit of ownership of a corporation. Each shareholder has one vote for each share of stock that he or she owns in the corporation. Shareholders cast their votes to elect a board of directors whose duty is to direct the corporation's business.

Advantages of a Corporation

There are several advantages in doing business as a corporation. For example, selling shares enables a corporation to tap into a large source of capital that is unavailable to partnerships and sole proprietorships. Each shareholder's liability is limited to the amount of money he or she paid for shares in the corporation. Another advantage of a corporation is that it is a legal entity, or a legal person, created by the state. Consequently, it has the power to make contracts, buy and sell goods, sue, and be sued. Another distinct advantage to the corporation is that it has continuity of existence. This means that a corporation continues to exist, regardless of the lifespans of its founders, shareholders, managers, and directors.

Disadvantages of a Corporation

Like sole proprietorships and partnerships, corporations have disadvantages. For instance, a corporation's income may be taxed more than once. This happens when a corporation distributes part or all of its profits, after taxes, to its shareholders in the form of dividends. The shareholders' dividends become part of their taxable income. In this way, profits of a corporation are taxed twice—once when earned by the corporation and again when shareholders receive their portion of the profit.

Corporations, especially larger ones, must also face extensive government regulation. Part of that regulation involves the actual formation of the corporation. The incorporation process must be followed exactly if the founders are to avoid legal difficulties, as outlined later in this chapter. Another disadvantage is that the original founders of the corporation can lose not only the control, but also the actual ownership of the corporation. Because of the prominence of some corporations, business decisions by their directors and officers are often subject to close scrutiny.

Legal Briefs

Although the shareholders of a corporation are the actual owners, they are not agents of the corporation. As a result, shareholders cannot commit the corporation to any contractual arrangements.

Types of Corporations

Corporations may be classified as public or private corporations, stock or nonstock corporations, and domestic or foreign corporations (see Figure 28.1). Public corporations include incorporated political units, such as towns, villages, cities, and school districts. Private corporations may be classified as profit or nonprofit corporations. Profit corporations, private corporations organized for the purpose of making money, are found in nearly every major field of economic activity,

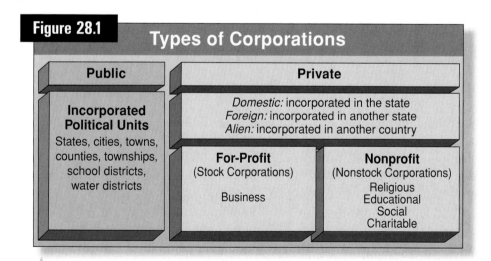

Figure 28.1

Types of Corporations

Public	Private	
Incorporated Political Units	*Domestic:* incorporated in the state *Foreign:* incorporated in another state *Alien:* incorporated in another country	
States, cities, towns, counties, townships, school districts, water districts	**For-Profit** (Stock Corporations) Business	**Nonprofit** (Nonstock Corporations) Religious Educational Social Charitable

TYPES OF CORPORATIONS
There are many different types of corporations, and each has a generally accepted label. *In your opinion, which of these corporate forms is the most effective?*

Social Studies
Imagine you have been operating a small business for several years. The business is growing, and you would like to expand. To expand quickly, you would like to set your business up as a corporation.

Research Activity
What procedures would you follow to set up a corporation in your state? What forms would you have to complete? What fees would you have to pay? Conduct research to find out. Then research the laws in another state. Compare and contrast the laws in both states.

including transportation, manufacturing, business, technology, entertainment, financial, and service fields. These corporations are regulated by the laws of the states in which they operate. If they are engaged in interstate commerce, they are also regulated by federal regulations. Any corporation formed for business purposes is operating for a profit and has capital stock. A bank, a railroad, and a trading firm are stock corporations.

Nonprofit corporations, such as the Red Cross, are formed for educational, religious, charitable, or social purposes. A nonprofit corporation in which membership is acquired by agreement, rather than by acquisition of stock, is also a nonstock corporation. Many nonprofit fraternal organizations are nonstock corporations.

Corporations may also be classified as domestic or foreign. A corporation is considered a domestic corporation in the state in which it is incorporated. In all other states in which it may operate, the corporation is considered a foreign corporation. A foreign corporation should not be confused with an alien corporation. An alien corporation is one that is incorporated in another country but is doing business in this country.

Forming a Corporation

Each state legislature has passed its own version of corporate law. Most state legislatures have followed the pattern established by the Model Business Corporation Act (MBCA). Other states have opted to follow the Revised Model Business Corporation Act (RMBCA), an updated version of the MBCA. Still other states have created their own statutes. Even those legislatures that have adopted either the MBCA or the RMBCA have made changes designed to fit the business climate, customs, and traditions of their states. This creates a great deal of variety among state incorporation laws. Despite this variety, some generalizations about the incorporation process can be made.

The Incorporation Process

A corporation cannot come into existence by itself—people must take the necessary steps to bring it into legal existence. Sometimes the owner of an existing sole proprietorship or the partners in an existing partnership will elect to incorporate. At other times, a business will start out from scratch as a corporation. Whatever the case, the as-yet-uncreated corporation will need promoters to direct the incorporation process. (See Figure 28.2).

Corporate Promoters A **promoter** carries out the incorporation process by taking the initial steps to organize and finance a business. These steps may include assembling investors, leasing office and warehouse space, purchasing supplies and equipment, and hiring employees.

Figure 28.2

THE INCORPORATION PROCESS

A corporation cannot come into existence spontaneously. It must be organized by people who take the steps outlined by a valid incorporation statute.

1 Choosing a Name

One of the first steps in setting up a new corporation is choosing a corporate name. Under most state statutes, the words *corporation, incorporated,* or *company,* or an abbreviation of one of the words, must be in the name.

2 Completing the Articles of Incorporation

Sometimes people who are already in business as sole proprietors or as partners decide to incorporate. Other times, people just starting out in business decide to incorporate. Whatever the case, the articles of incorporation must be filled out properly.

3 Receiving the Certificate of Incorporation

After the articles of incorporation have been approved by the secretary of state's office, a certificate of incorporation will be issued. At that time, the corporation has been officially formed.

Promoters are personally liable for the contracts they make in the name of the corporation. This liability can be avoided if the promoter convinces the corporation to officially adopt the contracts and remove the promoter from liability.

Corporate Name One of the first steps that the promoters take is to choose a corporate name. Under most state statutes, these words *corporation, incorporated,* or *company,* or an abbreviation of one of the words, must appear as a part of the corporate name. The corporation cannot use the name of an existing corporation, either foreign or domestic, or a name that is so similar to an existing name that people would be confused by that similarity. Even in situations where a specific state does not prohibit the use of similar names, the court will prevent such duplication if confusion or unfair competition results. Often the secretary of state's office can tell promoters if a name has been taken. It is also possible to reserve a name for a limited time, usually for a small fee. It is sometimes possible to obtain the permission of an existing corporation to use its name. Generally, written evidence of this consent must be filed with the secretary of state's office.

Articles of Incorporation Promoters are responsible for drawing up and filing the **articles of incorporation**, an application for incorporation of a business that describes a corporation's organization, powers, and authority (see Figure 28.3). Generally, this requirement can be met by obtaining a form from the office of the secretary of state. The articles of incorporation usually include the following information:

- Name of the corporation, including the words *company, incorporated,* or *corporation,* or appropriate abbreviations

- Proposed duration of the corporation
- Purpose or purposes of the corporation
- Number, classes, and value of corporate shares
- Shareholders' rights in relation to shares, classes of shares, and special shares
- Address of the original registered or statutory agent (person designated to receive service of process should the corporation be sued)
- Names and signatures of the initial directors
- Names and signatures of the incorporators

ARTICLES OF INCORPORATION
of

_____
(Name of Corporation)

The undersigned, desiring to form a corporation, for profit, under Sections 1701.01 et seq. of the Revised Code of Ohio, do hereby certify:

FIRST. The name of said corporation shall be _____

_____ .

SECOND. The place in Ohio where its principal office is to be located is

_____ , _____ County.
(City, Village, or Township)

THIRD. The purposes for which it is formed are:

To engage in any or all other lawful acts or activities for which corporations may be formed under Sections 1701.01 to 1701.98, inclusive, of the Ohio Revised Code.

FOURTH. The number of shares that it is authorized to have outstanding is 750 common shares.

FIFTH. The amount of stated capital with which the corporation shall begin business is five hundred dollars ($500.00).

IN WITNESS WHEREOF, We have hereunto subscribed our names, this

_____ day of _____ , 20_____ .

_____
(Name of Corporation)

_____

_____

_____

ARTICLES OF INCORPORATION
The principles for creating a corporation are essentially the same in all states. _What state office processes applications for incorporation?_

Some states have additional requirements, such as a minimum amount of capital on hand, often between $500 and $1,000, or a minimum number of incorporators.

Paying the filing fee completes the application. See Figure 28.4 for a list of the steps in the incorporation process. After the application is approved by the secretary of state, the corporation receives a certificate of incorporation. A **certificate of incorporation** is a corporation's official authorization to do business in the state. In some states, the certificate of incorporation is called a charter.

Structure of the Corporation   The initial shareholders of the newly formed corporation elect a board of directors who replace the original incorporators. Frequently, the original incorporators serve on the board.

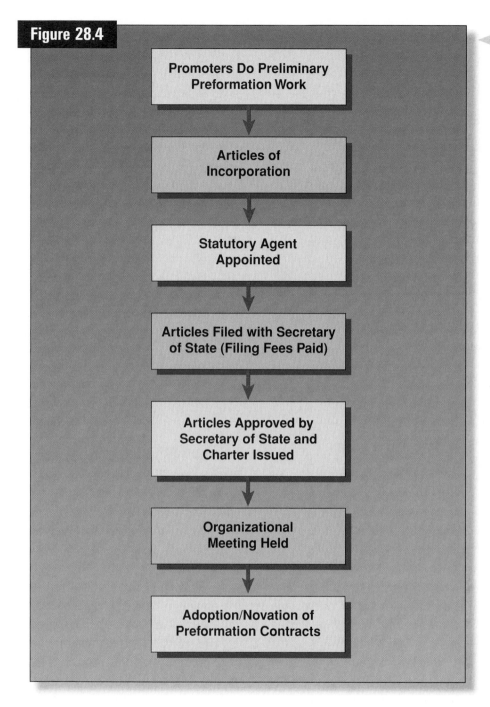

Figure 28.4

Promoters Do Preliminary Preformation Work

↓

Articles of Incorporation

↓

Statutory Agent Appointed

↓

Articles Filed with Secretary of State (Filing Fees Paid)

↓

Articles Approved by Secretary of State and Charter Issued

↓

Organizational Meeting Held

↓

Adoption/Novation of Preformation Contracts

STEPS IN THE INCORPORATION PROCESS
The incorporation process must be followed to create a legally formed corporation. *What term is used to designate a legally formed corporation?*

Some or all of the directors may be shareholders. Depending on the size of the company, there can be from one to about 35 directors. The board elects a chairman to speak for it. The directors, in turn, elect the top officers of the corporation to manage the company and carry out the board's policies and decisions. Officers can be members of the board, or they may be hired employees.

Corporate Financing

A corporation may seek financing through the sale of stock. Shares of stock represent a shareholder's interest in a corporation, and with shares in a corporation come certain rights. Companies may also seek funding through the sale of bonds, which are notes issued in return for money borrowed to fund various corporate activities.

Types of Stock　All public corporations issue common stock; it is the basic form of corporate ownership. Holders of **common stock** have voting rights in a corporation—as a group, they elect the corporation's board of directors. Common stock sometimes pays **dividends**, or profits, to the shareholders based on the corporation's performance. If the corporation does well, dividends will be high; if it does poorly, dividends will be low. Holders of common stock are the last shareholders to be paid. Common stock is sold on either at par or no-par value basis. Par value is the value printed on the stock certificates of some companies. In some states, par value is used as the basis for determining state incorporation taxes. Because the par value is arbitrary, most corporations issue no-par value stock.

The second type of stock a corporation issues is **preferred stock**. Holders of preferred stock have no voting rights. However, they do have the right to receive a fixed dividend. Holders of preferred stock have priority over holders of common stock; they are the first shareholders to be paid. There are two types of preferred stock: cumulative and noncumulative. If the shareholder owns cumulative preferred stock, and the corporation is unable to pay a dividend on time, it must make up the payment at a later date. Shareholders owning noncumulative shares do not have this right.

Stock Purchases　Purchasers of stock may buy the stock directly from the corporation or from individual owners of stock. They may buy stock personally or through agents called brokers. A broker fills the order to buy stock in one of two ways. The stock to be purchased may be traded on a stock exchange. A stock exchange is a continuous public auction in which stocks are bought and sold. The largest and best-known stock exchange is the New York Stock Exchange. Other exchanges include the Nasdaq Stock Market and the American Stock Exchange, as well as several regional exchanges. A broker may also purchase stocks over-the-counter, or outside the organized exchanges. Once the stocks are purchased, a stock certificate will be issued.

All stock is originally sold by the corporation itself. At the time the corporation is being organized, the promoters seek subscriptions from interested persons. These stock subscriptions are contracts to buy stock when the corporation completes its organization and is authorized by

Law Editor

In a democracy, laws must be effectively communicated to citizens. To do so, legislatures have created rigorous systems for reporting official versions of the law. The laws are then published so they can be used by lawyers and other citizens. Andrea Hansen helps make sure those official versions are correctly published in books and online, and that they are available for reference.

Hansen works as a senior editor for West Group, a law publisher head-quartered in Eagan, Minnesota. She is an attorney, although not all editors at the prominent publishing house have law degrees. Hansen works specifically on the laws created by the Missouri legislature—statutes known as the Missouri Code.

"After laws are passed by the legislature, they are written up and approved by the governor's office," she says. "We then publish them online and in books. A lot of my job is writing the historical and statutory notes that provide extra background information for lawyers."

The information Hansen provides is very important. She carefully studies the new law, compares it to the old, and then highlights important changes so lawyers, judges, scholars, and other citizens know what the law truly is. Hansen also informs readers of the date when a law takes effect.

What if legislators seem to pass laws that contradict one another? "Well, then we publish both versions and let the courts figure it out," Hansen says.

Skills	Reading, writing, teamwork, computer
Personality	Detail oriented, able to focus, comfortable doing the same thing for several months, able to meet deadlines
Education	At least a high school diploma, many with college and law degrees

For more information on editing and on state and federal codes, visit www.westgroup.com, **ubpl.glencoe.com**, or your public library.

the state to sell stock to the public. These subscriptions are similar to any other contract to sell, and the subscribers don't become stockholders until the organization is completed and stock certificates are issued to them. The corporation may continue to sell shares after its incorporation is complete, up to the number of shares authorized in its articles of incorporation. Like any other form of personal property, stocks may be transferred or assigned.

LIMITED LIABILITY COMPANIES
A new form of doing business that has become common today is known as the limited liability company. One of the chief advantages of a limited liability company is that it is taxed like a partnership. *What formalities must be followed to create a limited liability company?*

Corporate Bonds   A corporation may also finance its activities through bonds, which are notes issued for money that the corporation borrows. When a company makes bonds available, it is called a bond issue. Unlike stocks, bonds accrue interest and must be repaid in the future. If a company files for bankruptcy, bondholders' claims to company assets are paid before those of shareholders.

Forming a Limited Liability Company

A **limited liability company (LLC)** is a new type of business enterprise that has been adopted by all states. An LLC combines the best features of a partnership and a corporation. Like a corporation, it offers limited liability to its owners. Like the partners in a partnership, the owners of an LLC escape double taxation. LLCs are statutory entities, which means they can be formed only if the owners follow the legal steps required. The owners of an LLC are known as members, and the people who run the LLC are known as managers.

Generally, the law permits one legal person to form an LLC. The first step in forming an LLC is to draw up the articles of organization.

This can be done by obtaining the proper forms from the secretary of state's office. The articles of organization include the following:

- The name of the LLC, including either the words *limited liability company, limited,* or the abbreviations, *LLC* or *Ltd*
- The length of time that the LLC will exist
- The address where the operating agreement and the bylaws of the LLC are stored

Like a corporation, an LLC must also have a statutory agent for service of process. Filing fees must also be paid.

Members of a newly formed LLC will often want to draw up an operating agreement. An operating agreement will set up the bylaws under which the LLC will operate. Although some states permit oral operating agreements, it is best to express the terms of the operating agreement in writing.

Incorporation Problems

States differ in their interpretation of when the life of a corporation actually begins. Some states declare that the legal existence of a corporation begins when the articles have been filed. Others hold that a corporation begins when the articles have been approved by the secretary of state. Whatever the case, assuming that all formalities have been completed, once the legal existence of the corporation begins, it is said to be a *de jure* corporation. The term means "lawful" or "in law."

Sometimes, however, problems occur that disrupt the incorporation process. At other times people fail to incorporate, yet they act as if they

Virtual Law

Tax Law and Nonprofits

Nonprofit groups and charities are turning increasingly to the Internet for fund-raising. As they do so, the IRS is preparing to issue guidelines on applying tax law. These guidelines will have an effect on the taxes paid by nonprofits and charities on income received through online fund-raising. Charitable groups are also concerned with being taxed on sales from referring visitors to other Web sites, as well as the treatment of their tax exempt status. (Source: *New York Times*, p. B1, 2/12/01)

Connect Visit the Web site of a local or national charity. See what type of online activities they engage in that might affect their tax status.

Community Works

Prestigious List

Have you ever heard of a "Fortune 500 Company" but weren't quite sure what it is? The Fortune 500 is a list of America's largest corporations. Because it is considered to be a prestigious list, earning a place among the Fortune 500 is difficult. Other lists are being created that are held in a similar high esteem. The Global 500, America's Best Companies for Minorities, and the 100 Best Companies to Work For are lists that potential employees now consult to decide where they would like to invest their talents. *Which of these lists appeals to you? Would you use these lists as possible resources?*

Get Involved

Go online and investigate the companies listed under the titles mentioned above.

have incorporated. To deal with these problems, the courts have developed two doctrines: *de facto* corporations and corporation by estoppel. Other problems occur when a corporation has been properly formed but is not permitted by the owners to become an independent entity.

De Facto Corporation

Even while making a good faith attempt to incorporate, promoters sometimes inadvertently make an error in filing, or fail to complete the incorporation process. Technically, if the incorporation process is incomplete, the corporation doesn't legally exist. However, as long as the incorporators made a good faith attempt to incorporate under an existing state incorporation statute, and as long as the would-be corporation has acted like a corporation, few people can attack its existence. The law says that, although the corporation does not exist in law (*de jure*), it does exist in fact (*de facto*). This type of corporation is called a *de facto* corporation.

Some states have simplified the incorporation process and have abandoned the doctrine of *de facto* corporation. These states believe that there is little chance that the incorporation process will not be completed properly. The rule in these states is that if the incorporation process has been followed, then the corporation exists. However, if the incorporation process has not been followed, the corporation does not exist.

Corporation by Estoppel

Like other estoppel doctrines, corporation by estoppel stops people from denying the consequences of their own actions. Corporation by estoppel usually occurs when some party has been willing to treat a person or a group of people as a corporation, generally reaping some benefit from the relationship. When this happens, the court will not allow that party to then deny the existence of the corporation because doing so would be unfair.

Piercing the Corporate Veil

One of the primary advantages of forming a corporation is the limited liability of the individual shareholders. After incorporation is complete, shareholders reasonably expect to be insulated from the corporation's liabilities. Nevertheless, there are extreme circumstances in which the courts will deny shareholders the benefits of limited liability and hold them personally liable. Courts use colorful language to describe this situation, known as *piercing the corporate veil*. This expression means that the corporate entity, which is normally a veil shielding the shareholders from liability, will be pierced to reach the shareholders.

Depending on the facts, the court may rely on one of two theories to pierce the corporate veil:

- The alter ego theory
- The justice theory

The alter ego theory is used when the corporation has not been permitted to become an independent entity. The court looks at several things to determine whether a subsidiary is independent. For instance, the court looks at the management structure of the subsidiary and the parent company. If they shared the same directors and officers, and if decisions they made were always in the best interests of the parent company, it would suggest the need to pierce the corporate veil.

The justice theory is used when an individual or a parent corporation forms a corporation to defraud, to circumvent the law, to avoid paying a legally owed debt, or to violate the law in some way.

LAWS in Your Life

New and Hybrid Business Entities

A relatively new type of business is called a sub-chapter S corporation. In contrast with a corporation, an owner of an S corporation avoids double taxation at both the corporate and individual ownership levels. Rather, he or she is taxed only as an owner, meaning that losses can be deducted from work income in bad years and profits can only be taxed once during good years. To become an S corporation, a business must incorporate in the usual fashion and then apply to the Internal Revenue Service.

Another new business entity is the limited liability corporation (LLC). An LLC is a cross between a partnership and a corporation. Like a corporation, an LLC offers the protection of limited liability to its owners, and like a partnership, the owners' profits are only taxed once. An LLC is distinguished from an S corporation because unlike the latter, it does not have a limit to the number of shareholders.

In 1991, Texas created the limited liability partnership (LLP). This form was created to make it easier for existing partnerships to gain the advantages of an LLC, a process that hitherto had been complicated by the process of dissolving a partnership and recreating it as an LLC. Like an LLC, an LLP avoids double taxation and typically limits the liability of partners against torts committed by others involved in the partnership.

Research Activity Using the Internet, library, or other resource, research how each of these kinds of businesses are formed. Share your findings with the class.

Chapter Summary

Section 28.1 Corporations

- A corporation is an entity created by law to act as a single person. About 90 percent of all business in the United States is done by corporations. A corporation is authorized by law to act as a single person, distinct from its members or owners. Not all corporations are large. Approximately 40 percent of all corporations employ fewer than five employees. An individual who owns shares of a corporation is called a shareholder or stockholder. A share is a single unit of ownership of a corporation. A shareholder is entitled to one vote per share of stock that he or she owns in a corporation. Shareholders can cast their votes to elect a board of directors whose duty is to direct the corporation's business. The principal advantage of doing business as a corporation is the limited liability of the shareholders. Another advantage of a corporation is the fact that it has continuity of existence. This means that a corporation continues to exist, regardless of the lifespans of its founders, shareholders, managers, and directors.

- Public corporations are political units. Public corporations include towns, villages, cities, and school districts. Private corporations may be classified as profit or nonprofit corporations. Private corporations are not government run. Profit corporations are organized for the purpose of making money, and they have capital stock. Profit corporations are found in nearly every major field of economic activity, including transportation, manufacturing, business, technology, entertainment, financial, and service fields. These corporations are regulated by the laws of the states in which they operate. In contrast, nonprofit corporations are formed for educational, religious, charitable or social purposes, and membership is acquired by agreement rather than by acquisition of stock. Many nonprofit fraternal organizations are nonstock corporations. A corporation is deemed domestic in the state in which it is incorporated and is considered foreign in other states. An alien corporation is one that is incorporated in another country but is doing business in this country.

- A corporation cannot come into existence by itself—people must take the necessary steps to bring it into legal existence. A promoter carries out the incorporation process by taking the initial steps to organize and finance a business. These steps may include assembling investors, leasing office and warehouse space, purchasing supplies and equipment, and hiring employees. To create a corporation, the promoters must first choose a unique name and file the name with the secretary of state. Under most state statutes, the words corporation, incorporated, or company, or an abbreviation of one of the words, must appear as part of the corporate name. Articles of incorporation, which describe a corporation's organization, powers and authority, must also be filed with the secretary of state. Paying the filing fee completes the application process. After the application is approved by the secretary of state, the corporation receives a certificate of incorporation.

- A corporation is funded via subscription. At the time the corporation is being organized, the promoters seek out people who are interested in entering into contracts to buy stock when the corporation completes its organization and is authorized by the state to sell stock to the public.

- A limited liability company combines the best features of a partnership and a corporation. Like a corporation, it offers limited liability to its owners, and as do the partners in a partnership, the owners of an LLC escape double taxation.

Using Legal Language

Consider the key terms in the list below. Then use these terms to complete the following exercises.

corporation

shareholder

share

promoter

articles of incorporation

certificate of incorporation

dividends

limited liability company (LLC)

common stock

Understanding Business and Personal Law

Online

Self-Check Quiz Visit the *Understanding Business and Personal Law* Web site at **ubpl.glencoe.com** and click on Chapter 28: Forming and Financing a Corporation—Self-Check Quizzes to prepare for the chapter exam.

1. In groups of four, create a board game about corporations using all of the key terms. The purpose of the game will be to help the players develop an understanding of how to create, finance, and distinguish among various types of corporations.
2. Play your newly created game.
3. Present your game to the class.
4. As a class, vote to select the best game.
5. Play the winning game as a class.

The Law Review

Answer the following questions. Refer to the chapter for additional reinforcement.
6. What is a corporation? Who are its owners?
7. Discuss the advantages and disadvantages of forming a corporation.
8. What is the promoter's role in the incorporation process?
9. What must be included in the articles of incorporation?
10. What two kinds of stock are issued by a corporation?
11. What are the differences between these types of stock?
12. What are the two main types of corporations?
13. Identify new and hybrid business entities, including sub-chapter S corporations, limited liability partnerships, and limited liability corporations. Briefly explain each, and identify their distinguishing characteristics.
14. In Chapters 27 and 28, you learned about a variety of different business organizations: proprietorships, partnerships, corporations, and new and hybrid business entities such as an LLC or sub-chapter S corporation. Identify the duties and responsibilities for those interested in each type of business organization.
15. Under most state statutes, what words must be included in the name of a corporation?
16. What are dividends?
17. What is a stock exchange? What are some of the most prominent stock exchanges?

Linking School to Work

Acquiring and Evaluating Information
Consider the different business organizations.

18. Contrast the legal documentation required in forming different types of business organizations (proprietorship, partnership, and corporation).
19. Describe the significance of each type of documentation, noting the similarities and differences.
20. Name three businesses in your local community, and identify the type of organization that each exemplifies.

Let's Debate

Corporate Expansion
Tim and Eric own a small corporation called Be a Good Sport, Inc. Tim wants to keep the emphasis on court sports. Eric wants to expand by opening a subsidiary that would sell ski equipment and clothing.

Debate
21. What should Tim and Eric consider when trying to make this decision?
22. How can Tim and Eric resolve their differences without harming their relationship or their business?
23. Would the resolution be any different if their business were a partnership?
24. What would you recommend they do?

Grasping Case Issues

For the following cases, give your decision and state a legal principle that applies.

25. Ethel Holmes, Chris MacLeod, and Alicia Stevens decide to incorporate their printing business, naming it HMS, Inc. George Kitchel, their attorney, assures them that the articles will be approved. Because of a misunderstanding between Kitchel and a coworker, the articles are never filed. When William Blake is injured by an HMS delivery truck, he sues Holmes, MacLeod, and Stevens as individuals because the incorporation papers were not filed. How could the owners protect themselves?
26. Alice Pryor and Jessica Tunney operate their business for several years as a partnership. Pryor convinces Tunney that it would be a good idea to incorporate. Tunney agrees, so they change the name of the business to Pryor and Tunney, Inc. They do nothing further, although they tell their customers and creditors that they have formed a corporation. What would be their legal status if they were involved in a tort-based lawsuit?
27. Dennis Tharp and Merle Coffman decide to incorporate. They call their corporation Ford Motors because they figure that using a well-known name would attract business. They draw up the articles and include the corporation's name, proposed duration, and purpose; the number, classes and par value of corporate shares; and the names and signatures of the original directors and the incorporators. They then take the articles to the state attorney general's office for filing. Name four mistakes they made.
28. Martin Greenlawn, Gladys Chilcote, and Lillian Brunner decide to incorporate their flower shop, calling it the Hearts and Flowers Florist Shop, Inc. They file articles of incorporation with the appropriate state office, not knowing that they need a statutory agent. Through an oversight, a certificate of incorporation is issued. Eventually the state office discovers the error. Does the Hearts and Flowers corporation exist? Why or why not?

In each case that follows, you be the judge.

29. Choosing a Corporate Name

Legal Aid Services, Inc. was incorporated as a nonprofit organization providing free legal services. Four years later, American Legal Aid, Inc. was incorporated as a for-profit legal insurance corporation selling memberships to subscribers. When American Legal Aid began an extensive selling campaign, Legal Aid Services discovered that many people were confusing the two entities. The confusion hurt Legal Aid Services' image and threatened its funding. Consequently, Legal Aid Services sought an injunction prohibiting American Legal Aid from using the words *legal aid* in its corporate name. *Should Legal Aid Services be granted the injunction? Why or why not?*

American Legal Aid, Inc. v. Legal Aid Services, Inc., 503 P.2d 1201 (WY).

30. Personal Assets

In his role as a promoter for a new business, Spence purchased an employment agency from Huffman. The new corporation never generated enough money to pay Huffman. As a result, Huffman elected to sue Spence directly to obtain payment. Spence argued that his personal assets should not be placed at risk. *Was Spence correct? Why or why not?*

Spence v. Huffman, 486 P.2d 211 (AZ).

Legal Link

Bankruptcy Options

In our competitive, free-market system, some businesses are successful, while others are not. Sometimes businesses are dissolved because their owners are no longer interested or the market for its goods no longer exists. In other cases, a business cannot survive for financial reasons and goes bankrupt.

Connect

Using a variety of search engines, compare bankruptcy and dissolution options for different types of business organizations. Then answer the following questions.

31. What are some of the different kinds of bankruptcy, and in what ways do they apply or not apply to the different types of businesses?

32. Does bankruptcy always cause a business to dissolve? Explain your answer.

POWER READING STRATEGIES

33. **Predict** Why do you think 90 percent of all business in the United States is done by corporations?

34. **Connect** Do you own stock in a corporation? If so, what is the name of the corporation in which you own stock?

35. **Question** Can you explain the difference between public and private corporations?

36. **Respond** Explain the doctrine known as "piercing the corporate veil."

Operating a Corporation

**Understanding Business and Personal Law** *Online*

Chapter Overview Visit the *Understanding Business and Personal Law* Web site at ubpl.glencoe.com and click on Chapter 29: Operating a Corporation—Chapter Overviews to preview the chapter information.

The Opening Scene

Jakob and Aaron Kowalski and Cecilia Bronislawa are meeting in the boardroom of JAC Industries, Inc. They are discussing the corporation's upcoming shareholders meeting.

The Shareholders Meeting

CECILIA: Don't worry about the meeting. We've done a good job. We'll be reelected as directors. We always are.

JAKOB: Don't worry? Is that the best you can come up with?

AARON: That's the only thing she can come up with. Did you expect something more?

CECILIA: You two don't know anything about running a business. Look, you guys wanted to go public and sell stock to strangers. When you do that you've gotta be prepared for a shareholder proposal sometime.

JAKOB: A what?

CECILIA: You need to do some reading. You've never heard of a shareholder proposal? That's when our stockholders suggest changes in corporate policy.

AARON: That could be risky.

CECILIA: Maybe so, but the other shareholders still have to vote on it.

JAKOB: Hey, you're talking about everything we own. Let's be a little less cavalier about it.

AARON: So what's this shareholder proposal, anyway?

CECILIA: Something about human rights and doing business with countries that don't respect such rights.

JAKOB: What? I don't understand what the problem is. We don't do any business with those kinds of countries.

AARON: Someone thinks we do.

CECILIA: Look, we'll just state our position and let the shareholders vote.

JAKOB: So what's our position?

CECILIA: That all we're concerned with is making a profit for our shareholders.

JAKOB: What about the environment, the economy, the community? Shouldn't we talk about issues like that?

CECILIA: That means nothing to us. We're in business to make money.

AARON: Are you sure about that?

CECILIA: About as sure as I am about this shareholder lawsuit.

JAKOB: Shareholders can't sue their own corporation, can they?

CECILIA: Evidently. That's what this guy is doing. *(She tosses some papers toward Jakob.)*

AARON: Something about not granting him reemptive rights.

CECILIA: That's preemptive.

JAKOB: Whatever! Now I'm really worried! Did we or did we not do this?

CECILIA: Do what?

AARON: GRRRR! *(He storms out of the boardroom in frustration.)*

CECILIA: He's very high-strung, isn't he?

What Are the Legal Issues?

1. What do corporate directors do in relation to corporate management?
2. What responsibilities do corporate officers have?
3. What rights do corporate shareholders possess?
4. What is the business judgment rule?
5. What is the fairness rule?

Managing the Corporation

What You'll Learn

- How to define corporate director
- How to define corporate officer
- How to identify shareholders' rights
- How to identify shareholder voting techniques

Why It's Important

Understanding the nature of corporate management will help you protect your rights as a corporate shareholder.

Legal Terms

- directors
- officers
- shareholder
- proxy
- voting trust
- pooling agreement
- shareholder proposal
- direct suit
- derivative suit

Corporate Management

A corporation is just a legal concept: an artificial "person" created by the state and given many rights, powers, and duties. Managing a corporation is not simple. Unlike a sole proprietorship or a partnership, in which power is concentrated in the hands of a few individuals, power in a corporation is scattered among many individuals and institutions.

Board of Directors

Corporations are managed by a group of **directors**, who meet and vote as a board to set the policies. They are responsible for seeing that the corporation acts within its powers. The board might also suggest business policy. For example, it may decide to buy a new business site or build a new factory. It might vote to produce a new product or institute a new pension plan for employees. The board also oversees a wide range of employee-related policies.

You don't need special qualifications to be a director of a corporation, and usually the shareholders elect and also remove directors. However, a corporation's certificate of incorporation or its bylaws may specify that one director must be a shareholder and one must be a state resident.

Generally, directors serve for a set number of years and must then sit for reelection by the shareholders. Often, corporate bylaws call for staggered elections so that all of a corporation's directors are not elected at the same time. Directors meet regularly, at a time and place of their choosing.

Directors are not entitled to notice of regular meetings. However, they must be properly notified of any special meetings. If some of the directors hold a special meeting without notifying other directors, all actions taken at that meeting are invalid. The board of directors of a corporation is subject to the duty of due care and the duty of loyalty to the corporation.

Officers

Corporate **officers** are appointed by and can be removed by the corporation's directors. Officers include a president, vice-president(s), secretary, treasurer, assistant officers, and other agents. Officers' jobs are to implement the policies of the directors by carrying out day-to-day operations of the corporation. Officers are agents of the corporation, and principal-agent rules apply.

If the directors have decided to purchase a new business site, the corporation's officers would have authority to arrange the deal. This might involve a number of detailed steps, such as hiring an appraiser, employing an attorney, ordering a title search, and other tasks.

Like directors, officers are subject to the duties of loyalty and due care. Each officer's duties are generally spelled out in the corporation's by-laws. Managing a corporation can become complex because key figures often play more than one role. Often, directors are also officers and shareholders of the corporation.

CORPORATE MANAGEMENT
Most corporations are managed by a board of directors elected by the shareholders. *What is the relationship between the board of directors and the officers of a corporation?*

Shareholders

Corporations need money, called capital, which is obtained by selling units, or shares, of stock in the company. If you buy one or more shares, you become a **shareholder** (also called a stockholder), a member of the corporation.

Shareholders are sometimes called owners or investors in the corporation. It would be a mistake to use one label without the other, however, because shareholders of a corporation are really both owners and investors.

Shareholders are often individual people, but not always. A corporation can also be a shareholder in another corporation. General and limited partnerships can be shareholders in a corporation, and so can labor union retirement funds or a state workers' pension funds.

Shareholder Rights

Owners of stock in a corporation acquire certain rights. These rights include the following:

- The right to receive dividends as declared by the board of directors
- The right to receive and possess a stock certificate
- The right to have ready access to the corporate records
- The right to transfer all shares
- The right to maintain a proportionate share of stock in the corporation (preemptive rights)
- The right to exercise a vote for each share of stock owned

Right to Receive Dividends

Dividends are profits distributed to stockholders. They are usually payable when declared by the board of directors. Dividends must be distributed proportionately among shareholders.

Example 1. During its second year of operation, Holoscope Enterprises, Inc. made a nice profit. The board of directors declared a $38,000 dividend, to be divided among the 6,080 shares of common stock. Shareholders received $6.25 for each share of common stock they owned.

Directors do not have to declare a dividend when the corporation has made a profit. Sometimes they may feel that it's best to retain the profit. When a dividend is declared, it becomes a liability of the corporation, and shareholders can enforce payment of it. The dividend belongs to the shareholders of record, those listed as owning the stock on the date set down by the board. A dividend can be in the form of shares or cash.

Example 2. During Eurotech Corporation's fifth year of operation, a new venture resulted in tremendous profits. The board of directors declared a dividend to all shareholders of record on March 17. Everyone who owned shares on that date would participate in the dividend, even though they might sell their shares before the dividend is actually distributed.

Right to Receive a Stock Certificate

A stock certificate is proof that you own a part of the corporation, so the right to receive this document is considered an essential shareholder's right.

Right to Examine Books and Records

The law requires a corporation to keep accurate records of its business affairs. These records should include a list of all shareholders, an accurate accounting of all transactions, and the minutes of all meetings held by the directors and shareholders. Shareholders have a statutory right to see these records. To gain access to them, a shareholder must make a written request stating the purpose of the examination. As long as the request is made for a reasonable purpose, a shareholder cannot be denied access to records of a corporation.

Right to Transfer Shares of Stock

Another shareholder right is the ability to sell or transfer shares of stock. If you sell stock, you are the transferor, and the recipient is the

Figure 29.1

Shareholder Voting Powers

Voting Power	Definition
Proxy	One shareholder votes in place of another; regulated by SEC.
Shareholder Proposal	One shareholder adds proposal to annual shareholders meeting agenda; regulated by SEC.
Pooling Agreement	Shareholders agree to vote the same way; each retains own stock.
Voting Trust	Right to vote shares turned over to a trustee; usually irrevocable; time limit of 10 to 21 years.

SHAREHOLDER VOTING POWERS Shareholders' rights to vote depend on whether the stock held is nonvoting or voting stock. *Which type of stock is generally nonvoting?*

transferee. The transferee has the right to have the stock transfer recorded in the corporation's books. The transferee then becomes the shareholder and is entitled to all of the rights enjoyed by other shareholders.

Right to Maintain a Proportionate Share

Shareholders usually have the right to purchase a proportionate share of every new stock issue before the corporation offers it to the public. This right is called the shareholder's preemptive right. However, this right can be limited or denied by the corporation's certificate of incorporation, by its bylaws or regulations, or by state law. The idea behind preemptive rights is to prevent directors from taking control of the corporation by issuing more shares and buying them all themselves. Other shareholders can foil such attempts if they have the right to purchase enough shares to maintain the voting balance. Preemptive rights are common in small corporations, where control is an important issue.

EXERCISING SHAREHOLDER VOTING POWER Shareholders of corporate stock have voting power because their shares represent part ownership in the company. *How can shareholders exercise their voting power?*

Right to Vote

Because shareholders have voting powers as part owners, they can be involved in a corporation's management (see Figure 29.1 for a listing of shareholders' voting powers). A corporation can grant full voting rights only to holders of common stock. Holders of preferred stock usually have no voting rights, although they are sometimes granted limited voting rights.

The incorporation statutes of most states and the Model Business Corporation Act provide that a meeting of a corporation's shareholders be held annually. Most states allow the meeting to be held anywhere, and

Deutsche Telekom
Hauptversammlung 2001
Köln

many large corporations rent halls to encourage attendance. The purpose of the annual shareholders meeting is to elect the board of directors and to conduct other necessary business. The president or chairman of the board usually presides at shareholders meetings.

A majority of the shareholders must be present or represented by proxy before business can be conducted at a shareholders meeting. A **proxy** (see Figure 29.2) is the right to vote another shareholder's stock. It is a power of attorney, authorizing another to vote.

Proxy Voting   Sometimes shareholders try to control the election of the board of directors by buying a majority of the shares. If the shareholders do not have enough money to buy the necessary shares, or if they cannot find enough shares for sale, they solicit the proxies of other shareholders.

Voting Trusts   Under the terms of a **voting trust**, shareholders transfer their voting rights to a trustee. A voting trust attempts to control the corporation by concentrating voting power in the voting trustees. The voting trust generally cannot be changed for a specified time period. Most state limits run from 10 to 21 years. Voting trusts must be in

Figure 29.2

THE BACK-PACK CORPORATION
Proxy

The undersigned hereby appoints GEORGE KINNARD and MARY ANN CONNERLY and each of them, proxies, and with power of substitution (i.e., power to name replacements), to attend the Annual Meeting of shareholders of The Back-Pack Corporation, at the company's main office in Green Bay, Wisconsin, on April 15, 20--, commencing at 10 A.M. and any adjournment thereof, and there to vote all the shares of the undersigned for election of directors, and on any other business that may properly come before the meeting.

Dated: _March 20, 20—_   _Roberta J. Hogan_   (L.S.)
                                            Signature

Proxy # 125413   Roberta J. Hogan
                      37 Winona Lane
Account # 0590363   Des Moines, Iowa

PROXIES
A shareholder can appoint another shareholder to vote his or her shares of stock by signing a proxy. *Under what circumstances might a shareholder grant a proxy to another shareholder?*

writing and must be filed with the corporation. They ensure that future disputes will not prevent the participating shareholders from controlling the corporation.

Pooling Agreements   Instead of a voting trust, a group of shareholders may make a **pooling agreement**, or a contract to vote in a certain way on a particular issue. Pooling agreement are also called shareholder agreements or voting agreements. These agreements differ from proxies and voting trusts because the participating shareholders retain control of their own votes. Also, pooling agreements may be perpetual and may be kept secret.

Shareholder Proposals   Shareholders have the right to participate in shareholder meetings, including a chance to speak and offer proposals. A **shareholder proposal** is a resolution or policy suggested by a shareholder. It may be an amendment to the corporation's articles, a limit on the corporation's charitable contributions, a ceiling on the pay of the corporation's top executives, or some other suggestion.

Right to Sue

Shareholders have the right to sue the corporation to enforce their rights and to sue others on behalf of the corporation to enforce rights it has neglected.

Shareholders may bring a **direct suit** if they believe that they have been deprived of rights that belong to them. Shareholders may also bring a class action lawsuit against a corporation on behalf of all shareholders in their position.

In a **derivative suit**, shareholders sue the corporation's management on behalf of the corporation. A derivative suit is based on an injury to the corporation. The shareholders' right to sue is derived from the injury to the corporation. A shareholder may bring a derivative action suit against the chief executive officer on behalf of the corporation for the benefit of the corporation.

Example 3. Steve White is the president and chairman of the board of the OTTO Corporation. To cover several outstanding personal debts, he diverts money from the company. Because he controls the board of directors, they are not inclined to do anything. However, Rachel Kent, a shareholder of OTTO stock, decides to bring a derivative suit against the president on behalf of the corporation for the benefit of the corporation.

Derivative suits are more difficult to bring than direct suits because certain prerequisites must be met before a shareholder is eligible to file such suits. For example, the shareholder must have owned stock in the

Community Works

4-H
Joining clubs or groups is an easy way to meet people who share your interests. One club you may not know about is 4-H. The purpose of 4-H, whose name stands for the words *Head, Heart, Hands,* and *Health,* is to help young people discover and develop their potential. 4-H achieves this goal by encouraging you to set your own goals. The 4-H Member's Creed ends with this pledge: "I believe in my country, my state, my community, and in my responsibility for their development. In all these things I believe, I am willing to dedicate my efforts to their fulfillment." *Is this a pledge that you could make? Why or why not?*

Get Involved
Find out more information about a 4-H club in your area. Research the laws that government-financed clubs and organizations must obey.

corporation when the alleged injury occurred. This requirement is known as the rule of contemporaneous ownership. Without this rule, a person could search out a corporation whose activities he or she disliked, buy a few shares in that corporation, and then bring a derivative suit against the corporation's management.

Another prerequisite in bringing a derivative suit is that the shareholder must have exhausted all means of resolving the dispute by communicating with the board of directors and other shareholders.

In some states, a third prerequisite requires the shareholder to deposit a sum of money as security to cover the corporation's expenses in fighting the lawsuit. This rule discourages individuals who might hunt for corporations engaged in questionable activities, purchase several shares, and bring a derivative suit to win the damages awarded by the court, or alternatively, to force a large settlement from the corporation's management.

Example 4. Joe Rafferty owned shares in Synectech, Inc. He discovered that Karl Schmidt, Synectech's chief executive officer, had the corporation purchase several large tracts of overvalued real estate that were owned by Schmidt's brother. As a shareholder, Joe meets the prerequisite of contemporaneous ownership. However, before bringing a derivative suit, he must ask the board and the shareholders to take action to rescind Schmidt's deal or to require him to pay back any unjust profit made at the corporation's expense. Then Joe may be required to post a bond to cover corporate expenses in the lawsuit. After meeting these prerequisites, Joe will be allowed to bring suit.

Section 29.1 Assessment

Reviewing What You Learned

1. What is a corporate director?
2. What is a corporate officer?
3. What rights do shareholders possess?
4. How can shareholders exercise their right to vote their shares?

Critical Thinking Activity

Shareholder Rights Why should shareholders be able to sue their own corporation?

Legal Skills In Action

Shareholder Proposals Your cousin, Julianne, has decided to initiate a shareholder proposal in time for the next meeting of Yellowrock Pharmaceuticals, Inc. Write a letter to Julianne in which you remind her of all the requirements she will need to meet before presenting her proposal.

Management Responsibilities

The Duties of Directors and Officers

A corporation's directors and officers have a fiduciary relationship with the corporation. Recall that *fiduciary* means they are in a position of trust in relation to the corporation and the shareholders.

As agents of the corporation, the officers' fiduciary duties are similar to those of agents. Directors are a different matter, however. Their duties resemble those of agents and employees, but when they act as directors they are actually neither of the two. Directors must perform their duties in good faith and in a manner they believe will be in the best interests of the corporation. The duties are outlined in Figure 29.3.

The Business Judgment Rule

According to the Revised Model Business Corporation Act, a corporate manager must execute all responsibilities, "in good faith, with the care an ordinarily prudent person in a like position would exercise and in a manner he reasonably believes to be in the best interests of the corporation."

What does this requirement mean? The courts have tried to clarify the concept of due care to encourage competent people to become and remain corporate directors and officers. They have often given a liberal interpretation to the duty of due care, applying a formula known as the **business judgment rule**. This rule presumes that a board or a director acts with due care. The courts defer to managers' business decisions unless they find instances of fraud, a clear lack of good faith, an abuse of discretion, or an illegal act. In addition, there must be no conflict of interest in the decision. To prevent judges from becoming "Monday morning quarterbacks," the rule focuses not on whether a particular decision was the "right" decision but on how the decision was made.

Directors and officers are allowed to make mistakes as long as they act legally and in good faith and have not been negligent in performing their responsibilities. A few states add that directors and officers will be held liable only if they are grossly negligent in carrying out their duties. Directors and officers are not obligated to ensure that the corporation makes a profit. If the corporation suffers a loss from a transaction the board authorized, the directors are not liable to the shareholders unless they violate the business judgment rule.

What You'll Learn

- How to explain the business judgment rule
- How to explain the fairness rule
- How to define the corporate opportunity doctrine
- How to distinguish between a member-managed LLC and a manager-managed LLC

Why It's Important

Understanding the duties of corporate managers will help you judge how they conduct their businesses.

Legal Terms

- business judgment rule
- fairness rule
- insider trading
- corporate opportunity doctrine

Figure 29.3 — Duties of Corporate Managers

Rule	Situation	Explanation
Business judgment rule	Manager does not profit from decision.	Decision stands if it is made: (1) in good faith, (2) with due care within the law, and (3) in corporation's best interest.
Fairness rule	Manager profits from decision.	The decision must be fair to the corporation because managers must remain loyal to the corporation.
Insider trading rule	Manager possesses inside information not available to outsiders.	Manager must either reveal the information or refrain from trading on that information.
Corporate opportunity doctrine	Manager learns of a business opportunity that might reasonably interest the corporation.	Manager must offer the opportunity to the corporation before taking it for personal gain.

DUTIES OF CORPORATE MANAGERS
Directors and officers owe fiduciary duties to the corporation. *Are corporate managers required to show a profit every year to fulfill those fiduciary duties?*

How can directors or officers be negligent in performing their duties? One way is by not acting in a situation that demands action. For example, a director or officer who enters a deal with another corporation without doing research into the benefits and detriments of the transaction could be negligent. A director or officer who fails to take steps to remedy a major company problem also harms the corporation by not taking action.

Another way to be negligent is by making hasty management decisions. Negligent directors might spend only minutes reviewing reports and records about a proposed transaction, when they should have spent several days. In contrast, if the directors do their best and act carefully, their decisions will stand. Shareholders cannot fault directors for that error. Shareholders can, however, vote against these directors in the next corporate election at the annual shareholders meeting.

Some states have recently enacted antiliability statutes to limit the liability of directors. These statutes usually protect directors, rather than officers, because the directors are not involved in the day-to-day activity of the corporation. Still, some states have also extended the protection to officers.

The typical antiliability statute allows a corporation to add to its charter or bylaws a provision that will protect directors from liability

A Global Perspective: Laws Around the World

Argentina

We can't see or smell it, although we can sometimes feel and hear it. It can blast or ripple, and theorists say it would take only one percent of its force to generate enough electricity for the entire world. What is it? The wind!

Looking to the future, Argentina has enacted a wind energy law that was passed in 1998. Plans for building "wind parks" to power a number of the country's provinces are in the works. The new legislation also calls for connecting the national electrical system to the wind energy systems already in operation. The wind-power program not only offers economic benefits—jobs, investment opportunities, fair prices—but, for Argentina, it's an environmental landmark as well. "This law is an essential step to put Argentina on the road toward the development of clean energy sources; it will prove . . . that their implementation can be made possible by political will," says the campaign coordinator. Although a growing international trend today, harnessing the wind to make life easier is an idea that has been around for centuries. As far back as the seventh century, Persians used simple wind machines to grind grains. Here's a snapshot of Argentina.

Geographical area	**1,068,302 sq. mi.**
Population	**37,812,817**
Capital	**Buenos Aires**
Legal system	**Mix of U.S. and Western European systems**
Language	**Spanish**
Religion	**92% Roman Catholic**
Life expectancy	**75 years**

Critical Thinking Question List some of the reasons why using wind as an energy source is a better idea than using fossil fuels. For more information on Argentina, visit **ubpl.glencoe.com** or your local library.

for their decisions, provided there is no breach of loyalty, reckless or deliberate misconduct, illegal activity, or personal benefit to the director. Other antiliability statutes automatically extend this protection to directors, unless the shareholders amend the bylaws or the certificate of incorporation to exclude the protection.

Many antiliability statutes simply protect the directors from having to pay damages. The result is that shareholders can still bring a suit to force a reversal of the decision, but cannot collect compensation.

Duty of Loyalty and the Fairness Rule

Managers have a duty of loyalty to their corporation. Directors and officers must not exploit their positions for personal gain at the expense of the corporation. Their main motivation should be to act with the best interest of the corporation, and they should not engage in any activity that would deliberately damage the corporation. A director's or an officer's duty of loyalty may be questioned if he or she has a personal interest in a particular business decision.

Disclosure and Approval Requirements Note, however, that just because a director or an officer has an interest in the transaction, the courts should not automatically invalidate the decision. The transaction may stand despite the personal profit if one of three conditions is met. The first two conditions require the director or the officer to disclose involvement in the decision, including all the terms and how much profit he or she has made. If, after disclosure, the director or officer obtains

LAWS in Your Life

The Benefits of Nonprofit Status

There are many financial benefits to being a nonprofit corporation. For example, nonprofit corporations are tax exempt, meaning they do not have to pay certain taxes, such as income and property taxes. Tax exempt status also enables a nonprofit corporation to apply for public and private grants. A nonprofit corporation can solicit tax deductible contributions. This benefit allows donors to deduct their gifts from state and federal income tax returns.

Incorporating as a nonprofit organization also provides protection from personal liability. Like for-profit corporations, nonprofits can be sued, but the directors are protected from personal liability. This protection is especially useful when the nonprofit organization advocates an unpopular position. Other benefits of nonprofit status include reduced postal rates for mass mailings.

Research Activity Visit the library or the IRS Web site at www.irs.gov. How are nonprofit corporations taxed on "unrelated" activities?

the approval of a majority of the directors or the approval of the share-holders, then the decision will stand.

Fairness Rule   The third condition that could allow a director's decision to stand despite a personal interest in the transaction is the basic fairness of the decision to the corporation. If the director or officer has not met one of the disclosure and approval requirements, then he or she has the burden of proving that the decision is fair to the corporation. This requirement is called the **fairness rule**, but proving it can be a problem.

The director or officer can try to show that the decision in question would have had the same conditions, prices, or terms if it had been made between two disinterested parties. (This is called dealing at arm's length.) Beyond that, it is difficult to generalize about fairness, and most determinations of fairness are made on a case-by-case basis. Nevertheless, two corollaries of the fairness rule have evolved.

Insider Trading Rule

An insider typically is a corporate director or officer who has information about a publicly traded corporation that is not available to the public. He or she may not buy or sell shares in the corporation if the transaction is based on "inside" information. Any such transaction is referred to as **insider trading** and is unfair to the corporation and outsiders.

Some examples of insider trading include buying or selling stocks just before some major development occurs that will affect their price, or passing valuable information to an outsider who trades in the corporation's stock and subsequently repays the insider. Under the insider trading rules, directors or officers who possess inside information must either refrain from acting on it or reveal it publicly before acting on it.

> *Example 5.* Ervin Edwards, CEO of Treen Corporation, found out that Hiroshike Communications, Inc. planned to buy all of Treen's outstanding shares at a price far above the current market value. Without revealing this inside information to the public, Edwards bought as much Treen stock as he could and resold it to Hiroshike at an enormous profit. In doing so, Edwards violated the rule that forbids insider trading.

Corporate Opportunity Doctrine

Another extension of the duty of loyalty is the **corporate opportunity doctrine**. According to this doctrine, directors and officers cannot take a business opportunity for themselves if they have sure knowledge that the corporation would want to take that opportunity for itself. The directors must first present the opportunity to the corporation. If the corporation turns it down, then the directors or officers can take the opportunity for themselves.

It's a Question of Ethics

Revealing Relationships
Michael Appleby is one of seven directors on the board of Omega Corporation. When the position for chief financial officer became available, Michael lobbied for Joshua Stevens. Because of Michael's standing with other board members, Joshua was offered the job. A year later, during a conflict between the board and Joshua, the directors discovered that Joshua and Michael were cousins. While no rules were actually broken, the other directors were angry that this information had not been made known. *Were Michael and Joshua acting unethically? Why or why not?*

Example 6. Edward Costello, president of Doublestone Corporation, learned that Riversarian, Inc. was selling several lots of prime real estate at reduced prices. The president knew that Doublestone had been trying to buy the land to expand operations for several months, but he could not buy the land for himself without first telling the other officers and the directors of the opportunity.

The only exception to this rule is if the director or officer knows that the corporation is financially incapable of taking the opportunity, despite its interest. In such a situation, the director or the officer would be permitted to take the opportunity without violating the doctrine.

Managing a Limited Liability Company

In a limited liability company, the owners can either manage the firm on their own, or they can choose to enlist the services of outside administrators.

Member-Managed LLCs

As the name suggests, the owners themselves run member-managed LLCs. Management authority is apportioned based upon the money contributed by each member. The higher the capital contribution, the more authority that falls to a member manager. The member managers are actually acting as agents of the LLC. In this sense, they function very much like the partners of a general partnership. The LLC is therefore bound by any action performed by a member manager that falls within the apparent authority of the member. Nevertheless, some actions are outside the apparent authority of each member. Such actions would include submitting a claim of the LLC to arbitration and disposing of the firm's goodwill. Of course, recall that an LLC's operating agreement can change any of these arrangements.

Manager-Managed LLCs

Outside managers, hired by the members of the LLC, run manager-managed LLCs. In this scenario, the LLC is run much like a corporation. If one manager runs the LLC, he or she acts like the CEO of a corporation. If the members hire a group of managers, they would act like a board of directors. The business judgment rule and the fairness rule apply to the decisions of such managers.

Fiduciary Duties

Regardless of whether an LLC is run by the members themselves or by managers, a fiduciary duty still exists between those who run an LLC and the LLC itself. The same duty also exists between those who direct the LLC and the owners. However, it is a good idea to spell out the extent and nature of management duties in the operating agreement.

Section 29.2 Assessment

Reviewing What You Learned
1. What is the business judgment rule?
2. What is the fairness rule?
3. What is the corporate opportunity doctrine?
4. What is the difference between a member-managed LLC and a manager-managed LLC?

Critical Thinking Activity
Antiliability Statutes Why have some states passed antiliability statutes to protect directors?

Legal Skills in Action
The Fairness Rule You have decided to bring a lawsuit against the directors of a corporation in which you own stock, alleging that the officers gave themselves an overly large salary increase. Write a speech in which you explain how to apply the fairness rule to judge the conduct of corporate directors and officers.

Chapter Summary

Section 29.1 Managing the Corporation

- Corporate directors manage a corporation. They are responsible for broad policy decisions made by a corporation, and are subject to corporate bylaws and state laws regulating their behavior. You don't need special qualifications to be a director of a corporation, and usually the shareholders elect and remove directors. However, a corporation's certificate of incorporation or its bylaws may specify that one director must be a shareholder and one must be a state resident. Directors generally serve for a set number of years and then must sit for reelection by the shareholders. Often, corporate bylaws call for staggered elections so that all of a corporation's directors are not elected at the same time. Directors meet regularly, at a time and place of their choosing.

- Corporate officers carry out the day-to-day operations of the corporation. Officers are agents of the corporation and principal-agent rules apply. Like directors, officers are subject to the duties of loyalty and due care. Each officer's duties are generally spelled out in the corporation's bylaws.

- Shareholders are owners of stock in a corporation. They have the right to: (1) receive dividends as declared by the board of directors; (2) receive and possess a stock certificate; (3) have ready access to corporate records; (4) maintain a proportionate share of stock in the corporation; and (5) exercise a vote for each share of stock owned.

- To vote, a shareholder can attend the annual shareholders meeting in which the board of directors and officers present corporate business to be voted upon. Most states allow this meeting to be held anywhere, and many corporations rent halls to encourage attendance. The president or chairman of the board usually presides at shareholders meetings. A majority of the shareholders must be represented either in person or by proxy before business can be conducted. Shareholders can vote independently or under the terms of a voting trust or pooling agreement.

Section 29.2 Management Responsibilities

- The courts have tried to clarify the concept of due care to encourage competent people to become and remain corporate directors and officers. They have often given a liberal interpretation to the duty of due care, applying the business judgment rule. Corporate directors are presumed to be acting with due care, and the courts will defer to their judgment and decisions unless the directors lack good faith, commit illegal acts, or have conflicts of interest.

- A director's decision will stand, despite a conflict of interest in the transaction between the corporation and another party, if the director can prove that the decision would have involved the same conditions, price, or terms if it had been made at arm's length.

- An extension of the director's duty of loyalty to the corporation prohibits a director from taking a business opportunity for himself or herself if he or she has knowledge that the corporation would want to take that opportunity for itself. If the corporation turns down the opportunity, the director is then free to take it without conflict. The only exception to this rule is if the director or officer knows that the corporation is financially incapable of taking the opportunity, despite its interest. In such a situation, the director or officer would be permitted to take the opportunity without violating the doctrine.

- In a limited liability company, the owners can either manage the firm on their own, or they can choose to enlist the services of outside administrators. A member-managed LLC is one that is run by the owners themselves; a manager-managed LLC is one that is directed by an outside manager.

Using Legal Language

Consider the key terms in the list below. Then use these terms to complete the following exercises.

shareholder

directors

officers

proxy

voting trust

pooling agreement

shareholder proposal

direct suit

derivative suit

business judgment rule

fairness rule

insider trading

corporate opportunity
    doctrine

1. Form groups of four, and plan a mock shareholders meeting.
2. Role-play an election of the board of directors.
3. Vote on an issue.
4. Plan for a future event of your choosing.
5. Finally, write down a brief description of the shareholders meeting. With what did you have the most difficulty? What did you enjoy most?

Understanding Business and Personal Law Online

Visit the *Understanding Business and Personal Law* Web site at **ubpl.glencoe.com** and click on Chapter 29: Operating a Corporation—Self-Check Quizzes to prepare for the chapter exam.

The Law Review

Answer the following questions. Refer to the chapter for additional reinforcement.
6. Who elects the board of directors?
7. Are all shareholders individuals? Explain your answer.
8. Describe the two types of suits a shareholder might bring against a corporation.
9. Identify the people with legal responsibility for the acts (civil and criminal) of the business organization. What are the duties of directors and officers?
10. What is the insider trading rule? Give two examples.
11. Under what circumstances might a corporation decide not to issue a dividend?
12. What is a voting trust?
13. Why are the elections of corporate officers often staggered by corporate bylaws?
14. Describe the exception to the corporate opportunity doctrine.

Linking School to Work

Acquiring and Evaluating Information

School districts are often structured like corporations. For example, they have boards of directors (school boards) and officers. The citizens and parents are similar to the shareholders. Complete the following tasks:

15. Research the structure of the school district you attend.
16. Create a poster showing how it operates.
17. Write a one-page paper comparing your school district's operation to that of a corporation.

Let's Debate

Business Judgment

Yvette Ortiz serves as a director of Gordino Corporation, a maker of skin care products. After a short lunch meeting, Yvette made the decision to buy $1 million dollars worth of lotion from a friend whose company was going out of business. Unfortunately, the lotion's main ingredient was determined to be toxic, and Gordino Corporation had to dispose of the entire lot. The shareholders were upset and wanted to file a lawsuit against Yvette.

Debate

18. Will the business judgment rule protect Yvette?
19. Why or why not?

Grasping Case Issues

For the following cases, give your decision and state a legal principle that applies.

20. Josephine Sackman owns 50 shares of stock in Sinclair Industries, Inc. Sinclair declares a dividend on August 18. Josephine sells her shares to Chuck McManis on August 19. When the dividend is paid on August 25, Chuck claims it belongs to him. Is he correct? Explain you answer.

21. Marcia Quonset purchases 200 shares of common stock in Enright International, Inc. She becomes upset when she learns that Enright intends to close several plants. What options are available to her, besides exercising her voting power or bringing a suit against the managers?

22. Margie Fairfield, Louis Delaney, and Loretta Jacubekz are minority shareholders in Shelby Aluminum Corp. To consolidate their voting power, they decide to form a voting trust that would last for 25 years. They do not put the deal in writing or tell anyone at corporate headquarters. Have these shareholders formed a valid, binding voting trust? Explain your answer.

23. Oberlander Film Processing, Inc. recovers silver from used photographic negatives. Patricia Robinson, CEO of Oberlander, owns a photography studio that sells used negatives to Oberlander. Justine Shepherd, a shareholder in Oberlander, discovers that the CEO is overcharging the corporation for the used negatives. After voicing her concerns, Justine sues to compel Robinson to return her excessive profits to the corporation. What type of suit does she bring? What rule will be used to judge Robinson's conduct? Why?

24. The directors of Bibliotech, Inc. decided to raise funds to save their failing corporation by creating a subsidiary and selling shares. Unknown to investors, all the subsidiary's money would go directly into Bibliotech. When the subsidiary fails, will the investors have a cause of action against Bibliotech? Explain your answer.

In each case that follows, you be the judge.

25. Internal Remedies

Several shareholder derivative suits were brought by shareholders against the directors and officers of Public Service Company of New Hampshire to halt construction of a nuclear power plant. Robert Markewich wrote several letters of complaint to the board. Denied a personal appearance, Markewich sent the board another letter indicating his intent to sue. The board told Markewich that they would discuss the matter at an upcoming meeting. Markewich did not wait for the results of that meeting, but filed suit. *Did Markewich's letters constitute sufficient demand on the directors so that he had exhausted internal remedies? Why or why not?*
Seidel v. Public Service Company of New Hampshire, 616 F. Supp. 1342 (NH).

26. Duty of Loyalty

Norman Reisig, a shareholder in Normat Industries, Inc., became suspicious when company president Matthew Carter indicated continuing construction delays on a major condominium project. He discovered that the company owed more than $25,000 in construction fees, despite a recent loan of $200,000. Further investigation revealed that Carter had used the $200,000 to pay personal expenses. Reisig brought suit, claiming that Carter had breached his duty of loyalty to the company. *Is Reisig correct? Why or why not?*
Normat Industries, Inc. v. Carter, 477 So.2d 783 (LA).

Legal Link

Who's Who?

Boards of directors of major corporations are usually business and education executives with many years of experience. They often represent a variety of businesses such as banking, publishing, legal, retail, and manufacturing.

Connect

Using a variety of search engines, complete the following tasks:

27. Research a major corporation.
28. Find out the names, titles, and occupations of the board of directors.
29. Prepare a chart, spreadsheet, or other visual explaining your findings.

POWER READING STRATEGIES

30. **Predict** What do you think might happen if the board of directors began to dictate the day-to-day operations of the business?

31. **Connect** Do you own any stock? If not, do you think you will one day? Why or why not?

32. **Question** Why do you think the courts give a liberal interpretation to the duty of due care?

33. **Respond** Do you think there is a temptation for directors to take a lucrative business opportunity for themselves? Explain your answer.

CHAPTER 30

Corporate Regulation and Expansion

Understanding Business and Personal Law *Online*

Chapter Overview Visit the *Understanding Business and Personal Law* Web site at ubpl.glencoe.com and click on Chapter 30: Corporate Regulation and Expansion—Chapter Overviews to preview the chapter information.

The Opening Scene

Jakob and Aaron Kowalski and Cecilia Bronislawa are meeting in the boardroom of JAC Industries, Inc., discussing a possible merger with Collins Industries, Inc.

The Big Merger

AARON: Thanks for your cooperation, Cecilia and Jakob. I'm glad that we could meet on such short notice. We have some really important matters to discuss.

CECILIA: No problem. Of course I would make time for this meeting. We're facing the biggest decision of our corporate lives, and we don't have a clue what to do. I'm hoping this meeting will help us decide on the right course of action.

JAKOB: We'll figure something out. We always do. Plus, we can't feel too bad about ourselves. We're learning as we go along, and I don't think we're doing a bad job.

CECILIA: Thanks for the pep talk. I guess we better start discussing the matter at hand. What do you think we should do, Aaron?

AARON: What we need is a valuable asset to improve our bargaining position.

CECILIA: Look, we took the chance when you wanted to go public and sell stock, and it turned out great! Now we have to be prepared to take another chance. You can't expect to get anywhere in business if you're not prepared to take a few risks!

JAKOB: That's what you said about last month's shareholder proposal.

CECILIA: Well, was I wrong? I seem to remember that we survived that, didn't we?

AARON: Barely.

CECILIA: Yes, but we survived. Remember, let's focus on the positive!

AARON: Let's figure out one very important point first. What exactly does Collins want to buy?

CECILIA: What do you mean?

AARON: Do they want the assets of the company, its stock, or the entire company?

JAKOB: Wait a minute! Did either of you consider the idea that Collins may just be trying to eliminate competition? Sometimes companies buy out smaller companies in their industry just to get rid of competition.

CECILIA: I suppose it's possible, but that doesn't matter to us. Let's focus on how much money we could make.

JAKOB: Let's consider the legality of this whole situation. Do you think this merger would violate antitrust law? It's better to be safe than sorry. Maybe we should call the SEC.

AARON: I think you mean the FTC.

JAKOB: Whatever.

CECILIA: One thing's for sure—we need to consider all options carefully.

JAKOB: We're not completely vulnerable. Won't the business judgment rule protect us?

CECILIA: Maybe, but we still have to be fair to everyone involved.

JAKOB: Well, whatever happens, our lives will certainly be changed forever.

CECILIA: And hopefully we'll get rich!

What Are the Legal Issues?

1. What is the source of the federal government's power to regulate business?
2. What two statutes regulate the sale of securities?
3. What statutes regulate antitrust activities?
4. What are the differences among a merger, an asset acquisition, and a stock acquisition?

Government Regulation of a Corporation

Regulating Corporate Growth

The law generally views the growth and expansion of corporations as a good thing, as long as it does not restrain competition. Not everybody agrees, however. Some people feel that expanding a corporation does not necessarily increase productivity and may actually reduce competition. On the other hand, some claim that expansion allows for economies of scale, and may save a fading company that might not survive otherwise. Adding to the debate are the problems that arise when expansion takes place. Setting things right often falls on the shoulders of the government. The federal government has passed a series of acts to regulate corporate expansion. These acts seek to protect the interests of both corporations and shareholders.

THE SECURITIES AND EXCHANGE COMMISSION
The Securities and Exchange Commission was created by the Securities Exchange Act of 1934. *What is the primary role of the Securities and Exchange Commission?*

Business and the Constitution

The federal government derives its power to regulate business from the commerce clause of the United States Constitution. The **commerce clause** says Congress has the power to regulate commerce "among the several states," meaning the federal government has the power to regulate interstate commerce. During the last century, the U.S. Supreme Court gradually enlarged the scope of the government's power to regulate business. Now the federal government can regulate any business activity that affects interstate commerce, even one that occurs completely within the boundaries of a single state.

Securities Regulation

After the stock market crash of 1929, experts identified the sale and purchase of worthless securities as a major cause of the collapse. To combat this problem, Congress passed the Securities Act of 1933 and the Securities Exchange Act of 1934. These acts were intended to protect

LAWS in Your Life

Business Blues

Many small corporations are equally owned by two people. In such cases, it can be troublesome when one owner wants to sell the corporation and the other does not. The owner who wants to sell can't simply choose to dissolve the corporation. However, he or she can go to court to force a dissolution. This act is called an involuntary dissolution. Involuntary dissolutions are sometimes permitted when shareholders are hopelessly deadlocked.

To avoid deadlock, shareholders of small corporations should sign a buy-sell agreement at the time of the corporation's formation. Such an agreement would help avoid costly lawsuits.

Conduct Research Visit the library or use the Internet to research corporate law resources. In addition to deadlock, what other grounds for involuntary dissolution will courts consider?

investors by ensuring that purchasers can learn the true nature of securities they buy and by providing a way to discover fraud and unfair practices. The Securities Act defines a **security** as a money investment that seeks to make a profit solely because of another's efforts. Many things are included within this definition, such as corporate stocks, interests in savings and loans, interests in racehorses or sports teams, and even sales of coins.

The Securities Exchange Act created the **Securities and Exchange Commission (SEC)** in 1934 to administer federal securities law. The SEC is an independent agency consisting of five commissioners appointed by the president. The SEC employs lawyers, accountants, securities analysts, and others. It regulates sales of securities and the brokers, dealers, and bankers who sell securities. A crucial function of the agency is making sure that potential investors are informed about the nature of their investments. One way to accomplish this aim is through the registration requirement. Any company that falls under the jurisdiction of the SEC must file a registration statement and a prospectus with the agency before it offers securities for sale.

The **registration statement** is a general description of the securities and of the company making the offer. The **prospectus** contains a detailed view of the stock offering for potential investors. The corporation cannot offer stock for sale until the SEC has approved the registration statement. Violating this requirement by failing to file or by filing false information is punishable by fine and imprisonment. In addition, the SEC and the injured investors can bring suit. The SEC can seek an injunction to stop an offering already in progress and also has certain administrative remedies available. The registration process applies to a new stock issue, meaning the first time new stock is offered for sale. The SEC also functions as a watchdog over trading on the stock exchanges and regulates other corporate activities.

Antitrust Laws

During the 1800s, many large corporations in the United States attempted to form monopolies. One technique for seizing control of an industry was to form a trust, in which the voting power of the stock of various companies would be transferred to a single trustee. Eventually, the term "trust" came to describe all monopolies, even though many were not really trusts in the most accurate sense of the word. Figure 30.1 summarizes antitrust regulation enacted by Congress.

Sherman Antitrust Act

Congress passed the Sherman Antitrust Act in 1890 to try to stop the formation of monopolies. It worked for a short time. Then a case decided

Figure 30.1	Securities and Antitrust Legislation
Securities regulation:	
Securities Act of 1933	Regulates the issuance of new securities.
Securities Exchange Act of 1934	Established the Securities and Exchange Commission; deals with subsequent trading in securities.
Williams Act of 1968	Requires stricter reporting and procedural requirements.
Antitrust regulation:	
Sherman Antitrust Act of 1914	Prohibits contracts and combinations in restraint of trade; also prohibits monopolies, attempts to monopolize, and conspiracies to monopolize.
Clayton Antitrust Act of 1914	Prohibits specific practices such as tying agreements and interlocking directorates.
Federal Trade Commission Act of 1914	Established the Federal Trade Commission; promotes free and fair competition, and prohibits unfair and misleading practices.
Robinson-Patman Act of 1936	Deals with product pricing; advertising and promotional allowances.

SECURITIES AND ANTITRUST LEGISLATION
The federal government regulates many aspects of American business. *Where does the federal government get its power to regulate business?*

by the U.S. Supreme Court held that contracts or combinations would be illegal only if they formed an "unreasonable restraint of trade." This step displeased Congress, which took steps to counteract the negative effect.

Clayton Act

Congress passed the Clayton Act in 1914. In contrast to the Sherman Act, the Clayton Act made specific practices illegal. For example, a business could not sell goods to one company for less than the price it charged another company if the effect of the price difference was to reduce competition. It also became illegal to sell goods on the condition that a buyer would not buy products from the seller's competition.

Federal Trade Commission Act

Congress also passed the Federal Trade Commission Act in 1914. This measure was designed to protect businesses from the wrongful acts of other business firms. It stated, "Unfair methods of competition in commerce are hereby declared unlawful."

The Federal Trade Commission Act, however, does not define an unfair method of competition. Instead, it allows the courts to determine these methods on a case-by-case basis. The act also created the Federal Trade Commission (FTC) and charged it with preventing businesses from violating the Federal Trade Commission Act.

Robinson-Patman Act

The Robinson-Patman Act is an amendment to the Clayton Act. It says companies cannot sell goods at lower prices to high-volume purchasers without offering the same discount to smaller purchasers if this practice lessens or eliminates competition or creates a monopoly. The Robinson-Patman Act is not limited to discrimination on pricing. In general, it requires sellers to treat all buyers equally. Any fraud, such as preferential delivery schedules that help one seller but hurt others, has been outlawed.

Later Amendments

The Federal Trade Commission Act was amended in 1938 and 1975. The latest amendment provides protection to consumers as well as business people. The act now says, "Unfair methods of competition in or affecting commerce, unfair or deceptive acts or practices in or affecting commerce are hereby declared unlawful." The FTC also now has the power to make rules and regulations that define specific activities that are considered unfair and deceptive.

Sarbanes-Oxley Act of 2002

In 2001, the Enron Corporation, one of the world's largest traders in gas, electricity, and related commodities, collapsed in scandal and declared bankruptcy. Enron was accused of many crimes, including deceiving investors, inflating profits, and hiding debts. Arthur Anderson, the company's accounting firm, was later convicted of obstructing justice by shredding documents related to its work on Enron's accounting. Finally, WorldCom, then the world's second largest long-distance provider, suffered the largest bankruptcy in American history after it was revealed that it had improperly booked over $7 billion in earnings.

As a result of these high-profile scandals and to shore up faith in the American economy, President Bush signed the Sarbanes-Oxley Act of 2002. The act contains important rules affecting the reporting and corporate governance of public companies and their directors and officers. Major provisions include requiring CEOs and CFOs to certify periodic reports filed with the SEC. It also prohibits most loans to directors and executive officers, and forces company insiders to report changes in beneficial ownership within two days after a transaction has been executed.

Other Forms of Regulation

The government regulates corporate activities in ways other than through securities and antitrust regulation. These regulations include such things as the impact that corporate activities have on energy conservation and environmental protection.

Energy Regulation

The energy crisis of the 1970s drew the attention of the nation toward energy conservation. The federal government addressed the problem by creating the Department of Energy and the Federal Energy Regulatory Commission. The Nuclear Regulatory Commission regulates nuclear energy.

Federal Energy Regulatory Commission   The Federal Energy Regulatory Commission (FERC) controls the wholesale price of natural gas and electricity sold for use in interstate commerce. However, utility companies can apply to FERC if they believe an increase in prices is warranted. Intrastate prices are regulated by state utility agencies. The FERC also makes rules regulating interstate transportation of electricity and natural gas.

Nuclear Regulatory Commission   The Energy Reorganization Act created the Nuclear Regulatory Commission (NRC). The commission

Law & Academics

Social Studies
Corporations in the United States evolved as the nation grew. Federal charters for corporations were granted to both of the banks of the United States and to certain railroads after the Civil War. Laws were enacted as problems arose, and commissions were created to administer the laws. In general, the history of corporations in the United States has been marked by various federal regulations.

Research Activity
Using the medium of your choice, create a pictorial representation of corporate regulation in the United States. Include the laws, commissions, and governmental regulations affecting corporations.

THE ENVIRONMENTAL PROTECTION AGENCY
The Environmental Protection Agency exercises significant regulatory power over U.S. businesses. *What programs are covered by the EPA?*

regulates the licensing, constructing, and opening of nuclear reactors. The NRC also handles the possession, use, transportation, and disposal of nuclear material. The rules and regulations that govern licensed nuclear activities are made and carried out by the commission.

Environmental Protection Regulation

In the structure of the federal government, the responsibility for environmental protection falls on the shoulders of the Environmental Protection Agency (EPA). The EPA is an independent regulatory agency that is a part of the executive branch. One of its major jobs is to implement the Environmental Policy Act. However, the EPA is also responsible

POLLUTION CONTROL
The National Environmental Policy Act sets up a national program to fight pollution and clean up the environment. *What are some of the requirements for environmental protection established by the act?*

for implementation of other environmental laws that deal with air, water, solid waste, toxic substances, and noise pollution. The EPA also carries out executive orders related to the environment.

National Environmental Policy Act   Congress passed the National Environmental Policy Act in 1969 to establish a national program to fight pollution and clean up the environment. Under terms of the act, a detailed statement explaining the environmental consequences must precede any major federal governmental action that affects the quality of the environment. The statement must also include any alternatives that might be taken instead of the proposed action. The objective is to prevent or eliminate damage to the environment and protect the health and welfare of the public.

Environmental Protection Agency   In 1970, the EPA received the authority to administer all major federal antipollution programs dealing with air, solid waste, toxic substances, and pesticides. Under this authority, the EPA can do research, create and administer pollution control guidelines, and monitor programs to make sure that pollution abatement standards are met. The agency can also administer grants to help eliminate pollution under state-run programs. The EPA has the authority to act against entities that pollute the environment, even when a given act of pollution is unintentional.

Section 30.1   Assessment

Reviewing What You Learned
1. What is the source of the federal government's power to regulate business?
2. What are the two statutes that regulate the sale of securities?
3. What are the statutes that regulate antitrust activities?
4. What are the statutes that regulate energy and the environment?

Critical Thinking Activity
Contract Disputes The legal system impacts business by regulating its formation, operation, and expansion. Using the Internet, library, or other resource, evaluate the facts of a contract dispute involving a business and government regulations of energy and the environment. What are the facts of the case, how did the court rule, and why?

Legal Skills in Action
Responsibilities of the SEC Your grandfather is thinking about investing part of his savings in a new corporation that is about to place its stock for sale on the stock exchange. Write him an e-mail message in which you explain the responsibilities of the Securities and Exchange Commission. Make certain to mention the purpose and nature of a registration statement, as well as the purposes of a prospectus.

Corporate Expansion and Dissolution

Why It's Important

Understanding the nature of corporate expansion and dissolution will help you determine your rights as a shareholder.

Legal Terms

- merger
- asset acquisition
- stock acquisition
- tender offer
- suitor
- target

Increasing Shareholder Value

Investors buy shares in a corporation because they hope to make money through what is known as a return on their investment. The directors and officers of a corporation try to make the business earn a profit that can be returned as dividends to the shareholders, or to increase the value of the shares of the corporation so that those shares can be sold at a profit. One way to increase the value of a corporation's shares is to expand the business.

Types of Corporate Expansion

Ways for a corporation to expand include buying new land, building new manufacturing plants, opening new sales outlets, expanding product lines, and entering new fields of business. Growth and expansion can occur by joining with another corporation through a merger, an asset acquisition, or a stock acquisition (see Figure 30.2).

Merger and Consolidation

Merger and consolidation are common methods of business expansion. In a **merger**, one corporation continues its existence and absorbs another corporation, which gives up its corporate identity. By contrast, in a consolidation two or more companies join to form a new corporation. The new company is a composite of the old companies. As far as results are concerned, there is no significant difference between a merger and a consolidation, and the terms are often used interchangeably. Most of the time, the term merger is now used to describe both scenarios.

The boards of directors and shareholders of the corporations being joined together must approve the merger or consolidation. Generally, a two-thirds majority of the shareholders is required, although some state statutes require a super majority as high as four-fifths. Shareholders who dissent from a merger or a consolidation are entitled to be paid for their stock if they want to pull out of the new corporation.

Often, dissenters have to give written notice of their dissent before a vote is taken. The cost of paying these dissenters must be considered a cost of the merger. The assets, stock, and debts of the old corporation flow to the new or surviving corporation. Likewise,

Figure 30.2 — Corporate Expansion Techniques

Category	Description	Example	Liabilities
Merger and Consolidation	In merger, one company merges with another; in consolidation, two companies merge and a new company results.	Approval by boards and shareholders of both corporations.	Debts and product liability flow to the new or surviving company.
Asset Acquisition	One corporation buys all the property of another corporation.	Approval by board and shareholders of acquired company.	Debt usually does not flow to the buyer; product liability may flow to the buyer.
Stock Acquisition	One corporation (the suitor) makes a tender offer to the shareholders of another company (the target); if enough of the target shareholders accept and sell, the suitor takes control of the target.	Approval of enough shareholders to give the suitor control.	Debt and product liability flow to the suitor.

CORPORATE EXPANSION TECHNIQUES
Businesses are organized in the hope of expanding and making money. *If you were a shareholder, which expansion technique would you prefer?*

shareholders of the disappearing corporation become shareholders of the new corporation. Liabilities may also flow to the new corporation, including potential lawsuits, such as those for product defects or for dumping toxic waste.

Asset Acquisition

As the name suggests, in an **asset acquisition** one corporation agrees to purchase the assets or property of a second corporation. For instance, a corporation might sell its building and all of its equipment. The shareholders and the board of directors of the corporation selling the assets must approve this transaction. One advantage to asset acquisition is that, in general, the debts and the liabilities of the selling corporation do not transfer to the buying corporation. The reason is that the only thing actually transferred is ownership of the property. If a corporation is heavily in debt, it might decide to sell its assets to another corporation to raise cash quickly to pay off those debts.

Stock Acquisition

Another type of expansion is a **stock acquisition**, which occurs when an individual or a corporation purchases enough shares of stock in a corporation to control it. A stock acquisition often begins with a **tender offer** to shareholders of the corporation. This is an offer to buy a number of shares at a specified price. Tender offers are often referred to as takeover bids and are usually communicated to the prospective selling shareholders through a newspaper advertisement. The corporation making the tender offer is referred to as the **suitor**, and the corporation to be taken over is called the **target**. The suitor does not have to buy all the stock of the target, but just enough to control the election of directors. The suitor can also sidestep the directors and appeal directly to the shareholders.

> *Example 1.* Wentworth, a multimillionaire, has decided that he would like to purchase Radlech Electronics, Inc. He approaches the board of directors with his plan and finds that the directors are not interested. The next day, in *The Wall Street Financial*, he places an advertisement, offering to purchase shares of Radlech at $49 per share. The current market price of a share of Radlech is $35. Any and all shareholders who deal with Wentworth stand to make a big profit. Wentworth will not have to buy all the shares of Radlech. He needs to purchase only enough to allow him to control the election of directors. Wentworth has sidestepped the directors and appealed directly to the shareholders.

Because the suitor often wishes to restructure or even dismantle the target corporation, its directors and officers often object to a tender offer. They may fear the loss of their positions, or they may see the takeover bid as a threat to the very existence of the corporation. Under these conditions one of the first steps the managers often take is to launch a public relations campaign to discredit the suitor. In such a campaign, they may refer to the tender offer as a "hostile takeover bid" and to the suitor as a "corporate raider." They may also use other measures to combat a hostile takeover bid. These include techniques such as inviting a friendly suitor to purchase a valuable asset of the corporation to make it a less attractive target, offering to buy back the shares the hostile bidder has already purchased, but at a higher price, or inviting an individual or another corporation to outbid the hostile bidder.

Government Regulation of Corporate Expansion

A flurry of takeovers took place in the 1960s and 1980s. Many of these conglomerate mergers, which were valued in billions of dollars, involved bitter struggles between the suitors and the target companies. The activity created concerns that the mergers stifled competition, controlled markets and pricing, and discouraged innovation. As a result, Congress, state legislatures, and the courts have become involved in regulating the corporate takeover process.

Federal Regulation

A federal statute known as the Williams Act strictly controls takeover bids. Under this act, when a suitor offers to acquire more than five percent of a target, the suitor must file a statement with the SEC indicating where the money for the takeover is coming from, why the suitor is purchasing the stock, and how much of the target the suitor owns. The goal is to make certain shareholders know the qualifications and the intentions of the suitor. The Williams Act also gives shareholders who have purchased stock from the suitor 15 business days to change their minds. This provision takes some of the pressure off shareholders who may feel compelled to sell their shares to meet the suitor's deadline.

JUDICIAL SCRUTINY
The courts have taken the primary motive approach when applying the business judgment rule to corporate takeovers. *What are the problems with this approach?*

Careers in Law

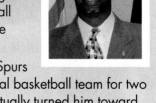

State Legislator

Oliver Robinson got a taste of fame at the tender age of 13. "I was a pretty good elementary school basketball player, and one day my name and picture landed in the Birmingham paper," says Robinson.

"Pretty good" eventually turned into "San Antonio Spurs good." The Alabama native played with the professional basketball team for two years, but Robinson's determination and ambition eventually turned him toward another competitive arena: politics. Today, the Birmingham businessman is a member of the Alabama House of Representatives.

After college, Robinson worked for several years for AmSouth Bancorps, where he eventually became vice president and manager for the company's office of community affairs. There he managed the large bank's community reinvestment program, guiding corporate investments in low- and moderate-income communities. He also handled AmSouth's public relations and dealt with federal regulators. Robinson says the experience he gained in each of these jobs helped him tremendously when he decided to start his own business, ABI Capital Management. ABI underwrites bonds for educational institutions.

Robinson also began to focus on state politics. The Alabama Democrat was elected to his first four-year term in 1998. Robinson enjoys his involvement in politics because it enables him to make a difference in the lives of others. He especially enjoys protecting the interests of the less fortunate. He represents Jefferson County and the eastern side of Birmingham and is a member of the Judiciary and Banking and Insurance Committees. He recently sponsored a bill to establish a police review board in Birmingham, a city that has a long history of civil rights advocacy.

"Even though the House didn't approve the bill," Robinson says, "I'm very proud of our efforts to get it through the legislature, and we'll keep trying until it is approved. It's an honor for me to represent the interests of the people I grew up with and try to improve their lives."

Skills	Negotiation, communication, public speaking, analytical
Personality	Able to compromise, adaptable, outgoing, sense of humor, concern for the welfare of others
Education	No specific education (although Robinson's background in political science and urban affairs has served him well)

For more information on legislators, visit **ubpl.glencoe.com** or your public library.

State Legislative Regulation

State legislatures have dealt with the concerns surrounding stock acquisitions in a number of ways. They have passed antiliability statutes to protect corporate directors whose companies are involved in takeovers. Several state legislatures have also enacted antitakeover statutes to discourage suitors from targeting companies within their states. One form of antiliability statute automatically gives directors the protection of the business judgment rule when the corporation is subjected to a takeover bid. This kind of law says that change of control in the corporation does not imply disloyalty or unfairness on the part of the directors. Another type of antiliability statute allows corporations to amend their bylaws to include this type of protection for their directors. This approach would permit the corporation to adopt the protection only if the shareholders gave their consent. A third type of statute extends this protection not only to directors but also to officers.

Judicial Scrutiny

Sometimes a corporation's directors and officers who successfully resist a takeover bid end up being sued by dissatisfied shareholders. Typically, the shareholders complain that the suitor's takeover would have been more profitable for them. These shareholders contend that the directors and officers selfishly sacrificed gains the shareholders could have made.

In such lawsuits, the courts must evaluate the decisions made by the corporation's directors and officers. One critical question courts must ponder is whether the business judgment rule should apply. Recall that the business judgment rule presumes that a director acts with due care and provides that a director's decision is immune to attack. However, the business judgment rule does not apply if the director acts illegally or based on a conflict of interest.

The obvious question in assessing resistance of a takeover bid is whether the manager's desire to maintain control of the corporation is too self-serving. Some courts have taken the primary motive approach in considering these cases. Under this approach, if the primary motive of the directors and officers is to maintain control of the corporation, they have a personal interest in the takeover and do not deserve the protection of the business judgment rule. The burden of proof is then on the directors to show that their decisions regarding the takeover were fair to the shareholders and corporation. The problem with the primary motive approach is that it is difficult to separate primary and secondary motives.

Dissolution of a Corporation

The government is as concerned about the end of a corporation as it is about the beginning of one. The end of a corporate entity is often referred to as the dissolution of the corporation, and it can come about

It's a Question of Ethics

Ethics and Advertising
The *Metro Daily News* receives 35 percent of its advertising revenue from Neuhaus Department Stores. In fact, Neuhaus is the single largest advertiser with the newspaper. When *Metro Daily News* published a story about discriminatory hiring practices at Neuhaus, the department store threatened to quit advertising. *What are the ethical issues?*

in two ways. The corporation can decide to end, or a corporation's dissolution can happen involuntarily. The law is also now concerned with the dissolution of limited liability companies.

Voluntary Dissolution

When a corporation ends, the demise must be reported to the government. The reason is that the government grants corporate charters and regulates the activities of all corporate entities. One way for a corporation to end voluntarily is through a unanimous vote of all of its shareholders. The directors may also vote for its end, provided they get the support of two-thirds of the shareholders. After the decision to end the corporation has been made, a statement of intent to dissolve must be filed with the secretary of state's office. The corporation must notify creditors by certified mail of its dissolution. The public must be notified by publication.

The creditors are the first to be paid when a corporation ends. If a surplus remains after the creditors have been paid, it goes to the shareholders. A receiver may be involved if the current assets cannot meet all obligations. A receiver is appointed by law and has the job of holding the property subject to all claims against the corporation. The receiver divides the assets among the creditors. Articles of dissolution must also be presented to the secretary of state.

Involuntary Dissolution

The secretary of state can ask the state attorney general to bring a *quo warranto* action against a corporation if the corporation has repeatedly conducted business illegally. If such an action is taken, the corporation could lose its charter and would no longer be authorized to do business in the state. The grounds for bringing such an action include failure by the corporation to file annual reports, failure to pay franchise taxes, or failure to maintain a statutory agent for service of process. A corporation may also be subject to a *quo warranto* action if it exceeds its authority or is formed fraudulently.

When a shareholder brings an action, the courts have the authority to liquidate the assets of the corporation. However, the shareholder must have appropriate grounds to seek the involuntary dissolution of the corporation. Such grounds include but are not limited to evidence of illegal actions, evidence of fraud, evidence of the waste of corporate assets, and evidence that a dissolution is needed to protect the shareholders' rights.

Dissolving a Limited Liability Company

State law also regulates the dissolution of a limited liability company. The reason is that an LLC is just as much a statutory entity as a corporation. State statutes generally outline the circumstances under which a limited liability company can be dissolved.

Circumstances of Dissolution The members of a limited liability company can initiate its dissolution by unanimous agreement. It is also possible for the dissolution to be triggered by the expulsion of a member. A member's bankruptcy and his or her withdrawal can also activate the dissolution. Many state statutes, however, now restrict a member's withdrawal, generally allowing it only if it is authorized by the LLC's operating agreement. It is also possible for the operating agreement to spell out the circumstances under which a limited liability company can be dissolved.

Effects of Dissolution The dissolution of the LLC does not stop the business of the LLC. A dissolution differs from a winding up. The winding up process, which effectively puts the LLC out of business, involves completing the company's business, selling its property, and satisfying the company's debts. A winding up need not follow a dissolution. The LLC can be continued if the remaining members choose to do so. The operating agreement can also say that unanimous consent of the members is not needed to continue the business of the LLC. On the other hand, it is not possible for the LLC to continue to operate if the number of members falls below that required by state statutory law.

Section 30.2 Assessment

Reviewing What You Learned
1. What are the differences among a merger, an asset acquisition, and a stock acquisition?
2. What is a tender offer?
3. What is the difference between a suitor and a target?
4. What is the difference between voluntary and involuntary dissolution of a corporation?
5. What are the circumstances under which a limited liability company can dissolve?

Critical Thinking Activity
Asset Acquisitions What advantages come with an asset acquisition?

Legal Skills in Action
Involuntary Dissolution You have just discovered that a corporation in which you hold stock is going to be subject to a *quo warranto* action. Write an entry in your Justice Journal outlining all of the possible reasons why the state may have decided to take this step against this company. Also remind yourself of the possible consequences of this action.

Chapter Summary

Section 30.1 Government Regulation of a Corporation

- The federal government derives its power to regulate business from the commerce clause of the U.S. Constitution. The federal government can regulate any business activity that affects interstate commerce, even one that occurs completely within the boundaries of a single state.

- Congress passed the Securities Act of 1933 and the Securities Exchange Act of 1934 to protect corporate investors by ensuring that information regarding securities is available before purchase. These acts protect purchasers by enabling them to learn the true nature of securities they buy and by providing a way to discover fraud and unfair practices.

- In 1890, Congress passed the Sherman Antitrust Act that declared monopolies to be illegal. In addition, Congress passed the Clayton Act in 1914, which made specific practices that foster the formation of monopolies illegal. To combat unfair competition, the Federal Trade Commission Act was passed to protect a business from the wrongful acts of unfairly competing companies. The Robinson-Patman Act made it illegal for companies to sell goods at lower prices to high-volume purchasers without offering the same discount to smaller purchasers.

- Among the federal acts that regulate energy and the environment are the Energy Reorganization Act and the National Environmental Policy Act. The Energy Reorganization Act created the Nuclear Regulatory Commission (NRC). The commission regulates the licensing, constructing, and opening of nuclear reactors. The NRC also handles the possession, use, transportation, and disposal of nuclear material. Under the terms of the National Environmental Policy Act, a detailed statement explaining the environmental consequences must precede any major federal government action that affects the quality of the environment.

Section 30.2 Corporate Expansion and Dissolution

- In a merger, one corporation continues its existence and absorbs another corporation, which gives up its corporate identity. In contrast, a consolidation of two or more companies is the formation of a new corporation. In an asset acquisition one corporation agrees to purchase the assets or property of a second corporation. A stock acquisition occurs when an individual or a corporation purchases enough shares in a corporation to control it.

- Before a stock acquisition, the buyer makes an offer to shareholders of a corporation to buy a number of shares at a specified price. A tender offer is also referred to as a takeover bid, and it is usually communicated to the prospective selling shareholders through a newspaper advertisement.

- A suitor is the party making the tender offer to buy shares to achieve a stock acquisition. The target is the corporation that is considered for takeover by the suitor.

- A corporation may dissolve itself voluntarily by a unanimous vote of all of its shareholders. The directors may also vote its end with the support of two-thirds of the shareholders. In contrast, the state can bring an action against a corporation for repeated wrongdoing and force its dissolution. In addition, a shareholder can bring an action to dissolve a corporation to protect the shareholders' rights from the consequences of destructive board decisions.

- The members of a limited liability company can initiate its dissolution by unanimous agreement, by the expulsion of a member, or by a member's bankruptcy and withdrawal from the company.

Using Legal Language

Consider the key terms in the list below. Then use these terms to complete the following exercises.

commerce clause

security

Securities and Exchange
  Commission (SEC)

registration statement

prospectus

merger

asset acquisition

stock acquisition

tender offer

suitor

target

1. Create a crossword puzzle using all of the key terms. Be sure to include an answer key.
2. Exchange puzzles with another student and solve each other's puzzles.
3. Check your partner's work and correct any mistakes that he or she made.

Understanding Business and Personal Law Online

Self-Check Quiz Visit the *Understanding Business and Personal Law* Web site at **ubpl.glencoe.com** and click on Chapter 30: Regulation and Expansion of a Corporation—Self-Check Quizzes to prepare for the chapter exam.

The Law Review

Answer the following questions. Refer to the chapter for additional reinforcement.

4. What are the four major federal antitrust laws? Give a brief description of what each law does.
5. What are the responsibilities of the Environmental Protection Agency (EPA)?
6. What happens when a shareholder dissents from a merger and desires to pull out of the new corporation?
7. How are takeover bids regulated?
8. Does the dissolution of a LLC stop the business of the LLC? Explain.
9. What was one of the major causes of the stock market crash of 1929?
10. What is a prospectus?
11. How does a merger differ from a consolidation?
12. What are the two ways that a shareholder can make money on his or her investment in a corporation?
13. Why might a corporation resist a suitor's attempt to take over the business through stock acquisition?

Linking School to Work

Acquiring and Evaluating Information

Using the newspaper, the Internet, or the local library, research a recent corporate merger. Explain:

14. The circumstances surrounding the merger.

15. Problems or issues that occurred during the merger process.

16. The advantages or disadvantages of the merger to the shareholders.

Write a two-page paper discussing your findings.

Let's Debate

Takeover or Merger?

In the 1990 movie *Pretty Woman*, Edward Lewis's company sets out to execute a takeover bid for James Morse's company. Lewis eventually decides on a merger rather than a takeover.

Debate

17. Assuming that Morse's company would have been dismantled and sold after the takeover, what effect might Lewis's decision have had?

18. What impact would Lewis's decision have had on both companies, their owners (shareholders), and their employees?

19. Do you think Lewis make the right decision? Why or why not?

Grasping Case Issues

For the following cases, give your decision and state a legal principle that applies.

20. Ilsa Garthwaite owns Future-graphics, Inc. a fashion-design business specializing in creating clothing for the super rich. She asks four of her best clients to choose a season's clothing line to sponsor. She suggests that each contribute $1 million and explains that the return on the investment would depend on Future-graphics's profits. Does Ilsa's sponsorship plan qualify as a security? Explain your answer.

21. Weldon Sackman and Frank Chandler are competitors and the only two farm equipment dealers in the county. They make an agreement to divide the county's territory, raise prices, and stop competing. If one breaches the agreement, may the other sue for breach of contract? Explain your answer.

22. Janet Juliano, an owner of stock in a corporation that merged with another corporation, claims she was not notified of the merger until after it was completed. Is this likely? Explain the usual procedure in a merger, and how a shareholder would be involved in the process.

23. Swallow & Ascot Books, Inc., a large children's book publisher, owns three percent of Pyatt, Inc., a leading comic-book publisher. Swallow decides to launch a takeover bid, with Pyatt as the target. Swallow offers the Pyatt shareholders $34 per share. The current market value is $22 per share. George Tackett sells his 50 shares, then changes his mind the next day. Is there anything he can do? Explain your answer.

24. The directors of the Mount Vernon Research Corporation sold tracts of land in its diamond mines under a series of land contracts. In return, the purchaser of each tract of land would be entitled to a return on his or her investment based on the year-end profits and in proportion to the number of land contracts that he or she owned. Would the SEC consider each of these contracts a security? Explain your answer.

In each case that follows, you be the judge.

25. Preferred Treatment

After being hired to build homes, the Centex-Winston Corporation contracted to purchase lumber, for resale, from Edward Hines Lumber Company. Hines consistently failed to deliver orders on time due to its preferential treatment of several Centex-Winston competitors. Centex-Winston sued Hines, claiming the preferential delivery violated the Robinson-Patman Act. *Is Centex-Winston correct? Why or why not?*

Centex-Winston v. Edward Hines Lumber Co., 447 F.2d 585 (7th Circuit).

26. True Intent

Irwin Lampert, Leonard Levy, and Paul Scuderi purchased more than 12 percent of General Aircraft's stock. Because the purchase exceeded 5 percent, they filed the SEC form required by the Williams Act, stating that the purchase was for investment purposes only. For the next year, Lampert, Levy, and Scuderi caused a great deal of trouble for General Aircraft's management. They eventually engineered a change on the board of directors, giving themselves more influence on corporate decision making. They then entered a proxy solicitation contest, challenging management for total corporate control. Management filed a complaint, claiming that the Williams Act filing had been fraudulent; the stock purchase had not been for investment purposes. The complaint asked the court to order Lampert, Levy, and Scuderi to amend their filing and to stop buying shares or soliciting proxies until the amendments had been properly processed. *Should the court order be granted? Why or why not?*

General Aircraft Corporation v. Lampert, 556 F.2d 90 (1st Circuit).

Legal Link

Another Crash?

On October 12, 1987, the Dow Jones Industrial Average plunged 508 points. When the closing bell rang, the market was worth 22 percent less than it had been that morning. It was the worst crash since 1929 and the Great Depression.

Connect

Using a variety of search engines:

27. Research the days leading up to October 12.
28. Develop a timeline of events that you think helped cause this event.

Then present to the class the reasons why you believe this stock market crash did not cause a major depression in the United States.

POWER READING STRATEGIES

29. **Predict** Do you think the growth and expansion of a business could actually reduce competition? Explain your answer.

30. **Connect** Can you think of a company that has not been able to expand because of the antitrust laws that are in place?

31. **Question** Is it the government's responsibility to protect the environment from pollution? Why or why not?

32. **Respond** When a corporation ends, why must you report the event to the government?

UNIT **6** Law Workshop:
Using Legal Tools

Do You Have an Idea for a Business?

Owning your own business can be financially and personally rewarding, but it demands a lot of work and dedication. Starting a business, whether it's a sole proprietorship, partnership, or corporation, also requires knowledge of business law.

Step A: Preparation

Problem: *How would you organize a corporation and convince others to invest in it?*

Objectives: In this workshop, you will work with partners to write the articles of incorporation for a business. You will also try to convince the class to buy your company's stock.

- **Research** and create a product idea.
- **Use technology** to prepare the articles of incorporation for your business.
- **Investigate** how to finance a corporation by selling stocks.
- **Present** your ideas, and try to persuade other members of your class to invest in your company.

Step B: Procedure

1. In groups of three or four, use the Internet and library to research new business ideas. Read business publications such as *BusinessWeek* or *The Wall Street Journal*.

2. Develop a product for your new business. Your company can offer goods, services, or both.

3. Write the articles of incorporation for your business. Use real-life information to create an interesting and realistic product.

4. Research how stocks are promoted by reading corporate annual reports and accessing Web sites for investor relations. Then give a sales presentation to the class, offering stock subscriptions for your corporation.

5. After all of the presentations have been given, vote for the three corporations that you would most likely invest in. Cast your ballots anonymously.

Step C: Creating a Model to Compare Corporations

As a class, count the ballots and list the results on the board. Make a chart that shows which three businesses received the most votes, along with the reasons that the businesses were chosen.

	Business #1	Business #2	Business #3
Reasons for choosing			

Step D: Workshop Analysis Report

Consider the information on the chart that the class has compiled, and answer the following questions:

1. What products were the top three businesses selling?
2. Is there any relationship among the three types of products? If so, what is it?
3. Compare the reasons given for choosing the businesses. Is there similarity among the reasons? If so, what is it?

Virginia Bankshares, Inc. v. Sandberg

U.S. Supreme Court

501 U.S. 1083 (1991)

Issue Can false statements phrased as opinions and beliefs in a proxy solicitation violate SEC Rule 14a-9, which prohibits the soliciting proxies by using materially false or misleading statements?

Facts Sandberg owned stock as a minority shareholder in First American Bank of Virginia. As part of a "freeze-out" merger, the bank directors of First American Bank of Virginia recommended that the bank merge into another bank, Virginia Bankshares, Inc., which was a subsidiary of the petitioner First American Bankshare, Inc. The directors solicited proxies for the merger proposal. A proxy is a document in which a shareholder appoints another person to act as his or her agent to vote the corporate stock. The directors stated "that they had approved the plan because of its opportunity for the minority shareholders to achieve a 'high' value . . . for their stock." The executive committee of First American Bank of Virginia, along with its board of directors, approved a price of $42 per share for the minority stockholders. After the merger was completed, the minority stockholders would lose their interest in the bank. Sandberg refused to give a proxy authorizing another person to vote for approval of the merger. Sandberg was not satisfied by the offer of $42 per share and did not believe that the statements made by the leadership of First American Bank of Virginia were fair to the minority stockholders.

After the merger was approved without her vote, Sandberg brought a civil action against both banking corporations and the directors of First American Bank. In her complaint, Sandberg alleged that the directors of First American Bank had not believed that the price offered for the stock was "high". Instead, she alleged that they made the recommendation for merger so that they could remain on the board of directors. Sandberg claimed that the directors violated the Rule 14a-9 of the SEC, which prohibits using materially false or misleading statements in soliciting proxies. At trial, the jury awarded Sandberg an additional $18 per share, the sum she would have received if the stock had been properly valued. The jury also informed Sandberg that she could prevail in her lawsuit without seeking to prove that she relied on First American Bank's misstatements. Rather, she only needed to prove that the misstatements were material and that the proxy solicitation was essential to the success of the merger.

Opinion The federal government created the Securities and Exchange Commission in response to the stock market crash of 1929. Prior to the stock market crash, worthless securities were being traded, and many investors fell victim to scams. The Securities Exchange Act of 1934 gave the Securities and Exchange Commission the authority to declare rules that regulate soliciting proxies. As a result, the SEC adopted Rule 14a-9, which prohibits soliciting proxies by using materially false or misleading statements.

Statements of Opinion

In this case, the bank directors stated in their proxy solicitation "that they had approved the plan because of its opportunity for the minority shareholders to achieve a 'high' value . . . for their stock." The bank directors argue that these phrases are merely statements of opinion and cannot be considered misstatements of material fact within the meaning of Rule 14a-9. They further argue that such statements of opinion do not violate Rule 14a-9 when included in a proxy solicitation that contains statements of fact from which shareholders can draw their own conclusions. The bank directors implied that they did not intend for the minority stockholders to rely heavily upon the statements included in the proxy solicitation, but instead assumed that stockholders would be guided by a variety of factors, including their own personal opinions and research, when making their decisions.

Reasonable Shareholder Reliance

In rejecting these arguments, the Court observed, "We think there is no room to deny that a statement or belief by corporate directors about a recommended course of action . . . can take on just that importance. Shareholders know that directors usually have knowledge and expertness far exceeding the normal investor's resources, and the directors' perceived superiority is magnified even further by the common knowledge that state law customarily obliges them to exercise their judgment in the shareholders' interest." In making misleading statements to protect their own interests, the directors had behaved unethically and had violated the rules issued by the Securities and Exchange Commission.

Holding Knowingly issuing false statements by directors of a corporation in a proxy solicitation, even when phrased as opinions and beliefs, may be materially misleading within the meaning of SEC Rule 14a-9. These types of statements are misleading because of the confidence placed in the opinions of directors by the shareholders as a result of the shareholders' perception of the directors' knowledge and expertise. The directors' positions and knowledge obligate them to make decisions that will benefit the corporation and its stockholders. Furthermore, shareholders expect the directors to act in the best interests of the shareholders, as required by state law.

Questions for Analysis

1. What is a proxy?
2. What is the Securities and Exchange Commission, and what is the source of its authority?
3. What does SEC Rule 14a-9 address?
4. Under the Court's decision, can a conclusory statement in a proxy solicitation be considered materially misleading within the meaning of SEC 14a-9?
5. Explain the Court's reasoning for concluding that statements of opinion by the directors of a corporation could be materially misleading to shareholders.

Web Resources

Go to the *Understanding Business and Personal Law* Web Site at **ubpl.glencoe.com** for information about how to access online resources for the Landmark Cases.

UNIT 7

UNIT OVERVIEW

Getting married, purchasing your first home, and planning for your retirement are important life events that many anticipate. It is necessary to know your legal rights and responsibilities when you reach these life events so that you can plan accordingly. In this unit, you will learn about the laws that govern the following topics:

- Marriage and divorce, and their legal consequences
- Renting and buying a residence
- Insurance protection
- Retirement and wills

Planning for the Future

Understanding Business and Personal Law *Online*

Chapter Overview Visit the *Understanding Business and Personal Law* Web site at ubpl.glencoe.com and click on Chapter 31: Marriage—Chapter Overviews to preview the chapter information.

The Opening Scene

Starting in this chapter, you will meet Robin Johnson, 22; her fiancé, Patrick Regan, 23; her sister, Tatiana, 15; and her brother, Dane, 17. Robin is arguing with her sister in the living room of the family's home.

Marriage Plans

TATIANA: I don't care what you say, Robin! You don't know what you're talking about. I'm going to marry Alan, even if he is 24 and I'm only 15. You know I'm very mature for my age! I don't want to just move in together—I really want to get married.

ROBIN: You are way too young to get married. How do you know that you'll even like this guy five years from now? You are mature for your age, but people change a lot in their late teens and early twenties. Plus, I don't understand why Alan can't find someone his own age. He's really strange. I guess I shouldn't worry too much, though. You can't get married without Mom and Dad's permission, anyway. There's no way they're going to go along with your plans.

TATIANA: It doesn't matter what Mom and Dad say. Alan said we could elope! I would be willing to elope if we had to! It's pretty romantic!

ROBIN: Tatiana, listen to me. Teenage marriages don't succeed very often. Wait until you're older. Finish high school and get more education, like Patrick and I are doing. Look at Pauline and Mark. They're waiting until they finish college to get married. That's a smart plan.

TATIANA: Yes, I know they're waiting, but Pauline says they'll have to go to another state to get married because they're first cousins. They won't be legally married here and can't even come back to this state to live!

ROBIN: That doesn't seem right. If they get legally married in another state, then that should make them married everywhere. *(Dane bounds into the house, drops his book bag on the floor, and opens the refrigerator door.)*

ROBIN: You're home later than usual. How was practice, Dane?

DANE: *(Ignoring the question.)* I found out something interesting at school today, Tatiana. Did you know that your boyfriend, Alan, lived with a girl for a year, and now she's claiming to be his common-law wife? She says he's the father of her child, too. I bet Alan didn't tell you any of that information. Alan is a real loser. I don't have any idea why you like him.

ROBIN: Oh, no!

TATIANA: *(Stunned.)* Alan never mentioned anything about living with a woman and having a child. I'm sure it's not true. You must be kidding! I know that Alan wouldn't lie to me.

DANE: No, it's true. I heard it from someone who lives in Alan's apartment building. The guy that I talked to said that Alan has been living with this woman for the past year. He's even seen them take the baby places together. I think it's time to dump Alan.

TATIANA: But Alan wants to marry me! I still don't believe you.

DANE: He can't marry you if he's already married. That's bigamy! Anyway, you're too young to get married.

What Are the Legal Issues?

1. Can a 15-year-old girl marry without her parents' consent?
2. Is a marriage between first cousins legal?
3. Are first cousins related by affinity?
4. What is a common-law marriage and is it legal?
5. What is the name and legal effect of having two spouses at one time?

Marriage Formalities and Restrictions

What You'll Learn

- How to state when the marriage contract actually takes place
- How to describe the rights and duties involved in the marriage contract
- How to explain the requirements of a premarital agreement and state when they are important
- How to identify marriages that are prohibited by law

Why It's Important

The more you know about marriage laws and restrictions, the less likely you are to enter an unstable marriage.

Legal Terms

- premarital agreement
- consanguinity
- affinity
- bigamy
- polygamy

Government's Role in Marriage

Marriage is viewed by many as the basis of the family unit and is therefore considered vital to the preservation of values and culture. Each state is permitted, following U.S. Constitutional guidelines, to prescribe who is allowed to marry and how a marriage can be dissolved. However, each state must also recognize the laws and court decisions of other states. Eight states (Arizona, Colorado, Illinois, Kentucky, Minnesota, Missouri, Montana, and Washington) have adopted the Uniform Marriage and Divorce Act.

The Marriage Contract

Marriage is a personal relationship between a man and a woman, but it is also a civil contract that comes into existence when you become engaged. At the time of engagement, there is an agreement containing consideration (a promise to give up the legal right to remain single) between two parties who have the capacity to contract, by mutual consent and for a legal purpose. While a couple is engaged, the marriage contract is in its executory stage. The contract is executed when the wedding occurs. Under common law, if one of the parties failed to go through with the marriage after becoming engaged, the other party could sue for damages caused by breach of the marriage contract. However, this is no longer the law in most states today.

Example 1. Ramon Hernandez asked Dulce Torres to marry him, and she accepted. A few months later, Dulce changed her mind and called off the engagement. If the parties lived in a state that still follows common law on this point, Ramon could sue Dulce for any damages he suffered because of the breach of contract.

In some states, a man is entitled to the return of the engagement ring when a marriage is called off. The theory is that the ring is a contingent gift, dependent upon the realization of the marriage. In other states, however, courts have allowed a woman to keep the ring if the man ended the engagement.

Rights and Duties

When you enter into an ordinary contract, your rights and duties are created by agreement. The marriage contract, however, changes your

▶ **BEING ENGAGED**
The marriage contract comes into existence at the time of the engagement. *If the engagement falls through, must the engagement ring be returned?*

legal status, and the law gives both husband and wife new rights and duties, which are intended to provide protection to both parties. People who live together without being married do not receive this special protection. The following rights are some of the rights given by law when you marry:

- The right to support by your spouse when necessary
- The right to inheritance from your deceased spouse

Virtual Law

Marriage and the Internet

Do you have friends or relatives who would be unable to attend your wedding because of travel, cost, health, or distance? The Internet now makes it possible for people anywhere in the world with access to a computer to see your wedding in real time. All you need is a Web camera, a computer, and an Internet connection, or to hire a company that can provide this service for you. You can also place video clips from your wedding on the Internet and wedding pictures in an online photo album.

Connect Using your favorite search engine, research some of the other ways in which the Internet might be used for purposes of preparing for a wedding.

LAWS in Your Life

Domestic Violence

Unfortunately, domestic abuse sometimes occurs in a marriage. Victims of domestic abuse may pursue several legal options to address the situation. One such option involves filing a criminal complaint against the abuser with the local prosecutor's office.

Suing the abuser in civil court for damages related to injuries received is also an option. When someone harms another, the harmful act is called a tort. Torts include the act of battery or the unlawful use of bodily force against another. In the case of domestic abuse, the abuser may be subject to punishment in both criminal and civil courts.

In the past, most states did not allow family members to sue each other for torts. The idea was that this might lead to a breakdown in family relationships. Today, almost all states allow such civil suits to be filed against family members. Some states still prohibit family members from suing each other except in the case of intentional torts. The courts nearly always view acts of domestic violence as intentional torts. As such, lawsuits against the abuser are usually allowed to proceed.

Conduct Research Using the library or the Internet, find out more about legal help available to victims of domestic abuse.

- The right to property if the marriage ends
- The right to compensation to continue your standard of living if the marriage ends
- The right to file a joint income tax return

Most employers also give certain rights to their employees' spouses. These rights normally include health insurance coverage and retirement benefits.

The primary duty that arises from the marriage contract is the duty of being faithful to your spouse. This duty cannot be relinquished, even by agreement. Other duties, in general, flow from the rights previously discussed. If your spouse has the right to receive support, for example, then you have the duty to provide it.

All people, married or not, must refrain from causing bodily harm to those they live with. In addition, both parents, whether married or not, have the duty to support their children.

Premarital Agreements

Sometimes, before they marry, people enter into written agreements concerning the real and personal property they will own during their marriage. They set forth how their property interests will be handled if the marriage ends by death or divorce. A **premarital agreement**, also called an antenuptial or prenuptial agreement, is made between prospective spouses in contemplation of marriage and becomes effective upon marriage. Figure 31.1 shows a sample premarital agreement. In making a premarital agreement, you must make honest statements, and you and your partner must fully disclose your assets to each other. In some states, a different attorney must represent each party.

A premarital agreement must be in writing and signed by both parties. Although laws vary from state to state, parties to a premarital agreement generally may contract with respect to the following issues:

- The rights and obligations of each of the parties with regard to any of the property of either or both of them
- The right to buy, sell, manage, and control real and personal property
- The disposition of real and personal property upon separation, divorce, or death
- The change or elimination of support

RESOLVING POTENTIAL PROBLEMS
Second or third marriages can involve many decisions and responsibilities. *How would a premarital agreement help a couple resolve some of these details?*

Premarital Agreement

Agreement made this 10th day of June, 20--, between Joseph Taft of 1273 Holly Lane, Amesburgh, PA, and Susan Jacobs, of 299 Oak Lane, Amesburgh, PA.

Whereas a marriage is shortly to be solemized between the parties hereto;

Whereas Susan Jacobs now owns a large amount of property and expects to acquire from time to time additional property under a trust established by her uncle, Henry Jacobs;

Whereas Joseph Taft has agreed that all of the property now or in the future owned by Susan Jacobs, or her estate, shall be free of all rights that he might acquire by reason of his marriage to her; it is agreed as follows:

1. Susan Jacobs shall have full right and authority, in all respects the same as she would have if unmarried, to use, enjoy, manage, convey, mortgage, and dispose of all of her present and future property and estate, of every kind and character, including the right and power to dispose of same by last will and testament.

2. Joseph Taft releases to Susan Jacobs, her heirs, legal representatives, and assigns, every right, claim, and estate that he might have in respect to said property by reason of his marriage to Susan Jacobs.

IN WITNESS WHEREOF the parties have hereunto set their hands and seals the day and year first above written.

Joseph Taft

Susan Jacobs

PREMARITAL AGREEMENT
Married people have certain economic rights and duties that a premarital agreement may exclude. *When does a premarital agreement become effective?*

- The making of a will
- Ownership of and benefits from life insurance policies

People who have children from other relationships often enter into prenuptial agreements to protect their children. For instance, upon the death of the biological parent, the assets of that parent can pass to the new spouse, and in effect, disinherit the children of the deceased parent.

Written agreements are also important for people who live together without being married. In such arrangements, people don't receive the protection that is given automatically to those who are married. Written agreements can address such issues as financial responsibility and property ownership, as well as the other issues mentioned previously.

Prohibited Marriages

Certain types of marriages are illegal because they are opposed to public policy. Prohibited marriages are those between certain relatives, marriages by one party to two or more people at the same time, and in most states, marriages between persons of the same sex.

Marriage Between Relatives

Statutes in many states prohibit marriage between certain persons who are related by **consanguinity** (blood) or **affinity** (marriage). In these states, such marriages are void. Some states base their law on the common law, which made it illegal to marry certain relatives. Figure 31.2 shows which relatives it is illegal to marry under the common law.

If you married any relatives listed in Figure 31.2, then the marriage would be void, and any children born of the union would be illegitimate. Under the common law, it would be illegal to marry a person related by affinity, even after the relationship that binds the parties ends by death or divorce.

Legal Briefs

Under the Napoleonic Code, people under 30 years of age could not marry without their father's permission. In addition, a father could have his child incarcerated for as long as six months based on his word alone.

Figure 31.2	
Consanguinity	**Affinity**
Mother or Father	Stepmother or Stepfather
Grandmother or Grandfather	Step-grandmother or Step-grandfather
Daughter or Son	Stepdaughter or Stepson
Granddaughter or Grandson	Step-granddaughter or Step-grandson
Aunt or Uncle	Mother–in-law or Father-in-law
Sister or Brother	Grandmother-in-law or Grandfather-in-law
Niece or Nephew	Daughter-in-law or Son-in-law
	Granddaughter-in-law or Grandson-in-law

MARRIAGES BETWEEN RELATIVES
Marriage to these relatives was prohibited by common law. Many states have changed this law. *How is being related by consanguinity different from being related by affinity?*

Example 2. Gerard Ingels and Ramona Parker, whose marriage lasted for six months, were divorced. Ramona later wanted to marry Gerard's father, a widower. In a state that follows the common-law rule regarding marriage between family members related by affinity, they could not marry.

Although the marriage of first cousins is allowed under common law, many states prohibit such relationships. Almost half the states have no prohibition against marriage of persons related by affinity.

A marriage between close family members constitutes more than a social stigma or legal dilemma. Children born to blood relatives are more likely to suffer from birth defects because there is a greater chance that the two parents could share and pass on harmful genes.

Bigamy and Polygamy

A marriage that is contracted while either party is already married is void in all states, unless the prior marriage is ended by annulment. **Bigamy** is the act of having two spouses at the same time. **Polygamy** is the act of having more than two spouses at once. Any children born of a man and woman whose marriage is void are illegitimate. Bigamy and polygamy are crimes under the laws of every state in this country.

In some states, if one of the parties entered into the marriage without knowing the other party was married, the second marriage may become valid on the death or divorce of the partner to the first marriage.

Section 31.1　Assessment

Reviewing What You Learned
1. When does the marriage contract actually come into existence? Explain your answer.
2. List five rights that are given by law to people when they marry.
3. What is a premarital agreement, and why is it important?
4. Provide three examples of marriages that are prohibited by law.

Critical Thinking Activity
Fairness Ian and Rochelle decided to break their engagement of six months because they believed that they just weren't right for each other. By law in their state, Ian is entitled to the return of the engagement ring. Do you think this is fair? Why or why not?

Legal Skills in Action
The Role of Marriage In Your Life Marriage is a personal relationship arising out of a civil contract. It is a serious contract that most people believe will last forever. In 2–3 paragraphs, describe the role, if any, that marriage might play in your future life.

Marriage Laws

The Requirements of Marriage

Each state has its own laws regulating marriage. Figure 31.3 summarizes marriage laws in the different states.

Age Requirements

With exceptions in Mississippi and Nebraska, you can be married at age 18 without your parent's consent. You can be married at a younger age if a parent or guardian gives permission. In some states, the permission of the court is also required if you are below a certain age.

Example 3. Joseph Klein wanted to marry Krista Ogden, 14. Under Massachusetts law, the couple could marry only if one of Krista's parents and the probate court judge gave permission. If Krista's parents or the judge denied permission, the couple would have to wait until Krista turned 18 to marry.

Marriages between teenagers are more likely to end in divorce. As a result, the law requires parental permission to prevent minors from entering into foolish or otherwise unsuitable marriages.

Common-Law Marriage

In England, under the common law, people did not need to have a formal ceremony to bind them in wedlock. Instead, they only had to agree between themselves that they were married. No witnesses were required, and the agreement could be either oral or written. This informal type of marriage, called a **common-law marriage**, came to America with the early colonists. Today, 11 states and the District of Columbia still recognize common-law marriages.

With a few exceptions, the states that recognize the common-law marriage require the following elements:

- The parties must agree, by words in the present tense, that they are husband and wife.
- The parties must cohabit, or live together, for a certain time period, which varies among the states. The parties must represent themselves as being husband and wife so that the public recognizes their marital status. This representation may be accomplished by actions such as introducing your partner as your spouse, and by sharing a joint bank account.

What You'll Learn

- How to describe the marriage laws in your state with regard to age requirements, ceremony, medical exams, and license
- How to differentiate between a common-law marriage and a ceremonial marriage

Why It's Important

Understanding the various marriage laws will make you better prepared when the time comes to choose a spouse.

Legal Terms

- common-law marriage
- solemnize
- marriage license
- proxy marriage

Figure 31.3

U.S. Marriage Laws Summary Table

State	Age Requirement for License	Waiting Period for License	Blood Test	Cost	Validity of License	Residency
Alabama	18	None	None	$25	30 Days	None
Alaska	18	3 Days	None	$25	90 Days	None
Arizona	18	None	None	$50	1 Year	None
Arkansas	18	None	None	$30	60 Days	None
California	18	None	None	$50-$80	90 Days	None
Colorado	18	None	None	$20	30 Days	None
Connecticut	18	Varies	Varies	$35	25-35 Days	None
Delaware	18	24 Hours	Yes	$35	30 Days	None
District of Columbia	18	3 Days	Yes	$35	Indefinitely	None
Florida	18	3 Days	None	$56-$88.50	60 Days	None
Georgia	18	None	Yes	$40	None	None
Hawaii	18	None	None	$50	30 Days	None
Idaho	18	None	None	$28	Indefinitely	None
Illinois	18	None	None	$15-$20	60 Days	None
Indiana	18	None	None	$18	60 Days	Yes
Iowa	18	3 Days	None	$30	None	None
Kansas	18	3 Days	None	$50	6 Months	None
Kentucky	18	None	None	$34.50	29 Days	None
Louisiana	18	3 Days	None	$25	30 Days	None
Maine	18	3 Days	None	$20	90 Days	None
Maryland	18	2 Days	None	$55	6 Months	None
Massachusetts	18	3 Days	Yes	$25	60 Days	None
Michigan	18	3 Days	None	$20-$35	33 Days	None
Minnesota	18	None	None	$70	6 Months	None
Mississippi	21	3 Days	Yes	$21	90 Days	None
Missouri	18	3 Days	None	$50	30 Days	None
Montana	18	3 Days	None	$50	30 Days	None

MARRIAGE LAWS
Marriage laws differ from state to state and often change. *How would you find out your state's current marriage requirements?*

A few states do not regard the last two elements as essential to a valid common-law marriage. If a common-law marriage is properly entered into in a state that recognizes such relationships, then it will be regarded as a valid marriage in any other state, as Robin suggests in The Opening Scene.

Example 4. Henry Lewiston and Elka Swenson say to each other that they are married. They cohabit in the state of Rhode Island and introduce themselves as husband and wife to people they meet. However, they have never had a marriage ceremony. Later, they move to Massachusetts, which does not recognize the common-law marriage. That state would nonetheless regard Henry

Figure 31.3 (Continued)

U.S. Marriage Laws Summary Table

State	Age Requirement for License	Waiting Period for License	Blood Test	Cost	Validity of License	Residency
Nebraska	19	None	Some	$15	1 Year	None
Nevada	18	None	None	Varies	Indefinitely	None
New Hampshire	18	3 Days	None	$45	90 Days	None
New Jersey	18	72 Hours	None	$28	30 Days	None
New Mexico	18	None	None	$25	Indefinitely	None
New York	18	1 Day	None	$20-$30	60 Days	None
North Carolina	18	None	None	$40	60 Days	None
North Dakota	18	None	None	$35	60 Days	None
Ohio	18	None	None	$45	60 Days	None
Oklahoma	18	None	Yes	$25	10 Days	None
Oregon	18	3 Days	None	$60	60 Days	None
Pennsylvania	18	3 Days	None	$25-$40	60 Days	None
Rhode Island	18	None	None	$24	3 Months	None
South Carolina	18	1 Day	None	$25	Indefinitely	None
South Dakota	18	None	None	$40	20 Days	None
Tennessee	18	None	None	$31	30 Days	None
Texas	18	3 Days	None	$36	30 Days	None
Utah	18	None	None	$40	30 Days	None
Vermont	18	None	None	$20	60 Days	None
Virginia	18	None	None	$30	60 Days	None
Washington	18	3 Days	None	$52	60 Days	None
West Virginia	18	None	None	$23	Indefinitely	None
Wisconsin	18	5 Days	None	$50-$60	30 Days	Yes
Wyoming	18	None	None	$25	Indefinitely	None

*Please use the above information as a guideline. Verify all information by contacting your local county clerk.

and Elka as legally married because the Rhode Island law, which allows the common-law marriage, was properly followed.

A divorce is required to end a common-law marriage. Henry and Elka, in Example 4, would have to go through a formal divorce procedure if they decide to end their common-law marriage.

Ceremonial Marriage

From early colonial times, a marriage ceremony could only be officiated by a cleric or magistrate. Today, most states still require some kind of ceremony or other serious rite to **solemnize** marriage. However, as long as the parties declare that they take each other as husband

A Global Perspective: Laws Around the World

India

To know India, you must understand Hinduism, one of the world's oldest faiths and the major religion of India. Even in contemporary India, which especially in urban areas has experienced rapid technological development and modernization, the ancient tenants of Hinduism remain important influences on a follower's life.

One of traditional Hinduism's most important structures is the caste system, which divides society into a hierarchy of separate classes. At the top of the caste system are the Brahmans, traditionally the priests and scholars. Next are the Kshatriyas, the rulers, warriors, and landowners, followed by the Vaisyas, the artisans and merchants. The lowest caste is the Sudras, the farmers and peasants. Beneath these four main castes are the so-called "untouchables," which include beggars, butchers, and sweepers. Traditionally, the higher one's caste, the greater one's rights and privileges. Over time, India has expanded the caste system to include thousands of castes based on these original divisions.

Today, India is a democratic and politically secular country, and discriminating against a person based on caste is legally forbidden. The practice of "untouchability" was officially abolished under India's constitution in 1950, and the government has passed numerous laws to help educate and employ people who might have otherwise suffered discrimination under the traditional caste system. The government also passed social legislation such as the Hindu Marriage Act, allowing an Indian to marry a person of a different caste. Although the traditional caste system is still important, especially in rural areas, modern India offers its citizens more freedom, mobility, and opportunity than ever before. Here's a snapshot of India.

Geographical area	**1,269,346 sq. mi.**
Population	**1,045,845,226**
Capital	**New Delhi**
Legal system	**Based on English common law**
Language	**Hindi, 14 other official languages, English**
Religion	**81.3% Hindu; 12% Muslim**
Life expectancy	**63 years**

Critical Thinking Question List several U.S. laws that help minorities or the disadvantaged get ahead, and briefly describe each. For more information about India, visit **ubpl.glencoe.com** or your local library.

and wife in the presence of a person authorized by state law to solemnize marriages, no particular form must be followed. Some courts have held that a marriage that is properly solemnized is valid even when a marriage license was not obtained before the ceremony.

Covenant Marriage

The covenant marriage, adopted in Arkansas, Arizona, and Louisiana, is an attempt to reduce divorce and protect children. The parties to a covenant marriage must undergo counseling before the wedding and during the marriage to solve conflicts. In most cases, the couple can divorce only after a specified period of separation, or if one spouse is guilty of adultery, spousal or child abuse, abandonment, or a felony.

Marriage License

It is generally necessary to get a license to be joined in a ceremonial marriage. A **marriage license** is a certificate issued by a government office that gives permission to two people to marry. Once issued, the license becomes effective after any waiting period required by state law. The license will expire if the couple doesn't marry during the prescribed time period.

Waiting Period

Under common law, notice of a forthcoming marriage had to be published and posted to give people who might oppose the marriage the

PLANNING A MARRIAGE
To get married, a couple will have to follow certain steps. *What steps are usually included in this process?*

Law & Academics

Social Studies

Arranged marriages are common in India. Citing the high divorce rate in the United States, many Indians argue that arranged marriages are more successful than romantic marriages. Many Indians believe that romantic love alone does not necessarily lead to a good marriage. Instead, they feel that true love flows from a properly arranged union between two compatible people.

Research Activity

Research arranged marriages in India. Find out who makes the arrangement and if the prospective bride and groom meet or date before entering marriage.

chance to object. These notices were called marriage banns. Today, most states have a waiting period before a license is issued, instead of requiring that marriage banns be published.

Why do states require a waiting period? The motivation is to give the man and woman time to reconsider their decision. In addition, a waiting period may allow evidence of fraud, force, or jest to be uncovered. The delay also gives interested parties, such as the parents of the prospective marriage partners, an opportunity to object on other grounds.

Blood Test/Physical Examination

Some states require a blood test or physical examination before a marriage license is issued. These tests may screen prospective spouses for such conditions as AIDS, venereal disease, sickle cell anemia, rubella (German measles), and infectious tuberculosis. The type of test and particular conditions involved vary from state to state. Under a typical state statute, if a venereal disease, such as syphilis, is found and is in the non-communicable stage, both parties are informed about the disease and the possibility of transmitting such an infection to the marital partner or to their children. If syphilis is found to be in the communicable stage, a marriage license is not issued.

In a state that tests for rubella, the test must certify that the female, if she is of childbearing age, is immune to rubella infection. If she

BLOOD TEST

Some states require a blood test or physical examination before issuing a marriage license. If a venereal disease in a communicable stage is found, the license will not be issued. *Do you think there are any other reasons that a marriage license should not be issued?*

refuses the test, the doctor must advise her of the risks of contracting rubella during childbearing years and of the vaccine available to eliminate or protect against such risks.

Example 5. William Matera and Lynn Newkirk decided to get married. They went to the clerk's office in their town and applied for a marriage license. They were told they would have to wait at least three days before the license could be issued and that they would have to have their blood tested.

Proxy Marriage

In a **proxy marriage**, one or both of the parties can't be present for the wedding, and an agent acts on their behalf. Such a marriage, which is allowed in some states, still requires a ceremony. The Uniform Marriage and Divorce Act provides that a person who can't come to the solemnization of his or her marriage may authorize, in writing, a third person to act as proxy. The person solemnizing the marriage must be satisfied that the absent party is unable to be present and has consented to the marriage.

Use of Various Names

Under common law, people may use any name provided they do not do so to commit fraud. A wife does not have to adopt her husband's surname (last name), for example. Although widely followed, this practice came about through custom and was not required by common law. Today, many married women continue to use their maiden names or they hyphenate it with their husband's surnames.

Section 31.2 Assessment

Reviewing What You Learned

1. Under today's law, at what age may a person in most states marry without parental consent?
2. What is the difference between a common-law marriage and a ceremonial marriage?

Critical Thinking Activity

Surnames Are there any reasons why a husband and wife having different surnames would be impractical? Explain your answer.

Legal Skills in Action

Marriage Laws Using a software program, design a table of the marriage laws in your state that you need to consider before getting married. Do your best to address all the laws discussed in this chapter.

Chapter Summary

Section 31.1 Marriage Formalities and Restrictions

- Each state is permitted, following U.S. Constitutional guidelines, to prescribe who is allowed to marry and how a marriage can be dissolved. However, each state must also recognize the laws and court decisions of other states. Marriage is a civil contract that comes into existence when you become engaged. At the time of engagement, there is an agreement containing consideration (a promise to give up the legal right to remain single) between two parties who have the capacity to contract, by mutual consent and for a legal purpose. While a couple is engaged, the marriage contract is in its executory stage. The contract is executed when the wedding occurs. Under common law, if one of the parties failed to go through with the marriage after becoming engaged, the other party could sue for damages caused by breach of the marriage contract. However, this is no longer the law in most states today.

- The marriage contract imposes rights and duties that provide financial protection to both parties to the marriage. If you are married, you have the following rights: (1) the right to support by your spouse when necessary; (2) the right to inheritance from your deceased spouse; (3) the right to property if the marriage ends; (4) the right to compensation to continue your standard of living if the marriage ends; and (5) the right to file a joint income tax return. The primary duty that arises from the marriage contract, however, is the duty of being faithful to your spouse.

- A premarital agreement must be in writing and signed by both parties prior to getting married. In making a premarital agreement, you must make honest statements, and you and your partner must fully disclose your assets to each other. In some states, a different attorney must represent each party. Although laws vary from state to state, parties to a premarital agreement generally may contract with respect to the following issues: (1) the rights and obligations of each of the parties with regard to any of the property of either or both of them; (2) the right to buy, sell, manage, and control real and personal property; (3) the disposition of real and personal property upon separation, divorce, or death; (4) the change or elimination of support; (5) the making of a will; and (6) the ownership of and benefits from life insurance policies.

- Certain types of marriage are prohibited, including marriages between relatives, marriages that result in bigamy or polygamy, and marriages between persons of the same sex. Bigamy is the act of having two spouses at the same time. Polygamy is the act of having more than two spouses at the same time.

Section 31.2 The Requirements of Marriage

- Most states require a marriage to be solemnized. In most states, a person can be married at the age of 18 without a parent's consent and at a younger age with permission. Most states have a waiting period before a marriage license is issued, and some states require a blood test to screen for certain infectious diseases or conditions affecting childbirth.

- Eleven states and the District of Columbia recognize common-law marriage. In those jurisdictions, a common-law marriage occurs when the parties agree, by words in the present tense, that they are husband and wife. They must cohabit for a certain time period, and they must present themselves to the rest of the world as husband and wife. A divorce is required to end a common-law marriage. A ceremonial marriage is solemnized by a ceremony or serious rite.

Using Legal Language

Consider the key terms in the list below. Then use these terms to complete the following exercises.

premarital agreement

consanguinity

affinity

bigamy

polygamy

common-law marriage

solemnize

marriage license

proxy marriage

1. As a review activity, create an original speech explaining the main points outlined in this chapter. Use as many of the review terms as possible. Refer to this chapter for extra help if necessary.
2. Working with a partner, practice delivering your speech.
3. Deliver your speech to the class.
4. As a class, choose the best speech. Make sure that the speech selected correctly uses the key terms.

Understanding Business and Personal Law Online

Self-Check Quiz Visit the *Understanding Business and Personal Law* Web site at **ubpl.glencoe.com** and click on Chapter 31: Marriage—Self-Check Quizzes to prepare for the chapter exam.

The Law Review

Answer the following questions. Refer to the chapter for additional reinforcement.

5. What is the primary duty that arises from the marriage contract?
6. What is consanguinity? affinity? How are marriages between those related by consanguinity and affinity viewed by the law?
7. What is bigamy? polygamy? How does law view bigamy and polygamy?
8. Describe a covenant marriage? Where has it been adopted?
9. What is the purpose of a waiting-period requirement?
10. Why do most states require parental permission if a child below a certain age wishes to marry?
11. What is a marriage license?
12. What is a proxy marriage?
13. Why do most states impose a waiting period before a marriage license is issued?

Linking School to Work

Interpreting and Communicating Information

Write a one-page paper comparing the rights and duties that arise when you enter into a marriage contract with the rights and duties that come about when you enter into a regular contract.

14. What are the similarities?

15. What are the differences?

Let's Debate

Curtis and Myrna are engaged to be married early next year. They are madly in love and are planning a large church wedding. Curtis wants to write a premarital agreement in case their marriage ends in divorce. Myrna is opposed to this idea because she believes marriage is forever.

Debate

16. Do Curtis and Myrna need a premarital agreement? Explain why or why not.

17. How would you answer Myrna when she says, "We don't need one; marriage is forever"?

18. Do you believe that all engaged couples should have premarital agreements? Why or why not?

Grasping Case Issues

For the following cases, give your decision and state a legal principle that applies.

19. Vadim Petrenko asks Lada Nureyev to marry him and presents her with a diamond engagement ring. Lada accepts. Three months later, Lada cancels the engagement. Vadim threatens to sue for breach of contract. May he do so?

20. Garrett Robins and Mary Lyman lived together in Vermont as husband and wife for 20 years. They agreed that they were married and presented themselves to others as husband and wife. They had no marriage ceremony. When Garrett died without leaving a will, Mary claimed she should inherit his assets because she was his common-law wife. Do you agree?

21. Brigitte Samuels wants to marry her uncle, Raynard Prost. Will their marriage be valid? What will be the legal status of any children of the marriage?

22. Tsong Lee, 22, wants to marry Mei-Gui Yan, 14. They both live in Massachusetts. Mei-Gui's parents refuse to give permission for the marriage. Can the couple legally marry? Why or why not?

23. Five years after Carlos Soledad and Novia Chavez marry, Novia discovers that Carlos never divorced his first wife, who is living and still uses the surname Soledad. Is the marriage between Carlos and Novia valid? Explain your answer.

24. Michelle Weibel was married to Albert Weibel for twelve years. Several years after Albert's death in an automobile accident, Michelle received a marriage proposal from Albert's widowed stepfather, Terry. Is Michelle free to marry Terry? Explain your answer.

25. Jacqueline Pesci recently married Marvin Leary. A resolute feminist, Pesci asks her husband to assume her maiden name as a surname. Leary is willing to assume the name Pesci but is unsure of the legality of using his wife's surname. What are Leary's legal rights in this situation?

In each case that follows, you be the judge.

26. Broken Promise

Charles Gill gave Dianne Shively an engagement ring, worth $3,600, when they became engaged. Less than a month later, Shively told Gill that she was not ready for marriage. Gill requested that Shively return the engagement ring, but she refused to do so. *Is Gill entitled to the return of the ring? Why or why not?*

Gill v. Shively, 330 So.2d 415 (FL).

27. Too Many Wives

Two months after divorcing Bobby Gunter, Gloria Gunter married Edward Peters. Gunter was not well acquainted with Peters and assumed that he was not married. She later learned that Peters was still married and had deceived her into thinking he was divorced. *What legal wrong did Peters commit? What is the legal effect of Gunter's marriage to Peters?*

Gunter v. Gunter, 418 N.E.2d 149 (IL).

Legal Link

Wedding Bells

After dating for a few years and discussing it with their families, Meena and Manoj want to get married in your state. However, they are not sure of the laws governing marriage.

Connect

28. Using a variety of search engines, help Meena and Manoj find the following information:
    - The required ceremony to solemnize the marriage
    - The necessary waiting period
    - Blood tests/physical exam requirements
    - Age requirements and exceptions

POWER READING STRATEGIES

29. **Predict** Why do you think we need laws governing marriage in this country?

30. **Connect** How old do you think you will be when you get married, and what factors will you consider in making the decision to get married? Explain your answer.

31. **Question** Do you think it is necessary to have laws that prohibit certain types of marriages?

32. **Respond** Do you think covenant marriages should be adopted in all 50 states? Why or why not?

Divorce and Its Legal Consequences

Understanding Business and Personal Law *Online*

Chapter Overview Visit the *Understanding Business and Personal Law* Web site at ubpl.glencoe.com and click on Chapter 32: Divorce and Its Legal Consequences—Chapter Overviews to preview the chapter information.

The Opening Scene

Robin Johnson and her fiancé, Patrick Regan, are talking in the living room of the Johnson residence.

Caught in the Middle

ROBIN: Has Bill had any luck finding a job since he got laid off?

PATRICK: Didn't I tell you? This will blow your mind! Bill left Betty and the twins and moved to Alaska.

ROBIN: Bill and Betty split up? What a shocker! I never would've thought that could happen. They seemed to have such a strong marriage. When did he go?

PATRICK: About two weeks ago. I think losing his job was just too much for Bill to handle. I heard he was pretty depressed. Betty's devastated about the situation. I hear she's gonna file for divorce this week on grounds of desertion.

ROBIN: Isn't that rushing things? Maybe he'll come back. How could he leave those beautiful twins? Why, he took care of them all of the time after he lost his job.

PATRICK: True. When Betty went back to work, Bill stayed home.

ROBIN: I don't understand what's happening these days. So many people are getting divorced! It's really discouraging!

PATRICK: Either that or they're having their marriages annulled.

ROBIN: Whatever. Isn't an annulment the same as a divorce?

PATRICK: I'm not sure.

(Six months later, Robin meets Betty at the supermarket. The twins are sitting in the grocery cart. Betty looks tired and unhappy.)

ROBIN: Hi, Betty. The twins are so big I hardly recognized them!

BETTY: Well, you'd better take a good look. They may not be here much longer.

ROBIN: I don't understand! What do you mean? Are you moving?

BETTY: No, I'm staying right where I am. But Bill is trying to get custody of the twins. I thought that mothers always have the right to keep their children.

ROBIN: I don't know how the courts decide things like that. But you probably don't have to worry. Everyone knows you're a great mother. Don't let this worry you.

BETTY: Thanks, Robin. I appreciate that.

ROBIN: Things must be pretty tough for you right now. Does Bill send you anything for support?

BETTY: That's another problem. Bill says he won't pay the support payment the judge ordered if he doesn't have custody. How can I force him to pay when he's in Alaska?

ROBIN: I see what you mean.

BETTY: Well, the twins are getting restless. I'd better finish my shopping. It's nice to see you, Robin.

ROBIN: Thanks, Betty. It's good to see you, too. Good luck!

What Are the Legal Issues?

1. Can a spouse file for a divorce on the grounds of desertion two weeks after the other spouse has left home?
2. What is the difference between a divorce and an annulment?
3. Do mothers always have the right to custody of their children?
4. Does the law provide a method for obtaining support payments from spouses who live out of state?

Ending a Marriage

What You'll Learn

- How to describe an annulment, a legal separation, and a divorce
- How to list the general grounds for an annulment
- How to contrast a legal separation with a divorce
- How to name and describe the most common grounds for divorce
- How to distinguish between one's residence and one's domicile and discuss what this means in a divorce proceeding

Why It's Important

Learning about divorce laws will help you better deal with the process should you ever be involved in a divorce.

Legal Terms

- annulment
- legal separation
- divorce
- no-fault divorce
- adultery
- desertion
- domicile
- residence

How Marriages End

A marriage comes to an end in one of three ways: the death of one of the parties, annulment, or divorce. An **annulment** is a declaration by the court that the marriage was never effective; it was void from the beginning. Although the laws vary from state to state, marriages generally can be annulled on the grounds of duress and fraud. When someone is forced to marry against his or her will, it is considered duress. When a person is persuaded to marry by misrepresentation, it is fraud. Some common examples of fraud that are grounds for annulment include being below the state age to marry, secretly intending never to have children, or concealing pregnancy by someone other than the husband.

Legal Separation and Divorce

A **legal separation**, also called a limited divorce or a separation from bed and board, is a court judgment ending the right to cohabitation. In making a separation judgment, the court will temporarily decide the issues of child custody and support, but you and your spouse remain married until there is an absolute (final) divorce.

In contrast, a **divorce** (called dissolution of marriage in some states) is a declaration by the court that a valid marriage has come to an end.

BECOMING DIVORCED
Nearly half of marriages today eventually end in divorce. *Why do you think this is so?*

Grounds for Divorce

The grounds for divorce vary among the states. Figure 32.1 summarizes the divorce laws of different states.

No-Fault Divorce

Almost all states have a **no-fault divorce** law, which eliminates the need to prove that one party is to blame. States give different names to the breakdown of the marriage relationship, including *incompatibility, irretrievable breakdown,* and *irreconcilable differences.*

The Uniform Marriage and Divorce Act, which has been adopted by Arizona, Colorado, Illinois, Kentucky, Minnesota, Missouri, Montana, and Washington, has eliminated the traditional grounds for divorce in favor of the no-fault approach. In these states, the procedure is referred to as a *dissolution* rather than a divorce, and the grounds for a dissolution is called *irretrievable breakdown.*

A few states have for many years allowed divorce on the grounds of incompatibility. One spouse does not have to prove that the other spouse is at fault. All that is required is evidence indicating that the couple has a personality conflict so deep that there is no chance for a reconciliation.

Many states require that you live apart from your spouse for a period of time before a divorce is allowed. Reconciliation bureaus have been established in some states in an attempt to reunite couples and save marriages, and various states have established procedures for couples to seek reconciliation. Some states have enacted simplified dissolution of marriage procedures that end marriages quickly, often without the need for a lawyer.

Traditional Grounds for Divorce

The grounds for divorce vary from state to state. In most states, however, you only need to prove that the marriage relationship has broken down to get a divorce.

Adultery   Having a voluntary sexual relationship with someone other than your spouse is called **adultery**. It is a crime in some states, in addition to being grounds for divorce. Because of its private nature, adultery is most commonly proven by circumstantial evidence (evidence that is indirect). It is often proven by showing the person charged had the opportunity to commit adultery and the inclination or tendency to do so. Establishing these two elements is usually enough for a court to grant the complaining party a divorce. However, criminal adultery must be proven beyond a reasonable doubt.

Community Works

Alcohol Abuse
As you learned in this chapter, alcoholism is grounds for divorce in most states. This disease affects millions of Americans. A person who is dependant on alcohol suffers increased risks for cancer, heart disease, liver disfunction, and depression. *Did you know that many teens suffer from alcoholism? What can you do if you suspect that one of your friends suffers from an alcohol-related problem?*

Get involved
Learn the signs that indicate a potential problem with alcohol. Volunteer at a teen crisis center that specializes in chemical abuse issues.

Figure 32.1

Grounds for Divorce and Residency Requirements

STATE	No Fault Sole Ground	No Fault Plus Traditional	Incompatibility Available	Parties Must Live Apart	Legal Separation Available	Must Live in State
Alabama		x	x	2 years	x	6 months
Alaska	x		x	2 years	x	6 months
Arizona	x	x[1]			x	90 days
Arkansas		x		18 mos.	x	60 days
California	x				x	6 months
Colorado	x				x	90 days
Connecticut		x		18 mos.	x	1 year
Delaware		x	x	6 mos.	x	6 months
District of Columbia	x			1 year	x	6 months
Florida	x					6 months
Georgia		x				6 months
Hawaii	x			2 years[1]	x	6 months
Idaho		x			x	6 weeks
Illinois		x		2 years	x	90 days
Indiana			x		x	60 days
Iowa	x				x	1 year
Kansas			x		x	60 days
Kentucky	x			60 days	x	180 days
Louisiana		x[2]		6 months[3]	x	6 months
Maine		x			x	6 months
Maryland		x		1 year		1 year
Massachusetts		x				None
Michigan	x				x	6 months
Minnesota	x				x	180 days
Mississippi		x				6 months
Missouri		x		1–2 years	x	90 days
Montana	x		x	180 days	x	90 days
Nebraska	x				x	1 year

DIVORCE LAWS

Most states have other divorce laws in addition to those listed here. Divorce laws can change, however, and a check of current state laws is advised. *How would you learn about your state's current divorce laws?*

Example 1. Ralph Aronson sought a divorce from his wife, June, in Illinois. He charged that she committed adultery with David Bernhardt, who roomed in the same house with them. There was evidence that a sexual relationship between Ralph and June had not existed for many years, and that June often visited bars and went on dates with other men. The court granted the divorce, saying that both the opportunity and the inclination to commit adultery existed.

In Example 1, if June had been charged with criminal adultery, the circumstantial evidence would not have been enough to convict her. To

Figure 32.1 Continued

Grounds for Divorce and Residency Requirements

STATE	No Fault Sole Ground	No Fault Plus Traditional	Incompatibility Available	Parties Must Live Apart	Legal Separation Available	Must Live in State
Nevada			x	1 year	x	6 weeks
New Hampshire		x		2 years		1 year
New Jersey		x		18 mos.		1 year
New Mexico		x	x		x	6 months
New York		x		1 year	x	1 year
North Carolina		x		1 year	x	6 months
North Dakota		x			x	6 months
Ohio		x	x	1 year		6 months
Oklahoma			x		x	6 months
Oregon	x				x	6 months
Pennsylvania		x		2 years		6 months
Rhode Island		x		3 years	x	1 year
South Carolina		x		1 year	x	3 months (both residents)
South Dakota		x			x	None
Tennessee		x		2 years	x	6 months
Texas		x		3 years		6 months
Utah		x		3 years	x	90 days
Vermont		x		6 months		6 months
Virginia		x		1 year	x	6 months
Washington	x					1 year
West Virginia		x		1 year	x	1 year
Wisconsin	x				x	6 months
Wyoming		x	x		x	60 days

1. Grounds are either marriage irretrievably broken or two years separation.
2. Covenant marriage statutes establish specific grounds for divorce for covenant marriages.
3. Two years for covenant marriages.

convict someone of any crime, the state must prove the defendant guilty beyond a reasonable doubt.

Cruelty   Until the introduction of no-fault divorce laws, cruelty was the most common ground for divorce. Generally, to prove cruelty, you must show that there has been personal violence that endangers your life or health and that makes living together unsafe or unbearable. Usually, more than one act of violence is required. Sometimes, however, it is possible to obtain a divorce because of mental suffering alone. In these cases, you must prove that the mental suffering was caused by your spouse and that it damaged your health.

Example 2. Elise Carruthers persisted in going out with other men against the objections of her husband, Stan. He became so upset over her conduct that his health deteriorated. The court granted a divorce on the grounds of cruelty, even though there was no physical violence.

Desertion   The unjustified separation of one spouse from the other with the intent of not returning, for a time set by law (normally one year) is called **desertion**. The spouse seeking the divorce must want the other spouse to return. He or she cannot consent to the other spouse's absence.

Alcoholism or Drug Addiction   Habitual intoxication, either with alcohol or drugs, is grounds for divorce in many states. The habit must be confirmed, persistent, voluntary, and excessive. It is the abuse of alcohol or drugs, rather than the mere use of them, that is grounds for divorce.

Nonsupport   If you seek a divorce for nonsupport, you must show that your spouse had the ability to provide economic support but

LAWS in Your Life

Claim Your Name

When a man and woman marry, the woman sometimes chooses to follow established custom by taking the husband's last name. Upon divorce, the woman may decide to change back to her former name and also change the last name of her children. In most states, the judge hearing the divorce will also entertain a petition to restore a spouse's former name. If the judge orders such restoration in the divorce decree, that's all the paperwork needed to apply for a name change on personal records and identification. If the divorce decree does not address this issue, a name change can usually be accomplished informally by resuming use of the former name consistently. Then the spouse can request that it be changed on all personal records.

A child's name may be changed from that of the father only upon petition to the court. The court will order a name change if it is in the best interest of the child. The court weighs factors such as whether the mother is remarrying and the need to identify with a new family unit.

Conduct Research Research your state laws regarding name changes for children. How does a name change affect parental rights and responsibilities?

NONSUPPORT
Nonsupport is one of the traditional grounds for divorce still available in some states. *What must a spouse seeking such a divorce prove in court?*

willfully failed to do so. In the past, nonsupport could be used as grounds for divorce only by the wife and only in the states that recognized it. In recent years, however, more states have begun to allow the husband to use nonsupport as grounds for divorce.

Conviction of a Felony   Many states allow a divorce if either party is convicted of a felony, an infamous (disgraceful) crime, or a crime of moral turpitude (one that is morally wrong). Some states also permit a divorce if one spouse is imprisoned for a certain number of years after the marriage occurs.

Domicile and Residence Requirements

For a court to hear a case, it must have the authority, or jurisdiction. In a divorce case, the court's jurisdiction is based on where the person seeking the divorce makes his or her home.

Domicile

The person asking for the divorce must be domiciled within the geographic area over which the court has jurisdiction. A **domicile** is your principal place of abode. It is the place to which, when you are absent, you have the intent of returning. A domicile cannot be abandoned or

Careers in Law

Fingerprint Expert

Kevin Teddy is an expert in fingers and toes. For the last 16 years, the Michigan State Police officer has helped convict hundreds of criminals by identifying the unique patterns of loops, arches, and whorls on their fingers—and sometimes, their toes.

"The use of forensic DNA is an up-and-coming science," says Teddy, who recently was appointed director of the Michigan State Police Forensic Science Division's Grayling Lab. "But in most investigations, fingerprints are still the number one piece of evidence."

Despite the identification of hundreds of thousands of fingerprints during the last century, no two have ever been found to be identical. In fact, Teddy says, each of the fingerprints from a single individual is unique.

Investigating officers collect fingerprints by dusting the surface of an object with special fine powders that enhance the natural oils left behind by a hand. The print is photographed and then "lifted" with an adhesive strip. A clear, rigid piece of plastic is attached to the adhesive strip to preserve the fingerprint as evidence. The item is identified according to where the print was found, the date and time, and the officer's initials.

Although the best surfaces for fingerprinting are hard and shiny, Teddy has gotten good prints from paper, tightly woven cloth, and even a tomato. As a full-time fingerprint specialist, he identified more than 300 suspects per year through the patterns on their fingers or toes.

"Before I became the head of the lab, I examined thousands of prints every day," Teddy says. "I love it—it's a science that's part art. You need to be able to see patterns and form an opinion as well as understand the technical and scientific aspects. And I like the fact that I'm providing a service to people by catching the bad guys."

Skills	Standard and digital photography; computer; artistic
Personality	Patient, meticulous, dedicated
Education	Degree in chemistry for fingerprinting techniques; police academy training and crime scene experience.

For more information on fingerprinting, visit the International Association for Identification, www.theiai.org/; the Web site of the Southern California Association of Fingerprint Officers, www.scafo.org; **ubpl.glencoe.com**; or your public library.

surrendered until another domicile is acquired. You may have several residences, but you can have only one domicile at any given time.

Members of the military are presumed to retain the domicile of their home state, unless they are able to prove otherwise. Under the Uniform Marriage and Divorce Act, however, a member of the armed services may obtain a divorce in the place where he or she is stationed.

Residence Requirements

A **residence** is a place where you actually live, or reside. It may or may not be your domicile.

Example 3. While attending college, Kathleen Zacharias lived in a dormitory in California (her residence). She spent the summer working at Yellowstone National Park in Wyoming (another residence). Her domicile during this entire period, however, was her home in Kansas because it was her principal place of abode and she intended to return there to live in the future.

In addition to requiring that persons seeking divorces be domiciled in their jurisdiction, most states have particular residence requirements.

Example 4. Myrna Clouser lived with her husband, Pete, in Arizona. When marital difficulties arose, she left and went to live with her parents in New Mexico. Upon seeking a divorce in that state, however, she was told she would have to live in New Mexico for at least six months before bringing the divorce action.

It's a Question of Ethics

Child Support and Visitation
Louis Ingram's parents are divorced. His mother has custody of him and his two sisters, and his father has visitation rights. Last month Mr. Ingram lost his job, and he stopped paying child support. Louis's mother refuses to allow his father further visitation. *Should Louis's mother allow visitation? Should his father pay something toward child support?*

Section 32.1 Assessment

Reviewing What You Learned

1. What is the difference between an annulment, a legal separation, and a divorce?
2. Explain the general grounds for an annulment.
3. In legal terms, contrast a legal separation with a divorce.
4. Describe the common grounds for divorce.
5. How does distinguishing between one's residence and one's domicile relate to a divorce proceeding?

Critical Thinking Activity

No-Fault Divorce Why do you think most states have a no-fault divorce law?

Legal Skills in Action

Divorce Law Several top lawyers from around the country have been debating the current divorce laws. Imagine you have a chance to add to their discussion. Write a letter to the lawyers explaining what you would like to see changed about the current divorce laws in this country.

Divorce Settlement

What You'll Learn

- **How to identify factors considered in determining alimony payments**
- **How to describe the way marital property is distributed when a couple divorces**
- **How to explain the laws regarding custody and support of children**

Why It's Important

Understanding the laws about alimony, property distribution, custody, and support can help you through a difficult divorce.

Legal Terms

- **alimony**
- **equitable distribution laws**
- **sole custody**
- **joint custody**

Alimony

The word *alimony* comes from Latin and means "sustenance," or "nourishment." In the legal context of divorce, **alimony** is an allowance for support and maintenance made to a divorced person by a former spouse. It is not intended as a penalty.

Temporary alimony is granted to one of the spouses while he or she is waiting for a divorce or separate support action to be completed. It is sometimes called *alimony pendent lite*, meaning "alimony pending a lawsuit." Usually, the spouse who is found to have been at fault during the marriage will not be awarded alimony.

> **Example 5.** Stephen Gagne obtained a divorce from his wife, Eliza, on grounds of cruelty. The court did not order him to pay anything to Eliza because her misconduct during the marriage (her cruelty to Stephen) eliminated her entitlement to alimony.

There is no fixed rule for determining the amount of alimony. Such factors as your income and earning capacity, financial resources, future prospects, current obligations, the number of dependents, and the number of former or subsequent spouses are taken into consideration. Also considered are your spouse's situation in life, earning capacity, separate property, contribution to your property, age, health, obligations, and number of dependents.

If a spouse who is receiving alimony gets married again, that doesn't necessarily end the obligation to pay. Usually, however, the court will change its order relative to alimony in such a circumstance. In most states, the death of either party ends the obligation to pay alimony. The laws of a few states require the deceased husband's estate to continue paying alimony.

Marital Property

Most states have laws intended to assure equitable distribution of marital property when a couple divorces. **Equitable distribution laws** allow judges to distribute property equitably, or fairly, between a husband and wife, regardless of who has title to the property. In dividing the property, judges consider such things as the age and individual earning power of each spouse, the length of the marriage, and the contributions of each spouse to the marriage, including the value of homemaking services.

On divorce, property is distributed differently depending upon whether a state is community or non-community property state. In non-community states, assets and earnings gained during marriage are divided equitably; that is, as the court deems fair. For example, the higher wage earner might take two-thirds of the assets and the lower wage earner may receive only one-third. In community property states, each spouse is said to own a one-half interest in property acquired during the marriage. Property owned before marriage or received as a gift remains separate property unless it is commingled with community property or treated as such.

Custody and Support of Children

When marriages fail, the custody and support of the couple's children is a major concern of society. Many states have passed laws to protect children in such circumstances.

Custody of Children

The parents of children born within a marriage are considered to be joint guardians of their offspring. If they break up, each parent has an equal right to custody of the children, and state law governs most custody matters. Most states divide custody into two parts: legal custody and physical custody. Legal custody is the parent's right to make major decisions about the child's health, education, and welfare. Physical custody deals with the daily living arrangements of the child.

Sole custody gives all parental rights, duties, and powers to one parent. **Joint custody** divides the rights, duties, and powers between the parents. Under sole custody, the children live with the custodial parent, and visitation rights are given to the noncustodial parent. Under joint custody, the children live with each parent at different times.

In awarding custody, the court attempts to determine what is in the best interests of the child. Parents are allowed to compete for custody on an equal footing, but the decision is based on the child's needs. Some states favor awarding custody to the primary caretaker in the marriage. The primary caretaker is the parent who spent the most time caring for the child. Many states also give great weight to the child's wishes in determining custody.

CHILD CUSTODY
When parents break up, each parent has an equal right to his or her child's custody. *What does the court attempt to determine when awarding custody?*

"Divorce.Com"

The Internet is a vast source of information. Almost any legal topic can be researched on the Internet. Some Web sites focus only on one specific legal issue, such as divorce. There are several Web sites that offer information on divorce laws in each of the states. These sites also offer ways to allow consumers to calculate child support. Consumers can also go to these sites to get divorce document packages. (Source: *New York Times*, February 22, 2001)

Connect Search the Internet for Web sites that offer legal information pertaining to divorce. Determine the extent of advice available.

Support of Children

Child support is a basic obligation of every parent. This obligation exists regardless of which parent has custody.

State Guidelines Federal regulations require that every state adopt child support guidelines. The guidelines must:

- Take into consideration all earnings and income of the noncustodial parent.
- Have specific criteria and a mathematical formula that determine the support obligation.
- Provide for the children's healthcare needs, through insurance coverage or other means.

Federal regulations also recommend that states adhere to the following principles in their establishing guidelines:

- Both parents should share responsibility for support of their children in proportion to their income.
- The subsistence needs of each parent should be considered, but the child support obligation should never be set at zero.
- Child support must cover a child's basic needs, plus ensure that the child is entitled to share in a parent's standard of living.
- Each child has an equal right to share in his or her parent's income, subject to the child's age, the parent's income, income of a current spouse, and other dependents.
- Each child is entitled to support, even if the parents were not married at the time of his or her birth.
- A guideline should encourage the involvement of both parents in the child's upbringing.

Enforcement A legal order for child support is necessary to assure enforcement of child support. The legal order can be obtained from a judge, or in some courts, from an administrative hearing officer. The support order must follow the state guidelines previously mentioned.

The Uniform Interstate Family Support Act (UIFSA) allows support orders of one state to be enforced in every state. The act also provides for the registration of support orders in different states so that people who do not pay can be found more easily. Out-of-state employers can withhold support payments from an employee's paycheck for child support. Federal and state income tax refunds can also be sidetracked to pay for support, and liens can be placed on out-of-state real estate. Passports may also be denied to enforce child support orders.

CHILD SUPPORT
States are required to adopt child support guidelines that take into consideration all earning and income of the absent parent. *How should parents share responsibility for supporting their children?*

Section 32.2 Assessment

Reviewing What You Learned
1. What factors are taken into consideration when determining the amount of alimony to be awarded?
2. Explain the equitable distribution laws.
3. Describe the difference between sole and joint custody.

Critical Thinking Activity
Enforcement What do you think might happen if the Uniform Reciprocal Enforcement Support Act were not enforced in all states?

Legal Skills in Action
Asset Distribution Milka and Marvin are divorcing after 25 years of marriage. Together they own a home worth $125,000, furniture worth $56,500, and two cars worth $22,300, and they have approximately $45,630 in cash. Based on the contributions of each spouse to the marriage, the judge has ruled that Milka will receive 66.6 percent of their total assets. What is the dollar value of Milka's distribution?

Chapter Summary

Section 32.1 Ending a Marriage

- A marriage comes to an end in one of three ways: the death of one of the parties, annulment, or divorce. An annulment is a declaration by the court that a marriage was never valid. Although the laws vary from state to state, marriages generally can be annulled on the grounds of duress and fraud. In contrast, a divorce is a declaration by the court that a valid marriage has come to an end. A legal separation declares that husband and wife no longer have the right to cohabit, but they are still considered married. In making a separation judgment, the court will temporarily decide the issues of child custody and support, but you and your spouse remain married until there is an absolute (final) divorce.

- Although laws vary from state to state, a marriage generally can be annulled when someone is forced to marry against his will or when someone is persuaded to marry by the use of a misrepresentation. When a person is persuaded to marry by misrepresentation, it is fraud. Some common examples of fraud that are grounds for annulment include being below the state age to marry, secretly intending never to have children, or concealing pregnancy by someone other than the husband.

- A legal separation is a court judgment ending the right to cohabit, but the parties remain married until the absolute divorce.

- The grounds for divorce vary from state to state. In most states, however, you only need to prove that the marriage relationship has broken down to get a divorce. The most common grounds for divorce are no-fault, adultery, cruelty, desertion, alcohol or drug addiction, nonsupport, conviction of a felony, and withholding knowledge of the desire not to have children.

- For a court to hear a case, it must have the authority, or jurisdiction. In a divorce case, the court's jurisdiction is based on where the person seeking the divorce makes his or her home. A person asking for the divorce must be domiciled where the court is located. A domicile is the principal place of abode, and the place to which, when you are absent, you have the intent of returning. A residence is a place where you actually live, which may or may not be your domicile. A domicile cannot be abandoned or surrendered until another domicile is acquired. You may have several residences, but you can have only one domicile at any given time.

Section 32.2 Divorce Settlement

- Alimony is not intended as a penalty. Usually, the spouse who is found to have been at fault during the marriage will not be awarded alimony. There is no fixed rule for determining the amount of alimony. Some factors in determining an award of alimony include each spouse's income and earning capacity, financial resources, future prospects, separate property, current obligations, the number of dependents, age, health, and the number of former spouses.

- Equitable distribution laws allow judges to distribute property equitably, or fairly, between a husband and wife, regardless of who has title to the property. In determining equitable distribution of marital property when a couple is divorced, the court considers the age and earning power of each spouse, the length of the marriage, and the contributions of each spouse to the marriage.

- When spouses divorce, each parent has an equal right to the children's custody. The court will award the form of custody that is in the best interest of the child. Every state has adopted child support guidelines, and to enforce child support, a legal order is necessary.

Using Legal Language

Consider the key terms in the list below. Then use these terms to complete the following exercises.

annulment	adultery
residence	sole custody
legal separation	desertion
alimony	joint custody
divorce	domicile
equitable distribution laws	no-fault divorce

Understanding Business and Personal Law Online

Self-Check Quiz Visit the *Understanding Business and Personal Law* Web site at **ubpl.glencoe.com** and click on Chapter 32: Divorce and Its Legal Consequences—Self-Check Quizzes to prepare for the chapter exam.

1. Your best friend's parents are getting a divorce. Using the legal terms provided, role-play a conversation you might have with your friend discussing the legal aspects of divorce.
2. Share your feelings of this discussion in a paragraph. Was this an easy conversation? Do you believe you could assist a friend whose parents are getting a divorce? Why or why not?
3. With your partner, discuss other general issues relating to divorce. Why has the rate of divorce increased dramatically in recent decades? How can divorce be prevented? What are the long-term societal implications of divorce?

The Law Review

Answer the following questions. Refer to the chapter for additional reinforcement.

4. Is circumstantial evidence enough to prove criminal adultery? Why or why not?
5. What kind of cruelty may be grounds for divorce?
6. When a divorced spouse remarries, how might his or her alimony be affected?
7. When dividing marital property, what do judges usually consider?
8. Name the three ways custody arrangements can be made. Must the court approve them all?
9. What is a no-fault divorce?
10. How has the Uniform Interstate Family Support Act (UIFSA) helped to protect children of divorced parents?

Linking School to Work

Interpreting and Communicating Information

Interview a local divorce attorney, mediator, family court advocate, or someone else who works with the divorce laws in your state.

11. Ask questions regarding the specifics of the law such as annulment, legal separation, grounds for divorce, adultery, alimony, and custody issues.
12. Prepare an oral presentation of your findings.
13. Share your report with the class.
14. As a class, discuss any surprising or disturbing information.

Let's Debate

Choosing Between Parents

After 15 years of marriage, your aunt and uncle have decided to divorce. They have asked their two children to decide with whom they want to live. Your cousins don't want to choose because they don't want to hurt either parent's feelings. They ask you for help in deciding what they should do.

Debate

15. What would you ask your cousins to think about when making their decision?
16. What would you advise them to do and upon what grounds would you base your recommendation?
17. What would you do if you were in your cousins' shoes?

Grasping Case Issues

For the following cases, give your decision and state a legal principle that applies.

18. Roger Bates believes that his divorce from his wife, Lisa, will not affect his ownership of the house because the title is in his name only. Is he correct? Why or why not?
19. Mike Trudeau divorces his wife, Eileen, on grounds of her adultery. Eileen seeks alimony from Mike. Is the court likely to award it to her? Explain your answer.
20. Henry and Gloria O'Brien divorce. Henry is ordered to pay $200 a week toward support of their children. He moves to another state and stops making payments. Can Gloria enforce the court order? Why or why not?
21. Jean Darnelle, whose domicile is in Michigan, wants to divorce her husband, Philip. She is planning to spend a month vacationing in Florida and thinks it would be a good idea to get the divorce while she is there. Can she do so? Explain your answer.
22. Marta Pastore believes that her husband, Vicente, has committed adultery. She knows he often goes to a bar and leaves with a woman, and that they often go to the woman's apartment. When Marta threatens to divorce Vicente on grounds of adultery, he claims she can't prove it and therefore can't divorce him on those grounds. Do you agree? Why or why not?
23. To convince Jennifer Lind to marry him, Robert Crane informs Lind that he is a multimillionaire. During the couple's courtship, Crane showers Lind with expensive gifts and promises to pay off all of her debts. However, after marrying Crane, Lind discovers that he is destitute. On what grounds, if any, may Lind seek an annulment of the marriage?

In each case that follows, you be the judge.

24. Alimony

Francis and June Connor were divorced. Although Francis was permanently and totally disabled and unable to support himself, the court ordered him to turn over his half of their house to June as alimony. Francis appealed the decision and asked the appellate court to order June to pay him alimony. *Should the appellate court reverse the lower court's decision? Why or why not?*
Connor v. Connor, 372 So.2d 130 (FL).

25. Custody Rights

Prior to their divorce, Tammy and John Tropea entered into a child custody agreement that was made part of the divorce judgment. Tammy was to have sole custody of their children, and John was granted visitation on holidays and "at least three days of each week." The judgment barred the parties from relocating outside of their home county of Onondaga, New York, without court approval. A year later, Tammy asked the court for permission to relocate with the children to the Schenectady area, which is over two hours away. She planned to marry an architect who had an established firm there. She stated that she was willing to cooperate in a liberal visitation schedule that would afford John frequent contact with his children. She would also drive the children to and from their father's home. *In awarding custody, what does the court attempt to determine?*
Tropea v. Tropea, 665 N.E.2d 145 (NY).

Legal Link

Transfer of Property

In Section 32.2, you were introduced to the different property laws in community and non-community states. Using the Internet, research and outline the process of transferring property ownership of real property in community property states. Then outline the process of transferring property ownership of real property in non-community property states.

Connect

26. In community property states, can property acquired during marriage be transferred without the consent of both spouses? Why or why not?

27. In non-community property states, how is property transferred after a marriage ends in divorce?

POWER READING STRATEGIES

28. **Predict** Should the government make it difficult to get a divorce? Why or why not?

29. **Connect** What do you think couples can do before they are married to reduce their chances of a divorce?

30. **Question** Why do you think the grounds for divorce are different in each state?

31. **Respond** Do you think it is right that employers can withhold money from employees' paychecks for child support?

Renting a Place to Live

Understanding Business and Personal Law *Online*

Chapter Overview Visit the *Understanding Business and Personal Law* Web site at ubpl.glencoe.com and click on Chapter 33: Renting a Place to Live—Chapter Overviews to preview the chapter information.

The Opening Scene

Robin and Patrick, whose wedding date is rapidly approaching, are looking for a place to live. In this scene, they pull up in front of a two-family house.

Apartment Mishaps

ROBIN: I'm really beat. Every place we've seen has been too expensive or too run-down.

PATRICK: Or it's already been rented.

ROBIN: Can you believe that place where the owner said he never rented to young couples because they might have children?

PATRICK: How about the one who wouldn't allow dogs? Dusty has never bothered anyone. He's just a big, lovable softie.

ROBIN: I guess some people don't like Great Danes.

PATRICK: *(Knocking on the door.)* This place looks pretty good from the outside.

OWNER: (Opening the door.) Hello, can I help you?

PATRICK: Hi. We'd like to look at the apartment you advertised. Is it still available?

OWNER: Yes, it is. Come on in. I have two apartments upstairs, and the one on the right is vacant. I'll show it to you. *(On the way up, Robin stumbles and Patrick grabs her.)* Watch out for that broken step! A couple of nails came out. I'm gonna fix it next week. *(Unlocking the door.)* Here you are, take a look around.

ROBIN: It's nice!

PATRICK: I don't like that light fixture. The rest of the place looks good, though.

OWNER: This place never stays empty long.

PATRICK: Is it okay to have a dog?

OWNER: Sure. I like little critters.

(After a careful inspection, Patrick and Robin tell the landlord they will take the apartment.)

OWNER: I'll need a security deposit and the first and last months' rent.

PATRICK: Do we need to sign a lease?

OWNER: No way. I don't bother with that written stuff.

(A few weeks later, Robin and Patrick are now married and settling into the apartment.)

PATRICK: It's great to have our own place!

ROBIN: It's wonderful! That new light fixture is just perfect. You did such a good job wiring. I wonder if we should have thrown out the old fixture, though.

(A month later, Patrick and Robin are sitting in the dark with candles burning.)

ROBIN: I can't believe the landlord shut off our electricity just because he doesn't like Dusty. He said he's going to keep the light fixture and our security deposit, too—all because of Dusty!

PATRICK: I'm going downstairs to set him straight! *(Patrick rushes out the door, but he trips on the loose board on the stairs and tumbles to the bottom of the stairway.)* Oooh! I think my leg's broken!

ROBIN: Oh, no!

What Are the Legal Issues?

1. Is it against the law to refuse to rent to people who might have children in the future?
2. Must the rental of an apartment be evidenced by a writing, or may it be oral?
3. May a landlord legally shut off a tenant's electricity?
4. May a landlord keep a security deposit because he or she doesn't like a tenant's dog?
5. Who owns fixtures that are installed by the tenant?
6. Is the landlord or the tenant responsible for injuries caused by a defect in a common area of an apartment building?

The Rental Agreement

What You'll Learn

- **How to define the main types of tenancies available to persons who rent real property**
- **How to describe some of the common covenants found in a lease**
- **How to summarize rent control laws**

Why It's Important

Knowing all you can about rental agreements and the types of tenancies will help you choose a place to live and know how to address disputes that may arise.

Legal Terms

- lessee
- lessor
- tenancy
- tenancy for years
- periodic tenancy
- rent day
- tenancy at will
- tenancy at sufferance
- lease
- sublease

Tenancy

If you rent real property, such as an apartment or house, you are a tenant. If you own real property and rent it to someone else, you are a landlord. The contract between a tenant and landlord is called a lease. In a lease, the tenant is known as the **lessee**, and the landlord is the **lessor**.

Types of Tenancies

Although they rent from someone else, tenants own an interest in the real estate they lease, called a leasehold estate or **tenancy**. The types of tenancies are tenancy for years, periodic tenancy, tenancy at will, and tenancy at sufferance. Figure 33.1 shows some considerations to keep in mind when renting an apartment.

Figure 33.1

What to Look for in Selecting an Apartment

Location
- Near school, work
- Near church, mosque, synagogue
- Near shopping
- Near public transportation
- Near recreation: parks, museums

Finances
- Amount of monthly rent
- Amount of security deposit
- Cost of utilities
- Length of lease

Building
- Condition of building and grounds
- Parking facilities
- Recreation on premises
- Security system
- Condition of hallways, stairs, and elevators
- Access to mailboxes

Layout and Facilities
- Size and condition of unit
- Type and controls of heating and cooling systems
- Plumbing and water pressure
- Type and condition of appliances
- Condition of doors, locks, windows, closets, and floors

APARTMENT SEARCH
Many considerations go into renting an apartment. *Which of the four broad categories listed here would be most important to you?*

Tenancy for Years

A **tenancy for years** is the right to occupy property for a definite or fixed period of time. It may be for 1 week, 6 months, 1 year, 5 years, 99 years, or any other period of time, as long as the time period is definite. A tenancy for 100 years or more has the effect of transferring absolute ownership to the tenant. For this reason, leases are occasionally written for 99-year periods. Some states require a tenancy for years to be in writing because it is a transfer of an interest in real property. Other states require a tenancy to be in writing only if it's for longer than a year.

Periodic Tenancy

A **periodic tenancy**, also called a tenancy from year to year (or month to month, or week to week), is a tenancy that continues for successive fixed periods. One of the parties may terminate this tenancy by giving advance notice to the other party. If such proper notice is not given, the tenancy continues for another like period. The notice requirement differs from state to state, but it is often the period between rent days. The **rent day** is the day on which the rent is due.

Example 1. Enrica Pastore rented an apartment on a year-to-year lease, which expired on December 31. On November 15, she told her landlord she wanted to terminate the lease. In her state, however, three months' notice is required to terminate a year-to-year tenancy, so Enrica's landlord could hold her to an additional year.

Tenancy at Will

A **tenancy at will** is an interest in real property that continues for an indefinite period of time. No written agreement is required to create this tenancy. It is terminated when either the landlord or the tenant gives the notice required by state law, which is usually 30 days.

Tenancy at Sufferance

A **tenancy at sufferance** arises when a tenant doesn't leave the premises after his or her tenancy has expired. This situation often occurs when a tenancy for years expires or when a tenancy at will has been properly terminated by the landlord but the tenant remains in possession. A tenant at sufferance, also called a holdover tenant, is a wrongdoer who no longer has legal interest in the property. Generally, a tenant at sufferance is not entitled to notice to vacate but is liable to pay rent for the period of occupancy.

TENANCY AT WILL
A tenancy at will continues for an indefinite period of time. *How is a tenancy at will terminated?*

If a landlord accepts rent from a tenant after a tenancy has expired, a periodic tenancy or a tenancy at will may come about instead of a tenancy at sufferance.

The Lease Agreement

A written agreement between a lessor and a lessee is called a **lease**. The lease creates the landlord-tenant relationship. It provides the tenant with exclusive possession and control of the real property of the landlord. The general rules of contract law apply to this form of agreement. Figure 33.2 shows a sample lease.

Terms in a Lease

The terms of a lease, known as covenants, set forth the rights and duties of the landlord and the tenant. The basic right that the tenant wants is possession and a continued occupancy, free from interference or annoyances. The landlord wants rent and possession of the property in good condition at the term's end.

Security Deposit In addition to the first month's rent, landlords often require you to pay a security deposit and the last month's rent at the beginning of a tenancy. These requirements are intended to secure the payment of rent or repairs for damages to the property. The security

Figure 33.2

A Typical Lease Agreement

Description of the property, including its address	**RENTAL AGREEMENT OF PROPERTY AT 4744 LEMONA STREET, EAST TROY, WISCONSIN 53120**
Names of owners and tenants	Parties in agreement are Corey Lucas and Paula Yates. Corey has rented the second-floor apartment to be used as a private residence, for his or her (one person) use only and for no other purpose, for a term of six months.
Dates during which the lease is valid	The term of this agreement will be from June 1, 20--, to November 30, 20--, at which time another six-month agreement will be drawn.
Amount of the security deposit	The rent will be $540 per month. There will be a security of one and one-half months' rent, for a total of $810. The monies held as security will be held until such time that the tenant desires to move or until he/she is asked to vacate the premises. The security deposit along with any interest it accrues will be returned to the tenant, minus any monies held for repair or damages, rubbish removal, or cleaning to be done.
Amount and due date of monthly rent and penalties for late payment	Rent will be due from the tenant on the first of each month and not later than five days after the first of each month. A late penalty of 5% of the monthly rent will be assessed for any rent not paid by the end of the five-day grace period. The tenant is personally responsible for paying the monthly expenses, including electric, telephone, and cable service. These expenses are not included in any monthly rent payment.
List of restrictions regarding pets, remodeling, activities, and so on	The tenant was advised that there is to be NO SMOKING in the apartment while he/she is in residence at this address. There will be no pets allowed at any time in the apartment while he/she resides here. If the tenant or landlord decides that the tenant must vacate the apartment, a thirty (30) day notice must be given before the first of the month.
Tenant's right to sublet the rental unit	The tenant may not sublease (rent to another person) this property without the landlord's written permission. The tenant must provide his/her own insurance on the contents of the apartment, such as furniture, jewelry, clothes, etc. The tenant will not hold the landlord or landlord's agent responsible in the event of a loss.
Conditions under which the landlord may enter the apartment	The tenant agrees to let landlord enter property at reasonable hours to inspect or repair the property. Landlord will notify the tenant 24 hours in advance and give the time and reason for the visit. This place of residence shall be occupied by no more than (1) person.
Charges to the tenant for damage, moving out of the unit early, or refusing to pay rent	At the expiration of the tenancy, the tenant will surrender the premises to the landlord in as good condition as when received. The tenant will remove all rubbish from the premises. If he or she fails to do so, the tenant will forfeit part of the security deposit in order for the landlord to pay for removal. If the tenant breaks the lease for any reason, the landlord may keep the security deposit. This agreement is between Corey Lucas and Paula Yates. On this day, this agreement is signed by both parties.

Corey Lucas   6/10/--   *Paula Yates*   6/10/--

Tenant   Date   Landlord   Date

deposit often equals one month's rent. Some states limit the amount of a security deposit and require that interest be paid on it on an annual basis.

Decoration and Repairs The landlord has no obligation to decorate the premises, unless the lease says so or unless it is required by statute or local ordinance. The landlord, however, must make any repairs

LEASE

A lease is the agreement between the lessor and lessee that puts in writing the details of the landlord-tenant relationship. *Which components of a lease are likely to be most negotiable?*

necessary to keep the premises fit for living. For instance, a landlord would be required to address a major repair such as a leaky roof or a broken furnace. This obligation is known as the implied warranty of habitability. Basically, the tenant owns the property for the stated period and is obligated to maintain the premises and make any repairs that are not the obligation of the landlord.

Assignment and Subletting An assignment of a lease occurs when you transfer the remaining period of time in a lease to someone else. A **sublease** occurs when you transfer part of the term of a lease, but not the remainder of it, to someone else.

Example 2. Charles and Nancy Olson held a three-year lease on a house in Wellesley. The house was near the college campus where their daughter went to school. One summer, while the lease was still in effect, the Olsons went on an extended vacation. They sublet their house to a friend, John Bennis, who had been hired by the college for the summer. John and his family lived at the house until the Olsons returned in the fall.

SECURITY DEPOSIT
Most leases for apartments call for a security deposit to protect the lessor against nonpayment or property damage. *What is the usual amount of a security deposit?*

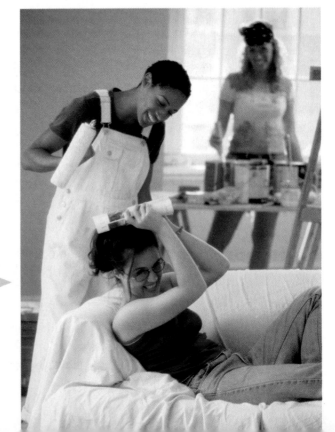

DECORATING AND REPAIRING
The landlord has no obligation to decorate the premises unless it is provided for in the lease. *In what condition must the premises be when the tenant leaves?*

A Global Perspective: Laws Around the World

Australia

In 1982, Eddie Koiki Mabo, a native leader of Murray Island just north of Queensland, stood in Australia's High Court. He and several neighbors sought legal rights to land their ancestors had occupied for generations. The islanders disputed the claim of *terra nullius* (land belonging to no one), which was the concept used by the British Crown to possess the Australian continent. It took 10 years, but on June 3, 1992, the Court ruled that the islanders were entitled to the "possession, occupation, use and enjoyment" of their land. The Mabo decision changed the relationship between Aboriginal natives and European settlers. For the first time, Aboriginal people could claim title to land that they believed was rightfully theirs.

In response to the High Court decision, the Australian government enacted the Native Title Act of 1993. During its passage through Parliament, Australia's Prime Minister said, ". . . we give the indigenous people of Australia, at last, the standing they are owed; as original occupants of this continent . . . as workers, soldiers, explorers, artists, sportsmen and women, . . . as people who have survived the loss of their land and the shattering of their culture." Here's a snapshot of Australia.

Geographical area	2,966,153 sq. mi.
Population	19,546,792
Capital	Canberra
Legal system	Based on English common law
Language	English, indigenous languages
Religion	87% Christian
Life expectancy	80 years

Critical Thinking Question The Aboriginal people will never reclaim all the land that belonged to their ancestors. Think of several ways the Australian government might help compensate them for their loss. For more information on Australia, visit **ubpl.glencoe.com** or your local library.

If a landlord doesn't want a tenant to assign or sublet the property, a covenant in the lease must say that. Otherwise, a tenant may either assign or sublet the property to someone else. However, the original tenant is still responsible to the landlord for the rent.

Legal Briefs

When renting, keep the volume on your stereo low. Most leases contain a "quiet enjoyment" clause that basically says you can't disrupt your neighbors, and if you do, you could be in violation of the terms of your lease. Your landlord could very well go to court to evict you for playing your stereo too loudly.

Cases in some states have held that an implied covenant of good faith and fair dealing exists in every lease of business property. Under this rule, landlords may not withhold consent to the sublease or assignment of long-term leases to commercial premises without a good reason.

Option to Renew or to Purchase Many leases contain a provision allowing renters the option to renew the lease for one or more additional periods. This provision gives renters the right to a new lease, under the same terms, for an additional period. Similarly, a renter can be given an option to purchase the property. This is an agreement by the lessor to sell the property to the lessee for a stated price. To exercise an option, a renter must notify the lessor on or before the date set forth in the lease.

Rent Control

Some large communities have passed rent control laws to keep rent within an affordable range. These laws limit what landlords can charge for rental property and also often contain procedures that must be followed before tenants can be evicted. In a number of areas, rent control laws have caused landlords to turn their apartments into condominiums, leading to shortages in rental apartments. Such laws differ from place to place. Some states, including Massachusetts, have done away with rent control laws altogether.

Section 33.1 Assessment

Reviewing What You Learned
1. What is the difference between a tenancy for years, a periodic tenancy, and a tenancy at will?
2. Name the common covenants found in a lease.
3. Explain rent control laws.

Critical Thinking Activity
Elements of a Contract Use the Internet, library, or other resource to find a copy of a standardized lease for an apartment. Then explain the elements of legal contracts as they apply in the context of renting a place to live.

Legal Skills in Action
Maintaining the Premises The grounds surrounding the apartment complex where you live are full of trash. The grass hasn't been mowed for weeks, and it looks pretty shabby. You've mentioned the problem to the landlord, but no action has been taken. Write a petition to circulate among the tenants to ask the landlord to hold a meeting to discuss the difficulty.

Responsibilities of Landlord and Tenant

The Landlord's Duties

Landlords have specific duties imposed by law, in addition to those found in a lease. These duties include refraining from practicing discrimination in renting property, maintaining the premises, and delivering peaceful possession.

Refrain from Discrimination

In selecting tenants, landlords are bound by various laws against discrimination. Laws such as the Civil Rights Act place special emphasis on human needs and rights. In nearly all states, it is against the law for a landlord to refuse to rent or lease property to any person because of race, religion, color, national origin, sex, age, ancestry, or marital status. Refusing to rent to a member of the armed forces, a blind person, or a person who might have children in the future is also against the law.

Maintain the Premises

Rental property offered for dwelling purposes must be fit for human habitation. This means that it must be relatively clean, properly heated, furnished with utilities, and safe.

In some states, if you think the premises are not fit for human habitation and violate the sanitary code, you may pay rent to the court instead of the landlord, pending correction of conditions. In other states, after giving notice to the landlord, you can correct the defect at your own expense and withhold rent up to the amount of that expense.

Deliver Peaceful Possession

Tenants are entitled to the exclusive peaceful possession and quiet enjoyment of the rental premises. **Quiet enjoyment** is your right to undisturbed possession of the property. The landlord cannot interfere with these rights as long as you abide by the conditions of the lease and those imposed by law.

The Tenant's Duties

Tenants have the duties of paying rent, abiding by the terms of the lease, avoiding waste, and returning fixtures.

Abiding by the Terms of the Lease

As a tenant, you have the duty to pay rent to the landlord when it is due. You must also observe the valid restrictions contained in the lease.

What You'll Learn

- How to explain the duties of landlords and tenants
- How to describe eviction proceedings
- How to identify tort liability of landlords and tenants to third parties

Why It's Important

The better you understand the responsibilities of landlords and tenants, the better prepared you will be when you rent or lease property.

Legal Terms

- quiet enjoyment
- waste
- fixtures
- trade fixtures
- eviction
- constructive eviction

CHOOSING RENTAL HOUSING
Renting involves more than just finding a desirable apartment. *In what ways do these steps protect the rights of both tenant and landlord?*

Failure to abide by the restrictions gives the landlord the right to seek eviction. Figure 33.3 shows some smart steps that tenants can follow to make sure their rights are protected.

Avoid Waste

Tenants also have a duty to avoid damaging or destroying the property, acts also known as committing waste. **Waste** is defined as substantial damage to premises that significantly decreases the value of the property. You must return the premises to the landlord in as good a condition as when you moved in, except for reasonable wear and tear. If you have been guilty of waste, you must pay the landlord for the damage.

Example 3. While renting a house in Public Square, Connie Mayles placed an electric heater in one of the rooms. The unit's thermostat was broken, and the heater became red hot, burning a hole in the floor. This damage was not the result of ordinary wear and tear. Connie will be held responsible for having the floor repaired.

Return Fixtures

The tenant must turn over to the landlord all fixtures in the premises at the expiration of the tenancy. **Fixtures** are items of personal property attached to real property, such as built-in stoves and dishwashers, kitchen cabinets, and ceiling light fixtures. Unless otherwise agreed,

---

Figure 33.3 — Finding and Living in Rental Housing

Step 1: The Search
- Choose a location and a price that fit your needs.
- Compare costs and features among possible rental units.
- Talk to people who live in the apartment complex or the neighborhood.

Step 2: Before Signing a Lease
- Be sure that you understand and agree with all aspects of the lease.
- Note the condition of the rental unit in writing. Have the unit's owner sign it.

Step 3: Living in Rental Property
- Keep the place in good, clean condition.
- Notify the owner of any necessary repairs.
- Respect the rights of neighbors.
- Obtain renter's insurance to protect personal belongings.

Step 4: At the End of the Lease
- Leave the unit in at least as good condition as it was when you moved in.
- Tell your landlord where to send your refunded security deposit.
- Ask that any deduction from your deposit be explained in writing.

▲ FIXTURES
Unless otherwise agreed, fixtures become part of the real property and belong to the landlord, even when installed by the tenant. *What are some examples of fixtures?*

they become part of the real property and belong to the landlord, even when installed by the tenant.

In determining whether an item is a fixture, courts consider the following questions:

- Has there been a temporary or permanent installation of the personal property?
- Can the fixture be removed without damaging the building?
- What was the intent of the parties at the time the attachment was made?

When fixtures are installed in such a way that their removal would ruin the appearance of a room or building, they become part of the real property and cannot be removed.

Example 4. Rene Fox rented an apartment from Tower Gardens. She did not like the light fixtures in the apartment and had them replaced with ones she liked better. Rene also replaced the wall-to-wall carpeting that covered a plywood floor in the living room. Both items would now be considered fixtures and would belong to the landlord when Rene moved out.

Roomies

When two or more people sign a rental agreement, they become cotenants. This arrangement means that they share the same rights and responsibilities under the lease. If one tenant behaves badly, it can have a negative effect on all the other cotenants.

Under a cotenancy, each tenant is "jointly and severally" liable under the terms of the lease. In other words, a landlord can hold all tenants or just a single tenant responsible for meeting the terms of the lease, including payment of rent. For example, if one tenant skips on the rent, the other tenants are still obligated to pay the full amount due to the landlord. If one tenant violates the lease in some way, all tenants can be evicted.

One way to avoid potential problems with irresponsible roommates is to have a written agreement covering issues that are likely to arise during the term of the lease. Such issues include rent, space allocation, household chores, food sharing, noise, overnight guests, and moving out. Landlords aren't bound by such agreements, and courts may not enforce anything but the financial terms. However, roommate agreements help put all parties on notice of the expectations.

Writing What issues might be covered in a roommate agreement? Draft some sample terms.

Trade fixtures are items of personal property brought to the premises by the tenant that are necessary to carry on the trade or business to which a rental property will be devoted. For example, if you leased a storefront for a small mending business, you might install sewing machines, special lights, and perhaps a refrigerator to keep food. When you leave at the conclusion of the lease, you could take these items with you. Contrary to the general rule, trade fixtures remain the personal property of the tenant and can be removed at the end of the term of occupancy.

Eviction Proceedings

Eviction occurs when a landlord deprives a tenant of the physical possession of the premises. You can be evicted for things such as not paying rent, remaining after the expiration of the lease, damaging the premises (commission of waste), and violating provisions in the lease.

It is illegal in every state, however, for a landlord to use force to evict a tenant. The landlord must first obtain a court order. The court will generally appoint a sheriff or other authorized officer to carry out the eviction order.

A **constructive eviction** occurs when a landlord breaches a duty under the lease. This breach may take place if the landlord deprives you of heat, electricity, or some other fundamental service that was called for under the lease. When constructive eviction occurs, you may consider the lease terminated, leave the premises, and stop paying rent. Deciding whether a constructive eviction has occurred, however, is usually a matter handled by a court.

Tort Liability

When someone is injured on rented or leased property, both the landlord and the tenant may be liable. Whoever is in control of the area where the injury occurs is generally liable if the injury is caused by negligence. The landlord can be liable for injury caused by a defect in the common areas over which he or she has control, such as hallways or stairways. Likewise, as a tenant, you can be liable for injury caused by defects in the portion of the premises over which you have control.

Law & Academics

Mathematics
When renting an apartment or house, you should read and understand the lease you are about to sign. You should also investigate all the costs involved.

Research Activity
Research apartments in your area. Select one that you would like to rent. Find out how much it would cost to actually live there. Include costs such as first and last month's rent, security deposits, and utilities deposits and installations. Prepare a budget by using spreadsheet software to record your findings.

Section 33.2 Assessment

Reviewing What You Learned
1. What are the duties of the landlord? What are the duties of the tenant?
2. Under what circumstances may a landlord evict a tenant? How must eviction be carried out?
3. Who is liable when someone is injured due to a defect in an apartment house stairway? Why?

Critical Thinking Activity
Reasonable Wear and Tear What do you think is considered reasonable wear and tear on an apartment you have rented for one year? five years?

Legal Skills in Action
Landlord Liabilities You have rented a second-story apartment at the beach for the summer. The complex has a common picnic area with barbeque grills, a swimming pool, and tennis courts. You know you will have visitors all summer long and wonder what might happen if someone gets hurt. Make a list of the parts of the premises where the landlord would be liable for injuries to one of your guests.

Chapter Summary

Section 33.1 The Rental Agreement

- Several types of tenancies exist. A tenancy for years is the right to occupy property for a definite or fixed period of time. It may be for 1 week, 6 months, 1 year, 5 years, 99 years, or any other period of time, as long as the time period is definite. A tenancy for 100 years usually has the effect of transferring absolute ownership to the tenant. For this reason, leases are occasionally written for 99-year periods. Some states require a tenancy for years to be in writing because it is a transfer of an interest in real property. A periodic tenancy continues for successive fixed periods, subject to termination by advance notice. One of the parties may terminate this tenancy by giving advance notice to the other party. If such proper notice is not given, the tenancy continues for another like period. The notice requirement differs from state to state, but it is often the period between rent days. A tenancy at will is the right to occupy for an indefinite period of time, and it is subject to termination when either the landlord or tenant gives requisite notice. No written agreement is required to create this tenancy. A tenancy at sufferance arises when a tenant doesn't leave after the expiration of her or his tenancy. A tenant at sufferance, also called a holdover tenant, is a wrongdoer who no longer has legal interest in the property. Generally, a tenant at sufferance is not entitled to notice to vacate but is liable to pay rent for the period of occupancy. If a landlord accepts rent from a tenant after tenancy has expired, a periodic tenancy or a tenancy at will may come about instead of a tenancy at sufferance.
- Some covenants found in a lease are the following: (1) the landlord requires a monetary deposit as security deposit; (2) the landlord must make repairs necessary to keep the premises fit for living; (3) a tenant may assign or sublet the leased property; and (4) the tenant may renew the lease or purchase the property.
- To keep rent affordable, some communities have rent control laws that limit the amount of rent that landlords can charge. These laws also include certain procedures that must be followed to evict tenants.

Section 33.2 Responsibilities of Landlord and Tenant

- Landlords have several duties. They must refrain from practicing discrimination in renting their property. In nearly all states, it is against the law for a landlord to refuse to rent or lease property to any person because of race, religion, color, national origin, sex, age, ancestry, or marital status. Refusing to rent to a member of the armed forces, a blind person, or a person who might have children in the future is also against the law. Landlords must also keep property for dwelling purposes fit for human habitation. Tenants are entitled to the exclusive peaceful possession and quiet enjoyment of the property. Duties belonging to tenants include the duty to pay rent when it is due and the duty to observe the valid restrictions contained in the lease. Tenants also have a duty to avoid damaging or destroying the property, acts known as committing waste. Waste is defined as substantial damage to premises that significantly decreases the value of the property.
- A tenant can be evicted for failing to pay rent, remaining after the expiration of the lease, committing waste, and violating the provisions of a lease. It is illegal in every state for a landlord to use force to evict a tenant.
- The landlord can be liable for injuries caused by defects in the common areas of leased property. The tenant can be liable for injuries that occur in the area over which he or she has control.

Using Legal Language

Consider the key terms in the list below. Then use these terms to complete the following exercises.

lessee

lessor

tenancy

tenancy for years

periodic tenancy

tenancy at will

tenancy at sufferance

sublease

quiet enjoyment

waste

fixtures

trade fixtures

eviction

constructive eviction

Understanding Business and Personal Law Online

Self-Check Quiz Visit the *Understanding Business and Personal Law* Web site at **ubpl.glencoe.com** and click on Chapter 33: Renting a Place to Live—Self-Check Quizzes to prepare for the chapter exam.

1. Imagine you are a landlord of a small apartment complex. Using as many of the key terms as possible, write a lease for someone who is planning to rent one of the apartments.
2. With a partner, role-play a scenario in which a prospective, first-time tenant asks questions about various parts of the lease. Try to be as realistic as possible.
3. Present your skit to the class.
4. As a class, vote to select the best skit.

The Law Review

Answer the following questions. Refer to the chapter for additional reinforcement.

5. How does a tenant become a tenant at sufferance?
6. How does an implied warranty of habitability affect the landlord? the tenant?
7. How does assigning a lease differ from subletting?
8. In deciding a case that involves a dispute over ownership of a fixture, what factors should a judge consider?
9. When constructive eviction occurs, what may a tenant consider about the lease?
10. What are some factors that you should consider when renting an apartment?
11. Why do most landlords require tenants to submit a security deposit?
12. If a landlord does not a want a tenant to sublet his or her property, how can he or she convey this restriction?
13. What is meant by the expression *quiet enjoyment*?
14. What are trade fixtures?

Linking School to Work

Participating as a Member of a Team
Obtain a standard lease form. With a partner, identify and explain the clauses that benefit the landlord and the clauses that benefit the tenant, then:

15. Compare leases with another team in your class.
16. Look for similarities and differences in the leases.
17. Choose the lease that you would prefer if you were seeking to rent. Justify your choice in a brief paragraph.

Let's Debate

Apartment Maintenance
Pete is a junior in college. He rents an apartment in a complex near the university where he attends classes. Pete always pays his rent on time. However, each month there are more maintenance problems that go unfixed. The hot water heater has been broken for two weeks, and the front door really needs painting. Pete is becoming frustrated and wants to break his lease and find a new place to live.

Debate
18. Can Pete legally break his lease? Why or why not?
19. What else could Pete do besides move? Evaluate his various options with the help of your classmates.
20. If you were Pete, what would you do?

Grasping Case Issues

For the following cases, give your decision and state a legal principle that applies.

21. Chanda Epstein rents an apartment for $500 a month. She does not sign a lease, and nothing is said about the length of her stay. Can Chanda end the tenancy whenever she wishes, without giving notice to the landlord? Why or why not?
22. Bruce Yerkes rents an apartment from Scenic Acres, Inc., signing a three-year lease. After living there for one year, Bruce assigns his lease to Pamela Pelletier and notifies Scenic Acres, Inc. of the assignment. Pamela, however, fails to pay the rent for three months. Can Scenic Acres, Inc. legally collect from Bruce? Explain your answer.
23. Maria Manzueta rents an apartment to Gregory Shenker for $450 per month. Gregory loses his job and falls behind in his rent payments. Maria threatens to throw him out if he does not leave. Can Maria forcibly evict Gregory? Why or why not?
24. The furnace that heats Elizabeth Cain's apartment breaks down. She notifies the landlord, but the furnace is not repaired. Winter is approaching. On what legal ground may Elizabeth seek relief?
25. Michael Fernandez signs a one-year lease for an apartment in the Executive Suites. During the winter, ice and snow pile up over the front entrance to the building, and the janitor makes no effort to remove it. A friend who visits Michael slips and falls on the ice, suffering a serious injury. The landlord claims that Michael is liable for the injury. Do you agree? Explain your answer.

In each case that follows, you be the judge.

26. Injury Liability

The Kings lease a residential dwelling from a partnership called JA-SIN. The lease agreement provides that the tenants are to "take good care of the house" and "make, at their own expense, the necessary repairs caused by their own neglect or misuse." A guest of the Kings trips on a loose tread on an outside stairway and is injured. *Who is responsible, the landlord or the tenant? Explain your answer.*
Ford v. JA-SIN, 420 A.2d 184 (DE).

27. Eviction

Lolita Pentecost rents an apartment from M. Harward, an apartment manager. According to Harward, Pentecost did not pay her rent. Pentecost alleges that Harward forcefully evicted her and her two children and kept her furniture and possessions. Harward claims that he kept Pentecost's possessions because she did not pay the rent. *Can a landlord forcefully evict a tenant and keep the tenant's possessions for nonpayment of rent? Why or why not?*
Pentecost v. Harward, 699 P.2d 696 (UT).

Legal Link

Texas Bound

Selina has received a huge promotion at work, and as part of her new job duties, she is being transferred to Austin, Texas. She will be renting an apartment in Austin for at least a year and needs to find a new place to live.

Connect

Using a variety of search engines:

28. Help Selina research apartments online.
29. Use apartment locator services and online apartment guides as a place to start.

POWER READING STRATEGIES

30. **Predict** Why do you think it is important to have a written lease when you rent a place to live?

31. **Connect** Who is liable if the apartment you sublet to a friend is damaged?

32. **Question** Do you think a landlord has the right to enter the premises you rent? Explain your answer.

33. **Respond** What can you do to make sure the premises where you live are as safe as possible?

CHAPTER 34

Buying a Home

Understanding Business and Personal Law Online

Chapter Overview Visit the *Understanding Business and Personal Law* Web site at ubpl.glencoe.com and click on Chapter 34: Buying a Home—Chapter Overviews to preview the chapter information.

The Opening Scene

Robin and Patrick are sitting in their car in front of a house with a "For Sale" sign on the front lawn.

Home Base

ROBIN: We're really lucky. Not many people inherit enough money for a down payment on a house. Your Aunt Florence was really generous to us.

PATRICK: She always did have a soft spot for me.

ROBIN: This house is really cool.

PATRICK: Yes. It's nice. And the property around here is well kept. That garage next door looks brand new.

(A car drives up and stops behind their car.)

BROKER: *(Getting out of the car.)* I see you found it all right. Isn't this a beauty? Come on, I'll show you the inside. *(They walk into the house.)*

BROKER: You're going to love this place. It has three bedrooms, an updated kitchen, and a nice little yard. Best of all, there's a little apartment over the garage that you can rent out.

(After looking through the house, Patrick and Robin decide to buy it.)

BROKER: You won't be sorry. This house is the best buy I've had in a long time. Sign right here.

PATRICK: Shouldn't we have our lawyer look at this contract before we sign it?

BROKER: That's up to you, but you better hurry. This opportunity won't last long.

ROBIN: What kind of deed will we get?

BROKER: The best kind—a quitclaim deed.

PATRICK: Will the house be in both our names?

BROKER: It sure will. You'll own it as tenants in common. That way, if one of you should pass away, the other will own the house outright.

(Two months later, Patrick is measuring the length of the front yard with a tape measure. A car stops in front of the house, and a man gets out.)

PATRICK: Hello.

BUILDING INSPECTOR: Hello. I'm a building inspector. I saw your "Apartment for Rent" sign.

PATRICK: Yes. We have an apartment for rent over the garage.

BUILDING INSPECTOR: You can't rent an apartment here. This part of town is zoned for single families only.

PATRICK: Really? We didn't know that.

BUILDING INSPECTOR: Sorry. *(He drives off.)*

NEXT-DOOR NEIGHBOR: *(Approaching.)* Hi, Patrick! How's everything?

PATRICK: I just found out that we can't rent our apartment over the garage.

NEIGHBOR: Is that right?

PATRICK: And I've just measured my front yard, and it doesn't seem to come out right. My deed says that our front yard is 150 feet, but from that boundary over there, it goes two feet into your garage.

NEIGHBOR: Are you sure? They built my garage on part of your land?

PATRICK: It looks that way.

What Are the Legal Issues?

1. Is it important to have a lawyer check an agreement to buy a house before signing?
2. Is a quitclaim deed the best kind of deed to have?
3. What does owning property as tenants in common mean?
4. Do people always have the right to rent out an apartment in their house?
5. Can someone gain title to another's real property by placing a garage on it?

Evaluating Housing Alternatives

Why It's Important

Being able to evaluate housing alternatives will help you to decide whether to purchase a home.

Legal Terms

- mortgage
- equity
- debt ratio
- cooperative
- condominium

Deciding to Buy a Home

Buying a home may be the most important purchase you will ever make. You will need to weigh the advantages and disadvantages of home ownership, consider how much you can afford, and determine the type of home that will best fit your needs (see Figure 34.1). You will probably consider taking out a mortgage to help you with the costs. A **mortgage** is a written instrument by which the buyer (the mortgagor) pledges real property to the lender (the mortgagee) as security for a loan.

Advantages to Home Buying

A key advantage of owning your home is the ability to do with it as you wish without having to answer to another owner. The gradual increase in **equity**, or the difference between the fair market value and the mortgage, in the property is another important advantage of home ownership. Equity increases as you pay off the mortgage and as the property increases in value. Except during times of recession, you can often sell a house for more than you paid for it. You can also deduct property taxes and interest paid on your mortgage from your income tax return.

Disadvantages to Home Buying

There are some disadvantages to owning a house. They include the inconvenience and cost of upkeep, as well as the inability to move easily and quickly if necessary.

How Much Can You Afford?

The first step in buying a house is determining the price range that you can afford. This information can be obtained by talking with a loan officer at a bank. The officer can give you an idea of the amount of down payment you will need and the approximate amount you can borrow, based on your income and expenses.

Down Payment Down-payment requirements range from zero to 30 percent of the purchase price. Qualified veterans can obtain a Veteran's Administration (VA) loan to buy a house up to $240,000 with no down payment. Mortgages backed by federal agencies, such as Fannie Mae and Freddy Mac, are available with a 3 percent down payment.

Figure 34.1

Evaluating Housing Alternatives

	Advantages	Disadvantages
Renting an Apartment	Easy to move; low maintenance responsibility; low financial commitment.	No tax advantage; limitations on activities; less privacy.
Renting a House	Easy to move; low maintenance responsibility; low financial commitment; more space.	Higher utility expenses; some limitations on activities; no tax advantage.
Owning a House	Pride of ownership; plenty of space; tax benefits.	Financial commitment; high living expenses; limited mobility.
Owning a Condominium	Pride of ownership; fewer maintenance costs or responsibilities than a house; tax benefits; access to recreation and businesses.	Financial commitment; less privacy than in a house; need to get along with others; typically small and limited space; may be hard to sell.
Owning a Mobile Home	Less expensive than other ownership options.	May be hard to sell; possible poor construction quality.

HOUSING ALTERNATIVES
Choosing a type of housing is a decision that involves many trade-offs. *What are the three advantages or disadvantages on this list that seem most important to you right now?*

FHA loans (loans insured by the Federal Housing Administration) can be obtained with a down payment of 3 to 5 percent. Conventional bank loans require down payments ranging from 10 to 30 percent. See Figure 34.2 for more information on loans.

Loan Qualifications A lender will judge your ability to repay your loan based on your credit report and your **debt ratio**, or the amount of your monthly payments compared to your monthly income. Your mortgage payment, including taxes and insurance, should not exceed 28 percent of your monthly gross income. Total monthly debt payments (including your new mortgage, credit cards, car payments, and so on) should not exceed 36 percent of your income.

> *Example 1.* Ariel's gross pay is $40,000 a year ($3,333 a month). The most she can afford for a monthly mortgage payment at 28 percent is $933. Her total monthly debt payments at 36 percent should not exceed $1,200.

Figure 34.2

The Mortgage Professor's Web Site

The amount you can spend on a house depends on your income, the amount of cash you can allocate to the transaction, and the mortgage terms available in the market at the time you are shopping. These include interest rates, points, term, down payment requirements, and the maximum allowable ratio of housing expense to income. In addition, affordability may be affected by your existing indebtedness if this is higher than the indebtedness that lenders are willing to accept, and by closing costs which vary from one part of the country to another.

The table below provides some ballpark estimates of how much house you can afford with a 7.5 percent 2 point mortgage for 30 years. For each of 7 sale prices, the table shows the total cash required to meet down payment requirements and settlement costs, the total monthly housing expense, the minimum income required to cover housing expenses, and the maximum amount of debt service allowable on the minimum income.

How Much House Can You Afford With a 7.5 Percent 30-Year Mortgage

To Spend This Amount on a House...	You Need At Least This Gross Monthly Income...	To Cover This Monthly Housing Expense...	Other Monthly Debt Payments Should Not Exceed...	And You Need at Least This Much Cash...	For the Down Payment Lenders Are Likely to Require...	And the Closing Costs
$400,000	$11,290	$3,160	$903	$59,200	$40,000	$19,200
350,000	10,260	2,871	820	51,800	35,000	16,800
300,000	8,790	2,461	703	44,400	30,000	14,400
250,000	7,330	2,051	586	37,000	25,000	12,000
200,000	6,280	1,756	502	19,800	10,000	9,800
150,000	4,710	1,317	376	14,850	7,500	7,359
100,000	3,230	903	258	7,940	3,000	4,940

Notes: Minimum monthly income is based on a ratio of monthly housing expense to income of 28 percent. Closing costs excluding points are assumed to total 3 percent of the sale price. The maximum monthly debt service payment is assumed to be 8 percent of minimum monthly income. Monthly housing expense includes principal and interest, mortgage insurance, taxes, and hazard insurance. Taxes and hazard insurance are assumed to be 1.825 percent of sale price. The down payment requirement is assumed to be 10 percent on prices of $250,000–400,000, 5 percent on $150,000–200,000, and 3 percent on $100,000. Mortgage insurance premium rates are .9 percent with 3 percent down, 78 percent with 5 percent down, and .52 percent with 10 percent down.

AFFORDING A MORTGAGE
Your financial condition and the value of the property you wish to buy determines how much you can afford for a house. *How much in other monthly debt payments, in addition to your mortgage, can you have if you buy a $100,000 house?*

A HAPPY DAY
The day you buy your first house will be a memorable occasion. *Why is your debt ratio important when you buy a house?*

Types of Home Ownership

You have many choices in selecting a home, depending on how much you can afford and the desired size of the house and its location. See Figure 34.3 for more information on buying a home.

BUYING A HOUSE
Purchasing a house is a complicated process. *What are some possible results of not thinking through all the elements discussed in this chapter?*

Single- and Multifamily Homes

Single-family homes are the most popular type of home. They offer the most privacy and usually have more overall usable space than other types of housing.

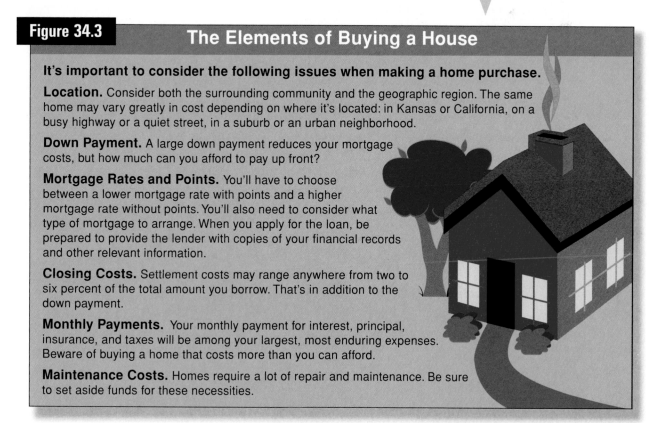

Figure 34.3

The Elements of Buying a House

It's important to consider the following issues when making a home purchase.

Location. Consider both the surrounding community and the geographic region. The same home may vary greatly in cost depending on where it's located: in Kansas or California, on a busy highway or a quiet street, in a suburb or an urban neighborhood.

Down Payment. A large down payment reduces your mortgage costs, but how much can you afford to pay up front?

Mortgage Rates and Points. You'll have to choose between a lower mortgage rate with points and a higher mortgage rate without points. You'll also need to consider what type of mortgage to arrange. When you apply for the loan, be prepared to provide the lender with copies of your financial records and other relevant information.

Closing Costs. Settlement costs may range anywhere from two to six percent of the total amount you borrow. That's in addition to the down payment.

Monthly Payments. Your monthly payment for interest, principal, insurance, and taxes will be among your largest, most enduring expenses. Beware of buying a home that costs more than you can afford.

Maintenance Costs. Homes require a lot of repair and maintenance. Be sure to set aside funds for these necessities.

Careers in Law

Criminal Court Judge

When Dianne Jones puts on her judge's robes each morning and strides into Dallas County Criminal Court, she brings years of knowledge and experience with her.

"Before I became a judge," Jones says, "I tried and defended many cases as an attorney. You have to be quick on your feet when you are in charge of a courtroom, and criminal litigation helps you gain that ability."

Jones' court handles misdemeanor cases, half of which concern family violence misdemeanors. This category of crime includes stalking, violations of protective orders, and some kind of assault. She is especially interested in these kinds of cases because they allow her to affect the lives of children.

"It's wonderful to think you might make a difference in these situations," Jones says. "I try to bring together defendants, victims, lawyers, and sometimes other family members to try to resolve the family problems for the long term."

Often this means court-ordered counseling for the defendant. For most first-time offenses, Jones places the convicted individual on probation and requires them to participate in regular counseling. If an individual does not fulfill these requirements, Jones can be tough.

"People on probation must show that they have seriously participated in the required counseling within one month of my sentence," she says. "If they can't do so, they have violated their probation." That usually means jail time.

Jones prefers that people do fulfill her requirement for counseling. "The more people we catch at the front end of a misdemeanor," she says, "the less likely the misdemeanor will become violent. It's important to save children from being exposed to this kind of behavior—both to protect them now and to keep them from growing up to repeat the kind of adult behavior they have witnessed."

Because Jones' judicial position is an elected office, she also is very involved in the political process. Every four years, she must campaign for re-election—a process that includes public speaking, raising campaign funds, and listening to the issues brought by people in the Dallas community.

Skills	Public speaking; quick thinker; lots of litigation experience, if possible as a prosecutor and a defense attorney
Personality	Relaxed, but firm; willingness to listen to all sides; comfortable letting attorneys try their cases without micromanaging.
Education	Undergraduate degree; law degree; practical experience as a trial lawyer.

For more information about judges, visit **ubpl.glencoe.com** or visit your public library.

Multifamily dwellings are less expensive to own because of the income from nonowner-occupied units. The owner's monthly mortgage and tax payments can often come from rental income. Ownership of a multifamily dwelling can be a way to afford your first house.

Mobile Homes

Mobile homes represent a sizable portion of the dwellings in this country. Mobile homes, also known as manufactured homes, are less expensive to purchase than other types of houses and cost less to keep up. They usually can be sold quickly and easily.

Cooperatives

A **cooperative** (co-op) is a form of home ownership in which buyers purchase shares in the corporation that owns an apartment building and holds the mortgage on it. Shareholders have a proprietary lease that gives them the right to their individual units. Each shareholder has the right of possession of an apartment and must pay a share of the operating expenses, mortgage, and taxes.

Condominiums

In a **condominium** (often called a condo), each owner has an absolute individual interest in an apartment unit and an undivided common interest in the common areas of the condo project. These common areas include stairways, yards, swimming pools, parking areas, elevators, heating systems, and the like. An association made up of the condominium owners manages the condominium.

Section 34.1 Assessment

Reviewing What You Learned
1. What are the advantages and disadvantages of buying a home?
2. Is it possible to buy a home with no down payment? Explain your answer.
3. Describe the five types of home ownership.

Critical Thinking Activity
Lender Criteria If you were planning to borrow money to buy a home, why would your employment history be important to a lender?

Legal Skills in Action
Calculating the Down Payment Using the following scenarios, determine the down payment required on a house that costs $240,000. (Assume all other costs are already included.)
- VA loan to a qualified veteran
- Fannie Mae loan: 3 percent
- FHA loan: 4.5 percent
- Conventional loan: 15 percent

The Home Buying Process

Contracting to Buy a House

When you have found a house you like that is within your price range, the next step is to enter into a purchase and sale agreement with the seller (see Figure 34.4). The agreement should be subject to your getting a mortgage to purchase the property. To obtain the best legal protection, have a lawyer review the agreement before signing it.

Applying for a Mortgage

Lenders need security, a way of getting their money back in case the borrower does not pay. Satisfying this need is the purpose of a mortgage. If the buyer, or mortgagor, pays the money back as agreed, then the mortgage is discharged, and the homeowner owns the property

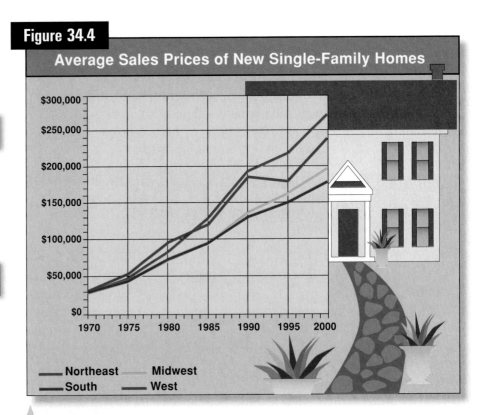

Figure 34.4

Average Sales Prices of New Single-Family Homes

Legend: Northeast, Midwest, South, West

SELLING PRICE
The average selling price of homes in the United States has risen steadily since 1970. *Which region of the country experienced the greatest gain? the lowest?*

Don't Fence Me In

When property boundaries are in dispute, it is usually because a neighbor wants to build a fence or cut down a tree close to the property line. One easy way to resolve such conflict is to hire a land surveyor to mark off the proper lines. However, this option may be expensive. It can cost between $300 and $3,000 for a land survey, depending on the market and the complexity of the project.

A less costly way to resolve such disputes is to agree on where you want the boundary to be located. Then it's simply a matter of signing deeds that properly describe the new boundary. It is helpful to have an attorney draft the description to appear in the deed. Doing so will help avoid any potential problems with property transfer in the future, especially if there is a mortgage on the property. After the deed is signed, it should be recorded at the county office of land records. Recording the deed will put others on notice of the new legally recognized boundary.

Research Activity Visit your County Recorder's Office (sometimes called the Land Registry Office) and ask about how they record deeds. Describe the process.

---

outright. If the mortgagor does not pay the money back according to the terms of the agreement, the lender, or mortgagee, can have the property sold to pay off the loan.

Types of Mortgages

Because different lenders charge different interest rates, you can save money by shopping around for a mortgage. Because home buyers typically mortgage large sums of money, even a slightly lower interest rate can translate into thousands of dollars of savings. There are various types of mortgage loan plans available. A conventional mortgage typically offered by a bank involves no government backing by either insurance or guarantee. The loan is made by a private lender who exclusively carries the risk of loss. Such a loan usually requires a sizable down payment, and interest rates vary from one lender to another. Although conventional loans are often written for a 30-year period, a shorter period reduces the cost of the loan.

Example 2. Monica and James Dipirro took out a mortgage loan of $80,000 at 9.5 percent for 30 years. They paid $672.68 each month for principal and interest. The total cost of the loan over the 30-year period was $162,165. Had they taken a 20-year loan instead, their monthly payments would have been $745.70, but the cost of the loan over the 20-year period would have been $98,968—a savings of $63,197.

To help meet borrowers' needs, there is a variety of creative financing available (see Figure 34.5). A fixed-rate mortgage stays the same throughout the life of the mortgage, but it requires a large down payment. An adjustable-rate mortgage (ARM) has an interest rate that moves up and down, following an index to which it is tied. A graduated-payment mortgage has a fixed interest rate during the life of the mortgage, but the

DIFFERENT MORTGAGES
Real estate loans are made with a variety of financing plans. *What type of mortgage allows lower monthly payments at the beginning of the loan when your income is lowest, and increases as your income rises?*

Figure 34.5	Some Methods of Financing a Home
Type	**Description**
Fixed Rate Mortgage	Fixed interest rate, usually long-term; equal monthly payments, including principal and interest, until debt is paid in full
Adjustable Rate Mortgage	Interest rate changes based on a financial index, resulting in possible changes in monthly payments, loan term, and/or principal; some plans have rate or payment caps
Balloon-Payment Mortgage	Monthly payments based on fixed interest rate, usually short-term; payments may cover interest only with principal due in full at term's end
Graduated-Payment Mortgage	Lower monthly payments rise gradually then level off for duration of term; with flexible interest rate, additional payment changes possible if index changes
Shared-Appreciation Mortgage	Below-market interest rate and lower monthly payments in exchange for a share of profits when property is sold or on a specified date; many variations
Assumable Mortgage	Buyer takes over seller's original, below-market rate mortgage
Seller Take-Back Mortgage	Seller provides all or part of financing with a first or second mortgage
Wraparound Mortgage	Seller keeps original low-rate mortgage; buyer makes payments to seller who forwards a portion to the lender holding original mortgage; offers lower effective interest rate on total transaction

monthly payments increase over the life of the loan. A balloon-payment mortgage has relatively low fixed payments during the life of the mortgage, but it is followed by one large final (balloon) payment. There are also other creative ways of financing the purchase of real property.

Example 3. Joan Ackley wants to borrow $100,000 to expand her business. She owns a valuable building on which there is already an existing mortgage of $50,000 at 8 percent interest. Ackley does not want to disturb this mortgage because the interest rate is so low. Henry Baker agrees to loan Ackley $150,000 at 11 percent. Baker will give Ackley only $100,000 cash, however, and take over her payments on the $50,000 first mortgage. Ackley will pay $150,000 plus interest back to Baker over the life of the loan. The mortgage that Ackley gives Baker is called a wraparound mortgage because it includes the first mortgage in its payment plan.

Federal Protection

The Real Estate Settlement Procedures Act (RESPA), a federal law, gives you protection when you apply for a loan. Under this law, the lender must give you a copy of a booklet that explains the real estate settlement procedure. The lender must also give you an estimate of the costs that you will incur in obtaining the loan. Later, a uniform settlement statement must be filled out, which will show you the exact cost of the settlement. You have a right to see the completed form on the day before the closing if you wish. The lender must also give you a truth-in-lending statement showing the true costs of the interest and finance charge on the mortgage loan.

A HOME AT LAST
There are different types of co-ownership of real property. *Which type of co-ownership allows title to pass automatically to the co-owner if the other owner dies?*

Taking Ownership

Ownership of property can be taken in your name alone or with someone else as a co-owner. There are different types of co-ownership as well as different types of deeds in common use.

Co-ownership

There are three main forms of co-ownership of real property. These include tenancy in common, joint tenancy, and tenancy by the entirety.

Tenancy in Common   **Tenancy in common** is a type of co-ownership in which two or more people own an interest in the whole property. An owner may deed away his or her interest without permission of the other owners. An owner's heirs inherit that person's share of the property upon death.

> *Example 4.* Wendy Chow, Beverly Rojas, and Mark Rojas owned real property as tenants in common. When Chow died, her one-third share of the property was inherited by her husband and two children, giving each of them a one-ninth interest in the property. They became tenants in common with the Rojases, who each still owned a one-third interest in the property.

Joint Tenancy   **Joint tenancy** (also called joint tenancy with the right of survivorship) is a type of ownership in which two or more people

Virtual Law

Online Mortgage Providers

Applying for a home loan online is becoming a popular way to get a mortgage. Online loans are subject to the same disclosure laws that govern traditional home loans. After a borrower that uses the Internet receives a loan offer from a lender, that lender is required to make the loan. Some online mortgage lenders are experimenting with automated approval systems. These software programs would apply all the normal rules of loan decisions to a given situation. The idea is to imitate the human decision-making process and make the loan approval procedure much more efficient. (Source: *New York Times*, February 26, 2001, p. C5)

Connect Visit the Web site of a major mortgage lender. See if they have an online loan application process.

own an interest in the whole property. An owner may deed away his or her interest without permission of the other owners. Upon the death of one joint tenant, the entire ownership goes to the other joint tenants.

Example 5. If Wendy Chow, Beverly Rojas, and Mark Rojas, in Example 4, had owned the property as joint tenants instead of tenants in common, there would have been a different result after Chow's death. The Rojases would have assumed ownership of the entire property as joint tenants. Chow's husband and children wouldn't have received any interest in the property.

Tenancy by the Entirety   Only a husband and wife may hold a **tenancy by the entirety**. This kind of tenancy is based on a common-law doctrine that held that a husband and wife are regarded by the law as one. In theory, each spouse owned the entire property, which neither could transfer without the other's consent. The husband, however, had the entire control over the property. He alone had the right to enter the premises and the right to receive the rent and profits from it. When either spouse died, the property was owned outright by the surviving spouse. The advantage of this type of ownership is that the property cannot be taken away from one of the spouses, even by a court, unless both spouses are sued together.

Example 6. Harry and Wanda Quinn owned their residence as tenants by the entirety. Mrs. Quinn was involved in an automobile accident that injured another driver. Suit was brought against Mrs. Quinn but not against Mr. Quinn. Their home could not be taken from them in court to sell to satisfy a judgment, even if Mrs. Quinn was held to be responsible, because the couple owned the property as tenants by the entirety.

Some states have updated this law to give women and men equal rights to possession of the property, as well as to the rent and profits from it. Other states have done away with this type of ownership altogether.

Deeds

A **deed** is a written instrument that transfers ownership of real property. The person transferring ownership is the grantor. The one to whom ownership is given is the grantee. Title is transferred when the deed is signed and delivered. The deed should be recorded in a public office to give notice to the public that the grantee now owns the property.

A general warranty deed contains express warranties that title to the property is good. The warranties are the personal promises of the grantor that if title is discovered to be faulty, the grantor will make up for any

Jordan is a small, rural town. Although many people live in the country, the school is located in town. Most of the students take the bus to school, but there are also some people living in town who want to walk to school. Unfortunately, there are no sidewalks that lead to the school, and parents are afraid it is unsafe for children to walk along the road. The city council of Jordan refuses to exercise its right to eminent domain and claim the property necessary to construct sidewalks. They say they will only build the sidewalks if the property owners agree to have the sidewalks built. *Do you agree with the parents or the city council? What is the ethical issue in this case?*

loss suffered by the grantee. A general warranty deed is the most desirable form of deed because it gives the grantee the most protection.

A special warranty deed contains express warranties that no defect arose in the title during the time that the grantor owned the property but not before. Unlike a general warranty deed, no warranties are made as to defects arising before the grantor owned the property. See Figure 34.6 for an example of a deed.

A bargain and sale deed transfers title to property without giving warranties. A bargain and sale deed requires consideration to be valid. As a result, it cannot be used to make a gift of real property.

A quitclaim deed transfers whatever interest the grantor has in the property, but it does not warrant that the grantor has any interest. It merely releases the grantor's rights to the property.

Example 7. Rebecca Hartney learned that several years ago the seller of the house she had purchased had given a neighbor the right in a deed to cut across the rear of the property. Hartney didn't want the neighbor to continue this practice. In return for a small consideration, the neighbor gave up the right by signing a quitclaim deed.

Limitations on Property Use

There are often limitations on property use that you should be aware of when becoming a homeowner. These limits may affect how you build on your land, as well as how you can use the land that you own. See Figure 34.7 for more information.

Zoning Laws

Communities use ordinances and bylaws to regulate the use of real property within their boundaries. Most cities and towns have **zoning laws** that prescribe the use that may be made of property in specified areas. One area, for example, might be zoned for single-family houses only, another for multifamily dwellings, and another for business and industry.

When a zoning law is enacted, it does not apply to existing uses of the property. These uses are called nonconforming uses and may continue, although they cannot be expanded.

Eminent Domain

Eminent domain is the right of the government to take private land, with compensation to its owners, for public use. The government can take private land for such things as public buildings, highways, school buildings, power projects, housing projects, parks, and many other public uses. The private owner must be paid the fair value of the land taken.

Figure 34.6

Deed

I, Mae Lee Pete, of Georgetown, Essex County, Massachusetts, for consideration paid and in full consideration of $186,500, grant to Rodrigo Martinez and Conchita Martinez, husband and wife, of 72 Lakeshore Drive, Georgetown, MA 01833, as tenants by the entirety, with warranty covenants the land with the buildings thereon situated at 72 Lakeshore Drive, Georgetown, Massachusetts bounded and described as follows:

EASTERLY: by Georgetown Lake Drive, seventy-five (75) feet;

NORTHERLY: by the north portion of Lot #116 on Plan hereinafter referred to approximately one hundred twenty-four and 5/10 (124.5) feet;

WESTERLY: by land now or formerly of Georgetown Lakeshores Inc. fifty-nine (59) feet; and

SOUTHERLY: by Lot #117 on said plan one hundred twenty-three (123) feet.

Being lot #117 and the south half of Lot #116 as shown on a plan entitled "Georgetown Lake Shores" Section 1, surveyed by Clinton F. Goodwin, Reg. Eng., recorded with the Essex South District Registry of Deeds in Plan Book 27, Page 72 on May 31, 1986.

Being the same premises conveyed to me by deed of Wayne B. Gadsby and Deidre J. Gadsby, date May 31, 1996, and recorded with Essex South District Registry of Deeds in Book 12739, page 218.

Witness my hand and seal this 12th day of August, 20 --.

Mae Lee Pete
Mae Lee Pete
The Commonwealth of Massachusetts

Essex, ss   Aug. 12, 20 --

Then personally appeared the above-named MAE LEE PETE and acknowledged the foregoing instrument to be her free act and deed, before me

Harvey X. Silva
Harvey X. Sylva, Notary Public
My commission expires 6/28/--

DEED
A deed is a written instrument that transfers ownership of real property. *Which is the most desirable form of deed?*

Figure 34.7

The Nature of Real Property

Real property is the ground and everything permanently attached to it. Included are buildings, fences, trees, and perennial plants on the surface; earth, rocks, and minerals under the surface; and the airspace above the surface.

1 Air Rights

You own the airspace above your property to as high as you can effectively use. Leaning walls, projecting building eaves, and electric and telephone wires that extend over another's land have all been held to be trespasses. It is also unlawful to fire shots over the land of a neighbor.

2 Trees

A tree belongs to the person on whose land the trunk is located. You can trim the branches of your neighbor's tree that overhang your property, but only up to your property line.

3 Vegetation

Flowers, shrubs, vineyards, and field crops that grow each year without replanting (perennials) are considered real property. They belong to the new owners when real property is sold.

4 Subterranean Rights

You own the ground below the surface of your property to the center of the earth. Property owners sometimes sell *subterranean rights* if their property is in an area where mines or wells are operated.

5 Riparian Rights

Different owners of land on the opposite sides of a stream own to the bank if the stream is navigable, and to the stream's midpoint if it is not navigable. Owners do not have title to the water or to the fish that swim in the water.

Adverse Possession

Ownership of real property can be lost by **adverse possession**. This loss occurs when someone who doesn't own property takes possession of it for a period set by state statute, such as twenty years. The possession must be open, not secretive, with a claim that it is being done rightfully. The continuous possession by others, one after the other, without interruption by the real owner, is counted toward this time period.

Example 8. Bruce and Jennifer Lue bought a house and lived in it for 25 years. Later, they discovered that the property line ran through the middle of their house. Their neighbor actually owned the land under half their house. The Lues could petition the court for title to the land under their house by adverse possession.

Liens, Licenses, and Easements

Property use can be limited by liens, licenses, or easements. A lien is a right in another's property as security for a financial obligation. For example, in Chapter 17, we saw that a hotel keeper has a lien over a guest's property. A license is a temporary, revocable right to limited use of another's land. An **easement** is an irrevocable right to make limited use of another's land. It might be a right to cross someone else's land at a particular place, such as a driveway, or for a particular purpose, such as drainage. An easement is a property interest that, once established, cannot be terminated without the consent of the owner of the right. Usually, an easement is bought and paid for, either in money or by some other consideration.

Section 34.2 Assessment

Reviewing What You Learned

1. Describe legal aspects of a mortgage. Include information on the types of mortgages and the federal protection offered to borrowers.
2. Describe the differences among a fixed-rate, an adjustable-rate, a graduated-payment, and a balloon-payment mortgage.
3. Examine the forms of co-ownership of real property. Briefly describe each form.
4. What types of deeds are discussed in this chapter? How are they alike? How are they different?
5. Distinguish between liens, licenses, and easements.

Critical Thinking Activity

Zoning Laws Why do you think most communities have zoning laws to stipulate the use of property in certain areas?

Legal Skills in Action

Contracts to Purchase a Home Imagine you are a lawyer hired by Robin and Patrick (from The Opening Scene). Write a letter to them explaining what they should have done before signing the contract to purchase their home.

Chapter Summary

Section 34.1 Evaluating Housing Alternatives

- Advantages of owning a house include the ability to do with it as you wish, the gradual buildup of equity in the property, and the ability to deduct taxes and interest from your income tax return. Disadvantages include the inconvenience and cost of upkeep and the inability to move easily and quickly.

- Down-payment requirements vary between zero to 30 percent of the purchase price depending on the type of loan for which you qualify. Qualified veterans can obtain a Veteran's Administration (VA) loan to buy a house up to $203,000 with no down payment. Mortgages backed by federal agencies, such as Fannie Mae and Freddie Mac, are available with a 3 percent down payment. FHA loans (loans insured by the Federal Housing Administration) can be obtained with a down payment of 3 to 5 percent. Conventional bank loans require down payments ranging from 10 to 30 percent. The amount you can borrow also varies depending on how much you earn. A lender will also judge your ability to repay your loan based on your credit report and your debt ratio. Your debt ratio is the amount of your monthly payments compared to your monthly income.

- The types of home ownership include a single-family home, a multifamily home, a mobile home, a cooperative, and a condominium. Single-family homes are the most popular type of home. They offer the most privacy and usually have more overall usable space than other types of housing. Multifamily homes are less expensive to own because of the income from nonowner-occupied units. The owner's monthly mortgage and tax payments can often come from rental income. Mobile homes, also known as manufactured homes, are less expensive to purchase than other types of houses and cost less to keep up. A cooperative is a form of home ownership in which buyers purchase shares in the corporation that owns an apartment building and holds the mortgage on it. In a condominium, each owner has an absolute individual interest in an apartment unit and an undivided common interest in the common areas of the condo project.

Section 34.2 The Home Buying Process

- The purchase and sale agreement should be subject to your getting a mortgage and should be reviewed by a lawyer before being signed.

- The types of mortgages include conventional, fixed rate, adjustable rate, graduated payment, and balloon payment.

- Co-owners may take title as tenants in common, joint tenants, or if husband and wife, as tenants by the entirety. Tenancy in common is a type of ownership in which two or more people own an interest in the whole property. An owner's heirs inherit that person's share of the property upon death. Joint tenancy is a type of ownership in which two or more people own an interest in the whole property. Upon the death of one joint tenant, the entire ownership goes to the other joint tenants. Only a husband and wife can own property by tenancy by the entirety. In theory, each spouse owns the entire property, which neither can transfer without the other's consent.

- The principal kinds of deeds are a general warranty, a special warranty, a bargain and sale deed, and a quitclaim deed. A general warranty deed contains express warranties that title to the property is good. A special warranty deed contains express warranties that no defect arose in the title during the time that the grantor owned the property, but not before. A bargain and sale deed grants no warranties. A quitclaim deed releases the grantor's rights to the property.

- Property owners can lose title to their property by eminent domain, adverse possession, and by giving easements to others.

Using Legal Language

Consider the key terms in the list below. Then use these terms to complete the following exercises.

equity	tenancy by the entirety
debt ratio	deed
cooperative	zoning laws
condominium	eminent domain
mortgage	adverse possession
tenancy in common	easement
joint tenancy	

1. Using the local real estate section of your newspaper as a guide, write a brief description of the home in which you would like to live. Be sure to include the cost, the location, and the size of the home.
2. With a partner, role-play a scenario between a real estate attorney and a person who is buying a home. Use as many of the key terms as possible in your role-play exercise.
3. Present your role-play to the class.

Understanding Business and Personal Law Online

Self-Check Quiz Visit the *Understanding Business and Personal Law* Web site at **ubpl.glencoe.com** and click on Chapter 34: Buying a Home— Self-Check Quizzes to prepare for the chapter exam.

The Law Review

Answer the following questions. Refer to the chapter for additional reinforcement.

4. What information does a lender use to judge your ability to repay your mortgage loan?
5. What type of home ownership is the most popular? Explain your answer.
6. What is the purpose of the Real Estate Settlement Procedures Act (RESPA)?
7. What common law doctrine is tenancy by entirety based upon? What is the advantage of this type of ownership?
8. Why do local governments and public utilities usually obtain easements?
9. What is a debt ratio?
10. Why are single-family homes more popular than other types of housing?
11. Distinguish between liens, licenses, and easements.

Linking School to Work

Acquiring and Evaluating Information

Create a picture of your dream home. Include a detailed description of both the interior and exterior, and then:

12. Look at the real estate ads in the newspaper.
13. Compare your dream home with the homes that are advertised. Based on the prices of the homes in the ads, how much would you be able to sell your home for?

Let's Debate

Buying a Home?

You agree to buy Kyle Chilcote's house. He gives you a purchase and sale agreement and asks you to sign it. You ask your attorney to review the contract, and he suggests some changes. You ask Kyle to put the suggested changes into the contract. Kyle refuses.

Debate

14. What are your options?
15. You really want the house. What could you do to convince Kyle to add the changes to the contract?
16. What might have happened if you had signed the contract without your attorney reviewing it?

Grasping Case Issues

For the following cases, give your decision and state a legal principle that applies.

17. Henry DiRito and Oskar Henrich own a parcel of real property as tenants in common. When Henrich dies, who owns the property? Explain your answer.
18. Cordero and Miel Rueda want to buy a house that costs $100,000. How much monthly income would they need to afford a 7 percent, 30-year mortgage (see Figure 34.2)?
19. How much of a down payment would Cordero and Miel need in Case 2 to obtain a mortgage?
20. Assume the Ruedas in Cases 2 and 3 take title to a property as tenants by the entirety in a state that follows the common-law doctrine on that subject. One day, Cordero refuses to allow Miel to enter the premises. Is Cordero within his legal rights? Explain your answer.
21. Two years after Smith starts raising pigs on her property, the neighborhood in which she lives is rezoned. The new zoning law prohibits raising of certain animals, including pigs. Must Smith stop raising pigs? Why or why not?
22. Rob and Lucy Whitney, newlyweds, are interested in buying a home. Their income is relatively small right now, but they expect to make more money in the future, when Lucy finishes law school. What type of mortgage might Rob and Lucy wish to consider?
23. The county government has determined that Shrewsbury needs another elementary school. Martha Jones owns a large tract of land in the area in which the school is needed. The government offers to purchase the land from Jones for a fair price. Jones, however, refuses the offer and claims that she does not have to sell her property. What rights, if any, does Jones have in resisting the government's offer?

In each case that follows, you be the judge.

24. Transferring Interest in Property

Walter and Emma Barrett jointly executed a warranty deed conveying three lots of land to Chandler and Jean Clements as joint tenants with the right of survivorship. Six years later, Jean Clements conveyed her one-half undivided interest in the property to Wheeler. Chandler claimed that Jean could not sell her interest to another person without his approval. *Was Chandler correct? Why or why not?*
Clements v. Wheeler, 314 So.2d 64 (AL).

25. Adverse Possession

George Woodruff owned a land lot in Beatrice, Nebraska. For seven years, he planted a vegetable garden on a vacant lot next to his land, with the owner's permission. Later, he placed a fence about three feet beyond his property line, on the vacant lot. He planted a row of cedar trees on a line appearing to be a continuation of the fence line. *Is it possible for Woodruff to obtain title to the three-foot strip of land next to his lot? Why or why not?*
Hadley v. Ideus, 374 N.W.2d 231 (NE).

Legal Link

Confusion Abounds

Rochelle and Octavio are planning to purchase their first home. After reviewing their income and debt, they believe they can purchase a home in the range of $85,000. Now it is time to research mortgage loans. Rochelle and Octavio are confused and have asked you for help.

Connect

Using a variety of search engines, explore the Web sites for Fannie Mae and Freddie Mac mortgages. Find out the following information:

26. The purpose of Fannie Mae and Freddie Mac.
27. The similarities and differences between the two organizations.
28. Whether Rochelle and Octavio would be able to secure a mortgage backed by Fannie Mae or Freddie Mac.

POWER READING STRATEGIES

29. Predict Why do you think people consider home ownership the "Great American Dream"?

30. Connect Do you plan to own a house one day? Why or why not?

31. Question Do you think you would be able to obtain a mortgage while you are still in high school?

32. Respond How would you feel if the government decided to take your land for public use? Is that really fair?

Insurance Protection

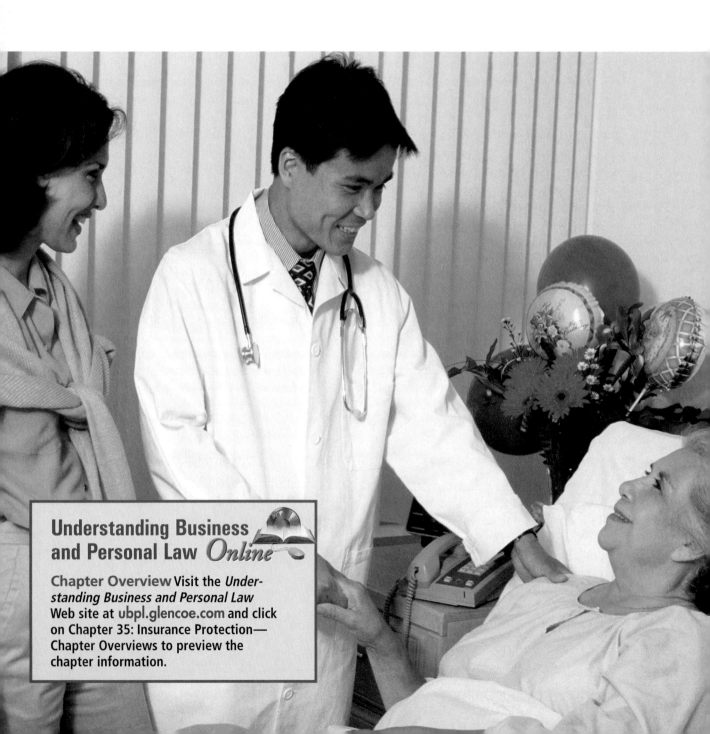

Understanding Business and Personal Law *Online*

Chapter Overview Visit the *Understanding Business and Personal Law* Web site at ubpl.glencoe.com and click on Chapter 35: Insurance Protection—Chapter Overviews to preview the chapter information.

The Opening Scene

Robin and Patrick are about to sit down at their dining room table. They have invited their neighbors, Liz and Jeff, to join them for dinner.

The Neighbors

ROBIN: It's great to get together with you guys.

LIZ: Did you hear what happened while you were away yesterday?

ROBIN: No. What happened?

JEFF: We had a fire in the neighborhood, and there was a shootout!

ROBIN: A shootout?

JEFF: Yeah. The police came with a warrant to arrest Mrs. Vicker's son, Robert. The Vickers live up the street, you know. The police wanted Robert for armed robbery.

PATRICK: Mrs. Vickers is a nice lady, but I've never met her son.

JEFF: Well, when Robert saw the police outside the house, he started shooting out the window.

ROBIN: I don't believe it!

LIZ: He wounded two officers, and the officers finally had to kill him.

ROBIN: Oh my. Poor Mrs. Vickers!

JEFF: And later in the day, Steve and Linda's house caught on fire.

LIZ: Yeah, Steve lit the grill on the back porch and went inside for a minute. When he came out, the porch was on fire.

PATRICK: Did it do much damage?

JEFF: It ruined the porch and damaged the kitchen quite a bit.

ROBIN: I hope their insurance will cover it.

PATRICK: Steve and I were talking about our fire insurance coverage just last week. He said his house was insured for about half its value.

ROBIN: That should cover any fire damage, then.

PATRICK: Say, I just remembered something. I loaned Steve my laptop last week. I hope it wasn't destroyed in the fire.

JEFF: Your homeowner's insurance should cover that.

PATRICK: Speaking of insurance, I don't know whether it's better to get term life insurance or straight life insurance.

JEFF: I think term insurance is best. I heard it builds up a loan value that you can borrow from.

ROBIN: Dinner's almost ready. I can smell the steak cooking on the grill.

PATRICK: I hope you're watching it! We don't want our house to burn down!

JEFF: Hey, here's an idea! Why don't Liz and I take out life insurance on your two lives, and you take it out on ours. That way, if you get killed in a shootout, we can collect.

LIZ: Don't joke about that, Jeff. It's not funny.

ROBIN: Poor Mrs. Vickers. I hope she had insurance on her son's life.

What Are the Legal Issues?

1. Is the full amount of a loss covered when a house is insured for half its value?
2. Does a homeowner's policy cover damage to personal property left at someone else's house?
3. Can policyholders borrow money on a term insurance policy?
4. Can people take out life insurance on anyone they want?
5. Is an insurance company liable if the insured is killed while trying to avoid capture by the police?

The Insurance Contract

What is Insurance?

Our lives are filled with risks, including the loss of property, loss of health, loss of income, and loss of our lives. Insurance can protect you against such losses (see Figure 35.1). The basic purpose of insurance is to spread the losses among a greater number of people. **Insurance** is a contract under which, for consideration, the **insurer**, or the insurance company, agrees to compensate you for a specific loss.

Insurance Terms

The **policy** is the written contract between a person buying insurance and the insurance company that sells it. When you buy the policy, you are the **policyholder**. The **insured** is the person whose life or property is insured. The **beneficiary** is the person named in the policy to receive benefits paid by the insurer in the event of a loss. A **rider** is an attachment to an insurance policy that modifies the policy's terms.

Figure 35.1 — Examples of Risk Management Strategies

Risks: Personal Events	Risks: Financial Impact	Strategies for Reducing Financial Impact
Disability	• Loss of Income • Increased expenses	• Savings and investments • Disability insurance
Death	• Loss of income	• Life insurance • Estate planning
Property Loss	• Catastrophic storm damage to property • Repair or replacement • Cost of theft	• Property repair and upkeep • Auto insurance • Homeowner's insurance • Flood or earthquake insurance
Liability	• Claims and settlement costs • Lawsuits and legal expenses • Loss of personal assets and income	• Maintaining property • Homeowner's insurance • Auto insurance

MANAGING RISKS
Risk management strategies help reduce the financial impact of various risks. *Can you think of any other strategies that would apply to the risks mentioned in the chart?*

The Need for Home Inventory

When buying a house, the lender will require that hazard insurance be acquired before the loan is finalized. This insurance protects the bank's investment in the event of fire, falling trees, wind, vandalism, theft, and other such acts. Homeowner's insurance policies cover damage to the physical structure, as well as loss or damage to personal items and home furnishings.

When personal belongings are stolen or destroyed, you will have a much better chance of full recovery if you have prepared an inventory of your belongings. One way to put together an inventory is by taking photographs and noting specific characteristics of each item of value. Itemize such things as jewelry, music CDs, electronic equipment, bikes, tools, furniture, and collectibles. Make sure you record any serial numbers, model numbers, or other identifying marks. This information might assist the authorities in the recovery of your property. Also keep a record of receipts, appraisals, and other documents that reflect the monetary value of each item. When the inventory is complete, make sure you keep it in a safe place and update it when necessary.

Conduct Research Visit the Web site of an insurance company or contact your family's insurance agent. What guidance is available for doing an inventory?

You can't take out insurance unless you have an **insurable interest** in the person or property you want to insure. Consequently, you can only take out insurance on a person or property if the loss of that person or property would pose a financial burden to you. For life insurance, the insurable interest must exist at the time you buy the insurance. For property insurance, the insurable interest must exist at the time of loss.

Example 1. If you lend $10,000 to a friend, to be repaid at the end of three years, you create an insurable interest in your friend's life to the extent of $10,000 for three years. You should be able to get an insurance policy on your friend's life for $10,000, if he or she can pass the required physical examination and meet all the other requirements of the policy.

Risk is the peril, loss, or event insured against, such as fire, theft, or death. An insurance policy lists the coverage, or amount and extent of risk, that the insurance company will cover.

INSURABLE INTEREST You cannot take out insurance unless you have an insurable interest in the person or property insured. *For life insurance, when must the insurable interest exist?*

The **premium** is the amount of money you pay to the insurance company for insurance coverage. Proceeds are payments by insurance companies to beneficiaries for losses covered by the policy.

The **face value** is the amount of protection stated in a life insurance policy, meaning the amount of money a beneficiary would receive if the insured died. This amount is also called the death benefit or proceeds. It usually includes interest added to the face value of the policy and deductions for outstanding loans. The **cash value** of a life-insurance policy is the amount of money you can take by either borrowing against or cashing in the policy. When a policy is cashed in, the death benefit no longer applies.

Section 35.1 Assessment

Reviewing What You Learned
1. What is the purpose of insurance?
2. Explain why insurance is a contract.
3. What is the difference between the policyholder and the beneficiary?

Critical Thinking Activity
Life Insurance Why do you think you can't take out insurance on anyone you want?

Legal Skills in Action
Elements of a Contract Use the Internet, library, or other resource to find a copy of a standardized insurance contract. Then explain the elements of legal contracts as they apply in the context of an insurance policy.

Life and Health Insurance

Life Insurance

Life insurance is an insurance contract that provides monetary compensation for losses suffered as a result of someone's death. Premiums for life insurance are based on several factors, including the age and health of the insured, coverage, and type of policy. It is less expensive to buy life insurance when you are young because the death rate for young people is very low, and their health is usually at its peak (see Figure 35.2).

Straight Life Insurance

Straight life insurance, also called ordinary life insurance and whole life insurance, requires the payment of premiums throughout the insured's life. The premiums remain constant throughout the policy. Upon the insured's death, the beneficiary is paid the face value of the policy. Because straight life insurance builds up a cash and loan value, it provides savings as well as protection.

Universal life insurance, a form of straight life insurance, allows policyholders to change the terms of the policy as their needs change. Coverage can be increased or decreased, and cash can be withdrawn without canceling the policy. The premiums vary according to the changes in the policy.

Limited-Payment Life Insurance

Limited-payment life insurance allows you to stop paying premiums after a stated length of time—usually 10, 20, or 30 years. The beneficiary will receive the amount of the policy upon the death of the insured, whether it occurs during the payment period or after.

Endowment Insurance

Endowment insurance provides protection for a stated time, generally 20 to 30 years. The face value of the policy is paid to the insured at the end of the agreed period. If the insured dies before the end of the agreed period, the full amount is paid to the beneficiary at the time of death.

Example 2. Don Ray purchased a $10,000, 20-year endowment policy naming his wife, Rose, as beneficiary. He died after the policy had been in force only three years, at which time Rose

What You'll Learn

- How to describe the main types of life insurance
- How to recognize risks that are not covered by insurance
- How to explain the main types of health insurance and the plans that are available

Why It's Important

Knowing how to determine your life and health insurance needs will help you handle your finances when dealing with unexpected events.

Legal Terms

- life insurance
- straight life insurance
- universal life insurance
- limited-payment life insurance
- endowment insurance
- annuity
- term insurance
- Medicare
- Medicaid

Figure 35.2

Life Expectancy Table, All Races, 1996

Age	Both Sexes	Male	Female	Age	Both Sexes	Male	Female
0	76.9	74.1	79.5	50	30.0	27.9	31.8
1	76.4	73.7	79.0	55	25.7	23.8	27.4
5	72.5	68.8	75.1	60	21.6	19.9	23.1
10	67.6	64.9	70.1	65	17.9	16.3	19.2
15	62.6	59.9	65.2	70	14.4	13.0	15.5
20	57.8	55.2	60.3	75	11.3	10.1	12.1
25	53.1	50.6	55.4	80	8.6	7.6	9.1
30	48.3	45.9	50.6	85	6.3	5.6	6.7
35	43.6	41.3	45.8	90	4.7	4.1	4.8
40	38.9	36.7	41.0	95	3.5	3.1	3.5
45	34.4	32.3	36.3	100	2.6	2.4	2.7

LIFE EXPECTANCY

This table helps insurance companies determine insurance premiums. *Use the table to find the average number of additional years a 15-year-old male and female are expected to live.*

received the $10,000 proceeds. If Don had lived until the policy had been in effect for 20 years, the insurance company would have paid the $10,000 to him at that time.

Annuity

An **annuity** is a guaranteed retirement income that is purchased by paying either a lump-sum premium or making periodic payments to an insurer. You may choose to receive an income for a certain fixed number of years, with a beneficiary receiving what is left of the annuity when you die. Alternatively, you may choose to receive payments as long as you live, losing what is left of the annuity upon death.

Accidental Death and Dismemberment Insurance

Accidental death and dismemberment insurance provides benefits only when the insured is killed in an accident, loses the use of one or more limbs, or loses sight in one or both eyes. Commonly, if one hand, one foot, or the sight in one eye is lost, the policy pays half the benefit that would be paid for loss of life. Some policies contain a double indemnity clause. If the insured dies accidentally, the beneficiary receives double the amount of the face value of the policy. A policy may also provide monthly payments to the insured for becoming totally disabled. There is often a waiver of premium provision, which means that premiums do not have to be paid as long as the insured is disabled.

ACCIDENT INSURANCE

Accident insurance policies only pay benefits when the insured dies or is injured in an accident. *How much do accident insurance policies commonly pay when an insured loses one hand in an accident?*

Term Insurance

Term insurance is issued for a particular period, usually five or ten years. It is the least expensive kind of life insurance because it has no cash or loan value. Premiums for term insurance increase at the end of each term because the insured is older and is considered a greater risk (see Figure 35.3).

Figure 35.3	Term Life Insurance Premiums					
	Twenty-Year Guaranteed Level Premium Term Insurance Nonsmoker Premiums					
	$300,000 Policy		$400,000 Policy		$500,000 Policy	
Age	Annual	Monthly	Annual	Monthly	Annual	Monthly
25	192.00	16.70	236.00	20.53	280.00	24.36
30	216.00	18.79	268.00	23.32	320.00	27.84
35	270.00	23.49	340.00	29.58	410.00	35.67
45	540.00	46.98	700.00	60.90	860.00	74.82
55	1,140.00	99.18	1,500.00	130.50	1,860.00	161.82

TERM INSURANCE PREMIUMS

Premiums for term insurance increase at the end of each term. *Why is term insurance the least expensive kind of life insurance?*

When buying term life insurance, you should select a policy that can be renewed at the end of each term, regardless of your health. You should also ask for a convertible policy, one that can be exchanged for a cash value policy at a later date, regardless of the state of your health. Term insurance offers protection alone, in contrast to straight life insurance, which combines protection with a savings plan.

Exemptions from Risk

Some states do not allow beneficiaries to receive life insurance proceeds if the insured is legally executed or if the insured is killed by the police while trying to avoid capture. In most cases, the courts allow a beneficiary to receive benefits under a life insurance policy when the insured is murdered, except when the murderer is the beneficiary.

Sometimes people lie about their age to obtain insurance at a lower premium. In such cases, the insurer will still be required to pay a claim, but only based on the amount of insurance that could have been purchased on the basis of the true age of the insured for the premiums that were paid.

The insurer may cancel the policy if the insured makes false statements. It is unjust and unlawful, however, for the insurer to collect premiums for many years and then, upon the death of the insured, refuse to pay because of misrepresentation.

Virtual Law

Insurance Online

Entering into agreements to buy insurance is sometimes frustrating. Shopping for the right coverage on the Internet can be convenient. It can also be confusing because there are so many companies out there. Several major insurance companies have recently joined forces to create one "market place" site. This site will allow consumers to compare coverage offered by these companies. Customers will be able to immediately buy coverage from this site with a credit card. Until now, customers had to hop from one company's Web site to another. Then they had to contact the company directly. The new site promises a more convenient way to shop for insurance. (Source: *New York Times*, February 14, 2001)

Connect Visit the Web sites of a large insurance company to see if it is part of this new way of shopping for insurance.

Health Insurance

Basic health insurance often includes the following benefits:

- Inpatient and outpatient hospital care
- Physician care
- Surgery
- Prescription drugs
- Dental and vision care

Major medical coverage pays for expenses beyond those covered by a basic plan, including long-term hospitalization and the cost of catastrophic illness.

Insurance Plans

Health insurance companies offer a variety of health insurance plans to make some degree of health insurance coverage available to most people. The type of coverage people carry depends on the their individual situations.

Group Plans Many people get their health insurance through a group insurance plan where they work. Insurance companies can offer lower premiums to large groups, and many employers pay part of the premium for each employee. See Figure 35.4 for a listing of basic features that all types of health insurance should offer.

A federal law known as the Consolidated Omnibus Budget Reconciliation Act (COBRA) allows employees to keep their group insurance for a specific period of time after being laid off. Under COBRA,

Community Works

Helmet Laws
Bicycling is a great way to exercise outdoors, but like any sport, there is a chance of injury. Concerned about the possibility of head injuries to cyclists, some states have passed mandatory helmet laws. There are many arguments for and against these laws. *Do you think there is a need for mandatory helmet laws?*

Get Involved
Find out which states have mandatory helmet laws. Write your congressperson a letter telling him or her how you feel about helmet legislation for your state.

Figure 35.4	Health Insurance Must Haves

A health insurance plan should:

- Offer basic coverage for hospital and doctor bills.
- Provide at least 120 days' hospital room and board in full.
- Provide at least a $1 million lifetime maximum for each family member.
- Pay at least 80 percent for out-of-hospital expenses after a yearly deductible of $500 per person or $1,000 per family.
- Impose no unreasonable exclusions.
- Limit your out-of-pocket expenses to no more than $3,000 to $5,000 a year, excluding dental, vision care, and prescription costs.

HEALTH INSURANCE
Although health insurance plans vary greatly, all plans should have the same basic features. *Would you add anything to this list of must haves?*

employees who have been laid off pay their own premiums but can shift to another group plan upon starting a new job.

Individual Plans People who work for a company that does not offer health insurance or who are self-employed can buy individual health insurance. This insurance is more expensive than group insurance because the cost cannot be spread among a large group of people.

HMOs and PPOs

When you sign up for health insurance, you often have a choice between enrolling in an HMO and PPO plan.

Health Maintenance Organizations Health Maintenance Organizations (HMOs) contract with doctors and other healthcare professionals to provide healthcare services for their members. Members pay monthly premiums and must choose from a list of doctors provided by the HMO. HMOs encourage their members to have regular checkups, immunizations, and other forms of early treatment. In this way, it is hoped that people will be less likely to require more expensive kinds of treatment. Many different kinds of organizations sponsor HMOs, including doctors, community groups, insurance companies, labor unions, and corporations.

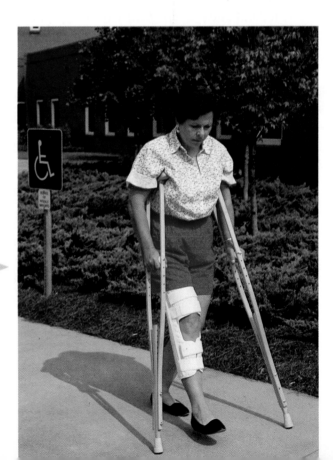

DISABLED
Disability insurance pays benefits when those insured are unable to work. *What is the difference between partial and total disability insurance coverage?*

Preferred Provider Organizations   A Preferred Provider Organization (PPO) is a group of healthcare providers, such as doctors or hospitals, who provide care for groups of employees at reduced rates. PPOs are usually sponsored as part of an employer's group health plan. Employees choose among the healthcare providers on the PPO list when they need treatment. Choosing a non-PPO provider reduces the benefits paid to the insured under the plan.

Government Health Care Plans

People over 65 who are covered by social security are eligible for **Medicare**, a federally funded health insurance program. Medicare Part A helps pay for inpatient hospital care. Medicare Part B pays for 80 percent of doctors' and other medical services. Many people buy their own medigap insurance to cover the 20 percent not covered by Medicare.

Medicaid is a healthcare plan for low-income people. State governments administer Medicaid, which is funded by both state and federal funds.

Disability Insurance

Disability insurance pays you benefits when you can't work because of a disability. It can be purchased from a private insurer. Most often, however, it is paid in whole or in part by the employer. Total, or long-term, disability pays if you can't perform normal job duties for a year or longer; partial, or short-term, disability pays for a few months of being disabled.

Law & Academics

Language Arts
An HMO is a type of prepaid medical service in which members pay a fee for all health services, including hospitalization. A health policy analyst, Dr. Paul Ellwood, coined the term "health maintenance organization" in the early 1970s. The costs to patients are fixed in advance, so preventive medicine is stressed.

Research Activity
HMOs were controversial from the start, and the debate continues all the way to the federal legislators in Washington, D.C. Research HMOs and prepare a debate on the pros and cons of this type of health coverage.

Section 35.2   Assessment

Reviewing What You Learned
1. What are the principal types of life insurance? Briefly describe each one in your own words.
2. What risks are generally not covered by insurance?
3. What benefits are provided by basic health insurance? major medical?

Critical Thinking Activity
Life Insurance Who needs life insurance? Explain your answer.

Legal Skills in Action
Calculating Future Premiums Kim Lee has decided to purchase dental and vision insurance. Her agent quoted her a price of $250 per year but told her the price will probably increase a little each year. If it increases three percent per year every year, what will her premium be 10 years from now?

Property Insurance

What You'll Learn

- How to identify what kinds of loss are covered by homeowner's insurance and fire insurance
- How to calculate the amounts recoverable by homeowners under coinsurance clauses
- How to describe the coverage of marine insurance

Why It's Important

Understanding property insurance will help you protect your property at the lowest cost.

Legal Terms

- property insurance
- binder
- floater policy
- homeowner's insurance
- renter's insurance
- fire insurance
- coinsurance
- ocean marine insurance
- inland marine insurance

Property Insurance

Property insurance is a contract in which the insurer promises, for a stated premium, to pay you a sum of money if a particular piece of real or personal property is damaged or destroyed. The policy becomes effective as soon as the insurer accepts your application, or even sooner if a binder is issued. A **binder** gives you temporary protection until a policy is issued.

A **floater policy** is one that insures property that cannot be covered by specific insurance because it is constantly changing in value or location. A personal property floater, for example, can cover a bicycle, portable stereo, or laptop computer, no matter where the items are located.

Homeowner's and Renter's Insurance

Many insurance companies offer a combination policy known as a homeowner's policy. **Homeowner's insurance** protects against most types of losses and liabilities related to home ownership, including fire, windstorm, vandalism, burglary, and injuries suffered by other persons while on the property. See Figure 35.5 for a more complete listing of some of the losses covered by homeowner's insurance. With certain limitations, homeowner's policies cover your personal property anywhere in the world. **Renter's insurance** protects you against loss of personal property, liability for a visitor's

▲ PROPERTY INSURANCE
Most private property can be insured to reduce the risk of loss. *What are some kinds of protection that are covered by homeowner's insurance?*

Figure 35.5

Losses Covered by Homeowner's Policy

Basic (HO-1)	Basic (HO-2)	Comprehensive (HO-5)
1. Fire or lightning	12. Falling objects	All perils
2. Loss of property removed from premises endangered by fire or other perils	13. Weight of ice, snow, sleet	EXCEPT: earthquake, landslide, flood, surface water, waves, tidal water or tidal wave, the backing up of sewers, seepage, war, and nuclear radiation
3. Windstorm or hail	14. Collapse of building(s) or any part thereof	
4. Explosion	15. Sudden and accidental tearing asunder, cracking, burning, or bulging of a steam or hot water heating system or of appliances for heating water	
5. Riot or civil commotion		
6. Aircraft		
7. Vehicles		
8. Smoke	16. Accidental discharge, leakage, or overflow of water or steam from within a plumbing, heating, or air-conditioning system, or domestic appliance	
9. Vandalism and malicious mischief		
10. Theft	17. Freezing of plumbing, heating, and air conditioning systems, and domestic appliances	
11. Breakage of glass constituting a part of the building	18. Sudden and accidental injury from artificially generated current electrical appliances, devices, fixtures, and wiring	

personal injury, and liability for negligent destruction of the rented premises.

Fire Insurance

Fire insurance covers loss resulting directly from an unfriendly or hostile fire. Damages that result from trying to put out a fire, or from theft or breakage while attempting to remove insured goods to a safe location are considered directly related to the fire and are usually covered by a fire insurance policy. Damage caused by soot, smoke, water, or heat from a nearby burning building is also covered by fire insurance most of the time.

Coinsurance Clauses

Coinsurance is a provision in an insurance policy that limits your recovery for a loss if the property is not insured for its full replacement value. For example, if your insurance policy has an 80 percent coinsurance clause, your house must be insured for 80 percent of its replacement value to receive full reimbursement for a loss (see Figure 35.6).

HOMEOWNER'S INSURANCE
Categories of insurance policies are determined by the number of perils they insure against. *Can homeowner's insurance cover you against all perils?*

A Global Perspective:
Laws Around the World

The Netherlands

Do people who are incurably ill have the right to die? In a landmark decision, in the first year of the second millennium, the Dutch said yes. The Netherlands has become the world's first country to legalize euthanasia.

Greek for "good death," *euthanasia* is defined as the practice of painlessly ending the lives of individuals with incurable or painful diseases or severe handicaps. Although the Dutch "have shut a blind eye" to the practice of euthanasia for many years, a bill passed by Parliament's lower house has made euthanasia legal.

The procedural guidelines are strict:

1. The attending doctor must be sure that the patient's request is voluntary, well thought-out, and that he or she is "facing unremitting and unbearable suffering."
2. The patient and doctor must agree that there is no other acceptable option.
3. The doctor must consult with at least one other doctor who has examined the patient.
4. The procedure must be carried out in a medically acceptable way.

Euthanasia is a subject that not many people agree on. Advances in medical science that prolong life indefinitely, have made it an issue that's not going to go away. Here's a snapshot of the Netherlands.

Geographical area	**16,023 sq. mi.**
Population	**16,067,754**
Capital	**Amsterdam**
Legal system	**Civil law system incorporating French penal theory**
Language	**Dutch**
Religion	**31% Roman catholic**
	21% Protestant
	4.4% Muslim
Life expectancy	**79 years**

Critical Thinking Question Oregon is the only U.S. state that sanctions euthanasia for terminally ill patients. Euthanasia has never been carried out in this state, however, because of court opposition. List some of the reasons why you think people would oppose euthanasia. Then state your opinion about euthanasia. Do you think it should be legal or illegal? Why? For more information on the Netherlands, visit **ubpl.glencoe.com** or your local library.

COINSURANCE CLAUSE

"The insurance company will pay that part of a loss that the insurance carrier bears to 80 percent of the replacement cost of the building."

It would cost $100,000 to replace Zelia's house. If she insured it for $60,000, the insurance company would pay only three-fourths of any loss, computed as follows:

$$\frac{\$60,000}{80\% \text{ of } \$100,000} = \frac{\$60,000}{\$80,000} = \frac{3}{4}$$

A fire partially destroys the building, causing $40,000 worth of damage. Because of the coinsurance clause, Zelia would recover $30,000 (3/4 of the loss) from the insurance company.

COINSURANCE CLAUSE Coinsurance limits the insurer's liability for a loss if the property is not insured for its full replacement value. *What fraction of any loss would the insurance company pay if the house in this example would cost $150,000 to replace?*

Marine Insurance

Marine insurance is one of the oldest kinds of insurance coverage, dating back to Venetian traders who sailed the Mediterranean Sea. **Ocean marine insurance** covers ships at sea. **Inland marine insurance** covers goods that are moved by land carriers such as trains, trucks, and airplanes. Inland marine insurance also covers such items as jewelry, fine arts, musical instruments, and wedding presents. Customers' goods in the possession of bailees, such as fur-storage houses and dry cleaners, are also covered by inland marine insurance.

Section 35.3 Assessment

Reviewing What You Learned

1. What types of losses are covered by homeowner's insurance? fire insurance?
2. What is a coinsurance clause? What does it mean if your policy has an 80 percent coinsurance clause?
3. Explain marine insurance coverage.

Critical Thinking Activity

Renter's Insurance If you decide to go away to college, you will probably rent a dorm room or an apartment. Should you buy renter's insurance? Why or why not?

Legal Skills in Action

Insurance Coverage Lois and Ed carry homeowner's and fire insurance. One day, they put a small pizza in their toaster oven and went outside to chat with neighbors. They forgot about the pizza, which caused a fire in the kitchen. The kitchen was destroyed and the rest of the house was damaged by smoke and ash. With a partner, debate whether Lois and Ed's loss will be covered by either policy.

Chapter Summary

Section 35.1 The Insurance Contract

- The basic purpose of insurance is to spread the losses among a greater number of people. Insurance is a contract under which, for consideration, the insurer, or the insurance company, agrees to compensate you for a specific loss.
- A policy is the written contract between the policyholder and the insurance company that sells it on behalf of the insured, the one whose life or property is being insured. The beneficiary is the person named in the policy to receive the proceeds paid by the insurer in the event of a loss. A rider is an attachment to an insurance policy that modifies the policy's terms. The premium is the amount of money the policyholder pays to the insurance company for insurance coverage.

Section 35.2 Life and Health Insurance

- Straight life insurance requires you to pay premiums throughout your life. Universal life insurance allows you to change the terms of the policy as your needs change. Limited payment life insurance provides that premiums stop after a stated length of time. The proceeds of an endowment policy are paid to the beneficiaries upon the insured's death, or to the insured if alive at the end of an agreed period. An annuity is a guaranteed retirement income paid for either by a lump-sum premium or by periodic payments. Accidental death and dismemberment insurance provides benefits only when you are killed in an accident, lose the use of one or more limbs, or lose sight in one or both eyes. Term insurance covers you for a particular time period, usually five or ten years. Term insurance is the least expensive kind of life insurance because it has no cash or loan value. Premiums for term life insurance increase at the end of each term because the insured is older and considered a greater risk.

- Insurers are exempt from paying when an insured is legally executed, or when the beneficiary murders the insured. Usually beneficiaries can recover for death caused by suicide under a policy that's at least two years old.
- Basic health insurance coverage covers hospital and medical expenses. Major medical insurance pays for medical expenses beyond those covered by a basic plan. Group plans are insurance plans offered through a place of work. Individual plans are for people whose companies do not offer health insurance or for those who are self-employed. People can also opt for coverage by a Health Maintenance Organization (HMO), which is a group of healthcare professionals. A Preferred Provider Organization (PPO) is a group of healthcare providers, such as doctors or hospitals, who provide care for groups of employees at reduced rates. Medicare is the federally funded health insurance program for those over 65, and Medicaid is a healthcare plan for low-income people.

Section 35.3 Property Insurance

- Property insurance covers losses to specific property for a stated premium. A homeowner's policy protects against losses and liabilities related to home ownership. Fire insurance covers loss resulting directly from an unfriendly or hostile fire.
- Coinsurance limits your liability for a loss if the property is not insured for its full replacement value. If the coinsurance clause provides for 80 percent coinsurance, then your house must be insured for 80 percent of its replacement value to receive full reimbursement for a loss.
- Ocean marine insurance covers ships at sea. Inland marine insurance covers goods that are moved by carrier.

Consider the key terms in the list below. Then use these terms to complete the following exercises.

insurance

limited-payment life insurance

policyholder

beneficiary

rider

insurable interest

premium

face value

cash value

life insurance

coinsurance

inland marine insurance

insurer

universal life insurance

endowment insurance

annuity

term insurance

Medicare

Medicaid

property insurance

binder

floater policy

ocean marine insurance

Understanding Business and Personal Law Online

Self-Check Quiz Visit the *Understanding Business and Personal Law* Web site at **ubpl.glencoe.com** and click on Chapter 35: Insurance Protection— Self-Check Quizzes to prepare for the chapter exam.

1. With a partner, create an agenda for an imaginary meeting with an insurance agent. Use as many of the key terms as possible.
2. With a partner, role-play a conversation with an insurance agent to discuss your insurance needs.
3. Present your discussion to the class.

The Law Review

Answer the following questions. Refer to the chapter for additional reinforcement.

4. Would it be possible for you to take out an insurance policy on your teacher's car? Why or why not?
5. What is the difference between the face value and the cash value of a life insurance policy?
6. Why is it usually less expensive to buy life insurance when you are young?
7. Which features should you look for when you purchase term insurance?
8. What is the purpose of a binder?

Linking School to Work

Participating as a Member of a Team
In small groups, create an imaginary person with property who will need insurance. Be as realistic as possible. Negotiate with your team members about what kinds of insurance will be required to protect the person and his or her property interests. Next:

9. Contact four different insurance agents, and ask for premium quotes on life, health, and property insurance.
10. Negotiate with the agents, and review their quotes to determine which agent made the best overall offer.

Be prepared to answer the agents' questions about the imaginary person and property that you created.

Let's Debate

No Need for Insurance?
Arlen is a risk taker. He is a professional stuntman and loves to jump out of burning buildings, drive fast cars, and live from paycheck to paycheck. Recently, his friend Pam asked Arlen about the insurance he carries. Arlen just laughed—he doesn't believe in insurance. "It is a waste of money," he says.

Debate
11. Explain the importance of life, health, and property insurance to Arlen.
12. What type of insurance would you recommend that Arlen purchase first? Explain your answer.

Grasping Case Issues

For the following cases, give your decision and state a legal principle that applies.

13. Al Zuni Trading, Inc. purchased a $1 million life insurance policy on the life of Thomas McKee, one of its officers. McKee resigned from the company three months later, and died two years after that. Is Al Zuni Trading, Inc. entitled to the million dollars? Explain your answer.
14. Antoinette Gareau is seriously ill and needs to be hospitalized. A friend recommends a certain hospital that specializes in treating her illness. An HMO provides Antoinette's health insurance. Will it cover services in any hospital that she chooses? Why or why not?
15. Alphonse Weible purchased a straight life insurance policy on his life. After paying premiums regularly for six years, he lost his job and stopped making payments. After a grace period, the insurance company canceled the policy. Is Alphonse entitled to a refund of some of the money he paid to the insurance company? Explain your answer.
16. Yang Pak insured his house for $32,000, under a fire insurance policy that contains an 80 percent coinsurance clause. The house is worth $80,000. An accidental fire caused $10,000 of damage to the house. How much money will Yang receive from the insurance company?
17. Zane Lewis stated in his application for life insurance that he was 22 years old, when he was actually 28. After paying premiums for five years, Zane died, and the insurance company discovered his correct age. The company refused to settle on the policy, claiming material misrepresentation. Will the insurance company have to pay the claim? Explain your answer.

In each case that follows, you be the judge.

18. Life Insurance

Chester Henrikson, Sr. purchased a $10,000 life insurance policy on the life of his son, Chester, Jr. For the first nine years of the policy's life, Chester, Sr. and his wife were listed as primary beneficiaries of the policy. In the tenth year, Chester, Sr. had his wife's name removed. Two years later, Chester, Sr. was found guilty of the voluntary manslaughter of Chester, Jr. *Is Chester, Sr. entitled to the proceeds of the insurance policy? Why or why not?*
New York Life Insurance Co. v. Henrikson, 415 N.E.2d 146 (IN).

19. Accident Insurance

William Galindo, Jr. suffered a broken neck while playing in a high school football game. As a result of that injury, Galindo is a quadriplegic. The high school had an accident insurance policy that paid the following: $10,000 for the loss of both hands or both arms and $10,000 for the loss of both feet or both legs. The policy also contained the following words: "Maximum Dismemberment Benefit $10,000." *Is Galindo entitled to these insurance proceeds? If so, how much? Explain your answer.*
Galindo v. Guarantee Trust Life Insurance Co., 414 N.E.2d 265 (IL).

Legal Link

Life in the Mile High City

Denise has recently graduated from college and is working in Denver, Colorado. She is renting an apartment. As she is settling in to her new job and life, she thinks she might need some insurance. She would especially like to protect against risks to her health, life, and personal belongings.

Connect

Using a variety of search engines, find out:

20. What types of insurance Denise can purchase online.
21. How to obtain quotes for life, health, and renter's insurance through a Web site.

POWER READING STRATEGIES

22. **Predict** Why do you think people buy insurance? Why wouldn't they just save for a problem that might occur?

23. **Connect** Is there any type of insurance you think you should have at your age? Explain.

24. **Question** Insurance companies rely on statistics to determine the cost they charge policyholders. Is this fair? Why or why not?

25. **Respond** Do you think it is the government's responsibility to provide health insurance for those over 65 years of age?

Retirement and Wills

Understanding Business and Personal Law Online

Chapter Overview Visit the *Understanding Business and Personal Law* Web site at ubpl.glencoe.com and click on Chapter 36: Retirement and Wills— Chapter Overviews to preview the chapter information.

The Opening Scene

Patrick is working on his laptop computer as Robin arrives home with her sister, Tatiana.

Bright Future

PATRICK: Hi, honey! How was your interview?

ROBIN: Wonderful! I got the job!

PATRICK: Great! Will you be doing the same kind of work you do now?

ROBIN: No, even better—I'm starting as a supervisor. It's a young company, so there should be lots of room for advancement. They were impressed with the fact that I have a college degree.

PATRICK: I knew that would make a difference.

TATIANA: How's the pay?

ROBIN: My starting salary will be $5,000 more than what I make now! The benefits are good, too. They even have a noncontributory pension plan.

TATIANA: Is that important?

ROBIN: The one I have now is contributory.

PATRICK: You have two years of pension benefits already accumulated.

ROBIN: Yes, and I hope I don't lose them by changing jobs. With our social security and my pension, we should have a long, happy retirement.

PATRICK: I hope it won't be like Mr. Kulak's. He worked hard all his life and collapsed a week after he retired. It must be hard for his daughter, Martha. I can't imagine what it must be like to lose your father and mother in the same year!

TATIANA: She's the only one left in their family now. Did you know that she was adopted?

PATRICK: I hope she doesn't have trouble inheriting from her father's estate, being adopted. I wonder if he had a will.

ROBIN: A lady in the grocery store told me that if you die without a will, the state takes everything. I hope that doesn't happen to Martha! Mr. Kulak worked so hard all those years, and his daughter should receive his money.

TATIANA: I hope she does.

ROBIN: Speaking of wills, Patrick, you and I don't have wills.

PATRICK: I had a will once, before we were married. I have no idea what happened to it. I'll look around for it.

ROBIN: You probably left everything to your old girlfriend.

TATIANA: *(Laughing.)* Ha! That would be something if your old girlfriend inherited everything instead of Robin.

ROBIN: That's what you think! There's a lawyer in the building where I work. Maybe I'll stop in to see her tomorrow about our wills.

PATRICK: That's a good idea. I hope you don't have some old boyfriend in mind to leave things to.

ROBIN: No. I'm going to leave everything to you, Patrick. If you're not alive when I die, everything will go to Tatiana.

TATIANA: Whenever you're ready, sis, I'll be the first witness!

What Are the Legal Issues?

1. How does a contributory pension plan differ from a noncontributory pension plan?
2. May workers transfer pension benefits from one job to another?
3. From whom do adopted children inherit?
4. Does the state take the property of a person who dies without a will?
5. Is a surviving spouse given any legal protection when omitted from a deceased spouse's will?

Retirement Income

What You'll Learn

- **How to describe the main features of social security**
- **How to discuss the retirement benefits offered by employer pension plans**
- **How to explain the pension rights given to employees under ERISA**
- **How to distinguish among the various personal retirement plans**

Why It's Important

Learning about different types of retirement plans will help you predict what your financial situation and needs will be when you retire.

Legal Terms

- **pension plan**
- **401(k) plan**
- **vesting**
- **portability**
- **Individual Retirement Account (IRA)**
- **Keogh Plan**

Public Pension Plans

The federal government administers social security, railroad pensions, military pensions, and civil service pensions. Many state and local governments also provide pensions for their employees.

Social Security

Social security provides income to people when their regular income stops because of retirement, disability, or the death of someone who had provided them with income (see Figure 36.1). You and your dependents become eligible for social security benefits when you work at a job that is covered by social security. While working at such a job, you receive work credits—units that stand for a specific amount of money earned during a calendar quarter. A worker can earn four work credits in one year.

Example 1. Carlos earned $3,640 during the first quarter (three months) of 2001, $790 during the second quarter, $900 during the

Figure 36.1	Retirement Age to Receive Social Security Benefits	
People Born in	**Receive Full Benefits At Age**	
1938	65 and 2 months	
1939	65 and 4 months	
1940	65 and 6 months	
1941	65 and 8 months	
1942	65 and 10 months	
1943–54	66	
1955	66 and 2 months	
1956	66 and 4 months	
1957	66 and 6 months	
1958	66 and 8 months	
1959	66 and 10 months	
1960 or later	67	

GETTING SOCIAL SECURITY
Most people receive social security benefits when they retire. *At what age will you be able to receive full social security benefits?*

SOCIAL SECURITY
BENEFITS
Social security is an
important source of
income for many retired
people. *How are social
security benefits
calculated?*

Community
Works

Retired Hire
Did you ever wonder
why some elderly indi-
viduals are working
instead of enjoying
their retirement? Some
enjoy being in the
public, but others need
extra money because
their retirement income
isn't enough to cover
their expenses. Many
teens think they are
too young to worry
about retirement.
However, according to
Merrill Lynch, if you
started a Roth IRA at
age 16 and maximized
your yearly contribu-
tions, when you turned
46, you would have
an after-tax salary of
$25,480 for the next
20 years. *What do
you think is the best
age to start saving
for retirement?*

Get involved
Get a part-time job and
begin saving a small
percentage of your
salary each month.
Investigate other
relatively risk free
money market options.

third quarter, and nothing during the fourth quarter. In 2001, workers covered by social security received one credit for $830 of earned income in a calendar quarter. Carlos received two social security work credits for the year 2001—one for the first quarter and one for the third quarter.

With certain exceptions, workers need 40 work credits to become eligible for social security benefits. Forty work credits equal ten years of contributions to the fund. However, the ten work years do not need to be consecutive. The actual amount to be paid by social security will depend on your average earnings over a period of years. The more you earn, the more you receive in benefits, up to a certain limit.

People born before 1938 can retire at the age of 65 and receive full benefits, or they can retire at 62 and receive reduced benefits. The minimum age at which you can retire and still receive full benefits is gradually increasing.

Workers are entitled to disability benefits under the social security law if they have a physical or mental condition that prevents them from doing substantial, gainful work and if the condition has lasted (or is expected to last) for at least 12 months. Workers are also considered disabled if they have any condition that is expected to result in death.

Employer Retirement Plans

A **pension plan** is a retirement plan that is funded at least in part by an employer. The company where you work may offer a pension plan to supplement social security. If it is financed entirely by the employer,

Chapter 36: *Retirement and Wills* **773**

it is called a noncontributory pension plan. Most employer pension plans, however, are contributory pension plans financed by employees alone or by the combined contributions of employers and employees.

Under a **401(k) plan**, employees agree to forgo a bonus or take a salary reduction to invest in a retirement plan. Employers sometimes match the amount contributed by employees. A similar plan for employees of nonprofit organizations is known as a 403(b) plan. Funds in either plan are not taxed until the money is withdrawn, but the money cannot be withdrawn without penalty before the age of 59 1/2. Lower income workers are entitled to tax credits when they save for retirement.

Defined-Benefit Plans

Defined-benefit plans are the most common type of employer pension plan. Under this type of plan, employees receive a definite, predetermined amount of money upon retirement or disability. The fixed amount is based on an employee's years of service; the amount of the monthly benefit is an amount of money fixed in advance for each year of service. For example, a plan may pay $30 per month for each year of service. If you worked 20 years for the company, your pension would be $600 per month. Payments may also be calculated based on a percentage of your wages over the years. The employer must contribute necessary amounts to ensure that benefits will be paid at retirement.

Defined-Contribution Plans

In defined-contribution plans, an employer pays a certain amount into a pension fund every month (or every year) for each employee. The amount contributed is usually a fixed percentage of the employee's wages or salary.

Employee Retirement Income Security Act

The Employee Retirement Income Security Act (ERISA) places many controls on the management of pension funds and gives certain rights to workers. Under the act, employers must place employees' pension contributions into a pension trust, independent of the employer. Workers are guaranteed the right to receive pension benefits regardless of whether they are working under the plan at the time of retirement.

Under ERISA, employees' contributions vest immediately, and all pension benefits must vest after a worker has been on the job for three years. The **vesting** of retirement benefits is the act of giving a worker a guaranteed right to receive a future pension.

Workers may transfer benefits from one company's pension plan to the plan of another company, from one company's pension plan to an individual retirement plan, or from an individual retirement plan to a company plan. The ability to transfer pension benefits from one job to another is called **portability**.

It is important to investigate and take advantage of the retirement options afforded by your employer, even early in your career. Your willingness to start early in preparing for retirement can make a significant difference in your level of future income (see Figure 36.2).

Virtual Law

Teachers' Fund Invests in High Technology

In 2002, the Teachers' Retirement System of Louisiana filed a lawsuit against software maker Siebel Systems, Inc. The lawsuit alleged that the firm's directors violated the company's rules for granting stock options by exceeding the limits set on the number of stock options it was allowed to grant and by issuing options at below market value without correctly expensing the difference in price. At the time, Siebel's stock price had fallen. The Teachers' Retirement System claimed that they suffered financial losses because the excessive stock option grants diluted the value of their shares and contributed to the fall in price.

Connect Visit the Web site of your state's public employees' retirement system. See if it mentions whether the fund invests in high-tech companies.

Tax-deferred investments, such as IRAs, can grow considerably by the time you retire if you start investing in them early. *In this figure, which person contributed more money to the retirement plan? Which one earned more by age 65? Why?*

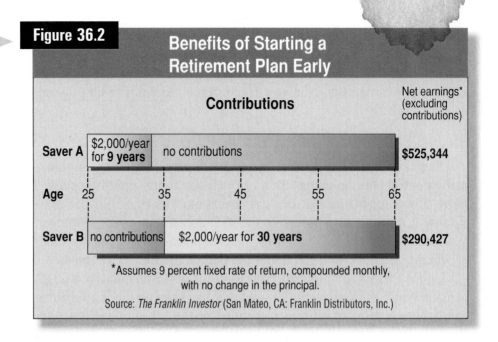

Figure 36.2

Benefits of Starting a Retirement Plan Early

	Contributions		Net earnings* (excluding contributions)
Saver A	$2,000/year for **9 years**	no contributions	**$525,344**
Age	25　　　　35　　　　45　　　　55　　　　65		
Saver B	no contributions	$2,000/year for **30 years**	**$290,427**

*Assumes 9 percent fixed rate of return, compounded monthly, with no change in the principal.

Source: *The Franklin Investor* (San Mateo, CA: Franklin Distributors, Inc.)

Personal Retirement Plans

Self-employed persons and employees who are not covered by company pension plans have the same retirement needs as others. However, unlike employees of a large business, self-employed persons are unable to share the burden of setting up a retirement plan with a group of people. The retirement funds must come from their own pockets.

Individual Retirement Accounts

An **Individual Retirement Account (IRA)** is an individual's own personal pension plan (see Figure 36.3 for a summary of the various types of IRAs). It is a system of providing for retirement by saving part of your earnings every year. The earlier you start saving, the more you will have when you retire. Investing early also allows you to take greater advantage of compound interest, which is interest earned on both the principle amount in the account and the interest already earned on the account, or interest on the interest.

ROTH IRA

A Roth IRA is an attractive way to save for retirement. *What are some of the benefits of this type of IRA?*

Figure 36.3	Various Types of IRAs
Type of IRA	**Features**
Regular IRA	• Tax-deferred interest and earnings • $3,000* annual limit • Limited eligibility for tax-deductible contributions • Contributions do not reduce current taxes
Roth IRA	• Tax-deferred interest and earnings • $3,000* annual limit on individual contributions • Withdrawals are tax-free in specific cases • Contributions do not reduce current taxes
Simplified Employee Pension Plan (SEP-IRA)	• "Pay yourself first" payroll reduction contributions • Pre-tax contributions • Tax-deferred interest and earnings
Simple IRA	• Contributions by employer and employee • $7,000 ($10,000 by 2005) maximum employee annual contribution • Tax-deferred interest and earnings • Subject to same rules as Regular IRA
Spousal IRA	• Tax-deferred interest and earning • Both working spouse and nonworking spouse can contribute up to $3,000 each year • Limited eligibility for tax-deductible contributions • Contributions do not reduce current taxes
Rollover IRA	• Traditional IRA that accepts rollovers of all or a portion of your taxable distribution from a retirement plan • You can rollover to a Roth IRA
Coverdale Education Savings Account	• Tax-deferred interest and earning • 10% early withdrawal penalty is waived when money is used for higher-education expenses • $2,000 annual limit on individual contributions • Contributions do not reduce current taxes

*Increases to $4,000 in 2005, $5,000 in 2008, and indexed for inflation thereafter.

Traditional IRA Amounts up to $3,000 (increasing to $5,000 by 2008) may be set aside annually for retirement under a traditional IRA. Contributions are tax deductible if your income is below a certain amount, and interest is tax deferred until the money is withdrawn. Unless used for certain home purchases and higher education costs, funds cannot be withdrawn without penalty before you reach the age of $59 \frac{1}{2}$. When you become $70 \frac{1}{2}$ years old, you must begin taking minimum required distributions and paying taxes on the money you withdraw.

CHOOSING AN IRA
IRAs can be a good way to save money for retirement. *What are the features of the Coverdale Education Savings Account?*

Roth IRA   A Roth IRA is an attractive way to save for retirement. Distributions (withdrawals) are not required during your lifetime. When taken after age 59 1/2, distributions are tax free if you have had the account for five years.

Coverdale Education Savings Account   A Coverdale Education Savings Account can be established for a child under eighteen by anyone who wants to save for the child's college education. The interest on the savings is tax free and there is no early withdrawal penalty. The amount saved for each child may not exceed $2,000 a year.

Simplified Employee Pension Plan   A Simplified Employee Pension Plan (SEP) is an IRA funded by an employer. Money is withheld from an employee's pay and placed in the IRA account. Employers may contribute up to 25 percent of the employee's pay or $41,000—whichever is lower. The money invested in the plan is not taxed until it is withdrawn and cannot be withdrawn without penalty before the age of 59 1/2.

Keogh Plans

A **Keogh plan** is a retirement plan for self-employed people and their employees. Contributions to the plan are tax deductible, and the interest earned is tax-deferred until the money is withdrawn. The savings can build to age 70 1/2, at which time the retiree must begin to withdraw the money.

Section 36.1   Assessment

Reviewing What You Learned

1. What is the purpose of social security?
2. Explain the difference between a noncontributory and a contributory pension plan.
3. What are the pension rights given to people under ERISA?
4. Describe a traditional IRA, a Roth IRA, a Coverdale Education Savings Account, a Simplified Employee Pension Plan, and a Keogh plan.

Critical Thinking Activity

Preparing for Retirement Many Americans believe that if they are covered under an employer's retirement plan, they will have a satisfactory income after they retire. Explain the flaw in this reasoning.

Legal Skills in Action

Evaluating Retirement Plans As you think about your future career, the retirement plan that a job offers is an important benefit to consider. Evaluate the different types of plans discussed in this section and choose the one you think is best for you. With a partner, explain the reasons for your selection.

Estate Planning

Making a Will

A **will** is a document that is signed during your lifetime that provides for the distribution of your property upon death. Each state has its own requirements for making a will. Figure 36.4 shows a sample will.

A person who dies with a will is said to die **testate** and is called a testator (male) or a testatrix (female). A gift of personal property that is made by will is called a **bequest**, or legacy. A gift of real property that is made by will is called a **devise** in most states. Some states refer to a gift in a will of both real and personal property as a devise. Those who receive property by will are referred to as beneficiaries. They are also known (in most states) as legatees if they receive personal property and as devisees if they receive real property under a will. The term **heir** refers to one who inherits property under a will or from someone dying without a will.

Who May Make a Will

Any person of sound mind who has reached the age of adulthood (eighteen years) may make a will. You reach eighteen on the day before your eighteenth birthday (see Chapter 7). To be of sound mind, you must have sufficient mental capacity to do the following:

- Understand the nature and extent of your property
- Know who would be the natural persons to inherit your property, even though you may leave your property to anyone you choose
- Know that you are making a will
- Be free from delusions that might influence the dispensation of your property

Formal Requirements of a Will

To be valid, a will must conform exactly to the law of the state where it is made. A will that is legally made in one state will be recognized as valid in every state.

With the exception of nuncupative (oral) wills of personal property by soldiers and mariners, a will must be in writing. It must be signed and witnessed by the number of witnesses required by state law—usually two. A signature can be any mark (such as an X) that is intended by the testator to be a signature. When a testator is paralyzed and cannot write, someone else can sign in the testator's presence and with the testator's

LAST WILL AND TESTAMENT
OF
JANET L. SCANLON

I, JANET L. SCANLON, of Groveland, County of Essex, Commonwealth of Massachusetts, make this my Last Will and Testament, hereby revoking all earlier wills and codicils.

ARTICLE I

I give, devise, and bequeath all my estate, real, personal, and mixed and wherever situated to my husband, Mathew A. Scanlon, if he is living on the thirtieth day after my death.

ARTICLE II

If my husband, MATHEW A. SCANLON is not living on the thirtieth day after my death, I give and devise all of my property of every kind and wherever located that I own at the time of my death or to which I am then in any way entitled in equal shares to my children, RYAN M. SCANLON and COREY L. SCANLON, but if either of them shall not be living, his share thereof shall pass to his issue then living by the right of representation, and in default of such issue then his share shall pass to the survivor of them.

I, the undersigned testator, do hereby declare that I sign and execute this instrument as my last will, that I sign it willingly in the presence of each said witnesses, and that I execute it as my free and voluntary act for the purposes herein expressed, this 15th day of January 20--.

_____
Janet L. Scanlon

We, the undersigned witnesses, each do hereby declare in the presence of the aforesaid testator that the testator signed and executed this instrument as her last will and in the presence of each of us, that she signed it willingly, that each of us hereby signs this will as witness in the presence of the testator, and that to the best of our knowledge the testator is eighteen (18) years of age or over, of sound mind, and under no constraint or undue influence.

_____   _____
(Witness)   (address)

_____   _____
(Witness)   (address)

COMMONWEALTH OF MASSACHUSETTS
COUNTY OF ESSEX

Subscribed, sworn to, and acknowledged before me by the said testator and witness this 15th day of January 20--.

_____
Carl Pierce, Notary Public

SAMPLE WILL
A will must be signed and witnessed by the number of witnesses required by state law. *In whose presence did the testatrix and the witnesses sign this will?*

consent. In many states, a holographic will, that is, a will written entirely in the handwriting of the testator, is valid without witnesses.

Revoking or Changing a Will

In some states, a will may be revoked by burning, tearing, canceling, or obliterating the will with intent to revoke it; executing a new one; and marrying after the will was created. A divorce usually revokes gifts made under a will to a former spouse. A **codicil** is a formal document used to supplement or change an existing will. It must be signed and witnessed just like a will to be valid.

Family Protection

State laws contain provisions designed to protect surviving family members when a spouse dies. Some states provide for a family allowance, or money taken from the decedent's estate to meet the family's needs while the estate is being settled. Another family protection is the homestead exemption, which puts the family home beyond the reach of creditors up to a certain limit. Still another protective device in some states is exempt property, which is certain property of a decedent that passes to the surviving spouse or children and is beyond the reach of creditors. In some states, for example, $3,500 worth of personal property passes automatically to the surviving spouse, or if none exists, to surviving children equally.

Protection of Spouses

A surviving spouse who doesn't like the provisions of a deceased spouse's will may choose to take a different portion of the estate set by state statute. This is known as a surviving spouse's elective or forced share.

▶ PEACE OF MIND
Preparing a will can make things easier for your family after your death and ensure that your estate is distributed according to your wishes. *Although you cannot make a will before you are 18 years old, what would happen if you were to die without a will after that age?*

Law & Academics

Computer Technology
Where will your life lead you? You can predict what your life might be like in the next few years, but it is difficult to imagine what the future will really hold. Technology is similar. It changes so fast and sometimes takes turns we don't expect.

Research Activity
Imagine what your life will be like in 20 years. How will technology affect your life? What impact will it have on your career, your living arrangements, and your leisure activities? How will it change the way you plan for your retirement? Create a computerized presentation explaining your vision for the future.

Careers in Law

Legal Columnist

When the topic is the First Amendment, lawyers, judges, and legal scholars around the country read and heed the opinions of Charles Levendosky. Levendosky's newspaper columns have been published in the *Los Angeles Times,* the *Atlanta Journal-Constitution,* the *Baltimore Sun,* and the *International Herald-Tribune.*

In fact, Levendosky has little formal training or education relating to the law. Levendosky majored in physics, math, and secondary education and has published almost a dozen books of poetry. He studies the First Amendment because it protects the rights of writers and artists to express their opinions.

"Writers shine a little light on the human condition," says Levendosky, who has served as Wyoming's poet-in-residence for over a decade. He became interested in free speech issues after two families attempted to censor books in Wyoming schools.

Levendosky began educating himself by studying every First Amendment decision written by the Supreme Court, reading books by First Amendment scholars, and talking with experts. In 1994, the *Casper Star-Tribune* asked him to write a cyber column about First Amendment issues. Once a year, the newspaper, which was one of the earliest to expand to the Internet, sends Levendosky to Washington, D.C. to hear oral arguments before the Supreme Court. Seeing the Supreme Court in action has given Charles Levendosky added perspective on First Amendment issues.

"I see my role as helping people find answers about their First Amendment rights, or putting them in touch with the experts who can," he says from his home office in Casper.

Skills	Analytical, communication, computer, willingness to listen to sources you disagree with
Personality	Must have a passion for what you do; a self-starter, never satisfied with "just okay"
Education	"High school students should start educating themselves by understanding the Supreme Court decisions about children's First Amendment rights and how those decisions affect them. It's important for students to know that even though their rights are not the same as those of adults, young people have fought for their own rights and changed the law."

For more information on legal columnists, visit **ubpl.glencoe.com**, or your public library.

FAMILY PROTECTION
State laws have provisions to protect surviving family members when a spouse dies. *What are some of the family-protection devices?*

Laid-Off or Early Retirement

Manolo is 55 years old. He has worked for the past 15 years as a fork-lift operator in a ware-house and hopes to work for several more years. However, his company is "downsizing," and his employer told him that he could either take early retirement or be laid off. By taking early retirement, Manolo would have access to his retirement funds and perhaps pay hefty taxes on them. By being laid off, Manolo's retirement would stay with the company, and he would have very little income until he could find another job, which could be difficult for a man his age. *In your opinion, What does Manolo owe the company? What does the company owe Manolo?*

Protection of Children

Children who can prove that they were mistakenly left out of a parent's will are protected by the laws of most states. Forgotten children will receive the same share that they would have received if their parent had died without a will. Children who are intentionally omitted from a parent's will do not have this protection.

Example 2. Edward Morley's will gave a large sum of money to charity and provided nothing for his son, Dennis. The will contained a clause stating, "I intentionally omit to provide for my son, Dennis Morley." Because Edward's intent was clear, Dennis will receive nothing from his father's estate.

Adopted children are treated, in most states, as though they were the naturally born children of their adoptive parents. They inherit from their adoptive parents rather than from their natural parents.

Dying Without a Will

A person who dies without a will is said to have died **intestate**. The deceased's personal property is distributed according to the laws of intestate succession of the state in which the deceased was domiciled.

Figure 36.5

Distribution of Intestate Property Under a Typical State Statute*

If you are survived by:	Your estate is distributed:
1. Spouse and child(ren)	One half to spouse, one half to children
2. Spouse, no children, but next of kin (including parents, siblings, niece, nephew, aunt, uncle, cousin, etc.)	Where the estate is less than $200,000, all to spouse. If the estate is larger than $200,000, the first $200,000 plus one half of everything in excess of $200,000 to spouse. The remainder to next of kin in this order: parents(s), siblings, nieces and nephews, grandparents, uncles and aunts, cousins.
3. Spouse, no child, no next of kin	All to spouse
4. No spouse, one or more children	All to children
5. No spouse, no child, but next of kin	All to next of kin, in the order described above in 2.
6. No spouse, no child, no next of kin	All "escheats" to the state, that is, all turned over to the state because there are no heirs or beneficiaries.

*Massachusetts Law of Descent and Distribution Law of Intestate Succession (G.L. c. 190 §1)

INTESTATE SUCCESSION
Each state has its own law of intestate succession. *What does such a law determine?*

In contrast, the real property passes according to the law where the property is located. Figure 36.5 shows Massachusetts' laws of intestate succession. Dying without a professionally drafted and legally valid will can have serious consequences. Not only are the intentions of the deceased subject to question and legal challenge, but beneficiaries may be forced to pay significant administrative fees, legal costs, and estate taxes. As a result, it is usually wise to have a valid will, especially if you are married, have children, or there are others who are dependent upon you for support.

In general, the surviving spouse is entitled to one-third or one-half of the estate. The balance of the estate is usually divided equally among the deceased's children. If any children are deceased, then grandchildren share equally in their deceased parent's share of their grandparent's estate. If all children are deceased, all grandchildren share equally in their grandparent's estate. If there are no children or grandchildren, the property goes to the decedent's parents, if living, and if not, to brothers and sisters of the decedent. The children of any deceased brothers or sisters (nieces and nephews) take their parent's share of the estate.

If there are no brothers or sisters or nieces or nephews, uncles and aunts inherit the property. If no uncles or aunts survive the decedent, cousins become the heirs. It is only when a person is survived by no blood relatives that the property will escheat; that is, become the property of the state.

Settling an Estate

When people die owning assets, their estate must be probated; that is, it must be settled under the supervision of the probate court. The first job of the probate court is to establish the validity of the will. If no one opposes the probating of the will, this can be a simple matter. Sometimes, however, heirs who are left out of a will may contest it.

A will usually names a personal representative called an **executor** (male) or **executrix** (female) to carry out the terms of the will. If there is no will, or if the executor or executrix named in the will fails to perform, someone must petition the court to settle the estate. That person, when appointed, is called an administrator or administratrix. The executor or administrator gathers the estate assets, pays the debts and taxes, and distributes the remainder of the assets according to the terms of the will or state law.

Section 36.2   Assessment

Reviewing What You Learned

1. Who may make a will?
2. What are the formal requirements of a will?
3. How can a will be changed or revoked?
4. Explain how surviving family members are protected legally when a spouse dies.
5. What happens when a person dies without a will?
6. Discuss the legal procedure that must be followed when someone dies owning property.

Critical Thinking Activity

Power of Attorney Reconsider what you learned about the power of attorney in Chapter 18, and think about how it relates to what you have learned about wills in this chapter. Identify methods of conducting transactions in spite of an incapacity or death, via power of attorney or will.

Legal Skills in Action

Calculating Estate Distribution According to Doug's will, his widow will receive one-half of his estate and each of his two children will receive one-third of the remainder. Doug's best friend will receive three-fourths of the balance of his estate, and his favorite charity will receive the remainder. Assuming that Doug's estate totals $300,000, how much will each party receive?

Chapter Summary

Section 36.1 **Retirement Income**

- Social security provides income to people when their regular income stops because of retirement, disability, or the death of someone who had provided them with income. You and your dependents become eligible for social security benefits when you work at a job that is covered by social security.

- A pension plan is a retirement plan that is funded at least in part by an employer. If the plan is financed entirely by the employer, it is called a noncontributory pension plan. A plan that is financed by the combined contributions of employers and employees is a contributory pension plan. Most employer pension plans are contributory, and many employers match the amount contributed by the employee. Under a 401(k) plan, an employee invests in a retirement plan, which is not taxed until the money is withdrawn. Under a defined-benefit plan, an employee receives a predetermined amount of money upon retirement or disability. Under a defined-contribution plan, an employer pays a certain amount into a pension fund every month, which is paid upon retirement or disability.

- The Employee Retirement Income Security Act (ERISA) requires that the employer place his or her employees' pension contributions into a pension trust.

- Individual retirement accounts (IRAs) allow you to provide for retirement by saving a part of your earnings every year into an account with favorable tax implications. Funds in a Roth IRA are free from tax when withdrawn after age 59 1/2. The interest in an Education IRA is tax free, and there is no early withdrawal penalty. Contributions to a Keogh plan are tax deductible and the interest is tax deferred.

Section 36.2 **Estate Planning**

- Any person of a sound mind who has reached the age of adulthood may make a will. To be of sound mind means you have sufficient mental capacity to understand the nature and extent of your property, know the natural persons to inherit your property, know that you are making a will, and be free from delusions.

- To be valid, a will must be in writing, signed, and witnessed.

- In some states, wills may be revoked by burning, tearing, canceling, or obliterating the document with the intent of revoking it; by executing a new will; and by changing marital status. A will is changed by making a new will or by adding a codicil.

- Surviving family members are protected from an unfavorable will by such things as family allowance, homestead exemption, and exempt property. A surviving spouse who does not like the provisions of a deceased spouse's will may choose to take a different portion of the estate, as determined by state law. Children who are mistakenly omitted from a parent's will may receive the share they would have received had the parent died without a will.

- The personal property of a person who dies intestate goes to that person's heirs according to the law of the state where the decedent was domiciled. Real property passes according to the law where the property is located. If there are no surviving blood relatives, the property goes to the state. The personal property of a person who dies testate is distributed according to the instructions in that person's will.

- When someone dies owning assets, the executor or administrator gathers the assets, pays the debts and taxes, and distributes the remainder according to the terms of the will or state law.

Using Legal Language

Consider the key terms in the list below. Then use these terms to complete the following exercises.

401(k) plan
vesting
portability
Individual Retirement
   Account (IRA)
Keogh Plan
will

testate
bequest
devise
heir
codicil
intestate
executor/executrix

1. Write a letter to a relative, and make recommendations to him or her about saving for retirement and making a will. Use as many of the key terms as possible in your letter. Make sure to emphasize the benefits of starting a retirement savings plan as early as possible.
2. Exchange letters with a partner and write a response to your partner's letter. Be sure to correct any mistaken or confusing uses of the key terms.
3. Save your letter, and share it with your relative.

Understanding Business and Personal Law Online

Self-Check Quiz Visit the *Understanding Business and Personal Law* Web site at **ubpl.glencoe.com** and click on Chapter 36: Retirement and Wills— Self-Check Quizzes to prepare for the chapter exam.

The Law Review

Answer the following questions. Refer to the chapter for additional reinforcement.
4. How do you become eligible for social security benefits?
5. Saving for your retirement is extremely important. What might be the advantages of contributing to a contributory retirement plan? What might be the disadvantages?
6. What are the requirements to be "of sound mind"?
7. In general, how much of an estate is a surviving spouse entitled to when his or her spouse dies?
8. What is the difference between an executor/executrix and an administrator/administratrix?

Linking School to Work

Acquiring and Evaluating Information
Establishing a plan for your retirement savings is important.
9. Interview someone who has retired.
10. Find out how that person prepared for retirement.
11. Ask for any advice he or she would offer a young person preparing to enter the workforce.

As a class, analyze the advice given and prepare a "Top 10" list of the best suggestions.

Let's Debate

No Need for a Will?
Justin is 30 years old and single. He works as a network technician for a large company and is vested in his employer's pension plan. Justin just bought his first home, drives a red sports car, and has several thousand dollars in savings. Justin doesn't have a will; he doesn't think he needs one because he isn't married and only has one nephew.

Debate
12. Would you recommend Justin make a will? Why or why not?
13. What would happen to Justin's assets and debts if he were to die without a will?
14. At what age do you think someone should make a will?
15. When do you plan on making your first will?
16. Do your parents have wills? If no, why not?

Grasping Case Issues

For the following cases, give your decision and state a legal principle that applies.
17. After working for Datatech Corporation for 10 years, Harry Bailey took a position with another company. Datatech Corporation notified Bailey that his pension benefits under the noncontributory pension plan terminated when he left. Does Bailey have any legal rights? Explain your answer.
18. Darius Pelzer lived on a small income he had from property he inherited. After he reached 65 years of age, however, inflation made it difficult for him to live on this income. He applied for social security benefits. Will he get the benefits? Why or why not?
19. After Peter Ramirez's death, two wills that he had made were found. One was dated May 20, 1986, and the other was marked June 17, 2001. Which should be accepted by the court? Explain your answer.
20. Betsy Addis signs her will and has Paula Cantini, a friend, sign as a witness. Is this will valid? Explain your answer.
21. Bertha Bogart made her will according to the laws of her state. Six months later, she decided to leave a favorite uncle $2,000. She orally notified the executor named in her will, but she did not change her will. May the executor give Bogart's uncle the $2,000? Why or why not?
22. Jean Johnson became angry at her son and tore up the original copy of her will, which had included a generous bequest to the son. She made a new will, leaving her son $1. After Johnson's death the son tried to have the will set aside in favor of the previous will, a copy of which was found among Johnson's papers. Do you think the son will succeed? Why or why not?

In each case that follows, you be the judge.

23. Social Security

Carmen Ciciretti filed his application for retirement benefits under the Social Security Act and died 10 days later. The Social Security Administration, unaware of his death, sent him a check for $677.60. The executor of Ciciretti's estate returned the check to the Social Security Administration, asking for a check made payable to him as the executor of the estate. The Administration sent a check to Ciciretti's wife in Italy instead. *Was the Social Security Administration correct? Why or why not?*
Guarino v. Celebrezze, 336 F.2d 336 (3rd Circuit).

24. Witness Signatures

Joseph Katz signed his will in the presence of two witnesses. The witnesses, however, printed their names in the place provided for signature instead of signing. After Katz's death, the will was presented for probate, and the witnesses signed an affidavit stating that they did witness the will. The question arose as to whether printing the name at the end of the will qualified as signature. *How would you decide this case? Explain your answer.*
Will of Katz, 494 N.Y.S.2d 629 (NY).

Legal Link

History Lesson

Francesca has worked for 10 years and contributed each year to social security. She knows she will be eligible to collect benefits when she retires. Francesca is interested in learning more about the history of social security and has asked you to help.

Connect

25. Using a variety of search engines, research the history of social security. What situation gave rise to social security, and why does it remain important today? Write a two-page paper explaining your findings.

POWER READING STRATEGIES

26. **Predict** Why do you think there is an age requirement for collecting social security?

27. **Connect** Will an employer pension plan be a factor when you are looking for a job? Why or why not?

28. **Question** When should you make a will? Is writing a will something that you should do even when you are young? Why or why not?

29. **Respond** What are some advantages of having a will when you die?

UNIT 7 Law Workshop:
Using Legal Skills

How Might a Landlord Create a Lease for Young Tenants?

Young adults don't always make the best tenants. Many are in college or are otherwise only temporary tenants. Some cannot afford to pay rent because of low income. Others are noisy or do not have sufficiently good credit. Too many people sharing a house or indifference to rented property can result in damage to the property.

Step A: Preparation

Problem: *How would you legally represent a landlord who rents to young adults?*

Objectives: In this workshop, you will work with a partner to create a lease for a landlord who rents to young adults.

- **Research** types of tenancies and lease agreements.
- **Investigate** reasons for legal disputes among tenants and landlords in your community.
- **Use technology** (e.g., word processing or spreadsheet applications) to prepare a lease agreement.
- **Analyze** lease agreements for issues that relate to tenants in a college community and address the legal issues that pertain especially to young adult tenants.

Step B: Procedure

1. Choose a partner, and review the information on tenancies and lease agreements in Chapter 33.
2. Use newspaper archives or court records to research landlord/tenant disputes in your area.

3. Decide the type of tenancy and the terms of a lease agreement that you would recommend to your client.
4. Based on your research, present your lease to the class, and explain how it addresses college tenant issues.

Step C: Create a Model to Compare Lease Agreements

Prepare a chart that shows how the type of tenancy and the terms of the lease address issues related to having college students as tenants. As a class, display all of the charts.

	Type of Tenancy	General Covenants	Security Deposit	Renewals	Decoration and Repairs	Assignment and Subletting	Termination of the Lease
Lease Agreement Chart							
Brief Description							
What issue does this address?							

Step D: Workshop Analysis Report

Compare the information presented on the different charts, and answer the following questions:

1. Many college students do not attend school during summer. How can a lease address this issue?
2. Do you think the security deposit should be raised because of the age of the tenants? If so, why?
3. Do you think the lease should contain special decoration and repair terms? Why or why not?

Jones v. Mayer Co.

U.S. Supreme Court

392 U.S. 409 (1968)

Issue Does a private company's refusal to sell a house to an African-American man violate 42 U.S.C § 1982, which prohibits racial discrimination in real estate transactions?

Facts Joseph Lee Jones, an African-American, filed a complaint alleging that Alfred H. Mayer Co. had refused to sell him a house because of his color. In his complaint, Jones alleged that such action violated 42 U.S.C § 1982 (Title 42, Section 1982 of the U.S. Code), which provides:

> All citizens of the United States shall have the same right, in every State and Territory, as is enjoyed by white citizens thereof to inherit, purchase, lease, sell, hold, and convey real and personal property.

The trial court granted Mayer Co.'s motion to dismiss. The appellate court affirmed the dismissal, concluding that Section 1982 does not apply to private real estate transactions.

Opinion In plain and clear language, 42 U.S.C § 1982 prohibits racial discrimination by private citizens, as well as public authorities. In citing a previous case, the Court stated, "[A] citizen who is denied the opportunity to purchase the home he wants '[s]olely because of [his] race and color'. . . has suffered the kind of injury that 1982 was designed to prevent." The Court rejected the Mayer Company's argument that Congress could not have intended such a literal reading of the statute.

The Historical Context

The Court observed that the statute had originally been part of the Civil Rights Act of 1866. After reviewing comments of U.S. Senators made on the floor of the Senate, the Court noted, "We think that history leaves no doubt that, if we are to give [the law] the scope that its origins dictate, we must accord it a sweep as broad as its language."

Comparison to Recent Legislation

In addressing the case, the Court also made it clear that the case did not involve a comprehensive open housing law. Unlike recent legislation, Section 1982 did not address a variety of issues involving discriminatory housing practices. The Court compared Section 1982 to the Fair Housing Title (Title VIII) of the Civil Rights Act of 1968, Pub. L. 90-284, 82 Stat. 81. Section 1982 differed from Fair Housing Title in that it dealt only with racial discrimination and did not address discrimination that might occur as a result of an individual's religion or national origin. Section 1982 also did not address discrimination with regard to services or facilities that might accompany the sale or rental of property, nor did section 1982 forbid advertising that indicated discriminatory practices. Unlike the Fair Housing Title Act, section 1982 also did not address discrimination in providing brokerage services or permit the federal government or Attorney General to intervene to assist parties that had been treated unjustly. Finally, the court observed that section 1982 did not include a provision that authorized a federal court to order the payment of damages.

Despite the fact that section 1982 did not address the majority of the issues included in the approved Civil Rights Act of 1968, the court felt that "it would be a serious mistake to suppose that 1982 in any way diminishes the significance of the law recently enacted by Congress."

Examining Precedent

The Court also considered relevant previous cases. *Hurd v. Hodge*, U.S. 24, had given the Court a recent opportunity to examine section 1982. *Hurd v. Hodge* arose when property owners in the District of Columbia tried to impose restrictive covenants against the African-American residents of their block. A federal district court held that the deeds of the African-American residents were void, thus enforcing the restrictive covenants.

In rendering a decision on *Hurd v. Hodge*, the Court adopted a broad view of section 1982 and held that the enforcement of the restrictive covenants would have denied the African-Americans "the same right as is enjoyed by white citizens . . . to inherit, purchase, lease, sell, hold, and convey real and personal property." The Court felt that to decide differently would be to "reject the plain meaning of language." Furthermore, the Court stated that it made no difference if an African-American were denied the right to rent or purchase property by a private party; that African-American would still be unable to enjoy the same rights as a white citizen, regardless of the source of the discrimination.

Constitutionality

The Court concluded that the statute is constitutional in its purpose to enforce the Thirteenth Amendment, which abolished slavery. Section 1 of the Amendment states:

Neither slavery nor involuntary servitude, except as punishment for crime whereof the party shall have been duly convicted, shall exist within the United States, or any place subject to their jurisdiction.

Section 2 of the Amendment provides that "Congress shall have the power to enforce this article by appropriate legislation." 42 U.S.C § 1982 is just such legislation.

Holding

The provisions of 42 U.S.C § 1982 prohibit all racial discrimination, private as well as public, in the sale or rental of property.

Questions for Analysis

1. What federal statute prohibits racial discrimination in the sale and rental of real estate?
2. On what basis did the intermediate appellate court affirm the trial court's decision to dismiss the action?
3. From what act did this statute originate?
4. What process did the Court utilize to assist it in interpreting the meaning of the statute?
5. What Amendment to the U.S. Constitution does the statute enforce?

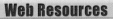

The Constitution of the United States

Preamble

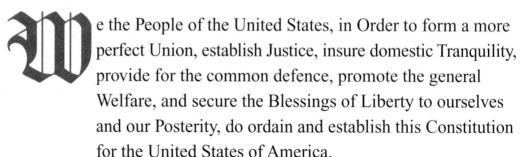

e the People of the United States, in Order to form a more perfect Union, establish Justice, insure domestic Tranquility, provide for the common defence, promote the general Welfare, and secure the Blessings of Liberty to ourselves and our Posterity, do ordain and establish this Constitution for the United States of America.

Article I

Section 1 ■ All legislative Powers herein granted shall be vested in a Congress of the United States, which shall consist of a Senate and House of Representatives.

Section 2 ■ The House of Representatives shall be composed of Members chosen every second Year by the People of the several States, and the Electors in each State shall have the Qualifications requisite for Electors of the most numerous Branch of the State Legislature.

No Person shall be a Representative who shall not have attained to the Age of twenty five Years, and been seven Years a Citizen of the United States, and who shall not, when elected, be an Inhabitant of that State in which he shall be chosen.

*Representatives and direct Taxes shall be apportioned among the several States which may be included within this Union, according to their respective Numbers, which shall be determined by adding to the whole Number of free Persons, including those bound to Service for a Term of Years, and excluding Indians not taxed, three fifths of all other Persons. The actual Enumeration shall be made within three Years after the first Meeting of the Congress of the United States, and within every subsequent Term of ten Years, in such Manner as they shall by Law direct. The Number of Representatives shall not exceed one for every thirty Thousand, but each State shall have at Least one Representative; and until such enumeration shall be made, the State of New Hampshire shall be entitled to chuse three, Massachusetts eight, Rhode-Island and Providence Plantations one, Connecticut five, New-York six, New Jersey four, Pennsylvania eight, Delaware one, Maryland six, Virginia ten, North Carolina five, South Carolina five, and Georgia three.

When vacancies happen in the Representation from any State, the Executive Authority thereof shall issue Writs of Election to fill such Vacancies.

The House of Representatives shall chuse their Speaker and other Officers; and shall have the sole Power of Impeachment.

Section 3 ■ The Senate of the United States shall be composed of two Senators from each State, chosen by the Legislature thereof, for six Years; and each Senator shall have one Vote.

Immediately after they shall be assembled in Consequence of the first Election, they shall be divided as equally as may be into three Classes. The Seats of the Senators of the first Class shall be vacated at the Expiration of the second Year, of the second Class at the Expiration of the fourth Year, and of the third Class at the Expiration of the sixth Year, so that one third may be chosen every second Year; and if Vacancies happen by Resignation, or otherwise, during the Recess of the Legislature of any State, the Executive thereof may make temporary Appointments until the next Meeting of the Legislature, which shall then fill such Vacancies.

---

* Text of the Constitution represented in gray and crossed out indicates that it has been amended and is no longer in effect.

No Person shall be a Senator who shall not have attained to the Age of thirty Years, and been nine Years a Citizen of the United States, and who shall not, when elected, be an Inhabitant of that State for which he shall be chosen.

The Vice President of the United States shall be President of the Senate, but shall have no Vote, unless they be equally divided.

The Senate shall chuse their other Officers, and also a President pro tempore, in the Absence of the Vice President, or when he shall exercise the Office of President of the United States.

The Senate shall have the sole Power to try all Impeachments. When sitting for that Purpose, they shall be on Oath or Affirmation. When the President of the United States is tried, the Chief Justice shall preside: And no Person shall be convicted without the Concurrence of two thirds of the Members present.

Judgment in Cases of Impeachment shall not extend further than to removal from Office, and disqualification to hold and enjoy any Office of honor, Trust or Profit under the United States: but the Party convicted shall nevertheless be liable and subject to Indictment, Trial, Judgment and Punishment, according to Law.

Section 4 ■ The Times, Places and Manner of holding Elections for Senators and Representatives, shall be prescribed in each State by the Legislature thereof; but the Congress may at any time by Law make or alter such Regulations, except as to the Places of chusing Senators.

The Congress shall assemble at least once in every Year, and such Meeting shall be on the first Monday in December, unless they shall by Law appoint a different Day.

Section 5 ■ Each House shall be the Judge of the Elections, Returns and Qualifications of its own Members, and a Majority of each shall constitute a Quorum to do Business; but a smaller Number may adjourn from day to day, and may be authorized to compel the Attendance of absent Members, in such Manner, and under such Penalties as each House may provide.

Each House may determine the Rules of its Proceedings, punish its Members for disorderly Behaviour, and, with the Concurrence of two thirds, expel a Member.

Each House shall keep a Journal of its Proceedings, and from time to time publish the same, excepting such Parts as may in their Judgment require Secrecy; and the Yeas and Nays of the Members of either House on any question shall, at the Desire of one fifth of those Present, be entered on the Journal.

Neither House, during the Session of Congress, shall, without the Consent of the other, adjourn for more than three days, nor to any other Place than that in which the two Houses shall be sitting.

Section 6 ■ The Senators and Representatives shall receive a Compensation for their Services, to be ascertained by Law, and paid out of the Treasury of the United States. They shall in all Cases, except Treason, Felony and Breach of the Peace, be privileged from Arrest during their Attendance at the Session of their respective Houses, and in going to and returning from the same; and for any Speech or Debate in either House, they shall not be questioned in any other Place.

No Senator or Representative shall, during the Time for which he was elected, be appointed to any civil Office under the Authority of the

United States, which shall have been created, or the Emoluments whereof shall have been encreased during such time; and no Person holding any Office under the United States, shall be a Member of either House during his Continuance in Office.

Section 7 ■ All Bills for raising Revenue shall originate in the House of Representatives; but the Senate may propose or concur with Amendments as on other Bills.

Every Bill which shall have passed the House of Representatives and the Senate, shall, before it become a Law, be presented to the President of the United States; If he approve he shall sign it, but if not he shall return it, with his Objections to that House in which it shall have originated, who shall enter the Objections at large on their Journal, and proceed to reconsider it.

If after such Reconsideration two thirds of that House shall agree to pass the Bill, it shall be sent, together with the Objections, to the other House, by which it shall likewise be reconsidered, and if approved by two thirds of that House, it shall become a Law. But in all such Cases the Votes of both Houses shall be determined by yeas and Nays, and the Names of the Persons voting for and against the Bill shall be entered on the Journal of each House respectively. If any Bill shall not be returned by the President within ten Days (Sundays excepted) after it shall have been presented to him, the Same shall be a Law, in like Manner as if he had signed it, unless the Congress by their Adjournment prevent its Return, in which Case it shall not be a Law.

Every Order, Resolution, or Vote to which the Concurrence of the Senate and House of Representatives may be necessary (except on a question of Adjournment) shall be presented to the President of the United States; and before the Same shall take Effect, shall be approved by him, or being disapproved by him, shall be repassed by two thirds of the Senate and House of Representatives, according to the Rules and Limitations prescribed in the Case of a Bill.

Section 8 ■ The Congress shall have Power To lay and collect Taxes, Duties, Imposts and Excises, to pay the Debts and provide for the common Defence and general Welfare of the United States; but all Duties, Imposts and Excises shall be uniform throughout the United States;

To borrow Money on the credit of the United States;

To regulate Commerce with foreign Nations, and among the several States, and with the Indian Tribes;

To establish an uniform Rule of Naturalization, and uniform Laws on the subject of Bankruptcies throughout the United States;

To coin Money, regulate the Value thereof, and of foreign Coin, and fix the Standard of Weights and Measures;

To provide for the Punishment of counterfeiting the Securities and current Coin of the United States;

To establish Post Offices and post Roads;

To promote the Progress of Science and useful Arts, by securing for limited Times to Authors and Inventors the exclusive Right to their respective Writings and Discoveries;

To constitute Tribunals inferior to the supreme Court;

To define and punish Piracies and Felonies committed on the high Seas, and Offences against the Law of Nations;

To declare War, grant Letters of Marque and Reprisal, and make Rules concerning Captures on Land and Water;

To raise and support Armies, but no Appropriation of Money to that Use shall be for a longer Term than two Years;

To provide and maintain a Navy;

To make Rules for the Government and Regulation of the land and naval Forces;

To provide for calling forth the Militia to execute the Laws of the Union, suppress Insurrections and repel Invasions;

To provide for organizing, arming, and disciplining, the Militia, and for governing such Part of them as may be employed in the Service of the United States, reserving to the States respectively, the Appointment of the Officers, and the Authority of training the Militia according to the discipline prescribed by Congress;

To exercise exclusive Legislation in all Cases whatsoever, over such District (not exceeding ten Miles square) as may, by Cession of particular States, and the Acceptance of Congress, become the Seat of the Government of the United States, and to exercise like Authority over all Places purchased by the Consent of the Legislature of the State in which the Same shall be, for the Erection of Forts, Magazines, Arsenals, dock-Yards, and other needful Buildings; And

To make all Laws which shall be necessary and proper for carrying into Execution the foregoing Powers, and all other Powers vested by this Constitution in the Government of the United States, or in any Department or Officer thereof.

Section 9 ■ The Migration or Importation of such Persons as any of the States now existing shall think proper to admit, shall not be prohibited by the Congress prior to the Year one thousand eight hundred and eight, but a Tax or duty may be imposed on such Importation, not exceeding ten dollars for each Person.

The Privilege of the Writ of Habeas Corpus shall not be suspended, unless when in Cases of Rebellion or Invasion the public Safety may require it.

No Bill of Attainder or ex post facto Law shall be passed.

No Capitation, or other direct, Tax shall be laid, unless in Proportion to the Census or Enumeration herein before directed to be taken.

No Tax or Duty shall be laid on Articles exported from any State.

No Preference shall be given by any Regulation of Commerce or Revenue to the Ports of one State over those of another: nor shall Vessels bound to, or from, one State, be obliged to enter, clear, or pay Duties in another.

No Money shall be drawn from the Treasury, but in Consequence of Appropriations made by Law; and a regular Statement and Account of the Receipts and Expenditures of all public Money shall be published from time to time.

No Title of Nobility shall be granted by the United States: And no Person holding any Office of Profit or Trust under them, shall, without the Consent of the Congress, accept of any present, Emolument, Office, or Title, of any kind whatever, from any King, Prince, or foreign State.

Section 10 ■ No State shall enter into any Treaty, Alliance, or Confederation; grant Letters of Marque and Reprisal; coin Money; emit Bills of Credit; make any Thing but gold and silver Coin a Tender in Payment of Debts; pass any Bill of Attainder, ex post facto Law, or Law impairing the Obligation of Contracts, or grant any Title of Nobility.

No State shall, without the Consent of the Congress, lay any Imposts or Duties on Imports or Exports, except what may be absolutely necessary for executing it's inspection Laws: and the net Produce of all Duties and Imposts, laid by any State on Imports or Exports, shall be for the Use of the Treasury of the United States; and all such Laws shall be subject to the Revision and Controul of the Congress.

No State shall, without the Consent of Congress, lay any Duty of Tonnage, keep Troops, or Ships of War in time of Peace, enter into any Agreement or Compact with another State, or with a foreign Power, or engage in War, unless actually invaded, or in such imminent Danger as will not admit of delay.

𝒜RTICLE II

Section 1 ■ The executive Power shall be vested in a President of the United States of America. He shall hold his Office during the Term of four Years, and, together with the Vice President, chosen for the same Term, be elected, as follows

Each State shall appoint, in such Manner as the Legislature thereof may direct, a Number of Electors, equal to the whole Number of Senators and Representatives to which the State may be entitled in the Congress: but no Senator or Representative, or Person holding an Office of Trust or Profit under the United States, shall be appointed an Elector.

~~The Electors shall meet in their respective States, and vote by Ballot for two Persons, of whom one at least shall not be an Inhabitant of the same State with themselves. And they shall make a List of all the Persons voted for,~~ ~~and of the Number of Votes for each; which List they shall sign and certify, and transmit sealed to the Seat of the Government of the United States, directed to the President of the Senate. The President of the Senate shall, in the Presence of the Senate and House of Representatives, open all the Certificates, and the Votes shall then be counted. The Person having the greatest Number of Votes shall be the President, if such Number be a Majority of the whole Number of Electors appointed; and if there be more than one who have such Majority, and have an equal Number of Votes, then the House of Representatives shall immediately chuse by Ballot one of them for President; and if no Person have a Majority, then from the five highest on the List the said House shall in like Manner chuse the President. But in chusing the President, the Votes shall be taken by States, the Representation from each State having one Vote; A quorum for this Purpose shall consist of a Member or Members from two thirds of the States, and a Majority of all the States shall be necessary to a Choice. In every Case, after the Choice of the President, the Person having the greatest Number of Votes of the Electors shall be the Vice President. But if there should remain two or more who have equal Votes, the Senate shall chuse from them by Ballot the Vice President.~~

The Congress may determine the Time of chusing the Electors, and the Day on which they shall give their Votes; which Day shall be the same throughout the United States.

No Person except a natural born Citizen, or a Citizen of the United States, at the time of the Adoption of this Constitution, shall be eligible to the Office of President; neither shall any Person be eligible to that Office who shall not have attained to the Age of thirty five Years, and been fourteen Years a Resident within the United States.

In Case of the Removal of the President from Office, or of his Death, Resignation, or Inability to discharge the Powers and Duties of the said Office, the Same shall devolve on the Vice President, and the Congress may by Law provide for the Case of Removal, Death, Resignation or Inability, both of the President and Vice President, declaring what Officer shall then act as President, and such Officer shall act accordingly, until the Disability be removed, or a President shall be elected.

The President shall, at stated Times, receive for his Services, a Compensation, which shall neither be encreased nor diminished during the Period for which he shall have been elected, and he shall not receive within that Period any other Emolument from the United States, or any of them.

Before he enter on the Execution of his Office, he shall take the following Oath or Affirmation: "I do solemnly swear (or affirm) that I will faithfully execute the Office of President of the United States, and will to the best of my Ability, preserve, protect and defend the Constitution of the United States."

Section 2 ■ The President shall be Commander in Chief of the Army and Navy of the United States, and of the Militia of the several States, when called into the actual Service of the United States; he may require the Opinion, in writing, of the principal Officer in each of the executive Departments, upon any Subject relating to the Duties of their respective Offices, and he shall have Power to grant Reprieves and Pardons for Offences against the United States, except in Cases of Impeachment.

He shall have Power, by and with the Advice and Consent of the Senate, to make Treaties, provided two thirds of the Senators present concur; and he shall nominate, and by and with the Advice and Consent of the Senate,

shall appoint Ambassadors, other public Ministers and Consuls, Judges of the supreme Court, and all other Officers of the United States, whose Appointments are not herein otherwise provided for, and which shall be established by Law: but the Congress may by Law vest the Appointment of such inferior Officers, as they think proper, in the President alone, in the Courts of Law, or in the Heads of Departments. The President shall have Power to fill up all Vacancies that may happen during the Recess of the Senate, by granting Commissions which shall expire at the End of their next Session.

Section 3 ■ He shall from time to time give to the Congress Information of the State of the Union, and recommend to their Consideration such Measures as he shall judge necessary and expedient; he may, on extraordinary Occasions, convene both Houses, or either of them, and in Case of Disagreement between them, with Respect to the Time of Adjournment, he may adjourn them to such Time as he shall think proper; he shall receive Ambassadors and other public Ministers; he shall take Care that the Laws be faithfully executed, and shall Commission all the Officers of the United States.

Section 4 ■ The President, Vice President and all civil Officers of the United States, shall be removed from Office on Impeachment for, and Conviction of, Treason, Bribery, or other high Crimes and Misdemeanors.

ARTICLE III

Section 1 ■ The judicial Power of the United States, shall be vested in one supreme Court, and in such inferior Courts as the Congress may from time to time ordain and establish. The Judges, both of the supreme and inferior Courts, shall hold their Offices during good

Behaviour, and shall, at stated Times, receive for their Services, a Compensation, which shall not be diminished during their Continuance in Office.

Section 2 ■ The judicial Power shall extend to all Cases, in Law and Equity, arising under this Constitution, the Laws of the United States, and Treaties made, or which shall be made, under their Authority; to all Cases affecting Ambassadors, other public Ministers and Consuls; to all Cases of admiralty and maritime Jurisdiction;—to Controversies to which the United States shall be a Party;—to Controversies between two or more States; between a State and Citizens of another State;—between Citizens of different States, between Citizens of the same State claiming Lands under Grants of different States, and between a State, or the Citizens thereof, and foreign States, Citizens or Subjects.

In all Cases affecting Ambassadors, other public Ministers and Consuls, and those in which a State shall be Party, the supreme Court shall have original Jurisdiction. In all the other Cases before mentioned, the supreme Court shall have appellate Jurisdiction, both as to Law and Fact, with such Exceptions, and under such Regulations as the Congress shall make.

The Trial of all Crimes, except in Cases of Impeachment, shall be by Jury; and such Trial shall be held in the State where the said Crimes shall have been committed; but when not committed within any State, the Trial shall be at such Place or Places as the Congress may by Law have directed.

Section 3 ■ Treason against the United States, shall consist only in levying War against them, or in adhering to their Enemies, giving them Aid and Comfort. No Person shall be convicted of Treason unless on the Testimony of two Witnesses to the same overt Act, or on Confession in open Court.

The Congress shall have Power to declare the Punishment of Treason, but no Attainder of Treason shall work Corruption of Blood, or Forfeiture except during the Life of the Person attainted.

Article IV

Section 1 ■ Full Faith and Credit shall be given in each State to the public Acts, Records, and judicial Proceedings of every other State. And the Congress may by general Laws prescribe the Manner in which such Acts, Records and Proceedings shall be proved, and the Effect thereof.

Section 2 ■ The Citizens of each State shall be entitled to all Privileges and Immunities of Citizens in the several States.

A Person charged in any State with Treason, Felony, or other Crime, who shall flee from Justice, and be found in another State, shall on Demand of the executive Authority of the State from which he fled, be delivered up, to be removed to the State having Jurisdiction of the Crime.

No Person held to Service or Labour in one State, under the Laws thereof, escaping into another, shall, in Consequence of any Law or Regulation therein, be discharged from such Service or Labour, but shall be delivered up on Claim of the Party to whom such Service or Labour may be due.

Section 3 ■ New States may be admitted by the Congress into this Union; but no new State shall be formed or erected within the Jurisdiction of any other State; nor any State be formed by the Junction of two or more States, or Parts of States, without the Consent of the

Legislatures of the States concerned as well as of the Congress.

Clause 2: The Congress shall have Power to dispose of and make all needful Rules and Regulations respecting the Territory or other Property belonging to the United States; and nothing in this Constitution shall be so construed as to Prejudice any Claims of the United States, or of any particular State.

Section 4 ■ The United States shall guarantee to every State in this Union a Republican Form of Government, and shall protect each of them against Invasion; and on Application of the Legislature, or of the Executive (when the Legislature cannot be convened) against domestic Violence.

Article V

The Congress, whenever two thirds of both Houses shall deem it necessary, shall propose Amendments to this Constitution, or, on the Application of the Legislatures of two thirds of the several States, shall call a Convention for proposing Amendments, which, in either Case, shall be valid to all Intents and Purposes, as Part of this Constitution, when ratified by the Legislatures of three fourths of the several States, or by Conventions in three fourths thereof, as the one or the other Mode of Ratification may be proposed by the Congress; Provided that no Amendment which may be made prior to the Year One thousand eight hundred and eight shall in any Manner affect the first and fourth Clauses in the Ninth Section of the first Article; and that no State, without its Consent, shall be deprived of its equal Suffrage in the Senate.

Article VI

All Debts contracted and Engagements entered into, before the Adoption of this Constitution, shall be as valid against the United States under this Constitution, as under the Confederation.

This Constitution, and the Laws of the United States which shall be made in Pursuance thereof; and all Treaties made, or which shall be made, under the Authority of the United States, shall be the supreme Law of the Land; and the Judges in every State shall be bound thereby, any Thing in the Constitution or Laws of any State to the Contrary notwithstanding.

The Senators and Representatives before mentioned, and the Members of the several State Legislatures, and all executive and judicial Officers, both of the United States and of the several States, shall be bound by Oath or Affirmation, to support this Constitution; but no religious Test shall ever be required as a Qualification to any Office or public Trust under the United States.

Article VII

The Ratification of the Conventions of nine States, shall be sufficient for the Establishment of this Constitution between the States so ratifying the Same.

Done in Convention by the Unanimous Consent of the States present the Seventeenth Day of September in the Year of our Lord one thousand seven hundred and Eighty seven and of the Independence of the United States of America the Twelfth In witness whereof We have hereunto subscribed our Names,

G. O. Washington—Presidt.
and deputy from Virginia

[Signed also by
the deputies of twelve States.]

Amendment I

Congress shall make no law respecting an establishment of religion, or prohibiting the free exercise thereof; or abridging the freedom of speech, or of the press; or the right of the people peaceably to assemble, and to petition the Government for a redress of grievances.

Amendment II

A well regulated Militia, being necessary to the security of a free State, the right of the people to keep and bear Arms, shall not be infringed.

Amendment III

No Soldier shall, in time of peace be quartered in any house, without the consent of the Owner, nor in time of war, but in a manner to be prescribed by law.

Amendment IV

The right of the people to be secure in their persons, houses, papers, and effects, against unreasonable searches and seizures, shall not be violated, and no Warrants shall issue, but upon probable cause, supported by Oath or affirmation, and particularly describing the place to be searched, and the persons or things to be seized.

Amendment V

No person shall be held to answer for a capital, or otherwise infamous crime, unless on a presentment or indictment of a Grand Jury, except in cases arising in the land or naval forces, or in the Militia, when in actual service in time of War or public danger; nor shall any person be subject for the same offence to be twice put in jeopardy of life or limb; nor shall be compelled in any criminal case to be a witness against himself, nor be deprived of life, liberty, or property, without due process of law; nor shall private property be taken for public use, without just compensation.

Amendment VI

In all criminal prosecutions, the accused shall enjoy the right to a speedy and public trial, by an impartial jury of the State and district wherein the crime shall have been committed, which district shall have been previously ascertained by law, and to be informed of the nature and cause of the accusation; to be confronted with the witnesses against him; to have compulsory process for obtaining witnesses in his favor, and to have the Assistance of Counsel for his defence.

Amendment VII

In suits at common law, where the value in controversy shall exceed twenty dollars, the right of trial by jury shall be preserved, and no fact tried by a jury, shall be otherwise reexamined in any Court of the United States, than according to the rules of the common law.

Amendment VIII

Excessive bail shall not be required, nor excessive fines imposed, nor cruel and unusual punishments inflicted.

Amendment IX

The enumeration in the Constitution, of certain rights, shall not be construed to deny or disparage others retained by the people.

Amendment X

The powers not delegated to the United States by the Constitution, nor prohibited by it to the States, are reserved to the States respectively, or to the people.

Amendment XI

The Judicial power of the United States shall not be construed to extend to any suit in law or equity, commenced or prosecuted against one of the United States by Citizens of another State, or by Citizens or Subjects of any Foreign State.

Amendment XII

The Electors shall meet in their respective states and vote by ballot for President and Vice-President, one of whom, at least, shall not be an inhabitant of the same state with themselves; they shall name in their ballots the person voted for as President, and in distinct ballots the person voted for as Vice-President, and they shall make distinct lists of all persons voted for as President, and of all persons voted for as Vice-President, and of the number of votes for each, which lists they shall sign and certify, and transmit sealed to the seat of the government of the United States, directed to the President of the Senate; the President of the Senate shall, in the presence of the Senate and House of Representatives, open all the certificates and the votes shall then be counted; The person having the greatest number of votes for President, shall be the President, if such number be a majority of the whole number of Electors appointed; and if no person have such majority, then from the persons having the highest numbers not exceeding three on the list of those voted for as President, the House of Representatives shall choose immediately, by ballot, the President. But in choosing the President, the votes shall be taken by states, the representation from each state having one vote; a quorum for this purpose shall consist of a member or members from two-thirds of the states, and a majority of all the states shall be necessary to a choice. And if the House of Representatives shall not choose a President whenever the right of choice shall devolve upon them, before the fourth day of March next following, then the Vice-President shall act as President, as in case of the death or other constitutional disability of the President.

The person having the greatest number of votes as Vice-President, shall be the Vice-President, if such number be a majority of the whole number of Electors appointed, and if no person have a majority, then from the two highest numbers on the list, the Senate shall choose the Vice-President; a quorum for the purpose shall consist of two-thirds of the whole number of Senators, and a majority of the whole number shall be necessary to a choice. But no person constitutionally ineligible to the office of President shall be eligible to that of Vice-President of the United States.

Amendment XIII

Section 1 ■ Neither slavery nor involuntary servitude, except as a punishment for crime whereof the party shall have been duly convicted, shall exist within the United States, or any place subject to their jurisdiction.

Section 2 ■ Congress shall have power to enforce this article by appropriate legislation.

𝔄mendment XIV

Section 1 ■ All persons born or naturalized in the United States, and subject to the jurisdiction thereof, are citizens of the United States and of the State wherein they reside. No State shall make or enforce any law which shall abridge the privileges or immunities of citizens of the United States; nor shall any State deprive any person of life, liberty, or property, without due process of law; nor deny to any person within its jurisdiction the equal protection of the laws.

Section 2 ■ Representatives shall be apportioned among the several States according to their respective numbers, counting the whole number of persons in each State, excluding Indians not taxed. But when the right to vote at any election for the choice of electors for President and Vice-President of the United States, Representatives in Congress, the Executive and Judicial officers of a State, or the members of the Legislature thereof, is denied to any of the male inhabitants of such State, being twenty-one years of age, and citizens of the United States, or in any way abridged, except for participation in rebellion, or other crime, the basis of representation therein shall be reduced in the proportion which the number of such male citizens shall bear to the whole number of male citizens twenty-one years of age in such State.

Section 3 ■ No person shall be a Senator or Representative in Congress, or elector of President and Vice-President, or hold any office, civil or military, under the United States, or under any State, who, having previously taken an oath, as a member of Congress, or as an officer of the United States, or as a member of any State legislature, or as an executive or judicial officer of any State, to support the Constitution of the United States, shall have engaged in insurrection or rebellion against the same, or given aid or comfort to the enemies thereof. But Congress may by a vote of two-thirds of each House, remove such disability.

Section 4 ■ The validity of the public debt of the United States, authorized by law, including debts incurred for payment of pensions and bounties for services in suppressing insurrection or rebellion, shall not be questioned. But neither the United States nor any State shall assume or pay any debt or obligation incurred in aid of insurrection or rebellion against the United States, or any claim for the loss or emancipation of any slave; but all such debts, obligations and claims shall be held illegal and void.

Section 5 ■ The Congress shall have the power to enforce, by appropriate legislation, the provisions of this article.

Amendment XV

Section 1 ■ The right of citizens of the United States to vote shall not be denied or abridged by the United States or by any State on account of race, color, or previous condition of servitude.

Section 2 ■ The Congress shall have the power to enforce this article by appropriate legislation.

Amendment XVI

The Congress shall have power to lay and collect taxes on incomes, from whatever source derived, without apportionment among the several States, and without regard to any census or enumeration.

Amendment XVII

The Senate of the United States shall be composed of two Senators from each State, elected by the people thereof, for six years; and each Senator shall have one vote. The electors in each State shall have the qualifications requisite for electors of the most numerous branch of the State legislatures.

When vacancies happen in the representation of any State in the Senate, the executive authority of such State shall issue writs of election to fill such vacancies: *Provided*, That the legislature of any State may empower the executive thereof to make temporary appointments until the people fill the vacancies by election as the legislature may direct.

This amendment shall not be so construed as to affect the election or term of any Senator chosen before it becomes valid as part of the Constitution.

Amendment XVIII

Section 1 ■ After one year from the ratification of this article the manufacture, sale, or transportation of intoxicating liquors within, the importation thereof into, or the exportation thereof from the United States and all territory subject to the jurisdiction thereof for beverage purposes is hereby prohibited.

Section 2 ■ The Congress and the several States shall have concurrent power to enforce this article by appropriate legislation.

Section 3 ■ This article shall be inoperative unless it shall have been ratified as an amendment to the Constitution by the legislatures of the several States, as provided in the Constitution, within seven years from the date of the submission hereof to the States by the Congress.

Amendment XIX

The right of citizens of the United States to vote shall not be denied or abridged by the United States or by any State on account of sex. Congress shall have power to enforce this article by appropriate legislation.

Amendment XX

Section 1 ■ The terms of the President and the Vice President shall end at noon on the 20th day of January, and the terms of Senators and Representatives at noon on the 3d day of January, of the years in which such terms would have ended if this article had not been ratified; and the terms of their successors shall then begin.

Section 2 ■ The Congress shall assemble at least once in every year, and such meeting shall begin at noon on the 3d day of January, unless they shall by law appoint a different day.

Section 3 ■ If, at the time fixed for the beginning of the term of the President, the President elect shall have died, the Vice President elect shall become President. If a President shall not have been chosen before the time fixed for the beginning of his term, or if the President elect shall have failed to qualify, then the Vice President elect shall act as President until a President shall have qualified; and the Congress may by law provide for the case wherein neither a President elect nor a Vice President shall have qualified, declaring who shall then act as President, or the manner in which one who is to act shall be selected, and such person shall act accordingly until a President or Vice President shall have qualified.

Section 4 ■ The Congress may by law provide for the case of the death of any of the persons from whom the House of Representatives may choose a President whenever the right of choice shall have devolved upon them, and for the case of the death of any of the persons from whom the Senate may choose a Vice President whenever the right of choice shall have devolved upon them.

Section 5 ■ Sections 1 and 2 shall take effect on the 15th day of October following the ratification of this article.

Section 6 ■ This article shall be inoperative unless it shall have been ratified as an amendment to the Constitution by the legislatures of three-fourths of the several States within seven years from the date of its submission.

Amendment XXI

Section 1 ■ The eighteenth article of amendment to the Constitution of the United States is hereby repealed.

Section 2 ■ The transportation or importation into any State, Territory, or Possession of the United States for delivery or use therein of intoxicating liquors, in violation of the laws thereof, is hereby prohibited.

Section 3 ■ This article shall be inoperative unless it shall have been ratified as an amendment to the Constitution by conventions in the several States, as provided in the Constitution, within seven years from the date of the submission hereof to the States by the Congress.

Amendment XXII

Section 1 ■ No person shall be elected to the office of the President more than twice, and no person who has held the office of President, or acted as President, for more than two years of a term to which some other person was elected President shall be elected to the office of President more than once. But this Article shall not apply to any person holding the office of President when this Article was proposed by Congress, and shall not prevent any person who may be holding the office of President, or acting as President, during the term within which this Article becomes operative from holding the office of President or acting as President during the remainder of such term.

Section 2 ■ This article shall be inoperative unless it shall have been ratified as an amendment to the Constitution by the legislatures of three-fourths of the several States within seven years from the date of its submission to the States by the Congress.

Amendment XXIII

Section 1 ■ The District constituting the seat of Government of the United States shall appoint in such manner as Congress may direct:

A number of electors of President and Vice President equal to the whole number of Senators and Representatives in Congress to which the District would be entitled if it were a State, but in no event more than the least populous State; they shall be in addition to those appointed by the States, but they shall be considered, for the purposes of the election of President and Vice President, to be electors appointed by a State; and they shall meet in the District and perform such duties as provided by the twelfth article of amendment.

Section 2 ■ The Congress shall have power to enforce this article by appropriate legislation.

Amendment XXIV

Section 1 ■ The right of citizens of the United States to vote in any primary or other election for President or Vice President, for electors for President or Vice President, or for Senator or Representative in Congress, shall not be denied or abridged by the United States or any State by reason of failure to pay poll tax or other tax.

Section 2 ■ The Congress shall have power to enforce this article by appropriate legislation.

Amendment XXV

Section 1 ■ In case of the removal of the President from office or of his death or resignation, the Vice President shall become President.

Section 2 ■ Whenever there is a vacancy in the office of the Vice President, the President shall nominate a Vice President who shall take office upon confirmation by a majority vote of both Houses of Congress.

Section 3 ■ Whenever the President transmits to the President pro tempore of the Senate and the Speaker of the House of Representatives his written declaration that he is unable to discharge the powers and duties of his office, and until he transmits to them a written declaration to the contrary, such powers and duties shall be discharged by the Vice President as Acting President.

Section 4 ■ Whenever the Vice President and a majority of either the principal officers of the executive departments or of such other body as Congress may by law provide, transmit to the President pro tempore of the Senate and the Speaker of the House of Representatives their written declaration that the President is unable to discharge the powers and duties of his office, the Vice President shall immediately assume the powers and duties of the office as Acting President.

Thereafter, when the President transmits to the President pro tempore of the Senate and the Speaker of the House of Representatives his written declaration that no inability exists, he shall resume the powers and duties of his office unless the Vice President and a majority of either the principal officers of the executive department or of such other body as Congress may by law provide, transmit within four days to the President pro tempore of the Senate and the Speaker of the House of Representatives their written declaration that the President is unable to discharge the powers and duties of his office. Thereupon Congress shall decide the issue, assembling within forty-eight hours for that purpose if not in session. If the Congress, within twenty-one days after receipt of the latter written declaration, or, if Congress is not in session, within twenty-one days after Congress is required to assemble, determines by two-thirds vote of both Houses that the President is unable to discharge the powers and duties of his office, the Vice President shall continue to discharge the same as Acting President; otherwise, the President shall resume the powers and duties of his office.

Amendment XXVI

Section 1 ■ The right of citizens of the United States, who are eighteen years of age or older, to vote shall not be denied or abridged by the United States or by any State on account of age.

Section 2 ■ The Congress shall have power to enforce this article by appropriate legislation.

Amendment XXVII

No law, varying the compensation for the services of the Senators and Representatives, shall take effect, until an election of representatives shall have intervened.

The Declaration of Independence

In Congress, July 4, 1776. the Unanimous Declaration of the thirteen united States of America.

When in the Course of human events, it becomes necessary for one people to dissolve the political bands which have connected them with another, and to assume among the powers of the earth, the separate and equal station to which the Laws of Nature and of Nature's God entitle them, a decent Respect to the Opinions of Mankind requires that they should declare the causes which impel them to the separation.

We hold these truths to be self-evident, that all men are created equal, that they are endowed by their Creator with certain unalienable Rights, that among these are Life, Liberty and the Pursuit of Happiness. That to secure these rights, Governments are instituted among Men, deriving their just powers from the consent of the governed, that whenever any Form of Government becomes destructive of these Ends, it is the Right of the People to alter or to abolish it, and to institute new Government, laying its foundation on such principles, and organizing its Powers in such form, as to them shall seem most likely to effect their Safety and Happiness. Prudence, indeed, will dictate that Governments long established should not be changed for light and transient causes; and accordingly all experience hath shewn, that mankind are more disposed to suffer, while evils are sufferable, than to right themselves by abolishing the forms to which they are accustomed. But when a long train of abuses and usurpations, pursuing invariably the same Object, evinces a design to reduce them under absolute Despotism, it is their right, it is their duty, to throw off such Government, and to provide new Guards for their future security. Such has been the patient Sufferance of these Colonies; and such is now the necessity which constrains them to alter their former Systems of Government. The history of the present King of Great Britain is a history of repeated injuries and usurpations, all having in direct object the Establishment of an absolute Tyranny over these States. To prove this, let Facts be submitted to a candid world.

He has refused his Assent to Laws, the most wholesome and necessary for the public good.

He has forbidden his Governors to pass Laws of immediate and pressing importance, unless suspended in their operation till his Assent should be obtained; and when so suspended, he has utterly neglected to attend to them.

He has refused to pass other Laws for the accommodation of large districts of people, unless those people would relinquish the right of Representation in the Legislature, a right inestimable to them, and formidable to tyrants only.

He has called together legislative bodies at places unusual, uncomfortable, and distant from the depository of their public Records, for the sole purpose of fatiguing them into compliance with his measures.

He has dissolved Representative Houses repeatedly, for opposing with manly firmness his invasions on the rights of the people.

He has refused for a long time, after such dissolutions, to cause others to be elected; whereby the Legislative powers, incapable of the Annihilation, have returned to the People at large for their exercise; the State remaining in the mean time exposed to all the dangers of invasion from without, and the convulsions within.

He has endeavoured to prevent the population of these States; for that purpose obstructing the Laws for Naturalization of Foreigners; refusing to pass others to encourage their migrations hither, and raising the conditions of new Appropriations of Lands.

He has obstructed the Administration of Justice, by refusing his Assent to Laws for establishing Judiciary powers.

He has made Judges dependent on his Will alone, for the Tenure of their offices, and the amount and payment of their salaries.

He has erected a multitude of New Offices, and sent hither swarms of Officers to harrass our people, and eat out their substance.

He has kept among us, in times of peace, Standing Armies, without the Consent of our Legislatures.

He has affected to render the Military independent of and superior to the Civil power.

He has combined with others to subject us to a jurisdiction foreign to our constitution, and unacknowledged by our laws; giving his Assent to their Acts of pretended Legislation:

For quartering large bodies of armed troops among us:

For protecting them, by a mock Trial, from punishment for any Murders which they should commit on the Inhabitants of these States:

For cutting off our Trade with all parts of the world:

For imposing Taxes on us without our Consent:

For depriving us, in many Cases, of the benefits of Trial by Jury:

For transporting us beyond Seas to be tried for pretended Offences:

For abolishing the free System of English Laws in a neighbouring Province, establishing therein an Arbitrary government, and enlarging its Boundaries so as to render it at once an example and fit instrument for introducing the same absolute rules into these Colonies:

For taking away our Charters, abolishing our most valuable Laws, and altering fundamentally the Forms of our Governments:

For suspending our own Legislatures, and declaring themselves invested with power to legislate for us in all cases whatsoever.

He has abdicated Government here, by declaring us out of his Protection and waging War against us.

He has plundered our Seas, ravaged our Coasts, burnt our towns, and destroyed the lives of our people.

He is at this time transporting large Armies of foreign Mercenaries to compleat the works of death, desolation, and tyranny, already begun with circumstances of Cruelty and perfidy scarcely paralleled in the most barbarous ages, and totally unworthy the Head of a civilized nation.

He has constrained our fellow Citizens taken Captive on the high Seas to bear Arms against their Country, to become the executioners of their friends and Brethren, or to fall themselves by their Hands.

He has excited domestic insurrections amongst us, and has endeavoured to bring on the inhabitants of our frontiers, the merciless Indian Savages, whose known rule of warfare, is an undistinguished destruction, of all ages, sexes and conditions.

In every stage of these Oppressions we have Petitioned for Redress in the most humble terms: Our repeated Petitions have been answered only by repeated injury. A Prince, whose character is thus marked by every act which may define a Tyrant, is unfit to be the ruler of a free people.

Nor have We been wanting in attentions to our British brethren. We have warned them from time to time of attempts by their legislature to extend an unwarrantable jurisdiction over us. We have reminded them of the circumstances of our emigration and settlement here. We have appealed to their native justice and magnanimity, and we have conjured them by the ties of our common kindred to disavow these usurpations, which, would inevitably interrupt our connections and correspondence. They too have been deaf to the voice of justice and of consanguinity. We must, therefore, acquiesce in the necessity, which denounces our Separation, and hold them, as we hold the rest of mankind, Enemies in War, in Peace, Friends.

We, therefore, the Representatives of the united States of America, in General Congress, Assembled, appealing to the Supreme Judge of the world for the rectitude of our intentions, do, in the Name, and by Authority of the good People of these Colonies, solemnly publish and declare, That these United Colonies are, and of Right ought to be, Free and Independent States; that they are absolved from all Allegiance to the British Crown, and that all political connection between them and the State of Great Britain, is and ought to be totally dissolved; and that as Free and Independent States, they have full Power to levy War, conclude Peace, contract Alliances, establish Commerce, and to do all other Acts and Things which Independent States may of right do. And for the support of this Declaration, with a firm reliance on the protection of divine Providence, we mutually pledge to each other our Lives, our Fortunes, and our sacred Honor.

Signed by Order and in Behalf of the Congress, JOHN HANCOCK, President.

Attest. CHARLES THOMSON, Secretary.

Philadelphia: Printed by JOHN DUNLAP.

GLOSSARY

abandoned When an emancipated minor gives up the protection afforded to them as minors. (p. 148)

abandoned property Property that has been discarded by the owner without the intent to reclaim ownership. (p. 363)

acceptance The second party's unqualified willingness to go along with the first party's proposal. (p. 109)

acceptor Drawee who has agreed to a draft by accepting the written word on a draft and signing his or her name. (p. 509)

accord The acceptance by the creditor of less than what has been billed to the debtor. (p. 170)

accord and satisfaction Contract is discharged when one party to an agreement agrees to accept performance from the other party that is different from what was agreed upon in the original contract. (p. 230)

actual damages Damages directly attributable to another party's breach of contract. (p. 251)

actual harm The proof that a plaintiff suffered physical injuries, property damage, or financial loss. (p. 90)

actual notice In terminating an agency relationship, this type of notice is given to third parties when the third party has given credit to the principal through the agent. Notice by certified mail is the best way to give actual notice. (p. 427)

adhesion contract Standard contract used by car dealers. A sentence on the front says that the buyer agrees to terms on the reverse side. The back of the form contains a full page of small-print terms that favor the seller. (p. 347)

administrative law Rules and procedures that are established by regulatory agencies. (p. 21)

administrator/administratrix Male or female who is appointed to petition the courts on the behalf of those named in the will. (p. 785)

adulterated A food or drug that contains any substance that may make it harmful to the health of the consumer; also, a product that contains any substance mixed or packed with it to reduce its quality or strength below the prescribed minimum standards. (p. 329)

adultery Act of having a voluntary sexual relationship with someone other than a spouse. (p. 695)

adverse possession Title to real property obtained by taking actual possession of the property openly, notoriously, exclusively, under a claim of right, and continuously for a period of time set by state statute. (p. 745)

affinity Related by marriage. (p. 679)

agency by estoppel Agency created when a principal is prevented from claiming that an agent was unauthorized. Such an agency occurs if the principal has misled a third party into thinking that the agent did have authority. (p. 405)

agency Relationship in which one person represents another person in some sort of business transaction with a third party. (p. 392)

agent One who represents another person in negotiating business deals, entering into contracts, and performing a variety of other business tasks for the principal. (p. 392)

alien Person who is living in this country but owes his or her allegiance to another country. (p. 157)

alimony An allowance or support and maintenance payment to a divorced person by a former spouse. (p. 702)

alternative dispute resolution The process, outside of the usual system, by which parties may attempt to solve their disputes by using creative settlement techniques. (p. 34)

annual percentage rate (APR) The true interest rate of the loan. (p. 330)

annuity Guaranteed retirement that is purchased by paying either a lump-sum premium or making periodic payments to an insurer. (p. 756)

annulment Declaration by a court that a marriage was never effective and was void from the beginning. (p. 694)

answer The defendant's response to the allegations filed by the plaintiff in the complaint. (p. 36)

anticipatory breach Parties to a contract notify the other party that they will not go through with the contract before the time for performance. (p. 250)

apparent authority Exists when the principal has somehow led a third party to believe that a non-agent is an agent, or that an agent has a power that he or she does not truly have. (p. 417)

appellate courts The United States courts of appeals. (p. 29)

appellate jurisdiction Any party to a suit decided in a federal district court may appeal to the federal court of appeals in the circuit where the case was tried. (p. 29)

arraignment Procedure in which the accused is brought to court, is read the indictment containing information regarding the crime, and is asked to plead guilty or not guilty. If the person pleads not guilty, the case proceeds to trial. If the person pleads guilty, the judge may impose sentencing. (p. 45)

arrest Action when a person is deprived of his or her freedom by a police officer. (p. 43)

arson The willful and malicious burning of a building. (p. 68)

articles of incorporation Application for the incorporation of a business; describes a corporation's organization, powers, and authority. (p. 610)

articles of partnership Statement of agreement of all partners that is required to form a general partnership; also called a partnership agreement or articles of copartnership (p. 588)

assault The attempt to commit a battery such as pointing or shooting a gun at someone. (p. 64)

asset acquisition Occurs when one corporation agrees to purchase the assets or property of a second corporation. (p. 655)

assignment The transfer of rights under a contract. (pp. 242, 542)

assumption of risks Defense in which the defendant shows that the plaintiff knew of the risk involved in an activity and still took the chance of being injured. (p. 92)

auction without reserve The auctioneer must sell the goods to the highest bidder. (p. 273)

auction with reserve The auctioneer does not have to sell the goods for the highest bid if it is lower than the reserve amount (what the seller wishes to get for the item). (p. 273)

bad check Check that is drawn on an account in which there are insufficient funds. (p. 526)

bail Money or other property that is left with the court to assure that a person who has been arrested, but released, will return to trial. (p. 43)

bailee One who holds the personal property of another for a specific purpose. (p. 368)

bailment The transfer of possession and control of personal property to another with the intent that the same property will be returned later. (p. 368)

bailor The person who transfers property. (p. 368)

bait and switch Advertising bargains that do not exist to lure customers to a store so that they will buy more expensive merchandise. (p. 321)

bank draft Check drawn by a bank against funds the bank has on deposit. (p. 513)

bankruptcy Legal process by which a debtor can make a fresh start through the sale of assets to pay off creditors. (p. 496)

bankruptcy laws Set procedures for discharging a debtor's obligations. The obligations still exist, but the debtor can no longer be imprisoned for failure to pay. (p. 235)

bargained-for exchange A promise is made in return for another promise, an act, or a promise not to act. (p. 165)

battery The unlawful touching of another person that usually involves the forceful use of a person's hand, knife, or gun against another. Battery also may be committed by giving poison or drugs to an unsuspecting victim, spitting in someone's face, commanding a dog to attack, or even kissing someone who does not want to be kissed. (p. 63)

bearer paper Instrument that is payable to bearer or cash and may be negotiated by delivery alone without an indorsement. (p. 544)

beneficiary Person who is named in an insurance policy to receive benefits paid by the insured in the event of a loss. (p. 752)

benefit Something that a party was not previously entitled to receive. (p. 164)

bequest Gift of personal property that is made by a will. (p. 779)

best evidence rule The requirement that the original copy of a written agreement be submitted into evidence. (p. 216)

bigamy Act of having two spouses at one time. (p. 680)

bilateral contract A two-sided contract that contains two promises. (p. 111)

GLOSSARY

bilateral mistake Occurs when both parties to a contract are mistaken about some important fact. (p. 135)

bill of lading Receipt for shipment of goods given by a transportation company to a shipper when the carrier accepts goods for shipment. (p. 281)

bill of sale Formal evidence of ownership. (p. 276)

binder Offers temporary protection until a policy is issued. (p. 762)

blank indorsement Act of signing an order instrument on the back. By doing so, the payee is in effect saying that the instrument may be paid to anyone. (p. 546)

bodily injury liability Insurance that protects the insured against claims or lawsuits for death or injury caused by negligence. (p. 352)

bona fide occupational qualification (BFOQ) The defense an employer has against the charge of disparate treatment; allows the employer to show that the qualification in question is a *bona fide* (good faith) employment qualification that may justify discrimination. (p. 468)

breach of contract Wrongful failure to perform one or more promises. (p. 207)

breach of duty The failure to use the degree of care that would have been used by a reasonable person. (p. 88)

bulk transfer Transfer of all merchandise and supplies at once. (p. 274)

burglary The breaking into, and entering of, a dwelling house or place with the intent to commit a felony. (p. 67)

business judgment rule Presumes that a board of directors acts with due care. Courts defer to managers' business decisions unless they find instances of fraud, a clear lack of good faith, an abuse of discretion, or an illegal act. This rule focuses not on whether a particular decision was right, but on how the decision was made. (p. 633)

business necessity Defense that employers have against a charge of disparate impact; allows that if an employer can show that the qualification in question is required to perform the job, it may be permitted despite its disparate impact on a protected class. (p. 468)

Buyer's Guide Information required by the FTC to be posted on each used vehicle a dealer has for sale; gives warranty protection information. (p. 344)

capacity The legal ability to enter a contract. (pp. 109, 147)

carrier A transportation company. (pp. 278, 376)

cash value Amount of money a person can take by either borrowing against or cashing in an insurance policy. (p. 754)

cashier's check Check drawn by a bank upon itself. (p. 531)

caveat emptor Latin phrase meaning "let the buyer beware." (p. 316)

caveat venditor Latin phrase meaning "let the seller beware." (p. 316)

cease and desist orders Legally binding orders to stop a practice that would mislead the public. (p. 320)

certificate of deposit (CD) Note provided by a bank that is a bank's written receipt of money and its promise to pay the money back, usually with interest on the due date. (p. 508)

certificate of incorporation Corporation's official authorization to do business in a state. (p. 612)

certified check Check that is guaranteed by the bank. (p. 529)

check Type of a draft drawn on a bank and payable on demand. (p. 509)

child labor laws Laws that control the work that children are permitted to do and the hours they are permitted to work. (p. 445)

Civil Rights Act The Civil Rights Act of 1964 prohibits discrimination in employment based on race, color, religion sex, sexual preference, or national origin. (p. 465)

closed shop Business or company that requires a person to be a member of a union before being hired. (p. 444)

closed-end credit Credit that is given for a specific amount of money and that cannot be increased by making additional purchases. (p. 484)

codicil Formal document used to supplement or change an existing will. It must be signed and witnessed to be valid. (p. 781)

coinsurance Provision in an insurance policy that limits your recovery for a loss if the property is not insured for its full replacement value. (p. 763)

collateral Something of value you use to obtain a secured loan. The creditor obtains an interest in this item and can secure payment with it if you do not pay the loan. (p. 485)

collective bargaining agreement Contract negotiations between the employer and representatives of the labor union covering issues related to employment. (p. 434)

collision insurance Insurance that covers damage to a vehicle when it is in an accident, regardless of who was at fault. (p. 353)

commerce clause Clause in the U.S. Constitution that states that the United States Congress has the power to regulate commerce "among several states." (p. 647)

common carrier Carrier that is compensated for providing transportation to the general public. (p. 376)

common law Decisions of the early law courts developed in England, based on customs. They are characterized by the practice of deciding cases on precedent. (p. 17)

common-law marriage Informal type of marriage in which the parties agree either in writing or orally that they are married and live as man and wife. (p. 681)

common stock Basic form of corporate ownership. (p. 614)

comparative negligence The process by which the negligence of each party is compared and the amount of the plaintiff's recovery is reduced by the percent of his or her negligence. (p. 92)

compassion Sympathy towards the difficulties of others. (p. 11)

competitive bidding The process by which rivals submit bids for a project. (p. 197)

complaint Formal papers filed with the court by the plaintiff and defendant that express the plaintiff's allegations, or claims. (p. 36)

complete performance When all the terms of a contract have been carried out properly and completely. (p. 224)

comprehensive insurance Insurance that covers damages to a vehicle from sources other than collision, including fire, theft, lightning, flood, hail, windstorm, riot, and vandalism. (p. 354)

computer crime Crimes committed through the use of computers. (p. 71)

concealment Occurs when an individual makes a false representation by choosing not to reveal important information. (p. 129)

conditional indorsement Type of restrictive indorsement that makes the rights of the indorsee subject to a specific event or condition. (p. 548)

condominium Form of home ownership in which each owner has absolute individual interest in an apartment unit and an undivided common interest in the common areas of the building. (p. 735)

consanguinity State of being related by blood. (p. 679)

consequential damages Losses that do not flow directly from an act but only from some of the consequences or results of the act. (p. 305)

consideration The exchange of things of value. (p. 109); The exchange of benefits and detriments by parties to an agreement. (p. 164)

conspiracy Agreement to commit a crime for a promised consideration. (p. 186)

Constitution Document that spells out the principles by which the government operates. (p. 14)

constructive eviction Occurs when a landlord breaches a duty under the lease. (p. 723)

consumer Someone who buys or leases goods, real estate, or services for personal, family, or household purposes. (p. 316)

contract Any agreement enforceable by law. (p. 106)

contract to sell Agreement that involves the immediate sale of goods. (p. 268)

contributory negligence Behavior by the plaintiff that helps cause his or her injuries. (p. 91)

GLOSSARY

cooling-off rule Provision that gives customers three business days to cancel contracts for most purchases made away from the seller's regular place of business. (p. 322)

cooperation The act of working together toward a common end. (p. 420)

cooperative Form of home ownership in which buyers purchase shares in the corporation that owns an apartment building and holds the mortgage on it. (p. 735)

copyright Right granted to an author, composer, photographer, or artist to exclusively publish and sell an artistic or literary work. (p. 365)

corporate opportunity doctrine Directors and officers cannot take a business opportunity for themselves if they have knowledge that the corporation would want to take that opportunity for itself. (p. 637)

corporation A body formed and authorized by law to act as a single person. (p. 606)

cosignature A second person's act of signing a loan contract, thereby agreeing to pay the loan if necessary. (p. 488)

counteroffer Any change in the terms of the offer that means the offeree has not really accepted the offer. (p. 117)

credit Arrangement through which a person may receive cash, goods, or services immediately, and pay for them in the future. (p. 484)

creditor Party who sells the goods or lends the money. (p. 484)

crime An offense against the public at large, which is therefore punishable by the government. (p. 80)

crime against property Crimes including burglary, robbery, arson, and embezzlement. (p. 66)

crimes involving controlled substances Acts in which a person commits a crime either under the influence of drugs or alcohol, or is involved in the illegal sale of those substances.(p. 71)

damages Payment recovered in court by a person who has suffered an injury. (p. 251)

debit card Card used to electronically subtract money from a bank account to pay for goods or services. (p. 534)

debtor Party who buys goods on credit or borrows money. (p. 484)

debt ratio Amount of the monthly payments on a mortgage compared to the income of the debtor. (p. 731)

deed Written instrument that transfers ownership of real property. (p. 741)

defamation The wrongful act of injuring another person's reputation by making false statements. (p. 84)

defendant The person accused of a crime. (p. 56)

definite time paper Instruments that are payable on or before the stated date. (p. 514)

delegation The transfer of a duty. (p. 243)

delinquent child A minor child under a certain age (generally 16–18) who has committed an adult crime. (p. 31)

demand paper Instrument that is payable on demand when it is so stated, or an instrument that is payable "on sight" or "on presentation." (p. 514)

depository bank The first bank to which an item is transferred for collection; the depository bank may also be the payor bank. (p. 545)

derivative suit Suit brought against a corporation's management by the shareholders on behalf of the corporation. (p. 631)

desertion Unjustified separation of one spouse from the other with the intent of not returning. (p. 698)

destination contract The place that goods are required to be delivered. (p. 279)

detention hearing Hearing in which a judge learns whether there are good reasons to keep the accused in custody. (p. 47)

detriment Any loss suffered from an agreement. (p. 164)

devise Gift of real property that is made by a will. (p. 779)

direct suit Lawsuit that may be brought against a corporation by stockholders to enforce their rights. (p. 631)

directors Persons responsible for seeing that a corporation acts within its powers, and who suggest business policy and oversee a wide variety of employee-related policies. (p. 626)

disability Any physical or mental impairment that substantially limits one or more of the major life activities. (p. 470)

disability insurance Insurance that pays a person when he or she is unable to work because of a physical or mental disability. (p. 761)

discharged When a contract ends. (p. 224)

disclaimer A statement holding that, regardless of any provisions, policies, or oral promises to the contrary, an employment-at-will situation exists between the employee and the employee. (p. 439)

discrimination Unequal treatment of individuals based on sex, sexual preference, age, race, nationality, or religion. (p. 465)

dishonored An instrument that a party refuses to pay or accept. (p. 570)

disparate impact Occurs when an employer has an employment policy or criteria that appears neutral on the surface but has an unfair impact on the members of one or more of the protected classes. (p. 468)

disparate treatment Occurs when an employer intentionally discriminates against an individual or a group of individuals belonging to one of the protected classes. (p. 466)

dissolution Legal detachment. (p. 597)

diversity of citizenship Cases that involve citizens of different states and in which the amount of money in dispute exceeds $75,000. (p. 28)

dividends Profits paid to shareholders based on a corporation's performance. (p. 614)

divorce Declaration of a court that a marriage has come to an end. (p. 694)

domestic violence Any reckless form of physical or mental abuse within a family or household. (p. 64)

domicile Principle place of abode; the place to which you have the intent of returning when you are absent. (p. 700)

donee Person who receives a gift. (p. 362)

donor Person who gives a gift. (p. 362)

draft An order to pay money that involves three parties: the drawer, the drawee, and the payee. (p. 509)

drawee Party that is ordered by the drawer to pay money to the payee. (p. 509)

drawer Party that orders the drawee to pay money to the payee. (p. 509)

duplicate original Copy of the original written agreement. (p. 216)

duress Overcoming a person's will by the use of force, or by threat of force or bodily harm. (p. 137)

duty of care The duty not to violate the rights of others. (p. 88)

duty to account Obligation of an agent to keep a record of all the money collected and paid out and to report this to the principal. (p. 419)

duty to notify To succeed in a claim for breach of warranty, the buyer must satisfy his or her duty to notify. This duty requires the buyer to notify the seller within a reasonable time after a defect is discovered. (p. 308)

easement The right to make use of someone else's land. (p. 742)

economic duress Consists of threats to a person's business or income that cause him or her to enter a contract without real consent. (p. 137)

electronic commerce The buying and selling of goods and services, or the transfer of money, over the Internet (p. 284)

electronic fund transfer (EFT) Banking method that uses computers and electronic technology as a substitute for checks and other paper forms of banking. (p. 534)

electronic signature Method of signing an electronic message that identifies a particular person as the source of the message. (p. 286)

emancipated Minors who are no longer under the control of their parents and are responsible for their own contract. (p. 148)

embezzlement The wrongful taking of another person's property by a person who is entrusted with that property. (p. 68)

eminent domain The right of the government to take private land, with compensation to its owners, for public use. (p. 745)

employer identification number A number that is assigned to an employer for tax purposes. (p. 585)

employment-at-will General rule governing employment in most states. (p. 434)

endowment insurance Provides protection for a stated time, generally 20 to 30 years. The face value of the policy is paid to the insured at the end of the agreed-upon period. (p. 755)

Equal Credit Opportunity Act Ensures that both businesses and consumers are given an equal chance to obtain credit. (p. 493)

equal pay rule States that employers engaged in interstate commerce must pay women the same rate of pay as men; covers hourly workers, executives, administrators, professional employees, and outside salespeople who receive salaries and/or commission. (p. 456)

equitable distribution laws Allow a judge to distribute property fairly between a divorcing husband and wife, regardless of who has title to the property. (p. 702)

equity Difference between the fair market value of a home and the mortgage. (p. 730)

estoppel Restraint on a person to prevent him or her from contradicting a previous act. (p. 175)

ethics Means for determining what a society's values ought to be. (p. 6)

eviction Occurs when a landlord deprives a tenant of the physical possession of the premises that they have been renting. (p. 722)

executor/executrix Male or female named in the will to carry out the wishes of the deceased. (p. 785)

express authority Includes all of the orders, commands, or directions a principal directly states to an agent when the agency relationship is first created. (p. 415)

express contract A contract stated in words that may be either oral or written. (p. 111)

express warranty An oral or written statement, promise, or other representation about the quality, ability or performance of a product. (p. 294)

face value Amount of protection stated in a life insurance policy, meaning the amount of money a beneficiary would receive if the insured died. (p. 754)

Fair Credit Billing Act Allows consumers to contest charges on their credit cards within a stated time frame. (p. 493)

Fair Credit Reporting Act Prohibits the abuse of a valuable consumer asset—credit. This act deals with unfavorable reports issued by credit bureaus. (p. 493)

Fair Debt Collection Act Asserts that it is illegal for debt collectors to threaten consumers with violence, use obscene language, or contact consumers by telephone at inconvenient times or places. Debt collectors also are not allowed to impersonate government officials or attorneys, obtain information under false pretenses, or collect more than is legally owed. (p. 494)

fairness rule Requirement that an officer or director prove that a business decision he or she made was fair to the corporation. (p. 637)

fair use doctrine The right to use copyrighted material without permission in certain cases. The amount and use of the material must be reasonable and not harmful to the copyright owner. (p. 365)

false imprisonment When the police arrest someone without probable cause or the proper warrant. (p. 83)

family farmer One who receives more than one-half of his or her total income from a farm. (p. 497)

featherbedding Requiring an employer, usually by a union, to keep unneeded employees, to pay employees for not working, or to assign more employees to a given job than are needed. (p. 444)

federal statutes Laws that are passed by the United States Congress and signed by the president. (p. 18)

Federal Trade Commission (FTC) Federal commission whose job it is to prevent businesses from violating the Federal Trade Commission Act. (p. 287)

felony A major crime punishable by imprisonment or death. (p. 56)

fictitious name Made-up name that a sole proprietor uses. (p. 584)

finance charge The cost of a loan in dollars and cents. (p. 338)

financial responsibility law Requires vehicle owners to prove they can pay for damages or injury caused by an automobile accident. (p. 251)

fire insurance A type of insurance policy that covers loss resulting directly from an unfriendly or hostile fire. (p. 763)

firm offer An irrevocable offer (p. 176); also, a merchant's written promise to hold an offer open for the sale of goods. (p. 270)

fixtures Items of personal property attached to real property such as built-in stoves and dishwashers. Unless otherwise stated in the lease, fixtures become part of the real property and belong to the landlord, even when installed and paid for by the tenant. (p. 721)

floater policy Policy that insures property that cannot be covered by specific insurance because it is constantly changing in value or location. (p. 762)

f.o.b. Stands for "free on board," and means that goods will be delivered from the shipping point to the destination. (p. 278)

forbearance Not doing something that you have the legal right to do. (p. 164)

forgery False signature on a check or other document. (p. 527)

401(k) plan Retirement plan whose funds are not taxed until the money is withdrawn, but the money cannot be withdrawn without penalty before the age of 59. Employees agree to forgo a bonus or take a salary reduction in order to invest in this plan. Employers sometimes match the amount contributed by employees. (p. 774)

fraud A deliberate deception intended to secure an unfair or unlawful gain. (p. 128)

fraudulent misrepresentation Any statement that deceives the buyer. (p. 318)

full warranty Promises to fix or replace a defective product at no charge to the consumer. (p. 295)

future goods Crops that are not yet grown, or other items that have not yet been manufactured. (p. 278)

general agent Person who has been given the authority to perform any act within the scope of a business. (p. 402)

general jurisdiction A general trial court that handles criminal and civil cases. All cases that involve major crimes and large amounts of money must begin in one of these courts. (p. 31)

general partnership Two or more parties combine their money, labor, and skills for the purpose of carrying on a lawful business. (p. 588)

genuine agreement A valid offer that is met by a valid acceptance. (p. 109)

good faith To deal honestly with another party with no intent to seek advantage or to defraud. (pp. 418, 561)

goods Moveable items including specially manufactured items such as furniture, books, livestock, cultivated crops, clothing, automobiles, and personal effects of any kind. (p. 213)

gratuitous Free. The law does not enforce free agreements. (p. 164)

gratuitous agreement Free agreement that does not involve consideration. The law usually refuses to enforce free agreements. (p. 164)

gratuitous bailment Property is transferred to another person without either party giving or asking for payment. (p. 369)

grievance procedure Establishes a series of steps that an employee must follow to appeal the decisions of an employer who may have violated the collective bargaining agreement. (p. 435)

gross negligence Very great negligence. (p. 370)

guardian Someone who is appointed to protect the rights of a mentally impaired person or a child. (p. 157)

hate crime Any act that uses symbols, writings, pictures, or spoken words to create fear or anger in people solely because of their race, religion, color, sexual preference, or gender. (p. 65)

Health Maintenance Organizations (HMOs) Organizations that contract with doctors and other healthcare providers to offer healthcare services for members. Members pay monthly premiums and must choose from a list of doctors provided by the HMO. (p. 760)

heir Person who inherits real or personal property. (p. 779)

holder Person who possesses a negotiable instrument payable to the order of the person holding it or to the bearer. (p. 543)

holder in due course Holder who takes an instrument for value in good faith and without notice. (p. 560)

holographic will Will written entirely in the handwriting of the testator(rix). It is valid without witnesses. (p. 781)

homeowner's insurance A type of insurance policy that protects against most types of losses and liabilities related to home ownership, including fire, windstorm, vandalism, burglary, and injuries suffered by other persons while on the property. (p. 762)

homestead exemption Debtors filing bankruptcy can keep a maximum of $16,150 in equity in a personal residence. (p. 499)

honesty Character trait of a person who is open and truthful in dealing with others. (p. 11)

hostile working environment A workplace that has become a distressing, humiliating, or hostile place because of a pattern of severe and pervasive sexually demeaning behavior. (p. 469)

identified goods Goods that presently exist and have been set aside for a contract. (p. 278)

illusory promise A contract that appears at first glance to be a contract, but on further scrutiny is revealed to be hollow. (p. 177)

implied authority Powers that can be understood from the express terms of an agency agreement. (p. 415)

implied contract A contract that comes about through the actions of the parties. (p. 111) An employer says, writes, or does something to lead the employee to the reasonable belief that he or she is not an at-will employee. (p. 438)

implied covenant Exception to employment-at-will doctrine that holds that in any employment relationship, there is an implied promise that employer and employee will be fair and honest in their dealings with one another. (p. 441)

implied warranty Guarantee of quality imposed by law. (p. 300)

impossibility of performance Situation in which it is legally impossible to fulfill the obligations of the agreement. (p. 230)

incidental damages Any reasonable expenses, resulting from a breach, that have been incurred by the buyer. (p. 251)

indemnification Entitlement to repayment of the amount lost. (p. 420)

independent contractor Person who works for, but is not under the control of, a proprietor. (p. 394)

indictment A written accusation to charge an individual that is issued after the grand jury hears evidence and testimony of witnesses. This issuance does not mean that the person is guilty, but that the grand jury believes there is enough evidence to show that there is a possibility that the person is guilty. (p. 45)

Individual Retirement Account (IRA) An individual's own personal pension plan that is a system of providing for retirement. (p. 776)

indorsement Act of placing one's signature on an instrument, usually on the back, to transfer it to another. (p. 544)

injunction Order a plaintiff seeks to prevent the defendant from taking action, or to stop an action that has already begun. (pp. 41, 255)

inland marine insurance Insurance coverage for goods that are moved by land carriers such as trains, trucks, and airplanes. (p. 765)

insider trading An illegal practice in which an officer or director buys or sells shares in a corporation based on information obtained as a result of his or her position in the company. (p. 637)

insurable interest A person's right to take out insurance on another person because that person can show he or she would suffer financial loss or hardship in the event of the death of the insured or a loss of property. (p. 753)

insurance Contract under which, for consideration, the insurance company agrees to compensate the insured for a specific loss. (p. 752)

insured Person whose life or property is insured who may or may not be the policyholder. (p. 752)

insurer Company that agrees, for a consideration, to compensate the insured for a specific loss. (p. 752)

intangible personal property Property that has no substance and cannot be touched, such as money that is owed. (p. 362)

integrity Willingness to do the right thing regardless of personal consequences. (p. 12)

intellectual property An original work fixed in a tangible medium of expression. (p. 365)

intentional tort Occurs when a person knows and desires the consequences of his or her act. (p. 81)

interest The fee a borrower pays to the lender for using the money. (p. 189)

intermediate courts The courts between the lower and higher courts. (p. 29)

interstate commerce Business activities that touch more than one state. (p. 297)

intestate The act of dying without a will. (p. 783)

intrastate sales Sales that take place within a state. (p. 330)

invasion of privacy Interfering with a person's right to be left alone, which includes the right to be free from unwanted publicity and interference with private matters. (p. 86)

invitation to negotiate An invitation to deal, trade, or make an offer. (p. 114)

joint custody Divides the rights, duties, and powers of parenting between the parents. Under this arrangement the children live with each parent at different times. (p. 703)

joint liability In the event of a lawsuit, all the partners must be sued together. (p. 597)

joint tenancy Type of ownership in which two or more people own an interest in the whole property. (p. 740)

judgment The court's determination or decision in a case. (p. 41)

jurisdiction The power and authority given to a court to hear a case and to make a judgment. (p. 28)

justice Ability to treat all people fairly. (p. 11)

Keogh plan Retirement plan for self-employed people and their employees. (p. 778)

kidnapping The unlawful removal or restraint of a person against his or her will. (p. 63)

larceny The unlawful taking and carrying away of the personal property of another with the intent to deprive the owner of the property. (p. 68)

law System of rules of conduct established by the government of a society to maintain stability and justice. (p. 12)

lease Written agreement between a lessor and a lessee that creates the landlord-tenant relationship. It provides the tenant with exclusive possession and control of the real property of the landlord. (p. 714)

legal age The age of majority which, in most states, remains 18. (p. 148)

legality The final element of a contract. (p. 109)

legal separation A court judgment ending the right to cohabitation. (p. 694)

legal tender U.S. coin or currency. (p. 229)

legislature The body of lawmakers of each state that is responsible for making statutory laws. (p. 19)

lemon law Protects consumers when they buy defective vehicles, either new or used. (p. 348)

lessee The tenant of an apartment or house that is owned by another person. (p. 712)

lessor The owner of a house or apartment that is for rent or lease. (p. 712)

libel False statements in written or printed form that injure another's reputation or reflect negatively on that person's character. (p. 84)

license A legal document stating that the holder has permission from the proper authorities to carry on a certain trade or profession. (p. 191)

lien A claim that one has against the property of another. (p. 304)

life insurance Contract that provides monetary compensation for losses suffered as a result of someone's death. (p. 755)

limited jurisdiction Local courts that handle minor matters such as misdemeanors and civil actions involving small amounts of money. (p. 30)

limited liability company (LLC) Combines the best features of a partnership and a corporation. Like a corporation, it offers limited liability to its owners, and the ability to escape double taxation. (p. 616)

limited partner Partner or investor who has no control in managing the partnership and whose name may not appear in the partnership name. (p. 599)

limited partnership Partnership formed by two or more persons having one or more general partners and one or more limited partners. (p. 599)

limited-payment life insurance Allows a person to stop paying premiums after a stated length of time—usually 10, 20, or 30 years. (p. 755)

limited warranty Any written warranty that does not meet the requirements for a full warranty. A limited warranty does not promise free repair, and commonly covers only parts, not labor. (p. 298)

line of credit Maximum amount of money made available to the buyer. (p. 484)

lottery A game that consists of drawing lots, typically tickets with different combinations of numbers printed on them, in which prizes are distributed to the winners among persons buying a chance. (p. 190)

majority Occurs when a person has reached the legal age of adulthood. (p. 148)

maker Person agreeing in writing to pay money to another. (p. 506)

manslaughter The unlawful killing of another human being without malice aforethought; can be divided into two categories, voluntary or involuntary. (p. 62)

marriage license Certificate issued by a government office that gives permission to two people to marry. It becomes effective after the couple has met the state's requirement for a waiting period, and will expire if the couple does not marry during the prescribed time period. (p. 685)

master Person who has the right to control the conduct of another who is performing a task for the benefit of the master. (p. 394)

material fact A fact that is important to one of the parties in presenting a case of fraud. (p. 129)

Medicaid Healthcare plan for low-income people that is funded by both state and federal funds and administered by the state. (p. 761)

medical payments insurance Pays for medical and sometimes funeral expenses resulting from bodily injury to anyone occupying the policyholder's car in an accident. (p. 352)

Medicare Federally funded health insurance program. (p. 761)

memorandum Written evidence of an agreement. (p. 207)

merchant Business or person who deals regularly in the sale of goods or who has a specialized knowledge of goods. (p. 269)

merger Occurs when one company continues its existence and absorbs another corporation that gives up its corporate identity. (p. 654)

minor A person who has not reached the age of legal adulthood. (p. 148)

minority Age of a person below the age of majority. (p. 148)

mirror image rule States that the acceptance of an offer must not change the terms of the original offer in any way. (p. 117)

misdemeanor A crime less serious than a felony that is punishable by a fine or a brief imprisonment in a county or city jail. (p. 56)

misrepresentation Occurs when a person makes an innocent statement that later turns out to be false. (p. 132)

mitigation of damages Obligation of the injured party to protect the other party from any unnecessary losses. (p. 253)

money order Draft that substitutes for a check and may be purchased for a fee from banks, post offices, stores, travel offices, and automobile clubs. Instead of being drawn on an individual's account, a money order is drawn on the funds of the organization that issues it. (p. 531)

morality Values that govern a society's attitude toward right and wrong. (p. 6)

mortgage A written instrument by which the buyer pledges real property to the lender as security for a loan. (p. 730)

motor vehicle violations The breaking of traffic laws through willful acts or ignorance of the law. (p. 70)

murder The unlawful killing of another human being with *malice aforethought*, which means the killer had evil intent. (p. 62)

mutual release An agreement between two parties to end an agreement. (p. 230)

mutuum Occurs when goods are loaned with the understanding that they will be used and replaced with different identical goods at a later date. (p. 368)

necessaries Food, clothing, shelter, and medical care. (p. 156)

neglected or abused child A child who is homeless, destitute, or without adequate parental care. (p. 32)

negligence An accidental or unintentional tort, and the failure to exercise the degree of care that a reasonable person would have exercised in the same situation. (p. 88)

negotiable instrument Written document giving special legal rights to the transferee that may be transferred by endorsement or delivery. (p. 506)

negotiation Transfer of an agreement in such a way the transferee becomes a holder. (p. 542)

no-fault divorce Eliminates the need to prove that one party is to blame for the failure of the marriage. (p. 694)

no-fault insurance Regardless of who caused the accident, all drivers involved collect money from their own insurance companies. (p. 355)

note Written promise by one person to pay money to another person. (p. 506)

notice by publication In terminating an agency relationship, this type of notice is given to third parties when the third party has given credit to, but also has done a cash business with, the agent or knows that the other persons have dealt with the principal through the agent. Posting a notice in a newspaper is usually sufficient for this type of notice. (p. 427)

novation The agreement whereby the original party to a contract is replaced by a new party. (p. 248)

nuisance Anything that interferes with the enjoyment of life or property. (p. 83)

obedience An agent must obey all reasonable orders and instructions within the scope of the agency agreement. (p. 417)

Occupational Safety and Health Administration (OSHA) The agency within the federal government that sets safety and health standards for many companies within the United States. (p. 454)

ocean marine insurance Insurance coverage for ships at sea. (p. 765)

offer A personal proposal by one party to another intended to create a legally binding agreement. (p. 109)

officers Persons who are appointed, and can be removed by, the corporation's directors. Officers include a president, vice-president(s) and other agents who are responsible for implementing the policies of the directors, and carrying out the day-to-day operations of the corporation. (p. 627)

online privacy Part of a person's general right to privacy. (p. 286)

open-end credit Can be increased by the debtor by continuing to purchase goods or services on credit, up to a certain limit. (p. 484)

operation of law A contract is discharged by a court because it is in the best interest of society. (p. 233)

option When an offeree gives consideration to an offeror in exchange for a promise from the offeror to keep an offer open for a specified period of time. (p. 176)

order paper Instrument that says something such as "pay to the order of." (p. 543)

ordinary negligence Failing to use the care that a reasonable person would use under the same circumstances. (p. 371)

original jurisdiction Authority of a court to try a case the first time it is heard. (p. 28)

output contract Agreement to buy all of a merchant's goods. (p. 272)

outstanding checks Checks that have been written that have not yet been returned to the bank. (p. 523)

parol evidence rule States that evidence of oral statements made before signing a written agreement that cannot be presented in court to change or add to the terms of that written agreement. (p. 215)

partnership by estoppel Arrangement in which someone does or says something that leads a third party to believe a partnership exists. (p. 591)

partnership by proof of existence A partnership that forms regardless of the label given to the enterprise or the intent of the parties involved. (p. 590)

GLOSSARY

passenger People being legally transported. (p. 378)

past consideration Consideration that took place in the past or that is given for something that has already been done. (p. 177)

patent Gives an inventor the exclusive rights to make, use, or sell an invention for 17 years. (p. 365)

payee Person to whom a maker agrees to make monetary payment. (p. 507)

pension plan Retirement plan established by an employer or a union that is designed to provide income to employees after they retire. (pp. 456, 773)

performance The parties fulfill the terms of the contract by doing what they had earlier promised. (p. 224)

periodic tenancy The right to occupy from year to year, month to month, or week to week; a tenancy that continues for successive fixed periods. (p. 713)

perjury Making a false statement under oath. (p. 207)

personal defenses Negotiable instrument defenses that can be used against a holder, but cannot be used against a holder in due course. (p. 563)

personal property Anything that can be owned other than real estate. (p. 362)

plaintiff The party that accuses a person of a crime. (p. 56)

policy Written contract between a person buying insurance and the insurance company; states exactly what losses will be compensated for, and the amount of compensation. (p. 752)

policyholder Individual or group of people who have purchased insurance. (p. 752)

polygamy Act of having more than two spouses at one time. (p. 680)

pooling agreement A contract to vote in a certain way on a particular issue. (p. 631)

portability Ability to transfer pension benefits from one job to another. (p. 776)

precedent A judge is required to follow an earlier court decision when deciding a case with similar circumstances. Also called the doctrine of *stare decisis*. (p. 17)

preexisting duties An existing legal obligation to do something. (p. 177)

preferred stock Stocks issued by a corporation to owners who have no voting rights but who have the right to receive a fixed dividend. (p. 614)

premarital agreement Agreement made between prospective spouses in contemplation of marriage that becomes effective upon marriage. It must be in writing and signed by both parties and usually pertains to the rights and obligations of each of the parties with regard to any of the property of either or both. (p. 677)

premium Amount of money paid to an insurance company for insurance coverage. (p. 754)

presentment Demand made by a holder to pay or accept an instrument. (p. 569)

price Set amount of money that is to be paid for goods. (p. 268)

price fixing Occurs when competitors agree on certain price ranges within which they set their prices. (p. 197)

primary liability The absolute liability to pay. (p. 568)

principal Person who is represented by an agency in the negotiations of business deals, and the entry into contracts. The principal is normally legally bound by those agreements. (p. 392)

privacy contract Contracting directly with another person. (p. 306)

privity of contract Determines who can sue whom over a question of performance required by a contract. (p. 248)

product liability law Manufacturers, sellers, and suppliers of goods can be held responsible if a product proves to be unsafe and someone is injured. (p. 327)

promissory Containing or consisting of a promise. (p. 175)

promissory estoppel Principle that bars a party from taking back certain types of promises, such as charitable subscriptions, on which another party relies. (p. 175)

promoter Person who carries out the incorporation process by taking the initial steps to organize and finance a business. (p. 608)

property damage liability insurance Insurance that applies when a person damages the property of others, including such things as another car, a house, a telephone pole, or a tree. (p. 353)

property insurance Contract in which the insurer promises, for a stated premium, to pay a sum of money if a particular piece of real estate is damaged or destroyed. (p. 762)

prosecutor The government attorney who presents the case in court against the person accused. (p. 56)

prospectus Document containing a detailed view of the stock offering for potential investors. (p. 648)

proximate cause The legal connection between unreasonable conduct and the resulting harm. (p. 90)

proxy Right to vote another shareholder's stock. (p. 630)

proxy marriage Occurs when one or both of the parties cannot be present for the wedding, and an agent acts on their behalf. (p. 687)

public policy tort Allows a fired employee to recover compensatory and punitive damages if he or she can prove that the firing violated public policy. (p. 440)

qualified indorsement Indorsement in which words have been added to the signature to limit the liability of the indorser. (p. 549)

quid pro quo harassment Occurs when one worker demands sexual favors from another worker in exchange for some employment-related privileges, such as a raise or promotion. (p. 469)

quiet enjoyment The right of a tenant to the undisturbed possession of the property that he or she is renting. (p. 719)

ratification Occurs if the principal, with full knowledge of the facts, accepts the benefits of the unauthorized act. (p. 407)

ratify The approval of a contract. (p. 154)

real defenses Defenses that can be used against a holder in due course. (p. 566)

real property Land and anything permanently attached to it. (p. 213)

reasonable care The degree of care that a reasonably prudent person would have used under the same circumstances and conditions. (p. 371)

reasonable time The time that is suitable, fair, and proper to the objective in view. (p. 224)

rebuttable presumption The presumption of a person's legal ability to enter into a contract. (p. 147)

registered limited liability partnership (RLLP) Designed to eliminate a disadvantage of a general partnership, namely joint and several liability. Under this statute, partners can escape joint and several liability for the torts, wrongful acts, negligence, or misconduct of other partners by registering with the appropriate state office. (p. 598)

registration statement General description of securities and of the company that is making the securities available for sale. (p. 648)

reimbursement Repayment by the principal to the agent for money the agent spends from his or her own funds for the principal's benefit. (p. 420)

rejection A refusal of an offer by the offeree, which brings the offer to an end. (p. 120)

release An agreement not to sue. (p. 168)

rent day The day on which rent is due. (p. 713)

renter's insurance Protects a person against loss of personal property, liability for a visitor's personal injury, and liability for negligent destruction of the rented premises. (p. 762)

repossess To take back. (p. 346)

requirement contract Occurs when a seller agrees to supply the needs of a buyer. (p. 272)

rescind A person who has been induced to enter into a contract by fraud may cancel the contract. (p. 128)

residence Place where a person actually lives or resides. (p. 701)

respondeat superior Latin phrase meaning "let the master respond"; typically refers to situations in which the hired servant has acted in an injurious manner, and the master may also be held responsible. (p. 397)

restraint of trade An unreasonable limitation on the full exercise of doing business with others. (p. 195)

restrictive covenant A promise not to compete. (p. 197)

restrictive indorsement Indorsement in which words have been added, in addition to the signature of the transferor, to limit its use. (p. 548)

revocation Taking back of an offer by the offeror. (p. 120)

rider Attachment to an insurance policy that modifies the policy's terms. (p. 752)

right-to-work laws State laws that prohibit union shops. (p. 444)

risk of loss The responsibility for loss or damage to goods. (p. 278)

robbery The wrongful taking and carrying away of the personal property of another through violence or threats. (p. 68)

sale Contract in which ownership of goods is transferred. (p. 268)

Sarbanes-Oxley Act of 2002 An important act that contains rules regarding the reporting and corporate governance of publicly traded companies. (p. 651)

satisfaction The agreed-to settlement as contained in the accord. (p. 170)

seal A mark or an impression placed on a written contract indicating that the instrument was executed and accepted in a formal manner. (p. 173)

secondary liability Liability to pay only after certain conditions have been met. (p. 568)

secured loan Loan in which creditors obtain an interest in something of value from which they can secure payment if the debtor does not pay. (p. 485)

secured party The lender or seller who holds the security interest. (p. 485)

Securities and Exchange Commission (SEC) Independent agency created in 1934 that regulates the sales of securities and the brokers, dealers, and bankers who sell them. (p. 648)

security Money investment that seeks to make a profit solely because of another person's efforts. (p. 648)

security interest Interest that is given to creditors. (p. 485)

servant Person whose conduct in the performance of a task is subject to the control of another. (p. 394)

severance pay Set amount of money to compensate employees for being discharged. (p. 435)

sex offense Any act in which a victim is sexually violated against his or her will. (p. 64)

share A single unit of ownership of a corporation. (p. 606)

shareholder Person who buys one or more shares of a corporation. (pp. 606, 626)

shareholder proposal A suggestion submitted by a shareholder about a broad company policy or procedure. (p. 631)

shelter provision States that a holder who receives an instrument from a holder in due course acquires the rights of the holder in due course, even though he or she does not qualify as a holder in due course. (p. 562)

shipment contract A contract under which a seller turns goods over to a carrier for delivery to a buyer. Both the title and risk of loss pass to the buyer when the goods are given to the carrier. (p. 278)

shoplifting The act of stealing goods from a store. (p. 69)

sight draft Draft that is payable as soon as it is presented to the drawee for payment. (p. 509)

slander A false statement that is made orally to a third party. (p. 85)

slight negligence Failure to use the care that persons of extraordinary prudence and foresight use. (p. 371)

smart card Data card with a computer chip that can store a large amount of data. Smart cards can hold debit and credit card balances and identification information. (p. 492)

Social Security Act The Social Security Act of 1935 and its amendments set up a social insurance program funded by contributions from both employers and employees. Employers must automatically deduct a certain amount from employee's paychecks, contribute an equal amount, and send both contributions to the Internal Revenue Service. (p. 460)

sole custody Gives all the parental rights, duties, and powers to one parent. Under sole custody the children live with one parent, and visitation rights are given to the noncustodial parent. (p. 703)

sole proprietorship Form of business that is owned and operated by one person. (p. 584)

solemnize Ceremony or rite that formally recognizes an event such as a marriage. (p. 683)

special agent Person who is employed to accomplish a specific purpose or to do a particular job. (p. 402)

special indorsement Made by writing the words "pay to the order of," or "pay to," followed by the name of the person to whom the instrument is to be transferred and the signature of the indorser. (p. 547)

specific performance A judgment in a civil trial in which the defendant is asked to comply with the terms he or she promised in a contract with the plaintiff (p. 41); also, if money from a settlement is not enough to repay a breach of contract, one party may sue the other by asking the court to order the other party to do specifically what he or she originally agreed to do. (p. 254)

stale check Check that a bank refuses to pay because it is more than six months old. (p. 522)

statute Law specifically passed by a governing body that has been created for a stated purpose. (p. 18)

Statute of Frauds State laws requiring that certain contracts be evidenced in writing. (p. 207)

statute of limitations The law that specifies the time within which a contract may be legally enforced. (p. 233)

stock acquisition Occurs when an individual or a corporation purchases enough shares of stock in a corporation to control it. (p. 659)

straight life insurance Requires the payment of premiums throughout the insured's life and pays its face value to the beneficiary. (p. 755)

strict liability An injury caused by an individual's participation in an ultra-hazardous activity (p. 88); also, manufacturers or suppliers are responsible for selling goods that are unreasonably dangerous. (p. 327)

sublease Occurs when a person transfers part of the term of a lease, but not the remainder of it, to someone else. (p. 716)

substantial performance Slightly less than full performance. Someone has fulfilled the major requirements of a contract in good faith, leaving only minor details incomplete. (p. 224)

suitor Company making a tender offer. (p. 656)

Taft-Hartley Act Created to equalize the power of labor and management. This act provided, among other things, the provision that the President of the United States could postpone a strike for up to 60 days if the strike would endanger the nation's health or safety. (p. 444)

tangible personal property Something that has substance and can be touched, such as CD players, vehicles, and food. (p. 362)

target Corporation that is to be taken over by a suitor. (p. 656)

telemarketers People who try to sell products by telephone. (p. 323)

tenancy A renter's right to hold interest in the property that is being rented. (p. 712)

tenancy at sufferance When a tenant wrongfully remains in possession of the premises after the tenancy has expired. (p. 714)

tenancy at will An interest in real property that continues for an indefinite period of time. (p. 714)

tenancy by the entirety Tenancy based on the common law doctrine that held that a husband and wife are regarded by the law as one. In theory each spouse owned the entire property, which neither could transfer without the other's consent. (p. 741)

tenancy for years The right to occupy property for a definite or fixed period of time. (p. 713)

tenancy in common Type of co-ownership in which two or more people own an interest in the whole property. (p. 740)

tenancy in partnership Limits the use or transfer of property by partners without the permission of the other partners. (p. 594)

tender An offer to do what you have agreed to do under the terms of a contract. (p. 229)

tender offer An offer to buy a number of shares at a specified price. (p. 656)

term insurance Insurance that is issued for a particular period, usually five or ten years. It has no cash or loan value, and the premiums increase at the end of each term because the insured is older and is considered a greater risk. (p. 757)

testate The act of dying with a will. (p. 779)

testator(rix) Man or woman who makes a will. (p. 779)

third-party beneficiary Person who is not a party to a contract, but still benefits from the contract. (p. 249)

time draft Draft that is not payable until the lapse of the particular time period stated on the draft. (p. 509)

GLOSSARY

title The formal written right of ownership of goods. (p. 276)

tort A private wrong committed by one person against another involving one person's interference with another person's rights. (p. 80)

tortfeasor Person who commits a tort. (p. 82)

tortious bailee Person who wrongfully keeps the lost property of another or who knowingly possesses stolen property. (p. 371)

trade fixtures Items of personal property brought to the rented premises by the tenant that are necessary to carry on the trade or business to which a rental property will be devoted. (p. 722)

trademark Distinctive symbol, mark, or slogan used by a business to identify and distinguish its goods from products sold by others. (p. 365)

traveler's check An instrument that requires the buyer to pay the full amount of the checks, and the offering institution guarantees the funds. (p. 531)

trespass The wrongful damage to, or interference with, the property of another. (p. 82)

unconscionable An agreement or contract that is considered completely out of line. (p. 166)

unconstitutional Any action or law that goes against the United States Constitution. (p. 19)

underinsured motorist insurance Insurance that protects the insured when he or she is involved in an automobile accident and the other driver does not have enough insurance to pay for any injuries. (p. 352)

undue influence Occurs when a person uses unfair and improper persuasive pressure to force another person to enter into an agreement. (p. 138)

unemployment compensation System of government payments to people who are out of work and looking for a job. Payments are made from an unemployment insurance fund financed by payroll taxes in employers or unemployment insurance premiums paid by employees. (p. 461)

unenforceable A contract that the court will not uphold, generally because of some rule of law, such as the statute of limitations. (p. 111)

unenforceable contract A contract the court will not uphold. (p. 111)

unfair and deceptive practices An act that misleads consumers. (p. 317)

Uniform Commercial Code (UCC) Collection of laws that govern the various types of business transactions. (p. 268)

unilateral contract A contract that contains a promise by only one person to do something if and when the other party performs some act. (p. 112)

unilateral mistake An error on the part of one of the parties to the contract. (p. 133)

uninsured motorist insurance Insurance that provides protection when the insured is injured in an automobile accident that is caused by a driver who has no insurance. (p. 352)

unintentional tort Occurs when a person does not have the mental determination of the consequences of his or her acts. (p. 81)

union Organization of employees that is formed to protect the welfare of its members. (p. 434)

union shop Business or company in which a worker must join the union within 30 days after being employed. (p. 444)

universal life insurance Allows policyholders to change the terms of the policy as their needs change. (p. 755)

unlimited liability A business owner is responsible for all losses experienced by the business. (p. 587)

unruly child A minor who has done something that is inappropriate that is not considered an adult crime. (p. 31)

usage of trade Method of dealing commonly used in a particular field. (p. 270); also, an implied warranty arising from the customary ways in which the parties have dealt in the past. (p. 303)

Used Car Rule Requires all used car dealers to place a large sticker in the window of each vehicle explaining the "as is" warranty and any other specific warranty protection provided. (p. 344)

usury Charging more than the maximum legal interest rate. (p. 189)

uttering Crime that results when an offeror deliberately submits a forged instrument to another. (p. 528)

valid contract A contract that is legally good. (p. 110)

value Agreed-upon consideration given or accepted in payment of a debt. (p. 561)

vandalism The willful and or malicious damage to property. (p. 69)

verdict The decision made by members of a jury after they deliberate. (p. 41)

vesting Act of giving a worker a guaranteed right to receive a future pension. (p. 775)

voidable contract A contract that a party to it is able to void or cancel for some legal reason. (p. 110)

voidable title If goods are acquired through fraud, a mistake, or undue influence, the title may be voided if the injured party elects to do so. (p. 276)

void contract A contract that has no legal effect. (p. 110)

voting trust Transfer of voting rights of a shareholder or trustee. (p. 630)

Wagner Act First law addressing collective bargaining, established guidelines for determining which employment concerns had to be included in the collective bargaining process. (p. 442)

warehouse receipt Document given to a customer by the warehouse that is storing his or her goods. (p. 281)

warrant of merchantability The merchant warrants that the goods being sold are merchantable; given only when the seller regularly sells goods of that kind. (p. 302)

warranty Another name for a guarantee. (p. 294)

warranty of fitness The seller warrants by implication that the goods will be fit for the purpose for which they are to be used. This warranty exists whether the seller is a merchant or a private party. (p. 301)

warranty of title The seller warrants that the title being conveyed is good and that the transfer is lawful. (p. 303)

waste Substantial damage to rental property that significantly decreases the value of the property. (p. 720)

will Document that is signed during a person's lifetime that provides for the distribution of his or her personal property upon his or her death. (p. 779)

words of negotiability The words to the order of and to bearer on a negotiable instrument. (p. 514)

worker's compensation Insurance program that provides income for workers who are injured or develop a disability or disease as a result of their jobs. (p. 464)

zoning laws Limitations on property use in specified areas, as prescribed by cities and towns. (p. 742)

CASE INDEX

A

American Legal Aid, Inc. v. Legal Aid Services, Inc., 623

Amstead v. United States, 195

Automobile Workers v. Johnson Controls, Inc., 478–479

B

Bagge's Case, 451

Bayer v. Travelers Indemnity, 359

Beach v. Ocwen Federal Bank, 578–579

Bierlein v. Alex's Continental Inn, Inc., 335

Blackstone v. State Ex. Rel. Blackstone, 259

Booker v. Revco, 29

Butler v. Lovoll, 221

C

Centex-Winston v. Edward Hines Lumber Co., 665

Cipollone v. Liggett Group, Inc., 100–101

Clements v. Wheeler, 749

Coleman v. Duncan, 291

Com. v. Ashcraft, 25

Connor v. Connor, 709

Cousineau v. Walker, 143

D

Denny v. Ford Motor Co., 386–387

Doe v. Oceola, 383

E

EEOC v. The Wyoming Retirement System, 475

Elliot v. Ohio Department of Rehabilitation and Correction, 411

Everett v. Bucky Warren, Inc., 335

Ewing v. Board of Regents of the University of Michigan, 25

F

Fazio v. Loweth, 519

Florida v. Riley, 53

Fleer Corporation v. Topps Chewing Gum, Inc., 203

Ford v. JA-SIN, 727

G

Galindo v. Guarantee Trust Life Insurance Co., 769

General Aircraft Corporation v. Lampert, 665

Gentile v. MacGregor Mfg. Co., 313

Gill v. Shively, 691

Guarino v. Celebrezze, 789

Gunter v. Gunter, 691

H

Hadley v. Ideus, 749

Hall v. Horizon House Microwave, Inc., 221

Hanes v. Giambrone, 603

Hoddesons v. Koos Brothers, 411

Humberto Decorators, Inc. v. Plaza National Bank, 557

I

Inside Radio/Radio Only, Inc. v. Board of Review, 475

J

Jones v. Mayer Co., 792–793

Juergens v. Stahl, Klubnik, and Associates, Inc., 451

K

Koedding v. N.B. West Contracting Co., Inc., 183

L

La Sara Grain v. First National Bank of Mercedes, 557

Leeper v. Pennsylvania Higher Education Assistance Agency, 503

Lefkowitz v. Great Minneapolis Surplus Store, 125

Leo v. Maro Display, 161

Liarkos v. Mello, 359

M

Marvin v. Marvin, 216

Mastrobuono v. Shearson Lehman Hutton, Inc., 262–263

Meyers v. Washington Times Co., 259

Miranda v. Arizona, 43

Myers v. Forest City Enterprises, Inc., 29

N

National Bank v. Refrigerated Transp., 575

New York Life Insurance Co. v. Henrikson, 769

Normat Industries, Inc. v. Carter, 643

O

Office of Disciplinary Counsel v. Lloyd, 431

Olmstead v. United States, 195

P

Parker v. Arthur Murray, Inc., 239

Pentecost v. Harward, 727

P.P. Inc. v. McGuire, 519

Q

Quinn v. Stuart Lakes Club, Inc., 203

R

R.A.V. v. St. Paul, 77

Richardson v. Girner, 575

Richmond v. Croson Co., 53

Romedy v. Willett Lincoln-Mercury, Inc., 313

Rothenbeucher v. Tockstein, 125

Russel v. Transamerica Ins. Co., 291

S

Sanchez v. Sanchez, 161

Schnell v. Nell, 168

Scott v. Purser Truck Sales, Inc., 383

Selman v. Manor Mortgage Co., 503

Siedel v. Public Service Company of New Hampshire, 643

Siegel v. New England Merchants National Bank, 539

Simandl v. Simandl, 603

Spence v. Huffman, 623

Stahl v. LePage, 431

State v. Reese, 77

T

Trisko v. Vignola Furniture Co., 183

Tropea v. Tropea, 709

V

Virginia Bankshares, Inc. v. Sandberg, 668–669

W

Wagner v. State, 143

Weaver v. Grafio, 239

Will of Katz, 789

Y

Yates v. Commercial Bank and Trust Co., 539

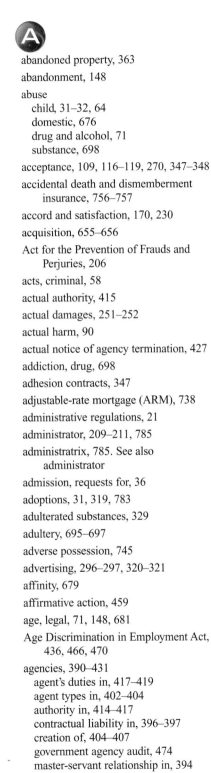

INDEX

INDEX

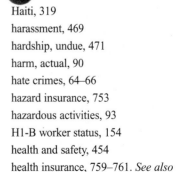

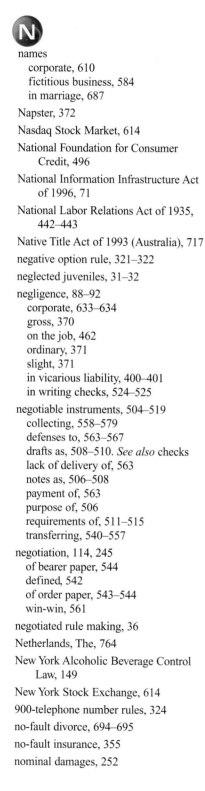

INDEX

INDEX

Photo Credits

Cover Photography: Lester Lefkowitz/Corbis Stock Market(tl); Tom McCarthy/PhotoEdit (br)